Lecture Notes in Computer Science 4308

Commenced Publication in 1973
Founding and Former Series Editors:
Gerhard Goos, Juris Hartmanis, and Jan van Leeuwen

Soma Chaudhuri   Samir R. Das
Himadri S. Paul   Srikanta Tirthapura (Eds.)

Distributed Computing and Networking

8th International Conference, ICDCN 2006
Guwahati, India, December 27-30, 2006
Proceedings

 Springer

Volume Editors

Soma Chaudhuri
Iowa State University
Department of Computer Science
230 Atanasoff Hall, Ames, IA 50011, USA
E-mail: chaudhur@cs.iastate.edu

Samir R. Das
Computer Science Department, SUNY at Stony Brook
Stony Brook, NY 11794-4400, USA
E-mail: samir@cs.sunysb.edu

Himadri S. Paul
Indian Institute of Technology, Guwahati
Department of Computer Science & Engineering
Guwahati-781039, India
E-mail: hspaul@iitg.ernet.in

Srikanta Tirthapura
Iowa State University
Department of Electrical and Computer Engineering
Ames, IA, 50010, USA
E-mail: snt@iastate.edu

Library of Congress Control Number: 2006938041

CR Subject Classification (1998): C.2, D.1.3, D.2.12, D.4, F.2, F.1, H.4

LNCS Sublibrary: SL 1 – Theoretical Computer Science and General Issues

ISSN	0302-9743
ISBN-10	3-540-68139-6 Springer Berlin Heidelberg New York
ISBN-13	978-3-540-68139-7 Springer Berlin Heidelberg New York

Springer is a part of Springer Science+Business Media

springer.com

© Springer-Verlag Berlin Heidelberg 2006
Printed in Germany

Typesetting: Camera-ready by author, data conversion by Scientific Publishing Services, Chennai, India
Printed on acid-free paper   SPIN: 11947950   06/3142   5 4 3 2 1 0

Message from the General Chairs

The *Eighth International Conference on Distributed Computing and Networking*, which was held in Guwahati, India in December 2006, is an outgrowth and a continuation of the sequence of workshops titled *International Workshop on Distributed Computing (IWDC)"*. Since its modest start in 1999, this annual event has grown rapidly in scope, volume, quality and visibility. Being traditionally situated in the different academic centers in India, it has also reflected the high-level research carried out in India in the area of distributed computing, and has helped to nourish and strengthen research interconnections among researchers in India itself as well as with distributed computing researchers throughout the world.

During the seventh meeting of IWDC, held last December in Kharagpur, the Steering Committee noted with deep satisfaction how the once small workshop has gradually grown, through the efforts of a dedicated group of academics in the area, and acquired the stature and recognition of a leading international conference. Subsequently, the Steering Committee decided to reflect this development by changing the title of the meeting from a *Workshop* to a *Conference*. At the same time, it was also recognized that the recent shifts in research interests within the area of distributed computing, and particularly the recent focus on topics related to distributed networking and on links bridging between distributed computing and networking, should also be reflected in the new name. The conference was thus renamed the *International Conference on Distributed Computing and Networking (ICDCN)*. It should be stressed that while the new name entails a certain departure from the traditional track outlined by the seven previous IWDC meetings, with an eye towards further expansion in size, scope and competitiveness, the underlying intention is still to maintain and preserve the special character of IWDC, as well as many of the features that contributed to its past success, and particularly the pleasant and informal atmosphere, facilitating close interactions and academic discussions.

Organizing a large conference is not a trivial task, and we are indebted to many. First and foremost, we are thankful to our generous sponsors, IBM, HP India Ltd., The Department of Science and Technology and The Department of Information Technology of the Government of India, for their benevolent support which was vital to making the conference a success.

The Program Committee made arduous efforts in reviewing the numerous submissions and selecting an impressive collection of high-quality papers for presentation. Our sincere thanks are due to the Program Chairs, Soma Chaudhuri and Samir R. Das, for coordinating and leading this effort, culminating in an exciting and well-balanced program. We are grateful to the Keynote Chair, Sajal K. Das, for arranging five high-quality keynote talks by eminent leaders in the field. Following the tradition of previous years, we set up four advanced tutorials on topics of interest, relevant to the realm between distributed computing and networking, namely, Modeling Biological Networks, Network Security, Algorithmic Issues in Wireless Sensor Networks, and Optical Networking. This was made possible by the efforts of the Tutorial Chairs, Sridhar Iyer and Pinaki Mitra.

The Organizing Committee worked hard to ensure that the participants enjoyed a comfortable stay and the technical meetings proceeded as smoothly as possible. We are grateful to the General Vice Chair, Sukumar Nandi, for arranging to hold the conference in Guwahati and for all he did to make the conference a success. Thanks are due to the Publicity Chairs, P. K. Das and Sriram V. Pemmaraju, for their great work in publicizing the event both locally and internationally, to the Publication Chairs, H. S. Paul and Srikanta Tirthapura, for their tremendous efforts in compiling the final proceedings, and to the Organizing Chair, D. Goswami, the Finance Chair, J. K. Deka, and the Scholarship Chair, S. V. Rao, for their hard work.

We are grateful to the Indian Institute of Technology Guwahati for extending the logistic support to the conference. We thank Sukumar Ghosh, the head of the ICDCN Steering Committee, for his guidance, continuous support and advice.

Last but not least, we extend our heartfelt thanks to the authors, reviewers and participants of the conference, for their vital contribution to the success of this conference. It is our sincere hope that this event becomes another invaluable link in the sequence of IWDC and ICDCN meetings and a useful outlet for knowledge dissemination within the distributed computing and networking communities.

December 2006   Gautam Barua
                                                              IIT Guwahati
                                                          Guwahati, India

                                                              David Peleg
                                          Weizmann Institute of Science
                                                          Rehovot, Israel

Message from the Technical Program Chairs

Welcome to the Proceedings of the Eighth *International Conference on Distributed Computing and Networking (ICDCN)*, 2006! This event was previously known as *IWDC* or *International Workshop on Distributed Computing*. It is great to see that a small workshop that grew out of the interests of a dedicated group of enthusiasts now has gained the stature of a truly international conference, covering most aspects of distributed computing and networking.

This year we received 245 paper submissions continuing on the growth trend that we observed in recent years. We received submissions from all over the world. The electronic submission system (WIMPE) registered authors from India, USA, China, Korea, UK, Canada, Iran, Germany, Greece, Netherlands, France, Italy, Israel, Lebanon, Turkey, Ireland, and Poland, reflecting a true international nature of the conference. A good fraction of submitted authors are from outside India, a fact also reflected in the conference program and the content of these proceedings.

Similar to the geographical diversity, the topical diversity of the submissions was noteworthy. All topics mentioned in the Call for Papers were covered. The 50 members of the Technical Program Committee along with a team of external reviewers worked hard on the reviews under a very strict timeline. At the end of the review period, the Program Chairs selected 29 regular papers and 30 short papers for inclusion in the proceedings and presentation in the conference.

We were also fortunate to have an array of keynote speakers – Faith Ellen (University of Toronto), Nicola Santoro (Carleton University), Eli Gafni (UCLA), Shay Kutten (Technion), Manindra Agrawal (IIT-Kanpur), Anurag Kumar (Indian Institute of Science). Their talks provided us with the unique opportunity to hear the leaders of their fields. Their papers related to the talks are also included in these proceedings.

The main conference program was preceded by a day of tutorial presentations. We had an array of four tutorials, presented by Kalyan Basu (University of Texas at Arlington), Indranil Sen Gupta (IIT, Kharagpur), Sriram Pemmaraju (University of Iowa) and Ashwin Gumaste (IIT, Bombay), on biological networks, network security, sensor networks and optical networks, respectively.

We thank all authors for their interest in ICDCN 2006, and all Program Committee members and external reviewers for their commitment in spite of a tight schedule and a high review load. We hope that you will find the IDCDN proceedings to be technically rewarding.

December 2006

Soma Chaudhuri
Iowa State University
Ames, Iowa, USA

Samir R. Das
Stony Brook University
Stony Brook, New York, USA

Organization

Executive Committee

Steering Committee chair

Sukumar Ghosh, University of Iowa, USA

General Co-chairs

Gautam Barua, IIT Guwahati, India
David Peleg, Weizmann Institute of Science, Israel

General Vice-Chair

Sukumar Nandi, IIT Guwahati, India

Keynote Chair

Sajal K. Das, University of Texas at Arlington, USA

Tutorial Co-chairs

Sridhar Iyer, IIT Bombay, India
Pinaki Mitra, IIT Guwahati, India

Program Co-chairs

Soma Chaudhuri, Iowa State University, USA
Samir R. Das, Stony Brook University, USA

Publicity Co-chairs

P. K. Das, IIT Guwahati, India
Sriram V. Pemmaraju, University of Iowa, USA

Publication Co-chairs

Himadri Sekhar Paul, IIT Guwahati, India
Srikanta Tirthapura, Iowa State University, USA

Organising Chair

D. Goswami, IIT Guwahati, India

Finance Chair

J. K. Deka, IIT Guwahati, India

Scholarship Chair

S. V. Rao, IIT Guwahati, India

Program Committee

Chairs

Soma Chaudhuri	Iowa State University
Samir R. Das	Stony Brook University

Committee Members

Mustaque Ahmad	Georgia Institute of Technology
Nilanjan Banerjee	Motorola India Research Lab
Amiya Bhattacharya	New Mexico State University
Ying Cai	Iowa State University
Jiannong Cao	Hong Kong Polytechnic University
Nabanita Das	Indian Statistical Institute, Kolkata
Koustuv Dasgupta	IBM India Research Lab
Anwitaman Datta	EPFL Zurich
D. M. Dhamdhere	Indian Institute of Technology, Bombay
Christof Fetzer	University of Dresden
Faith Ellen	University of Toronto
Pierre Fraigniaud	University of Paris
Ayalvadi Ganesh	Microsoft Research, Cambridge
Ratan K. Ghosh	Indian Institute of Technology, Kanpur
Arobinda Gupta	Indian Institute of Technology, Kharagpur
Indranil Gupta	University of Illinois, Urbana-Champaign
Sandeep Gupta	Arizona State University
Sridhar Iyer	Indian Institute of Technology, Bombay
Prasad Jayanti	Dartmouth College
Sanjay Jha	The University of New South Wales
Ajay Kshemkalyani	University of Illinois at Chicago
Joy Kuri	Indian Institute of Science, Bangalore
Shay Kutten	Technion, Israel
Richard Ladner	University of Washington
Yonghe Liu	University of Texas at Arlington
B.S. Manoj	University of California, San Diego
Mahesh Marina	University of California, Los Angeles
Marios Mavronicolas	University of Cyprus
Prasant Mohapatra	University of California, Davis
Sukumar Nandi	Indian Institute of Technology, Guwahati
Asis Nasipuri	University North Carolina, Charlotte
Sriram Pemmaraju	University of Iowa
Sushil Prasad	Georgia State University
C Pandu Rangan	Indian Institute of Technology, Madras
S V Rao	Indian Institute of Technology, Guwahati
Debashis Saha	Indian Institute of Management, Kolkata

G Sajith   Indian Institute of Technology, Guwahati
Mukesh Singhal   University of Kentucky
Bhabani Sinha   Indian Statistical Institute, Kolkata
Arunava Sen   Arizona State University
Arun Somani   Iowa State University
Pradip Srimani   Clemson University
Wallapak Tavanapong   Iowa State University
Srikanta Tirthapura   Iowa State University
Philippas Tsigas   Chalmers University, Sweden
Mark Tuttle   Intel
Nitin Vaidya   University of Illinois, Urbana-Champaign
Roger Wattenhofer   ETH, Zurich
Jennifer Welch   Texas A&M University
Taieb Znati   University of Pittsburg

Additional Reviewers

The following reviewers external to the Program Committee participated in the review process. We greatly acknowledge their contributions.

Bikas Agarwalla   Boris Koldehofe
Keno Albrecht   Rajeev Kumar
Amihood Amir   Gad Landau
Jon A Preston   Li Lao
James Aspnes   Abhijit Lele
Janaka Balasooriya   Moshe Lewenstein
A. Banerjee   Y. Liu
Adrish Banerjee   Zvika Lotker
Subbarao Bhagavati   Ritesh Maheshwari
Subhasis Bhattacharjee   Subhamoy Maitra
Subir Biswas   Srilaxmi Malladi
Christina Christara   Elad Michael Schiller
Umesh Deshpande   Sumit Mittal
Salih Ergut   Vishnu Navda
Anders Gidenstam   Adam O'Neill
Anurag Goyal   Saurav Pandit
Phuong Ha   Himadri Sekhar Paul
Ted Herman   Imran Pirwani
Ivan Howitt   Rajiv Ranjan
Shweta Jain   Raul Santelices
Linda Jiang Xie   Stefan Schmid
Avinash Joshi   Onn Schori
Seung Jun   Naresh Sharma
Anand Kashyap   Aameek Singh

Mudhakar Srivatsa
Arun Subbiah
Anand Prabhu Subramanian
Anthony Sulistio
Shamik Sural

Lakshmi Venkatraman
Srikumar Venugopal
Weigang Wu
Zhiguo Xu

Table of Contents

Keynote Talk II

Session II A: Security

Session II B: Grid and P2P Computing

A.K. Choudhury Memorial Lecture

Keynote Talk III

Session III A: Ad Hoc Networks II

Session III B: Performance Evaluation I

Keynote Talk IV

Session IV: Distributed Computing and Algorithms II

Keynote Talk V

Session V A: Internetworking Protocols and Applications

Session V B: Ad Hoc Networks III

Session VI A: Performance Evaluation II

Session VI B: Optical Networks and Multimedia

Session VII A: Sensor Networks

Session VII B: Wireless Networks

Distributed Security Algorithms by Mobile Agents

Paola Flocchini[1] and Nicola Santoro[2]

[1] University of Ottawa
flocchin@site.uottawa.ca
[2] Carleton University
santoro@scs.carleton.ca

Abstract. Mobile Agents have been extensively studied for several years by researchers in Artificial Intelligence and in Software Engineering. They offer a simple and natural way to describe distributed settings where mobility is inherent, and an explicit and direct way to describe the entities of those settings, such as mobile code, software agents, viruses, robots, web crawlers, etc. Further, they allow to express immediately notions such as selfish behaviour, negotiation, cooperation, etc arising in the new computing environments. As a programming paradigm, they allow a new philosophy of protocol and software design, bound to have an impact as strong as that caused by that of object-oriented programming. As a computational paradigm, mobile agents systems are an immediate and natural extension of the traditional message-passing settings studied in distributed computing.

In spite of all this, mobile agents systems have been largely ignored by the mainstream distributed computing community. It is only in the last few years that several researchers, some motivated by long investigated and well established problems in automata theory, computational complexity, and graph theory, have started to systematically explore this new and exciting distributed computational universe.

In this paper we describe some interesting problems and solution techniques developed in this investigations.

1 Introduction

The use of *mobile agents* is becoming increasingly popular when computing in networked environments, ranging from Internet to the Data Grid, both as a theoretical computational paradigm and as a system-supported programming platform.

In networked systems that support autonomous mobile agents, a main concern is how to develop efficient agent-based *system protocols*; that is, to design protocols that will allow a team of identical simple agents to cooperatively perform (possibly complex) system tasks. Example of basic tasks are *wakeup, traversal, rendez-vous, election*. The coordination of the agents necessary to perform these tasks is not necessarily simple or easy to achieve. In fact, the computational problems related to these operations are definitely non trivial, and a great deal of theoretical research is devoted to the study of conditions for the solvability of

S. Chaudhuri et al. (Eds.): ICDCN 2006, LNCS 4308, pp. 1–14, 2006.

these problems and to the discovery of efficient algorithmic solutions; e.g., see [1,2,4,5,6,7,17,18,20,45].

At an abstract level, these environments can be described as a collection of autonomous mobile *agents* (or *robots*) located in a graph G. The agents have computing capabilities and bounded storage, execute the same protocol, and can move from node to neighboring node. They are *asynchronous*, in the sense that every action they perform (computing, moving, etc.) takes a finite but otherwise unpredictable amount of time. Each node of the network, also called *host*, provide a storage area called *whiteboard* for incoming agents to communicate and compute, and its access is held in fair mutual exclusion. The research concern is on determining what tasks can be performed by such entities, under what conditions, and at what cost.

At a practical level, in these environments, *security* is the most pressing concern, and possibly the most difficult to address. Actually, even the most basic security issues, in spite of their practical urgency and of the amount of effort, must still be effectively addressed (for a survey, see [50]).

Among the severe security threats faced in distributed mobile computing environments, two are particularly troublesome: *harmful agent* (that is, the presence of malicious mobile processes), and *harmful host* (that is, the presence at a network site of harmful stationary processes).

The former problem is particularly acute in unregulated non-cooperative settings such as Internet (e.g., e-mail transmitted viruses). The latter not only exists in those settings, but also in environments with regulated access and where agents cooperate towards common goals (e.g., sharing of resources or distribution of a computation on the Grid. In fact, a local (hardware or software) failure might render a host harmful. In this paper we concentrate on two security problems, one for each type: *locating a black hole*, and *capturing an intruder*.

2   Black Hole Search

2.1   The Problem and the Model

The problem posed by the presence of a harmful host has been intensively studied from a programming point of view (e.g., see [41,54,56]). Obviously, the first step in any solution to such a problem must be to *identify*, if possible, the harmful host; i.e., to determine and report its location; following this phase, a "rescue" activity would conceivably be initiated to deal with the destructive process resident there. Depending on the nature of the danger, the task to identify the harmful host might be difficult, if not impossible, to perform.

Consider the presence in the network of a *black hole*: a host which *disposes* of visiting agents upon their arrival, leaving *no observable trace* of such a destruction. Note that this type of highly harmful host is not rare; for example, the undetectable crash failure of a site in a asynchronous network turns such a site into a black hole. The task is to unambiguously determine and report the location of the black hole by a team of mobile agents. One can easily see that the problem can also be formulated as an exploration problem. In fact, the black hole can be located only after the whole network has been visited, and all nodes but one are found to be safe. Clearly, in this process some agents have disappeared in the black hole). The searching agents start from the same safe site (the homebase); the task is successfully completed if, within finite time, at least one agent survives, and all surviving agents know the location of the black hole. The research concern is to determine under what conditions and at what cost mobile agents can successfully accomplish this task, called *Black-Hole Search*. The main complexity measures for this problem are: the *size* of the solution (i.e., the number of agents employed), the *cost* (i.e., the number of moves performed by the agents executing a size-optimal solution protocol). Sometimes also bounded *time* complexity is considered.

In general no assumptions are made on the time for an agent to move on a link, except that it is finite; i.e., the system is asynchronous. Moreover, agents communicate by writing and reading on whiteboards located at the nodes.

2.2   A Background Problem: Safe Exploration

The problem of exploring and mapping an unknown environment has been extensively studied in a *safe* environment, due to its various applications in different areas (navigating a robot through a terrain containing obstacles, finding a path through a maze, or searching a network).

Most of the previous work on exploration of unknown graphs has been limited to single agent exploration. Studies on exploration of *labelled* graphs typically emphasize minimizing the number of moves or the amount of memory used by the agent (e.g., see [1,17,19,51,52]). Exploration of *anonymous* graphs is possible only if the agents are allowed to mark the nodes in some way; except when the graph has no cycles (i.e. the graph is a tree [20,37]). For exploring arbitrary anonymous graphs, various methods of marking nodes have been used by different authors. Pebbles that can be dropped on nodes have been proposed first in [9] where it is shown that any strongly connected directed graph can be explored using just one pebble (if the size of the graph is known) and using $O(\log \log n)$ pebbles, otherwise. Distinct markers have been used, for example, in [29] to explore unlabeled undirected graphs. Yet another approach, used by Bender and Slonim [10] was to employ two cooperating agents, one of which would stand on a node, while the other explores new edges. Whiteboards have been used by Fraigniaud and Ilcinkas [38] for exploring directed graphs and by Fraigniaud et al. [37] for exploring trees. In [20,38,39] the authors focus on minimizing the amount of memory used by the agents for exploration (they however do not require the agents to construct a map of the graph).

There have been few results on exploration by more than one agent. A two agent exploration algorithm for directed graphs was given in [10], whereas Fraigniaud et al. [37] showed how k agents can explore a tree. In both these cases, the agents start from same node and they have distinct identities. In [7] a team of dispersed agents explores a graph and constructs a map. The graph is anonymous but the links are labeled with sense of direction; moreover the protocol works if the size n of the network or the number of agents k are co-prime and it achieves a move complexity of $O(km)$ (where m is the number of edges). Another algorithm with the same complexity has been described in [15], where the requirement of sense of direction is dropped. In this case the agents need to know either n or k, which must be coprime. The solution has been made "effective" in [16], where effective means that it will always terminate, regardless of the relationship between n and k reporting a solution whenever the solution can be computed, and reporting a failure message when the solution cannot be computed.

The map construction problem is actually equivalent to some others basic problems, like *Agent Election*, *Labelling* and *Rendezvous*. Among them rendezvous is probably the most investigated; for a recent account see [2,46].

2.3   Basic Properties for Black Hole Search

When considering the black hole search problem, some constraints follow from the asynchrony of the agents. For example [21]:

- For asynchronous agents to locate the black hole, G must be 2-node-connected.
- For asynchronous agents to locate the black hole, the number of nodes of G must be known.
- For asynchronous agents it is impossible to verify if there is a back hole.

Moreover, since one agent may immediately wander into the black hole, we have:

- At least two agents are needed to locate the black hole.

How realistic is this bound? How many agents suffice? The answers vary depending on the a priori knowledge the agents have about the network, and on the consistency of the local labelings.

2.4   Impact of Knowledge

Topological Ignorance. Consider first the situation of *topological ignorance*; that is when the agents have no a priori knowledge of the topological structure of G. Then any generic solution needs at least $\Delta + 1$ agents, where Δ is the maximal degree of G, even if the agents know Δ and the number n of nodes of G. Interestingly, in any *minimal* generic solution (i.e., using the minimum number of agents), the agents must perform $\Omega(n^2)$ moves in the worst case [23]. Both these bounds are *tight*. In fact there is a protocol that correctly locates the black hole in $O(n^2)$ moves using $\Delta + 1$ agents that know Δ and n [23]. The algorithm essentially performs a collective "cautious" exploration of the graph until all nodes but one are considered to be safe. The whiteboard on the homebase is used to store information about the nodes that have been already explored and the agents move back and forth from the homebase to continue their job. If the black hole is a node with maximum degree, there is nothing to prevent Δ agents disappearing in it.

Sense of Direction. Consider next the case of topological ignorance in systems where there is *sense of direction* (SD); informally, sense of direction is a labeling of the ports that allows the nodes to determine whether two paths starting from a node lead to the same node, using only the labels of the ports along these paths (for a survey on Sense of Direction see [34]). In this case, two agents suffice to locate the black hole, regardless of the (unknown) topological structure of G. The proof of [23] is constructive, and the algorithm has a $O(n^2)$ cost. This cost is optimal; in fact, it is shown that there are types of sense of direction that, if present, impose an $\Omega(n^2)$ worst-case cost on any generic two-agent algorithm for locating a black hole using SD. As for the topological ignorance case, the agents perform an exploration. The algorithm is similar to the one with topological ignorance (in fact it leads to the same cost); sense of direction is however very useful to decrease the number of casualties. The exploring agents can be only two: a node that is being explored by an agent is considered "dangerous" and by the properties of sense of direction, the other agent will be able to avoid it in its exploration, thus insuring that one of the two will eventually succeed.

Complete Topological Knowledge. Consider the case of *complete topological knowledge* of the network; that is, the agents have a complete knowledge of the edge-labeled graph G, the correspondence between port labels and the link labels of G, *and* the location of the source node (from where the agents start the search). This information is stronger then the more common *topological awareness* (i.e., knowledge of the class of the network, but not of its size nor of the source location – e.g. being in a mesh, starting from an unknown position).

Also in this case, two agents suffice [23]; furthermore the cost of a minimal protocol can be reduced in this case to $O(n \log n)$, and this cost is worst-case optimal. The technique here is quite different and it is based on a partitioning of the graph in two portions, which are given to the two agents to perform the exploration. One will succeed in finishing its portion and will carefully move to help the other agent finishing its own.

Topology-Sensitive Universal Protocols. Interestingly, it is possible to considerably improve the bound on the number of moves without increasing the team size. In fact, there is a recent *universal* protocol, *Explore and Bypass*, that allows a team of *two* agents with a map of the network to locate a black hole with cost $O(n + d \log d)$, where d denotes the diameter of the network [25].

This means that, without losing its universality and without violating the worst-case $\Omega(n \log n)$ lower bound, this algorithm allows two agents to locate a black hole with $\Theta(n)$ cost in a very large class of (possibly unstructured) networks: those where $d = O(n / \log n)$.

Importantly, there are many networks with $O(n/logn)$ diameter in which the previous protocols [23,24] fail to achieve the $O(n)$ bound. A simple example of such a network is the *wheel*, a ring with a central node connected to all ring nodes, where the central node is very slow: those protocols will require $O(n \log n)$ moves.

Variations with Complete Topological Knowledge. A very simple algorithm that works on any topology (a-priori known by the agents) is shown in [27]. The algorithm, based on the pre-computation of an open vertex cover by cycles of the network, uses the optimal number of agents (two); its cost (number of moves) depends on the choice of the cover and it is optimal for several classes of networks. These classes include all Abelian Cayley graphs of degree three and more (e.g., hypercubes, multi-dimensional tori, etc,), as well as many non-Abelian cube graphs (e.g., CCC, butterfly, wrapped-butterfly networks, etc.). For some of these networks, this is the only algorithm achieving such a bound.

Using Tokens. Recently the problem has been investigated also in a different, weaker model where there are no whiteboards at the nodes but each agent has an identical token that the agent can place on (or remove from) a node [26,28]. Surprisingly, the black hole search problem can be solved also in this model. Furthermore, this can be done using a minimal team size and performing a polynomial number of moves; not surprisingly, the protocol is quite complex. Also the case of the ring has been studied in details in [28].

2.5 Special Topologies

A natural question to ask is whether the bounds for arbitrary networks with full topological knowledge can be improved for networks with special topologies by topology-dependent proptocols.

Rings. The problem has been investigated and its solutions characterized for *ring* networks [21]. A $Omega(n \log n)$ lower bound holds since $\Omega(n \log n)$ moves are needed by any two-agents solution [21]. An agent and move optimal solution exists, based on a partitioning of the ring and on a non-overlapping exploration by the agent. There exists an optimal trade-off between time complexity and number of agents. In fact, increasing the number of agents the number of moves cannot decrease, but the time to finish the exploration does [21]. Notice that the lower bound for rings implies an $\Omega(n \log n)$ lower bound on the worst case cost complexity of any *universal* protocol.

   The ring has been investigated also to perform another task: *rendezvous* of k anonymous agents, in spite of the presence of a black hole. The problem is studied in [22] and a complete characterization of the conditions under which the problem can be solved is established. The characterization depends on whether k or n is unknown (at least one must be known for any non-trivial rendezvous). Interestingly, it is shown that, if k is unknown, the rendezvous algorithm also solves the black hole location problem, and it does so with a bounded time complexity of $\Theta(n)$; this is a significant improvement over the $O(n \log n)$ bounded time complexity of [21].

Interconnection Networks. The negative result for rings does not generalizes. Sometimes the network has special properties that can be exploited to obtain a lower cost network-specific protocol. For example, two agents can locate a black hole with only $O(n)$ moves in a variety of highly structured interconnection networks such as *hypercubes*, square *tori* and *meshes, wrapped butterflies, star graphs* [24]. These strategies are based on the construction of a special walk in the graph and by using this walk to explore the network.

2.6   Synchronous Networks

The Black Hole search problem has been studied also in synchronous settings, where the time for an agent to traverse a link is assumed to be unitary.

When the system is synchronous the goals and strategies are quite different from the ones reviewed in the previous sections. In fact, one of the major problem when designing an algorithm for the asynchronous case is that an agent cannot wait at a node for another agent to come back; as a consequence, agents must always move, and have to do it carefully. When the system is synchronous, on the other hand, the strategies are mostly based on waiting the right amount of time before performing a move. The algorithm becomes the determination of the shortest traversal schedule for the agents, where a traversal schedule is a sequence of actions (move to a neighbouring node or stay at the current node). Furthermore, for the black hole search to be solvable, it is no longer necessary that the network is 2-node connected; thus, the black hole search can be performed by synchronous agents also in trees.

In synchronous networks tight bounds have been established for some classes of trees [13]. In the case of general networks the problem of finding the optimal strategy is shown to be NP-hard [14,44] and approximation algorithms are given in [13] and subsequently improved in [43,44]. The case of multiple black holes have been very recently investigated in [12] where a lower bound on the cost and close upper bounds are given.

3   Intruder Capture and Network Decontamination

A particularly important security concern is to protect a network from unwanted, and possibly dangerous intrusions. At an abstract level, an intruder is an alien process that moves on the network to sites unoccupied by the system's agents "contaminating" the nodes it passes by. The concern for the severe damage intruders can cause has motivated a large amount of research, especially on detection (e.g., see [3,36,55]).

3.1   Decontamination and Related Problems

Assume the nodes of the network are initially *contaminated* and we want to deploy a team of agents to *clean* (or decontaminate) the whole network. The cleaning of a node occurs when an agent transits on the node; however, when a node is left without protection (no agents on it) it might become *re-contaminated* according to a recontamination rule. The most common recontamination rule is that as soon as a node without an agent on it has a contaminated neighbour, it will become contaminated again.

A variation of the decontamination problem described above has been extensively studied in the literature under the name of *graph search* (e.g., see [30,42,47,49,53]). The graph search problem has been studied for many classes of graphs, and determining the optimal number of searchers (called *search number*) has been proved to be NP-complete in general.

In the classical graph search problem the agents can be arbitrarily moved from a node "jumping" to any other node in the graph. The main difference in the setting described in this survey is that the agents, which are pieces of software, *cannot be removed from the network*; they can only move from a node to a *neighboring* one. This additional constraint has been introduced and first studied in [5] resulting in a *contiguous, monotone, node search* or *intruder capture* problem. With the contiguous assumption the nature of the problem changes considerably and the classical results on node and edge search do not generally apply. The problem of finding the optimal number of agents is still NP-complete for arbitrary graphs. As we will survey below, the problem has been studied mostly in specific topologies. Also the arbitrary topology has been considered; in this case, some heuristics have been proposed [35] and a move-exponential optimal solution has been given in [11]. Investigations on the relationship between the contiguous model and the classical one for graph search (where the agents can "jump") has been studied, for example, in [8,40].

In this survey we use the term *decontamination* to refer to contiguous monotone node search as defined in [8].

3.2   The Models for Decontamination

Initially, all agents are located at the same node, the *homebase*, and all the other nodes are contaminated; a decontamination strategy consists of a sequence of movements of the agents along the edges of the network. The agents can communicate when they reside on the same node.

Starting from the classical model employed in [5] (called *Local Model*), additional assumptions have sometimes been added to study the impact that more powerful agents' or system's capabilities have on the solutions of our problem.

1) In the *Local Model* an agent located at a node can "see" only local information, like the state of the node, the labels of the incident links, the other agents present at the node.
2) *Visibility* is the capability of the agent to "see" the state of its neighbors; i.e., an agent can see whether a neighboring node is guarded, whether it is clean, or contaminated. Notice that, in some mobile agent systems, the visibility power could be easily achieved by "probing" the state of neighboring nodes before making a decision.
3) *Cloning* is the capability, for an agent, to clone copies of itself.
4) *Synchronicity* implies that local computations are instantaneous, and it takes one unit of time (one step) for an agent to move from a node to a neighboring one.

The efficiency of a strategy is usually measured in terms of number of agents, number of moves performed by the agents, and ideal time.

We say that a cleaning strategy is *monotone* if once a node is clean, it will never be contaminated again. All the results reported here apply for monotone strategies.

3.3   Results in Specific Topologies

Trees. The tree has been the first topology to be investigated in the Local Model [5]. In the paper, the authors show a linear distributed algorithm to determine the minimum number of agents necessary to decontaminate an arbitrary given tree and describe a decontamination strategy. The determination of the optimal number of agents is done through a saturation where appropriate information about the structure of the tree are collected from the leaves and propagated along the tree, until the optimal is known for each possible starting point. In the worst case (complete binary tree) the number of agent is $O(\log n)$, where n is the number of nodes in the tree.

Hypercubes. It has been shown in [32] that to decontaminate a hypercube of size n, $\Theta(\frac{n}{\sqrt{\log n}})$ agents are necessary and sufficient. The employ of an optimal number of agents in the Local Model has an interesting consequence; in fact, it implies that $\Theta(\frac{n}{\sqrt{\log n}})$ is the search number for the hypercube in the classical model, i.e., where agents may "jump".

In the algorithm for the Local Model one of the agents acts as a *coordinator* for the entire cleaning process. The cleaning strategy is carried out on the broadcast tree of the hypercube. The main idea is to place enough agents on the homebase and to have them move, level by level, on the edges of the broadcast tree, leaded by the coordinator in such a way that no recontamination may occur. The number of moves and the ideal time complexity of this strategy are indicated in Table 1.

The visibility assumption allows the agents to make their own decision regarding the action to take solely on the basis of their local knowledge. In fact, the agents are still moving on the broadcast tree, but they do not have to follow the order imposed by the coordinator. The agents on node x can proceed to clean the children of x in the broadcast tree when they "see" that the other neighbors of x are either clean or guarded. With this strategy the time complexity is drastically reduced (since agents move concurrently and independently), but the number of agents increases. Other variations of those two models have been studied and summarized in Table 1.

A characterization of the impact that these additional assumptions have on the problem is still open. For example: an optimal move complexity in the Local Model with Cloning has not been found, and it is not clear whether it exists; when the agents have Visibility, synchronicity has not been of any help although it has not been proved that it is indeed useless; the use of an optimal number of

Table 1. Decontamination of the Hypercube. The star indicates an optimal bound.

		Agents	Time	Moves
Local	Local	$(\star)\ O(\frac{n}{\sqrt{\log n}})$	$O(n \log n)$	$O(n \log n)$
	Local, Cloning, Synchronicity	$n/2$	$(\star)\ \log n$	$(\star)\ n-1$
Visibility	Visibility	$n/2$	$(\star)\ \log n$	$O(n \log n)$
	Visibility and Cloning	$n/2$	$(\star)\ \log n$	$(\star)\ n-1$

agents in the weaker Local Model is obtained at the expenses of employing more agents and it is not clear whether this increment is necessary.

Chordal Rings. The Local and the Visibility Models have been subject of investigation also in the Chordal Ring topology in [33].

Let $C(\langle d_1 = 1, d_2, ..., d_k\rangle)$ be a chordal ring network with n nodes and link structure $\langle d_1 = 1, d_2, ..., d_k\rangle$, where $d_i < d_{i+1}$ and $d_k \leq \lfloor\frac{n}{2}\rfloor$. In [33] it is first shown that the smallest number of agents needed for the decontamination does not depend on the size of the chordal ring, but solely on the *length* of the longest chord. In fact, any solution of the contiguous decontamination problem in a chordal ring $C(\langle d_1 = 1, d_2, ..., d_k\rangle)$ with $4 \leq d_k \leq \sqrt{n}$, requires at least $2 \cdot d_k$ searchers ($2 \cdot d_k + 1$ in the Visibility Model).

In both models, the cleaning is preceded by a deployment stage after which the agents have to occupy $2d_k$ consecutive nodes. After the deployment, the decontamination stage can start. Also in the case of the chordal ring, the visibility assumption allows the agents to make their own decision solely on the basis of their local knowledge: an agent move to clean a neighbour only when this is the only contaminated neighbour. The complexity results in the two Models are summarized in Table 2.

Table 2. Results for the Chordal Ring. The $(\star)$ indicates an optimal bound.

Chordal Ring	Agents	Time	Moves
Local	$2d_k + 1\ (\star)$	$3n - 4d_k - 1$	$4n - 6d_k - 1$
Visibility	$2d_k\ (\star)$	$\frac{n-2d_k}{2(d_k-d_{k-1})}$	$n - 2d_k\ (\star)$

Consistently to the observations for the Hypercube, also in the case of the chordal ring the visibility assumption allows to drastically decrease the time complexity (and in this case also the move complexity). In particular, the strategies for the visibility model are optimal both in terms of number of agents and in terms of number of moves; as for the time complexity, visibility allows some concurrency (although it does not bring this measure to optimal as was the case for the hypercube).

Tori. A lower bound for the torus has beed derived in [33]. Any solution of the decontamination problem in a torus $T(h, k)$ with $h, k \geq 4$ requires at least

$2 \cdot min\{h, k\}$ agents; in the *Local model* it requires at least $2 \cdot min\{h, k\} + 1$ agents. The strategy that matches the lower bound is very simple. The idea is to deploy the agents to cover two consecutive columns and then keep one column of agents to guard from decontamination and have the other column move along the torus. The complexity results are summarized in Table 3. As for the other topologies, Visibility decreases time and slightly increases the number of agents. In the case of the torus it is interesting to notice that in the Visibility model all three complexity measures are optimal.

Table 3. Results for the 2-dimensional Torus with dimensions h, k, $h \leq k$

Torus	**Agents**	**Time**	**Moves**
Local	$2h + 1$ $(\star)$	$hk - 2h$	$2hk - 4h - 1$
Visibility	$2h$ $(\star)$	$\lceil \frac{k-2}{2} \rceil$ $(\star)$	$hk - 2h$ $(\star)$

Finally, these simple decontamination strategies can be generalized to d-dimensional tori (although the lower bounds have not been generalized). Let $T(h_1, \ldots, h_d)$ be a d-dimensional torus and let $h_1 \leq h_2 \leq \ldots \leq h_d$. Let N be the number of nodes in the torus and let $H = \frac{N}{h_d}$. The resulting complexities are reported below.

Table 4. Results for a d-dimensional Torus $T(h_1, h_2, \ldots, h_d)$

d-dim Torus	**Agents**	**Time**	**Moves**
Local	$2\frac{N}{h_d} + 1$	$N - 2\frac{N}{h_d}$	$2N - 4\frac{N}{h_d} - 1$
Visibility	$2\frac{N}{h_d}$	$(\lceil h_d - 2 \rceil)/2$	$N - 2\frac{N}{h_d}$

3.4 Different Contamination Rules

In [48] the network decontamination problem has been considered under a new model of *immunity* to recontamination: a clean node, after the cleaning agent has gone, becomes recontaminated only if a weak majority of its neighbours are infected. This recontamination rule is called *local immunization*. The paper studies the effects of this level of immunity on the nature of the problem in tori and trees. More precisely, it establishes lower-bounds on the number of agents necessary for decontamination, and on the number of moves performed by an optimal-size team of cleaners, and it proposes cleaning strategies. The bounds are tight for trees and for synchronous tori; they are within a constant factor of each other in the case of asynchronous tori. It is shown that with local immunization only $O(1)$ agents are needed to decontaminate meshes and tori, regardless of their size; this must be contrasted with e.g. the $2\min\{n, m\}$ agents required to decontaminate a $n \times m$ torus without local immunization [33]. Interestingly, among tree networks, binary trees were the worst to decontaminate without local immunization, requiring $\Omega(\log n)$ agents in the worst case [5]. Instead, with local immunization, they can be decontaminated by a *single* agent.

References

1. S. Albers, M. Henzinger. "Exploring unknown environments". *Proc. 29th Annu. ACM Sympos. Theory Comput.*, 416–425, 1997.
2. S. Alpern, S. Gal. *The Theory of Search Games and Rendezvous.* Kluwer, 2003.
3. M. Asaka, S. Okazawa, A. Taguchi, S. Goto. "A method of tracing intruders by use of mobile agent". *INET*, www.isoc.org, 1999.
4. B. Awerbuch, M. Betke, M. Singh. Piecemeal graph learning by a mobile robot. *Information and Computation* 152, 155–172, 1999.
5. L. Barrière, P. Flocchini, P. Fraigniaud, N. Santoro. "Capture of an intruder by mobile agents". *Proc. 14th ACM-SIAM Symp. on Parallel Algorithms and Architectures (SPAA)*, 200-209, 2002.
6. L. Barrière, P. Flocchini, P. Fraigniaud, N. Santoro. "Can we elect if we cannot compare?" In *Proc. 15th ACM Symp. on Parallel Algorithms and Architectures (SPAA)*, 200–209, 2003.
7. L. Barriere, P. Flocchini, P. Fraigniaud, N. Santoro. "Election and rendezvous in fully anonymous systems with sense of direction". In *Theory of Computer System*, to appear.
8. L. Barrière, P. Fraigniaud, N. Santoro, D.M. Thilikos. "Searching is not jumping". *Proc. 29th Int. Workshop on Graph Theoretic Concepts in Computer Science (WG)*, LNCS 2880, 34-45, 2003.
9. M. Bender, A. Fernandez, D. Ron, A. Sahai, S. Vadhan. "The power of a pebble: Exploring and mapping directed graphs". In *Proc. 30th ACM Symp. on Theory of Computing (STOC)*, 269–287, 1998.
10. M. Bender, D. K. Slonim. "The power of team exploration: two robots can learn unlabeled directed graphs". In *Proc. 35th Symp. on Foundations of Computer Science (FOCS)*, 75–85, 1994.
11. L. Blin, P. Fraigniaud, N. Nisse, S. Vial. " Distributed chasing of network intruders by mobile agents". *Proc. of the 13th Int. Coll. on Structural Information and Communication Complexity (SIROCCO)*, 70–84, 2006.
12. C. Cooper, R. Klasing, T. Radzik "Searching for black-hole faults in a network using multiple agents". *Proc. 10th Int. Conf. on Principle of Distributed Systems (OPODIS)*, 2006.
13. J. Czyzowicz, D. Kowalski, E. Markou, A. Pelc. "Searching for a black hole in tree networks". *Proc. 8th Int. Conf. on Principle of Distributed Systems* (OPODIS), 35-45, 2004.
14. J. Czyzowicz, D. Kowalski, E. Markou, A. Pelc. "Complexity of searching for a black hole". *Fundamenta Informaticae*, 71(2-3), 229-242, 2006. 35-45, 2004.
15. S. Das, P. Flocchini, A. Nayak, N. Santoro. "Exploration and labelling of an unknown graph by multiple agents" *Proc. 12th Int. Coll. on Structural Information and Communication Complexity, (SIROCCO)*, 99-114, 2005.
16. S. Das, P. Flocchini, A. Nayak, N. Santoro. "Effective elections for anonymous mobile agents". *Proc. 17th Int. Symp. on Algorithms and Computation (ISAAC)*, 2006.
17. X. Deng, C. H. Papadimitriou, "Exploring an unknown graph". *J. of Graph Theory* 32(3), 265–297, 1999.
18. A. Dessmark, P. Fraigniaud, A. Pelc. "Deterministic rendezvous in graphs". In *Proc. 11th European Symp. on Algorithms (ESA)*, 184–195, 2003.
19. A. Dessmark, A. Pelc. "Optimal graph exploration without good maps". In *Proc. 10th European Symp. on Algorithms (ESA)*, 374–386, 2002.

20. K. Diks, P. Fraigniaud, E. Kranakis, A. Pelc. "Tree exploration with little memory". *Journal of Algorithms*, 51:38–63, 2004.
21. S. Dobrev, P. Flocchini, G. Prencipe, N. Santoro". "Mobile search for a black hole in an anonymous ring". *Algorithmica*, to appear.
22. S. Dobrev, P. Flocchini, G. Prencipe, N. Santoro. "Multiple agents rendezvous in a ring in spite of a black hole". *Proc. 6th Int. Symp. on Principles of Distributed Systems* (OPODIS) 34-46, 2003.
23. S. Dobrev, P. Flocchini, G. Prencipe, N. Santoro. "Searching for a black hole in arbitrary networks: optimal mobile agents protocols". *Distributed Computing*, to appear.
24. S. Dobrev, P. Flocchini, R. Kralovic, G. Prencipe, P. Ruzicka, N. Santoro. "Optimal search for a black hole in common interconnection networks". *Networks*, 47 (2), p. 61-71, 2006.
25. S. Dobrev, P. Flocchini, N. Santoro. "Improved bounds for optimal black hole search in a network with a map. *Proc. 10th Int. Coll. on Structural Information and Communication Complexity* (SIROCCO), 111-122, 2004.
26. S. Dobrev, P. Flocchini, R. Kralovic, N. Santoro. "Exploring a dangerous unknown graph using tokens". *Proc. 5th IFIP Int. Conf. on Theoretical Computer Science* (TCS), 131-150, 2006.
27. S. Dobrev, P. Flocchini, N. Santoro. "Cycling Through a Dangerous Network: A Simple Efficient Strategy for Black Hole Search". *Int. Conf. on Distributed computing Systems* (ICDCS), 2006.
28. S. Dobrev, R. Kralovic, N. Santoro, W. Shi. "Black Hole Search in Asynchronous Rings Using Tokens". *Proc. 6th Conf. on Algorithms and Complexity* (CIAC), 139-150, 2006.
29. G. Dudek, M. Jenkin, E. Milios, D. Wilkes. "Robotic exploration as graph construction". *Transactions on Robotics and Automation*, 7(6):859–865, 1991.
30. J. Ellis, H. Sudborough, J. Turner. "The vertex separation and search number of a graph". *Information and Computation*, 113(1):50–79, 1994.
31. P. Flocchini, E. Kranakis, D. Krizanc, N. Santoro, C. Sawchuk. "Multiple mobile agent rendezvous in a ring". *Proc. 6th Latin American Theoretical Informatics Symp.* (LATIN), 599–608, 2004.
32. P. Flocchini, M.J. Huang, F.L. Luccio. "Contiguous search in the hypercube for capturing an intruder" *Proc. 18th IEEE Int. Parallel and Distributed Processing Symp.* (IPDPS), 2005.
33. P. Flocchini, M.J. Huang, F.L. Luccio. "Decontamination of chordal rings and tori". *Proc. 8th Workshop on Advances in Parallel and Distributed Computational Models (APDCM)*, 2006.
34. P. Flocchini, B. Mans, N. Santoro. "Sense of direction in distributed computing". *Theoretical Computer Science*, vol. 291, 29-53, 2003.
35. P. Flocchini, A. Nayak, A. Shulz. " Cleaning an arbitrary regular network with mobile agents" *Proc. of the 2nd Int. Conf. on Distributed Computing & Internet Technology (ICDCIT)*, 132-142, 2005.
36. N. Foukia,J. G. Hulaas, J. Harms. "Intrusion Detection with Mobile Agents". *INET*, www.isoc.org, 2001.
37. P. Fraigniaud, L. Gasieniec, D. Kowalski, A. Pelc. "Collective tree exploration". *Networks*, to appear.
38. P. Fraigniaud, D. Ilcinkas, "Digraph exploration with little memory". *Proc. 21st Symp. on Theoretical Aspects of Computer Science* (STACS), 246–257, 2004.
39. P. Fraigniaud, D. Ilcinkas, G. Peer, A. Pelc, D. Peleg. "Graph exploration by a finite automaton". *Theoretical Computer Science*, to appear.

40. P. Fraigniaud, N. Nisse. "Monotony Properties of Connected Visible Graph Searching". *Proc. 32nd Int. Workshop on Graph-Theoretic Concepts in Computer Science* (WG)22-24, 2006.
41. F. Hohl. "Time limited blackbox security: Protecting mobile agents from malicious hosts". In *Proc. of Conf on Mobile Agent Security*, LNCS 1419, pages 92–113, 1998.
42. L. Kirousis, C. Papadimitriou. "Searching and pebbling". *Theoretical Computer Science*, 47(2):205–218, 1986.
43. R. Klasing, E. Markou, T. Radzik, F. Sarracco. "Approximation bounds for black hole search problems". *Proc. 9th Int. Conf. on Principle of Distributed Systems* (OPODIS), 2005.
44. R. Klasing, E. Markou, T. Radzik, F. Sarracco. "Hardness and approximation results for black hole search in arbitrary graphs". *Proc. 12th Int. Coll. on Structural Information and Communication Complexity* (SIROCCO), 200-215, 2005.
45. E. Kranakis, D. Krizanc, N. Santoro, C. Sawchuk. "Mobile agent rendezvous in a ring". In *Int. Conf. on Distibuted Computing Systems (ICDCS)*, 592–599, 2003.
46. E. Kranakis, D. Krizanc, S. Rajsbaum. "Mobile agent rendezvous". *Proc. 13th Int. Coll. on Structural Information and Communication Complexity* (SIROCCO), 1–9, 2006.
47. A. Lapaugh. "Recontamination does not help to search a graph". *Journal of the ACM* 40(2), 224–245, 1993.
48. F. Luccio, L. Pagli, N. Santoro. "Network decontamination with local immunization". *Proc. 8th Workshop on Advances in Parallel and Distributed Computational Models (APDCM)*, 2006.
49. N. Megiddo, S. Hakimi, M. Garey, D. Johnson, C. Papadimitriou. "The complexity of searching a graph". *Journal of the ACM* 35(1), 18–44, 1988.
50. R. Oppliger. "Security issues related to mobile code and agent-based systems". *Computer Communications*, 22(12):1165 – 1170, 1999.
51. P. Panaite, A. Pelc, "Exploring unknown undirected graphs". *Journal of Algorithms*, 33 281-295, 1999.
52. P. Panaite, A. Pelc. "Impact of topographic information on graph exploration efficiency". *Networks*, 36, 96–103, 2000.
53. T. Parson. "The search number of a connected graph". In the 9th *Southeastern Conf. on Combinatorics, Graph Theory and Computing*, Utilitas Mathematica, 549–554, 1978.
54. T. Sander, C. F. Tschudin. "Protecting mobile agents against malicious hosts". In *Proc. of Conf on Mobile Agent Security*, LNCS 1419, pages 44–60, 1998.
55. E. H. Spafford, D. Zamboni. "Intrusion detection using autonomous agents". *Computer Networks*, 34(4):547–570, 2000.
56. J. Vitek, G. Castagna. "Mobile computations and hostile hosts". In D. Tsichritzis, editor, *Mobile Objects*, pages 241–261. University of Geneva, 1999.

A Real-Time Guarantee Scheme Based on the Runtime Message Scheduling and Error Control for the Dual Wireless Ad Hoc Sensor Network[*]

Mikyung Kang[1], Abhijit Saha[1], Junghoon Lee[1],
Gyung-Leen Park[1], and Hanil Kim[2,**]

[1] Dept. of Computer Science and Statistics, [2] Dept. of Computer Education,
Cheju National University,
690-756, Ara 1 Dong, Jeju City, Jeju Do, Republic of Korea
{mkkang, abhijit298, jhlee, glpark, hikim}@cheju.ac.kr

Abstract. This paper proposes and analyzes a real-time guarantee scheme for time-sensitive messages on ad hoc sensor network built on top of dual channels, each of which exploits a time-slotted channel access mechanism synchronized across the dual channels. Each message is evenly partitioned to produce two identical message sets for the coordinator to determine the polling schedule according to the EDF policy. The slot rearrangement step maximizes the number of switchable pairs so that the scheduled polls can be switched dynamically between the channels in response to the current channel status. By the runtime slot exchange procedure that reclaims slots reserved but not used due to channel error, the deadline meet ratio can be further improved. Simulation results show that the proposed scheme improves the real-time performance by up to 12.5 % compared with global EDF or NCASP.

1 Introduction

The IEEE 802.11 MAC (Medium Access Control), a contention based medium access protocol, has been successfully deployed in WLAN (Wireless Local Area Network) and has also been implemented in many wireless testbeds and simulation packages for wireless multi-hop networks[1]. As both speed and capacity of wireless media increase, so does the demand for supporting time-sensitive high-bandwidth applications and peer-to-peer applications such as VoIP, mobile video conferencing, and so on. Particularly, wireless ad hoc sensor networks are mainly applied to emergency, disaster recovery, rescue, exploration, and military action. However, it is widely recognized that the MAC in multihop ad hoc sensor networks is not only inefficient but also suffers from the quality degradation as well as the connection instability originated from the ad hoc mobility.

A wireless ad hoc network is a self-configuring network of mobile routers and associated hosts connected by wireless links, forming an arbitrary topology. The

---

[*] This research was supported by the MIC, Korea, under the ITRC support program supervised by the IITA (IITA-2005-C1090-0502-0009).
[**] Corresponding author.

S. Chaudhuri et al. (Eds.): ICDCN 2006, LNCS 4308, pp. 15–26, 2006.

routers are free to move randomly and organize themselves in an unfixed pattern. Thus, the network's wireless topology may change rapidly and unpredictably. Such a network may operate in a stand-alone mode, or may be connected to the larger backbone network such as Internet. Minimal configuration and quick deployment make ad hoc networks suitable for emergency situations. Each sensor station has wireless communication capability and some level of intelligence for signal processing and networking of the data.

The time-sensitive message has a hard real-time constraint that it should be transmitted within a bounded delay as long as there is no network error. Otherwise, the data are considered to be lost, and the loss of a hard real-time message may jeopardize the correctness of execution result or system itself. Accordingly, a real-time message stream needs the guarantee from the underlying network that its time constraints are always met in advance of the system operation or connection setup. However, just the guarantee scheme is not sufficient to satisfy such time constraints as the wireless ad hoc network is subject to unpredictable location-dependent and bursty errors, which make a real-time traffic application fail to send or receive some of its real-time packets[2].

In spite of such error characteristics, the wireless network has an advantage that it can be easily duplicated, or a cell is able to operate dual channels. The dual channel networks have doubled network bandwidth, so intuitively such a network should be able to accommodate twice as much real-time traffic as a single network. However, real-time scheduling for dual or multiple resource system is known to be an NP-hard problem[3], while the uniprocessor system has optimal scheduling solutions such as RM (Rate Monotonic) for static scheduling as well as EDF (Earliest Deadline First) for dynamic scheduling. Applying RM or EDF method to multiple resource system is not optimal in scheduling preemptable jobs due to its work conserving nature[4]. However, the network transmission has no data dependency between each message, so the optimality of EDF scheme can be preserved also for the dual networks if we view the given message set as two independent (identical) message sets.

Moreover, the dual channels can cope with network errors without violating the time constraints of messages, if the transmission order is rearranged to alleviate the situation that the same stream is scheduled on the time slots cobegining at both channels. If the simultaneous slots are allocated to different stations, the allocation can be switched between the channels when the coordinator cannot reach the station via the originally scheduled channel. With these assertions, we are to propose and analyze the performance of a bandwidth allocation scheme for real-time sensor messages on the dual channel wireless networks, aiming at sustaining the optimality of EDF scheduling scheme as well as maximizing the capability of coping with wireless channel errors. In this paper, the ad-hoc mode IEEE 802.11 WLAN is assumed to be the target communication architecture[1].

The rest of this paper is organized as follows: Section 2 introduces the related works. With the description on the dual wireless ad hoc network in Section 3,

Section 4 describes the proposed real-time message scheduling scheme in detail. After exhibiting the performance measurement result in Section 5, Section 6 concludes this paper with a brief summarization and the description of future works.

2 Related Works

Several MAC protocols have been proposed to provide bounded delays for real-time messages along with non-real-time data over a wireless channel. Most protocols that do not conform to the IEEE standard, are typically based on a frame-structured access which completely removes the contention part. For example, Choi and Shin suggested a unified protocol for real-time and non-real-time communications in wireless networks[5]. In their scheme, a BS (Base Station) polls a real-time mobile station according to the non-preemptable EDF policy. The BS also polls the non-real-time message according to the modified round-robin scheme regardless of a standard CSMA/CA (Carrier Sense Multiple Access with Collision Avoidance) protocol to eliminate message collision. M. Caccamo and et. al proposed a MAC that supports deterministic real-time scheduling via the implementation of TDMA (Time Division Multiple Access), where the time axis is divided into fixed size slots to apply the EDF discipline to wireless local area network[6]. Referred as *implicit contention*, it makes every station simultaneously run the common real-time scheduling algorithm to determine which message can access the medium.

Most works that conform to the IEEE standard are aiming at enhancing the ratio of timely delivery for soft multimedia applications, rather than providing a hard real-time guarantee. For example, DBASE (Distributed Bandwidth Allocation/Sharing/Extension) is a protocol to support both synchronous and multimedia traffics over IEEE 802.11 *ad hoc* WLAN[7]. The basic concept is that each time real-time station transmits its packet it will also declare and reserve the needed bandwidth at the next collision-free period. Every station collects this information and then calculates its actual bandwidth at the next cycle. This scheme can be applied to WLAN standard, but it is not essentially designed for hard real-time message streams. Also, EDCF (Enhanced Distributed Contention Function) provided no guarantee of service, but it establishes a probabilistic priority mechanism to allocate bandwidth based on traffic categories, while HCF (Hybrid Coordination Function) replaced centralized polling based access mechanism that a hybrid controller polls stations during a contention-free period[8].

The dual network architecture is analogous to the dual processor system, as both network and processor can be considered as an active resource. According to the IEEE 802.11 standards, at any instance a maximum of three channels can be used simultaneously as the channels overlap each other[9][10]. In this system, each node can be equipped with two or more (transmitter, receiver) pairs, giving the flexibility to transmit and receive simultaneously on both channels. Traditionally, there have been two approaches for scheduling periodic tasks in dual or multiprocessors, namely, *partitioning* and *global scheduling*[3].

The partitioning scheme assigns each stream to a single network, on which messages are scheduled independently. The main advantage of partitioning approaches is that they reduce a multiprocessor scheduling problem to a set of uniprocessor ones. However, finding an optimal assignment to networks is a bin-packing problem, which is NP-hard in the strong sense. In addition, Lee et al. have proposed a bandwidth allocation scheme for real-time traffic on dual channel WLANs. This scheme decides the polling vector based on the weighted round robin policy for contention-free period[11]. Accordingly, their scheme can not only efficiently overcome the deferred beacon that declines the schedulability in WLAN, but also reduce the worst case waiting time. However, it did not consider how to overcome the channel error at all.

In global scheduling, all eligible tasks are stored in a single priority-ordered queue while the global scheduler selects for execution of the highest priority task from this queue. For example, CASP (Contiguous Algorithm for Single Priority) maintains an allocation vector A, where A_i represents the partial sum of slots currently allocated to channel i[12]. For a given request, the scheduling algorithm allocates the request contiguously on the channel which has the least partial sum of allocation. Additionally, NCASP (Non-continuous Algorithm for Single Priority) defines an overflow amount Φ, and if an assignment makes A_i exceed Φ, it is split and then the overflown part is assigned to another resource. However, how to decide Φ brings another complex case-sensitive problem.

3   Dual Wireless Ad Hoc Network

3.1   IEEE 802.11 WLAN

The WLAN operates on both CP (Contention Period) and CFP (Contention Free Period) phases alternatively in BSS (Basic Service Set) as shown in Fig. 1. Each CFP and CP are mapped to PCF (Point Coordination Function) and DCF (Distributed Coordination Function), respectively[1]. PC (Point Coordinator) node, typically AP (Access Point), sequentially polls each station one by one during CFP. Even in the *ad hoc* mode, it is possible to designate a specific node to play a role of PC in a target group. The PC attempts to initiate CFP by broadcasting a *Beacon* at regular intervals derived from a network parameter of *CFPRate*. Only the polled node is given the right to transmit its message for a predefined time interval, and it always responds to a poll immediately whether it has a pending message or not.

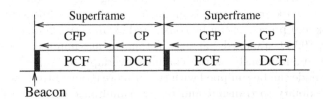

Fig. 1. Time axis of wireless LAN

3.2 Ad Hoc Network

IEEE 802.11 MAC specification allows for two modes of operation: ad hoc and infrastructure modes[1]. In ad hoc mode, two or more stations recognize each other through beacons and establish a peer-to-peer communication without any existing infrastructure. In smart-rooms and hot-spot networks where wireless access-enabled stations are located close in a small area enough to form a direct connection without preplanning, ad hoc mode is known to have many advantages including the low management cost[13]. Oppositely, in infrastructure mode there is a fixed entity called an AP that bridges all data between the mobile stations associated to it. Applying the DCF to ad hoc network leads to uncertainties to each node's access to the medium. Unfortunately, these uncertainties sum up over multiple hops, hence throughput and end-to-end delay can suffer from large variations, impacting against time-sensitive real-time applications. As a result, to support a certain level of QoS, some kind of coordination function is indispensable.

To support the multihop and mobile characteristics of wireless ad hoc networks, the rapid deployment of network and dynamic reconstruction after topology changes are efficiently implemented by cluster management. There are several algorithms used to divide the network into clusters. The most widely used clustering algorithms are LIDCA (Lowest IDentifier Clustering Algorithm) and HCCA (Highest Connectivity Clustering Algorithm) [14]. Nodes in the network have a unique identifier. LIDCA organizes the network based on this identifier, giving the role of a cluster-head to the node with the lowest ID in a neighborhood. The operation of HCCA is similar to LIDCA, but it divides the network according to the connectivity of each node, thus selects the nodes with highest connectivity - those with most neighbors - as cluster-heads. In both algorithms, every cluster is identified using the ID of its cluster-head. Upon deployment, nodes transmit their position in a single TDMA frame, with enough power to reach all the other nodes. In the ad hoc mode, this cluster-head node can designate to play a role of PC to schedule the transmission.

3.3 Network and Message Model

In ad hoc network, each cell or cluster is assumed to consist of a PC and multiple sensor stations, and each of them is capable of transmitting and receiving at the same time using two transceivers while the adjacent channels are separated by guard bands. Every station shares medium on the common frequency band and accesses according to the predefined MAC protocol. Each flow is ether an uplink or downlink, while PC coordinates the overall network operations. This paper exploits the contention-free TDMA style access policy as in [2,3,5], for the real-time guarantee, as the contention resolution via packet collisions consumes the precious communication energy.

As the real-time guarantee cannot be provided without developing a deterministic access schedule, the network time is divided into a series of equally sized slots to eliminate the unpredictability stemmed from access contention.

Accordingly, the allocation scheme assigns each slot to real-time streams so as to meet their time constraints. The slot equals the basic unit of wireless data transmission and the other non-real-time traffic is also segmented to fit the slot size. Therefore, a preemption occurs only at the slot boundary. The time slots of both networks are synchronized, that is, every time a slot on one network begins, the other network also starts its slot. This network access can be implemented by making PC poll each station according to the predefined schedule during the CFP.

The traffic of sensory data is typically *isochronous* (or synchronous), consisting of message streams that are generated by their sources on a continuing basis and delivered to their respective destinations also on a continuing basis[4]. This paper follows the general real-time message model which has n streams, namely, S_1, S_2, ..., S_n, and each S_i generates a message less than C_i at each beginning of its period P_i. Each packet must be delivered to its destination within D_i time unit from its generation or arrival at the source, otherwise, the packet is considered to be lost. Generally, D_i coincides with P_i to make the transmission complete before the generation of the next message. As is the case of other works, we begin with an assumption that each station has only one stream, and this assumption can be generalized with virtual station concept[4].

3.4   Error Model

The 802.11 radio channel is modeled as a Gilbert channel[13]. We can denote the transition probability from state *good* to state *bad* by p and the probability from state *bad* to state *good* by q, as shown in Fig. 2. The pair of p and q representing a range of channel conditions, has been obtained by using the trace-based channel estimation. The average error probability and the average length of a burst of errors are derived as $\frac{p}{p+q}$ and $\frac{1}{q}$, respectively. A packet is received correctly if the channel remains in state *good* for the whole duration of packet transmission. Otherwise, it is received in error. Channels between the PC and respective stations are independent of one another in their error characteristics, and both channels between the PC and a station have no relationship as they use different radio frequency. For all transmissions, senders expect acknowledgment for each transmitted frame and are responsible for retrying the transmission. After all, error detection and recovery is up to the sender station, as positive acknowledgments are the only indication of success.

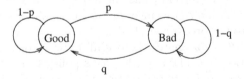

Fig. 2. Error model

4   Message Scheduling

4.1   Bandwidth Allocation Procedure

As the most prominent dynamic priority scheduling mechanism for the uniprocessor real-time system, EDF algorithm assigns priorities to individual jobs in the tasks according to their absolute deadlines. The schedulability of message streams can be tested by the following sufficient condition[6]:

$$\forall_i,\ 1 \le i \le n,\quad \sum_{k=1}^{i} \frac{C_k}{P_k} + \delta \le 1.0, \tag{1}$$

which assumes that all the messages are sorted by increasing relative deadlines and that there are n streams, while P_i and C_i denote the period and maximum transmission time of stream S_i, respectively. The δ denotes the overhead term originated from the network management such as polling/probing overhead, beacon packet broadcast, interframe space, and so on.

Since the invocation behavior of a set of periodic tasks repeats itself once every T time units, where T, called the *planning cycle* of the task set, is the least common multiple of the periods of all periodic tasks, we only need to consider all the task invocation in a planning cycle. Let $< f_i^1, f_i^2 >$ be the i-th slot assignments of channel 1 and channel 2. If f_i^1 and f_i^2 are allocated to different streams, say A and B, respectively, their transmission channels can be switched without violating their time constraints. We define a *switchable pair* if f_i^1 and f_i^2 are allocated to different streams. The $< f_i^1, f_i^2 >$ is also a switchable pair if any one of f_i^1 and f_i^2 is left unassigned. The purpose of bandwidth allocation, or slot assignment is to maximize the number of switchable pairs, as it can overcome channel errors.

To inherit the optimality of EDF in a single resource system, the allocation scheme first partitions the given stream set into two identical sets so that each of them has the same period set but the transmission time of every stream is reduced by half. Namely,

$$\Theta : \{(P_i, C_i)\} \rightarrow \Theta_1 : \{(P_i, \frac{C_i}{2})\}, \Theta_2 : \{(P_i, \frac{C_i}{2})\} \tag{2}$$

Next, the schedule for Θ_1 and Θ_2 is determined by EDF policy, both schedules being identical. And then, the allocation in Θ_2 is rearranged to maximize the number of switchable pairs. When the allocation scheme generates the schedule of Θ_2, it also creates the list of range to which an allocation can be migrated. The earliest time of movement, E_t, is the arrival time of message that occupies slot t, while the amount of backward movement is marked as its laxity, L_t. The E_t and L_t of unassigned slot are set to 0 and $T - (t+1)$, respectively, as it can be relocated anywhere within the planning cycle. From the last slot, f_t^1 and f_t^2 are checked whether they are equal, namely, they are allocated to the same station. If so, the rearrangement procedure attempts to change f_t^2 as follows:

> for slot i from E_t to t
>   if ($f_i^2 == f_t^2$) continue; // same station
>   if ($L_i + i < t$) continue; // cannot be deferred
>   else exchange f_i^2 and f_t^2 and break;

[**Example 1**]. This example shows the bandwidth allocation for the given stream set. The stream set consists of 3 streams, A(6,2), B(3,2), and C(4,4). Their utilization is 2.0, the length of planning cycle being 12. The schedule for both networks is identical as they follow the same EDF scheduling policy after partitioning the stream set into $\Theta_1 : \{(6,1), (3,1), (4,2)\}$ and $\Theta_2 : \{(6,1), (3,1), (4,2)\}$ as shown in Fig. 3(a). The figure also shows that the earliest relocatable slot and slack time by which the allocation can be deferred. The rearrangement procedure begins from slot 11 backward to slot 0. As shown in Fig. 3(a), f_{11}^1 and f_{11}^2 are both C, so it is desirable to relocate C in f_{11}^2. Among slots from 8 (decided by E_{11}) to 11, as f_8^2 is A and $L_8 + 8 \geq t$, f_8^2 and f_{11}^2 are exchanged, making $< f_{11}^1, f_{11}^2 >$ a switchable pair. This procedure will be repeated down to slot 0 and Fig. 3.(b) shows the final allocation. In this example, every slot pair turned into the switchable one.

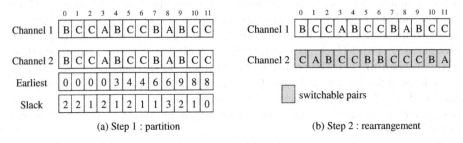

Fig. 3. Scheduling procedure

4.2   Runtime Scheduling and Error Control

Before polling a station, the PC transmits a probing control packet to the scheduled station, which then returns the control packet to the PC. If the PC does not receive the probing control packet correctly from the station, the channel is estimated to be bad. Even though the probing indicates the channel is good, the ensuing transmission can fail if a state transits to the bad state during the transmission. For simplicity, this paper disregards the overhead terms including channel probing, polling overhead, mandatory ACK/NAK, and so on, but the amount is bounded and constant for all slots, so it can be merged into transmission time.

Let's assume that PC is to start slot i which is originally allocated to A on channel 1 as well as B on channel 2, namely, $< A, B >$. PC first probes the channel status from itself to A and B on all two channels. Table 1 shows the probing result and corresponding actions. As shown in row 1 (case No.1), PC can reach A on channel 1 and also B on channel 2, so PC polls each station as scheduled. In row 2, by switching polls between the two channels, PC can save the 2 transmissions that might fail on ordinary schedule. PC can reversely reach A only on channel 2 while B on channel 1. In row 3, all connections from PC are bad except the one to A through channel 2. If PC switch $< A, B >$ to $< B, A >$, only A can send on channel 2. In row 4, only A can send on channel 1 as scheduled. In row 7, all scheduled connections from PC are bad.

Table 1. Channel status and transmission

No.	Ch1–A	Ch2–B	Ch1–B	Ch2–A	Ch1	Ch2	save
1	Good	Good	X	X	A	B	0
2	Bad	Bad	Good	Good	B	A	2
3	Bad	Bad	Bad	Good	–	A	1
4	Good	Bad	Good	Bad	A	–	0
5	Bad	Bad	Good	Bad	B	–	1
6	Bad	Good	Bad	Good	–	B	0
7	Bad	Bad	Bad	Bad	–	–	0

X : don't care

The polling table in Table 1 has some entries marked as '-', which means PC cannot poll A or B. This means that the scheduled transmission of corresponding stream is invalidated and the slot would be wasted without the further rearrangement. To improve the network throughput, it seems better to poll another station. Let $S_i^{n,a}$ be channel status of allocated message a (A, B, or C) on channel n (1 or 2) at i-th slot time. Among the next pending messages, the coordinator will pick and try those meet the following constraints: First, arrival time, E_i, lies prior to the current slot time. Second, slot time lies prior to the deadline of invalidated message. This enables the postponed message to be retransmitted within its deadline.

```
if (S_t^{1,a1} and S_t^{2,a2} are Good) continue;
else if (S_t^{1,a2} and S_t^{2,a1} are Good)
       exchange f_t^1 and f_t^2 and break;
else
       if (there is a good pair when f_t^1 is switched with f_t^2 )
              allocate corresponding one good pair (channel-message);
       for slot i from (t + 1) to (t + L_t) // bad time slot t
              if (f_i^n == f_t^n) continue; // same station
              if (E_i^n > t) continue; // cannot be advanced
              else exchange f_i^n and f_t^n and break;
       if (S_t^{bn,ba} is still Bad) allocate failed message.
```

[**Example 2**]. This example shows the runtime scheduling for the given stream set. As shown in Fig. 4, the channel status and transmission are as follows: In slot time 0 (case No.1), PC can reach B on channel 1 and also C on channel 2, so PC can poll as scheduled. In slot time 1 (case No.2), C and A messages can meet time constraints by switching polls between the two channels. In slot time 3 and 10 (case No.3 and No.4), corresponding message can improve network throughput by exchanging messages between the two channels or two slots satisfying the condition.

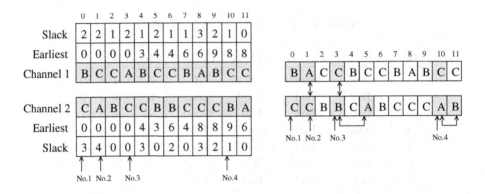

Fig. 4. Runtime scheduling procedure

The slot length, say L, is as large as the basic unit of wireless data transmission and every traffic is also segmented to fit the slot size. Each invocation needs $\lceil \frac{C_i}{L} \rceil$ slots, so every packet should be received correctly to be reassembled at the receiver. When the failed packets are managed and allocated to reclaim the unused slot, we consider the probability that the entire message can be correctly received. The only one message is selected among the failed messages according to the following rules: It has the higher probability of the success ratio by being allocated one more slot. If we let N be the number of successfully transmitted slots until now, the message whose $\frac{N}{\lceil \frac{C_i}{L} \rceil}$ value is the largest one, is selected.

5   Performance Evaluation

This section measures the performance of the proposed scheme in terms of deadline meet ratio according to the packet error rate via simulation using ns-2 event simulator[15]. We fixed the length of planning cycle to 24 as well as the number of streams to 3, and generated every possible stream sets whose utilization ranges from 0.2 to 2.0, to measure how much the rearrangement scheme can improve network throughput. Fig. 5 shows the deadline meet ratio according to the packet error rate to demonstrate the effect of runtime slot exchange. The curve marked as *Switch* represents the result of switching pairs while that marked as *Reclaim* shows the effect of reclaiming unused slots. The success ratio means the fraction of timely delivery of real-time packet. The packet error rate is the function of packet length and bit error rate, so we make it range from 0.0 to 0.5, considering the error-prone wireless channel characteristics. As shown in Fig. 5, the deadline meet ratio is improved by around 12.5 % when the packet error rate is over 0.4 and the number of switchable pairs is 24. Fig. 6 plots the result of runtime scheduling and error control scheme based on the example described in section 4.

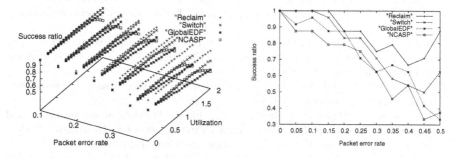

Fig. 5. Success ratio   **Fig. 6.** Success ratio

6 Conclusion

This paper has proposed and analyzed the performance of a real-time guarantee scheme for time-sensitive applications using message scheduling and error control on the dual channel ad hoc networks. Basically, simultaneous use of dual channels increases the available bandwidth of the network and satisfies the ever-increasing demand of higher bandwidth. After dividing the network time into fixed size slots synchronized across the two channels, polling schedule is determined according to the optimal EDF policy. In addition, slot rearrangement scheme makes it possible to maximize the number of switchable pairs, making it possible for the coordinator to select an error-free channel, as well as rearrange polling order to reclaim the reserved but not used channel.

Simulation results show that the proposed scheme improves the schedulability by 12.5 % for real-time messages using the runtime slot exchange scheme. Also, it allocates more bandwidth to messages as it can enhance achievable throughput for the given stream sets. As a future work, we will extend the message model to the personalized real-time applications mainly targeted to the telematics system which provides streaming information service to the users of high-mobility[16].

References

1. IEEE 802.11-1999: Part 11-Wireless LAN Medium Access Control (MAC) and Physical Layer (PHY) Specifications (1999)
2. Adamou, M., Khanna, S., Lee, I., Shin, I., Zhou, S.: Fair real-time traffic scheduling over a wireless LAN. Proc. IEEE Real-Time Systems Symposium (2001) 279–288

3. Carpenter, J., Funk, S., Holman, P., Srinivasan, A., Anderson, J., Baruah, S.: A categorization of real-time multiprocessor scheduling problems and algorithms. Handbook of Scheduling: Algorithms, Models, and Performance Analysis. Chapman Hall/CRC Press (2003)
4. Liu J.: Real-Time Systems. Prentice Hall (2000)
5. Choi, S., Shin, K.: A unified wireless LAN architecture for real-time and non-real-time communication services. IEEE/ACM Trans. on Networking **8** (2000) 44–59
6. Caccamo, M., Zhang, L., Sha, L., Buttazzo, G.: An implicit prioritized access protocol for wireless sensor networks. Proc. IEEE Real-Time Systems Symposium (2002)
7. Sheu, S., Sheu, T.: A bandwidth allocation/sharing/extension protocol for multimedia over IEEE 802.11 ad hoc wireless LANS. IEEE Journal on Selected Areas in Communications **19** (2001) 2065–2080
8. Mangold, S., et. al.: IEEE 802.11e wireless LAN for quality of service. Proceedings of the European Wireless (2002)
9. Rangnekar, A., Wang, C., Sivalingam, K., Li, B.: Multiple access protocols and scheduling algorithms of multiple channel wireless networks. Handbook of Algorithms for Mobile and Wireless Networking and Computing (2004)
10. Han, D., Jwa, J., Kim, H.: A Dual-Channel MAC Protocol Using Directional Antennas in Location Aware Ad Hoc Networks. Lecture Notes in Computer Science, Vol. 3983. (2006) 594–602
11. Lee, J., Kang, M., Park, G.: Design of a hard real-time guarantee scheme for dual ad hoc mode IEEE 802.11 WLANs. Lecture Notes in Computer Science, Vol. 3738. Springer-Verlag, Berlin Heidelberg New York (AdHocNow 2005) (2005) 141–152
12. Damodaran, S., Sivalingam, K.: Scheduling algorithms for multiple channel wireless local area networks. Computer Communications (2002)
13. Shah, S. H., Chen, K., Nahrstedt, K.: Dynamic bandwidth management for single-hop ad hoc wireless networks. ACM/Kluwer Mobile Networks and Applications (MONET) Journal **10** (2005) 199-217
14. Kai, L., Jiandong, L.: Mobile Cluster Protocol in Wireless Ad Hoc Networks. Proc. Intl. Conf. on Commun. Tech. (WCC-ICCT 2000), 1 (2000)
15. Fall, K., Varadhan, K.: Ns notes and documentation. Technical Report. VINT project. UC-Berkeley and LBNL (1997)
16. Kang, E., Kim, H., Cho, J.: Personalization Method for Tourist Point of Interest (POI) Recommendataion. accepted at Knowledge-Based & Intelligent Information & Engineering Systems (2006)

ADIAN: A Distributed Intelligent Ad-Hoc Network

Saeed Shahbazi[1], Gholamreza Ghassem-Sani[2], Hamidreza Rabiee[2],
Mohammad Ghanbari[3], and Mehdi Dehghan[4]

[1] Iran Telecommunication Research Center, Tehran, Iran
shahbazi@ce.sharif.edu
[2] Computer Engineering Department, Sharif University of Technology, Tehran, Iran
{sani, rabiee}@sharif.edu
[3] Department of Electronic Systems Engineering, University of Essex, United Kingdom
ghan@essex.ac.uk
[4] Computer Engineering Department, Amirkabir University of Technology, Tehran, Iran
dehghan@ce.aut.ac.ir

Abstract. Mobile Ad-hoc Networks are networks that have a dynamic topology without any fixed infrastructure. To transmit information in ad-hoc networks, we need robust protocols that can cope with constant changes in the network topology. The known routing protocols for mobile ad-hoc networks can be classified in two major categories: proactive routing protocols and reactive routing protocols. Proactive routing protocols keep the routes up-to-date to reduce delay in real-time applications but they have high control overhead. The control overhead in reactive routing protocols is much less than proactive routing protocols; however, the routes are discovered on demand, which is not suitable for real-time applications. In this paper, we have introduced a new routing system for mobile ad-hoc networks called ADIAN, which is based on the concepts of Distributed Artificial Intelligence (DAI). In ADIAN, every node acts as an independent and autonomous agent that collaborates with other agents in the system. Our experimental results have verified the efficiency and robustness of ADIAN under dynamic conditions of ad-hoc networks.

Keywords: Mobile Ad-hoc Networks, Routing, and Distributed Artificial Intelligence.

1 Introduction

A Mobile Ad-hoc Network (MANET) is a network consisting of wireless devices that make a self-configured network together. There is no fixed communication infrastructure in MANETs. Since wireless devices' broadcasting range is limited, communication in MANETs depends on the intermediate nodes. Therefore, each node in the network acts as a router. In these networks the topology changes constantly due to the mobility of the nodes. Furthermore, new nodes may be added to the network, existing nodes may leave the network, or some nodes may go to the sleep mode, dynamically. Due to special characteristics of these networks, the main problem is how to setup an

S. Chaudhuri et al. (Eds.): ICDCN 2006, LNCS 4308, pp. 27–39, 2006.

effective routing mechanism to deliver data packets. Another problem involves power consumption. Since most of the nodes are battery operated and have limited power, power consumption of nodes should be minimized.

Distributed nature and dynamicity of MANETs, make it suitable for applying Distributed Artificial Intelligence (DAI) techniques. Many routing protocols have already been designed for MANETs; however, most of them use simple assump-tions to model the mobility of the nodes. What is more, they have a modular structure containing object codes. Intelligent agents embody stronger notion of autonomy than objects. Likewise, the agents are capable of flexible behavior, and the standard object model has nothing to say about such types of behavior. Moreover, cooperation of a set of autonomous and intelligent agents can tolerate and handle potential failures in MANETs.

In this paper we introduce a new routing system called A Distributed Intelligent Ad-hoc Network (ADIAN), where network nodes are considered as intelligent agents and the agents discover routes to deliver information. Agents in ADIAN are autonomous and act in a plausible way. In this system, the routing overhead, which has an important impact on the performance of the MANETs is aimed to be minimized. This point is discussed further in section 4-3.

The remainder of the paper is organized as follows: sections 2 and 3 briefly present the existing routing protocols of two major categories: proactive and reactive routing. The weakness of the existing routing protocols and the motivation for using DAI techniques is then discussed in the section 3. Section 4 includes a detailed description of ADIAN. In section 5 the simulation results are presented. Finally, section 6 concludes the paper.

2   Routing in Ad-Hoc Networks

Dynamic nature of a MANET due to the mobility of its nodes causes a high degree of unpredictability in the network topology. This unpredictability makes the task of routing for transfer of information very complex. Design of a robust routing algorithm in these networks is an important and active research topic. Various routing protocols have already been introduced and evaluated in different environments and traffic conditions [5-6]. An extensive review and comparison of routing protocols for MANETs can be found in [7].

Environment and features of the MANETs, such as mobility and limited energy and bandwidth, requires an efficient use of available resources. In other words, to preserve the power, the routing overheads should be minimized and routing loops need to be avoided. Other important issues include: scalability, directional link support, security, reliability, and QoS [13-15].

The existing routing protocols of MANETs are divided into two major categories: 1) proactive routing protocols and 2) reactive routing protocols [5]. Proactive routing protocols constantly keep the routes between each pair of nodes up-to-date, by using periodic broadcasts. Since routing information is kept in some routing tables, these protocols are sometimes called table-driven protocols. On the other hand, reactive routing protocols discover a route only when it is required. Moreover, discovery process of a route is often initiated by the source node [5, 14].

The main feature of the proactive routing protocols is to maintain fixed routes to every pair of node in the network. Creating and maintaining routes are performed through periodic and event-driven messages (such as triggered messages when a link is broken) [5, 14]. Some of the proactive routing protocols include: DSDV[1], CGSR[2], WRP[3], TBRPF[4,] and FSR[5] [16-18, 21-24].

In reactive routing protocols, in order to reduce the routing overhead, routes are discovered only when they are needed. Some of the reactive routing protocols include: DSR[6], AODV[7], TORA[8], ABR[9], and SSR[10] [25-28].

3 Application of DAI in Routing in Ad-Hoc Networks

Distributed and dynamic nature of the MANETs makes this domain suitable for applying DAI techniques. Most of the ad-hoc routing protocols do not use these techniques. Since there are a few routing protocols that use artificial intelligence, having a new system in which the intelligent agents can collaborate for routing has motivated us to apply some of the DAI techniques to the routing problem in the ad-hoc networks. Multi-agent systems offer production systems that are decentralized rather than centralized, emergent rather than planned, and concurrent rather than sequential.

In this section we briefly explain two routing protocols that have used simple DAI techniques. Moreover, there are some related works that try to use artificial intelligence techniques in [29-32], but they do not exploit autonomous agents in their algorithms.

3.1 ARAMA

ARAMA is based on the concepts in biology [1]. The idea of designing ARAMA is based on the Ant Colony. Forward packets (Forward Ants) are used to collect information and backward packets (Backward Ants) are used to update the routing information in the nodes. Motivation of the algorithm is based on similarity between the MANETs and the ant routing algorithm (i.e., both of them have similar features such as their self-built, self-configured, and distributed nature). Some of the advantages of this algorithm are: fast response to the changes, local solution, employing both of

---

[1] Destination Sequenced Distance Vector.
[2] Cluster-head Gateway Switch Routing.
[3] Wireless Routing Protocol.
[4] Topology Dissemination Based on Reverse-Path Forwarding.
[5] Fisheye State Routing.
[6] Dynamic Source Routing.
[7] Ad hoc On-demand Distance Vector.
[8] Temporally Ordered Routing Algorithm.
[9] Associatively Based Routing.
[10] Signal Stability Routing.

reactive and proactive advantages, discovering multiple routes, reliable routes, ability to control the updates and the broadcasts.

3.2 Ant-AODV

One of the disadvantages of AODV is the lack of ability to handle real-time applications. Moreover, the ant type routing algorithms can not work well in highly dynamic networks with weak routes. Since nodes are dependent on ants for collecting information, in some cases the nodes carrying ants may leave the network unpredictably. This is caused by nodes mobility, and sleep mode of the mobile hosts. In this case, the number of ants in the network is decreased, which results in ineffective routing [2].

Ant-AODV is designed to solve the existing weaknesses of AODV and the ant routing. Some of its characteristics are: decreasing end-to-end and route discovery delay. Unlike other routing protocols, it does not waste bandwidth used for routing overhead, either.

Ant-AODV and ARAMA use swarm intelligence as one of the DAI methods. In the swarm intelligence, each agent can not solve the problem or even part of it alone. In other words, these protocols do not act autonomously and do not have the ability to make decision in various domains and different situations independently.

Therefore, none of the existing routing protocols for MANETs is suitable for all the conditions. In other words, each protocol is usually designed for a special purpose and for a special domain.

In the rest of this paper we will focus on a new routing system called ADIAN, which has been implemented as a framework to test different conditions. We can test various situations in topology and size of the network in order to determine the important criteria in robustness of the network.

4   ADIAN

ADIAN discovers the routes on-demand and is based on nodes negotiation as intelligent agents. Agents act autonomously in ADIAN. Routing in ADIAN is based on agents' negotiation to deliver data packets. The negotiation protocol between agents ADIAN is to some extend similar to that of CNET [9]. Moreover, each node has uncertain and limited knowledge about the agents in other nodes, which are represented in a way similar to meta-knowledge of MINDS algorithm [10]. Finally, the routing process is achieved through cooperating agents. Furthermore, the agent's knowledge is updated through negotiation with other agents, and by data packets' transmission.

4.1   Knowledge Store in ADIAN

In ADIAN, each agent stores its knowledge in four tables that consist of: State Table, Routing Table, Neighborhood Table, and Belief Table. The "State Table" includes the latest agent's information. The "Routing Table" contains the latest information about the destination agents and the appropriate neighbor agents that are used to deliver data packets to the desired destination. The "Neighborhood Table" includes a list of neighbors, which is updated periodically. The subsection 4.2 explains how these tables are used in ADIAN.

The Belief Table contains information about every node, which is accompanied by a belief degree about the accuracy of the information, and an updating time of each record. There are some other fields in this table including: Destination Agent, Belief Degree, Position of the agent, Remained Power, and the other important resources such as: CPU Load, Congestion Level, and whether or not the agent is busy. This table is used to choose the best neighbor to negotiate for delivering data packets to a desired destination.

Each agent in ADIAN learns the status of other agents through communication. Whenever a new agent enters into the system, it will construct its own belief table. The information in this table is later updated based on the information of the received data packets from other agents. At the start point of adding a new record, the belief degree value is set to the value of sender's belief degree. Then, through a punishment/reward mechanism, the degree of each agent belief, which indicates the accuracy of its meta-knowledge, gradually converges to a stable state.

The position information of nodes in ADIAN is assumed to be supplied by a GPS. Note that the information of each agent is local and no agent has a full view of the whole system. In order to know the position of other agents, each agent has to rely on its meta-knowledge about others.

In Figure 1, the typical knowledge of the first agent about the second agent is represented. This knowledge-base shows that agent 1 is 80% certain about the accuracy of its information about agent 2. This uncertainty gradually reduces through negotiation between the agents, and by transmission of data packets through the network.

							Belief Table						
ID	Source Node	Destin. Node	belief	Power	pos X	pos Y	Transmission Delay	Band Width	Congestion Level	CPU Load	Is Busy	Time
1	agent1	agent2	80%	178	5	1	0.1ms	128K B	2%	18%	No	27

Fig. 1. Format of the Belief Table – each agent has knowledge about the other agents with a belief degree

4.2 Routing in ADIAN

The ADIAN routing includes the three following phases.

1) Route Discovery
The new routes are found in this phase. Agents are responsible for delivery of data packets from a source node to a destination node, while trying to find an optimal route. Therefore, they go through a negotiation process to find a suitable route to deliver the data packets. If an agent intends to deliver a packet, and it does not find any neighbor in its routing table, it will search its neighborhood table based on its

own information about the destination that exist in its Belief Table to choose the best neighbor. The selection is based on the following factors: Euclidean Distance, Belief Degree, Remained Power, and Updating Time using the following equation:

$$Distance = \frac{Euclidean\ Distance}{\frac{1}{3}\left(\alpha\dfrac{updatingtime}{currenttime}+\beta*belief+\delta*power\right)} \tag{1}$$

Where α represents the importance of updating time in choosing a route, β is the belief's importance level, and δ is the remained power importance degree.

The effectiveness of α, β, and δ is discussed in section 5.2, and simulation results compare their effectiveness.

During route discovery, the agent that has the least distance is chosen to negotiate. Then a message is sent to the chosen agent for cooperating in transmission of the data packets. This agent evaluates the received information as indicated below.

(a) Information about the destination accompanied with the belief degree of the source agent regarding that information.

(b) Some other information such as delivery priority of the data packets used to increase the system performance.

Agents in ADIAN can accept/reject the negotiation autonomously. In some cases, if there is any congestion or limited resource in the selected agent, it will deny to cooperate in routing that ends in having a balanced network and a robust routing.

As an example, consider Figure 2, where agent A decides to send some data packets to agent E. It assesses its neighbors, and uses its knowledge about E that is found in its Belief Table to calculate the distances between itself and its neighbors, using the above equation. In this example, the least distance belongs to the agent B; therefore, it is chosen for negotiation.

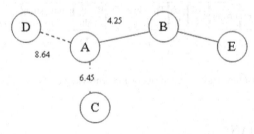

Fig. 2. Topology of a sample ad-hoc network – agent A is trying to send its packets to agent E

If B has enough power to deliver packets, it will evaluate the received information for inconsistencies. If there is any inconsistency between its knowledge and the received information, it will return the correct information to A, and will not accept the negotiation. Agent A will then correct its knowledge. Otherwise, it will send a message in order to inform A that it can cooperate with it.

In ADIAN, data packets are also used to update information that agents have about each other. In other words, each data packet carries some extra information regarding a limited number of lastly visited agents. Besides, if an agent accepts to cooperate with another agent, it will send back its information to the requested agent. The initial performance of ADIAN might be low due to local and inaccurate knowledge of its agents. However, this exchange of information facilitates the gradual convergence of ADIAN to a stable and acceptable performance.

As it was explained earlier, the knowledge of ADIAN agents is gradually refined via their communications. The performance of ADIAN is highly dependent on the accuracy of its agents' knowledge. Therefore, in the cases where only few agents communicate, the system might not have a reasonable performance. To handle this problem, a periodic broadcasting scheme is used. To reduce the overhead, the broadcasting is done only if an agent remains idle for a certain period of time.

2) Route Maintenance
The second phase of routing is the route maintenance which is responsible for maintaining the routes during the transmission task. In ADIAN, there is no need to send additional control packet to maintain routes. Data packets in their journey are used to update the knowledge of the visited agents; therefore, agents receive up-to-date information about each other.

Another problem is to prevent routing loops. ADIAN prevents routing loops using a list of illegal neighbors. If a data packet passes through a node, then it adds the previously visited node to its list. Agents are not allowed to use the nodes in their illegal list for routing.

3) Failure Handling
The third phase of routing is about handling the potential failures, which are often due to mobile nodes, and sometimes are due to having low battery in nodes that contribute to a transmission task. If a link between two nodes fails, the related information in their routing table will be deleted and the current agent tries to negotiate with another agent. If there is no suitable agent for routing, a backward routing will be performed to the previously visited agent.

4.3 ADIAN Features

ADIAN satisfies the following requirements that have been specified in [19] such as:

– The process of routing need to be performed cooperatively.
– Routing loops should be prevented.
– Routing should be initiated on-demand.
– The possibility of having a *sleep mode* need to be considered (i.e., when the power of agents are less than a threshold, they deny cooperation in delivering packets).
– Agents' knowledge about the world and one another is local, limited, and uncertain.
– In distributing the tasks through the network, the load balancing should be considered.
– The routing algorithm should be complete (i.e., if there exists a route to a destination, the algorithm would find it).

In addition, there is no need to use control packets in ADIAN, so that the bandwidth is preserved and the ADIAN Overhead is low.

5 Simulation Results

To assess the performance of the proposed protocol, that consists of a Multi Agent Systems (MAS), called ADIAN, we have used various simulations in a typical mobile Ad-hoc network environment, as described below.

5.1 Simulation Model

In order to demonstrate the effectiveness of ADIAN, we evaluate our proposed protocol and compare its performance to the DSR and AODV. We have implemented ADIAN using the GLObal MObile SIMulation (GLOMOSIM) library [33].

The number of the nodes in the simulation world is 40; however, the size of the simulation world including the number of nodes, and the mobility pattern of nodes could be simply configured by adjusting the simulation parameters. In addition, system parameters such as available power, updating time, and beliefs in choosing the next hop are all configurable, and have been tested in different states.

The details of the ADIAN's simulation model, including the transmission primitives, mobility and traffic model, are reported next.

5.1.1 Transmission Primitives

Here, an ideal scheduler controls the packet transmissions and each agent uses a FIFO buffer. The size of the buffer is limited to 20 packets. A broadcast packet is initiated after the channel is free for a Random Assessment Delay (RAD) randomly chosen in the range [0, 1, 2, ..., 250] milliseconds (ms) with a transmission radius of R = 250 meter. By notifying a packet reception to the contractor (i.e. the selected sender's neighbor for delivering data packets) about remaining for the whole duration of the transmission within the transmission range, no collisions with other transmissions would be occurred, simultaneously.

The required time to detect a link breakage is simulated by considering a typical re-transmission mechanism with an exponential back-off. The nominal transmission speed is set to 8 Mbps. This simplified model would present the main behavior of a typical wireless link layer in our simulations.

5.1.2 Traffic

Packets are generated by 20 Constant Bit Rate (CBR) sources at the rate of 5 packets/sec. The size of data packets is different and is chosen from a source file. The parameters in the source file records are: "time", "source agent", "destination agent", and "data packet size", where each field is separated by a special delimiter. Note that the scenario for the simulation is fixed. However, we can change the scenario easily. The number of simultaneous sources at any time can be more than one by defining more sources that have the same time field value.

5.1.3 Mobility

Agents can move in an n * m kilometer (km) region according to the random waypoint mobility model with a zero pause time.

The default values were set to n = m = 1 km. At the beginning of simulations the agents were placed randomly inside the region. Each agent then selects a new point and moves towards it at a constant speed, that is chosen in the range of $[1, 2, ..., V_{max}]$ m/s, uniformly at random. When the agent arrives at the destination, it would repeat the same behavior.

5.1.4 Performance Metrics
The following metrics have been considered during the simulations.
- *Delivery Rate*; ratio of the number of data packets delivered to the destinations generated by the traffic sources.
- *Time Cost*; lasting time to deliver data packets to the destination.
- *Physical Distance*; Euclidean distance among hops.

5.2 Comparison Between Different Scenarios

In the simulations, the cost includes temporal and physical distance. The temporal cost is related to the negotiations (1 per negotiation) and sending the packets to the next hop (2 per sending). For calculating the physical distance, the Euclidean distance is used. The simulation model is similar to the one described in section 5.1. The pause time for each agent to settle down and then move was set to 100 seconds.

In this section, different experiments have been performed to determine the desired coefficients of the system parameters. In the simulations, we have evaluated three parameters including: delivery rate, time cost, and physical distance cost. Here, the agents move randomly such that some links maybe formed to increase performance, or vise versa. In other words, a suitable topology maybe formed, that increases the performance, or conversely, an undesired link may occur, which decreases the per-formance. To minimize the effect of this phenomenon, we have forced the desired pattern by statistical analysis.

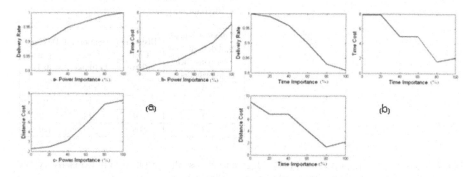

Fig. 3. (a) The effect of importance of power to choose best next hop: a- Delivery rate (%), b- Time Cost (10ms), c- Physical distance (20m), (b) The effect of importance of updating time to choose the best next hop: a- Delivery rate (%), b- Time Cost (10ms), c- Physical distance (20m)

Figure 3(a) shows that when the level of importance of power choosing the next hop increases, the delivery rate will also increase. In other words, the probability of

36   S. Shahbazi et al.

having no power for each node, which leads to go to sleep mode, will decrease. This fact is shown in Figure 3(a)-a. According to Figures 3(a)-b and 3(a)-c, there is a trade-off between increasing delivery rate and increasing the costs. By using the results of these experiments one can determine the desired parameters for the desired perform-ance for different applications.

In Figure 3(b), the importance of updating time factor is shown. When the updated time factor is given more importance the effects of power and the delivery rate will decrease (Figure 3(b)-a). According to the Figures 3(b)-b and 3(b)-c, the costs de-crease by increasing the importance of the updating time. This is because, more up-to-date routes means less backtracks in the routing process. Therefore, agents need to have fewer negotiations.

Figure 4 shows the result of experiments where the degree of agents' belief regard-ing other agents was gradually given a higher priority. Similar to the updated time effect, by increasing the importance of belief degree, the importance of the power decreases. Therefore, the delivery rate will decrease. This fact is shown in Figure 4(a). According to Figures 4(b) and 4(c), the costs decrease by increasing the importance of the belief degree, which is due to the fact that transmissions face less deadlock (i.e., paths and cooperating agents are chosen more accurately).

Our experimental results showed that the power and the belief degree factors have more effects on the system than the updating time.

We have also performed some experiments regarding the levels of information car-ried with the data packets, as shown in Table 1. In the first set of experiments, which is shown in row 1 of the table, there is no additional information in the data packets. The results of carrying information about 1, 2, and 3 last visited nodes are shown in rows 1, 2, and 3 of the table, respectively. According to Table 1, increasing the number of visited nodes in data packets that carry information will increase the performance.

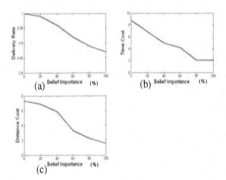

(a) Belief Importance (%)
(b) Belief Importance (%)
(c) Belief Importance (%)

Table 1. Experimental results of effects of added information to data packets on system performance

# of visited nodes that data packets carrying their information	Distance Cost (×20m)	Temporal Cost (×10ms)	Delivery Rate (0-1)
0	4.97	7.28	0.8
1	3.9	3.16	0.9
2	3.04	3.13	0.96
3	2.05	2.27	0.99

Fig. 4. The effects of importance of belief degree to choose the best next hop: (a) Delivery rate (%), (b) Time Cost (10ms), (c) Physical distance (20m)

5.3 Comparison with Other Protocols

To show the effectiveness of ADIAN, comparisons with two typical proactive (DSDV) and reactive (AODV) routing protocols were made. The first one compares the overhead of the protocols, and the other one is about the measurement of

"GOODPUT". The conditions of the simulation remain the same, as expressed in section 5.1. Furthermore, the coefficients of ADIAN in section 5.2 are set to 33.33%.

Figure 5(a) shows the comparison results of ADIAN, DSDV, and AODV Delivery Rate. The results indicate that ADIAN has the best performance in correctly delivering the data packets. This is due to the agents' negotiations to find a path to the destination, as was explained earlier in section 4.2.

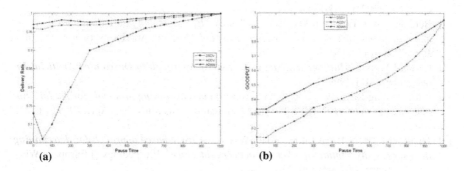

(a)   (b)

Fig. 5. (a) Delivery rate comparison of ADIAN, AODV, and DSDV. (b) GOODPUT comparison of ADIAN, AODV, and DSDV.

The comparison of "GOODPUT" factor is shown in Figure 5(b). This is a measure that shows the probability or the rate of successfully received packets with no cell loss that causes packet loss at the receiver. The results show that the GOODPUT factor of ADIAN is the best. This is the consequence of ADIAN's low overhead that was discussed earlier, in section 4.2.

6 Conclusions

Ad-hoc networks are flexible networks that do not have any pre-installed infrastructure. By recent developments in wireless technology and peripheral devices, the application of such networks has been rapidly increased. However, the routing problem in ad-hoc networks due to mobility of nodes is still a challenging issue.

In this paper, we have presented a new routing system called ADIAN, for ad-hoc networks. In ADIAN, routing is performed by the help of DAI methods, and each node in the network is regarded as an autonomous agent. Therefore, we have achieved to design a robust routing algorithm by using intelligent agents. Moreover, we have been successful to decrease the routing overhead.

In this paper, the simulation results were based on various parameters such as the life of power supply, update time, and agents' belief about other agents. The results show that, in different conditions, ADIAN gradually converges to the desired point of operation by minimizing the costs and the resource consumptions. This gradual convergence is due to inaccurate knowledge of its distributed agents in the early stages of the routing algorithm.

References

[1] O. Hussein, T. Saadawi, "*Ant Routing Algorithm for Mobile Ad-hoc networks (ARAMA)*" Source: IEEE International Performance, Computing and Communications Conference, Proceedings, 2003, p 281-290.

[2] Shivanajay Marwaha, Chen Khong Tham, Dipti Srinivasan, "*Mobile Agents based Routing Protocol for Mobile Ad- hoc Networks*", IEEE Global Telecommunications Conference, v 1, 2002, p 163-167.

[3] Belding-Royer, Elizabeth M., Perkins-Charles, "*Evolution and future directions of the ad hoc on-demand distance-vector routing protocol*". Source: Ad Hoc Networks, v 1, n 1, July, 2003, p 125-150.

[4] Gerhard Weiss, "*Multiagent Systems A Modern Approach to Distributed Artificial Intelligence*", MIT 1999.

[5] E.M. Belding-Royer, C.-K. Toh, "*A review of current routing protocols for Ad hoc mobile wireless networks*", IEEE Personal Communications Magazine (April 1999) v 6, n 2, p 46–55.

[6] Jean-Pierre Ebert, Brian Burns, Adam Wolisz, "*A trace based approach for determining the energy consumption of a WLAN network interface*", Proceedings of European Wireless, February 2002, pp. 230–236.

[7] C.E. Perkins, "*Ad hoc Networking*", Addison-Wesley, Reading, MA, 2000.

[8] Alex L. G. Hayzelden, John Bigham, "*Software Agents for Future Communication Systems*", Springer, 1999.

[9] Randall Davis, Reid G. Smith, "*Negotiation as a Metaphor for Distributed Problem Solving*", Artif. Intell., vol 20, pp. 63-109, 1983.

[10] Uttam Mukhopadhyay, Larry M. Stephens, Michael N. Huhns, Ronald D. Bonnell, "*An intelligent system for document retrieval in distributed office environments*", Journal of the American Society for Information Science, Vol. 37, Issue 3 (May 1986), pp. 123-135.

[11] Alex L. G. Hayzelden, Rachel A. Bourne, "*Agent Technology for Communication Infrastructures*" Wiley, 2001.

[12] Ryokichi Onishi, Saneyasu Yamaguchi, Hiroaki Morino, Hitochi Aida, Tadao Saito, "*The Multi-agent System for Dynamic Network Routing*", IEICE Transactions on Communications, v E84-B, n 10, October, 2001, p 2721-2728.

[13] R. Beraldi, R. Baldoni, "*Unicast routing techniques for mobile Ad hoc networks*", in: M. Ilyas (Ed.), Handbook of Ad hoc Networks, CRC Press, New York, 2003 (Chapter 7).

[14] Elizabeth Belding-Royer, "*Routing approaches in mobile Ad hoc networks*", in: S. Basagni, M. Conti, S. Giordano, I. Stojmenovic (Eds.), Ad hoc Networking, IEEE Press Wiley, New York, 2003.

[15] M.S. Corson, J. Macker, "*Mobile Ad hoc networking (MANET): routing protocol performance issues and evaluation considerations*", RFC 2501, IETF, January 1999.

[16] C.E. Perkins, P. Bhagwat, "*Highly dynamic destination sequenced distance-vector routing (DSDV) for mobile computers*", Computer Communications Review (October 1994) 234–244.

[17] C.-C. Chiang, H.K. Wu, W. Liu, M. Gerla, "*Routing in clustered multi hop, mobile wireless networks with fading channel*", in: Proceedings of IEEE SICON_97, April 1997, pp. 197–211.

[18] S. Murthy, J.J. Garcia-Luna-Aceves, "*An efficient routing protocol for wireless networks*", ACM Mobile Networks and Applications (MONET) Journal, Special Issue on Routing in Mobile Communication Networks, October 1996, pp. 183–197.

[19] Joseph P. Macker and M. Scott Corson. *"Mobile Ad hoc networking and the IETF"*. Mobile Computing and Communications Review, 2(1):9.14, 1998.

[20] B. Bellur, R.G. Ogier, F.L. Templin, *"Topology broadcast based on reverse-path forwarding (TBRPF)* ", IETF Internet Draft, draft-ietf-manet-tbrpf-01.txt, March 2001.

[21] *"APE: Ad hoc Protocol Evaluation test bed"*, Department of Computer Systems at Uppsala, Sweden., ACM/Kluwer Mobile Networks and Applications Journal 6 (3) (2001) 211–222.

[22] L. Kleinrock, K. Stevens, *"Fisheye: a lens like computer display transformation"*, Technical Report, UCLA, Computer Science Department, 1971.

[23] P.F. Tsuchiya, *"The Landmark Hierarchy: a new hierarchy for routing in very large networks"*, Computer Communications Review 18 (4) (1988) 35–42.

[24] G. Pei, M. Gerla, X. Hong, *"LANMAR: landmark routing for large scale wireless Ad hoc networks with group mobility"*, in: Proceedings of IEEE/ACM MobiHOC 2000, Boston, MA, August 2000, pp. 11–18.

[25] D.B. Johnson, D.A. Maltz, *"Dynamic source routing in Ad hoc wireless networks"*, in: T. Imielinski, H. Korth (Eds.), Mobile Computing, Kluwer Academic Publishers, Dordrecht, 1996, pp. 153–181.

[26] C.E. Perkins, E.M. Royer, *"Ad hoc on-demand distance vector routing"*, in: Proceedings of 2nd IEEE Workshop on Mobile Computing Systems and Applications, February 1999.

[27] V.D. Park, M.S. Corson, *"A highly adaptive distributed routing algorithm for mobile wireless networks"*, in: Proceedings of INFOCOM _97, April 1997.

[28] R. Dube, C. Rais, K.-Y. Wang, S. Tripathi, *"Signal stability based adaptive routing for Ad hoc mobile networks"*, IEEE Personal Communications, February 1997, pp. 36–45.

[29] Zheng, Xiangquan; Guo, Wei; Liu, Renting, *"An ant-based distributed routing algorithm for ad-hoc networks"* Source: 2004 International Conference on Communications, Circuits and Systems, v 1, 2004, p 412-417.

[30] Ohtaki, Yoshitaka; Wakamiya, Naoki; Murata, Masayuki; Imase, Makoto, *"Scalable ant-based routing algorithm for ad-hoc networks"* Source: Proceedings of the Third IASTED International Conference on Communications, Internet, and Information Technology, 2004, p 50-55.

[31] Ahmed, Tarek H., *"Simulation of mobility and routing in ad hoc networks using ant colony algorithms"* International Conference on Information Technology: Coding and Computing, ITCC, v 2, Proc. ITCC 2005, p 698-703.

[32] Shen, Chien-Chung; Huang, Zhuochuan; Jaikaeo, Chaiporn, *"Ant-based distributed topology control algorithms for mobile ad hoc networks"* Source: Wireless Networks, v 11, n 3, May, 2005, p 299-317.

[33] UCLA Parallel Computing Laboratory and wireless Adaptive Mobility Laboratory, *"GloMoSim: A Scalable Simulation Environment for Wireless and Wired Network"*.

A Mobility Tolerant Cluster Management Protocol with Dynamic Surrogate Cluster-Heads for a Large Ad Hoc Network

Parama Bhaumik[1] and Somprokash Bandyopadhyay[2]

[1] Dept. of Information Technology, Jadavpur University,
Kolkata, India
parama@it.jusl.ac.in
[2] MIS group, Indian Institute of Management, Calcutta, India
somprokash@iimcal.ac.in

Abstract. It is not a trivial job to maintain clusters in a highly mobile ad hoc scenario where changes in node activity status cause frequent and unpredictable topological changes. It requires continuous and efficient management protocol for frequent up-dation and re-clustering which are costly in a resource-poor environment. In this context, we describe a convenient cluster management protocol that incurs very little communication overhead for maintaining a stable cluster structure. Our protocol defines a geographical boundary for each cluster using GPS information that enables the mobile nodes to get alarmed while crossing the cluster boundary. Here a cluster-head is also free to leave the cluster after delegating the leadership to a member-node, which will then act as a surrogate cluster-head of the cluster. The simulation results indicate that this mechanism reduces as much as 30% of the overhead traffics involved in cluster maintenance.

1 Introduction

The clustering is always of significant importance for network management, routing methods, QoS, resource allocation, topology update effect and in this context, they should be maintained and managed efficiently. This task becomes complicated in a highly mobile scenario and results in much overhead with increase in cluster size [2, 3, 4]. Existing periodic trigger based clustering management protocol incorporates large intra and inter-cluster traffic that degrades the performance of the network as a whole.

Here we describe a convenient and a low cost cluster management protocol for large mobile networks. We assume that the locations of the nodes are available directly using GPS (Global Positioning System). Clusters are formed initially using a modified Max-Min-D-cluster formation algorithm [1] and we propose to construct a static geographical boundary for each cluster using GPS of the boundary nodes. In this protocol the nodes are free to move from one cluster to another keeping the cluster structure entirely stable within the defined region boundary. This boundary information is available with all the members of a cluster. Our technique enables all the nodes of a cluster

S. Chaudhuri et al. (Eds.): ICDCN 2006, LNCS 4308, pp. 40–45, 2006.

to get alarmed while crossing the cluster boundary and is able to generate a timely request for unbind and bind with old and new cluster-head respectively.

This paper also proposes a novel optimistic cluster head-surrogating scheme for achieving efficiency in mobile cluster management process. In this scheme a cluster-head is also free to leave its cluster after delegating the leadership to any member-node of its current cluster. This member-node now will act as a surrogate cluster-head of the cluster. The process actually duplicates a copy of headship program and related member information list to the selected surrogate-head. This particular technique of defining the clusters with fixed boundaries has following advantages.

1. The cluster structure becomes robust in the face of topological changes caused by node motion, node failure and node insertion /removal.
2. Conventional beacon-based cluster management algorithms require the entire network to reconfigure continuously, while in GPS based cluster management protocol the impact of node mobility has been localized within the cluster and its immediate neighboring clusters.
3. The ability of surrogating cluster headship from a mobile cluster head to any of its neighbor.
4. Independent and autonomous cluster control and maintenance by the mobile members only.
5. No performance degradation of the network due to cluster management protocol.

2   GPS Bounded Cluster Structure Algorithm

To obtain the initial set of clusters, we referred a leader election algorithm - Max-Min D–Cluster Formation algorithm proposed by Alan D. Almis, Ravi Prakash, Vuong Duong and T. Huynh [1]. There are several advantages for using Max-Min D–Cluster Formation algorithm over other existing clustering algorithms like the nodes can asynchronously run the heuristics so no need for synchronized clocks, we can customize the number of clusters as a function of d.

In our proposed GPS based clustering algorithm we have used the initial leader election part of the Max-Min D–Cluster algorithm in the first phase. In the second phase the elected leader or the cluster head will be able to recognize its boundary by getting the GPS information from all of its member nodes and will announce this boundary location values within d hop. Thus all the member nodes get alarmed about the current cluster boundary and will utilize this value while going out of this cluster. The cluster boundary algorithm can be explained in two phases.

Phase I: Max-Min D–Cluster Formation Algorithm
1. At some common epoch each node initiates **2d** rounds of flooding of information exchange (**node id**) where d is the given heuristic. Each node maintains a logged entry of two arrays, **WINNER** and **SENDER** to store the results of each flooding round.
2. Initially each node sets its winner to be equal to its own node id.
3. This is the phase for **FLOODMAX** where a node chooses the largest value among its own **WINNER** array and this process continues for d rounds.

4. This **FLOODMIN** phase follows **FLOODMAX** where a node chooses the smallest rather than the largest value as its new **WINNER** to reclaim some of their territory.
5. After these two d rounds of information exchange a node is able to determine its cluster-head.

The existing Max-Min D–Cluster Formation algorithm can be stopped here and as the head selection procedure is over we can now proceed to define a static geographical boundary for the clusters. This geographic boundary can be easily defined with the absolute coordinate position (GPS) of the nodes lying at the boundaries.

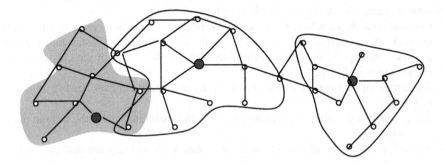

Fig. 1. Initial Cluster structures formed with Max - Min -D Clustering

Phase II: Cluster Boundary Formation Algorithm
1. The cluster head broadcasts get_**Position_ forAll** ( ) request message along with its own GPS to get percolated within d hop.
2. All member nodes in turn unicasts back the message **node_GPS** ( ) to the cluster-head using geographical routing.
3. Cluster-head receives all the GPS values of its members and calculates the maximum limiting coordinates for Left, Right, Up and Down values to define its boundary.
4. The cluster head then broadcasts the message **get_Boundary_values( )** within the d hop transmission range to notify all the member nodes about the cluster boundary.
5. All the member nodes become alarmed about the rectangular cluster boundary information that can be verified while changing their positions.

Thus our GPS based clustering algorithm will partition the network into a number of geographically overlapping clusters. These cluster boundaries are static, and are not required to be redefined with the mobility of the boundary nodes. This boundary value will be once notified to all the members of a cluster and will remain fixed until all the nodes move away from this region. In that case only the cluster–head will recall the initial clustering algorithm to remain connected and the cluster boundary does not exists any more.

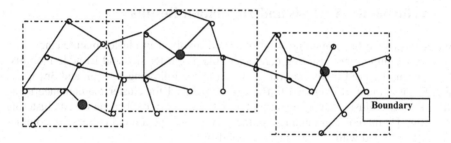

Fig. 2. Cluster boundaries formed with GPS of the boundary nodes

3   Cluster Management Protocol

For periodic beacon based cluster maintenance protocols if a cluster member is moving out of the transmission range of the CH, the member node searches for the new head by detecting the new CH beacon signal. There is no other intelligent way to track the mobility of a member node. Here we have proposed a cluster maintenance protocol using GPS technology, which is able to maintain a stable cluster structure even in presence of high mobility incurring little overhead. In this protocol any node including the cluster head automatically gets alarmed while crossing the geographical boundary of a cluster using the program which continuously compares the current GPS value of the node with that of the boundary values. Thus it is quite easy for a departing node to make a timely arrangement for rebinding with a new CH and unbind with the old one.

4   Mobility Management of Cluster Heads Through Selection of Surrogate Heads

The entire process of surrogating actually involves the transfer of cluster head information and re-announcement of new cluster head within the cluster. We have considered different schemes for selecting surrogate head considering different aspects of the network performance like number of cluster head change in the near future or the overhead traffic involved in transferring the headship.

We have found that if the surrogate head can be selected from the middle of the cluster then, the chance of this new cluster head to cross the cluster boundary gets reduced and as such the duration of a node to remain as cluster head increases remarkably. This particular scheme though yields better stability of a cluster [fig .4] but the traffic overhead involved for handover of headship is much higher due to multihop data transfer. In the second scheme, when the departing head can select any of its 1- hop neighbors as surrogate head and as such there is no need to concern about their positions. Here the initial overhead for head transfer is much less due to 1 hop data transfer. But as the surrogate head lies within the vicinity of cluster boundary the chance of change of cluster head in near future also gets increased.

5 Performance Analysis and Simulation Results

We first analyze the communication overhead involved in cluster maintenance with varying the important clustering parameters like i) cluster size and ii) node mobility. It has been observed in all the graphs shown in the following fig [3a and 3b] that a significant amount of overhead traffic can be reduced for cluster maintenance using the GPS based cluster management protocol. For the periodic beacon based clustering algorithm [1] there is a gradual rise in the curves showing a rapid increase in communication overhead with cluster size and mobility.

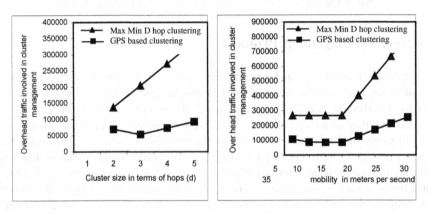

Fig. 3. Average overhead involved in cluster maintenance with a) varying cluster size b) varying node mobility

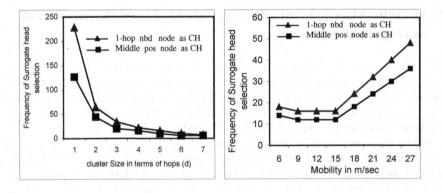

Fig. 4. Frequency of cluster head surrogating using the two selection schemes with a) varying cluster size b) varying node mobility

The cluster topology stability can be measured by determining the number of times each cluster head has attempted and given up its role as cluster head. So in the second part of our simulation results we have tried to show the performance of the surrogate head selection schemes. We have counted the number of cluster changes with varying cluster size and varying the node mobility, and the results give the efficiency of selection scheme used.

6 Conclusion

Here we have tried to minimize the frequency of re-clustering by proposing a GPS based stable cluster maintenance protocol. We have shown that using a one time absolute geographical boundary for a cluster, it can be kept stable over a region for a long period. In this protocol the mobility can be managed locally and as such the communication overhead gets heavily reduced. The cluster belonging ness can be determined once by using the deterministic GPS based approach and any further modifications in the member belongingness can be taken care locally without having a little impact on the rest of the network. This GPS based robust approach together with the support of Surrogate cluster-head makes this approach highly deployable in an extremely mobile environment.

Acknowledgments. This research work is partially sponsored by the Centre for Mobile Computing and Communication, Jadavpur University, India under the UGC Scheme "Universities with Potential for Excellence".

References

[1] Alan D. Amis Ravi Prakash Thai H.P. Vuong Dung T. Huynh. Max-Min D-Cluster Formation in Wireless Ad Hoc Networks. IEEE INFOCOM, March, 2000.
[2] John Sucec and Ivan Marsic Rutgers University. Clustering Overhead for Hierarchical Routing in Mobile Ad hoc Networks. IEEE INFOCOM 2002.
[3] I-Shyan Hwang, Chih-Kang Chien and Chiung-Ying Wang. A Novel GPS-Based Quorum Hybrid Routing Algorithm (GPS-QHRA) for Cellular-Based Ad Hoc Wireless Networks. Journal of Information Science and Engineering, Volume 21, Number 1, January 2005.
[4] P. Basu, N. Khan, and T.D.C.Little. A Mobility Based Metric for Clustering in Mobile Ad Hoc Networks. Proc IEEE ICDCS 2001 Workshop on Wireless Networks.

Prediction Based QoS Routing in MANETs

Shahram Mohrehkesh, Mahmoud Fathy, and Saleh Yousefi

Department of Computer Engineering,
Iran University of Science and Technology, Tehran, Iran
Cmsmohrehkesh_sh@comp.iust.ac.ir,
{mahfathy, syousefi}@iust.ac.ir

Abstract. The aim of this work is to propose a QoS routing algorithm in MANETs. The proposed algorithm predicts the future states of nodes including buffer level and position. Predicting the future state of node, the algorithm could decide whether a node is a good selection as a router or not. Through this algorithm, more stable and lower buffer level nodes are selected and hence QoS routing parameter could be satisfied. The proposed algorithm outperforms even in high speed and high load network conditions. Simulation shows routing performance has been improved, especially in terms of end-to-end delay.

Keywords: Mobile Ad hoc Network, QoS Routing, Prediction, buffer, positon.

1 Introduction

Mobile Ad hoc Networks (MANETs) are typically heterogeneous networks with various types of mobile nodes. Many applications are running in MANETs that need different levels of quality. Qualities of Service (QoS) parameters are mostly bandwidth, delay, jitter, and packet loss. Providing end-to-end support for QoS guarantees is a central and crucial issue in designing future multimedia MANETs. Quality of Service is more difficult to guarantee in MANETs than in other types of networks because of a limited bandwidth resource, limited power abilities and the absence of a fixed structure coupled with the ability of nodes to move freely.

Some works have been done in QoS routing in ad hoc networks. So far, some algorithms such as Flexible QoS Model for MANET (FQMM) [1] as well as QoS extensions of AODV[2], DSR[3], TORA[3], DSDV[3] and OLSR [4] are proposed. In addition, Multi-Path QoS Routing protocol relying on the ticket-based probing technique has been proposed in [5]. However, these algorithms did not propose a mechanism to reduce delay as a QoS requirement.

Some QoS routing algorithms which consider delay as QoS requirement have been proposed in literature such as Predictive location-based [6], VGAP [7] and AQOR [8]. In [6] a predictive location-based algorithm is proposed which finds path based on updated location of nodes. Although this protocol seems promising, the overhead in maintaining and updating tables is high. Moreover, the prediction accuracy is highly dependent on the previous states of mobile nodes which might be misleading. VGAP [7] could guarantee statistical end to end delay. However, it seems that it did not outperform in high traffic conditions because it uses only cluster heads to transmit

S. Chaudhuri et al. (Eds.): ICDCN 2006, LNCS 4308, pp. 46–51, 2006.
© Springer-Verlag Berlin Heidelberg 2006

traffic and limits the available bandwidth usage. AQOR [8] also proposes a method to compute end to end delay for a path. But, this algorithm not only did not operate very well in high traffic and high speed nodes conditions but also did not select a stable path and paths may be broken immediately.

This paper proposes a new QoS routing algorithm which focuses on delay as the main QoS parameter. This paper shows that the new algorithm, Prediction based QoS Routing, PQR, takes the impact of the speed, location, and buffer level of nodes into its account to reduce end-to-end delay. In the following section, the new proposed algorithm, PQR, is described. Simulation analysis is presented to show the performance of PQR algorithm in section III. Finally, the conclusions are presented in section IV.

2 PQR

In a wired network, if nodes adopt a WFQ-like service discipline and the source traffic is constrained by a leaky bucket, an upper bound on the end-to-end delay and bandwidth guarantees can be provided [9]. However, when fair queueing algorithms are used over wireless networks, the delay bound may not hold due to the bursty and location dependent channel errors of a wireless link.

2.1 Structure of PQR

PQR tries to predict future states of nodes and decide whether to choose a node as a forwarder or not. The future state of node includes its future buffer occupancy percentage as well as its future location in relation to its downstream node.

Buffer: Occupancy percentage of a node's buffer is the buffer level. If the buffer level of a particular node is high, this implies that a large number of packets are queued up for forwarding, which in turn implies that a packet routed through this node would have to experience high queueing delays.

To predict future buffer level, a Minimum Mean Square Error Predictor (MMSE predictor) is used. By using this predictor, there is no need to know the underlying structure of traffic; therefore, it can be used for on-line prediction purposes [10]. MMSE is a well known method which its effective performance is shown in many literature such as [11], [12].

Let $\{X_t\}$ denotes a linear stochastic process and suppose that the next value of $\{X_t\}$ can be expressed as a linear combination of current and previous observations. That is

$$X_{t+1} = w_m X_t + ... + w_1 X_{t-m+1} + \varepsilon_t$$

where m is the order of regression.

In PQR, nodes which their estimated buffer level in future time is above 75% of the buffer size are high buffer level nodes and are not appropriate choice to be selected as a router. This is a heuristic value based on network resources performance.

Speed and node movement: If a node is moving with high speed, this would not be a good choice for packet forwarding. If it is selected as a router, after some seconds it will go away and its connection with its neighborhoods will be broken. So, it could not forward packets and many packets will be lost and must be generated and forwarded again. Consequently, delay in MAC layer is increased because of degradation of link quality. In addition, a route recovery should be performed which may last a few seconds and packets should be queued up until a new path is set. So, high speed movement causes increase of end-to-end delay. Indeed, node movement causes QoS violation and increases packet loss and packet delays as well as decreasing network throughput.

To decrease these kinds of QoS violation, PQR predicts whether a node's future position could have stable links to forward packets or not. Hence, node's position in relation to its downstream neighborhood is predicted. If two nodes will be in the range of each other in future, then the upstream node is selected as a router. To predict time duration which nodes will be in the range of each other, Link Expiration Time (LET) method has been proposed in [13] which is used here with a little modification because LET does not calculate the exact lifetime value expected.

Assume two mobile nodes that their speed and direction of their movement remain constant. Let the location of node i and node j at current time be given by (x_i, y_i) and (x_j, y_j). Also, let V_i, V_j be the speeds, and θ_i and θ_j be the directions of the nodes i and j respectively. If the transmission range of the nodes is r, then the Link Lifetime Duration (LLD) of the link between the two nodes will be based on t1 and t2 as shown below while in [13] LET is equal to t2.

$$a = v_i \cos \theta_i - v_j \cos \theta_j$$

$$t_{1,2} = \frac{-(ab+cd) \pm \sqrt{(a^2+c^2)r^2 - (ad-bc)^2}}{(a^2+c^2)}$$

$$b = x_i - x_j$$

$$c = v_i \sin \theta_i - v_j \sin \theta_j$$

$$d = y_i - y_j$$

Assume that always t1 is smaller than t2. If both t1 and t2 are greater than zero, then two nodes will be the in range of each other in future and LLD is set to t2-t1. If t1 is smaller than zero and t2 is greater than zero, it shows that two nodes are and will be in the range of each other until t2 time. So, LLD will be set to t2. If t1 and t2 are not defined or t1 and t2 are below zero, it means that two nodes will not be in range of each other. In these cases LLD is set to zero.

According to this prediction of future time, it is decided whether a node is a good choice to select as a router or not. Experimental results show that LLD value about 5 seconds is a desirable threshold. That is, when LLD is computed for a link between two nodes, if it is greater than the threshold, this is a good node to select as a router; otherwise, this node could not be a stable node in this path and will not be selected. Similar to the buffer threshold, the LLD threshold is also heuristic and is good for high speed scenarios (maximum mobile nodes' speed is 20 m/s). Obviously for lower speed, a higher threshold for LLD could be used to achieve better result.

To calculate LLD, the GPS information of upstream node should be sent to downstream node. Hence, some fields are added to route request messages. The fields contain node's speed, position and direction of movement. Adding the required information to route request message has two advantages: first, only when these information are required, they are transferred to downstream node; second, the most recently updated information is transferred, so LLD computation will be more accurate.

2.2 PQR Algorithm

We developed our PQR algorithm based on AODV routing protocol because of its on-demand features, recovery abilities and scalability. In PQR when downstream node receives a rout request message (e.g. RREQ in AODV) form node upstream, it predicts its future buffer level and its LLD in relation to upstream node. If its future buffer level is low (under 75%) and its LLD is greater than the threshold, downstream node will forward this RREQ to next hops; otherwise, it will drop the route request message. This repeats until route request message is received at the destination. Then, a route reply message is generated and sent to the destination as the same in AODV protocol. Note that considering future buffer and position status of nodes result to avoid the aggregation of traffic while selecting stable nodes simultaneously.

PQR, in fact, implements a call admission mechanism explicitly. For any request, it is checked whether there is a set of nodes which could make a desired path. Through PQR, we expect more stable paths are selected for routing so packets in this path will not experience long delays. Stable path means a path which has low breakage probability. Hence, QoS violation will be reduced and QoS guarantee will be provided with more probability. Meanwhile, including buffer as a selection criterion causes the distribution of load among paths. In addition, algorithm implementation is so simple. In the following section, the achieved results of simulations are explained.

3 Simulation

The following results were obtained by using Network Simulator (NS 2.28)[14]. 70 nodes were distributed randomly on a grid of 1000m *1000m with each node having a transmission range of 250m. Traffic sources are CBR (Constant Bit Rate). The data rate is varied between 50 to 400 packets per second with packet length of 512 bytes. Number of requests is 15 and they will enter randomly during the simulation time. The mobility model uses the random way point model. Nodes move with a randomly chosen speed (uniformly between 1 and 20 m/sec). Each node starts its movement from a random location to a random destination. Simulations were run for 1000 seconds and 10 times.

3.1 Performance Results

We compare the performance of our algorithm with AODV routing protocol which is our base protocol. PQR is compared with AODV within the following three key performance metrics:

-Average end-to-end delay of data packets - This includes all possible delays caused by buffering during route discovery latency, queuing at the interface queue, retransmission delays at the MAC, propagation and transmission times. As it is illustrated in Fig. 1, routing with proposed algorithm has a better end-to-end delay since the subset of forwarding nodes belongs to the set of nodes with more available buffer space as well as more stability with their neighborhoods.

-Packet delivery ratio - The ratio of the data packets delivered to the destination to those generated by the CBR sources. Fig. 2 shows a comparison of this metric for the AODV with PQR algorithm. Routing with PQR algorithm has a better packet delivery ratio because more stable and lower buffer level nodes are selected.

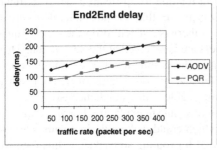

Fig. 1. Average end-to-end delay

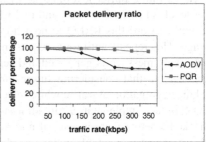

Fig. 2. Packet delivery ratio

-Call acceptance rate- It is the number of calls which a path is set for them to total number of calls. In PQR algorithm the call acceptance rate is reduced because for many calls there is not a stable path which could satisfy QoS requirements (Fig. 3).

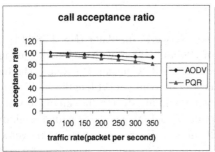

Fig. 3. Call acceptance ratio

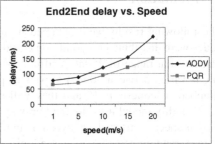

Fig. 4. Average e2e delay in various speeds

Thus, proposed algorithm did not accept it for admission to network. However, in AODV more calls are accepted but their QoS requirement are violated during their session.

Moreover, to show the efficiency of PQR in high speed and high traffic condition, we compare end to end delay of PQR with AODV in various speeds. Figure 4 shows end to end delay while maximum speed of nodes is varied between 1 to 20 m/s and traffic rate is set to 400 packet per seconds. As shown, PQR has a lower average end to end delay than AODV. It should be noted that PQR outperforms better in higher speed.

4 Conclusion

We introduced a Prediction based QoS Routing algorithm, PQR, to enhance on demand routing protocols to provide QoS routing, particularly in terms of end-to-end delay. The proposed algorithm predicts future states of nodes, and based on it, decides whether to select a node as a router or not. Through this algorithm, more stable and lower buffer level nodes are selected and hence end-to-end delay is reduced. Simulation results show the efficiency of the proposed algorithm.

References

1. H. Xiao, W. K. G. Seahand A. Lo, and K. C. Chua, "A flexible quality of service model for mobile ad-hoc networks," in IEEE VTC 2000-spring, Japon/Tokyo, 2000.
2. C. E. Perkins, E. M. Royer, S. R. Das, "Quality of Service for Ad hoc On-Demand Distance Vector Routing," draft-perkins-manet-aodvqos- 02.txt, IETF Internet Draft, work in progress, October 2003.
3. I. Jawhar and J. Wu, "Quality of Sevice Routing in Mobile Ad Hoc Networks," in Resource Management in Wireless Networking, M. Cardei, and D. -Z. Du (eds.), Kluwer, 2003.
4. Y.Ge, T.Kunz, L.Lamont, "Quality of Service routing in ad-hoc networks using OLSR," The 36th Hawaii International Conference on System Sciences (HICSS-36), Hawaii, USA, January 2003.
5. S. Chen and K. Nahrstedt, "Distributed Quality-of-Service Routing in Ad Hoc Networks," IEEE Journal on Selected Areas in Communications, 17(8):1488-1505, August 1999.
6. S.H. Shah, K. Nahrstedt, "Predictive location-based QoS routing in Mobile ad hoc networks," IEEE ICC 2002, Vol. 2, pp. 1022-1027.
7. J. N. Al-Karaki, A. E. Kamal," End-to-end support for statistical quality of service in heterogeneous mobile ad hoc networks," Journal of Computer Communications, 28(18): 2119-2132, November 2005.
8. Q. Xue, A. Ganz, "Ad hoc QoS On-demand Routing (AQOR) in Mobile Ad hoc Networks," Journal of Parallel and Distributed Computing (JPDC), vol 63, issue 2 pp 154 - 165, Feb. 2003.
9. A. Parekh, R.Gallager, "A Generalized Processor Sharing Approach to flow control in Integrated Services Networks- The Multiple Node Case," IEEE/ACM Transactions on Networking, Vol. 2, No.1, pp. 137-150, April 1994.
10. A. E. Albert and L. A. Gardner, Stochastic Approximation and Nonlinear Regression. MIT Press, 1967.
11. Gao, W., Wang, J., Chen, J., and Chen, S., ``PFED: a prediction-based fair active queue management algorithm," The 2005 International Conference on Parallel Processing (ICPP-05), pp. 485-491, 2005.
12. M. Ghaderi, "On the relevance of self-similarity in network traffic prediction," Tech. Rep. CS-2003-28, School of Computer Science, University of Waterloo, October 2003.
13. W. Su, S-J Lee, M. Gerla, "Mobility prediction and routing in ad hoc wireless networks," International Journal of Network Management, Vol. 11, Jan-Feb 2001, pp. 3-30.
14. K. Fall and K. Varadhan, NS notes and documentation, A Collaboration between researchers at US Berkley, LBL, USC/ISI, and Xerix PARC, available at http://www.isi.edu/nsnam/ns/.

MCDS Based Multicasting in Mobile Adhoc Networks

M. Shukla, M. Rai, G.S. Tomar⋆, and S. Verma

ABV Indian Institute of Information Technology and Management Gwalior
`raimrityunjay@gmail.com`

Abstract. Multicasting in resource constrained MANETs imposes a severe restriction on the message overhead for construction and maintenance of the multicast distribution tree. Algorithms based on minimum spanning trees (MST) or Steiner trees require reconstruction of the tree when members join or leave a multicast group in addition to change in network topology. In the present paper, multicasting based on MCDS with local repair is presented. The proposed MCDS algorithm tries to optimize the number of messages required for construction and maintenance of the multicast backbone. It is observed that when a node joins or leaves the multicast group, the time taken for repair with local route discovery is almost constant and is independent of multicast group size. Moreover, there is only a modest increase in the CDS size. The results are similar when a node that is not a member of the multicast group but forms a part of the MCDS moves away resulting in a change of the network topology.

1 Introduction

Adhoc wireless networks are resource constrained self-organizing, adaptive that do not have any established infrastructure or centralized administration. Sharing information and communication within a group necessitates that multicasting be employed for optimum utilization of resources such as bandwidth and energy. Multicasting techniques must address the issues of volatility of the network and resource constraints. In explicit multicasting [1], the destination information is listed in data packet headers. In [2] a shared mesh is established for each multicast group. The information of the position of a node and its neighbours has been utilised for position based multicasting in [3]. Multicast ZRP [4] proactively maintains a on-demand multicast shared tree membership for node's local routing zone at each node. In [4] conventional protocols are used to define a multicast group as a collection of hosts. In overlay multicasting [6], nodes participating in the multicast group exploit the multicast routing at application level. Multicasting requires construction and periodic reconstruction of MST or Steiner tree when members join/leave or the topology changes. To sustain communication, a minimum virtual backbone is required in the network. Different techniques

---

⋆ Jaypee Institute of Engineering and Technology.

S. Chaudhuri et al. (Eds.): ICDCN 2006, LNCS 4308, pp. 52–57, 2006.

have been proposed for the MCDS formation [7] [8] [9]. One set of algorithms [8] are based on the idea of creating a DS incrementally, other set of algorithms use initial set as CDS and recursively remove vertices using MST, steiner tree etc [9]. Some approaches [7] try to construct a MCDS by finding a maximal independent set, which is then expanded to CDS by adding connected vertices.

The rest of the paper is organized as follows. In Section II, an MCDS Algorithm has been proposed and the design of the related multicast protocol had been discussed. Section III contains the comparisons and simulation results. Section IV concludes the paper.

2   Proposed Scheme

In the proposed technique, source initiates the multicast group. It calculates the multicast routing tree and provides the other nodes with the required information. It also determines the bandwidth that the other nodes must be willing to provide in order to be a part of the multicasting group.

The source is aware of the routing information of all the nodes and uses an MCDS algorithm to calculate the multicasting tree. It then sends the routing information to all the nodes. Each node is only provided with the information it requires and does not have information for the entire multicast group.

After the initial construction of the multicasting group, whenever a node joins, leaves or moves away, a local route discovery process is initiated. A local repair process is initiated to maintain the tree.

2.1   MCDS Formation

The MCDS construction/modification is a resource intensive operation. To be efficient, it must require local information with minimal message exchange. The MCDS formation starts by hierarchically dividing the graph into Clusters. The clustered architecture of an ad-hoc network is a 2-level hierarchical network converts a dense network into sparse network and has node information locally which is suitable for scalability, so. Each cluster head computes its forward node that relays the broadcast packet, set to cover other cluster heads within its vicinity. The forward node set is computed such that all the cluster heads in network can be connected and broadcast packet is delivered to entire network. The information about the forward node set is also piggy-backed with the broadcast packet to further reduce its forward node set. The broadcast operation is restricted only to cluster heads and nodes in locally selected forward node sets.

Cluster heads are elected using election process based on Highest Connectivity. A gateway is a non-cluster head node in a cluster that has a neighbor in another cluster (i.e. gateways are needed to connect cluster heads together). The cluster heads and gateways together form a CDS of network. The cluster based broadcast algorithm only requires nodes in this CDS forward the broadcast packet while other nodes do not participate in packet forwarding process. In proposed work, Highest Connectivity of node is used for cluster head election.

The forward node set of the cluster head v is a subset of gateways by which the v connects to the cluster heads in $C(v)$ (adjacent cluster head set). v connects to a cluster head in $C^2(v)$ (cluster heads that are 2-hops away from v) via a 1-hop gateway and it connects to a cluster head in $C^3(v)$ (cluster heads that are 3-hops away from v) via two 2-hop gateways. At each cluster head, greedy algorithm is used to determine forward node set. The set of forward node set is selected as follows. The forward node set is organized as $\{f_1, f_2\}$ where f_1 is a 1-hop gateway used to connect to cluster heads in $C^2(v)$ and f_2 is a set of 2-hop gateways that are neighbors of f_1 and are used to connect to cluster heads in $C^3(v)$. f_2 may be empty if none in $C^3(v)$ is considered. The Core MCDS nodes and gateway or forwarding nodes together form the MCDS. The MCDS formation through this algorithm has the benefit that the number of cluster heads gets reduced; lesser number of MCDS nodes is formed as compared to other Algorithms.

2.2   The Multicast Protocol

The source initiates the multicast group as the group leader and the root of the multicast tree. It maintains a sequence number for the group and disseminates group information to all network nodes. The sequence number is incremented periodically by the group leader, and is used by the receiving nodes to determine the freshness of the group related messages. A node that wishes to join a multicast group will broadcast a Route Request message. Any on-tree node can respond to the this message with a Route Reply message via the reverse route. Other off-tree nodes will re-broadcast the Route Request message or unicast it to the group leader if the node has the group leader information and has a path to it. As the joining node may receive multiple replies, it activates the selected path by sending a Multicast Activation (MACT) message along the selected path to the multicast tree. The amount of bandwidth that the joining node must be ready to reserves is encapsulated in the request message. MACT message is then used to activate and reserve bandwidth on the selected path.

2.3   The Protocol Operations

Multicast Group Initialization. The source is aware of the members of the group and initiates the creation of the group. It uses the a query message to obtain routing table of the nodes. The nodes respond via query reply message. The MCDS is then deteremined. The source dessiminates the routing and bandwidth information to upstream and downstream neighbours to enable the nodes to maintain routing and reservation tables.

3   Results and Comparison

Case 1: Node Join. When a node joins, it is checked whether the node is connected to any on tree node. If so then the on tree becomes a part of the CDS and the node becomes a part of the tree. If not, a path to the tree is found. All the nodes on the path become a part of the CDS and the node becomes a part of the group.

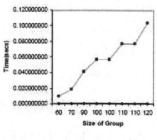

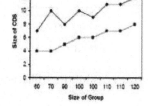

Fig. 1.   Fig. 2.

The graph in figure 1 shows the time taken for local route discovery (LR) and the time taken for constructing the new CDS for each of the eight cases. As can be seen the local route discovery is much faster than constructing the entire CDS again.

Figure 2 shows the number of nodes in the CDS for the local route discovery and the number of nodes when the MCDS is recalculated for each of the eight cases. There is an increase in the number of nodes in the CDS for the local route discovery. Only the source needs to maintain this information

Case 2: Leaving the Multicast Group. When a node leaves the multicast group, a local repair process is initiated. There are two possibilities. The leaving node may be part of the CDS or a simple on tree node. In the latter case no repair is needed. However, if it is part of the CDS then a repair process is initiated. As soon as any node discovers that there is link breakage with any of its neighbors it checks to see if it is still connected to any node in the CDS. If so no action is taken. If it not then a local route discovery process is initiated.

This is done for all the affected nodes. Once each node discovers a new path an message is sent to the source to maintain the multicast group information and compute the routing tables and other group related information.

In figure 3 shows the time taken for local route repair (LR) and the time taken for constructing the new CDS for each of the six cases. As can be seen the local route repair is much faster than constructing the entire CDS again.

The graph in figure 4 shows the number of nodes in the CDS for the local route repair and the number of nodes when the MCDS is recalculated for each of the six cases. There is an increase in the number of nodes in the CDS for the local route discovery. But only the source needs to maintain this information.

Case 3: Mobility of the Node. A node may move causing existing links to break. Whenever a node moves old links are broken and new links are formed. As a result a local route repair process is initiated.

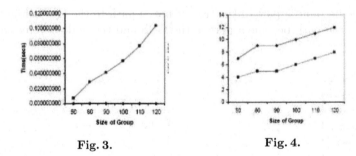

Fig. 3.   Fig. 4.

There are two possibilities. The node may be part of the MCDS or a simple on tree node.

If it is just a simple node, then the only affected node is the moving node itself. A local route discovery process is initiated and a path to the tree is found. All the nodes on the path are part of the CDS.

If the moving node is part of the MCDS then all the affected nodes have to recompute their routes. If the affected node is connected to any other node in the MCDS then nothing has to be done. Else a local route repair process is initiated and a path to the group is found.

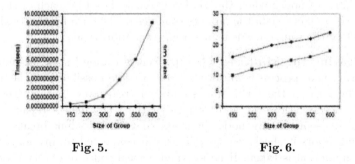

Fig. 5.   Fig. 6.

The graph in Fig 5 shows the time taken for local route repair (LR) and the time taken for constructing the new CDS for each of the six cases. As can be seen the local route repair is much faster than constructing the entire CDS again. It can be observed that the time taken for local route repair (LR) and the time taken for constructing the new CDS for each of the six cases. The local route repair is much faster than constructing the entire CDS again.

The graph in figure 6 shows the number of nodes in the CDS for the local route repair and the number of nodes when the MCDS is recalculated for each of the six cases. There is an increase in the number of nodes in the CDS for the local route discovery. However, only the source needs to maintain this information.

4 Conclusion

The proposed protocol integrates resource reservation with the routing protocol to provide multicasting. MCDS based algorithm is utilised to create the initial multicasting tree and uses local route discovery and route repair to manage removal of nodes and link breakages due to mobility.

The simulation results indicate the superiority of local route discovery and local route repair as opposed to reconstruction. The heuristic used to create the MCDS is simple and comparable to existing algorithms in terms of efficiency. The protocol is intuitively designed to work in adhoc networks with low mobility and low rates of addition. However, the efficacy of the protocol must be tested for networks having high mobility and high rates of nodes addition.

References

[1] L. Ji, M. Scott and J. Corson, "Explicit multicasting for mobile ad hoc networks", Mobile Networks and Applications Volume 8, Issue 5 (October 2003) Pages: 535 549 Year of Publication: 2003

[2] R. Vaishampayan and J.J. Garcia-Luna-Aceves, "Protocol for unified multicasting through announcements (PUMA)", Proceedings of the 1st IEEE International Conference on Mobile Ad-hoc and Sensor Systems (MASS), October 2004.

[3] M. Mauve, H. Fubler, J. Widmer, T. Lang "Position-Based Multicast Routing for Mobile Ad-Hoc Networks", Technical Report, Nr. TR-03-004, 2003.

[4] Z. Xiaofeng, J. Lillykutty, "Multicast Zone Routing Protocol in Mobile Ad Hoc Wireless Networks", 28th Annual IEEE International Conference on Local Computer Networks (LCN'03), pp. 150-152, 2003.

[5] Y. Ko and N. Vaidya, "Geocasting in Mobile Ad Hoc Networks: Location-Based Multicast Algorithms", Technical Report TR-98-018, Texas A&M University, September 1998.

[6] A. Detti, C. Loreti and P. Loreti, "Effectiveness of Overlay Multicasting,", IEEE Conf. On Mobile Ad-Hoc Network, 2004.

[7] S. Guha and S. Khuller, "Approximation algorithms for connected dominating sets", Algorithmica, 20(4), pp. 374-387, Apr. 1998.

[8] X. Cheng, X. Huang, D. Li, W. Wu, and D.-Z.Du, "Polynomial-Time Approximation Scheme for Minimum Connected Dominating Set in AdHoc Wireless Networks", Networks, Vol. 42, No. 4, pp. 202-208, 2003.

[9] J. Wu and H. Li, "On Calculating Connected Dominating Set for Efficient Routing in Ad Hoc Wireless Networks", Proceedings of the 3rd international workshop on Discrete algorithms and methods for mobile computing and communications, p.7-14, August 20-20, 1999, Seattle, Washington, United States.

Programmer-Centric Conditions for Itanium Memory Consistency

Lisa Higham[1], LillAnne Jackson[1,2], and Jalal Kawash[3,1]

[1] Department of Computer Science, The University of Calgary, Calgary, Canada
[2] Department of Computer Science, The University of Victoria, Victoria, Canada
[3] Department of Computer Science, American University of Sharjah, UAE
higham@ucalgary.ca, jackson@cpsc.ucalgary.ca, jkawash@aus.edu

Abstract. We formulate a programmer-centric description of the memory consistency model provided by the Itanium architecture. This allows reasoning about programs at a non-operational level in the natural way, not obscured by the implementation details of the underlying architecture. However, our definition is not tight. We provide two very similar definitions and show that the specification of the Itanium memory model lies between the two. These two definitions are motivated by slightly different implementations of load-acquire instructions.

Keywords: Programmer-centric memory consistency, Itanium multiprocessor.

1   Introduction

We contend that for programming purposes, a memory consistency model should be specified as a set of (ordering) rules on the *instructions* used by the programmer, rather than on a lower level collection of *operations*. Furthermore, the validity condition should be the natural notion of validity of sequences of these instructions acting on the objects of the system. For example, in a valid sequence of loads and stores, the value returned by each load instruction should be the value written by the most recent preceding instruction in the sequence that stored a value to the same memory location. Such a description is useful to a programmer of the system since she can reason about her code directly, and therefore we call it *programmer-centric*. Descriptions in terms of lower level operations specify an implementation (in hardware or on a virtual platform) and are useful for an architect who is building the system, but should not be confused with its specification. In this case these lower level implementations should be *proved* equivalent to the specification. A further advantage of our approach is that constructions can be composed. A high level specification of an object oriented system can be implemented by a succession of constructions, such that an implementation at one level is the specification for a still lower level, and each level of implementation is proved to correctly implement its specification. This, of course, is the familiar notion of abstraction; we simply extend it to weak models of memory consistency.

S. Chaudhuri et al. (Eds.): ICDCN 2006, LNCS 4308, pp. 58–69, 2006.

In previous work we established a framework for specifying programmer-centric memory consistency models and for proving such equivalences between specifications and implementations [7, 6]. This paper applies these ideas to the Intel Itanium architecture. That is, we aim for a programmer-centric specification of the memory consistency of the Itanium multiprocessor. As will be seen, we failed to realize this goal. Instead, we define two very similar programmer-centric memory consistency models, Itanium$_A$ and Itanium$_B$, and show that "official" Itanium memory consistency [9], henceforth referred to as Itanium (with no subscript), lies strictly between these two (Section 3). Itanium$_B$ and Itanium$_A$ differ only slightly in the ordering constraints involving Itanium load-acquire instructions, and each is motivated by a plausible hardware implementation. Several other plausible definitions also fail to exactly capture the Itanium memory consistency specification (Section 5). The main results of this paper are preceded, in Section 2, with an overview the Itanium architecture and a synopsis of its operational level memory consistency as described by Intel [9].

Several other frameworks for describing memory consistency have been proposed but are not central to this paper. The framework of Adir, Attiya and Shurek [1] is very similar to ours and precedes ours. Arvind and Maessem [3] provide a framework for serializable memory models. We are unaware, however, of how to use these frameworks to prove equivalence between systems. Yang et. al. [11, 12, 4] present a non-operational approach to specifying and analyzing shared memory consistency models and use it to provide a translation of the rules of Itanium specification. Adve and Gharachorloo [2] consider the question of programmer centricity of memory consisteny models and provide it by giving the illusion of sequentially consistent memory. The TLA work of Joshi et. al. [10] is a precise specification of Itanium and is the basis of the official specification [9].

2   Itanium Multiprocessors

2.1   Itanium Architecture

The Itanium specifications [9] are independent of specific machine implementations. Although we do not know of a concrete machine implementation that exactly captures the Itanium specifications, in this subsection we overview some of the architectural features of such a machine.

Itanium provides a distributed-shared memory (DSM) architecture where each processor maintains a replicated copy of the shared address space. The rules that govern processor execution and inter-processor communication are complicated and give rise to complex behaviors. Itanium also supports write-buffers with read by-passing, which further complicates the behavior of Itanium. Bypassing loads can complete before earlier buffered stores and give rise to an out-of-order execution. When a processor loads a variable that it never stores, however, (such as a single-writer variable owned by a different processor) the load returns the value from the local replica rather than from the local buffer. Itanium write buffers are guaranteed to be FIFO only per variable. Hence, two store instructions to different variables can be applied to a replica in the opposite order to that in which they occur in a processor's program.

To constrain out-of-order execution, Itanium supports the extensions of "acquire" and "release" to load and store instructions, respectively. A load-acquire instruction (denoted ld.acq) is always performed before any subsequent instruction in the program. A store-release (denoted st.rel) is always performed after every preceding instruction in the program. Store-releases also constrain interprocessor interaction. Specifically, incoming store-releases force earlier stores by the same processor to be applied remotely in the same order they are applied at the issuing processor. Acquires and releases also restrict the write buffer's behavior. For instance, when a release is buffered it forces all previously buffered stores to be removed from the buffer and applied to the local replicas before the release itself. A load-acquire can also force the buffer to be flushed, but this is not necessary in general.

2.2   Itanium Memory Consistency According to the Itanium Manual

Itanium memory consistency is specified in the Intel manual [9]. We paraphrase (and simplify) it here as concisely as possible, so that it can be compared to the programmer-centric version that we describe in Section 3. When the same things are named differently in the manual [9] and in our framework (Subsection 3.1), we use our terminology and notation, to simplify the comparisons. For example, what we call a computation is exactly what the manual calls an *execution*, and we denote program order by $\xrightarrow{prog}$ whereas the manual uses $\gg$. We also define a few additional terms to simplify notation. The symbol st[.rel] represents an instruction with store semantics (i.e. either st or st.rel), ld[.acq] represents a load instruction (i.e. either ld or ld.acq), and i represents any Itanium-based instruction.

Each Itanium-based instruction is decomposed into *operations* that either read values from or write values to memory locations. An instruction's operations correspond to different aspects of the visibility of the instruction for different processors. Specifically, ld[.acq] is "decomposed" into a single read operation R(ld[.acq]); st[.rel] by processor p is decomposed into $n+1$ write operations for an n-processor multiprocessor: a local write operation visible only to p denoted LV(st[.rel]) and a remote write operation for each processor q in the system denoted RV_q(st[.rel]). fence is "decomposed" into just one operation, F(fence). The operations of an instruction and the instruction itself *correspond*. For example, each of the operations $LV(st_p(x,v))$, $RV_p(st_p(x,v))$ and $RV_q(st_p(x,v))$ for every processor $q \neq p$ corresponds to the store instruction $st_p(x,v)$. The operation O is a *read operation* (respectively, *write operation*) if O corresponds to load (respectively, store) instruction.

We assume that memory locations with distinct names do not overlap. Let WR be a (write) operation corresponding to instruction st[.rel] and RD be a (read) operation corresponding to instruction ld[.acq]. The value stored by st[.rel] (respectively, written by WR) is denoted WrVal(st[.rel]) (respectively, WrVal(WR)).

Similarly, the value loaded by ld[.acq] (respectively, read by RD) is denoted Rd-Val(ld[.acq]) (respectively, RdVal(RD)). Every location b in memory has an *initial value*, denoted by InitVal(b), that will be returned to read operations when they occur before there are any write operations to that location.

Any computation of the basic Itanium processor family memory ordering model must have an associated *visibility order*, which linearly orders all the operations that correspond to all the instructions of the computation and satisfies the *Itanium rules* below. If there is no visibility order for a computation that satisfies all of these rules, the computation is not permitted by the architecture.

If an instruction i is by a processor p, we write $p = \text{Proc}(i)$. For any two operations O and U, $O \xrightarrow{V} U$ means that O precedes U in the visibility order V. If there is a store instruction $\text{st}_p(x, \cdot)$ and a load instruction $\text{ld}_p(x)$ such that $\text{LV}(\text{st}_p(x, \cdot)) \xrightarrow{V} \text{R}(\text{ld}_p(x)) \xrightarrow{V} \text{RV}_p(\text{st}_p(x, \cdot))$ then the operation $\text{R}(\text{ld}_p(x))$ is a *local read in* V and $\text{ld}_p(x)$ is a *local load in* V (or simply a local load or local read when V is clear).

Itanium Rules

(WO): Every store becomes visible locally before it becomes visible remotely.

For every store st[.rel] where $p=\text{proc}(\text{st}[.\text{rel}])$, $\text{LV}(\text{st}[.\text{rel}]) \xrightarrow{V} \text{RV}_p(\text{st}[.\text{rel}])$ and $\text{RV}_p(\text{st}[.\text{rel}]) \xrightarrow{V} \text{RV}_q(\text{st}[.\text{rel}])$ for $q \neq \text{Proc}(\text{st}[.\text{rel}])$.

(ACQ): Any instruction program-ordered after a ld.acq becomes visible after the ld.acq.

If $\text{ld.acq} \xrightarrow{prog} i$, A is a read operation corresponding to ld.acq, and O is an operation corresponding to i, then $A \xrightarrow{V} O$.

(REL): Any instruction program-ordered before a st.rel becomes visible before the st.rel.

- If $i \xrightarrow{prog} \text{st.rel}$, and i does not have store semantics, and O is an operation corresponding to i, then $O \xrightarrow{V} \text{LV}(\text{st.rel})$.
- If $\text{st}[.\text{rel}] \xrightarrow{prog} \text{st.rel}$ then $\text{LV}(\text{st}[.\text{rel}]) \xrightarrow{V} \text{LV}(\text{st.rel})$ and $\text{RV}_p(\text{st}[.\text{rel}]) \xrightarrow{V} \text{RV}_p(\text{st.rel})$ for each processor p.

(FEN): Instructions become visible in order with respect to fence instructions.

- If $\text{fence} \xrightarrow{prog} i$ and O is an operation corresponding to i, then $\text{F}(\text{fence}) \xrightarrow{V} O$.
- If $i \xrightarrow{prog} \text{fence}$ and O is an operation corresponding to i, then $O \xrightarrow{V} \text{F}(\text{fence})$.

(MD:RAW): Every load that is program-ordered after a store to the same location must become visible after that store.

- If st[.rel] and ld[.acq] access the same memory location and $\text{st}[.\text{rel}] \xrightarrow{prog} \text{ld}[.\text{acq}]$, then $\text{LV}(\text{st}[.\text{rel}]) \xrightarrow{V} \text{R}(\text{ld}[.\text{acq}])$.

(MD:WAR): Every store that is program-ordered after a load to the same location must become visible after that load.

- If ld[.acq] and st[.rel] access the same memory location and $\text{ld}[.\text{acq}] \xrightarrow{prog} \text{st}[.\text{rel}]$, then $\text{R}(\text{ld}[.\text{acq}]) \xrightarrow{V} \text{LV}(\text{st}[.\text{rel}])$.

(MD:WAW): Stores by a processor to a common location become visible to that processor in program order.

– If $st[.rel]_1$ and $st[.rel]_2$ access the same memory location and $st[.rel]_1 \xrightarrow{prog} st[.rel]_2$, then $LV(st[.rel]_1) \xrightarrow{V} LV(st[.rel]_2)$.

(COH): Stores to the same location become remotely visible in the same order for every processor.

– If $st[.rel]_1$ and $st[.rel]_2$ are stores to the same location and $Proc(st[.rel]_1) = Proc(st[.rel]_2)$ and $LV(st[.rel]_1) \xrightarrow{V} LV(st[.rel]_2)$ then $RV_p(st[.rel]_1) \xrightarrow{V} RV_p(st[.rel]_2)$.

– If $st[.rel]_1$ and $st[.rel]_2$ are stores to the same location and $RV_p(st[.rel]_1) \xrightarrow{V} RV_p(st[.rel]_2)$ for any processor p, then $RV_q(st[.rel]_1) \xrightarrow{V} RV_q(st[.rel]_2)$ for all processors q.

(WBR): Store-release instructions become remotely visible atomically.

– If $RV_p(st.rel) \xrightarrow{V} 0 \xrightarrow{V} RV_q(st.rel)$ then $0=RV_r(st.rel)$ for some processor r.

The remaining rules determine what value must be returned by a load, which depends on the placement of the read of the load within the low level write operations to the same location.

(RV1): Let $ld[.acq]$ be a local load of location x and $st[.rel]$ be a store to x, such that $Proc(st[.rel]) = Proc(ld[.acq])$. Suppose that $LV(st[.rel]) \xrightarrow{V} R(ld[.acq])$ and there is no other store, $st[.rel]'$, to x with $Proc(st[.rel]')= Proc(ld[.acq])$ where $LV(st[.rel]) \xrightarrow{V} LV(st[.rel]') \xrightarrow{V} R(ld[.acq])$. Then $RdVal(ld[.acq]) = WrVal(st[.rel])$.

(RV2): Let $ld[.acq]$ be a non-local load of location x and $p = Proc(ld[.acq])$. Suppose there is a store $st[.rel]$ to x such that $RV_p(st[.rel]) \xrightarrow{V} R(ld[.acq])$, and there is no other store $st[.rel]'$ to x with $RV_p(st[.rel]) \xrightarrow{V} RV_p(st[.rel]') \xrightarrow{V} R(ld[.acq])$. Then $RdVal(ld[.acq]) = WrVal(st[.rel])$.

(RV3): Let $ld[.acq]$ be a non-local load instruction of location x and $p = Proc(ld[.acq])$. Suppose there is no $st[.rel]$ to x such that $RV_p(st[.rel]) \xrightarrow{V} R(ld[.acq])$. Then $RdVal(ld[.acq]) = InitVal(x)$.

3 Programmer-Centric Itanium-Based Consistency

3.1 Framework

As each process in a multiprocess system executes, it issues a sequence of instruction invocations on shared memory objects.[1] For this paper the shared memory consists of only shared variables, and each *instruction invocation* is *Itanium-based*. That is, each instruction invocation is of the form $st_p(x, v)$ or $st.rel_p(x, v)$

---

[1] Parts of this section were first used in previous work (Section 2.2 of [5]); they are re-used in this work in a modified form.

meaning that process p writes a value v to the shared variable x, or $\mathrm{ld}_p(x)$ or $\mathrm{ld.acq}_p(x)$ meaning that process p reads a value from shared variable x, or fence_p meaning that process p invoked a memory fence instruction. Instruction invocations st and st.rel are referred to collectively as *store* instructions and have *store semantics*; ld and ld.acq are called *load* instruction invocations and have *load semantics*. It suffices (for this paper) to model each individual process p as a sequence of these instruction invocations and call such a sequence an *individual (Itanium-based) program*.[2] An *(Itanium-based) multiprogram* is a finite set of these individual programs.

An *instruction* is an instruction invocation completed with a response. In our setting the response of a store instruction invocation or a fence instruction invocation is an acknowledgment and is ignored. The response of a load invocation is the value returned by the invocation. A *(multiprocess) computation of an Itanium-based multiprogram*, P is created from P by changing each load instruction invocation, $\mathrm{ld}_p(x)$ (respectively, $\mathrm{ld.acq}_p(x)$) to $\nu \leftarrow \mathrm{ld}_p(x)$ (respectively, $\nu \leftarrow \mathrm{ld.acq}_p(x)$) where ν is either the initial value of x or some value stored to x by some store to x in the multiprogram.

Notice that the definition of a computation permits the value returned by each $\mathrm{ld}(x)$ or $\mathrm{ld.acq}(x)$ instruction invocation to be arbitrarily chosen from the set of values stored to x by the multiprogram. In an Itanium (or any other) multiprocessor, the values that might actually be returned are substantially further constrained by its architecture, which determines the way in which the processes communicate and that shared memory is implemented. A *memory consistency model* captures these constraints by specifying a set of additional requirements that computations must satisfy. Typically, these require the existence of a set of sequences of instructions that satisfy certain properties. A collection of such sequences for a computation C that meet all the requirements of memory consistency model $\mathcal{M}$ is called a set of $\mathcal{M}$-*verifying sequences for* C. We use $\mathcal{C}(P, \mathcal{M})$ to denote the set of all computations of multiprogram P that satisfy the memory consistency model $\mathcal{M}$. Memory consistency model $\mathcal{M}$ is *stronger than* $\mathcal{M}'$ if, for every Multiprogram P, $\mathcal{C}(P, \mathcal{M}) \subseteq \mathcal{C}(P, \mathcal{M}')$; $\mathcal{M}$ is *strictly stronger than* $\mathcal{M}'$ if $\mathcal{C}(P, \mathcal{M}) \subsetneq \mathcal{C}(P, \mathcal{M}')$ The terms *weaker* and *strictly weaker* are defined similarly.

The description of a memory consistency model is simplified by assuming that each store instruction invocation has a distinct value. Although it is technically straightforward to remove this assumption, without it, the description of the memory model is messy and its properties are consequently obscured.

For an Itanium-based computation C, $I(C)$ denotes all the instructions in C. $I(C)|p$ is the subset of $I(C)$ in processor p's program sequence; $I(C)|x$ is the subset of $I(C)$ applied to variable x; $I(C)|r$ is the subset containing only the load instructions; $I(C)|w$ is the subset containing only the store instructions; Let $I(C)|acq$ denote the subset containing all ld.acq instructions plus the memory fence instructions; let $I(C)|rel$ denote the subset containing all st.rel

---

[2] We have made some common simplifying assumptions such as memory locations do not overlap, memory is cacheable (i.e., WB) and semaphores are omitted.

instructions plus the memory fence instructions. The relation $(I(C), \xrightarrow{prog})$, called *program order*, is the set of all pairs (i, j) of instructions that are in the same individual computation of C and such that i precedes j in that sequence. For any partial order relation $(I(C), \xrightarrow{y})$, the notation $i \xrightarrow{y} j$ is used to mean $(i, j) \in (I(C), \xrightarrow{y})$.

A load instruction is *domestic* if the value it returns was stored into shared memory location x by a store instruction by the same processor; memory fence instructions and load instructions that are not domestic are *foreign*. If an instruction, i, with load semantics returns the value stored by an instruction, j, with store semantics then i and j are *causally related*.

3.2   Weak and Strong Itanium Memory Consistency

This section uses the framework of Subsection 3.1 to formulate two programmer-centric definitions of Itanium consistency and describe informally what the definitions are intended to capture. They differ only slightly in the constraints on ld.acq instructions.

Define the following partial orders. Let $i, j \in I(C)$ such that $i \xrightarrow{prog} j$.

Acquire A: $i \xrightarrow{Acquire\ A} j$ if and only if $i \in I(C)|acq$.

Acquire B: $i \xrightarrow{Acquire\ B} j$ if and only if $i \in I(C)|acq$ and i is foreign.

Acquire A describes a conservative implementation of ld.acq instructions, which requires any ld.acq to precede all instructions that follows it in the program. In the presence of buffers, certain architectural decisions can sacrifice this "text-book" behavior. For instance, Acquire B captures the situation when a ld.acq can be satisfied from the buffer (a domestic ld.acq). A ld that follows the ld.acq in program order could by-pass the buffer, or, a following st to a different variable could be committed to the local replica earlier than the buffered st that is used to satisfy the ld.acq. In these cases, the program order between the ld.acq and the subsequent ld or st is not necessarily preserved. There is one occurrence of each st in a processor's view, and these views are constructed based on the order in which stores occur in the local replicas. To maintain the intuitive notion of validity, the ld.acq must be delayed in the view until its causally-related st occurs in the local replica. Hence, a domestic ld.acq may occur in a view after a ld or a st that follows it in program order.

Acquire B allows this behavior, but prohibits it when the ld.acq is foreign (necessarily satisfied from the local replica rather than the buffer). It is also prohibited when ld.acq and the ld are applied to the same variable: if the ld.acq is satisfied from the buffer, then either the ld is also satisfied from the buffer or, if not, the st under consideration must have been applied to the local replica. This will be taken care of by the coherence requirement in the Itanium consistency definition.

One mechanism to prohibit a domestic ld.acq from occurring in a processor's view later than it should is to flush the buffer before the ld.acq is completed, ensuring that the ld.acq is always satisfied from the local replica. Such an architecture could achieve views satisfying Acquire A.

The following definition is parameterized by an arbitrary partial order on $I(C)$, denoted R, which will be replaced by various partial orders (such as Acquire A and B) to construct variants of Itanium consistency.

Definition 1. *A computation C satisfies Itanium$_R$ if for each $p \in P$ there is a total order $(I(C)|p \cup I(C)|w, \xrightarrow{S_p})$ such that S_p is valid and for every $i, j \in I(C)|p \cup I(C)|w$:*

1. *If $i \xrightarrow{R} j$ then $i \xrightarrow{S_p} j$ (R Order), and*
2. *If $i \xrightarrow{prog} j$ and $j \in I(C)|rel$ then $i \xrightarrow{S_p} j$ (Release Order), and*
3. *If $i \xrightarrow{prog} j$ and $i, j \in I(C)|x$ and $[(i \in I(C)|w$ or $j \in I(C)|w)$ or $(i \in I(C)|acq)]$ then $i \xrightarrow{S_p} j$ (Same Memory Order), and*
4. *If $i, j \in I(C)|x|w$ and $i \xrightarrow{S_p} j$ then $i \xrightarrow{S_q} j$, $\forall q \in P$ (Same Memory Agreement), and*
5. *If $i, j \in I(C)|rel$ and $i \xrightarrow{S_p} j$ then $i \xrightarrow{S_q} j$, $\forall q \in P$ (Release Agreement), and*
6. *If $i \in I(C)|rel$ and $j \in I(C)|st|p$ and $i \xrightarrow{S_p} j$ then $i \xrightarrow{S_q} j$, $\forall q \in P$ (Release to Store Agreement), and*
7. *There does not exist a cycle of $i_1, i_2 \ldots i_k \in I(C)|w$ where $i_j \in I(C)|p_j, \forall j \in \{1, 2, \ldots k\}$ and $k \le n$ such that: $i_k \xrightarrow{S_1} i_1$, and $i_1 \xrightarrow{S_2} i_2$, and $i_2 \xrightarrow{S_3} i_3 \ldots$ and $i_{k-1} \xrightarrow{S_k} i_k$ (Cycle Free Agreement).*

Itanium$_A$ abbreviates Itanium$_R$ when R = Acquire A. Itanium$_B$ is defined similarly (R = Acquire B). Section 5 defines additional Itanium models based on further variants of acquire orders.

Notice that a view of a processor consists of its own instructions in addition to the store instructions of all other processors. A specified Acquire Order is maintained by each view (item 1). The Release Order (item 2) is simply what a programmer expects: any instruction preceding a st.rel must maintain this order in the processors' views. Item 3 specifies the coherence requirement. The remaining items are requirements that establishing some agreement between the views of each processor. Since channels between processors are FIFO for each variable, the communicated store instructions to the same variable must appear in every view in the same order (item 4). A st.rel instruction occurs in all replicas atomically so item 5 requires the st.rel instructions to be seen in the same order by all processors. Furthermore, by item 6, if a st is seen by the storing processor after a st.rel, that st must be seen after the st.rel by all processors. Item 7 is a technical condition arising from timing considerations. Consider a store s_p by p and a store s_q by q. Since a store is visible to the storing processor before it is visible to others, it is not possible for p see s_q before s_p, and yet for q see s_p before s_q. Item 7 generalizes this to any number of processors.

4   Itanium Is Strictly Between Itanium$_A$ and Itanium$_B$

Because of space constraints, the proofs of our two major theorems, Theorems 1 and 2, are omitted but can be found elsewhere [8].

Theorem 1. Itanium$_A$ *memory consistency is strictly stronger than* Itanium *memory consistency.*

Theorem 2. Itanium *memory consistency is strictly stronger than* Itanium$_B$ *memory consistency.*

A couple of computations serve to illustrate the essential differences between Itanium$_B$, Itanium and Itanium$_A$. Computation 1 satisfies Itanium$_B$ consistency but not Itanium or Itanium$_A$ consistency.

Comp 1 $\begin{cases} p: 3 \leftarrow \text{ld}(x) \ \text{st}(x,2) \ \ 2 \leftarrow \text{ld.acq}(x) \ \text{st}(y,4) \\ q: 4 \leftarrow \text{ld.acq}(y) \ \text{st}(x,3) \end{cases}$

In Computation 1, $2 \leftarrow \text{ld.acq}_p(x)$ is domestic but $4 \leftarrow \text{ld.acq}_q(y)$ is foreign. $4 \leftarrow \text{ld.acq}_q(y)$ must be satisfied from the local replica and not the write-buffer, but it is possible for $2 \leftarrow \text{ld.acq}_p(x)$ to be satisfied from p's write-buffer while $\text{st}_p(x,2)$ is pending, waiting to be applied to p's local replica. Since the write-buffers are only FIFO per variable, it is possible for $\text{st}_p(y,4)$ to be applied to p's replica before $\text{st}_p(x,2)$. Hence, in p's view it is possible for $2 \leftarrow \text{ld.acq}_p(x)$ to occur after $\text{st}_p(y,4)$, a violation of the "text-book" implementation of ld.acq. Itanium$_B$ allows this behavior, which is captured by the following verifying sequences:

$\begin{cases} S_p: \text{st}_p(y,4) \ \text{st}_q(x,3) \ \ 3 \leftarrow \text{ld}_p(x) \ \text{st}_p(x,2) \ \ 2 \leftarrow \text{ld.acq}_p(x) \\ S_q: \text{st}_p(y,4) \ \ 4 \leftarrow \text{ld.acq}_q(y) \ \text{st}_q(x,3) \ \text{st}_p(x,2) \end{cases}$

Computation 1 does not satisfy Itanium because of the following cycle of operations:

$$R(3 \leftarrow \text{ld}_p(x)) \xrightarrow{MD:WAR} LV(\text{st}_p(x,2)) \xrightarrow{(MD:RAW)} R(2 \leftarrow \text{ld.acq}_p(x)) \xrightarrow{(ACQ)}$$
$$LV(\text{st}_p(y,4)) \xrightarrow{(WO)} RV_p(\text{st}_p(y,4)) \xrightarrow{(WO)} RV_q(\text{st}_p(y,4)) \xrightarrow{(RV2)} R(4 \leftarrow \text{ld.acq}_q(y))$$
$$\xrightarrow{(ACQ)} LV(\text{st}_q(x,3)) \xrightarrow{(WO)} RV_q(\text{st}_q(x,3)) \xrightarrow{(WO)} RV_p(\text{st}_q(x,3)) \xrightarrow{(RV2)} R(3 \leftarrow \text{ld}_p(x)).$$

Any verifying visibility sequence is a total order, so no such sequence could extend the orders of this cycle.

Also, Computation 1 does not satisfy Itanium$_A$, which requires $2 \leftarrow \text{ld.acq}_p(x)$ to precede $\text{st}_p(y,4)$ in p's view. However, this is not possible because S_p must extend:

$$\text{st}_q(x,3) \xrightarrow{valid} 3 \leftarrow \text{ld}_p(x) \xrightarrow{same\ memory} \text{st}_p(x,2) \xrightarrow{same\ memory} 2 \leftarrow \text{ld.acq}_p(x)$$
$$\xrightarrow{strong\ acquire} \text{st}_p(y,4).$$

The Cycle Free agreement requirement needs $\text{st}_q(x,3) \xrightarrow{S_q} \text{st}_p(y,4)$ because otherwise $\text{st}_q(x,3) \xrightarrow{S_p} \text{st}_p(y,4) \xrightarrow{S_q} \text{st}_q(x,3)$ which is not allowed. Thus, S_q contains the following cycle: $\text{st}_q(x,3) \xrightarrow{cycle\ free} \text{st}_p(y,4) \xrightarrow{valid} 4 \leftarrow \text{ld.acq}_q(y)$ $\xrightarrow{strong\ acquire} \text{st}_q(x,3)$.

While the "liberal" behavior of the ld.acq instructions in Itanium$_B$ allows computations that are otherwise prohibited under Itanium, the conservative behavior of the ld.acq instructions in Itanium$_A$ is too prohibitive.

Computation 2 satisfies Itanium consistency but not Itanium$_A$ consistency.

Comp 2 $\begin{cases} p:4 \leftarrow\text{ld.acq}(y) & \text{st}(x,5) & \text{st.rel}(z,2) \\ q:\text{st}(x,3) & 3\leftarrow\text{ld.acq}(x) & \text{st}(y,4)2\leftarrow\text{ld.acq}(z) & 3\leftarrow\text{ld}(x) \end{cases}$

Processor q can place $\text{st}_q(x,3)$ in its write-buffer, satisfy $3\leftarrow\text{ld.acq}(x)$ from the buffer, and then buffer $\text{st}_q(y,4)$. Since the write-buffers are only FIFO per variable it is possible for $\text{st}_q(y,4)$ to be applied to both replicas while $\text{st}_q(x,3)$ is still pending in the buffer. Processor p can perform $4\leftarrow\text{ld.acq}_p(y)$ and then apply $\text{st}_p(x,5)$ to q'a replica while $\text{st}_q(x,3)$ is still in q's buffer.

Formally, a sequence V that satisfies Itanium is:

$\text{LV}(\text{st}_q(x,3))$, $\text{R}_q(3\leftarrow\text{ld.acq}_q(x))$, $\text{LV}(\text{st}_q(y,4))$, $\text{RV}_q(\text{st}_q(y,4))$, $\text{RV}_p(\text{st}_q(y,4))$, $\text{R}_p(4\leftarrow\text{ld.acq}_p(y))$, $\text{LV}(\text{st}_p(x,5))$, $\text{LV}(\text{st.rel}_p(z,2))$, $\text{RV}_p(\text{st}_p(x,5))$, $\text{RV}_q(\text{st}_p(x,5))$, $\text{RV}_p(\text{st.rel}_p(z,2))$, $\text{RV}_q(\text{st.rel}_p(z,2))$, $\text{R}_q(2\leftarrow\text{ld.acq}_q(z))$, $\text{R}_q(3\leftarrow\text{ld}_q(x))$, $\text{RV}_q(\text{st}_q(x,3))$, $\text{RV}_p(\text{st}_q(x,3))$.

Itanium$_A$ does not allow Computation 2 since Itanium$_A$ requires all ld.acq instructions to be satisfied from the local replica rather than the buffer. Hence, $\text{st}_q(x,3)$ is guaranteed to be applied to q's replica before even $\text{st}_q(y,4)$ is buffered. p must see $\text{st}_q(y,4)$ before it buffers $\text{st}_p(x,5)$ because it sees the value in y through a ld.acq instruction. When p sees $\text{st}_q(y,4)$, the value of x in q's replica must be 3. p's $\text{st.rel}_p(z,2)$ forces $\text{st}_p(x,5)$ to be applied everywhere before the st.rel itself. When q sees $\text{st.rel}_p(z,2)$, it must also have seen $\text{st}_p(x,5)$. So the value of x in q's replica must be 5, overwriting the earlier value of 3. $3\leftarrow\text{ld}_q(x)$ must take place after $2\leftarrow\text{ld.acq}_q(z)$, since Itanium$_A$ requires the ld.acq to precede any following instruction. However, we have already argued that the value of x according to q cannot be 3.

Formally, the Itanium$_A$ sequence, S_p, must extend:

$\text{st}_q(y,4) \xrightarrow{valid} 4\leftarrow\text{ld.acq}_p(y) \xrightarrow{strong\ acquire} \text{st}_p(x,5) \xrightarrow{release} \text{st.rel}_p(z,2)$. The Cycle Free agreement requirement needs $\text{st}_q(y,4) \xrightarrow{S_q} \text{st}_p(x,5)$ because otherwise $\text{st}_q(y,4) \xrightarrow{S_p} \text{st}_p(x,5) \xrightarrow{S_q} \text{st}_q(y,4)$ which is not allowed. Thus, S_q must extend: $\text{st}_q(x,3) \xrightarrow{same\ memory} 3\leftarrow\text{ld.acq}_q(x) \xrightarrow{strong\ acquire} \text{st}_q(y,4) \xrightarrow{cycle\ free} \text{st}_p(x,5) \xrightarrow{release} \text{st.rel}_p(z,2) \xrightarrow{valid} 2\leftarrow\text{ld.acq}_q(z) \xrightarrow{strong\ acquire} 3\leftarrow\text{ld}_q(x)$. This makes the final $3\leftarrow\text{ld}_q(x)$ invalid.

5 Other Acquire Orders

Itanium$_B$ and Itanium$_A$ bound Itanium and the only difference between them is slight changes in the Acquire Order. So a natural question is: "Is there a definition of an Acquire Order that yields a programmer-centric memory consistency specification that is equivalent to Itanium?" This section examines several plausible Acquire Order definitions and compares their relative strengths. One interesting result is another memory consistency model that is weaker than Itanium$_A$ yet still strictly stronger than Itanium.

Define the *write-before-read* relation $(I(C), \xrightarrow{wbr})$ by: $i_1 \xrightarrow{wbr} i_2$ if, for some shared variable x, $i_1 \in I(C)|x|w$ and $i_2 \in I(C)|x|r$ and i_2 reads the same value written by i_1.

In addition to Acquire A and Acquire B defined in Subsection 3.2, define two additional acquire orders as follows. Let $i, j \in I(C)$ such that $i \xrightarrow{prog} j$.

Acquire C: $i_1 \in I(C)|acq$ and i_2 is a non-domestic load.
Acquire D: $i_1 \xrightarrow{wbr} i_3 \xrightarrow{prog} i_2$ and $i_3 \in I(C)|acq$

Acquire C models a possible implementation where two load instructions, $i_1 = $ ld.acq which is program ordered before $i_2 = $ ld or ld.acq, and i_1 checks the write-buffer and misses it, bypasses any pending stores, and returns its value from the local replica. Meanwhile i_2 hits the buffer and returns. The effect is that i_2 bypasses i_1 because when constructing the processor's view i_2 will be delayed until its causally-related buffered write is committed to the local replica. Acquire D restricts this behavior in which any instruction can similarly bypass an earlier (in program order) domestic ld.acq. The bypassing instruction cannot be moved too early in the processor's view. It must follow the st that is causally related to the bypassed ld.acq.

These two partial orders give rise to two new definitions for Itanium consistency, in particular Itanium$_C$ (Definition 1 with $R = $ Acquire C) and Itanium$_D$ (Definition 1 with $R = $ Acquire D).

More variants of the Itanium memory consistency model are defined by combining the four basic acquire orders based either on intersection or conjunction as follows. Let $\gamma, \beta \in \{A, B, C, D\}$.

Intersection: A computation C satisfies Itanium$_{\gamma \cap \beta}$ if C satisfies Itanium$_\gamma$ and Itanium$_\beta$.
Conjunction: A computation C satisfies Itanium$_{\gamma \wedge \beta}$ if C satisfies Itanium$_{\gamma \cap \beta}$ and there is a set of Itanium$_\gamma$-verifying sequences for C that are also Itanium$_\beta$-verifying sequences for C.

Note that the models Itanium$_{\gamma \cap \beta}$ allow the Itanium$_\gamma$-verifying sequences for C to be different from Itanium$_\beta$-verifying sequences for C. Hence, Itanium$_{\gamma \wedge \beta}$ is stronger than Itanium$_{\gamma \cap \beta}$.

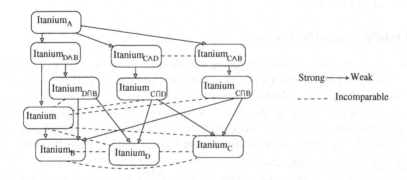

Fig. 1. Relative Strength of Various Systems

Since Itanium$_A$ is stronger than each of Itanium$_B$, Itanium$_C$, and Itanium$_D$, this introduces six new and distinct Itanium memory consistency models: Itanium$_{C \cap B}$, Itanium$_{C \cap D}$ Itanium$_{D \cap B}$ Itanium$_{C \wedge B}$, Itanium$_{C \wedge D}$ and Itanium$_{D \wedge B}$. Observe that Itanium$_A$ is also stronger than each of the models Itanium$_{C \wedge B}$, Itanium$_{C \wedge D}$ and Itanium$_{D \wedge B}$.

Figure 1 shows the relative strength of each system. The proofs are elsewhere [8].

A conclusion of this investigation is that Itanium$_{D \wedge B}$ is weaker than Itanium$_A$ but still stronger than Itanium. At present a programmer-centric consistency model that is equivalent to Itanium has not been identified. However, there is promise in this technique of strengthening the Acquire B order.

References

1. A. Adir, H. Attiya, and G. Shurek. Information-flow models for shared memory with an application to the PowerPC architecture. *IEEE Trans. on Parallel and Distributed Systems*, 14(5):502–515, 2003.
2. S. V. Adve and K. Gharachorloo. Shared memory consistency models: A tutorial. *IEEE Computer*, pages 66–76, December 1996.
3. Arvind and J.-W. Maessen. Memory model = instruction reordering + store atomicity. In *Proc. ISCA 2006*, to appear 2006.
4. G. Gopalakrishnan, Y. Yang, and H. Sivaraj. QB or not QB: An efficient execution verification tool for memory orderings. In *Proc. 16th International Conference on Computer Aided Verification (CAV'04)*, July 2004.
5. L. Higham and L. Jackson. Porting between Itanium and Sparc multiprocessing systems. In *18th ACM Symposium on Parallelism in Algorithms and Architectures (SPAA '06)*, to appear 2006.
6. L. Higham, L. Jackson, and J. Kawash. Specifying memory consistency of write buffer multiprocessors. *ACM Trans. on Computer Systems*. To appear.
7. L. Higham, L. Jackson, and J. Kawash. Capturing register and control dependence in memory consistency models with applications to the Itanium architecture. In *20th International Symposium on Distributed Computing (DISC 2006)*, to appear 2006. A longer version is available as Technical Report 2006-837-30, Department of Computer, The University of Calgary, Canada.
8. L. Higham, L. Jackson, and J. Kawash. Programmer-centric conditions for Itanium memory consistency. Technical Report 2006-838-31, Department of Computer Science, The University of Calgary, July 2006.
9. Intel Corporation. A formal specification of the Intel Itanium processor family memory ordering.
   http://www.intel.com/design/itanium/downloads/251429.htm/, Oct 2002.
10. R. Joshi, L. Lamport, J. Matthews, S. Tasiran, M. Tuttle, and Y. Yu. Checking cache-coherence protocols with tla, 2003.
11. Y. Yang, G. Gopalakrishnan, G. Lindstrom, and K. Slind. Analyzing the Intel Itanium memory ordering rules using logic programming and SAT. In *Proc. 12th Advanced Research Working Conference on Correct Hardware Design and Verification Methods (CHARME'03)*, pages 81–95, Oct 2003.
12. Y. Yang, G. Gopalakrishnan, G. Lindstrom, and K. Slind. Nemos: A framework for axiomatic and executable specifications of memory consistency models. In *Proc. 18th International Parallel and Distributed Processing Symposium (IPDPS'04)*, April 2004.

A Group Quorum System of Degree $1 + \sqrt{1 + \frac{n}{m}}$

Fouad B. Chedid

Department of Computer Science, Notre Dame University
P.O. Box: 72 Zouk Mikael, Zouk Mosbeh, Lebanon
`fchedid@ndu.edu.lb`

Abstract. The group mutual exclusion problem is a generalization of the ordinary mutual exclusion problem where each application process can be a member of different groups and members of the same group are allowed simultaneous access to their critical sections. Members of different groups must access their critical sections in a mutually exclusive manner. In 2003, Joung proposed a especially designed group quorum system for group mutual exclusion named the surficial system. Given the total number of manager processes in the system n and the number of groups sought m, the degree of the surficial system is $k = \sqrt{\frac{2n}{m(m-1)}}$, which means that up to k processes can be in their critical section simultaneously. In this paper, we propose a new group quorum system for group mutual exclusion of degree $k' = 1 + \sqrt{1 + \frac{n}{m}}$, which is much higher than k. Also, when $k = k'$, our system produces quorums of smaller size. This makes our system far more efficient and practical.

1 Introduction

Mutual exclusion is a fundamental problem in distributed systems. In this problem, access to a shared resource by concurrent processes must be synchronized so that only one process can use the resource at a time. The *group* mutual exclusion problem is a generalization of the ordinary mutual exclusion problem where each application process can belong to different groups and members of the same group are allowed simultaneous access to their critical sections. Members of different groups must access their critical sections in a mutually exclusive manner. Solutions for group mutual exclusion in shared memory models have been proposed in [2], [6], [10], [11]. In this paper, we consider processes that communicate via message passing. Solutions for group mutual exclusion in such networks have been proposed in [4], [15], [16].

Quorum-based solutions have been proposed for solving both ordinary and group mutual exclusion problems [1], [3], [5], [12], [13], [14]. The basic idea of this type of algorithms is to rely on a set M of *manager* processes to control access to the critical section. An *application* process that wishes to enter the critical section has to collect enough votes (permissions) from manager processes to form a quorum $Q \subseteq M$. Under the assumption that each manager process gives out its permission to at most one process at a time[1] (as in Maekawa's

---

[1] This assumption is made throughout the paper.

S. Chaudhuri et al. (Eds.): ICDCN 2006, LNCS 4308, pp. 70–81, 2006.

algorithm [12]), if quorums are made such that $\forall Q_i, Q_j \subseteq M, Q_i \cap Q_j \neq \phi$, then mutual exclusion is automatically guaranteed. It is known that quorum-based algorithms are resilient to node failures and network partitioning.

In 2003, Joung proposed a especially designed group quorum system for group mutual exclusion named the surficial system [8]. The main advantage of such approach is that it provides a way from which truly distributed quorum-based solutions for group mutual exclusion can be easily constructed [12]. Moreover, taking a purely mathematical perspective, we think that group quorum systems are an elegant object which study is well justified.

In an m-group quorum system over a set of manager processes P, there will be m groups (sets), each of which is a set of quorums of P such that every two quorums of different groups intersect. Intuitively, an m-group quorum system can be used to solve group mutual exclusion as follows: Each process i of group j, when attempting to enter its critical section, must acquire a quorum Q it has chosen from that group by obtaining permission from every member of Q. Upon exiting the critical section, process i returns the permission to the members of Q. By the intersection property, no two processes of different groups can enter their critical sections simultaneously.

Under the assumption that each manager process gives out its permission to at most one process at a time, a group quorum system has a main disadvantage: it limits the level of concurrency allowed by the system. This is true because the number of processes in a group that can enter their critical sections simultaneously is bounded above by the maximum number of pairwise disjoint quora in that group (also called the degree of the group). The theoretical upper bound on that degree, provided $m > 1$, is $OPT = \sqrt{n}$, where n is the number of manager processes in the system [8]. So, under the condition that no more than $\sqrt{n}$ processes of any group are to enter their critical sections simultaneously, group quorum systems are applicable. Now, if this is unacceptable for some applications, then by relaxing the above assumption, it is not difficult to equip a group quorum system with additional algorithms so that there is no limit on how many processes of the same group can be in their critical sections simultaneously. Such algorithms are described in [8].

Group quorum systems of optimal degree ($= \sqrt{n}$) are described in [9]. Unfortunately, the work in [9] requires n to be of the form x^2, where x is a power of a prime. To the author's knowledge, the only known group quorum system that works for any n and $m > 1$, named the surficial system, is described in [8]. The surficial system has degree $k = \sqrt{\frac{2n}{m(m-1)}}$, for some integer k, and produces quorums of size $s = (m-1)k$. In this paper, we describe a new group quorum system based on the notion of Cohorts, a concept introduced by Huang et $al.$ in 1993 [7]. Our system has degree $k' = 1 + \sqrt{1 + \frac{n}{m}}$, for some integer $k' > 2$, which is much higher than k for $m > 3$. Moreover, the quorum size in our system is $s' = m(k' - 2)$, which is smaller than s for the same degree $k' = k$ and for $m > k/2$. These improvements are significant because the degree of a system is related to its fault-tolerance and the level of concurrency it allows. The quorum size is related to the lower bound on the cost of communication imposed on any solution based on the system. Hence, our system is far more efficient and practical than the surficial system.

The rest of the paper is organized as follows. Section 2 gives basic definitions. Section 3 describes the group mutual exclusion problem and discusses the effectiveness of quorum-based solutions for it. Our contribution is included in Section 4. Section 5 is a conclusion.

2   Basic Definitions

The definitions and examples in this section are based on [7].

Definition 1. *Let* $P = \{1, ..., n\}$ *be a set of manager processes. A* **quorum system** *(also called* coterie*) over* P *is a set* $C \subseteq 2^P$ *of subsets of* P *satisfying the following requirements:*

intersection: $\forall Q_1, Q_2 \in C : Q_1 \cap Q_2 \neq \phi$.
minimality: $\forall Q_1, Q_2 \in C, Q_1 \neq Q_2 : Q_1 \nsubseteq Q_2$.

We call each $Q \in C$ a quorum. By the intersection property, a coterie can be used to develop algorithms for mutual exclusion in a distributed system. To enter a critical section, a process must receive permission from every member of some quorum. By the intersection property, mutual exclusion is guaranteed. The minimality property is not necessary but used rather to enhance efficiency. As it is clear that if $Q_1 \subseteq Q_2$, then a process that can obtain permission from every member of Q_2 can also obtain permission from every member of Q_1.

Definition 2. *A* k-coterie *C is a set of sets where each set* $Q \in C$ *is called a quorum. The following properties should hold for the quorums in a* k-coterie.

Intersection : *There are* k *quorums* $Q_1, Q_2, ..., Q_k$ *in* C *such that* $\forall i, j : 1 \leq i \neq j \leq k : Q_i \cap Q_j = \phi$ *(i.e., there exist* k *mutually disjoint quorums). But, there are no* $k + 1$ *mutually disjoint quorums.*
Minimality : $\forall Q_1, Q_2 \in C, Q_1 \neq Q_2 : Q_1 \nsubseteq Q_2$.

For example, $\{\{1, 3\}, \{1, 4\}, \{2, 3\}, \{2, 4\}\}$ is a 2-coterie because we can find two mutually disjoint quorums, but no three or four mutually disjoint quorums. By the intersection property, a k-coterie can be used to develop algorithms to achieve k-entry critical sections. To enter the critical section, a process is required to receive permission from all the members of some quorum in the system. Since no more than k quorums can be formed simultaneously, no more than k processes can be in their critical section at the same time.

Definition 3. *A* **Cohorts** $\mathbb{C}^{k,n} = \{C_1, C_2, ..., C_n\}$ *is a set of sets (also called cohorts*[2] *satisfying the following three properties:*

---

[2] The author acknowledges that the use of the term Cohorts to describe a set of cohorts is unnecessarily confusing, but we follow the same notation used in [7].

1. $n \geq k$.
2. $\forall i : |C_i| > k$.
3. $\forall i, j (i \neq j) : C_i \cap C_j = \phi$.

For example, $\mathbb{C}^{2,3} = \{\{1,2,3\}, \{4,5,6\}, \{7,8,9\}\}$ satisfies the above three properties.

With respect to a specific set Q, we define two types of cohorts: primary and supporting. Given a Cohorts $\mathbb{C}^{k,n}$, a cohort $C \in \mathbb{C}^{k,n}$ is Q's primary cohort if $|C \cap Q| = |C| - k + 1$. On the other hand, a cohort C is Q's supporting cohort if it yields exactly one element to Q; that is, if $|C \cap Q| = 1$. Clearly, a cohort C cannot be Q's primary and supporting cohort simultaneously.

A set Q is a quorum under $\mathbb{C}^{k,n}$ if it has one primary cohort C_i and all other cohorts $C_j (1 \leq j < i)$ are supporting cohorts of Q. Note that no supporting cohorts are needed when the primary cohort is C_1. It is known that quorums under $\mathbb{C}^{k,n}$ can form a k-coterie. For example, the following sets are quorums under $\mathbb{C}^{2,2} = \{\{1,2,3\}, \{4,5,6\}\}$:

$Q_1 = \{\underline{1,2}\}, Q_2 = \{1, \underline{4,5}\}, Q_3 = \{1, \underline{4,6}\}, Q_4 = \{1, \underline{5,6}\}, Q_5 = \{\underline{1,3}\}, Q_6 = \{2, \underline{4,5}\}, Q_7 = \{2, \underline{4,6}\}, Q_8 = \{2, \underline{5,6}\}, Q_9 = \{\underline{2,3}\}, Q_{10} = \{3, \underline{4,5}\}, Q_{11} = \{3, \underline{4,6}\}, Q_{12} = \{3, \underline{5,6}\}$,

where we have underlined for each quorum the elements from its primary cohort. The reader can check that those 12 quorums form a 2-coterie.

3   On Group Mutual Exclusion

In the group mutual exclusion problem, there is a set of resources (groups) $G = \{g_1, g_2, \ldots, g_m\}$ and a resource to be requested by a user may change dynamically (a user can be a member of different groups). Users wishing to use the same resource are allowed to access it (enter their critical sections) simultaneously. However, only one resource can be used at a time; that is, users of different groups (wishing to use different resources) must enter their critical sections in a mutually exclusive manner.

On Group Quorum Systems

Definition 4. *Let $P = \{1, ..., n\}$ be a set of manager processes. An m-group quorum system $\mathcal{C} = (C_1, ..., C_m)$ over P consists of m sets, where each $C_i \subseteq 2^P$ is a set of subsets of P satisfying the following properties:*

intersection: $\forall 1 \leq i, j \leq m, i \neq j, \forall Q_1 \in C_i, \forall Q_2 \in C_j : Q_1 \cap Q_2 \neq \phi$.
minimality: $\forall 1 \leq i \leq m, \forall Q_1, Q_2 \in C_i, Q_1 \neq Q_2 : Q_1 \not\subseteq Q_2$.

Each C_i is called a cartel and each $Q \in C_i$ a quorum.

The intersection property secures that no two processes of different groups can be in their critical sections simultaneously. The minimality property is used to enhance efficiency.

Define the *degree* of a cartel C_i, denoted $d(C_i)$, as the maximum number of pairwise disjoint quora in C_i. The degree of a group quorum system $\mathcal{C} = (C_1, ..., C_m)$, denoted $d(\mathcal{C})$, is defined as $d(\mathcal{C}) = min\{d(C_i)(1 \leq i \leq m)\}$. We say $\mathcal{C}$ is *regular* of degree k if all its cartels have the same degree k.

Under the condition that each quorum gives permission to only one process at a time, the number of processes of the same group that can be in the critical section simultaneously is bounded above by the degree of the cartel associated with that group. Moreover, following [8], we know that a group quorum system of degree k implies that every cartel contains at least an unhit quorum even if $k - 1$ manager processes have failed. So, high degree group quorum systems also provide for a better protection against faults. On the other hand, an m-group quorum system of degree k also implies that every quorum in the system has size at least k (unless $m = 1$). So, the higher the degree, the larger the quorum size is, which has a negative effect on the cost of communication when it comes to obtain (release) permissions from a quorum. So, in designing systems for group mutual exclusion, one has to try to reduce the quorum size while keeping the high degree of fault-tolerance.

4   The New Work

4.1   A New Group Quorum System Based on Cohorts

In this section, we introduce a new group quorum system based on the notion of Cohorts. First, we derive some basic facts about Cohorts in general.

Given a Cohorts $\mathbb{C}^{k,n} = \{C_1, ..., C_n\}$, properties 2 and 3 of a Cohorts imply that $\sum_{i=1}^{n} |C_i| > nk \geq k^2$ (by property 1). Moreover, if we let P denote the set $\cup_{i=1}^{n} C_i$, then $|P| \geq k^2$ or $k \leq \sqrt{|P|}$. This last inequality stimulates us to consider a Cohorts as a way to construct a regular group quorum system over P of degree k.

4.2   The Algorithm

Given the set of manager processes $P = \{1, ..., n\}$ and the number of groups sought m, we show how to use the notion of Cohorts to construct an m-group regular quorum system over P of degree k, where $n = mk(k - 2)$ (equivalently $k = 1 + \sqrt{1 + \frac{n}{m}}$), for some integer $k > 2$ and $m > \frac{k}{k-2}$.

Let $\mathfrak{C}$ denote the Cohorts $\mathbb{C}^{k,k} = \{C_1, ..., C_k\}$, where each cohort $C_i \subset P$, $|C_i| = m(k - 2) > k, \forall 1 \leq i \leq k$. Hence, $\cup_{i=1}^{k} C_i = P$; that is, all C_i are mutually disjoint. The reader can verify that $\mathbb{C}^{k,k}$ satisfies the properties of a Cohorts.

We know from the work of [7] that quorums under $\mathfrak{C}$ can form a k-coterie. Moreover, a simple way to construct a single group of k mutually disjoint quorums $Q_1, Q_2, ..., Q_k$ was described in [7]. It works as follows: For $1 \leq i \leq k$, make C_i the primary cohort of Q_i and a supporting cohort of Q_j ($i < j \leq k$). In the case of the Cohorts $\mathfrak{C}$, C_i yields exactly $m(k - 2) - k + 1$ elements to Q_i and exactly one element to each $Q_j (i < j \le k$. Because of property 3 of a Cohorts, it follows that those Q_i are mutually disjoint.

A main contribution of this paper is an algorithm which generalizes the method of [7] to construct an m-group regular quorum system over P of degree k. The algorithm, named Quorums, is described next.

Procedure Quorums (m: number of groups, k: degree)

1. Let $C = m(k-2)$; // common size of individual cohorts $C_1, \ldots, C_k$
2. Let $C_1, \ldots, C_k$ be k arrays of size C each. Initialize those arrays as follows.
   $C_1[] = \{1, \ldots, C\}$,
   $C_2[] = \{C + 1, \ldots, 2C\}$,
   $\ldots$
   $C_k[] = \{(k-1)C + 1, \ldots, kC = n\}$
3. Let $PC = C - k + 1$; // no. of elements drawn from primary cohort – referred to thereafter as the primary cohort elements of a quorum
4. Declare the array $Q[m][k][C]$ // to hold m groups of k quorums each; each quorum is of size C

5. For $i = 1$ to m do // ith group
6. Let $step = (i-1)(k-2)$ // step to move from one group to the next
7. For $j = 1$ to k do // jth quorum
8. For $p = 1$ to PC do // add elements drawn from primary cohort C_j
9. Let $l = step + p$
10. if $(l > C)$ then $l = l - C$ // lth value of the C_j cohort
11. Set $Q[i][j][p]$ to $C_j[l]$ // add a new member to the jth quorum of the ith group
12. End For $p = 1$
13. If $(j = 1)$ then // if first quorum of any group
14. Let $count = 1$
15. For $p = 2$ to k do // add elements drawn from secondary cohorts $C_2, \ldots, C_k$.
16. Let $l = step + C$
17. if $(l > C)$ then $l = l - C$
18. Set $Q[i][j][PC + count]$ to $C_p[l]$
19. Increment $count$
20. End For $p = 2$
21. Else // $j \ne 1$
22. Let $count = 1$
23. For $p = j - 1$ down to 1 do // add elements from secondary cohorts $C_1, \ldots, C_{j-1}$
24. Let $l = step + PC + count$
25. if $(l > C)$ then $l = l - C$
26. Set $Q[i][j][PC + count]$ to $C_p[l]$
27. Increment $count$
28. End For $p = j - 1$
29. Decrement $count$ // adjust count
30. For $p = k$ down to $j + 1$ do // add elements from secondary cohorts $C_{j+1}, \ldots, C_k$

31. Let $l = step + PC + count$
32. if $(l > C)$ then $l = l - C$
33. Increment $count$
34. Set $Q[i][j][PC + count]$ to $C_p[l]$
35. End For $p = k$
36. End Else
37. End For j
38. End For i

Denote the jth quorum of the ith group by Q_{ij}. Then, procedure Quorum places C elements in each Q_{ij} $(1 \leq i \leq m, 1 \leq j \leq k)$. Of those C elements, PC elements are drawn from Q_{ij}'s primary cohort $(= C_j)$ (this is done in steps $8 - 12$ of the algorithm). The remaining $(k - 1)$ elements are drawn from Q_{ij}'s (k-1) distinct secondary cohorts $(= C_1, \ldots, C_{j-1}, C_{j+1}, \ldots, C_k)$ (this is done either in steps $13 - 20$ if $j = 1$ or steps $21 - 36$ otherwise).

Next, we show that for any i, i', j, j' $(1 \leq i \neq i' \leq m, 1 \leq j, j' \leq k)$, the generated quorums Q_{ij} and $Q_{i'j'}$ have a nonempty intersection. We do this in three steps based on the values of j and j'.

Lemma 1. if $j = j'$, $k - 3 < |Q_{ij} \cap Q_{i'j'}| \leq (m - 2)(k - 2) - 1$.

Proof. By construction, the procedure Quorums visits each cohort $C_j, 1 \leq j \leq k$ to select the members of the k quorums of each group i $(1 \leq i \leq m)$. The primary cohort members of each Q_{ij} $(1 \leq i \leq m, 1 \leq j \leq k)$ are drawn from the cohort C_j. In particular, those members are $C_j[(i - 1)(k - 2) + 1], \ldots, C_j[(i - 1)(k - 2) + PC]$ (steps $8 - 12$ of the algorithm). In selecting members from C_j, the index value may have to be wrapped around to the beginning of C_j (this appears in steps $10, 17, 25$, and 32 of the algorithm). The step used by Quorums to move from one group to the next is $S = k - 2$. Figure 1 should help visualize our argument.

$$G_1 \qquad G_i \qquad\qquad G_{m-1} \qquad\qquad\qquad G_m$$
$$\downarrow \qquad \downarrow \qquad\qquad \downarrow \qquad\qquad\qquad\qquad \downarrow$$
$$C_1 : \{1, 2, \ldots, (i - 1)(k - 2) + 1, \ldots, PC - k + 4, \ldots, PC, PC + 1, PC + 2, \ldots, C\}$$

Fig. 1. Primary cohorts' elements of Q_{i1} $(1 \leq i \leq m)$

W.l.o.g., let $j = j' = 1$ and $i = 1$. Then, Q_{11} and $Q_{i'1}$ $(2 \leq i' \leq m-1)$ intersect using the primary cohort elements of those quorums. In particular, $|Q_{11} \cap Q_{21}| \geq PC - S$, $|Q_{11} \cap Q_{31}| \geq PC - 2S$, and $|Q_{11} \cap Q_{(m-1)1}| \geq PC - (m - 2)S = k - 3$. As for $i' = m$, the primary cohort elements of Q_{m1} consists of $S = k - 2$ elements from the end of C_1 and $PC - S$ elements from the beginning of C_1. Thus $|Q_{m1} \cap Q_{11}| = PC - S$. Thus, considering only the common elements in the primary cohort members, we have, $k - 3 < |Q_{ij} \cap Q_{i'j}| \leq PC - S = (m - 2)(k - 2) - 1$ for $1 \leq i \neq i' \leq m, 1 \leq j \leq k$. $\qquad\square$

Lemma 2. *If $j \neq j'$ but either $j = 1$ or $j' = 1$, $|Q_{ij} \cap Q_{i'j'}| \geq 1$.*

Proof. Let $j = 1$. W.l.o.g., let $i = 1$. Then, the $k - 1$ secondary cohorts elements of Q_{11} (steps $13 - 20$ of the algorithm) are: $C_2[C], C_3[C], \ldots, C_k[C]$ (See Fig. 2. Using those elements, Q_{11} intersects with all quorums $Q_{i'j'}$ for $3 \leq i' \leq m$ and $1 < j' \leq k$. This is true because all such quorums extend beyond the end of $C_{j'}$ when collecting their primary cohort elements. For $i' = 2$, the primary cohort elements of $Q_{2j'}$ $(1 < j' \leq k)$ are $C_{j'}[(k - 2) + 1] \ldots C_{j'}[(k - 2) + PC] = C_{j'}[(k - 2) + C - k + 1] = C_{j'}[C - 1]$, which means that the primary cohort elements of each $Q_{2j'}$ are one step short of the end of each $C_{j'}$. However, steps $21 - 36$ of the algorithm guarantee that $Q_{22} \cap Q_{11} = C_k[C]$, $Q_{23} \cap Q_{11} = C_2[C]$, and $Q_{2k} \cap Q_{11} = C_{k-1}[C]$. $\square$

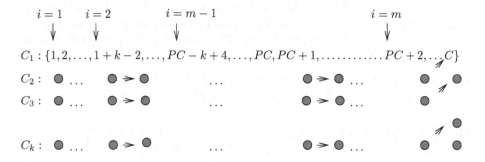

Fig. 2. Case of $j = 1 \neq j'$

Lemma 3. *If $j \neq j'$ and neither $j = 1$ nor $j' = 1$, $|Q_{ij} \cap Q_{i'j'}| \geq 1$.*

Proof. This is the most general of all three cases depicted pictorially in Fig. 3. W.l.o.g, let $i = 1$. In this case, Q_{1j} intersects with all quorums $Q_{i'j'}$ $(2 \leq i' \leq m - 1, 1 \leq j' \neq j \leq k)$. The intersection is between some of Q_{1j}'s secondary cohorts elements (steps $30 - 35$ of the algorithm, shown in Fig. 3 as the elements along the line of arrows from C_k to C_{j+1}) and $Q_{i'j'}$'s primary cohorts elements $(2 \leq i' \leq m - 1)$. For $i' = m$, the intersection may, in addition, involve the secondary cohorts elements of $Q_{mj'}$ (steps $23 - 28$ of the algorithm, shown in Fig. 3 for Q_{1j} as the elements along the line of arrows from C_{j-1} to C_1) and the primary cohort elements of Q_{1j}. $\square$

Summarizing all three lemmas, we conclude that $\forall i, i', j, j'$ $(1 \leq i \neq i' \leq m, 1 \leq j, j' \leq k)$, $1 \leq |Q_{ij} \cap Q_{i'j'}| \leq PC - S = m(k - 2) - 2k + 3$.

We have traced below the Quorums procedure for $P = \{1, \ldots, 32\}$ and $m = 4$. In this case, $k = 4$ and a 4-group regular quorum system over P of degree 4 can be constructed as follows. First, construct a Cohorts $\mathbb{C}^{4,4} = \{C_1, C_2, C_3, C_4\}$, where each $C_i \subset P$ and $|C_i| = m(k - 2) = 8$, $\forall 1 \leq i \leq 4$, and $\cup_{i=1}^{4} C_i = P$. Following the algorihm, let $C_1 = \{1, 2, 3, 4, 5, 6, 7, 8\}$, $C_2 = \{9, 10, 11, 12, 13, 14, 15, 16\}$, $C_3 = \{17, 18, 19, 20, 21, 22, 23, 24\}$, and $C_4 = \{25, 26, 27, 28, 29, 30, 31.32\}$.

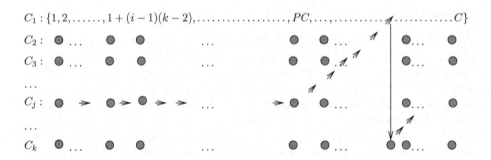

$$C_1 : \{1, 2, \ldots\ldots, 1 + (i-1)(k-2), \ldots\ldots\ldots\ldots\ldots, PC, \ldots, \ldots\ldots\ldots\ldots\ldots\ldots .C\}$$

Fig. 3. Members of Q_{1j}

In this case, each primary cohort yields exactly $m(k-2) - k + 1 = 5$ elements to its corresponding quorum. Applying our algorithm results in a 4-group regular quorum system over P of degree $k = 4$. The generated group quorum system $\mathcal{G} = \{G_1, G_2, G_3, G_4\}$ is as follows.

$\mathbf{G_1} = \{Q_1 = \{1, 2, 3, 4, 5, 16, 24, 32\}, Q_2 = \{9, 10, 11, 12, 13, 6, 30, 23\},$
$Q_3 = \{17, 18, 19, 20, 21, 14, 7, 31\}, Q_4 = \{25, 26, 27, 28, 29, 22, 15, 8\}\}$

$\mathbf{G_2} = \{Q_1 = \{3, 4, 5, 6, 7, 10, 18, 26\}, Q_2 = \{11, 12, 13, 14, 15, 8, 32, 17\},$
$Q_3 = \{19, 20, 21, 22, 23, 16, 1, 25\}, Q_4 = \{27, 28, 29, 30, 31, 24, 9, 2\}\}$

$\mathbf{G_3} = \{Q_1 = \{5, 6, 7, 8, 1, 12, 20, 28\}, Q_2 = \{13, 14, 15, 16, 9, 2, 26, 19\},$
$Q_3 = \{21, 22, 23.24, 17, 10, 3, 27\}, Q_4 = \{29, 30, 31, 32, 25, 18, 11, 4\}\}$

$\mathbf{G_4} = \{Q_1 = \{7, 8, 1, 2, 3, 14, 22, 30\}, Q_2 = \{15, 16, 9, 10, 11, 4, 28, 21\},$
$Q_3 = \{23, 24, 17, 18, 19, 12, 5, 29\}, Q_4 = \{31, 32, 25, 26, 27, 20, 13, 6\}\}$

4.3   Properties of the Proposed Group Quorum System

Given m and k, the procedure Quorums generates m groups of k quorums each, where each quorum is of size $m(k-2)$. Hence, the degree of the system is k and quorums belonging to the same group are mutually disjoint (recall $n = mk(k-2)$). Also, using the results of the previous section, we can state that quorums belonging to different groups have a non-empty intersection. In particular, if we let $\mathcal{G}(P) = (G_1, \ldots, G_m)$ be the set of groups generated by the algorithm, then $\forall 1 \leq i, j \leq m : i \neq j, \forall Q_1 \in G_i, \forall Q_2 \in G_j : 1 \leq |Q_1 \cap Q_2| \leq PC - S = m(k-2) - 2k + 3$.

Also, if we let n_p be the size of the multiset $\{Q \mid \exists 1 \leq i \leq m : Q \in G_i \text{ and } p \in Q\}$, then $n_p = m$. This is true because each group consists of k mutually disjoint quorums of size $m(k-2)$ each, drawn from a set $P = \{1, \ldots, n\}$, where $n = km(k-2)$. Thus, each manager process appears exactly once in each group. All these results are summarized in the following theorem:

Theorem 1. *Let $P = \{1, ..., n\}$ be a set of manager processes and m be a positive integer such that $m > 1$ and $n = mk(k-2)$ (equivalently $k = 1 + \sqrt{1 + \frac{n}{m}}$) for some integer $k > 2$ and $m > \frac{k}{k-2}$. Furthermore, let $\mathcal{G}(P) = (G_1, ..., G_m)$ be our proposed group quorum system. Then $\mathcal{G}(P)$ is an m-group regular quorum system over P of degree k. Moreover, $\mathcal{G}(P)$ satisfies the following properties:*

- $\forall 1 \leq i, j \leq m : |G_i| = |G_j| = k$.
- $\forall 1 \leq i, j \leq m, \forall Q_1 \in G_i, \forall Q_2 \in G_j : |Q_1| = |Q_2| = m(k-2)$.
- $\forall p, q \in P : n_p = n_q = m$, *where n_p is the size of the multiset $\{Q \mid \exists 1 \leq i \leq m : Q \in G_i \text{ and } p \in Q\}$, and similar for n_q.*
- $\forall 1 \leq i, j \leq m, i \neq j, \forall Q_1 \in G_i, \forall Q_2 \in G_j : 1 \leq |Q_1 \cap Q_2| \leq m(k-2) - 2k + 3$.

The first property of the theorem states that all groups have the same number of quora. This ensures fairness among different users wishing to access the critical section as members of different groups. Moreover, the size of each group is equal to the degree of the system; that is, all quora in a given group are mutually disjoint. The second property states that all quora have the same size $m(k-2)$. This implies that the number of permissions(messages) (i.e, cost of communication) needed per entry to the critical section is independent of the quorum a process chooses. The third property ensures that each manager process in the system shares the same responsibility (the load assumed by any process). As stated by Maekawa [12], these three properties are desired in a system from which truly distributed quorum-based algorithms for group mutual exclusion can be easily constructed. The last condition simply bounds the number of nodes that must be common to any two quora of different groups, thereby reducing the size of a quorum.

Finally, we explain the claim we made at the end of the Introduction section about our system being far more efficient and practical than the surficial system. Basically, our system requires n/m to be of the form $q^2 - 1$, for some positive integer q. This is far less stringent than the requirement of the surficial system of $\frac{2n}{m(m-1)} = q^2$ for some positive integer q. Also, when both systems are applicable, our system produces quorums of smaller size for a similar degree, assuming $m > k/2$.

We have compared in Table 1 the number of manager processes and the size of the quorum used in our system versus the surficial system for various values of m and k. In Table 1, $n(s)$ and $n'(s')$ refer to the number of manager

Table 1. Comparing number of processes and quorum size

$k = k$/	m	n/	s/	n	s
3	5	15	5	N/A	N/A
4	3	24	6	N/A	N/A
4	4	32	8	N/A	N/A
5	3	45	9	75	10
5	4	60	12	150	15
5	5	75	15	250	20

processes (size of the quorum) used in the surficial system and our system, respectively.

Note that there are entries in the table which are not applicable under the surficial system (denoted by N/A). The last entry in the table states that in order to construct a 5-group regular quorum system of degree 5, the surficial system uses 250 manager processes and produces quorums of size 20; our system uses 75 processes and produces quorums of size 15.

5   Conclusion

In this paper, we presented a new group quorum system for group mutual exclusion. Our system, which is based on the notion of Cohorts, is easy to construct and has nice properties from which truly distributed quorum-based algorithms for group mutual exclusion can be easily constructed.

Given the total number of manager processes n and the total number of groups m, our system has degree $k = 1 + \sqrt{1 + \frac{n}{m}}$, for some integer $k > 2$ and produces quorums of size $m(k - 2)$. This compares favorably to the surficial system of Joung [8], where the degree of the system is $\sqrt{\frac{2n}{m(m-1)}}$ and the size of the quorum is $(m - 1)k$.

References

1. Agrawal, D., El Abbadi, A.: An Efficient and Fault-Tolerant Solution for Distributed Mutual Exclusion. ACM Trans. Computer Systems, **9:1** (1991) 1–20
2. Alagarsamy, K., Vidyasankar, K.: Elegant Solutions for Group Mutual Exclusion Problem. Tech. Report, Dept. of Computer Science, Memorial Univ. of Newfoundland, Canada, (1999)
3. Barbara, D., Garcia-Molina, H.: Mutual Exclusion in Partitioned Distributed Systems. Distributed Computing, **1** (1986) 119–132
4. Cantarell, S., Datta, A.K., Petit, F., Villain, V.: Token Based Group Mutual Exclusion for Asynchronous Rings. Proc. 21th Intl. Conf. Distributed Computing Systems, (2001) 691–694
5. GarciarMolina, H., Barbara, D.: How to Assign Votes in a Distributed Systems. JACM, **32:4** (1985) 841–860
6. Hadzilacos, V.: A Note on Group Mutual Exclusion. Proc. 20th Ann. ACM Symp. Principles of Distributed Computing, (2001)
7. Huang, S.-T., Jiang, J.-R., Kuo, Y.-C.: K-Coteries for Fault-Tolerant Entries to a Critical Section. Proc. ICDCS, (1993) 74–81
8. Joung, Y.-J.: Quorum-Based Algorithms for Group Mutual Exclusion. IEEE Trans. On Parallel and Distributed Systems, **14:5** (2003) 205–215
9. Joung, Y.-J.: On Quorum Systems for Group Resources with Bounded Capacity. Proc. Distributed Computing (DISC), LNCS 3274, (2004) 86–101
10. Joung, Y.-J.: Asynchronous Group Mutual Exclusion (extended abstract). Proc. 17th Ann. ACM Symp. Principles of Distributed Computing, (1998) 51–60
11. Keane, P., Moir, M.: A Simple Local-Spin Group Mutual Exclusion Algorithm. Proc. 18th Ann. ACM Symp. Principles of Distributed Computing, (1999) 23–32

12. Maekawa, M.: A $\sqrt{N}$ Algorithm for Mutual Exclusion in Decentralized Systems. ACM Trans. Computer Systems, **3:2** (1985) 145–159
13. Manabe, Y., Park, J.: A Quorum-Based Extended Group Mutual Exclusion Algorithm Without Unnecessary Blocking. Proc. Tenth Int. Conference on Parallel and Distributed Systems (ICPADS) (2004)
14. Peleg, D., Wool, A.: Crumbling Walls: A Class of Practical and Efficient Quorum Systems. Distributed Computing, **10:2** (1997) 87–97
15. Ricart, G., Agrawala, A.K.: An Optimal Algorithm for Mutual Exclusion in Computer Networks. Comm. ACM, **24:1** (1981) 9–17
16. Wu, K.P., Joung, Y.-J.: Asynchronous Group Mutual Exclusion in Ring Networks. IEE Proc. Computer and Digital Techniques, **147:1** (2000) 1–8

An Efficient Non-intrusive Checkpointing Algorithm for Distributed Database Systems*

Jiang Wu and D. Manivannan

Department of Computer Science, University of Kentucky, Lexington, KY 40506

Abstract. Checkpointing distributed database systems is useful for recovery from failures as well as for audit purposes. In this paper, we present a non-intrusive checkpointing algorithm for distributed database systems. Our approach uses both checkpoints and transaction logs to capture a transaction-consistent state of the database which helps in reducing overall checkpointing overhead. Out approach is non-intrusive and hence does not block arriving or executing transactions during checkpointing.

Keywords: Checkpointing, distributed databases.

1 Introduction

It is a common practice to take checkpoints of a distributed database from time to time, and restore the database to the most recent checkpoint when a failure occurs. It is desirable that a checkpoint records a state of the database which reflects the effect of completed transactions only and not the results of any partially executed transactions. Such a checkpoint of the database is called a transaction-consistent (which we call from now on as tr-consistent) global checkpoint of the database [1].

A straightforward way to take a tr-consistent checkpoint of a distributed database is to block all newly submitted transactions, wait until all the currently executing transactions finish and then take a checkpoint of the whole database. Such a checkpoint is guaranteed to be tr-consistent, but this approach is not practical, since blocking newly-submitted transaction will increase transaction response time which is not acceptable for the users of the database. On the other hand, checkpointing the state of each data item independently and periodically without blocking any transactions is more desirable. However, if each data item in the database is checkpointed independently, then the checkpoints of the data items may not form a tr-consistent global checkpoint of the database and hence useless. Communication-induced checkpointing algorithms allow the data items to be checkpointed independently and also force the data items to take additional checkpoints to ensure each checkpoint of each data item to be part of a

---

* This material is based in part upon work supported by the US National science Foundation under Grant No. IIS-0414791. Any opinions, findings, and conclusions or recommendations expressed in this material are those of the authors and do not necessarily reflect the views of the National Science Foundation.

S. Chaudhuri et al. (Eds.): ICDCN 2006, LNCS 4308, pp. 82–87, 2006.

tr-consistent global checkpoint of the database. Baldoni et al. [2] presented two such protocols for distributed database systems.

The protocols presented by Baldoni et al. [2] may induce a large number of forced checkpoints, especially if the transactions access large number of data items. Such increase in checkpointing overhead will result in longer response time. They present two protocols, which we call Protocol A and Protocol B. Protocol B in [2] uses a lazy checkpointing approach to reduce checkpoints produced in Protocol A. In this paper, we propose an algorithm which uses both checkpoints of data items and transaction logs to determine a tr-consistent checkpoint of the database.

The remainder of this paper is organized as follows. In Section 2 we introduce the necessary background required for understanding the paper. In Section 3 we present our algorithm and simulation results. Section 4 concludes the paper.

2   Background

Similar to [2], we model a distributed database system as consisting of a finite set of data items, a set of transactions and a concurrency control mechanism for executing the transactions. We also assume the system is *deterministic*, in which the state of the database depends only on its initial state and the operations performed to it [3].

A data item is the smallest unit of data accessible to transactions. In this model, a non-empty set of data items resides at various sites. Sites exchange information via messages transmitted on a communication network, which is assumed to be reliable. Message transmission time is unpredictable but finite. The set of data items at each site is managed by a data manager (DM). For simplicity, we assume each data item x has a data manager DM_x. Each DM_x is responsible for controlling access to the data item, taking checkpoints periodically and performing other data maintenance (such as integration check) associated with that data item.

A transaction is defined as a partial order of read and write operations on various data items and terminates with a commit or an abort operation. Each transaction is managed by an instance of the transaction manager (TM) that forwards its operations to the scheduler which runs a specific concurrency control protocol. The TM with the help of the scheduler is responsible for the proper scheduling of the transaction in such a way that the integrity of the database is maintained.

The saved state of a data item is called a checkpoint. Each checkpoint on a data item is assigned a unique sequence number. We assume that the database consists of a set X of n data items $\mathbf{X} = \{x_i \mid 1 \leq i \leq n\}$. In addition, we denote by $C_x^{i_x}$ the checkpoint on x with sequence number i_x. The set of all checkpoints on data item x is denoted by $\mathbf{C_x} = \{C_x^{i_x} \mid i_x : i_x \geq 0\}$. When restoring a database from checkpoints, it is important that the set of checkpoints of the data items to which the database is restored forms a tr-consistent global checkpoint, that is, the checkpoints to which the database is restored represents the state of the database which reflects the effect of only completed transactions and not the results of any partially executed transactions.

A data item may take two types of checkpoints, namely, physical checkpoints and logical checkpoints [4]. A data item is said to have taken a physical checkpoint at time t_1 if the state of data item at time t_1 is available on the stable storage. A data item is said to have taken a logical checkpoint at time t_1 if adequate information is saved on the stable storage to allow the state of the data item at time t_1 to be recovered. A physical checkpoint is trivially a logical checkpoint, however, the converse is not true. One approach to take logical checkpoint at time t_1 is to take a physical checkpoint at some time $t_0 < t_1$ and log on stable storage all operations performed on the data item between t_0 and t_1. This approach can be summarized as [4]: *physical checkpoint + operation log = logical checkpoint.* This approach for taking a logical checkpoint may only be used for deterministic systems, because it implements a logical checkpoint using a physical checkpoint and the operation log.

3 Proposed Algorithm

Basically, the algorithms in [2] use forced checkpoints to prevent a specific condition from happening (refer to [2] and [5] for the concepts behind this approach) in the system. If all such conditions are prevented, it is guaranteed that for every checkpoint $C_x^{i_x}$ there exists a tr-consistent global checkpoint that includes $C_x^{i_x}$. First, we briefly review the two algorithms in [2] and discuss their drawbacks.

Baldoni et al. [2] assume that each data manager DM_x managing data item x has a variable ts_x, which stores the timestamp of the last checkpoint of x. Variable i_x denotes the index of the last checkpoint of x. Data managers can take basic checkpoints independently of each other periodically. To facilitate this function, a timer is associated with each data manager and when the timer expires, a checkpoint is taken and the timer is reset. In addition, whenever the condition that needs to be prevented is detected by means of comparing timestamps, data managers are directed to take additional forced checkpoints. The decision to take forced checkpoints is based on the control information (timestamps) piggybacked by commit messages of transactions.

Let R_{T_i} (repectivey, W_{T_i}) denote the set of read (respectively, write) operations issued by a transaction T_i, which is under the management of transaction manager TM_i [2]. Each time an operation of T_i is issued by TM_i to a data manager DM_x on data item x, besides the execution of the operation, DM_x returns the pair (identity of the data item x, value of its current timestamp ts_x). TM_i stores in $MAX\_TS_{T_i}$ the maximum value among the timestamps collected from all the data items that are read and/or written by T_i. When the transaction T_i is about to commit, the transaction manager TM_i sends a COMMIT message to each data manager DM_x involved in $R_{T_i}(W_{T_i})$. The COMMIT messages are piggybacked with $MAX\_TS_{T_i}$. Whenever a COMMIT message is received by DM_x, if $MAX\_TS_{T_i}$ piggybacked in COMMIT is greater than ts_x, a forced checkpoint is taken on data item x and the local ts_x is updated to the value of $MAX\_TS_{T_i}$. In addition, whenever a basic checkpoint is taken (when timer expires), the local ts_x is incremented by 1.

Based on how often the forced checkpoints are taken, two algorithms are introduced in [2]. In the first algorithm (we call it as Protocol A), a forced checkpoint is taken whenever the condition $MAX\_TS_{T_i} > ts_x$ holds. The second protocol (we call it as Protocol B) does not take forced checkpoints as often as Protocol A, because it skips taking some forced checkpoints that are suppose to be taken in Protocol A, as is called "lazy checkpointing" [6]. This protocol ensures that $\forall x$ (x is a data item) if there exists a checkpoint timestamped as $a \times Z$ (where $a \geq 0$ is an integer and Z is a control constant), then the global consistent checkpoint consisting that checkpoint exists. If a transaction T_i happens to access multiple data items and the value $MAX\_TS_{T_i}$ associated with the transaction happens to be greater than the timestamps of most of the data items it has accessed, it could result in large number of forced checkpoints concurrently.

Our algorithm tries to overcome this disadvantage. Our algorithms also maintains a variable ts_x for each DM_x, but it stores the timestamp of the last checkpoint of data item x, which may be a physical checkpoint or a marker in the log. i_x denotes the index value of the last physical checkpoint of data item x. In addition, we have a variable $ts_{physical}$ that stores the timestamp of the last physical checkpoint. In the log, a physical checkpoint is represented by $Checkpoint(ts_x, C_x^{ts})$, where C_x^{ts} is a link to the location of the physical checkpoint in the stable storage. This log entry means a checkpoint C_x^{ts} with timestamp ts_x has been taken. We usually use $Checkpoint.ts_x$ to refer to the first element in this tuple. The marker, on the other hand, uses a pair $\text{Marker}(ts_{physical}, ts_x)$. $ts_{physical}$ is the timestamp of the previous physical checkpoint that the marker depends on for recovery and ts_x is the current timestamp of the marker. Similarly, we use $Marker.ts_{physical}$ and $Marker.ts_x$ to refer to the first and second element in this tuple. We also use a variable called m_{num} to control the size of the consecutive markers within a reasonable range, called m_{max} and initialized as Z. If the number of consecutive markers exceeds $m_{max} = Z$, we will have to take a forced checkpoint rather than continue placing a marker into the log. The proposed checkpointing algorithm and the corresponding recovery algorithm is given in Table 1.

We simulated the performance of Protocol A, Protocol B in [2] and our algorithm (we denote our protocol as Protocol C) in a system with 10 data items, with the same value for Z and a series of random transactions. Figure 1 shows the total number of checkpoints taken (basic and forced) while the series of random transactions are processed. This shows that our algorithm (Protocol C) has less checkpointing overhead when compared to the two algorithms in [2].

4   Conclusion

Checkpointing has been traditionally used for handling failures in distributed database systems. An efficient checkpointing algorithm should be non-intrusive in the sense that it should not block the normal transactions while checkpoints

Table 1. Proposed Algorithm

Checkpointing Algorithm

- Initiation:
  $ts_x = 0$;
  $i_x = 0$;
  $ts_{physical} = 0$;
  $m_{num} = 0$;
  $m_{max} = Z$;
- Taking basic checkpoints, when the time expires:
  $i_x \leftarrow i_x + 1$;
  $ts_x \leftarrow ts_x + 1$;
  Take checkpoint $C_x^{ts_x}$;
  $ts_{physical} \leftarrow ts_x$;
  Write $Checkpoint(ts_x, C_x^{ts})$ into the log;
  $m_{num} \leftarrow 0$;
  Reset the local timer.
- Taking forced checkpoints or placing makers in the log, when DM_x receives
  $COMMIT(MAX\_TS_{T_i})$ from TM_i:
  if $ts_x < MAX\_TS_{T_i}$ and $m_{num} \leq m_{max}$ then
      $i_x \leftarrow i_x + 1$;
      $ts_x \leftarrow MAX\_TS_{T_i}$;
      Place a marker $Marker(ts_{physical}, ts_x)$ into the log;
      $m_{num} \leftarrow m_{num} + 1$;
      Reset the local timer;
  else if $ts_x < MAX\_TS_{T_i}$ and $m_{num} > m_{max}$ then
      $i_x \leftarrow i_x + 1$;
      $ts_x \leftarrow MAX\_TS_{T_i}$;
      $ts_{physical} \leftarrow ts_x$;
      Take forced checkpoint C_x^{ts};
      Write $Checkpoint(ts_x, C_x^{ts})$ into the log;
      $m_{num} \leftarrow 0$;
      Reset the local timer;
  endif
  process the COMMIT message.

Recovery Algorithm

- Whenever a data item x needs to rollback and initiates the recovery:
  Locate the latest checkpoint information in the log that is not damaged;
  if it is a checkpoint in the form of $Checkpoint(ts_x, C_x^{ts})$
    - Track through the link C_x^{ts} in $Checkpoint(ts_x, C_x^{ts})$ to the stable storage and restore the state of the data item;
    - Broadcast $Recovery(ts_x)$ message to all the data items in the distributed database system where $ts_x = Checkpoint.ts_x$
  else if it is a marker in the log in the form of $Marker(ts_{physical}, ts_x)$
    - Continue searching backward in the log until reaching a $Checkpoint(ts_x, C_x^{ts})$ entry where $Checkpoint.ts_x = Marker.ts_{physical}$;
    - Track through the link C_x^{ts} in the $Checkpoint(ts_x, C_x^{ts})$ to the stable storage and restore the state of the data item;
    - Redo all the operations in the log between $Checkpoint(ts_x, C_x^{ts})$ and $Marker(ts_{physical}, ts_x)$;
    - Broadcast $Recovery(ts_x)$ message to all the data items in the distributed database system where $ts_x = Marker.ts_x$;
  endif
  Resume normal database processing.
- Whenever a data item y receives $Recovery(ts_x)$ message:
  Track backward through all the checkpoint or marker entries in the log and locate the one with the smallest ts_y such that $ts_y \geq ts_x$;
  if it is a checkpoint in the form of $Checkpoint(ts_y, C_y^{ts})$
    - Track through the link C_y^{ts} in the $Checkpoint(ts_y, C_y^{ts})$ to the stable storage and restore the state of the data item;
  else if it is a marker in the log in the form of $Marker(ts_{physical}, ts_y)$
    - Continue searching backward in the log until reaching a $Checkpoint(ts_y, C_y^{ts})$ entry where $Checkpoint.ts_y = Marker.ts_{physical}$;
    - Track through the link C_y^{ts} in the $Checkpoint(ts_y, C_y^{ts})$ to the stable storage and restore the state of the data item;
    - Redo all the operations in the log between $Checkpoint(ts_y, C_y^{ts})$ and $Marker(ts_{physical}, ts_y)$;
  endif
  Resume normal database processing.

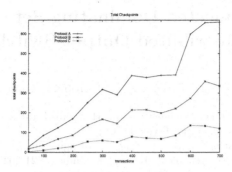

Fig. 1. Simulation Results - total checkpoints taken

are taken. In this paper, we presented an efficient non-intrusive checkpointing protocol that decreases the number of checkpoints taken while at the same time allows the individual data items to be checkpointed at any time.

References

1. Pilarski, S., Kameda, T.: Checkpointing for distributed databases: Starting from the basics. IEEE Transactions on Parallel and Distributed Systems **3** (1992) 602–610
2. Baldoni, R., Quaglia, F., Raynal, M.: Consistent checkpointing for transaction systems. The Computer Journal **44**(2) (2001)
3. Strom, R.E., Yemini, S.A.: Optimistic Recovery: an Asynchronous Approach to Fault-Tolerance in Distributed Systems. (1984)
4. Vaidya, N.H.: Staggered consistent checkpointing. IEEE Transactions on Parallel and Distributed Systems **10**(7) (July 1999) 694–702
5. Netzer, R.H.B., Xu, J.: Necessary and sufficient condition for consistent global snapshots. IEEE Trans. Soft. Eng. **6** (1999) 274–281
6. Wang, Y.M., Fuchs, W.K.: Lazy Checkpoint Coordination for Bounding Rollback Propogation. In: In Proc. 12th IEEE Int. Symp. on Reliable Distributed Systems, IEEE Computer Society Press (1993) 78–85

Adaptive Connected Dominating Set – An Exercise in Distributed Output Switching

Ankur Jain[1], Sushanta Karmakar[2], and Arobinda Gupta[2]

[1] Microsoft India Development Center, Hyderabad, India
ankurj@microsoft.com
[2] Department of Computer Science and Engineering
Indian Institute of Technology, Kharagpur, India – 721 302
{sushantak, agupta}@cse.iitkgp.ernet.in

Abstract. Switching between protocols based on environment is an elegant idea of enabling adaptation in distributed systems. In this paper, we give one approach of switching between two connected dominating set (CDS) construction protocols, one suitable for low load and the other suitable for higher load. In this method, the two connected dominating sets are computed in advance and switching is done between the two precomputed outputs. In addition, some CDS of the network is always maintained when switching is in progress.

1 Introduction

The performance of a distributed system depends on its environment. The environment may change with time. Hence a distributed system should be adaptive under changing environments. Adaptation is desirable in any distributed system since it helps the system to perform gracefully under different scenarios.

Most adaptive distributed algorithms are designed from scratch. However, it generally results in complex algorithms. Moreover, such algorithms are often application specific and are unable to change the main logic of the algorithm [1]. A more elegant way to achieve adaptation can be through protocol switching. If there exists multiple distributed algorithms for the same problem, each better suited to some particular environmental condition, then adaptation can be achieved by monitoring the environment and switching to the appropriate protocol depending on the environment.

In a network, protocol switching can be done using a centralized algorithm similar to the well-known two-phase commit protocol by asking nodes to stop working for some time and switch to another protocol. However this approach requires the whole network to freeze, thereby affecting the availability of the system. Moreover, it may be desirable to maintain some system property during the switching. For example, while switching between two distributed mutual exclusion algorithms, it is essential that no more than one process can enter the critical section. Similarly, while switching between two routing protocols, we would like to have each packet routed properly in spite of switching. Thus more sophisticated ways of protocol switching is needed.

S. Chaudhuri et al. (Eds.): ICDCN 2006, LNCS 4308, pp. 88–93, 2006.

Protocol switching has two components. The first one monitors the environment and helps in determining when a switch should be initiated. This can be done by forming a spanning tree of the network rooted at an initiator, and collecting the status of all nodes on a periodic basis. The second component deals with the procedure of actually switching between the protocols. In this paper, we concentrate on the second part and demonstrate one approach of protocol switching by designing a switching mechanism between two connected dominating set (CDS) construction protocols. A CDS of a graph $G = (V, E)$ is a set of nodes $V' \subseteq V$ such that for each $u \in V$, either $u \in V'$ or u is adjacent to some $v \in V'$, and the subgraph induced by V' is connected. A node $v \in V'$ is called a dominator. CDS is commonly used for routing in ad hoc networks. At low network load, a small CDS is preferable. However, at higher load, a degree-bounded CDS may be better to reduce the load on any one dominator. Thus the system can adapt to the network load by dynamically switching between the two CDS. Since CDS construction algorithms are non-reactive protocols, we assume that the two CDS are computed in advance and switching is done between the two precomputed CDS i.e. the outputs of the two CDS protocols. This may be termed as *output switching*. Given any two CDS algorithms, the output switching algorithm uses their outputs and combines them to provide an adaptive CDS to the upper layer. Moreover, the switching algorithm ensures that some CDS of the network is always maintained while switching is in progress, thereby providing some CDS at all times.

Arora et. al. [2] gave a distributed reset mechanism where a distributed system can switch from one global state to another without requiring a global freeze. This can be used for protocol switching but it will not guarantee any property during the switching and thus is not directly useful in our case. In [1], Liu et. al. discussed a switching method that can only be used on two protocols that are derived from the same abstract specification. Therefore it has limited applicability. In [3], Liu et. al. gave a way of switching between two protocols satisfying certain properties where a process delivers all messages for the old protocol before delivering any message for the new protocol. Moreover, all application layer messages are buffered at each node during switching and their delivery is delayed indefinitely till the switching is over. Thus the overhead is large.

The rest of the paper is organized as follows. Section 2 describes the switching algorithm and an outline of its correctness. We conclude the work in Section 3.

2 Switching Algorithm

We assume that the system is asynchronous with reliable and FIFO channels. Each node has a unique ID and it communicates only with its neighbors by sending messages. Also it is assumed that nodes or links do not fail at any time.

Without loss of generality, let the two CDS algorithms be associated with two colors, *white* and *black*. We shall refer to the two CDS as the *white CDS* and the *black CDS* respectively, and to the algorithms as the *whiteCDS* algorithm and the *blackCDS* algorithm respectively. Each node has a variable *color*. If

S_1: $I = 1 \wedge color = white \rightarrow I = 0$; $color = black$
$\qquad\qquad\qquad \forall u \in N(v)$, send $CHANGE\_OUT$ to u

S_2: $color = white \wedge b = 1 \wedge$ (received $CHANGE\_OUT$)
$\qquad\qquad \rightarrow color = black$
$\qquad\qquad\qquad \forall u \in N(v)$, send $CHANGE\_OUT$ to u

S_3: $color = white \wedge b = 0 \wedge w = 1 \wedge$ (received $CHANGE\_OUT$ from x)
$\qquad\qquad \rightarrow color = gray$; $g = 1$; $colorset[x] = black$
$\qquad\qquad\qquad \forall u \in N(v)$, send $UPDATE\_COLOR(v, color)$ to u

S_4: $color = white \wedge b = 0 \wedge w = 0 \wedge$ (received $CHANGE\_OUT$)
$\qquad\qquad \rightarrow color = black$
$\qquad\qquad\qquad \forall u \in N(v)$, send $UPDATE\_COLOR(v, color)$ to u

S_5: $color \neq black \wedge$ (received $UPDATE\_COLOR(x, c)$) $\rightarrow colorset[x] = c$

S_6: $color = gray \wedge$ (received $CHANGE\_OUT$ from x) $\rightarrow colorset[x] = black$

S_7: $color = gray \wedge (\forall u \in N(v), colorset[u] \neq white)$
$\qquad\qquad \rightarrow color = black$; $g = 0$
$\qquad\qquad\qquad \forall u \in N(v)$, send $UPDATE\_COLOR(v, color)$ to u

Fig. 1. Switching algorithm for node v

the network is currently using the output of the *whiteCDS* algorithm then at each node *color = white*, whereas if the output of the *blackCDS* algorithm is being used then at each node, *color = black*. Thus the aim of the switching algorithm is to change the color of all the nodes from *white* to *black* or *black* to *white* depending on the initial state. However during switching, some nodes can temporarily have an intermediate color *gray*. Each node maintains three boolean variables, w, b, and g. If $w = 1$ then the node is a dominator according to the *whiteCDS* algorithm, and if $b = 1$ then it is a dominator according to the *blackCDS* algorithm. Both these variables are set by the corresponding CDS algorithms at the beginning and never changed thereafter. The variable g, however, is set to 1 by the switching algorithm when the node's color is changed to *gray*. A gray node is considered as a temporary dominator. These gray dominators are needed to ensure that some CDS of the network is always maintained during the switching. At any instant of time, the CDS in the network is thus defined by all nodes with $(color = white \wedge w = 1)$ or $(color = black \wedge b = 1)$ or $(color = gray \wedge g = 1)$. Let $N(v)$ denote the set of neighbors of v.

The algorithm to switch from the white CDS to the black CDS is given in Fig. 1. The algorithm is shown in the form of guarded commands [4]. The algorithm to switch from the black CDS to the white CDS is the same with interchanging *white* and *black*, and w and b. There is a fixed node P that initiates the switching and is known as the initiator. The algorithm requires that the initiator must be a dominator of the CDS to which we want to switch. So to switch both ways it must be a dominator according to both the CDS algorithms (i.e. at initiator, $w = b = 1$). Thus we assume that there is at least one node that is a dominator according to both the algorithms. Later we will show how this assumption can be relaxed. There is a variable I at each node v which indicates whether it should initiate a switch. Initially $I = 1$ at the initiator and $I = 0$ at all other nodes. I can be set by the underlying monitoring protocol when a switch is necessary. The initiator, in S_1, changes its color to black and sends a message $CHANGE\_OUT$ to all its neighbors, asking them to switch. When a white node receives the $CHANGE\_OUT$ message it sets its *color* variable to either *black* or *gray* depending on w and b. In S_2, a white node with $b = 1$ becomes black upon receiving that message and it also forwards the $CHANGE\_OUT$ message to its neighbors. In S_3, if a white node is not a member of the black CDS but is a member of the white CDS, then upon receiving the $CHANGE\_OUT$ message, it becomes a temporary dominator by setting its *color* variable to *gray*, and it informs its new color to its neighbors by sending an $UPDATE\_COLOR$ message. Also each node remembers the color of its neighbors in the array *colorset*. In S_4, if a white node v, that is not a member of either CDS, receives the $CHANGE\_OUT$ message then it becomes black and informs its neighbors by sending an $UPDATE\_COLOR$ message. The node v does not temporarily become gray because the sender of the $CHANGE\_OUT$ message is its dominator and no other node needs v as its dominator or for connecting other dominators. S_5 and S_6 maintain the color information of all the neighbors which is used in S_7. In S_7, a gray node becomes black if and only if all its neighbors have color either gray or black.

2.1 Outline of Proof of Correctness

Lemma 1. *Each node receives the $CHANGE\_OUT$ message at least once.*

Proof. The initiator sends the $CHANGE\_OUT$ message to all its neighbors. By S_2, if a node with $b = 1$ receives the $CHANGE\_OUT$ message for the first time, it forwards the message to all its neighbors. Also the subgraph induced by the nodes with $b = 1$ is a CDS. Hence each node receives the $CHANGE\_OUT$ message at least once. □

Theorem 1 (Partial Correctness). *When the algorithm terminates, at each node color = black.*

Proof. After the algorithm terminates, let there be a node v with *color = white*. No action can change *color* from *gray* or *black* to *white*. Thus at v, *color* was always set to *white*. By Lemma 1, v must have received a $CHANGE\_OUT$ message. When v received it for the first time, it must have executed A_2, A_3, or A_4 and thereby changing *color* to either *black* or *gray*. This is a contradiction. Hence at each node, *color* is *black* or *gray*. Let there be a node v with *color = gray*. So G_7 must be enabled at v. This is again a contradiction since the algorithm has terminated. Thus *color* is *black* at each node. □

Theorem 2 (Termination). *The algorithm executes $O(e)$ actions before it terminates, where e is the total number of edges in the network.*

Proof. At a node v, each guard except G_5 and G_6 can be enabled at most once since the actions of those guards change the value of *color* and *color* can only change from *white* to *gray*, *white* to *black*, and *gray* to *black*. Thus *color* never attains any of its previous values again. Let us consider guard G_5. It is enabled only when $UPDATE\_COLOR(u, c)$ message is received. A node can send this message in A_3, A_4, or A_7, which can only execute at most once. This means that at node v, A_5 is executed $O(|N(v)|)$ times. Also any node can send $CHANGE\_OUT$ message at most once (in A_1 or A_2) and thus A_6 can be executed at most $|N(v)|$ times at a node v. Thus each node v executes $O(|N(v)|)$ actions. So the algorithm executes $O(e)$ actions before termination.   □

Lemma 2. *Some dominating set of the network is always maintained when switching is in progress.*

Proof. We prove that even during switching any node v, that is not a dominator, is adjacent to a dominator. There are two cases, depending on whether *color* is set to *white* or *black* at v, since a *gray* node is a dominator by definition.

Case 1: *color = black*. So v must have received a $CHANGE\_OUT$ message. The sender u of that message must have *color = black* and $b = 1$, i.e. u must be a dominator. Hence v is adjacent to a dominator. Also u will never change its *color* again and hence v remains adjacent to a dominator.

Case 2: *color = white*. If at v, $w = 1$ then v is a dominator. Otherwise v must have a neighbor u with $w = 1$ (due to white CDS). At u, if *color = black* then this implies that it executed A_2 since it could not have executed A_7 due to the neighboring *white* node v. From G_2 we get that at u, $b = 1$ and thus it is a dominator. If at u, *color = white* then again it is a dominator since at u, $w = 1$. Thus in any case u, a neighbor of v, is a dominator.   □

We call a node v a black dominator if (*color = black* $\land b = 1$) at v. Similarly, we call v a white dominator if (*color = white* $\land w = 1$) at v, and a gray dominator if (*color = gray* $\land g = 1$) at v.

Theorem 3. *Some connected dominating set of the network is always maintained when switching is in progress.*

Proof. By Lemma 2, we only need to show that any two dominators u and v are connected by a path containing only dominators. There are six possible cases.

Case 1: Both u and v are black dominators. The initiator P is a black dominator. Thus there exists a path between the initiator P and any black dominator x such that the path contains only black dominators. Thus u and v are connected through the path $u \rightsquigarrow P \rightsquigarrow v$.

Case 2: u is a black dominator and v is a gray dominator. A node can become gray only upon the receipt of a $CHANGE\_OUT$ message (in S_3). The sender of a $CHANGE\_OUT$ message is always a black dominator. Thus any gray dominator v is adjacent to a black dominator x. Using case 1, x is connected to u and hence so is v.

Case 3: Both u and v are gray dominators. From case 2, both u and v are connected to some black dominator and thus are connected to each other.

Case 4: u is a white dominator and v is a gray dominator. The initiator P becomes a black dominator. Since all the nodes with $w = 1$ form a CDS, so there exists a node x in $N(P) \cup \{P\}$ with $w = 1$. So there exists a path between u and x that contains only nodes with $w = 1$. Let one such path be u, u_1, u_2, u_3, ..., u_n, x. Traversing from u to x, consider the first node y with $color \neq white$. If there is no such y then this implies that u is connected to x through a path containing only white dominators. Since x is adjacent to P, u is connected to P and thus u is connected to the gray dominator v, using case 2. If y exists and $color = black$ at y then y must have become black after executing A_2 since it cannot execute A_7 due to the white node u_k to which it is adjacent. From G_2, we get that at y, $b = 1$ and thus it is a black dominator. So u is connected to a black dominator y (via u, u_1, u_2, ..., u_k, y). Using case 2, y is connected to v and thus so is u. However, if $color = gray$ at y then y is connected to v using case 3 and thus again so is u.

Case 5: Both u and v are white dominators. From case 4, both u and v are connected to some gray dominator and thus are connected to each other.

Case 6: u is a white dominator and v is a black dominator. Using case 2 and case 4, u and v are connected to some gray dominator and thus are connected to each other.   □

Theorem 4. *During switching, the total number of dominators is at most the size of the set formed by the union of the white CDS and the black CDS.*

Proof. During switching, any node with $w = b = 0$ never becomes a gray dominator. Hence the theorem is proved.   □

3 Conclusion

The switching algorithm assumed that the two CDS are not disjoint. If they are disjoint then there must exist at least one non-dominator which is adjacent to some dominator in both the CDS. Information can be passed through this node to initiate the switching in either way.

The precomputed output may become invalid due to failure of nodes or links. Protocol switching, as opposed to output switching, should be used in that case to recompute the CDS every time there is a switch. We plan to investigate this in future.

References

1. Liu, X., van Renesse, R.: Fast protocol transition in a distributed environment. In: ACM PODC. (2000)
2. Arora, A., Gouda, M.: Distributed reset. IEEE Transactions on Computers **43**(9) (1994)
3. Liu, X., van Renesse, R., Bickford, M., Kreitz, C., Constable, R.: Protocol switching: Exploiting meta-properties. In: International Workshop on Applied Reliable Group Communication (WARGC). (2001)
4. Dijkstra, E.W.: Guarded commands, nondeterminacy and formal derivation of programs. In: CACM. (1975)

An Efficient and Scalable Checkpointing and Recovery Algorithm for Distributed Systems

K.P. Krishna Kumar and R.C. Hansdah

Dept. of Computer Science & Automation, Indian Institute of Science,
Bangalore 560012, India
{krishna, hansdah}@csa.iisc.ernet.in

Abstract. In this paper, we describe an efficient coordinated checkpointing and recovery algorithm which can work even when the channels are assumed to be non-FIFO, and messages may be lost. Nodes are assumed to be autonomous, and they do not block while taking checkpoints. Based on the local conditions, any process can request the previous coordinator for the 'permission' to initiate a new checkpoint. Allowing multiple initiators of checkpoints avoids the bottleneck associated with a single initiator, but the algorithm permits only a single instance of checkpointing process at any given time, thus reducing much of the overhead associated with multiple initiators of distributed algorithms.

1 Introduction

Eighty percent of failures in computer systems are of non catastrophic nature, termed temporary faults. The checkpointing protocols described in the literature are mainly used to overcome these temporary faults. It is desirable that the checkpointing and recovery protocols (i) do not depend on a single central coordinator to avoid the bottleneck problem, (ii) do not assume that the communication channels are reliable and FIFO, (iii) are non-blocking at the time of taking checkpoints, (iv) permit nodes to take checkpoint at any point in time, i.e., nodes are autonomous, (v) have low space and message overhead,(vi) have a low recovery cost, and (vii) are adaptive in the sense that the smaller is the number of messages lost and the amount of interaction between the processes, the lower is the space and message overhead. Essentially, there are three categories of checkpointing and recovery protocols, viz., *coordinated, communication induced*, and *uncoordinated*. Communication induced and uncoordinated checkpointing protocols generally have high recovery cost and stable storage space required is also generally high. On the other hand, the centralized checkpoint initiator schemes like the algorithms in[1, 2] suffers from the bottleneck associated with a centralized initiator. For other distributed initiator schemes like Prakash and Singhal's algorithm[3], there may be multiple instances of checkpointing in the system at any given time. A detailed description of various checkpoint and rollback-recovery protocols can be found in [4, 5]. Our aim is to design a checkpointing algorithm with multiple initiators, but which has only one instance of checkpointing going on in the system at any point in time and has all of the

S. Chaudhuri et al. (Eds.): ICDCN 2006, LNCS 4308, pp. 94–99, 2006.

above features. The rest of the paper is organized as follows. Section 2 describes our checkpointing algorithm and in Section 3, we describe the rollback and recovery algorithm. In Section 4, the details of the performance evaluation are given, and finally, we conclude the paper in section 5.

2   The Checkpointing Algorithm

2.1   Informal Description

The system consists of a set of n processes $P_1, P_2, ..., P_n$ which communicate with each other using messages only. The channels are assumed to be non-FIFO, but messages may be lost. The faults are assumed to be transient. The transmission delays are unpredictable but finite. The messages, if they are delivered at the receiver's end, are delivered correctly. The processes are assumed to be asynchronous.

All the processes initiate a checkpoint before they start their computation. A process is initially nominated to be the coordinator. A coordinator for a checkpoint interval is responsible for coordinating the checkpointing activities for a particular checkpoint interval. Each checkpoint interval is given a unique checkpoint ID(CPID), and CPIDs are incremented sequentially. Application messages from the same node are also numbered sequentially. Both the sequence number of a message, and the current CPID are piggybacked on the message. If a process receives a message with a higher CPID than the current CPID, it takes a checkpoint before receiving the message. The concepts of CPID and sequence numbers are the same as those used in [2]. After a checkpointing process is initiated, the coordinator receives reports from all the processes regarding confirmation of having taken a checkpoint and a report of the count of all the messages they have sent and received. This is used by the coordinator to find out, whether all the processes have successfully taken a checkpoint and also that no messages sent in a particular checkpoint interval have been lost. For the next interval, some new processes may put their claim to be the coordinator and the present coordinator grants permission to one of them. It is assumed that the loss of control messages are handled using timeouts, and the failure of coordinator is handled using an election protocol.

2.2   Messages

There are two kinds of messages, viz., *application messages* and *control messages*. In this paper, the term message refers to application message only, unless stated otherwise. The various types of messages are as follows.

application_message: They are sent by the user application.
control_message: They are sent either by the processes or the coordinator as part of the checkpointing process. They include the following :
send_balance_report: They are sent by the coordinator to a process if the balance report from the process has not reached it after a certain time interval.

balance_report: These are forwarded by the processes to the coordinator when they take a checkpoint. It is the difference between the number of messages sent and received by a process during a checkpoint interval. Each process also sends a dependency list which gives the individual balance count with each of the other processes.

update_report: This message is sent by a process to the coordinator when it receives a message pertaining to a previous checkpoint interval.

reconcile_message: This message is sent by the coordinator to a processes which has received lesser number of messages than sent from a certain sender.

list_of_messages: The receiver process on getting the message *reconcile_message* from the coordinator, sends a list of message sequence numbers it has received from a given sender.

send_request_coord: This message is sent by the process requesting permission to initiate a new checkpointing process.

grant_permission_coord: This message is sent by the coordinator while granting permission to a process to be the coordinator for the next checkpoint interval.

2.3   The Algorithm

Algorithm at each process

Initially take a checkpoint before computation;
On receipt of an *application_message*:
   if(message.CPID > own CPID)
     take a checkpoint with new CPID;
   send *balance_report* to the coordinator;
if(message.CPID == own CPID)
  update the balance count;
if(message.CPID < own CPID)
  update balance count;
  send *update_report* to coordinator;
  log the message in stable storage;
On receipt of message *send_balance_report*:
   send the latest *balance_report* to coordinator;
On receipt of message *reconcile_message* :
   send the *list_of_messages* from the given process to the sender;
On receipt of message *list_of_messages* :
   send the missing messages to the receiver;
On requirement to initiate a checkpoint :
   send message *send_request_coord* to the present coordinator;
On receipt of message *grant_permission_coord*
   declare self as coordinator if indicated in the message;
   initiate checkpointing process;
To send an *application_message*;
   add the present CPID to the message header;
   log the message in volatile memory;

Algorithm at the coordinator process

On receipt of message *send_request_coord*:
   if the present checkpointing process is completed
   send message *grant_permission_coord* to the process;
On receipt of message *balance_report* from processes:
   update the overall balance count;
   update the overall process count;
   if(process count != 0 after scheduled timeout)
   send message *send_balance_report* to the concerned processes;

```
    if (( process count == 0) and (balance count != 0))
// all processes have taken fresh checkpoint.
    wait till time-out;
    send message request_balance_report to receiver processes with positive balance count;
// completion of checkpointing process
    if((process count == 0) and (balance count == 0))
    the checkpointing process is completed;
// to cater for any lost update messages
    if balance count != 0 after receipt of fresh balance report
    send message reconcile_message to the concerned receiver processes ;
```

3   Rollback Recovery

The processes maintain at most two checkpoints in the stable storage. One checkpoint is the fully completed one and the other one is the current checkpoint which
is being coordinated. The checkpoints with the same CPID form a recovery line.
In a modification to the Silva's algorithm [2], the rollback algorithm tries to minimize the number of processes which are required to rollback. On being informed
of a process's failure, the coordinator asks the processes to take a virtual checkpoint and forward the list of processes to which they have sent messages since
the checkpoint indicated in the coordinator's message. This checkpoint will be
the one coordinator knows has been completed. The processes, forward the list
as asked for and continue their computation. The virtual checkpoint does not
involve saving the state of the process. The processes are allowed to receive messages. But, processes are not allowed to send messages till further confirmation
is received from the coordinator. Using the lists provided by the processes, the
coordinator calculates the dependencies between processes. It finds out which
all processes have communicated with the failed process(es), either directly or
indirectly.

The rollback control messages are :

request_virtual_cp: This is sent by the coordinator to all the processes asking
them to forward their dependency lists. The processes further do not send any
more application messages, but continue to receive messages.

rollback_request: Message sent by the coordinator to the processes asking them
to rollback to a given CPID, and resume computation.

resume_request: Message sent by the coordinator to the processes asking them
to resume computation from the present state.

Algorithm at the coordinator process

```
On receipt of failure report of a process;
    take a virtual checkpoint;
    send request_virtual_cp message to all processes.
On receipt of message balance_report from the processes;
    calculate dependencies;
    send rollback_request message to dependent processes;
    send resume_request message to non-dependent processes;
```

Algorithm at each process

On receipt of message *request_virtual_cp*;
    take a virtual checkpoint;
    send *balance_report* to the coordinator;
    accept any incoming *application_message*;
    do not send any *application_message* ;
On receipt of message *rollback_request*;
    rollback to the indicated CPID;
    resume computation;
On receipt of message *resume_request*;
    resume computation from the present state;

4   Performance Evaluation

Extensive simulation was carried out to test the algorithms and measure various parameters. The simulations were done using discrete event simulation with the number of processes varying from 10 to 50. The error percentage of the channel was also varied from 0 to 10 percent. Exponential distribution was used for generation of messages. Each of the experiments were performed at least ten times, and the average values for all the measured parameters were taken.

In terms of checkpointing overhead, we have compared our checkpointing algorithm with uncoordinated algorithm that take periodic checkpointing and with uncoordinated algorithm that take a checkpoint prior to a message receipt event provided a message send event has occurred in the same checkpoint interval. We have also compared our algorithm with *communication induced checkpointing* algorithms,viz., Briatico, Ciuffoletti and Simoncini's(BCS) algorithm [6],

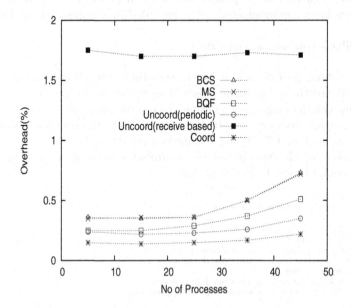

Fig. 1. Comparison of Checkpointing Overhead between different Algorithms

Manivannan and Singhal's (MS) algorithm [7] and the Baldoni, Quaglia and Fornara's(BQF) algorithm [8]. The comparison of the percentage overhead of the various classes of algorithm is shown in figure 1. The amount of saving in computation time in comparison to the situation in which all processes have to rollback as in [2] in the event of a failure is from 3 to 6% when the number of processes are upto 30. For further increase in number of processes, the saving is just over 1%. The saving is due to the fact that only those processes which have communicated with the failed process(es) are required to rollback.

5   Conclusion

In this paper, we have described an efficient checkpoint and recovery algorithm which tries to combine the advantages of coordinated, uncoordinated and the communication-induced protocols and which has all of the desirable features given earlier. Simulation results indicate that it performs well in terms of checkpointing overhead compared to other algorithms.

References

1. Koo, R., Toueg, S.: Checkpointing and rollback-recovery for distributed systems. IEEE Transactions on Software Engineering **13**(1) (1987) 23–31
2. Silva, L.M., Silva, J.G.: Global checkpointing for distributed programs. In: Proceedings of the 10th Symposium on Reliable Distributed Systems. (1992) 155–162
3. Prakash, R., Singhal, M.: Low cost checkpointing and failure recovery in mobile computing systems. IEEE Transactions on Parallel and Distributed Systems **7**(10) (1996) 1035–1048
4. Elnozahy, E., Johnson, D., Yang, Y.: A survey of rollback-recovery protocols in message passing systems. ACM Computing Surveys **34**(3) (2002) 375–408
5. Manivannan, D., Singhal, M.: Quasi synchronous checkpointing: Models, characterization and classification. IEEE Transactions on Parallel and Distributed Systems **10**(7) (1999) 206–216
6. Briatico, D., Ciuffoletti, A., Simoncini, L.: A distributed domino-effect free recovery algorithm. In: Proceedings of the IEEE International Symposium on Reliability, Distributed Software and Databases. (1984) 207–215
7. Manivannan, D., Singhal, M.: A low overhead recovery technique using quasi synchronous checkpointing. In: Proceedings of the IEEE International Conference on Distributed Computing Systems. (1996) 100–107
8. Baldoni, R., Quaglia, F., Fornara, P.: An index-based checkpointing algorithm for autonomous distributed systems. In: Proceedings of the IEEE International Conference on Distributed Computing Systems. (1999) 181–188

On Distributed Verification

Amos Korman and Shay Kutten

Faculty of IE&M, Technion, Haifa 32000, Israel

Abstract. This paper describes the invited talk given at the 8th International Conference on Distributed Computing and Networking (ICDCN 2006), at the Indian Institute of Technology Guwahati, India. This talk was intended to give a partial survey and to motivate further studies of distributed verification. To serve the purpose of motivating, we allow ourselves to speculate freely on the potential impact of such research.

In the context of sequential computing, it is common to assume that the task of verifying a property of an object may be much easier than computing it (consider, for example, solving an NP-Complete problem versus verifying a witness). Extrapolating from the impact the separation of these two notions (computing and verifying) had in the context of sequential computing, the separation may prove to have a profound impact on the field of distributed computing as well. In addition, in the context of distributed computing, the motivation for the separation seems even stronger than in the centralized sequential case.

In this paper we explain some motivations for specific definitions, survey some very related notions and their motivations in the literature, survey some examples for problems and solutions, and mention some additional general results such as general algorithmic methods and general lower bounds. Since this paper is mostly intended to "give a taste" rather than be a comprehensive survey, we apologize to authors of additional related papers that we did not mention or detailed.

1   Introduction

This paper addresses the problem of locally verifying global properties. This task complements the task of locally computing global functions. Since many functions cannot be computed locally [29, 42, 41], local verification may prove more useful than local computing - one can compute globally and verify locally.

In terms of sequential time, there exists evidence that verification is sometimes easier then computation. For example, verifying that a given color assignment on a given graph is a legal 3 coloring is believed to consume much less time than computing a 3 coloring [36]. As another example, given a weighted graph together with a tree that spans it, it is required to decide whether this tree is an MST of the graph. This *MST verification problem* was introduced by Tarjan in the sequential model. A linear time algorithm for computing an MST is known only in certain cases, or by a randomized algorithm [35, 37]. On the other hand, the sequential verification algorithm of [34] is (edge) linear.

In the context of distributed tasks, other measures of complexity are used, e.g., communication complexity. Still, one can ask a similar natural question. Given

S. Chaudhuri et al. (Eds.): ICDCN 2006, LNCS 4308, pp. 100–114, 2006.

a *distributed representation* of a solution for a problem (for example, each node holds a pointer to one of its incident edges), we are required to verify the legality of the represented solution (in the example, to verify that collection of pointed edges forms an MST). Does the verification consume fewer communication bits than the computation of the solution (e.g., the MST)?

Since faults are much more likely to occur in a distributed setting than in a sequential one, the motivation for verification in a distributed setting seems to be even stronger than in a sequential one. A common application of local distributed verification is in the context of self stabilization. See, for example, the *local detection* [31], or the *local checking* [9], or the *silent stabilization* [32]. Self stabilization deals with algorithms that must cope with faults that are rather sever, though of a type that does occur in reality [27, 28]. The faults may cause the states of different nodes to be inconsistent with each other. For example, the collection of pointed edges may not be a tree, or may not be an MST. Self stabilizing algorithm thus often use distributed verification repeatedly. If the verification fails, a (much heavier) global MST recomputation algorithm is invoked. An efficient verification algorithm thus saves repeatedly in communication. We discuss the use application of distributed verification to self stabilization in more length in Section 4.

In the *simple model* for local verification, all nodes are awakened simultaneously and start a computation. In a *t-local verification algorithm*, it is required that the represented solution is illegal iff after at most t time rounds, at least one processor outputs 0 (the rest may output 1). Since we want the locality parameter t to be independent of the network, it would be desired to have t be a constant.

Note, that for a constant t (even for $t = 1$), many representations can be trivially verified. For example, in the legal-coloring verification task, each node just checks that each of its neighbors has a different color than its own. As another example, in a distributed representation of a Minimal Independent Set (MIS), each node holds a flag indicating whether if belongs to the MIS or not. Clearly, such an MIS representation can be verified in one time round.

In a distributed representation of a subgraph of G, each node may point at some of its incident edges. The set of pointed edges forms a subgraph of G. In the *spanning tree* (respectively, *MST*) verification problem, it is required to check whether this subgraph is a spanning tree (resp., MST) of G or not. The following simple claim indicates that in a too simple model for local verification, the verifications of some basic representations require $\Omega(n)$ time rounds. (We do not describe the simple model explicitly).

Claim 1. *In the simple model for local verification, both the spanning tree and the MST verification problems require $\Omega(n)$ time rounds.*

Sketch of Proof: We show the result for the spanning tree case. Let $G = \{v_1, v_2, \cdots, v_n\}$ be a circle. For simplicity of presentation, we assume n is even. Consider three distributed representations of G as depicted in Figure 1. In the first representation, G_1, for each $1 \leq i \leq n - 1$, node v_i holds a pointer to

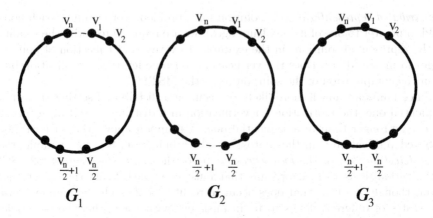

Fig. 1. The three representations of subgraphs in G. The thick edges correspond to the pointed edges and the dashed edges correspond to the non-pointed edges.

edge (v_i, v_{i+1}). Therefore, the pointed edges in G_1 are all the edges except for (v_n, v_1). In the second representation, G_2, for each $1 \le i \le n/2 - 1$ and each $n/2 + 1 \le i \le n$, node v_i holds a pointer to the edge (v_i, v_{i+1}) (mod $n + 1$). Therefore, the pointed edges are all the edges except for $(v_{n/2}, v_{n/2+1})$. Note that in both G_1 and G_2, the pointed edges form a spanning tree. In G_3, for each $1 \le i \le n$, node v_i holds a pointer to the edge (v_i, v_{i+1}). Therefore, the set of pointed edges consists of all edges in the circle.

First note that since the pointed edges in G_1 and G_2 form a spanning tree, no node in either G_1 or G_2 outputs 0. Assume by contradiction that the spanning tree verification can be accomplished in t time rounds, where $t < n/4$. In this case, a node can only gather information about the nodes at distance at most t from it. Therefore, for every $1 \le i \le n/4$ and every $3n/4 \le i \le n$, the output of v_i in G_3 is the same as the output of v_i in G_2. Similarly, for each $n/2 \le i \le 3n/4$, the output of v_i in G_3 is the same as the output of v_i in G_1. If follows that the output of each vertex in G_3 is not 0, contradicting the fact that the pointed edges in G_3 do not form a tree. □

In order to deal with verification tasks such as verifying spanning trees, the concept of *proof labeling schemes* was introduced in [40]. The formal definitions are given in Section 2. Informally, it is assumed that the *state* of every node has already been computed by some algorithm (in the above example, the state may consist of a pointer to an incident edge). The configuration (formed as the collection of states of all nodes) is supposed to satisfy some predicate (e.g., "the pointed edges form an MST of the underlying graph"). To enable local verification, labels are added to the nodes in preprocessing stage. To perform the verification, a node computes some *local* predicate, considering only its own state, as well as the above mentioned labels of its neighbors but not their states (!). The global configuration predicate is implied by the conjunction of the local predicates in the following manner. If the configuration is legal then each node outputs 1 (i.e., "I do not detect a problem"). However, if the configuration is not legal, then for *every* possible way of labeling the vertices, at least one node should detect a problem, i.e. output 0. This, in a way, means that if the configuration is not legal, the adversary cannot fool the verifier by changing the labels. The restriction of one time round can obviously be generalized to t time rounds (hopefully t being constant). However, all the results that have been previously established in the area of proof labeling schemes hold for the case $t = 1$.

Note, that there is some resemblance between the definition of proof labeling schemes and the notion of NP. Informally, the collection of assigned labels in the preprocessing stage can be considered a witness. If the configuration is legal then there exists a witness (labeling assignment) such that the legality of the configuration can be verified in one time round. Otherwise, if the configuration is not legal then there does not exist such a witness, i.e., for any labeling assignment, in one time round, at least one node should detect a problem.

We note that the number of bits in a label is the number of information bits a node needs to convey to its neighbors in the verification. Ideally, this number is as small as possible, even smaller than the state of the vertex. We evaluate a proof labeling scheme by its *label size*, i.e., the maximum number of bits assigned to a node of the graph in the preprocessing stage.

2   Model ([40])

We consider distributed systems that are represented by connected graphs. The vertices of the graph $G = \langle V, E \rangle$ correspond to the nodes in the system, and we use the words "vertex" and "node" interchangeably. The edges of G correspond to the links, and we use the words "link" and "edge" interchangeably. Denote $n = |V|$. Every node v has internal ports, each corresponding to one of the edges attached to v. The ports are numbered from 1 to $deg(v)$ (the degree of v) by an internal numbering known only to node v. If G is undirected, then for every vertex v let $N(v)$ denote the set of edges adjacent to v. If G is directed, then for any vertex v let $N(v)$ denote the set of edges incoming to v. In either case, for every vertex v let $n(v) = |N(v)|$. Unless mentioned otherwise, all graphs considered are undirected. For two vertices u and v in G, let $d_G(u, v)$ denote the unweighted distance between u and v.

Given a vertex v, let s_v denote the state of v and let $v_s = (v, s_v)$. A *configuration graph* corresponding to a graph $G = \langle V, E \rangle$ is a graph $G_s = \langle V_s, E_s \rangle$, where $V_s = \{v_s \mid v \in V\}$ and $(v_s, u_s) \in E_s$ iff $(v, u) \in E$. A *family of configuration graphs* $\mathcal{F}_s$ corresponding to graph family $\mathcal{F}$ consists of configuration graphs $G_s \in \mathcal{F}_s$ for each $G \in \mathcal{F}$. Let $\mathcal{F}_S$ be the largest possible such family when every state s is taken from a given set S. Unless mentioned otherwise, let S denote the set of integers. We sometimes refer to each state s_v of a configuration graph as having two fields: $s_v = (id(v), s'(v))$. Field $id(v)$ is v's *identity* and is encoded using $O(\log n)$ bits. When the context is clear we may refer to $s'(v)$ as the state of v (instead of to $s(v)$). A configuration graph G_s is *id-based* if for every pair of vertices v and u it is given that $id(u) \neq id(v)$. A graph whose identities are arbitrary (including possibly the case where all identities are the same) is termed *anonymous*. An id-based (respectively, anonymous) family is a family of id-based (respectively, anonymous) graphs. Let $\mathcal{F}^{all}$ be the collection of all directed strongly-connected and all undirected connected graphs with $O(n)$ vertices. Let $\mathcal{F}^{undirected}$ be the collection of all undirected connected graphs with $O(n)$ vertices. When it is clear from the context, we use the term "graph" instead of "configuration graph", "id-based graph" or "anonymous graph". We may also use the notation v instead of v_s. Given a family of configuration graphs $\mathcal{F}_s$, let $\mathcal{F}_s(W)$ denote the family of all graphs in $\mathcal{F}_s$ such that, when considered as weighted, the (integral) weight of each edge is bounded from above by W.

Many of the results in [40] deal with a distributed representation of subgraphs. Such a representation is encoded in the collection of the nodes' states. There can be many such representations. For simplicity, we focus on the case that an edge is included in the subgraph if it is explicitly pointed at by the state of an endpoint. That is, given a configuration graph G_s, the subgraph (respectively, directed subgraph) induced by the states of G_s, denoted $H(G_s)$ (respectively, $D(G_s)$), is defined as follows. For every vertex $v \in G$, if s_v includes an encoding of one of v's ports pointing to a vertex u, then the edge (respectively, directed edge) (v, u) is an edge in the subgraph. These are the only edges in the subgraph.

Consider a graph G. A distributed problem *Prob* is the task of selecting a state s_v for each vertex v, such that G_s satisfies a given predicate f_{Prob}. This induces the problem *Prob* on a graph family $\mathcal{F}$ in the natural way. We say that f_{Prob} is the *characteristic function* of *Prob* over $\mathcal{F}$.

This model tries to capture adding labels to configuration graphs in order to maintain a (locally checkable) distributed proof that the given configuration graph satisfies a given predicate f_{Prob}. Informally, a proof labeling scheme includes a *marker* algorithm M that generates a label for every node, and a *decoder* algorithm that compares labels of neighboring nodes. If a configuration graph satisfies f_{Prob}, then the decoder at every two neighboring nodes declares their labels (produced by marker M) "consistent" with each other. However, if the configuration graph does *not* satisfy f_{Prob}, then for *any possible* marker, the decoder must declare "inconsistencies" between some neighboring nodes in the labels produced by the marker. It is not required that the marker be distributed. However, the decoder is distributed and *local*, i.e., every node can check only the labels of its neighbors (and its own label and state).

More formally, A *marker* algorithm L is an algorithm that given a graph $G_s \in \mathcal{F}_s$, assigns a label $L(v_s)$ to each vertex $v_s \in G_s$. For a marker algorithm L and a vertex $v_s \in G_s$, let $N'_L(v)$ be a set of $n(v)$ fields, one per neighbor. Each field $e = (v, u)$ in $N'_L(v)$, corresponding to edge $e \in N(v)$, contains the following. (1) The port number of e in v; (2) the weight of e (if G is unweighted we regard each edge as having weight 1); (3) $L(u)$.

Let $N_L(v) = \langle (s_v, L(v)), N'_L(v) \rangle$. Informally, $N'_L(v)$ contains the labels given to all of v's neighbors along with the port number and the weights of the edges connecting v to them. $N_L(v)$ contains also v's state and label. A *decoder* algorithm $\mathcal{D}$ is an algorithm which is applied separately at each vertex $v \in G$.

When $\mathcal{D}$ is applied at vertex v, its input is $N_L(v)$ and its output, $\mathcal{D}(v, L)$, is boolean.

A *proof labeling scheme* $\pi = \langle \mathcal{M}, \mathcal{D} \rangle$ for some family $\mathcal{F}_s$ and some characteristic function f is composed of a *marker* algorithm $\mathcal{M}$ and a *decoder* algorithm $\mathcal{D}$, such that the following two properties hold:

1. For every $G_s \in \mathcal{F}_s$, if $f(G_s) = 1$ then $\mathcal{D}(v, \mathcal{M}) = 1$ for every vertex $v \in G$.
2. For every $G_s \in \mathcal{F}_s$, if $f(G_s) = 0$ then for every marker algorithm L there exists a vertex $v \in G$ so that $\mathcal{D}(v, L) = 0$.

We note that all the proof labeling schemes constructed so far use a polytime decoder algorithm. The *size* of a proof labeling scheme $\pi = \langle \mathcal{M}, \mathcal{D} \rangle$ is the maximum number of bits in the label $\mathcal{M}(v_s)$ over all $v_s \in G_s$ and all $G_s \in \mathcal{F}_s$. For a family $\mathcal{F}_s$ and a function f, we say that the *proof size* of $\mathcal{F}_s$ and f is the smallest size of any proof labeling scheme for $\mathcal{F}_s$ and f.

3   Basic Examples

To illustrate the definitions, we now present a basic proof labeling scheme [40] concerning agreement among all vertices. Note that v's neighbors cannot 'see' the state of v but they can see v's label. This is different than what is assumed e.g. in [31]. We note that the following lemma also demonstrates a connection between the notion of proof labeling scheme and that of communication complexity [43].

Lemma 2. *[40] The proof size of $\mathcal{F}_S^{all}$ and $f_{Agreement}$ is $\Theta(m)$.*

Proof. We first describe a trivial proof labeling scheme $\pi = \langle \mathcal{M}, \mathcal{D} \rangle$ of the desired size m. Given G_s such that $f_{Agreement}(G_s) = 1$, for every vertex v, let $\mathcal{M}(v) = s_v$. I.e., we just copy the state of node v into its label. Then, $\mathcal{D}(v, L)$ simply verifies that $L(v) = s_v$ and that $L(v) = L(u)$ for every neighbor u of node v. It is clear that π is a correct proof labeling scheme for $\mathcal{F}_S^{all}$ and $f_{Agreement}$ of size m. We now show that the above bound is tight up to a multiplicative constant factor even assuming that $\mathcal{F}_S^{all}$ is id-based. Consider the connected graph G with two vertices v and u. Assume, by way of contradiction, that there is a proof labeling scheme $\pi = \langle \mathcal{M}, \mathcal{D} \rangle$ for F_S^{all} and $f_{Agreement}$ of size less than $m/2$. For $i \in S$, let G_s^i be G modified so that both u and v have state $s(u) = s(v) = i$. Obviously, $f_{Agreement}(G_s^i) = 1$ for every i. For a vertex x, let $\mathcal{M}^i(x)$ be the label given to x by marker $\mathcal{M}$ applied on G_s^i. Let $L^i = (\mathcal{M}^i(v), \mathcal{M}^i(u))$. Since the number of bits in L^i is assumed to be less than m, there exist $i, j \in S$ such that $i < j$ and $L^i = L^j$. Let G_s be G modified so that $s_u = i$ and $s_v = j$. Let L be the marker algorithm for G_s in which $L(u) = \mathcal{M}^i(u)$ and $L(v) = \mathcal{M}^j(v)$. Then for each vertex x, $\mathcal{D}(x, L) = 1$, contradicting the fact that $f(G_s) = 0$. $\square$

Note, that the corresponding computation task, that of assigning every node the same state, requires only states of size 1.

By the above lemma, it is clear that for any m there exists a family $\mathcal{F}_s$ and a function f with proof size $\Theta(m)$. A somewhat stronger claim is presented in [40], namely, that a similar result exists also for *graph problems* (that is, problems where the input is only the graph topology).

Corollary 3. *For every function $1 \leq m < n^2$, there exists a graph problem on an id-based family with proof size $\Theta(m)$.*

Let us now show a family with a smaller proof size. The following example concerns the representation of various spanning trees in the system. The upper bound employs structures and ideas used in many papers including [3, 5, 31, 14, 4, 40]. The lower bound is taken from [40]. A lower bound in the different model of silent stabilization for one of the tasks below was presented in [32]. Consider five different problems, obtained by assigning states to the nodes of G so that $H(G_s)$ (respectively, $D(G_s)$) is a (respectively, directed) (1) forest; (2) spanning forest; (3) tree; (4) spanning tree; (5) BFS tree of G (for some root vertex r). Let $f_{No-cycles}$ (respectively, $f'_{No-cycles}$) be the characteristic function of either one of the five problems above.

Lemma 4. *[40] The proof size of $\mathcal{F}_S^{all}$ and $f_{No-cycles}$ (respectively, $f'_{No-cycles}$) is $\Theta(\log n)$.*

Proof. For proving the upper bound, construct the proof labeling scheme $\pi_{span} = \langle \mathcal{M}_{span}, \mathcal{D}_{span} \rangle$ for $\mathcal{F}_S$ and f being "$H(G_s)$ is a spanning tree". The other cases are constructed in a similar manner. Given G_s so that $f(G_s) = 1$, the marker algorithm $\mathcal{M}_{span}$ operates as follows. If $H = H(G_s)$ is a spanning tree, then it has $n - 1$ edges. Therefore, either there is only one vertex r in G_s whose state is not an encoding of one of its port numbers or there exist exactly two vertices whose states point at each other. In the second case let r be the vertex with the smaller identity among the two and in both cases r is considered as the root. Note that the state of each non-root vertex points at its parent in the rooted tree (H, r). Let $\mathcal{M}_{span}(v) = \langle id(r), d_H(v, r) \rangle$. For a vertex v_s and a marker algorithm L, the first field $L(v)$ is denoted by $L_1(v)$ and the second by $L_2(v)$. The decoder $\mathcal{D}_{span}(v, L) = 1$ iff all the following easy to verify events occur.

1. For every neighbor u of v, $L_1(u) = L_1(v) \in S$. I.e., all vertices agree on the identity of the root.
2. If $id(v) = L_1(v)$ then $L_2(v) = 0$.
3. If $id(v)$ is not $L_1(v)$ then s_v is an encoding of a port number of v leading to a vertex u such that $L_2(v) = 1 + L_2(u)$.
4. If $L_2(v) = 0$ then either s_v is not an encoding of a port of v or an encoding of a port of v leading to vertex u and $L_2(u) = 1$.

Obviously, the size of π_{span} is $O(\log n)$ so we only need to prove that the scheme is correct. Given G_s so that $f(G_s) = 1$. W show that $D_{span}(v, L) = 1$ for for all $u, v \in V$. The first fields of $\mathcal{M}_{span}(u)$ and $\mathcal{M}_{span}(v)$ are the same since they are both the identity of the root r. If $v \neq r$ then s_v is the identity of v's parent in the tree H, therefore $dist_H(v, r) = 1 + dist_H(s_v, r)$. Also, (2) above holds for r. Hence, $\mathcal{D}(v, \mathcal{M}_{span}) = 1$ for each vertex $v \in G$.

If, for some marker algorithm L, $\mathcal{D}(v, L) = 1$ for every vertex v, then by (1), all vertices must agree in the first field of their label. Denote this value x. Since the identities of the vertices are disjoint, there can be at most one vertex r

satisfying $id(r) = x$. Also, by (3), such a vertex must exist. By (3), for every vertex u such that $id(u) \neq x$ corresponds a directed edge leading to some vertex w and $L(u) - 1 = L(w)$. Therefore all directed paths must reach the special vertex r (satisfying $id(r) = x$). Therefore the edges corresponding to all vertices but r, form a spanning tree T and the only case to be inspected is whether the edge that correspond to r (if this edge exists), belongs to this tree. This is verified by (4). The upper bound for the case of a spanning tree follows.

In the case were f (respectively, f') is a "(respectively, directed) BFS tree", the decoder $\mathcal{D}(v, L)$ also checks that $|L_2(u) - L_2(v)| \leq 1$ for each (respectively, directed) neighbor u of vertex v.

Remark: a similar approach applies also to BFS trees on weighted id-based graphs except that the size of the scheme changes to $O(\log n + \log W)$. Note that in the above schemes if the decoder satisfies $\mathcal{D}(v, L) = 1$ for every v then $L_2(v) = d_G(v, r)$. Therefore, using this scheme we can also prove that each vertex holds its distance to the root.

Let us next prove the lower bound (the proof is essentially the same for all five problems). Let P be the horizontal path of n vertices. For the sake of analysis only, enumerate the vertices of P from left to right, i.e., $P = (1, 2, \cdots, n)$. For $i < n$, let s_i be the port number of the edge leading from vertex i to $i + 1$. Obviously, $f(P_s) = 1$ and $f'(P_s) = 1$. Assume, by way of contradiction, that there exists a proof labeling scheme $\pi = \langle \mathcal{M}, \mathcal{D} \rangle$ for $\mathcal{F}_s$ and either f or f' which is of size less than $\log(n/2) - 2$. Let $L(i)$ be the label given by $\mathcal{M}$ to vertex i in the above path P_s. Since the number of bits in each $L(i)$ is less than $\log(n/2) - 2$, there exist two pairs of vertices $(i, i+1)$ and $(j, j+1)$ where $1 < i$ and $i + 1 < j < n - 1$ so that $L(i) = L(j) = L'$ and $L(i+1) = L(j+1) = L''$. We now build the following ring R consisting of $j - i$ vertices whose identities are clockwise ordered from i to $j-1$. For $i \leq k < j-1$ let s_k be the port number of vertex k leading from k to $k+1$ and let s_{j-1} be the port leading from $j-1$ to i. Let us give R_s the same labeling L as $\mathcal{M}$ gives P_s, i.e., each vertex $i \leq k < j$ in R_s is labeled $L(k)$. By the correctness of π on P_s we get that for each vertex $v \in R_s$, $\mathcal{D}(v, L) = 1$. This is a contradiction to the fact that $f(R_s) = 0$ and $f'(R_s) = 0$.

Note that the proof applies to all the cases in the lemma, including the case that a (not necessarily spanning) subgraph does not have a cycle.   □

Note that the above lemma implies a lower bound of $\Omega(\log n)$ for proof labeling schemes for the Minimum Spanning Tree problem (MST). A proof in the spirit of the proof of lemma 2 was then used in [40] to increase this lower bound to $\Omega(\log n + \log W)$ where W is the maximum weight of an edge in the graph. This lower bound was later increased in [38] to $\Omega((\log n \log W))$. The proof of the lower bound in [38] is quiet involved. It uses a new combinatorial structure termed (h, μ)-*hypertrees* that is a combination between (h, μ)-trees and a hypercube. That is, an (h, μ)-hypertree is constructed by connecting (via a weighted path) every node in one $(h - 1, \mu)$-hypertree to the corresponding node in another $(h-1, \mu)$-hypertree. This doubling of the hypertree is partially responsible for the logarithmic behavior of the lower bound. The intuition behind this construction is that (1) the proof needed a structure with many cycles; and (2) the proof needed to make many nodes neighbors, since proof labeling schemes deal only with neighboring nodes. In the construction, h is the hight of the hypertree and μ is the weight of the weight of some edges that are crucial for the MST. That proof follows the general structure of [39] in the sense that labels for some $(h-1, \mu^2)$-hypertree H' are computed using the labels for some (h, μ)-hypertree H. However, the specifics are more complex and require some new tricks. For example, the verifier described in the construction for the lower bound, at any node v, has to *guess* labels for some other nodes.

Two general approaches to constructing proof labeling schemes are presented in [40]. One is a modular construction of a scheme from modules that are other schemes. The other is a simulation of the execution of a distributed algorithm that computes the function to be verified. The second method bears some similarity to the idea of the roll back compiler of [9], that is described briefly in Section 4. This method is used in [40] together with ad hoc improvements to derive an upper bound of $O(\log^2 n + \log n \log W)$ for the MST problem. This was improved later in [38] to match their improved lower bound.

Additional upper and lower bounds given in [40] for a number of graph problems, including many basic building block problems. Other results therein demonstrated the role and the cost of identities in this model. It was also shown that every predicate has a proof labeling scheme in id-based families of graphs.

4   Self Stabilization: An Application of Distributed Verification

In this section we mention the notion of self stabilizing algorithms. It turns out that distributed verification, in addition to its theoretical interest, can be very useful for the design of such algorithms.

The notion of self stabilization was suggested by Dijkstra in 1974 ([10], see also [12]). Dijkstra's paper later won the ACM-PODC influential paper award, that shortly after that became the Dijkstra Prize in Distributed Computing awarded by the ACM (the Association for Computing Machinery) at the Annual Symposium on the Principles of Distributed Computing (PODC). Starting in 2007, this prize will be given by the ACM and EATCS (the European Association for Theoretical Computer Science). It took some years until the importance of that paper became evident, as highlighted first by Lamport [17]. However, since then, a lot of attention has been invested in self stabilization, and this sub-area now even has its own conference (SSS).

In the above mentioned paper, Dijkstra studied the example of a token ring. This is a network of processors arranged in a circle, where each processor can "see" the whole state of one processor that immediately precedes it (e.g. in a clockwise order). The state of the processor (and of the preceding one) may imply that the processor "has a token", or that it "does not have a token". It is required that exactly one of the processors in the whole ring is in the state of "having a token" at any given time. A second requirement was that each node "passes the token" eventually to the processor succeeding it on the ring. When this action was taken, the passing processor no longer had a token, while the successor started to have one. Thus, the token circulates the ring.

This example was based on a commercial network where if two processors "had a token" their actions could have collided, while if no processor had a token the network could deadlock. Hence, if either more or less than one processor has a token, the network is in an illegal global state (configuration). The designers of the commercial network assumed that it could sometimes reach an illegal state because of either an incorrect initialization, or some equipment error, or bug, etc. (It was proven by [27] that in actual network, even simple and rather common faults may drive protocols into an arbitrary global state.) Hence, the commercial products had a mechanism to recover from an illegal state. This mechanism was based on a timing assumption- one processor serving as a leader (a "station") waited for a certain time ("timeout") to receive the token from each predecessor. If the token is not received, then it is assumed lost, and the leader generates a new token. A similar method is used to destroy a redundant token.

In some sense, the commercial solution involved a *global* verification. That is, the length of the timeout had to be large enough so that the token could visit every processor in the ring. Moreover, the decision about the size of the timeout had to take into account the durations the various processors needed to hold the token. For example, if some processors were slower than others, the decision about the timeout had to take this into consideration.

Dijkstra replaced the global timeout by a local action- each processor considered its own state and the state of its predecessor only, and acted. He showed that the network converged into a correct global state in spite of this distributed control. It is worth mentioning that Dijkstra's solution nevertheless involved a global computation. For example, assume that the network was in a legal state, and some adversary changes the state of one processor. In this case, it is possible to return to a correct global state by changing the state of one processor. However, Dijkstra's solution involves changes in the states of all the processors, as well as time that is long enough for all of them to be involved in the computation. (Moreover, a causal chain of events [18] of length $\Omega(n)$, where n is the number of the processors, may result.)

A part of the elegance in Dijkstra's algorithms was that they never really detected an illegal state. Instead, when the network was put in an illegal state, it "somehow" converged towards a legal state, and then stayed in the set of legal states. This was also a characteristic of many later algorithms. While elegant, this approach makes the design of algorithms difficult. Katz and Perry [16] suggested a method of partitioning the design of self stabilizing algorithms:

1. Design an algorithm- the *base algorithm*, that is not necessarily self stabilizing (this implies a definition of the legal global states).
2. Detect, in a self stabilizing manner, that the above algorithm reached an illegal state.
3. In the case that an illegal global state is detected, restart the execution of the algorithm from some global legal state.

In fact, they presented a method to perform the detection, given a leader node. The detection (distributed verification) was performed in a rather centralized manner. That is, their algorithm collected all the state information from all the nodes to the leader node. The leader then checked whether the collection of the states was a legal global state. (Collecting local states such that they form a consistent global state is not a trivial task even in a non- self stabilizing network, since in an asynchronous network local states are collected in different times, and may thus not be parts of the same global state [11].)

In terms of complexity, note, first, that the time complexity of the verification task above was linear in the number of nodes. Clearly, the communication cost for the above approach may be large.

The paradigm of *local detection* was developed independently in [31]. This can be viewed as replacing the second step above. The idea was to replace the definition of a correct global state by a collection of definitions for correct local states. Somewhat more formally, assume that the correctness of a global state is defined as a *global* predicate P, that is, P is defined over all the variables in all the states of the nodes in the network. Let us say that a predicate is *local* if it is defined only over the state of a single node v together with the states of all of v's neighbors. Now assume that the conjunction of local predicates implies P. If none of the local predicates is violated, then P holds.

The above allows to replace the detection step of the Katz and Perry's algorithm by a local detection. Each node collects the states of its neighbors and computes its local predicate repeatedly. If the local predicate is violated at any node, this node starts the recovery phase. The recovery may involve a computation that may not be local. However, the recovery may never be needed, while the attempt to detect an illegal state is performed infinitely often. Hence, it is much more important to have an efficient verification.

A self stabilizing algorithm for a spanning tree construction was presented in [31] for several purposes. First, it demonstrated the local detection by detecting potential cycles in the "tree" using the distance variables (see Section 3). Second, it demonstrated that the local detection could be used also for a dynamically changing state, as opposed to a state that contains already the desired spanning tree and thus is not supposed to change. Specifically, in the algorithm of [31], a node who wished to join a tree sent a message all the way to the tree root to ask for a permission. This message was forwarded by the nodes over the tree. In a self stabilizing environment, it is possible that the node never actually sent that request, even though it "remembers" in its state that it did. Hence, had the algorithm at the node just waited for an answer, a deadlock may have resulted, since such an answer may never arrive (e.g. if the request has never actually been sent). This non- local predicate- "a request message from node v is on its way to the root" is replaced in the algorithm of [31] by a set of local predicates at the nodes on the route of the request message. If the request message is not there, then some node on its assumed route would detect that illegal state.

Another motivation for the tree algorithm in [31] was to enable a self stabilizing *reset* instead of the third step of [16] (the recovery step). A distributed reset protocol restarts the base algorithm from a predetermined initial state. It was observed by Awerbuch, Patt-Shamir, Varghese, and Dolev [8] that it is not trivial to show that a general self stabilizing reset algorithm together with local detection can perform the transformation of any algorithm to a self stabilizing one correctly. However, it is rather easy to show that a self stabilizing reset that uses a spanning tree suffices. Several other self stabilizing tree algorithms were suggested independently. They defer in some of their properties (e.g., one assumed a leader, antoher used an upper bound on the number os nodes) but they too suggested, at least implicitly, the distributed verification of cycle freedom described in Section 3, see the work by Dolev, Israeli, and Moran, and by Arora and Gouda [13, 4].

The notion of *local checking* was presented in [9]. It bears similarities to the notion of local detection. Instead of a local predicate involving a node and all its neighbors, the local predicates in [9] are defined over the two endpoints of one edge. This has a potential of simplifying algorithms using these predicates. In [7], Awerbuch, Patt-Shamir, and Varghese extended the methodology of local detection and global correction to local detection and local correction. The methodology is applied in [7] to develop self-stabilizing interactive distributed protocols, such as, end-to-end communication and network reset.

As described above, the verification step using the method of [16] consumes $\Omega(n)$ time, while the verification using e.g. the approach of [31] takes $O(1)$ time. Methods suggested in [20, 15, 6, 21, 19] to detect cycles sacrificed some time efficiency in order to reduce the total sizes of variables used in the local predicates compared to that of [31]. This suggests the existence of a size- time trade-off. On the other hand, it is not clear whether the total communication cost for these methods is inherently smaller. Indeed, these algorithms communicate a smaller number of bits, but those are communicated to larger distances.

A specific subset of problems allows for a specific kind of self stabilization called *silent stabilization*. These are studied in Dolev, Gouda, and Schneider in [32]. Informally, when silent stabilization is obtained, the only activity a processor can be involved in is collecting the state information of its neighbors that appear in its local predicates, and computing its local predicates. In a sense, this too is a form of a local detection- if the desired property of the network does not hold (that is, if the network is in an illegal state) this should be detected at least by one node that will take additional actions to correct the state. This captures *input output* relations- for example, this can be useful for protocols that compute a spanning tree. When the tree is correct, no additional activity is required except for the checking. On the other hand, this does not capture an interactive problem, e.g. that of a token ring.

Some of the latter can be captured by the *Roll-back compiler* introduced by Awerbuch and Varghese in [9]. It can be applied to any deterministic protocol (however, if this protocol is not for an input-output problem, then the space used by the compiler may not be bounded). Each node maintains its own log of its events and states, and sends the log often to all its neighbors. Thus, every node can check every transition it made in the past, to see whether its view of this transition is consistent with the view of its neighbors. These are the local predicates. The global predicate $P_{history}$ is that "the current global state is a result of a legal run of the base algorithm". *Local checking* is also used in [9] for designing self stabilizing algorithms directly for several tasks such as shortest paths, topology update, leader election, and computing the maximum flow.

Beauquier, Delaet, Dolev, and Tixeuil(in [33]) assumed that only the part of the state meant to be visible to the outside can be read by other nodes. (The output is the part that appears in the specification of the task to be performed.) It was shown in [33] that this assumption may imply the need for a very large memory usage (e.g. for verifying a spanning tree).

Multiple self stabilizing algorithms have since used the idea of first detecting that the global state is illegal, and then correcting it. This makes a large body of work a potential application of distributed verification. We do not have the space here to survey them all. A rather comprehensive survey (but not up to date) of self stabilization by Herman and Johnen can be found in [1].

We note the following major difference between the model of proof labeling schemes and the ones used by past self stabilization algorithms. In the latter models, the design of the computation stage was intertwined with that of the verification stage, and the designers sought to design a computation process that will be easy for verification, and vice versa. This approach may lead to a low cost local verification. However, this approach might also have the disadvantage of making the design process less modular. In proof labeling schemes, it is assumed that the distributed representation of the structure or function at hand is already given, and the computed labels are required to verify this specific representation. This allows for more modular algorithm design and frees the algorithm designer to consider other goals when designing the distributed representation. The approach of proof labeling schemes may sometimes be useful also in verifying properties on existing structures, even when the original design of those structures was done without verification in mind.

To illustrate this difference, let us point out to one of the results in proof labeling schemes, which states that local checking sometimes requires labels that are longer even than the states (such as the states used in previous local checking methods). This occurs in the natural setting where vertices are required to have distinct states. For example, this can happen in an algorithm that hashes unique identities of nodes into shorter unique states. In the case where the underlying graph is an n-vertex path, the size of vertex labels that are required in order to verify that all the states are unique is $\Omega(n)$. This is longer than the state, which is $O(\log n)$. On the other hand, were we allowed to compute the states (rather than prove the given hashing), labels of size zero would have sufficed in the case of unique identities: just have the state equal the identity. (Since the identities are assumed in this example to be unique, the states "computed" in that way are unique too.) We note that in many other cases, "small" proof labeling schemes exist even under the stronger requirements that the state to prove was developed independently, and now it is required to develop the scheme.

References

1. A Comprehensive Bibliography on Self-Stabilization. A Working Paper in the CJTCS, http://cjtcs.cs.uchicago.edu/.
2. Y. Afek and G. M. Brown. Self-stabilization over unreliable communication media. *Distributed Computing Journal*, 7:27–34, 1993.
3. S. Aggarwal. Time optimal self- stabilizing spanning tree algorithms. M.Sc Thesis, MIT, May 1994.
4. A. Arora and M. Gouda. Distributed reset. In *Proc. of the 10-th FSTTCS: Springer-Verlag LNCS 472*, pp. 316–331, September 1990.
5. B. Awerbuch, S. Kutten, Y. Mansour, B. Patt-Shamir, and G. Varghese. Time optimal self stabilizing synchronization. In *Proc. 25th STOC*, pp. 652–661, May 1993.
6. B. Awerbuch and R. Ostrovsky. Memory efficient and self stabilizing network reset. In *PODC*, August 1994.
7. B. Awerbuch, B. Patt-Shamir, and G. Varghese. Self-stabilization by local checking and correction. In *Proc. of the 32nd IEEE FOCS* , pp. 268–277, October 1991.
8. B. Awerbuch, B. Patt-Shamir, G. Varghese, and S. Dolev. Self stabilization by local checking and global reset. in the Proc. of WDAG 94, Springer-Verlag LNCS, pp. 226–239, October 1994.
9. B. Awerbuch, , and G. Varghese. Distributed program checking: a paradigm for building self-stabilizing distributed protocols. In *32nd IEEE FOCS* , pp. 258–267, October 1991.
10. E. W. Dijkstra. Self-stabilizing systems in spite of distributed control. *CACM*, 17:643–644, November 1974.
11. K. Mani Chandy, Leslie Lamport. Distributed Snapshots: Determining Global States of Distributed Systems. ACM Trans. Comput. Syst. 3(1): 63-75 (1985).
12. E.W. Dijkstra. A belated proof of self-stabilization. *Distributed Computing*, 1(1):5-6, 1986.
13. S. Dolev, A. Israeli, and S. Moran. Self-stabilization of dynamic systems assuming only read/write atomicity. *Distributed Computing Journal*, 7, 1994.
14. S. Dolev, A. Israeli, and S. Moran. Uniform dynamic self-stabilizing leader election. IEEE Trans. Parallel Distrib. Syst. 8(4): 424-440 (1997).
15. G. Itkis, and L Levin. Fast and Lean Self-Stabilizing Asynchronous Protocols. In *Proc. of the 35th IEEE FOCS* , pp. 226-239, October 1994.
16. S. Katz and K. J. Perry. Self-stabilizing extensions. *Distributed Computing*, 7, 1994.
17. L. Lamport. Solved problems, unsolved problems and nonproblems in concurrency. Proceedings of the 3rd PODC, pp. 1-11August 1984.
18. Leslie Lamport: Time, Clocks, and the Ordering of Events in a Distributed System. Commun. ACM 21(7): 558-565 (1978).
19. A. Mayer, R. Ostrovsky, and M. Yung. Self-stabilizing algorithms for synchronous unidirectional rings. In *Proc. 7th SODA*, Jan. 1996.
20. A. Mayer, Y. Ofek, R. Ostrovsky, and M. Yung. Self-stabilizing symmetry breaking in constant space. In *Proc. 24th STOC*, pages 667-678, May 1992.
21. G. Parlati and M. Yung. Non-exploratory self stabilization for constant-space symmetry-breaking In *Proc. 2d ESA '94*, pages 183–201. LNCS 855 Springer Verlag.
22. M. Naor and L. Stockmeyer. What can be computed locally. In *Proc. 25th STOC*, pp. 185–193. ACM, May 1993.

23. Schieber and Snir. Calling names on nameless networks. *Information and Computation (formerly Information and Control)*, 113, 1994. also in: *Proc. of PODC 1989*, pp. 319–328, August 1989.
24. A. Segall. Distributed network protocols. *IEEE Trans. on Information Theory*, IT-29(1):23–35, January 1983.
25. J. Spinelli and R. G. Gallager. Broadcast topology information in computer networks. *IEEE Trans. on Comm.*, 1989.
26. G. Varghese. *Dealing with Failure in Distributed Systems*. PhD thesis, MIT, 1992.
27. G.M. Jayaram and Varghese. Crash failures can drive protocols to arbitrary states. PODC 1996, pp. 247-256.
28. M. Jayaram, G. Varghese. The Complexity of Crash Failures. *PODC 1997*, pp. 179-188.
29. M. Naor and L. Stockmeyer. What can be computed locally? *Proc. 25th STOC*, pp. 184–193, 1993.
30. R.G. Gallager, P.A. Humblet, P.M. Spira. A distributed algorithm for minimum-weight spanning trees. TOPLAS 5 (1983) 66-77.
31. Y. Afek, S. Kutten, and M. Yung. The Local Detection Paradigm and Its Application to Self-Stabilization. *Theor. Comput. Sci.* 186(1-2): 199-229 (1997).
32. S. Dolev, M. Gouda, and M. Schneider. Requirements for silent stabilization. *Acta Informatica*, 36(6): 447-462, 1999.
33. Beauquier, J., Delaet, S., Dolev, S., and Tixeuil, S., "Transient Fault Detectors". Proc. of the 12th DISC, Springer-Verlag LNCS:1499, pp. 62-74, 1998.
34. B. Dixon, M. Rauch, and R. E. Tarjan. Verification and Sensitivity Analysis of Minimum Spanning Trees in Linear Time. *SIAM Journal on Computing*, Vol. 21, No 6, pp. 1184-1192, December 1992.
35. M.L. Fredman and D.E. Willard. Trans-Dichotomous algorithms for minimum spanning trees and shortest paths. *Proc. 31st IEEE FOCS*, Los Alamitos, CA, 1990, pp. 719-725.
36. M. Garey and D. Johnson. Computers and Intractability. W.H. Freeman and Company, New York, 1979.
37. D. R. Karger, P.N. Klein, and R.E. Tarjan. A Randomized Linear-Time Algorithm to Find Minimum Spanning Trees. *JACM* Vol. 42, No. 2, pp. 3210328, 1955.
38. Amos Korman and Shay Kutten. "Distributed Verification of Minimum Spanning Trees". in Proc. *25th PODC 2006*, July 23-26 2006, Denver, Colorado, USA.
39. M. Katz, N.A. Katz, A. Korman, and D. Peleg. Labeling schemes for flow and connectivity. In *19th SODA*, Jan. 2002.
40. Amos Korman, Shay Kutten, and David Peleg. "Proof Labeling Schemes". Proceedings of the *24th PODC 2005*, Las Vegas, NV, USA, July 2005.
41. Nathan Linial. Distributive Graph Algorithms-Global Solutions from Local Data. FOCS 1987: 331-335.
42. Fabian Kuhn, Thomas Moscibroda, Roger Wattenhofer. What cannot be computed locally! PODC 2004: 300-309.
43. Andrew C. Yao. Some Complexity Questions Related to Distributed Computing. STOC 1979, 209-213.

The Price of Defense and Fractional Matchings[*]

Marios Mavronicolas[1], Vicky Papadopoulou[1], Giuseppe Persiano[2],
Anna Philippou[1], and Paul Spirakis[3]

[1] Department of Computer Science, University of Cyprus, Nicosia CY-1678, Cyprus
{mavronic, viki, annap}@ucy.ac.cy
[2] Dipartimento di Informatica ed Applicazioni "Renato M. Capocelli",
Università di Salerno, Italy
giuper@dia.unisa.it
[3] Research Academic Computer Technology Institute, Greece & Department of
Computer Engineering and Informatics, University of Patras, Greece
spirakis@ucy.ac.cy

Abstract. Consider a *network* vulnerable to security *attacks* and
equipped with *defense* mechanisms. How much is the loss in the provided
security guarantees due to the selfish nature of attacks and defenses?
The *Price of Defense* was recently introduced in [7] as a *worst-case* measure, over all associated *Nash equilibria*, of this loss. In the particular
strategic game considered in [7], there are two classes of confronting randomized players on a graph $G(V, E)$: ν *attackers*, each choosing vertices
and wishing to minimize the probability of being caught, and a single
defender, who chooses edges and gains the expected number of attackers
it catches.

In this work, we continue the study of the Price of Defense. We obtain
the following results:

- The Price of Defense is at least $\frac{|V|}{2}$; this implies that the *Perfect
  Matching Nash equilibria* considered in [7] are *optimal* with respect
  to the Price of Defense, so that the lower bound is *tight*.
- We define *Defense-Optimal graphs* as those admitting a Nash equi-
  librium that attains the (tight) lower bound of $\frac{|V|}{2}$. We obtain:
  - A graph is Defense-Optimal if and only if it has a *Fractional Per-
    fect Matching*. Since graphs with a Fractional Perfect Matching
    are recognizable in polynomial time, the same holds for Defense-
    Optimal graphs.
  - We identify a very simple graph that is Defense-Optimal but has
    no Perfect Matching Nash equilibrium.
- Inspired by the established connection between Nash equilibria and
  Fractional Perfect Matchings, we transfer a known bivaluedness re-
  sult about Fractional Matchings to a certain class of Nash equilibria.
  So, the connection to *Fractional Graph Theory* may be the key to
  revealing the combinatorial structure of Nash equilibria for our net-
  work security game.

[*] This work was partially supported by the European Union under IST FET Integrated
Project 015964 **AEOLUS**.

S. Chaudhuri et al. (Eds.): ICDCN 2006, LNCS 4308, pp. 115–126, 2006.

1 Introduction

Motivation, Framework and Summary. Consider a complex distributed system such as the Internet with security *attacks* and corresponding *defense* mechanisms. Assume that both attacks and defenses exhibit a selfish behavior, aiming at maximizing the security harm and the security protection, respectively. How much is the loss in security due to this selfish behavior? In a recent work, Mavronicolas *et al.* [7] introduced the *Price of Defense* as a *worst-case* measure for this loss.

More specifically, Mavronicolas *et al.* [7] focused on the concrete case where the distributed system is a network modeled as a graph $G(V, E)$; nodes are vulnerable to infection by ν threats, called *attackers*. Available to the network is a security software (or *firewall* [3]), called the *defender*, cleaning a limited part of the network. This model has been motivated by *Network Edge Security* [6], a new distributed firewall architecture. (For details on motivation, see [7, Section 1.1].) The model was introduced in [8] and further studied in [4,7,9].

Each *attacker* (called *vertex player*) targets a node of the network chosen via its own probability distribution on nodes; the *defender* (called *edge player*) chooses a single *edge* via its own probability distribution on edges. A node chosen by an attacker is harmed unless it is incident to the edge protected by the defender. The *Individual Profit* of an attacker is the probability that it escapes; the *Individual Profit* of the defender is the expected number of caught attackers. In a *Nash equilibrium* [12,13], no single player can unilaterally deviate from its randomized strategy in order to increase its Individual Profit. The *Price of Defense* is the worst case ratio, over all Nash equilibria, of the ratio of ν over the Individual Profit of the defender. For a particular Nash equilibrium, this ratio is called its *Defense Ratio*. The Price of Defense can be cast as the particular case of Price of Anarchy [5] induced by taking Social Cost to be the Individual Profit of the defender.

In this work, we continue the study of the Price of Defense. More specifically, we provide a *tight* lower bound on the Price of Defense, and we determine a characterization of graphs admitting a Nash equilibrium that attains this lower bound. The characterization establishes a connection to *Fractional Graph Theory* [14]; we further investigate this connection to shed some light into the combinatorial structure of Nash equilibria for our graph-theoretic network security game.

Contribution. We obtain the following results:

- We prove that the Price of Defense is at least $\frac{|V|}{2}$ (Theorem 5). This implies that the *Perfect Matching Nash equilibria*, a special class of Nash equilibria considered in [7] and known to have a Defense Ratio equal to $\frac{|V|}{2}$, are *optimal* with respect to the Price of Defense. It also naturally raises the question whether Perfect Matching Nash equilibria are the only such optimal Nash equilibria; more generally, which are the graphs that admit optimal Nash equilibria with respect to the Price of Defense?

- To address the last question, we introduce the class of Defense-Optimal graphs: a graph is *Defense-Optimal* if it admits a Nash equilibrium whose Defense Ratio is $\frac{|V|}{2}$. Clearly, the class of graphs admitting a Perfect Matching Nash equilibrium is contained in this class; an efficient characterization for that class is shown in [7, Theorem 6.2] (repeated as Theorem 2 in this paper). (This class is a strict subclass of the class of graphs with a Perfect Matching.) We have obtained the following results:

  - A graph is Defense-Optimal if and only if it has a *Fractional Perfect Matching* (Theorem 8). Our proof is constructive: Given a Fractional Perfect Matching, we construct a Defense-Optimal Nash equilibrium (Theorem 6), and vice-versa (Theorem 7). These dual constructions exhibit an interesting, perhaps unexpected connection between Nash equilibria for our graph-theoretic game and Fractional (Perfect) Matchings [14, Chapter 2] in graphs.

- We observe that the class of graphs admitting Perfect Matching Nash equilibria is strictly contained into the class of Defense-Optimal graphs. Towards this end, we identify the *simplest* Defense-Optimal graph that does not admit a Perfect Matching Nash equilibrium (Theorem 9).

- We further investigate the established equivalence between (Defense-Optimal) Nash equilibria and Fractional Perfect Matchings. Our starting point is a result from *Fractional Graph Theory* [14] stating that for any graph, there is a *Fractional Maximum Matching* with only two distinct (non-zero) values on edges [14, Theorem 2.1.5]. We establish a corresponding fact for *Defender Uniform* Nash equilibria. (These are Nash equilibria where the defender uses a uniform probability distribution on its support.) Specifically, we prove that from a Defender Uniform Nash equilibrium, one can obtain in polynomial time another (Defender Uniform) Nash equilibrium where the expected number of vertex players choosing each vertex may take only two distinct (non-zero) values (Theorem 11).

  We believe that a further investigation of the connection between Nash equilibria for our graph-theoretic game and Fractional Matchings will provide further key insights into the (yet not so well understood) combinatorial structure of these Nash equilibria.

Related Work and Significance. Our work continues the study of the game-theoretic virus model with attackers and a defender introduced by Mavronicolas et al. [8] and further studied in [4,7,9]. In particular, our work continues the study of the Price of Defense introduced in [7].

A different game-theoretic model of virus attack and propagation has been introduced by Aspnes et al. [1] and recently studied by Moscibroda et al. [11]. Moscibroda et al. [11] introduced the *Price of Malice* to quantify the impact of malicious players on the Price of Anarchy (without malicious players) for the game of Aspnes et al. [1]. Note that we do not consider malicious players for our game; we assume that all players are strategic. So, there is no apparent relation between Price of Malice and Price of Defense.

Our work is part of a currently major effort to introduce game-theoretic models in Computer Science in order to obtain insights into the reality of contemporary distributed systems such as the Internet. Work on game-theoretic analysis of complex distributed systems is now featured in major conferences of Distributed Computing.

2   Background, Definitions and Preliminaries

Graph Theory. Throughout, we consider an undirected graph $G = \langle V, E \rangle$ with no isolated vertices. We sometimes treat an edge as the set of its two vertices. For a vertex $v \in V$, denote as $\mathsf{Neigh}_G(v)$ the set of neighboring vertices of v in G; denote $\mathsf{Edges}_G(v)$ the set of edges incident to v. For a vertex set $U \in V$, $\mathsf{Neigh}_G(U) = \{v \in V \backslash U : u \in U \text{ and } (v, u) \in E\}$. For a vertex $v \in V$, denote $d_G(v)$ the *degree* of vertex v in G. For an edge set $F \subseteq E$, denote $G(F)$ the subgraph of G induced by F. For any integer $n \geq 1$, denote as K_n the *clique* graph of size n.

A vertex set $IS \subseteq V$ is an *Independent Set* if for all pairs of vertices $u, v \in IS$, $(u, v) \notin E$. A *Maximum Independent Set* is one that has maximum size; denote $\alpha(G)$ the size of a Maximum Independent Set of G. A *Vertex Cover* is a vertex set $VC \subseteq V$ such that for each edge $(u, v) \in E$ either $u \in VC$ or $v \in VC$. An *Edge Cover* is an edge set $EC \subseteq E$ such that for every vertex $v \in V$, there is an edge $(v, u) \in EC$. A *Matching* is a set $M \subseteq E$ of non-incident edges. A *Maximum Matching* is one that has maximum size. A *Perfect Matching* is a Matching that is also an Edge Cover.

A *Fractional Matching* is a function $f : E \to [0, 1]$ such that for each vertex $v \in V$, $\sum_{e \in \mathsf{Edges}(v)} f(e) \leq 1$. (If $f(e) \in \{0, 1\}$ for each edge $e \in E$, then f is just a Matching, or precisely, the indicator function of a Matching.) The *Fractional Matching Number* $\alpha'_F(G)$ of a graph G is the supremum of $\sum_{e \in E} f(e)$ over all Fractional Matchings f. A *Fractional Maximum Matching* is one that attains the Maximum Matching Number. It is a basic fact that $\alpha'_F(G) \leq \frac{|V|}{2}$ (see, for example, [14, Lemma 2.1.2]). A *Fractional Perfect Matching* is a Fractional Matching f with $\sum_{e \in \mathsf{Edges}(v)} f(e) = 1$ for all vertices $v \in V$. Hence, for a Fractional Perfect Matching f, $\sum_{e \in E} f(e)$ achieves the upper bound on $\alpha'_F(G)$, so that $\sum_{e \in E} f(e) = \frac{|V|}{2}$.

Note that the Fractional Matching Number of a graph can be computed in polynomial time by formulating (and solving) the Fractional Matching Number problem as a polynomial size (in fact, $|V| \cdot |E|$ size) Linear Program. (See, also, [2] for an efficient combinatorial algorithm.) Since a graph $G = (V, E)$ has a Fractional Perfect Matching if and only if its Fractional Matching Number is equal to $\frac{|V|}{2}$, it follows that the class of graphs with a Fractional Perfect Matching is recognizable in polynomial time.

Game Theory. We consider a *strategic game* $\Pi(G) = \langle \mathcal{N}, \{S_i\}_{i \in \mathcal{N}}, \{\mathsf{IP}\}_{i \in \mathcal{N}} \rangle$:

- The set of *players* is $\mathcal{N} = \mathcal{N}_{vp} \cup \mathcal{N}_{ep}$, where $\mathcal{N}_{vp}$ has ν *vertex* players vp_i, called *attackers*, $1 \leq i \leq \nu$ and $\mathcal{N}_{ep}$ has *edge* player ep, called *defender*.
- The *strategy set* S_i of vertex player vp_i is V, and the *strategy set* S_{ep} of the edge player ep is E. So, the *strategy set* $\mathcal{S}$ of the game is $\mathcal{S} = \left(\underset{i \in \mathcal{N}_{vp}}{\times} S_i \right) \times S_{ep} = V^\nu \times E$.
- Fix any *profile* $\mathbf{s} = \langle s_1, \ldots, s_\nu, s_{ep} \rangle \in \mathcal{S}$, also called a *pure profile*.
  - The *Individual Profit* of vertex player vp_i is a function $\mathsf{IP_s}(i) : \mathcal{S} \rightarrow \{0,1\}$ such that $\mathsf{IP_s}(i) = \begin{cases} 0, s_i \in s_{ep} \\ 1, s_i \notin s_{ep} \end{cases}$; intuitively, the vertex player vp_i receives 1 if it is not caught by the edge player, and 0 otherwise.
  - The *Individual Profit* of the edge player ep is a function $\mathsf{IP_s}(ep) : \mathcal{S} \rightarrow \mathbb{N}$ such that $\mathsf{IP_s}(ep) = |\{i : s_i \in s_{ep}\}|$; intuitively, the edge player ep receives the number of vertex players it catches.

A *mixed strategy* for player $i \in \mathcal{N}$ is a probability distribution over S_i. A *(mixed) profile* $\mathbf{s} = \langle s_1, \ldots, s_\nu, s_{ep} \rangle$ is a collection of mixed strategies, one for each player; $s_i(v)$ is the probability that vertex player vp_i chooses vertex v, and $s_{ep}(e)$ is the probability that the edge player ep chooses edge e.

The *support* of player $i \in \mathcal{N}$ in the mixed profile $\mathbf{s}$, denoted $\mathsf{Support_s}(i)$, is the set of pure strategies in its strategy set to which i assigns a strictly positive probability in $\mathbf{s}$. Denote $\mathsf{Support_s}(vp) = \bigcup_{i \in \mathcal{N}_{vp}} \mathsf{Support_s}(i)$. Set $\mathsf{Edges_s}(v) = \{(u,v) \in E : (u,v) \in \mathsf{Support_s}(ep)\}$. So, $\mathsf{Edges_s}(v)$ contains all edges incident to v that are included in the support of the edge player. For an edge $e = (u,v) \in E$, set $\mathsf{Vertices_s}(e) = \{w \in \{u,v\} : w \in \mathsf{Support_s}(vp)\}$.

A profile $\mathbf{s}$ is *Fully Mixed* [10] if for each vertex player vp_i, $\mathsf{Support_s}(i) = V$ and $\mathsf{Support_s}(ep) = E$; so, the support of each player is its strategy set. A profile $\mathbf{s}$ is *Uniform* if each player uses a uniform probability distribution on its support; that is, for every vertex player $vp_i \in \mathcal{N}_{vp}$ and $v \in \mathsf{Support_s}(i)$, $s_i(v) = \frac{1}{|\mathsf{Support_s}(i)|}$, and, for the edge player ep, for each $e \in \mathsf{Support_s}(ep)$, $s_{ep}(e) = \frac{1}{|\mathsf{Support_s}(ep)|}$.

A profile $\mathbf{s}$ is *Attacker Symmetric* [7] if for all vertex players $vp_i, vp_k \in \mathcal{N}_{vp}$, $s_i(v) = s_k(v)$, for each $v \in V$. An *Attacker Symmetric and Uniform* profile is an Attacker Symmetric profile where each attacker uses a uniform probability distribution on the common support; an Attacker Symmetric, Uniform and Fully Mixed profile is an Attacker Symmetric and Uniform profile where the common support is V. A profile is *Defender Uniform* [7] if the edge player uses a uniform probability distribution on its support.

For a vertex $v \in V$, the probability that the edge player ep chooses an edge that contains the vertex v is denoted by $P_{\mathbf{s}}(\mathsf{Hit}(v))$. So, $P_{\mathbf{s}}(\mathsf{Hit}(v)) = \sum_{e \in \mathsf{Edges_s}(v)} s_{ep}(e)$. For a vertex $v \in V$, denote as $\mathsf{VP_s}(v)$ the expected number of vertex players choosing vertex v according to $\mathbf{s}$; so, $\mathsf{VP_s}(v) = \sum_{i \in \mathcal{N}_{vp}} s_i(v)$.

Further, in an Attacker Symmetric and Uniform profile $\mathbf{s}$, for a vertex $v \in \mathsf{Support_s}(vp)$, $\mathsf{VP_s}(v) = \sum_{i \in \mathcal{N}_{vp}} s_i(v) = \frac{\nu}{|\mathsf{Support}_s(vp)|}$. For each edge $e = (u, v) \in E$, $\mathsf{VP_s}(e)$ is the expected number of vertex players choosing either the vertex u or the vertex v; so, $\mathsf{VP_s}(e) = \mathsf{VP_s}(u) + \mathsf{VP_s}(v)$. We provide a preliminary observation which will be useful later.

Lemma 1. *In a profile* $\mathbf{s}$, $\sum_{v \in V} P_{\mathbf{s}}(\mathsf{Hit}(v)) = 2$.

A mixed profile $\mathbf{s}$ induces an *Expected Individual Profit* $\mathsf{IP_s}(i)$ for each player $i \in \mathcal{N}$, which is the expectation according to $\mathbf{s}$ of the Individual Profit of player i. One may easily show that for the edge player ep, $\mathsf{IP_s}(ep) = \sum_{i \in \mathcal{N}_{vp}} (\sum_{v \in V} s_i(v) \cdot (P_{\mathbf{s}}(\mathsf{Hit}(v)))$; alternatively, $\mathsf{IP_s}(ep) = \sum_{v \in V} \mathsf{VP_s}(v) \cdot P_{\mathbf{s}}(\mathsf{Hit}(v))$.

The mixed profile $\mathbf{s}$ is a *(mixed) Nash equilibrium* [12,13] if, for each player $i \in \mathcal{N}$, it maximizes $\mathsf{IP_s}(i)$ over all mixed profiles that differ from $\mathbf{s}$ only with respect to the mixed strategy of player i. By Nash's result [12,13], there is at least one Nash equilibrium. We use a characterization of them from [8]:

Theorem 1 ([8]). *A profile* $\mathbf{s}$ *is a Nash equilibrium if and only if* (1) *for each vertex* $v \in \mathsf{Support}_s(vp)$, $P_{\mathbf{s}}(\mathsf{Hit}(v)) = \min_{v' \in V} P_{\mathbf{s}}(\mathsf{Hit}(v'))$, *and* (2) *for each edge* $e \in \mathsf{Support}_s(ep)$, $\mathsf{VP_s}(e) = \max_{e' \in E} \mathsf{VP_s}(e')$.

Call $\min_{v' \in V} P_{\mathbf{s}}(\mathsf{Hit}(v'))$ the *Minimum Hitting Probability* associated with $\mathbf{s}$.

We continue to introduce the class of Perfect Matching Nash equilibria from [7]. A *Covering profile* is a profile $\mathbf{s}$ such that (1) $\mathsf{Support}_s(ep)$ is an Edge Cover of G and (2) $\mathsf{Support}_s(vp)$ is a Vertex Cover of the graph $G(\mathsf{Support}_s(ep))$. It is shown in [8] that a Nash equilibrium $\mathbf{s}$ is a Covering profile, but not vice versa. An *Independent Covering profile* [8] is an Attacker Symmetric and Uniform Covering profile $\mathbf{s}$ such that (1) $\mathsf{Support}_s(vp)$ is an Independent Set of G and (2) each vertex in $\mathsf{Support}_s(vp)$ is incident to exactly one edge in $\mathsf{Support}_s(ep)$. In the same work, it was proved that an Independent Covering profile is a Nash equilibrium, called a *Matching Nash equilibrium* [8]. A *Perfect Matching Nash equilibrium* is a Matching Nash equilibrium such that the support of the edge player is a Perfect Matching of G. Call a graph *Perfect-Matching* if it admits a Perfect Matching Nash equilibrium. (This should not be confused with the strictly larger class of graphs with a Perfect Matching.) A characterization of Perfect-Matching graphs is provided in [7]:

Theorem 2 ([7]). *A graph* G *is Perfect-Matching if and only if* G *has a Perfect Matching and* $\alpha(G) = \frac{|V|}{2}$.

A *Defender Uniform Nash equilibrium* is a Defender Uniform profile that is a Nash equilibrium. Call a graph *Defender-Uniform* if it admits a Defender Uniform Nash equilibrium. We use a characterization from [7]:

Theorem 3 ([7]). *A graph* G *is Defender-Uniform if and only if there are non-empty sets* $V' \subseteq V$, *partitioned as* $V' = V_i' \cup V_r'$, *and* $E' \subseteq E$, *and an integer* $r \geq 1$ *such that:*

(1/a) *For each* $v \in V'$, $d_{G(E')}(v) = r$.
(1/b) *For each* $v \in V \backslash V'$, $d_{G(E')}(v) \geq r$.

(2/a) *For each $v \in V_i'$, for each $u \in \mathsf{Neigh}_G(v)$, it holds that $u \notin V'$.*
(2/b) *The graph $\langle V_r', \mathsf{Edges}_G(V_r') \cap E' \rangle$ is an r-regular graph.*
(2/c) *The graph $\langle V_i' \cup (V \backslash V'), \mathsf{Edges}_G(V_i' \cup (V \backslash V')) \cap E' \rangle$ is a $(V_i', V \backslash V')$-bipartite graph.*

An inspection of the proof of Theorem 3 in [7] implies a partial but more specific version of Theorem 3 that suffices for our purposes.

Theorem 4. *Consider a Defender Uniform Nash equilibrium s. Then, for the choices*

- $V' = \mathsf{Support}_s(vp)$, *with* (i) $V_i' := \{v \in V' \mid \mathsf{VP}_s(v) = \max_{e' \in E} \mathsf{VP}_s(e')\}$ *and* (ii) $V_r' := V' \backslash V_i'$;
- $E' = \mathsf{Support}_s(ep)$;
- $r = d_{G(\mathsf{Support}_s(ep))}(v)$ *for any vertex $v \in \mathsf{Support}_s(vp)$,*

the graph $\langle V_r', \mathsf{Edges}_G(V_r') \cap E' \rangle$ is an r-regular graph.

We prove a useful property of Defender Uniform Nash equilibria:

Lemma 2. *Consider a Defender Uniform Nash equilibrium s and the induced subgraph $\langle V_r', \mathsf{Edges}_G (V_r') \cap E' \rangle$, where $V_r' = V \backslash \{v \in V' \mid \mathsf{VP}_s(v) = \max_{e' \in E} \mathsf{VP}_s(e')\}$ and $E' = \mathsf{Support}_s(ep)$. Then, over all vertices v in each connected component of the subgraph, the variable $\mathsf{VP}_s(v)$ takes on at most two distinct (non-zero) values, which occur an equal number of times.*

For a Nash equilibrium s, the ratio $\frac{\nu}{\mathsf{IP}_s(ep)}$ is called the *Defense Ratio* of s. The *Price of Defense* [7], denoted PoD_G, is the *worst-case* Defense Ratio of s, over all Nash equilibria s. It is known that the Defense Ratio of every Perfect Matching Nash equilibrium is $\frac{|V|}{2}$ [7, Theorem 6.4]. Hence, restricted to Perfect Matching Nash equilibria, the Price of Defense is $\frac{|V|}{2}$.

3 A Lower Bound on the Price of Defense

We first use Theorem 1 to evaluate the Defense Ratio of a Nash equilibrium:

Proposition 1. *For a Nash equilibrium s,* $\frac{\nu}{\mathsf{IP}_s(ep)} = \frac{1}{\min_{v' \in V} P_s(\mathsf{Hit}(v'))}$.

Using Lemma 1 we show:

Proposition 2. *Assume a Nash equilibrium s. Then,* $\min_{v' \in V} P_s(\mathsf{Hit}(v')) \leq \frac{2}{|V|}$.

Theorem 5. *The Price of Defense is at least $\frac{|V|}{2}$.*

Proof. Consider any Nash equilibrium s. By Proposition 1, we get that $\frac{\nu}{\mathsf{IP}_s(ep)}$ $= \frac{1}{\min_{v' \in V} P_s(\mathsf{Hit}(v'))}$. By Proposition 2, this implies that $\frac{\nu}{\mathsf{IP}_s(ep)} \geq \frac{|V|}{2}$. Since $\mathsf{PoD}_G \geq \frac{\nu}{\mathsf{IP}_s(ep)}$, the claim follows. □

A Nash equilibrium **s** is *Defense-Optimal* if its Defense Ratio $\frac{\nu}{\mathsf{IP_s}(ep)}$ equals to $\frac{|V|}{2}$. A graph G is *Defense-Optimal* if it admits a Defense-Optimal Nash equilibrium. Proposition 1 immediately implies:

Corollary 1. *Consider a Defense-Optimal Nash equilibrium* **s**. *Then,* $\min_{v' \in V} P_\mathbf{s}(\mathsf{Hit}(v')) = \frac{2}{|V|}.$

Together with Proposition 2, Corollary 1 implies that Defense-Optimal Nash equilibria maximize the Minimum Hitting Probability.

4   Defense-Optimal Graphs

We provide a characterization of Defense-Optimal graphs. We first prove:

Theorem 6. *Assume that G has a Fractional Perfect Matching. Then, G is Defense-Optimal.*

Sketch of Proof. Consider a Fractional Perfect Matching $f : E \to [0, 1]$. Define an Attacker Symmetric, Uniform and Fully Mixed profile **s** as follows:

- For each edge $e \in E$, $s_{ep}(e) = \frac{2}{|V|} \cdot f(e)$.

It can be easily shown that s_{ep} is a probability distribution for the edge player. We first prove that **s** is a Nash equilibrium. It suffices to prove Conditions (1) and (2) in the characterization of Nash equilibria (Theorem 1).

- For Condition (1), consider any vertex $v \in V$. Clearly,

$$P_\mathbf{s}(\mathsf{Hit}(v))$$
$$= \sum_{e \in \mathsf{Edges_s}(v)} s_{ep}(e)$$
$$= \sum_{e \in \mathsf{Edges_s}(v)} \frac{2}{|V|} \cdot f(e)$$
$$= \frac{2}{|V|} \cdot \sum_{e \in \mathsf{Edges_s}(v)} f(e)$$
$$= \frac{2}{|V|} \qquad \text{(since } f \text{ is a Fractional Perfect Matching)}.$$

Thus, in particular, for any vertex $v \in \mathsf{Support_s}(vp)$, $P_\mathbf{s}(\mathsf{Hit}(v)) = \min_{v' \in V} P_\mathbf{s}(\mathsf{Hit}(v'))$ and Condition (1) holds.
- For Condition (2), consider any edge $e = (u, v) \in E$. Clearly,

$$\mathsf{VP_s}(e)$$
$$= \mathsf{VP_s}(u) + \mathsf{VP_s}(v)$$
$$= \frac{\nu}{|V|} + \frac{\nu}{|V|} \qquad \text{(since } \mathbf{s} \text{ is Attacker Symmetric, Uniform and Fully Mixed)}$$
$$= \frac{2\nu}{|V|}.$$

Thus, in particular, for any edge $e \in \mathsf{Support_s}(ep)$, $\mathsf{VP_s}(e) = \max_{e' \in E} \mathsf{VP_s}(e')$ and Condition (2) holds.

It follows that $\mathbf{s}$ is a Nash equilibrium. We finally prove that $\mathbf{s}$ is Defense-Optimal. Clearly, for any edge $e \in \mathsf{Support_s}(ep)$, $\mathsf{IP_s}(ep) = \mathsf{VP_s}(e)$, so that $\frac{\nu}{\mathsf{IP_s}(ep)} = \frac{\nu}{\mathsf{VP_s}(e)} = \frac{|V|}{2}$, so that $\mathbf{s}$ is Defense-Optimal. The claim follows. $\qquad\square$

Theorem 7. *Assume that G is Defense-Optimal. Then, G has a Fractional Perfect Matching.*

Sketch of Proof. Consider a Defense-Optimal Nash equilibrium $\mathbf{s}$ for G. By Proposition 1, $\min_{v' \in V} P_{\mathbf{s}}(\mathsf{Hit}(v')) = \frac{2}{|V|}$. By Lemma 1, $\sum_{v \in V} P_{\mathbf{s}}(\mathsf{Hit}(v)) = 2$. It follows that for each vertex $v \in V$, $P_{\mathbf{s}}(\mathsf{Hit}(v)) = \frac{2}{|V|}$. Define a function $f : E \to [0,1]$ as follows:

- For each edge $e = (u,v) \in E$, $f(e) = \frac{s_{ep}(e)}{P_{\mathbf{s}}(\mathsf{Hit}(v))}$.

Clearly, for each edge $e = (u,v) \in E$, $P_{\mathbf{s}}(\mathsf{Hit}(v)) \geq s_{ep}(e)$, so that $f(e) \leq 1$. Moreover, for each vertex $v \in V$,

$$\sum_{e \in \mathsf{Edges_s}(v)} f(e) = \sum_{e \in \mathsf{Edges_s}(v)} \frac{s_{ep}(e)}{P_{\mathbf{s}}(\mathsf{Hit}(v))}$$

$$= \frac{1}{P_{\mathbf{s}}(\mathsf{Hit}(v))} \cdot \sum_{e \in \mathsf{Edges_s}(v)} s_{ep}(e)$$

$$= 1.$$

Hence, f is a Fractional Perfect Matching, as needed. $\qquad\square$

Theorems 6 and 7 together imply:

Theorem 8 (Characterization of Defense-Optimal Graphs). *A graph is Defense-Optimal if and only if it has a Fractional Perfect Matching.*

Since the class of graphs with a Fractional Perfect Matching is recognizable in polynomial time, Theorem 8 immediately implies:

Corollary 2. *Defense-Optimal graphs are recognizable in polynomial time.*

By Theorem 2, the class of Perfect-Matching graphs is (strictly) contained in the class of graphs with a Perfect Matching. Since a Perfect Matching is a special case of a Fractional Perfect Matching, it follows that the class of Perfect-Matching graphs is (strictly) contained in the class of graphs with a Fractional Perfect Matching. Hence, Theorem 8 implies that the class of Perfect-Matching graphs is (strictly) contained in the class of Defense-Optimal graphs. We provide a particular example to demonstrate the strict inclusion.

Theorem 9. K_3 *is a Defense-Optimal graph but not a Perfect-Matching graph.*

5 Bivalued Nash Equilibria

Our starting point is a bivaluedness result about Fractional Maximum Matchings, which appears in [14, Theorem 2.1.5].

Theorem 10. *For any graph G, there is a Fractional Maximum Matching f such that for each edge $e \in E$, $f(e) \in \left\{0, \frac{1}{2}, 1\right\}$.*

We prove a game-theoretic analog of Theorem 10 with Nash equilibria (of Defender-Uniform graphs) in place of Fractional Maximum Matchings.

Theorem 11. *For a Defender-Uniform graph G, there is a Defender Uniform Nash equilibrium $\mathbf{s}$ such that for each $v \in \mathsf{Support}_\mathbf{s}(vp)$, $\dfrac{\mathsf{VP}_\mathbf{s}(v)}{\max_{e' \in E} \mathsf{VP}_\mathbf{s}(e')} \in \left\{\frac{1}{2}, 1\right\}$.*

Sketch of Proof. Transform a Defender Uniform Nash equilibrium $\mathbf{s}'$ for G into an Attacker Symmetric (and still Defender Uniform) profile $\mathbf{s}$:

---

1. $\mathbf{s}'_{ep} := \mathbf{s}_{ep}$.
2. For each player $vp_i \in \mathcal{NP}_{vp}$, for each vertex $v \in V$:

$$
s_i(v) := \begin{cases} \dfrac{\max_{e' \in E} \mathsf{VP}_{\mathbf{s}'}(e')}{\nu}, & \text{if } \mathsf{VP}_{\mathbf{s}'}(v) = \max_{e' \in E} \mathsf{VP}_{\mathbf{s}'}(e') \\[2mm] \dfrac{\max_{e' \in E} \mathsf{VP}_{\mathbf{s}'}(e')}{2\nu}, & \text{if } 0 < \mathsf{VP}_{\mathbf{s}'}(v) < \max_{e' \in E} \mathsf{VP}_{\mathbf{s}'}(e') \\[2mm] 0, & \text{if } \mathsf{VP}_{\mathbf{s}'}(v) = 0 \end{cases}
$$

Note that, by construction, $\mathsf{Support}_\mathbf{s}(ep) = \mathsf{Support}_{\mathbf{s}'}(ep)$ and $\mathsf{Support}_\mathbf{s}(i) = \mathsf{Support}_{\mathbf{s}'}(vp)$. We prove:

Lemma 3. *For each edge $e = (u, v) \in \mathsf{Support}_\mathbf{s}(ep)$, $\mathsf{VP}_\mathbf{s}(e) = \max_{e' \in E} \mathsf{VP}_\mathbf{s}(e')$.*

Lemma 4. $\sum_{v \in V} \mathsf{VP}_\mathbf{s}(v) = \nu$.

Sketch of Proof. By Theorem 4, the graph $G(E')$ is partitioned into two subgraphs: *(i)* the r-regular graph $\langle V'_r, \ \mathsf{Edges}_G(V'_r) \cap E' \rangle$, and *(ii)* the graph $\langle V'_i \cup (V \setminus V'), \mathsf{Edges}_G(V'_i \cup (V \setminus V')) \cap E' \rangle$. We will separately calculate the sums $\sum_{v \in V'_r} \mathsf{VP}_\mathbf{s}(v)$ and $\sum_{v \in V'_i \cup (V \setminus V')} \mathsf{VP}_\mathbf{s}(v)$.

We consider first the sum $\sum_{v \in V'_r} \mathsf{VP}_\mathbf{s}(v)$ and show that $\sum_{v \in V'_r} \mathsf{VP}_\mathbf{s}(v) = \sum_{v \in V'_r} \mathsf{VP}_{\mathbf{s}'}(v)$. We next consider the sum $\sum_{v \in V'_i \cup (V \setminus V')} \mathsf{VP}_\mathbf{s}(v)$ and show that $\sum_{v \in V'_i \cup (V \setminus V')} \mathsf{VP}_\mathbf{s}(v) = \sum_{v \in V'_i \cup (V \setminus V')} \mathsf{VP}_{\mathbf{s}'}(v)$. Thus,

$$
\begin{aligned}
\sum_{v \in V} & \mathsf{VP}_\mathbf{s}(v) \\
&= \textstyle\sum_{v \in V'_r} \mathsf{VP}_\mathbf{s}(v) + \sum_{v \in V'_i \cup (V \setminus V')} \mathsf{VP}_\mathbf{s}(v) \\
&= \textstyle\sum_{v \in V'_r} \mathsf{VP}_{\mathbf{s}'}(v) + \sum_{v \in V'_i \cup (V \setminus V')} \mathsf{VP}_{\mathbf{s}'}(v) \\
&= \qquad \textstyle\sum_{v \in V} \mathsf{VP}_{\mathbf{s}'}(v) \\
&= \qquad \nu \qquad\qquad\qquad \text{(since } \mathbf{s}' \text{ is a profile).} \qquad \square
\end{aligned}
$$

Lemma 5. s *is a profile.*

It remains to prove that **s** is a Nash equilibrium. We prove that **s** satisfies conditions (1) and (2) in the characterization of Nash equilibria (Theorem 1).

- By the construction of **s**, $s_{ep} = s'_{ep}$. This implies that for each vertex $v \in V$, $P_{\mathbf{s}}(\mathsf{Hit}(v)) = P_{\mathbf{s}'}(\mathsf{Hit}(v))$. Hence, in particular, $\min_{v' \in V} P_{\mathbf{s}}(\mathsf{Hit}(v')) = \min_{v' \in V} P_{\mathbf{s}'}(\mathsf{Hit}(v'))$.

  Consider any vertex $v \in \mathsf{Support}_{\mathbf{s}}(vp)$. Since $\mathsf{Support}_{\mathbf{s}}(vp) = \mathsf{Support}_{\mathbf{s}'}(vp)$, $v \in \mathsf{Support}_{\mathbf{s}'}(vp)$. Hence, by Condition (2) in the characterization of Nash equilibria (Theorem 1), $P_{\mathbf{s}'}(\mathsf{Hit}(v)) = \min_{v' \in V} P_{\mathbf{s}'}(\mathsf{Hit}(v'))$. Hence,

$$P_{\mathbf{s}}(\mathsf{Hit}(v)) = P_{\mathbf{s}'}(\mathsf{Hit}(v))$$
$$= \min_{v' \in V} P_{\mathbf{s}'}(\mathsf{Hit}(v'))$$
$$= \min_{v' \in V} P_{\mathbf{s}}(\mathsf{Hit}(v')),$$

  which proves Condition (1).
- Condition (2) is established in Lemma 3.

The proof is now complete. □

6 Epilogue

In this work, we continued the study of a network security game with attackers and a defender, introduced in [8]. We focused on the Price of Defense, introduced in [7] as a worst-case measure of security loss. We proved an optimal lower bound on the Price of Defense, and we provided an efficient characterization of graphs attaining the optimal lower bound. The characterization revealed a rich connection to Fractional Graph Theory, which we explored to show an interesting combinatorial (bivaluednsess) property of Nash equilibria.

Understanding the combinatorial structure of Nash equilibria for our network security game (and, more generally, for strategic games modeling security attacks and defenses) will provide key insights into the design of defense mechanisms. Quantifying the Price of Defense for other, more realistic variants of the network game remains a thrilling challenge. It will be interesting to see if Fractional Graph Theory will still be handy in this endeavor.

Extending Theorem 11 to the class of all graphs, or proving that such an extension is *not* possible, remains an interesting open problem.

References

1. J. Aspnes, K. Chang and A. Yampolskiy, "Inoculation Strategies for Victims of Viruses and the Sum-of-Squares Problem", *Proceedings of the 16th Annual ACM-SIAM Symposium on Discrete Algorithms*, pp. 43–52, 2005.

2. J.-M. Bourjolly and W. R. Pulleyblank, "König-Egerváry Graphs, 2-Bicritical Graphs and Fractional Matchings", *Discrete Applied Mathematics*, Vol. 24, pp. 63–82, 1989.
3. E. R. Cheswick and S. M. Bellovin, *Firewalls and Internet Security*, Addison-Wesley, 1994.
4. M. Gelastou, M. Mavronicolas, V. Papadopoulou, A. Philippou and P. Spirakis, "The Power of the Defender", *CD-ROM Proceedings of the 2nd International Workshop on Incentive-Based Computing*, July 2006.
5. E. Koutsoupias and C. H. Papadimitriou, "Worst-Case Equilibria", *Proceedings of the 16th Annual Symposium on Theoretical Aspects of Computer Science*, pp. 404–413, Vol. 1563, LNCS, 1999.
6. T. Markham and C. Payne, "Security at the Network Edge: A Distributed Firewall Architecture", *Proceedings of the 2nd DARPA Information Survivability Conference and Exposition*, Vol. 1, pp. 279-286, 2001.
7. M. Mavronicolas, L. Michael, V. G. Papadopoulou, A. Philippou and P. G. Spirakis, "The Price of Defense", *Proceedings of the 31st International Symposium on Mathematical Foundations of Computer Science*, pp. 717–728. Vol. 4162, LNCS, 2006.
8. M. Mavronicolas, V. G. Papadopoulou, A. Philippou and P. G. Spirakis. "A Network Game with Attacker and Protector Entities", *Proceedings of the 16th Annual International Symposium on Algorithms and Computation*, pp. 288–297, Vol. 3827, LNCS, 2005.
9. M. Mavronicolas, V. G. Papadopoulou, A. Philippou and P. G. Spirakis, "A Graph-Theoretic Network Security Game", *Proceedings of the 1st International Workshop on Internet and Network Economics*, pp. 969–978, Vol. 3828, LNCS, 2005.
10. M. Mavronicolas and P. Spirakis, "The Price of Selfish Routing", *Proceedings of the 33rd Annual ACM Symposium on Theory of Computing*, pp. 510–519, 2001.
11. T. Moscibroda, S. Schmid and R. Wattenhofer, "When Selfish Meets Evil: Byzantine Players in a Virus Inoculation Game", *Proceedings of the 25th Annual ACM Symposium on Principles of Distributed Computing*, pp. 35–44, 2006.
12. J. F. Nash, "Equilibrium Points in N-Person Games", *Proceedings of National Acanemy of Sciences of the United States of America*, pp. 48–49, Vol. 36, 1950.
13. J. F. Nash, "Non-Cooperative Games", *Annals of Mathematics*, Vol. 54, No. 2, pp. 286–295, 1951.
14. E. R. Scheinerman and D. H. Ullman, *Fractional Graph Theory*, Wiley-Interscience Series in Discrete Mathematics and Optimization, 1997.

Construction of Adaptive IDS Through IREP++ and ARM

Ramakrishna Raju S. and Sreenivasa Rao

College of Engineering, JNTU Anantapur
Andhra Pradesh, India
{srkr_swt, psrao_amp}@yahoo.co.in

Abstract. Many current IDSs are constructed by manual encoding of expert knowledge; changes to IDSs are expensive and slow. In this paper, we describe adaptively building Intrusion Detection (ID) models. The Central idea is to utilize auditing programs to extract an extensive set of features that describe each network connection or host session, and apply data mining programs to learn rules that accurately capture the behavior of intrusions and normal activities. We used an efficient algorithm for rule generation IREP++, which is able to produce rule sets more quickly and often express the target concept with fewer rules and fewer literals per rule resulting in a concept description that is easier for humans to understand. A new data structure (T-tree) for Association Rule Mining (ARM) is described.

1 Introduction

Currently building an effective IDS is an enormous knowledge engineering task. System builders rely on their intuition and experience to select the statistical measures for anomaly detection [1]. Experts first analyze and categorize attack scenarios and system vulnerabilities, and hand-code the corresponding rules and patterns for misuse detection. Because of the manual and ad hoc nature of the development process, current IDSs have limited extensibility and adaptability. Many IDSs only handle one particular audit data source, and their updates are expensive and slow.

Our research aims to develop a more systematic and automated approach in building IDSs. We are developing a set of tools that can be applied to a variety of audit data sources to generate intrusion detection models. We take a data-centric point of view and consider intrusion detection as a data analysis process. The central theme of our approach is to apply data mining programs to the extensively gathered audit data to compute models that accurately capture the *actual behavior* (i.e., patterns) of intrusions and normal activities. This automatic approach eliminates the need to manually analyze and encode intrusion patterns, as well as the guesswork in selecting statistical measures for normal usage profiles. More importantly, the same data mining tools can be applied to multiple streams of evidence, each from a detection module that specializes on a specific type(s) of intrusion or a specific component

S. Chaudhuri et al. (Eds.): ICDCN 2006, LNCS 4308, pp. 127–132, 2006.
© Springer-Verlag Berlin Heidelberg 2006

(e.g., a mission critical host) of the network system, to learn the combined detection model that considers all the available evidence. Thus our framework facilitates the construction of adaptive IDSs.

2 Systematic Frame Work

Data mining generally refers to the process of extracting descriptive models from large stores of data [2]. The recent rapid development in data mining has made available a wide variety of algorithms, drawn from the fields of statistics, pattern recognition, machine learning, and databases. Several types of algorithms are particularly useful for mining audit data:

We are developing a framework, first proposed in [3], of applying data mining techniques to build intrusion detection models. This framework consists of programs for learning classifiers and meta-classification [4], association rules [5] for link analysis, frequent episodes [6] for sequence analysis, and a support environment that enables system builders to interactively and iteratively drive the process of constructing and evaluating detection models. The end products are concise and intuitive rules that can detect intrusions, and can be easily inspected and edited by security experts when needed.

3 Mining Audit Data

In this section we describe our data mining algorithms, and illustrate how to apply these algorithms to generate detection models from audit data. Here audit data refers to pre-processed time-stamped audit records, each with a number of features.

3.1 Classification

In our approach, the learned rules replace the manually encoded intrusion patterns and profiles, and system features and measures are selected by considering the statistical patterns computed from the audit data. Meta-learning is used to learn the correlation of intrusion evidence from multiple detection models, and produce a combined detection models. IREP++ [7], a classification rule learning program, generates rules for the classifying the telnet records.

While RIPPER is a very fast algorithm, the training time was too long for an information assurance application of interest to the authors. Our application required an algorithm that could be trained on data sets with over one million training patterns and more than thirty features fast enough to be used in an interactive environment where training times of more than a few minutes would be unacceptable. We therefore used RIPPER as a starting point and attempted to develop an algorithm that achieved comparable accuracy but ran faster. The result of these efforts is IREP++. The algorithm has proven to have equivalent accuracy while being significantly faster at developing new rule sets. The speed improvements were achieved by making several changes to the RIPPER algorithm including a better pruning metric, some novel data structures, and more efficient stopping criteria. The algorithm is as shown below.

Algorithm 1: Algorithm Overview
Input: A training data set
Output: A rule set
LEARN(TrainingData)
(1) RuleSet NULL
(2) **repeat**
(3) (GrowSet, PruneSet) = SPLIT(TrainingData)
(4) NewRule GROWRULE(GrowSet)
(5) NewRule PRUNERULE(NewRule, PruneSet)
(6) **if** KEEP(NewRule)
(7) RuleSet RuleSet + NewRule
(8) TrainingData NOTCOVERED(RuleSet, TrainingData)
(9) **until** stopping criteria is met
(10) **return** RuleSet

3.2 Association Rules

There is empirical evidence that program executions and user activities exhibit frequent correlations among system features. For example, certain privileged programs only access certain system files in specific directories, programmers edit and compile C files frequently, etc. These consistent behavior patterns should be included in normal usage profiles. The goal of mining association rules is to derive multi feature (attribute) correlations from a database table. Given a set of records, where each record is a set of items, $support(X)$ is defined as the percentage of records that contain item set X. An association rule is an expression $X \rightarrow Y\ [C,S]$ [1]. Here X and Y are item sets, and $X \cap Y = \phi$; $s = support\ (X\ U\ Y)$ is the support of the rule, and $c = support(XUY)/support(X)$ is the confidence.

The most well-known ARM algorithm that makes use of the downward closure property is Agrawal and Srikant's Apriori algorithm. Agrawal and Srikant used a hash tree data structure, however, Apriori can equally well be implemented using alternative structures such as set enumeration trees [5]. Set enumeration trees impose an ordering on items and then enumerate the item sets according to this ordering. If we consider a data set comprised of just three records with combinations of six items: {1,3,4}, {2,4,5} and {2,4,6}(and a very low support threshold), then the tree would include one node for each large 1 (with its support count). The top level of the tree records the support for 1-itemsets, the second level for 2-itemsets, and so on. The implementation of this structure can be optimized by storing levels in the tree in the form of arrays, thus reducing the number of links needed and providing direct indexing. For the latter purpose, it is more convenient to build a "reverse" version of the tree, as shown in Fig. 1a. The authors refer to this form of compressed set enumeration tree as a T-tree (Total support tree). The implementation of this structure is illustrated in Fig. 1b, where each node in the T-tree is an object (TtreeNode) comprised of a support value (sup) and a reference (chldRef) to an array of child T-tree nodes.

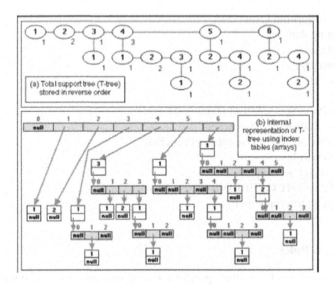

Fig. 1. Total Support Tree (T-tree)

4 Feature Construction

We apply the frequent episodes program to both normal connection data and intrusion data, and compare the resulting patterns to find the "intrusion only" patterns. The details of the pattern comparison algorithm are described in [6]. Briefly, since the number of patterns may be very large and there are rarely exactly matched patterns from two data sets, this heuristic algorithm considers two episodes related to two different sets of axis features as more different, and outputs (the user-specified) top percentage of the most "intrusion only" patterns. Here the attacker used may spoofed source addresses to send a lot of S0 connections (i.e., only the first SYN packet is sent) to a port (e.g., *http*) of the victim host in a very short time span (e.g., all in timestamp 1.1).

- A count of these connections;
- Let F_1 be *service, src dst* or *dst host* other than F_0. If the same F_1 value (e.g., "http") is in all the item sets of the episode, add a percentage of connections that share the same F_1 value as the current connection; otherwise, add a percentage of different values of F_1.
- Let V_2 be a value (e.g., "S0") of a feature F_2 (e.g.,*flag*) other than F_0 and F_1. If V_2 is in all the item sets of the episode, add a percentage of connections that have the same V_2; otherwise, if F_2 is a numerical feature, add an average of the F_2 values.

5 Audit Data and Intrusion Detection

We were provided with about 4 gigabyte of compressed *tcpdump* data of 2 weeks of network traffic. This data can be processed into about 5million of connection records of about 100 bytes each. kept only the filename extensions.

5.1 Misuse Detection

The training data includes "list files" that identify the timestamp, source host and port, destination host and port, and the name of each attack. We used this information to select intrusion data to perform pattern mining and feature construction, and to label each connection record with "normal" or an attack type to create training data for building classification models. Since the amount of audit data is huge, for example, some days have several millions of connection records due to the nasty DOS attacks; we did not aggregate all the connection records into a single training data set. Instead, we extracted all the connection records that fall within a surrounding time window of plus and minus 5 minutes of the whole duration of each attack to create a data set for each attack type. We also randomly extracted sequences of normal connections records to create the normal data set

5.2 User Anomaly Detection

"Insiders" misusing their privileges can be hard to detect since they don't normally need to break-in, and IDSs and security personnel tend to focus on guarding outside attacks. Insider problems are some of the most vexing problems for security personnel. (Indeed, who checks the checkers, i.e., the person to whom the IDS reports?)

   To analyze a user login session, we mine the frequent patterns from the sequence of commands during this session. This new pattern set is compared with the profile pattern set and a *similarity* score is assigned. Assume that the new set has n patterns and among them, there are m patterns that have "matches" (i.e., rules that they can be merged with) in the profile pattern set, then the similarity score is simply $m n$. Obviously, a higher similarity score means a higher likelihood that the user's behavior agrees with his or her historical profile.

Table 1. User Anomaly Description

User	Anomaly Description
programmer2	logs in from beta
secretary	logs in at night
sysadm	logs in from jupiter
programmer1	becomes a secretary
secretary	becomes a manager
programmer1	logs in at night
sysadm	**becomes a programmer**
manager1	becomes a sysadm
manager2	logs in from pluto

6 Conclusions

In this paper, we outline a data mining framework for constructing intrusion detection models. The key idea is to apply data mining programs to audit data to compute misuse and anomaly detection models, according to the observed.

We extend the traditional intrusion detection systems through automatic feature construction thus avoiding manual encoding, and used efficient data structures and algorithms to find the association rules like T-tree and IREP++.

References

[1] T. Lunt. Detecting intruders in computer systems. In Proceedings of the 1993 conference on Auditing and computer Technology, 1993

[2] U. Fayyad, G. Piatetsky-Shapiro, and P.Smyth. The KDD process of extracting useful knowledge from volumes of data. Communications of the ACM, 39(11)27-34, November 1996

[3] W. Lee and S.J.Stolfo. Data Mining Approach for Intrusion detection. In Proceedings of the 7th USENIX Security Symposium, San Antonio, TX, Jan 1998

[4] P.K. Chan and S.J. Stolfo. Toward parallel and distributed learning by meta-learning. In AAAI Workshop in Knowledge Discovery in Databases

[5] R. Agrawal, T.Imielinski, and A.Swami. Mining Association rules between sets of items in large data bases. In Proceedings of the ACM SIGMOD Conference on Management of Data

[6] H. Mannila, H.Toivonen, and A.I..Verkamo. Discovering frequent episodes in sequences. In Proceedings of the 1st International conference on Knowledge Discovery in Databases and Data Mining, Monteral, Canada, August 1995

[7] Leo Breiman, Jerome H. Friedman, Richard A. Olshen, and Charles J. Stone. *Classification and Regression Trees*. Chapman and Hall/CRC, Boca Raton, FL, 1984.

[8] Johannes Fürnkranz and Gerhard Widmer. Incremental reduced error pruning. In *Machine Learning: Proceedings of the Eleventh Annual Conference*, New Brunswick, New Jersey, 1994. Morgan Kaufmann.

[9] W. Lee, S. J. Stolfo, and K. W. Mok. A data mining framework for building intrusion detection models. In *Proceedings of the 1999 IEEE Symposium on Security and Privacy*, May 1999.

Proving Optimality of DWS(Distance-Weighted Sampling) Probability Function for FMS IP Trace-Back Technique

Jeankyung Kim[1], Jinsoo Hwang[1],
Byungryong Kim[2], and Kichang Kim[3]

[1] Department of Statistics, Inha University
jkkim@inha.ac.kr, jshwang@inha.ac.kr
[2] School of Computer Science and Engineering, Inha University
doolyn@inha.ac.kr
[3] School of Information and Communication Engineering, Inha University
kchang@inha.ac.kr

Abstract. A convergence time is the time to construct the attack path. In FMS, each router sends its IP by fragments, and the victim should wait until the last router sends its last IP fragment. Therefore, the convergence time is determined by the slowest router. Kim et al.[1] proposed a new sampling theory, so called Distance-Weighted Sampling that did not penalize the furthest router. They showed that the sampling probability $p = f(d)$ where the $f(d)$ is a decreasing function of distance d traveled by the target packet. Since the convergence time will be determined by the slowest router, we have to maximize the minimum number of IP fragments incoming at each router station. The optimal choice was stated as $f(d) = \frac{1}{2(d+1)}$ and a small sample simulation study supported their claim. In this article we are going to prove rigorously that $\frac{1}{2(d+1)}$ is indeed the optimal sampling probability under mild assumptions.

1 Introduction

Recently, an efficient IP trace-back technique called FMS (Fragment Marking Scheme) based on IP marking has been suggested[3,2]. FMS is efficient and allows automatic attack path discovery. However it suffers a long convergence time when building the attack path.

A convergence time is the time to construct the attack path. In FMS, each router sends its IP by fragments, and the victim should wait until the last router sends its last IP fragment. Therefore, the convergence time is determined by the slowest router. Kim et al.[1] proposed a new sampling theory, so called Distance-Weighted Sampling that did not penalize the furthest router. They showed that the sampling probability $p = f(d)$ where the $f(d)$ is a decreasing

S. Chaudhuri et al. (Eds.): ICDCN 2006, LNCS 4308, pp. 133–138, 2006.

function of distance d traveled by the target packet. Since the convergence time will be determined by the slowest router, we have to maximize the minimum number of IP fragments incoming at each router station. The optimal choice was stated as $f(d) = \frac{1}{2(d+1)}$ and a small sample simulation study supported their claim.

In this article we are going to prove rigorously that the chosen function is indeed the optimal one under mild assumptions. The rest of the paper is organized as follows: Section 2 explains some background concepts needed later, Section 3 gives the formal proof for the optimality of the probability function, and Section 4 provides concluding remarks.

2   Preliminary

Before embarking on the full proof, we need to clarify a few concepts. Let's assume that we have n routers ahead or n number of hops in the attack path, $R_1, R_2, \ldots, R_n$.

Whenever packets pass through a router, the router samples a part of them and overwrite IP fragments of its own. Rest of the packets' IP fragments are XORed with previous IP fragments, if any. If the router writes its own IP fragment, we define the distance of packets to be zero. If you do XOR, then those packets' distance increased by one. So the distance of packet tells you how far you have to trace back to find their origin. One can only trace back up to that number(distance) of past routers. Let's suppose R_1 is the first router in the possible attack path. All packets are marked with R_1's IP and having distance $d = 0$. Upon receiving these packets, R_2 samples them with probability $f(0) = f_0$ and overwrites its IP fragment and the rest are XORed with past R_1's IP fragment. So at R_2 we have two types of packets, $d = 0$ and $d = 1$, with probability f_0 and $1 - f_0$ respectively.

Now R_3 receives two kinds of packets: packets with $d = 0$ and $d = 1$. Under our new sampling scheme, different sampling probabilities f_0 and f_1 are applied to packets with $d = 0$ and $d = 1$, respectively. Let $R_m(d)$ denote the size of packet with distance d at router R_m. After sampling and marking process on router R_2, we have $R_3(0), R_3(1), R_3(2)$ packets at R_3 as follows:

$$R_3(0) = R_2(0) \times f_0 + R_2(1) \times f_1$$
$$R_3(1) = R_2(0) \times (1 - f_0)$$
$$R_3(2) = R_2(1) \times (1 - f_1).$$

The same fragment marking system and sampling process continues.

In order to achieve optimality, we try to maximize the number of the smallest distance packets at each router given the total number of packets fixed. Let $f_0, f_1, \ldots, f_n$ represent the sampling probability from packets with distances $d = 0, d = 1, \ldots, d = n$, respectively. At R_1, sampling probability f_0 should be $1/2$ to give equal number of packets of $R_2(0)$ and $R_2(1)$ to R_2. So the value of f_0 is determined. The rest of $f_i, i = 1, \ldots$ will be determined sequentially at each even numbered router under the principle of maximizing the minimum number of packets. The details will be shown in the next section.

3   Main Results

At router R_m, we have m different distance packets, $R_m(0), R_m(1), \ldots,$ $R_m(m-1)$ and the size of each packets is determined by the sampling probabilities, $f_0, f_1, \ldots, f_{m-2}$. Let $P_m(\cdot)$ denote the probability distribution at router R_m. That is, $P_m(i)$ is the probability of finding packets with distance i at R_m. Then by the law of probability $\sum_{i=0}^{m-1} P_m(i) = 1$.

We are going to determine the sampling probability distribution based on the strategy of maximizing the minimum of $P_m(\cdot)$ at each router R_m, i.e.,

$$\max_{f_0,\ldots,f_{m-1}} \min\{P_m(0), \ldots, P_m(m-1)\}.$$

Computation of $P_m(d)$ follows the rule mentioned in Kim et al.[1].

$$P_m(0) = \sum_{i=0}^{m-2} P_m(i) f_i \qquad (1)$$

$$P_m(d) = P_{m-1}(d-1)(1 - f_{d-1}) \quad \text{for} \ \ d = 1, \ldots, m-1. \qquad (2)$$

By following the rule above we can get the probability distribution easily for the first few routers. From the first few trials we can observe a few interesting points to note as follows.

- The sequence of the values of f_d's should be a nonincreasing sequence.
- The value of f_d is determined at even numbered router $R_{2(d+1)}$.
- The value of f_d determines the probabilitiy distribution $P_{d+2}(\cdot)$ of the router R_{d+2}, which are symmetric.

To generalize these findings, we employ the famous mathematical induction idea. Let A_k be the k-th statement of induction as follows:

$$A_k \ : \ f_{k-1} = \frac{1}{2k}, \quad P_{k+1}(\cdot) \ \text{has symmetric distribution}.$$

We have shown that A_k is true for $k = 1, 2, 3$. So if we can show that A_m is true under the assumption that A_k is true for $k = 0, \ldots, m-1$, then we can conclude that A_k is true for all nonnegative integer k.

The following theorem states the main result.

Theorem 1. *Under the condition that $f_0 \geq f_1 \geq f_2 \cdots$, the following statements are true. For nonnegative integer m,*

- *the optimal sampling probability $f_m = \frac{1}{2(m+1)}$,*
- *$P_m(\cdot)$ is symmetric i.e. $P_m(i) = P_m(m-i-1)$ for $i = 0, \ldots, m-1$.*

Proof: We would follow the mathematical induction on A_k's. Once we have proved that A_k is true for $k = 1, 2, 3$, we only need to follow the next steps:

1. Assume A_k is true for $k = 1, \ldots, m - 1$,
2. Set $P_{2m}(m - 1) = P_{2m}(m)$.
3. Determine f_{m-1}.
4. Symmetry of $P_{m+1}(\cdot)$ is obtained, which imply A_m.

Even though the proof goes slightly different for the cases that m is even or m is odd, the basic idea is the same, so we only follow the case of even number m closely.

From the assumption that $f_0 \geq f_1 \geq f_2 \cdots$, the ordering of bottom half of $P_{2m}(\cdot)$ is $P_{2m}(2m - 1) > P_{2m}(2m - 2) > \cdots > P_{2m}(m)$ and that of top half is $P_{2m}(0) > P_{2m}(1)$. We do not have enough information for complete ordering of $P_{2m}(\cdot)$ at this stage, however, from the fact that for $d = 1, \ldots, m - 2$,

$$P_{2m}(d) = P_{2m-d}(0)(1 - f_0) \cdots (1 - f_{d-1})$$

and $P_{2m-d}(0)$ includes one of $\{f_d : d = m, \ldots, 2m-2\}$, we know that $P_{2m}(m-1)$ is the only term determined by f_{m-1} among the top half of the router R_{2m}, and is an increasing function of f_{m-1}. Together with the fact that $P_{2m}(m)$ is the minimum among the bottom half of the router R_{2m} and is a decreasing function of f_{m-1}. it is natural to find the optimum sampling probability f_{m-1} by setting $P_{2m}(m - 1) = P_{2m}(m)$.

From the assumption that $f_k = \frac{1}{2(k+1)}$ for $k = 0, \ldots, m - 2$, for $m \geq 2$,

$$P_m(m - 1) = \prod_{i=0}^{m-2} (1 - f_i) = \frac{1}{2}\frac{3}{4} \cdots \frac{(2m - 3)}{(2m - 2)}.$$

Let $c_1 = 1$ and $c_d = P_d(d - 1)$ for $d = 1, \ldots, m$, then symmetry assumption of $P_d(\cdot)$ gives us $P_d(0) = P_d(d - 1) = c_d$.

From the symmetry of $P_m(\cdot)$, we can derive the following form at router R_{2m}:

$$P_{2m}(m - 1) = P_{m+1}(0)(1 - f_0) \cdots (1 - f_{m-2}) = P_{m+1}(0) \times c_m \qquad (3)$$
$$P_{2m}(m) = P_m(0)(1 - f_0) \cdots (1 - f_{m-1}) = c_m^2 \times (1 - f_{m-1}). \qquad (4)$$

By setting equations (3) and (4) are equal, we have

$$P_{m+1}(0) = c_m \times (1 - f_{m-1}). \qquad (5)$$

To solve this equation for f_{m-1}, we need to look at $P_{m+1}(0)$ closely. The probability $P_{m+1}(0)$ is obtained from the probability distribution $P_m(\cdot)$ of the previous router R_m as follows:

$$P_{m+1}(0) = P_m(0)f_0 + P_m(1)f_1 + \cdots + P_m(m - 2)f_{m-2} + P_m(m - 1)f_{m-1}.$$

By the symmetry assumption on $P_m(\cdot)$, we can get

$$P_m(k) = P_m(m - 1 - k) = P_{m-k}(0)(1 - f_0) \cdots (1 - f_{k-1}) = c_{m-k}c_{k+1} \qquad (6)$$

for $k = 0, \ldots, m - 1$, and hence

$$P_{m+1}(0) = c_m \left(\frac{1}{2} + f_{m-1} \right) + c_2 c_{m-1} \left(\frac{1}{4} + \frac{1}{2(m-1)} \right) + c_3 c_{m-2} \times$$
$$\left(\frac{1}{6} + \frac{1}{2(m-2)} \right) + \cdots + c_{\frac{m}{2}} c_{\frac{m}{2}+1} \left(\frac{1}{2(m/2)} + \frac{1}{2(m/2+1)} \right).$$

By plugging this in the equation (5), we have

$$2f_{m-1} = \frac{1}{2} - B$$

where

$$B = \frac{c_2 c_{m-1}}{c_m} \left(\frac{1}{4} + \frac{1}{2(m-1)} \right) + \frac{c_3 c_{m-2}}{c_m} \left(\frac{1}{6} + \frac{1}{2(m-2)} \right)$$
$$+ \cdots + \frac{c_{\frac{m}{2}} c_{\frac{m}{2}+1}}{c_m} \left(\frac{1}{m} + \frac{1}{m+2} \right).$$

Since $2f_{m-1} = \frac{1}{2} - B$ and B can be simplified to be $\frac{m-2}{2m}$, the optimal sampling probability is $f_{m-1} = \frac{1}{2m}$.

Now we are ready to prove the symmetry of $P_{m+1}(\cdot)$. Since $P_m(0) = P_m(m-1) = c_m$, from the equation (5) and $f_{m-1} = \frac{1}{2m}$, we get $P_{m+1}(0) = c_m(1 - \frac{1}{2m})$. And $P_{m+1}(m) = P_m(m-1)(1 - f_{m-1}) = c_m(1 - \frac{1}{2m})$, which shows $P_{m+1}(0) = P_{m+1}(m)$. For $i = 1, \ldots, m-1$, it is true that

$$P_{m+1}(i) = P_m(i-1)(1 - f_{i-1}) = c_{i+1} c_{m-i+1} = P_{m+1}(m-i),$$

by the equations (2) and (6). Therefore the symmetry of $P_{m+1}(\cdot)$ holds and our proof of theorem 1 is now completed.

4   Conclusion

FMS(Fragment Marking Scheme) is an important technique to track down the attacking path even under IP spoofing. However it suffers a long convergence time when computing the attack path. DWS(Distance-Weighted Sampling) has been suggested to minimize the convergence time by allowing close-to-equal chance for the marked IP fragments of each router to survive and reach the victim system. They achieved that by varying the sampling probability based on the distance the packet has traveled so far: packets traveled for longer path are favored over packets traveled shorter. They found an efficient probability function through experimentation. In this paper, we have proved rigorously that the function is indeed optimal.

Acknowledgements. This work was supported by INHA UNIVERSITY Research Grant.

138   J. Kim et al.

References

1. Byung-Ryong Kim. Ki-Chang Kim, Jin-Soo Hwang and Soo-Duk Kim. Tagged fragment marking scheme with distance-weighted sampling for a fast ip traceback. In *Lecture Notes in Computer Science 2642*, pages 442–452, Apr. 2003.
2. D. X. Song and A. Perrig. Advanced and authenticated marking schemes for ip traceback. In *in Proc. IEEE INFOCOM*, Apl. 2001.
3. A. K. Stefan Savage, David Wetherall and T. Anderson. Practical network support for ip traceback. In *in Proc. of ACM SIGCOMM*, pages 295–306, Aug. 2000.

A Mechanism for Detection and Prevention of Distributed Denial of Service Attacks

Jaydip Sen[1], Piyali Roy Chowdhury[2], and Indranil Sengupta[1]

[1] Department of Computer Science and Engineering
Indian Institute of Technology, Kharagpur-721302, India
[2] Department of Computer Science and Engineering
Future Institute of Engineering and Management, Kolkata-700150, India
sen_jaydip@yahoo.com, roychowdhury.piyali@gmail.com,
isg@iitkgp.ac.in

Abstract. With several critical services being provided over the Internet it has become imperative to monitor the network traffic to prevent malicious attackers from depleting the resources of the network. In this paper, we propose a mechanism to protect a web-server against a Distributed Denial of Service (DDoS) attack. Incoming traffic to the server is continuously monitored to immediately detect any abnormal rise in the inbound traffic. This detection activates a traffic-filtering rule that pushes down the network traffic to an acceptable level by discarding packets according to measured relative traffic levels of each of the active sources. The proposed mechanism does not affect legitimate users and is thus more effective and robust. We have presented simulation results to demonstrate the effectiveness of the proposed mechanism.

Keywords: DDoS, Buffer overflow, Security, Traffic level measurement.

1 Introduction

A *Denial of Service* (DoS) attack is an attempt by a malicious user to prevent legitimate users from availing the services by consuming the resources of a server or a network. DoS attacks, like SYN flooding, UDP flooding, DNS-based flooding, ICMP directed broadcast, Ping flood attack, IP fragmentation, and CGI attacks, typically involve flooding with a huge volume of traffic, thereby consuming network resources such as bandwidth, buffer space at routers, CPU time and recovery cycles of target servers. A DoS attack, when launched from multiple coordinating machines is referred to as *Distributed Denial of Service* (DDoS) attack, which owing to its distributed nature is very difficult to defend. In order to make the server resources available, it is highly critical to be able to detect such attacks as quickly as possible.

In this paper, we have proposed a robust mechanism to protect a web server from DDoS attack, utilizing some easily accessible information in the server, such that it is impossible for an attacker to disable the server by creating an overload. Moreover, as soon as the attempted overload disappears, the normal service quality resumes automatically. While the malicious attack is handled, the mechanism also minimizes the number of legitimate clients affected. This aspect of handling DDoS attacks is not taken into account in many of the current commercial solutions.

S. Chaudhuri et al. (Eds.): ICDCN 2006, LNCS 4308, pp. 139–144, 2006.
© Springer-Verlag Berlin Heidelberg 2006

The rest of the paper is organized as follows: Section 2 presents some related work in the area of protection against DoS attacks. Section 3 describes the major component of the proposed system and the algorithms for detection and prevention of attacks. Section 4 presents the simulation results and Section 5 concludes the paper.

2 Related Work

Several protection mechanisms have been proposed against DoS attack. *Network Ingress Filtering* [1] prevents attacks using spoofed source addresses. However, it is unable to curtail a flood attack originating from within a network. *Deterministic Packet Marking* (DPM) [2] relies on routing information that is inscribed in the packet header by the routers as the packet traverses the network, which linearly increases the size of IP packet header with the number of hops traversed, involving complex processing at the routers. *Probabilistic Packet Marking* [3] for IP Taceback improves DPM. Here each router probabilistically inscribes local path information onto a packet that traverses it. However, the increase in distributed nature of an attack makes it more difficult to localize the attacker. In *MULTOPS* [4], the routers detect bandwidth attacks based on packet sending rates. However, due to memory limitations, its efficiency degrades with randomized IP source addresses. *Client Side Puzzle* [5] is an effective tool to make protocols less vulnerable to resource depletion attacks, but in case of distributed attacks its effectiveness is an open question.

3 The Proposed System and Algorithms

In this section, we describe our traffic model and attack model on which we have developed our security system. A major system component - *interface* module is described with all the important algorithms for detection and prevention of attacks.

3.1 Traffic Model and Attack Model

In our model *packets* from the network means small independent queries to the server. We assume that every query causes same workload on the server, as with some enhancements (protocol enhancements, crypto hardware, caching etc.) the workload of different queries can be very similar. We also assume that the attacking machines use real addresses to establish two-way communication with the server just like a legitimate client. Let us suppose that there are $N(t)$ legal sources and $A(t)$ attacking sources in time slot t. The attacker reaches his goal only if attacking traffic is much higher than normal traffic. Several attacking machines could be used by the attacker, making it more difficult for the server to identify and foil them all. However, this makes it is more difficult for the attacker to hide. Hence, we assume that the attacker limits the number of attacking hosts, i.e., $A(t)$ is low. In fact, a tradeoff can be identified between the ability to hide and the efficiency of the attack.

3.2   The Interface Module

A DDoS *interface* module is attached to the server from the network side. This *interface* can be a software or a special-purpose hardware component of the server or an independent autonomous hardware component attached to the server. The incoming traffic enters a FIFO buffer. Traffic is modeled and analyzed over unit time slot using *discrete time* model. The server CPU empties μ packets per time slot from the buffer. Random traffic ensures a non-zero probability of buffer overflow situation. When a DdoS attack begins the buffer becomes full and most of the incoming packets are dropped, degrading the quality of service of the server. At this point, the *interface* module disrupts traffic from attacking sources effectively.

Let the attack begin at time t^* and at time $t^* + \delta$ the *interface* buffer become full. The first task is to detect the point of commencement of the attack, by accurately estimating t^*. The next task is to identify the sources of the attack, and to disrupt their traffic. The *interface* module can identify all active sources, measure the traffic generated by them and classify them into specific sets. The traffic level measurements are to be done in time slots between t^* and $t^* + \delta$. The effectiveness of the mechanism heavily depends on δ. Larger the value of δ, higher is the time for traffic measurements. It is achieved using a very large buffer. We propose that the buffer (L) is divided into two parts. The first part (L_1) is designed to serve the normal state of the server, and is chosen according to the service rate and the accepted probability of packet loss due to buffer overflow. The size of the second part (L_2) corresponds to the buffer introduced to gain enough time for traffic measurements during the start-up phase of the attack. Let $\hat{t}$ denote the expected value of t^*. It is also assumed that the set of active sources is constant during the period of the attack. Let $T_n(t)$ be the aggregate legal traffic and $T_a(t)$ be the aggregate attacking traffic. Λ_n and λ_a are the corresponding mean values, denoting the expected normal and expected attack traffics respectively. As t^* is earlier than the time of its detection ($\hat{t}$), we miss some time for efficient traffic measurements, which is minimized by estimating the aggregate traffic level continuously using sliding window method. The *interface* module handles two sliding time windows, a longer (with capacity of w_l slots) and a shorter (with capacity of w_s slots). This way we measure both a long time average level $\overline{\lambda}(t)$ and a short time average level $\hat{\lambda}(t)$, of incoming aggregate traffic per slot at time slot t.

3.3   Algorithms of the Interface Module

Four algorithms in the *interface* module are executed in the following order. Details of the algorithms are out of the scope of this paper due to space constraints.

1. Detection of attack: The beginning of an attack is assumed to take place at time $\hat{t}$. The determination of $\hat{t}$ can be done in any of the following two ways:

A. $\hat{t}$ is that point of time when the buffer L_1 becomes full.

B. $\hat{t}$ is that point of time when the following inequality holds:

$$\hat{\lambda}(\hat{t}) > (1+r)\overline{\lambda}(\hat{t}), \text{ where, r} > 0 \text{ is a design parameter.} \tag{1}$$

2. *Identification of attack sources:* The *interface* module distinguishes between the attacking traffic and the normal traffic by the corresponding means of their aggregate traffic (λ_a and λ_n), where $\lambda_a > \lambda_n$. It measures the traffic characteristics of all active sources by recognizing their network addresses and thereby identifies the attack sources.

3. *Disruption of traffic from attack sources:* Once the attacking sources are identified, the disruption of the traffic emanating from them is done by discarding all the incoming packets with source addresses in the set of clients identified as attackers.

4. *Checking the success of disruption of traffic:* On successful execution of above algorithms, the available buffer size should come back to the level of L_1 within a timeout interval. If this does not happen, more packets from active sources are to be discarded repeatedly until the buffer size is restored to the level of L_1.

4 Simulation and Results

The simulation program, written in *C* is executed on *Red Hat Linux* with a *MySQL* database that stores the traffic-data. The time interval is set at 10^{-6} seconds. Statistical data are collected in every second. The simulation is done with first 100 seconds as the normal traffic, attack starting at the 100th second and the attack continuing till 200th second. The simulation was ended with another 100 seconds of normal traffic to have an insight into the efficiency of the recovery function of the system.

Parameter setting for simulation: The arrival pattern at the *interface* module is modeled as a Poisson process. The *interface* module stores the packets in a buffer before passing them on to CPU for processing. The queue type is assumed to be *M/M/1*, with inter-arrival time and service time both following exponential distribution. The number of sources is kept constant throughout the simulation process. ICMP, NTP (Network time Protocol) and DNS clients send many small packets of constant size with uniformly distributed inter-packet arrival time. Thus these protocols resemble very close to our modeling assumptions. The number of simultaneous legitimate clients can vary over a broad range depending on the application scenario. We consider three different cases:

Case 1: For a small corporate server, $N(t)$ is low, say 5, and thus the average load on the server is low. In this case, $A(t)$ should be high, 40. Thus here $N(t) \ll A(t)$.

Case 2: For a server of medium size, say $N(t) = 50$, an attacker can launch a successful attack from a fewer number of hosts, say $A(t) = 50$. As in this case $N(t) \approx A(t)$, the attacker can easily hide himself.

Case 3: For a global portal server, $N(t)$ is very large, say 10000, making it difficult for the attacker to appropriately estimate $A(t)$. We assume that the attacker chooses $A(t) = 5000$ and a very high attacking rate: $\lambda_a = \lambda_n *10$. In this case, $N(t) > A(t)$.

Simulation 1: We have chosen a large number of hosts to test the effectiveness of our mechanism. The simulation parameters are listed in Table 1. With 10000 legal clients and $\lambda_n = 0.1$, the capacity of the server should be at least 1000. The attack is successful only when the service rate (μ) is less than 3000 ($\lambda_a *A(t) + \lambda_n*N(t)$). We have used $\mu = 1500$. We have taken the buffer size, $L_1 = 40$ (packets). As the normal traffic rate is 1000 packets/sec, we have taken a safe value of $L_2 = 3000$ (packets).

Table 1. Parameters for Simulation 1

Parameter	Value
Number of legal clients ($N(t)$)	10000
Number of attacking hosts ($A(t)$)	5000
Mean normal traffic rate (λ_n)	0.1
Mean attack traffic rate (λ_a)	0.4
Service rate (μ) (packets/sec)	1500
Sliding window size (w_s)	10 s
Tolerance for traffic jump (r)	0.6
Time frame for last correct value of λ	45 s

The estimation of δ is crucial, as the available time for traffic analysis depends on this. We have used a constant limit ($\hat{\delta} \le \delta$) for traffic analysis. Let us suppose that we know the total traffic is $T_n + T_a = 3000$. As $\mu = 1500$, we can expect L_1 to be full after $40/(3000-1500) \approx 0.3$ s. The whole buffer (L) will be full in $30040/(3000-1500) \approx 200$ s. We take $\delta = 10$. In real world, as we have no apriori knowledge about attacks, δ is estimated over a period of time. For simplicity, we set $w_s = \delta$.

Table 2 shows the results of the simulation on a large system with parameters mentioned in Table 1. It is observed that larger values of w_s make more accurate identification of attacks, though the system is more likely to enter into a buffer overflow situation. In an attack situation, the buffer will allow us to measure traffic only for 20 sec, after which, the attack identification algorithm will produce inaccurate and unpredictable results. Thus the value of w_s cannot be increased at our will. In summary, our mechanism provides good protection, if the parameters are well estimated and a large buffer size is available in the system.

Table 2. Results of simulation 1

Observed metrics	$\hat{\delta}(\hat{\delta}=w_s)$				
	5	10	20	30	40
Correctly identified attackers	2982	3784	4529	4784	4892
Filtered legal clients	1	557	260	132	59
Dropped packets	0	0	0	14251	28765
Max buffer level and corresponding timeframe	29717 (200 s)	14941 (110 s)	29732 (119 s)	30040 (120 s)	30040 (120 s)
Time to restore (after t^*)	149	104	73	71	81

Simulation 2: We have simulated a smaller system with parameters listed in Table 3. We have taken $L_1 = 40$ (packets), $L_2 = 160$ (packets) and $\delta = w_s = 10$. The experiments are repeated on 500 different sets of input data to obtain statistical information of the system. It was observed that the attack was detected by algorithm in Section *3.3 I A* in 4 cases. Algorithm in Section *3.3 I B* was faster in detecting the attack in 454 cases. In 42 cases, the attack was correctly identified by both these algorithms. Table 4 summarizes the simulation results.

Table 3. Parameters for Simulation 2

Parameter	Value
Number of legal clients ($N(t)$)	50
Number of attacking hosts ($A(t)$)	50
Mean normal traffic rate (λ_n)	0.1
Mean attack traffic rate (λ_a)	0.2
Service rate (μ) (packets/sec)	8

Table 4. Results of simulation 2

Observed metrics	Observed values		
	Minimum	Average	Conf. Intrvl. (95%)
Time to restore (after t^*)	49	114.732	1.942
Packets dropped	0	0.695	0.321
Normal user filtered (type II error)	1	7.115	0.231
Attackers filtered	21	32.413	0.235
Attack detection time (after t^*)	0	2.950	0.090

5 Conclusion

In this paper, we have presented a mechanism for detection and prevention of DDoS attacks on a server by inbound traffic analysis on it. We also described a simple yet robust model of solution for this problem. We have conducted simulation on our propose model. The simulation results confirm the effectiveness of our model and enable us to make a sensitivity analysis of the parameters of different algorithm for detection of an attack.

References

1. Ferguson, P. and Senie, D. Network Ingress Filtering: Defending Denial Of Service Attacks which Employ IP Source Address Spoofing. RFC 2827, May 2000.
2. Burch, H. and Cheswick, B. Tracing Anonymous Packets to Their Approximate Source. In Proceedings of the 14th Systems Administration Conference. Usenix LISA, December 2000, pp. 319-327.
3. Park, K. and Lee, H. On the Effectiveness of Probabilistic Packet Marking for IP Traceback Under Denial Of Service Attack. In Proceedings of IEEE- INFOCOM'01, Anchorage, Alaska, 2001, pp. 338-347.
4. Gil, T.M. MULTOPS: A Data-Structure for Bandwidth Attack Detection. M.S. Thesis, Virije Universiteit, Amsterdam, Netherlands, August 2000.
5. Bencsáth, B. Buttyan and L. Vajda, I. A Game Based Analysis of the Client Puzzle Approach to Defend Against DoS Attacks. In Proceedings of SoftCOM 2003, 11th International Conference on Software, Telecommunications and Computer Networks, pp. 763-767, University of Split, 2003.

Auction Based Resource Allocation in Grids

Sai Rahul Reddy P.[1] and Arobinda Gupta[2,3]

[1] Veveo (India) Pvt. Ltd, Bangalore
[2] School of Information Technology
[3] Department of Computer Science and Engineering
Indian Institute of Technology Kharagpur, India
sairahul@veveo.net, agupta@cse.iitkgp.ernet.in

Abstract. Auctions have been used as the market mechanism for allocating resources to users in a grid. However, most of the existing work either consider only homogeneous resources, or pick a resource randomly for bidding to increase the number of jobs finishing within their deadlines. Random selection does not consider resource capabilities and hence, do not optimize other important metrics like the average turnaround time and the average budget spent per job etc. In this paper, we consider the resource allocation problem in a grid with heterogeneous resources. We present allocation policies using sealed-bid auction that reduce the average turnaround time and the average budget spent per job, while still maintaining a high number of jobs finishing within their deadlines. Simulation results are presented to evaluate the performance of the policies.

Keywords: Grid, Resource, Allocation, Auction.

1 Introduction

Grid computing is defined as "coordinated resource sharing and problem solving in dynamic, multi-institutional virtual organizations"[7]. A grid allows the sharing of a wide variety of geographically distributed resources owned by different organizations [1]. Grid computing is generally used for problems with large computational, data storage, and/or collaboration requirement. Some applications of grid include simulations in astrophysics, climate modeling, modeling for drug design, high energy physics, infrastructure for multiplayer games etc. [2, 7, 8].

A grid may typically contain resources with comparable but different capability and availability. In such a system, it is necessary to assign each job to the most appropriate resource. Viewing the resources as suppliers and the users as consumers of services provided, markets for computing services/resources have been examined as a mechanism for allocating resources to jobs [12]. A market is where goods and services are bought and sold and a market mechanism is the process by which the market controls this buying and selling of goods [15]. There are several market mechanisms like commodity markets, tendering/contract net, auctions etc. [3]. Framing the resource allocation problem in economic terms is useful for several

S. Chaudhuri et al. (Eds.): ICDCN 2006, LNCS 4308, pp. 145–156, 2006.

reasons [13]. Resource usage may not be free and to make girds successful commercially, resource owners and users should get adequate rewards to motivate them to participate in the grid.

In this work, we investigate the use of auctions as the market mechanism for resource allocation in grids. The auction model supports one-to-many negotiation between a resource provider and multiple consumers. Auctions require little of global price information, are decentralized, and are easy to implement in grid settings [3]. There exist several studies on applying auctions to solve resource allocation problem in grids [6, 9, 10, 11, 13, 14]. Most of these works assume that the resources are homogenous. For example, most of them assume that all resources have the same speed and cost. But in a real world environment, resources can be heterogeneous and different parameters like resource type, resource speed, available memory, price of resource etc. need to be considered. The choice of a proper resource for an application will thus be based on various parameters. The studies in [9, 11] considered resources with different capabilities. However, resources are just selected randomly for bidding. The problem with random selection is that the resource capabilities are not considered for bidding and hence, important metrics like the average turnaround time and the average budget spent per job etc. increases.

In this paper, we consider resources with different capabilities (speeds) and prices. A set of users, each with a set of jobs, wish to use these resources. Each job has a deadline and an allowed maximum budget. We focus on two parameters, time and budget. The problem is to define resource allocation policies that allocate resources to the jobs while increasing the number of jobs finishing within their deadline and decreasing the average turnaround time and the average budget spent per job for these sets of jobs. We first present two simple policies that show better average turnaround time per job and average budget spent per job respectively compared with the random policy where a resource is chosen randomly for bidding. However, the number of jobs finishing within their deadlines is less in both these policies as compared to the random policy. We next present two parameterized policies that increase the number of jobs finishing within their deadlines while still maintaining a lower average turnaround time and average budget spent per job respectively. Simulation results are provided for all the policies to evaluate their performance.

In related work, Buyya et al. proposed Nimrod-G [4] which supports several economic models like commodity market, spot market, and contract net. It implements two resource selection policies for the above market models, time optimization, and budget optimization policies. However, they have not applied those policies to auctions. In auctions, we cannot directly use those policies.

The rest of this paper is organized as follows. Section 2 presents our system model. Section 3 presents two simple resource allocation policies that try to optimize time and budget respectively. Two modified policies are presented in Section 4. Finally, Section 5 concludes the paper.

2 System Model

The grid computational environment consists of resource consumers or users and resource providers. Resource consumers have jobs to be done and are willing to pay for it. Resource providers have computational resources and are willing to rent them for profit. We use sealed bid auction as our market mechanism. In the sealed bid auction, the auctioneer accepts bids from users in which the users will not know the other users' bid amount. At the end of the auction period, the auctioneer opens the bids and gives the resource to the highest bidder.

Each resource consumer or user has its corresponding resource broker and submits its jobs to the resource broker. A resource broker will search for a suitable resource provider and submit the job to it. Let U_1, U_2, U_3 ... U_N be the users participating in the grid and J_1, J_2, J_3 ... J_K be the corresponding jobs for each user. Each job specification J_i includes the job length, deadline, and budget. The jobs have to be completed within its deadline and its cost of execution must not exceed its allocated budget. The job length is specified in millions of instructions (MI). The deadline includes the time spent on the auctions also.

A resource provider executes jobs for resource consumers and charges them for usage of resource. Let R_1, R_2 ... R_M be the resources participating in the grid. Each resource R_i is modeled by a single processor with some speed and unit price. The capability of resources is expressed in terms of millions of instructions the resource can process in one second (MIPS). The unit price is the minimum amount a user must pay for using the resource for one second. In our work we considered resources with single processor. Each resource R_i will conduct auction A_i. Users who want to use the resource have to participate in the auction. In the rest of this paper, the speed of the resource R_i is referred to as $R_i.speed$, the start time for using the resource by a job is referred to as $R_i.resource\_usage\_start\_time$, and the unit price of the resource is referred to as $R_i.price$.

The main function of a resource broker is to find an appropriate resource according to the user policy and to bid for that resource. Let Rb_1, Rb_2 ... Rb_N be the resource brokers for the users U_1, U_2 ... U_N respectively. A user will specify which resource selection policy the resource broker has to use and the resource broker in turn selects resources to bid for accordingly. In the rest of the paper, we have used the terms resource broker and user interchangeably.

A *Grid Information Service* (*GIS*) contains complete information about current auctions. Each auction description A_i includes the resource provider id, the auction number, the starting time of resource usage, the auction end time, the reserve price, and the capability of the resource. It does not include the resource usage end time as that depends on the job it accepts in the auction. The resource broker will first contact the GIS for auction information. Resource providers will periodically update their auction information in the GIS.

Each resource provider will conduct sealed-bid auction and accept the bids until the end of the auction period. Here the bidding amount is in terms of cost/sec. The bidding amount should be greater than the reserve price for that resource. The exact bidding amount depends on the policy being used. At the end of the auction, the resource provider will open the bids and inform the resource brokers whether they won in the auction or not. The maximum bid amount is not revealed to others. This is to prevent resource brokers fro m behaving strategically. A resource broker may learn the bid amount to bid by participating in repeated auctions, but we do not consider it here. If no one participated in the bidding by the end of the auction, the above process is repeated. After the end of the current auction, the resource providers will start new auctions for the next available time slot. The starting time of the next usage is changed in accordance with the current accepted job.

$$S = \Phi$$
$$for\ i = 1\ to\ n\ do$$
$$\quad exec\_time = job\_length / R_i.speed$$
$$\quad completion\_time = R_i.resource\_usage\_start\_time + exec\_time$$
$$\quad if\ ((budget >= (R_i.price*exec\_time))\ AND\ (completion\_time <= deadline)\ )$$
$$\qquad S = S \cup R_i$$

Fig. 1. Algorithm to form resource set S for a job

$$sort\ S\ by\ price$$
$$select\ R_1\ from\ S$$
$$penalty = R_1.speed / max\_speed$$
$$min\_amount\_needed = (job\_length / R_1.speed)*R_1.price$$
$$bid\_amount = budget - (budget - min\_amount\_needed)*penalty$$
$$use\ bid\_amount\ to\ bid\ for\ R_1$$

Fig. 2. Algorithm for the *BudgetOptimized* policy

3   Two Simple Resource Selection Policies

In this section, we first implement two simple policies for resource allocation – *TimeOptimized* and *BudgetOptimized* policies. For each of the policies, the first step involves forming a set S of resources that can complete the job within its deadline and its allocated budget. The algorithm to form S is simple and is shown in Fig. 1. The variables *job_length* and *budget* refers to the length of the job and the budget allocated to it respectively.

After S has been formed, the two policies are defined as follows:

- *TimeOptimized Policy:* In the *TimeOptimized* policy, a user bids for a resource that can complete the job the earliest within the deadline and budget allocated for it. To do this, the resources in S are sorted in increasing order of completion time of the job, and the first resource in the list is bid for. The whole budget allocated to the job is used for bidding for the selected resource to maximize the chance of winning in the auction. If it fails in the current auction, it then chooses the next resource in the sorted list and bids for it. This continues until the job either finds a resource or misses its deadline.

- **BudgetOptimized Policy:** In the *BudgetOptimized* policy, a user will always bid for a resource that costs less but can still complete the job within the deadline and budget allocated for it. To do this, the resources in S are sorted in increasing order of their costs, and the first resource in the list (the lowest cost resource) is bid for. However, unlike the *TimeOptimized* policy, in the *BudgetOptimized* policy, the whole amount allocated to the job is not used for bidding. Instead, a *penalty* is calculated and the bid amount is obtained by reducing the allocated amount in proportion to the penalty. Here penalty is the degradation in performance a user is getting by choosing a lower speed resource. The penalty is high for low speed resources and low for high speed resources. So it bids less for a low speed resource and higher for a high speed resource. If it fails in the current auction, it then chooses the next higher cost resource from the sorted list. This continues until the job either finds a resource or misses its deadline. The pseudocode for the *BudgetOptimized* policy is shown in Fig. 2.

3.1 Simulation Results

We evaluate the above two policies by comparing it with the *Random* policy which has been used in the literature for heterogeneous resources. In the *Random* policy, a resource is chosen at random from the set *S* and is then bid for with the whole amount allocated to the job. If the user fails to win the resource, a resource is again chosen at random from *S* and the process is repeated.

We have used GridSim [5] for evaluating the proposed user selection policies. GridSim is a java based discrete event grid simulation toolkit. The simulated grid environment consists of 15 resources and 10 users. Resources have different processing speeds and reserve prices as given in Table 1. The reserve prices for these machines are chosen in such a way such that the price per MI is increasing when we go from low speed resource to high speed resource. The increase in the amount per MI is the premium paid to the resource for executing the job faster. If we have given the same price per MI for all resources, then the user will always choose high speed resources only. We assumed that each machine executes one job at a time. After completion of the present job it will again start a new auction. There are a total of 50 jobs for each user.

Table 1. MIPS and cost of each machine

M/c MIPS Rating	400	800	1200	1600	2000
Cost/Sec	2	6	10	14	18
No of machines	3	3	3	3	3

Incoming jobs for each user come according to Poisson distribution with mean λ. For all experiments we have taken λ to be 0.01. If we choose a higher λ then most of the jobs fail because of high load. The job deadline includes auction participation time, execution time of job, and waiting time at the resource end. For each job i, the deadline is set according to the following expression.

$$J_i.deadline = E_{ij} + Rand(E_{ij}) + \alpha \qquad (1)$$

where $J_i.deadline$ is the deadline for job i, E_{ij} is the execution time of J_i on R_j where R_j is the slowest resource available in the grid. Execution time is calculated as job length / MIPS of the resource, Rand(E_i) is a random value between 1 and E_{ij}, and α is positive constant. The constant is added to alleviate the effect of time spent on auctions. For all our experiments we took α as 30. This value is equal to the default auction time.

The budget for each job is distributed uniformly over the interval $[\mu_1, \mu_2]$ following other works in the literature. The lower limit μ_1 is given by the product of the smallest length of a job and the lowest reserve price of a resource while the upper limit μ_2 is given by the product of the largest length of a job and the highest reserve price of a resource.

In the first experiment, we implemented *Random, TimeOptimized,* and *BudgetOptimized* policies. The job length in this experiment varies from 10000 MI to 20000 MI. Fig. 3. and Fig. 4. show the number of jobs finishing within their deadlines and the average turnaround time per job in the *TimeOptimized* and the *Random* policies. Fig. 5. and Fig. 6. show the number of jobs finishing within their deadlines and the average budget spent per job in the *BudgetOptimized* and the *Random* policy.

From Fig. 3. and Fig. 4., it is clear that the *TimeOptimized* policy reduces the average turnaround time but the number of jobs finishing within deadline is less than that in the *Random* policy. Similarly, in the *BudgetOptimized* policy, the average budget spent per job is less than that in the *Random* policy but the number of jobs finishing within deadline is also less in the *BudgetOptimized* policy. The advantage of the *Random* policy is that as each user selects the resource randomly, overall there will be less contention for resources, so most of the time users will win in auctions. In the *TimeOptimized* policy there will be high contention for high speed resources and only one user wins in auction and the rest who participated in the auction will fail. These failed jobs again participate in a new auction. This process repeats and eventually many of the jobs miss their deadlines before winning any resource. However, the jobs that actually finish within their deadlines are done on higher speed resources, thereby reducing the average turnaround time. A similar phenomenon happens in the *BudgetOptimized* policy.

Thus the job success rate (the percentage of jobs finishing within their deadlines) in the *TimeOptimized* and the *BudgetOptimized* policies is less when compared with the *Random* policy. In the next section, we present two simple modifications of the *TimeOptimized* and the *BudgetOptimized* policies to improve their job success rate.

4   *k*-TimeOptimized and *k*-BudgetOptimized Policies

In this section we propose two new policies. The first one, *k-TimeOptimized*, tries to minimize the average turnaround time while increasing the number of jobs finishing within their deadlines. The second one, *k-BudgetOptimized*, tries to minimize the average budget spent per job while increasing the number of jobs finishing within their deadlines.

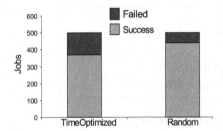

Fig. 3. Job success rate in TimeOptimized and Random policies

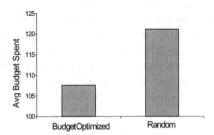

Fig. 4. Average turnaround time per job in TimeOptimized and Random policies

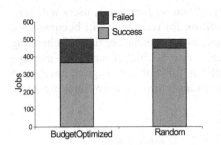

Fig. 5. Job success rate in BudgetOptimized and Random policies

Fig. 6. Average budget spent per job in BudgetOptimized and Random policies

4.1 k-TimeOptimized Policy

In the *k-TimeOptimized* policy, we sort the set S of resources in increasing order of completion time and then select one resource randomly from the top k resources for bidding. The value of k is specified by the user. For $k = 1$ this policy is equivalent to the *TimeOptimized* policy and for $k = n$ this policy is equal to the *Random* policy, where n is the total number of resources in the system. As k increases, the number of jobs finishing within their deadline increases, but the average turnaround time also increases. The pseudocode for this policy is shown in Fig. 7.

4.1.1 Simulation Results

We conducted the experiment for three different job lengths, 10000MI to 20000MI, 50000MI to 100000MI and 100000MI to 200000MI. For each experiment, we varied k from 1 to 15 and we measured the average turnaround time and job success rate. It shows how the job success rate and the average turnaround time vary when we move from the *TimeOptimized* policy to the *Random* policy. Fig. 8. and Fig. 9. show the job success rate and the average turnaround time respectively for different values of k and for different job lengths.

> *sort S by completion_time*
> *for i = k + 1 to S.length do*
>   *remove S_i from S*
> *select randomly one resource R_i from S*
> *use complete amount allocated to job to bid for R_i*

Fig. 7. Algorithm for the *k*-TimeOptimized policy

From Fig. 8. and Fig. 9., it is clear that when we go from $k = 1$ to $k = 15$, in general, the job success rate increases and at the same time the average turnaround time also increases. This is because, at $k = 1$, the behavior is exactly the same as that of the *TimeOptimized* policy. When we increase *k*, users will start choosing resources randomly and the competition for resources will become less. At the same time the average turnaround time is increasing because of choosing lower capability resources. The job success rate is higher and the average turnaround time is lower for lower job lengths as for high job lengths, once a job gets a resource, the resource stays busy for a longer time, thereby making some other jobs miss their deadlines.

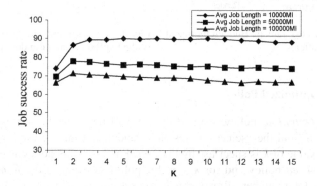

Fig. 8. Job success rate in *k*-TimeOptimized policy for different values of *k*

At $k = 4$ the success rate is fairly high as compared with that at $k = 15$. At $k = 15$ all the users will choose resources randomly and distribution of jobs is random. However, resources with high capability can execute more number of jobs than resources with lower capability. Ideally any policy should distribute more number of jobs to high capability resources and less number of jobs to low capability resources. But when we follow the *Random* policy, jobs will not get distributed in the above manner. So the number of jobs executing is higher at $k = 4$ than for say, $k = 15$.

4.2 k-BudgetOptimized Policy

In the *k-BudgetOptimized* policy, we sort the set S of resources according to cost and we select one resource randomly from the top *k* resources for bidding. At $k = 1$ this policy is equivalent to the *BudgetOptimized* policy, and at $k = n$ this is equal to the *Random* policy. As k increases, the number of jobs finishing within deadline increases but the average budget spent per job also increases. The pseudocode for the *k-BudgetOptimized* policy is shown in Fig. 10.

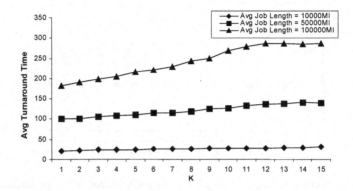

Fig. 9. Average turnaround time in *k*-TimeOptimized policy for different values of *k*

4.2.1 Simulation Results

Similar to the *k-TimeOptimized* policy, we conducted the experiment for three different job lengths. For each experiment, we changed k from 1 to 15 and we measured the average budget spent per job, the job success rate, and the average turnaround time. Fig. 11., Fig. 12., and Fig. 13. show how the average budget spent per job, the job success rate, and the average turnaround time vary when we move from the *BudgetOptimized* policy to the *Random* policy.

From Fig. 11., Fig. 12., and Fig. 13., we see that when we go from $k = 1$ to $k = 15$, the average budget spent per job increases slightly and the job success rate also increases. Similar to the *k-TimeOptimized* policy, at $k = 4$, the job success rate is high and at the same time the average budget spent per job remains low. The reason for this is the same as in the *k-TimeOptimized* policy. As we increase k, the competition

```
Sort S by price
max_speed = R_{S.length}
for i = k + 1 to S.length do
    remove S_i from S
select randomly one resource R_j from S
penalty = R_j.speed / max_speed
min_amount_needed = (job_length / R_1.speed)*R_1.price
bid_amount = budget – (budget –min_amount_needed)*penalty
use bid_amount to bid for R_i
```

Fig. 10. Algorithm for the *k*-BudgetOptimized Policy

for low cost resources will be decreased, so the number of jobs getting executed within their deadlines will be increased. As we increase k, we start choosing resources randomly so the budget spent per job will be increased. The average turnaround time is very high at $k = 1$ because of choosing low cost resources.

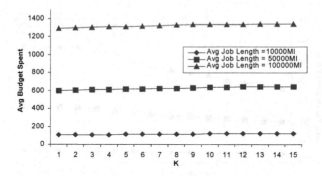

Fig. 11. Average budget spent per job in k-BudgetOptimized policy for different k

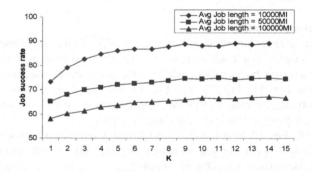

Fig. 12. Job success rate in the k-BudgetOptimized policy for different k

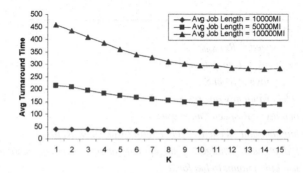

Fig. 13. Average turnaround time in the k-BudgetOptimized policy for different k

5 Conclusion

In this paper, we proposed and evaluated several auction based resource selection policies for users in grid. In all these policies we tried to optimize the average turnaround time, the average budget spent per job, and the job success rate. It would be interesting to investigate the case when the user provides his or her preference on the degree of importance he/she places on time over budget.

References

1. Baker M., Buyya R., and Laforenza D., "Grids and Grid Technologies for Wide-Area Distributed Computing", *Software: Practice and Experience*, Dec 2002, vol. 32, no. 15, pp. 1437-1466.
2. Berman F., Hey A. J. G., and Fox G., "Grid Computing: Making the Global Infrastructure a Reality", John Wiley & Sons, 2003.
3. Buyya R., Abramson D., Giddy J., and Stockinger H., "Economic Models for Resource Management and Scheduling in Grid Computing", *Concurrency and Computation: Practice and Experience*, Nov 2002, vol. 14, no. 13, pp. 1507-1542.
4. Buyya R., Abramson D., and Giddy J., "Nimrod/G: An Architecture for a Resource Management and Scheduling System in a Global Computational Grid", *4th International Conference on High Performance Computing in Asia-Pacific Region*, May 2000.
5. Buyya R. and Murshed M., "GridSim: A Toolkit for the Modeling and Simulation of Distributed Resource Management and Scheduling for Grid Computing", *Concurrency and Computation: Practice and Experience*, Nov. 2002, vol. 14, no. 13, pp. 1175-1220.
6. Chen M., Yang G., and Liu X., "Gridmarket: A Practical, Efficient Market Balancing Resource for Grid and P2P Computing", *2nd International Workshop on Grid and Cooperative Computing (GCC 2003),* Dec. 2003, Lecture Notes in Computer Science, vol. 3033, pp. 612–619.
7. Foster I., "The Anatomy of the Grid: Enabling Scalable Virtual Organizations", *International Journal of High Performance Computing Applications*, 2002, vol. 15, no. 3.
8. Gibbins H., Nadiminti K., Beeson B., Chhabra R., Smith B., and Rajkumar Buyya, "The Australian BioGrid Portal: Empowering the Molecular Docking Research Community", *3rd APAC Conference and Exhibition on Advanced Computing, Grid Applications and eResearch (APAC 2005)*, Sept. 2005.
9. Grosu D. and Das A., "Auction-Based Resource Allocation Protocols in Grids," *16th International Conference on Parallel and Distributed Computing and Systems*, Nov. 2004, pp. 20–27.
10. Kale L. V., Kumar S., Potnuru M., DeSouza J., and Bandhakavi S., "Faucets: Efficient Resource Allocation on the Computational Grid", *International Conference on Parallel Processing (ICPP 2004) "*, Aug. 2004, pp. 396–405.
11. Kant U., Grosu D., "Double Auction Protocols for Resource Allocation in Grids", *International Conference on Information Technology: Coding and Computing (ITCC'05),* 2005, vol. 1, pp. 366-371.
12. Nakai J., "Pricing Computing Resources: Reading between the Lines and Beyond," *Technical Report NAS-01-010, NASA Ames Research Center, Advanced Supercomputing Division,* Nov 2001.

13. Wolski R., Plank J. S., Brevik J., and Bryan T., "Analyzing Market-Based Resource Allocation Strategies for the Computational Grid". *International Journal of High Performance Computing Applications*, Aug. 2001, vol. 15, no. 3, pp. 258-281.
14. Xiao L., Zhu Y., Lionel M., Xu Z., "GridIS: An Incentive-Based Grid Scheduling", *19th IEEE International Parallel and Distributed Processing Symposium (IPDPS'05)*, 2005.
15. Deardorff's Glossary of International Economics, May 2006, http://www.personal.umich.edu/~alandear/glossary/m.html.

MLBLM: A Multi-level Load Balancing Mechanism in Agent-Based Grid

Mohsen Amini Salehi[1], Hossain Deldari[2], and Bahare Mokarram Dorri[3]

[1] Department of Software Engineering, Faculty of Engineering, Islamic Azad University,
Mashhad Branch, Iran
[2] Department of Software Engineering, Ferdowsi University, Mashhad, Iran
[3] Management and Planning Organisation of Khorasan, Mashhad, Iran
Amini@mshdiau.ac.ir, hd@ferdowsi.um.ac.ir, mokarram@mpo-kh.ir

Abstract. A computational grid is a widespread computing environment that provides huge computational power for large-scale distributed applications. Load balancing, has a considerable effect on the grid middleware performance. Current load balancing methods cannot satisfy all necessities for the grid. In this paper, a Multi-level Load Balancing Method (MLBM) is proposed. Cooperation among different levels in this method, removes disadvantages of each level, while satisfy most of load balancing requirements needed. Simulation results indicate that this new mechanism surpasses its predecessors in increasing efficiency and decreasing communication overhead.

1 Introduction

A computational grid is a hardware and software infrastructure that provides consistent, pervasive and inexpensive access to high end computational capacity. An ideal grid middleware should provide access to all the available resources seamlessly and fairly [1].

ARMS is an agent-based resource manger for grid computing which is aimed at provisioning scalability and adaptability [1]. In this system, agents cooperate with each other to achieve resource discovery. Each agent organizes all service information of a resource into Agent Capability Tables (ACTs). The agents are equipped with a performance prediction toolkit called PACE [1], [2] to predict available efficiency of resources. Experiments testify a high level of precision attained through PACE.

Considering the largeness, dynamic resources, and other specifications of the grid, it is impossible to utilize resources in equilibrium, unless using efficient load balancing methods. However, lack of a well-organized load balancing method is a crucial problem in most of grid resource managers, like ARMS.

Taking into account the ARMS specifications and the importance of load balancing, in this work, we attempt to propose a multi layer load balancing mechanism for ARMS.

Load balancing methods are designed essentially to spread the load on resources equally and maximize their utilization while minimizing the total task execution time [3]. Recently, some methods have been suggested for load balancing in the grid [1], [4], [5]. Heuristic approaches are applied in most of these methods.

S. Chaudhuri et al. (Eds.): ICDCN 2006, LNCS 4308, pp. 157–162, 2006.
© Springer-Verlag Berlin Heidelberg 2006

J. Cao implemented a load balancing method in ARMS [1]. As stated in [1], the efficiency of the mechanism highly depends on the number of cooperating ants *(n)* as well as their step count *(m)* which is defined by the grid user itself.

Some load balancing methods, like QLBVR [6], are periodical. It balances the extra load among neighboring nodes according to their average queue length and request arrival rate. This method uses *virtual routing* [6] method for checking the balancing profitability. Virtual routing changes the load balancing difficulty to an optimal routing problem by adding a virtual node in the network system.

In our proposed method, which is provided in the next section, we intend to use the advantages of both attitudes. Furthermore, there is an effective load balancing method in ARMS, which provides an optimal scheduling within a node [2]. We call this method a *'local-level'* load-balancing and we use it as the first level of load balancing in our new multi-layer approach, MLBM.

The rest of the paper is organized as follows: Section 2 contains a survey on current load balancing methods. In Section 3, different levels of MLBM method are described. Performance metrics and simulation results are included in Section 4. At last, we will present the conclusion as well as the relevant future works.

2   Proposed Method

In this section, firstly, a new load balancing method based on ant colony heuristic is proposed, and then a complementary method, which tries to compensate its defects, is suggested. Coupling these two methods with *local-level* will construct MLBM.

In this paper, the number of waiting jobs is considered as a criterion for measuring load in a node.

2.1   Grid-Level Load Balancing

In this level, an echo system of intelligent ants is suggested. Interactions between these ants will result in load balancing throughout the grid. Here, echo system means that the ants are created on demand to achieve load balancing. They may bear offspring or they commit suicide according to their environmental conditions. Every ant in the new mechanism hops *'m'* steps and then balances *'k'* overloaded nodes with *'k'* underloaded. In the next subsections, we will describe the grid-level method.

2.1.1   Creating, Moving and Deciding of Ants
If a node understands that it is overloaded, it can create a new ant with a few steps to balance the load quickly. A memory space, which is divided into an underloaded list *(Min-List)* and an overloaded list *(Max-List)*, is allocated to each ant in which the ant records specifications of the overloaded and underloaded nodes while wanders.

After entering a node, the ant should determine state of the node, i.e. overloaded, underloaded or equilibrium, using its acquired knowledge from the environment. As the state of the node is determined relative to the system conditions, decision making is performed adaptively by applying adaptive fuzzy logic. To make a decision, the ant deploys the node's current workload and its (i.e. the ant's) remained steps as two inputs to the fuzzy inference system. Then, the ant determines the state of the node.

Therefore, If the result is *"overloaded"* or *"underloaded"*, the node specifications must be added to the ant's *max-list* or *min-list*. Subsequently, the corresponding counter for *Max*, *Min*, or *Avg* increases by one.

In special circumstances, especially when an ant's life span is long while the ant is continuing its wandering, its memory may get full, but it still encounters nodes which are overloaded or underloaded. In this situation, if a node load is overloaded, the ant bears a new one with predefined steps. Here, adaptability translates into increasing the number of the ants automatically, whenever there are many overloaded nodes.

2.1.2   Load Balancing, Starting New Itineration

When the ant's hops end, it must start the balancing operation between its overloaded (*Max*) and underloaded (*Min*) elements gathered. After load balancing, the ant must reinitiate to begin a new itineration. One of the fields that must be initiated is the ant's step counts. However, the ant's step counts (*m*) must be relative to system conditions [1]. Therefore, if most of the nodes visited were underloaded or in equilibrium, the ant should prolong its wandering steps, i.e. decrease the load balancing frequency and vice versa. Doing this requires the ant's knowledge about the environment. Adaptive fuzzy logic is again used in determining the next itineration step counts. The controller determines the next step counts (*NextS*) based on the number of overloaded, underloaded and equilibrium nodes visited, along with the step counts during the last itineration (*LastS*). Actually, the former indicates recent condition of the environment, while later reports lifetime history of the ant. This fuzzy system can be stated as a relation as follows:

$$
\begin{aligned}
R_A &: MaxCnt < l,m,h > *MinCnt < l,m,h > *AvgCnt < l,m,h > \\
&* LastS < tl,l,m,h,th > \rightarrow NextS < tl,l,m,h,th,Dead >
\end{aligned}
\tag{1}
$$

If an ant's step counts extend to extreme values, its effect tends to be zero. Based on this premise, one can conclude that an ant with too long step counts does not have any influence on the system balance. In this circumstance, the ant must commit suicide i.e. *NextS* is fired in the *"Dead"* membership function.

2.2   Neighbor-Level Load Balancing

As mentioned before, we use neighbor-level load balancing as the second layer in MLBM. The algorithm of this level works as follows:

In ARMS, agents use PACE to obtain their resource capabilities information. Agents periodically exchange this information with their neighbors. An agent advertises its load information only among its neighbors. Load characteristics of the nodes could be attached to this exchanging information. Moreover, the receiver agent can estimate the time gap between sending and receiving the information as the transmission cost. The agents in the system exchange their status information at periodic interval of time T_s. We opportunistically append our favorite fields to them.

Based on the load information received in the last T_s, the agents estimate the current load of their neighbors in each interval. Then, the agent computes the average load on its neighboring agents. An agent calls itself *"overloaded"* if its load is greater than the average load of its neighbors. Neighbors, whose estimated load is less than the average, form an *active set*. However, because of the transmission cost, sending the agent load to all of the active set members might not be profitable [7]. We compass the problem of profitability using virtual routing [6].

2.3 MLBM: Multi-level Load Balancing Mechanism

Each of the two proposed methods has some defects. Neighbor-level method has a limited vision and grid-level method imposes too much communication overhead and is not fair. Combining these two methods with the *local-level*, would satisfy most of requirements for an ideal load balancing method. Now, MLBM works as follows:

Agents, periodically, exchange their state information in ARMS. Load information is attached to this exchanging data. Each agent uses *local-level* method to make its resources balance. Moreover, each overloaded agent uses *neighbor-level* method, to balance its load with adjacent neighbors. At the same time, some ants may pass through that agent and choose it for further balancing. However, if a node is overloaded, for several periods of time, and it has not been visited during this time, then the node itself creates a new ant to balance its load throughout a wider area.

Consider that in *neighbor-level* method, scattering radius is limited; however this flaw was compensated using ants. On the other side, using *neighbor-level*, the load inequality decreases. This causes fewer ants and less communication overhead. Moreover, as each node uses *neighbor-level* method, even if it is not visited by any ant, it can achieve load balancing. Thus the mechanism is fair.

3 Performance Evaluation

There are a number of performance metrics used to describe grid scheduling systems which are investigated. Let P be the number of agents of ARMS system and W_{pk} ($p=1$, $2... P$) be the workload of the agent p at period k. The average workload is:

$$\overline{W}_k = \frac{\sum_{p=1}^{P} W_{pk}}{P} \qquad (2)$$

The mean square deviation of W_{pk}, which characterizes the load balancing level of the system, is defined as (3). Let T_k be the total time spent in all agents to achieve a load balancing level L_k. Then, load balancing efficiency e_k, is calculated according to (4).

$$L_k = \sqrt{\frac{\sum_{p=1}^{P} (\overline{W}_k - W_{pk})^2}{P}} \qquad (3)$$

$$e_k = \frac{L_0 - L_k}{T_k} \qquad (4)$$

In this work, Agent system, Workload, and Resources are modeled as follows:

- *Agents.* Agents are mapped to a square grid. This simplification has been done in similar works [1], [4], and [5]. All of experiments described later include 400 agents.
- *Workload.* A workload value and corresponding distribution are used to characterize the system workload. The value is generated randomly in each agent.
- *Resources.* Resources are defined in the same way as workload.

4 Simulation Results

First experiment involves total network connections needed. As shown in Fig.1, total communication needed (C), in MLBM, is drastically less than the conditions only grid-level or seminal method [1] is used. It can be seen that the communication count goes flat in the last seconds, when the load balancing frequency decreases.

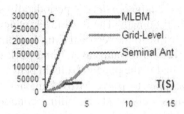

Fig. 1. Comparing communications needed (C) in MLBM, Grid-level, and Seminal method during the time ($T(s)$)

In second experiment, convergence speed is compared between the three methods.

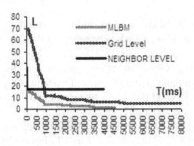

Fig. 2. Convergence speed in MLBM, Grid-level and Neighbor-level methods

For the sake of comparison, we examined balancing level (L) achieved during the time. The results are illustrated in Fig.2. As stated before, slow convergence speed was a defect in neighbor-level method. However, Fig.2 explains that the combination of the two methods cope the disadvantage.

In the last experiment, system efficiency is discussed. Efficiency (e) is calculated for MLBM, grid-level, and seminal ant method [1] during the time (T). Fig.3 proves that MLBM has the best efficiency between others.

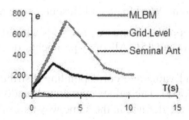

Fig. 3. Comparing efficiency (*e*) between MLBM, grid-level, seminal method in time (*T*)

5   Conclusion and Future Works

In this research, we proposed a multi-level load balancing method (MLBM) for grid environment; overloaded nodes get balances through these layers. In the first layer, which is *'node-level'*, an efficient scheduler tries to use node's resources equally. The second level, which is called *'neighbor-level'*, periodically scatters the extra load of overloaded nodes to a limited domain. The third level, which is *'grid-level'*, is a colony of intelligent ants which spread the regional extra load throughout the grid.

Cooperation of these layers in a multi-layer framework (MLBM) alleviates their disadvantages and, as exhibited in the paper, results in better efficiency.

In our future works, we plan to prove MLBM mathematically, promoting ant's intelligence and adaptation as well as adding billing contracts between resources as they exchange customer loads and overcome security considerations.

References

1. J. Cao: Self-Organizing Agents for Grid Load Balancing, Proc. 5th IEEE/ACM Int. Workshop on Grid Computing.
2. J. Cao, D. P. Spooner, S. A. Jarvis, S. Saini, and G. R. Nudd: Agent-Based Grid Load Balancing Using Performance-Driven Task Scheduling, in Proc. of 17th IEEE Int. Parallel and Distributed Processing Symp. Nice, (2003), 218-224.
3. A. Y. Zomaya and Y. The: Observations on using genetic algorithms for dynamic load-balancing, IEEE Trans. on Parallel and Distributed Systems, (2001), 899-911.
4. M. Amini, H. Deldari: Grid Load Balancing Using an Echo System of Ants, in Proc. Of 24th IASTED Int. Cnf, Innsbruck, (2006) 47–52.
5. M. Amini, H. Deldari: A Novel Load balancing Method in an Agent-based Grid, in Proc. Of IEEE Int. Cnf on Computing and Informatics, Kuala Lumpur, (2006).
6. Z. Zeng and B.Veeravalli: Rate-Based and Queue-Based Dynamic Load Balancing Algorithms in Distributed Systems, Proc. of the 10th Int. Cnf. on Parallel and Distributed Systems, (2004), 156-163.
7. S. Dhakal, B. S. Paskaleva, M. Hayat, E. Schamiloglu, C. T. Abdallah: Dynamical Discrete-Time Load Balancing in Distributed Systems in the presence of Time Delays, in Proc. 42nd IEEE Decision and Control Vol.5, (2003), 5128-5134.

Data Management for a Distributed Hash Table

Reshma Sonar and D.M. Thakore

BVCOE, Pune
RBedre@yahoo.com, deventhakur@yahoo.com

Abstract. This paper presents a new design and implementation of the DHash distributed hash table based on erasure encoding. This design is both more robust and more efficient than the previous replication-based implementation.

DHash uses erasure coding to store each block as a set of fragments. Erasure coding increases availability while saving storage and communication costs compared to a replication based design. DHash combines Chord's synthetic coordinates with the set of fragments to implement server selection on block retrieval.

Experiments with a 270-node DHash system running on the PlanetLab and RON testbeds show that the changes to DHash increase the rate at which the system can fetch data by a factor of six, and decrease the latency of a single fetch by more than a factor of two.The maintenance protocols ensure that DHash is robust without penalizing performance.

1 Introduction

DHTs have been proposed as a way to simplify the construction of large-scale distributed applications. DHTs store blocks of data on a collection of nodes spread throughout the Internet. Each block is identified by a unique key. The goals of these DHTs are to spread the load of storing and serving data across all the nodes and to keep the data available as nodes join and leave the system.

This paper presents a new design, based on erasure coding, for distributing and storing blocks within DHash, an existing DHT implementation. These changes make DHash a robust, efficient and practical DHT for demanding applications such as cooperative backup. Such an application requires that the DHT keep data available despite faults and that the DHT efficiently serve bulk data (unlike, for example, a naming system).

The main contribution of this paper is the way Dhash combines erasure encoded storage with the other techniques and properties of Chord to provide robust and efficient operation.These other techniques include proximity routing, server selection, and successor lists.

1.1 Peer-to-Peer Off-Site Backup

In order to help guide design decisions for DHash, we implemented a cooperative off-site backup system. The off-site backups are intended to complement conventional tape or disk- to-disk backups by adding an extra level of availability and providing a browse able archive of backups. The off-site backup system can be used alone if desired.

S. Chaudhuri et al. (Eds.): ICDCN 2006, LNCS 4308, pp. 163–168, 2006.
© Springer-Verlag Berlin Heidelberg 2006

The off-site backup system's goals are to support recovery after a disaster by keeping snapshots of file systems at other Internet sites. The system spreads the data over many sites in order to balance storage and network load. This striping also allows very large file systems to be backed up onto a set of hosts with individually limited disk space. The backup system performs daily incremental backups; each new backup shares storage with the unchanged part of the previous backups.

The intended users of the backup system are informal groups of people at geographically distributed sites who know each other; for example, colleagues at different university computer science departments. Each site is expected to make available spare disk space on workstations. These workstations are likely to be reasonably reliable and have fairly fast network connections.

Since the backup system sends file system copies over the Internet, communication performance is important; it must be possible to back up a full day's incremental changes to a typical server file system in a few hours. Performance is more sensitive to network throughput than to latency, since the backup system usually has large quantities of data that can be sent concurrently.

1.2 Background: Chord

DHash uses Chord to help determine on which host to store each piece of data. Chord implements a hash-like lookup operation that maps 160-bit data keys to hosts. Chord assigns each host an identifier drawn from the same 160-bit space as the keys. This identifier space can be viewed as a circle, in which the highest identifier is followed by zero.

Each Chord host maintains information about a number of other hosts, to allow it to efficiently map keys to hosts and to allow it to tolerate failures. Chord ensures that each host knows the identity (IP address, Chord identifier, and synthetic coordinates) of its successor: the host with the next highest identifier. This knowledge organizes the hosts into a circular linked list sorted by identifier.

In order to maintain the integrity of this organization if nodes fail, each node actually maintains a successor list, which contains the identities to the 'r' hosts that immediately follow the host in the identifier circle. If a node's successor is not responsive, the node replaces it with the next entry in its successor list.

1.2.1 Chord API
Get successor list(n) is a simple accessor method for the Chord node n. It is implemented as a single network RPC call. lookup(k, m), on the other hand, must send O(log N) RPC s in order to determine the m successors of key k.

Table 1.1. Chord API

Function	Description
Get successor list(n)	Contacts Chord node n and returns 's successor list. Each node in the list includes its Chord ID, IP address and synthetic coordinates
lookup(k, m)	Returns a list of at least m successors of key k. Each node in the list includes its Chord ID, IP address and synthetic coordinates

2 DHash: Distributed Hash Table

The DHash servers form a distributed hash table, storing opaque blocks of data named by the SHA-1 hash of their contents. Clients can insert and retrieve blocks from this hash table. The storage required scales as the number of unique blocks, since identical blocks hash to the same server, where they are coalesced.

DHash allows nodes to enter or leave the system at any time and divides the burden of storing and serving blocks among the servers. To increase data availability, DHash splits each block into 14 fragments using the IDA erasure code. Any 7 of these fragments are sufficient to reconstruct the block.

2.1 DHash API

Table 2.1. DHash API

Function	Description
put(k, b)	Stores the block b under the key k, where k = SHA-1(b).
Get(k)	Fetches and returns the block associated with the key k.

2.2 Block Availability

Like many fault-tolerant storage systems, DHash uses erasure coding to increase availability with relatively little cost in extra storage and communication. DHash uses the IDA erasure code. Given an original block of size s, IDA splits the block into f fragments of size s/k. Any k distinct fragments are sufficient to reconstruct the original block. Fragments are distinct if, in an information theoretic sense, they contain unique information.

IDA has the ability to randomly generate new, probabilistically distinct fragments from the block alone; it does not need to know which fragments already exist. From f randomly generated fragments, any k are distinct with probability greater than (p-1 / p), where p is the characteristic prime of the IDA implementation.

2.3 Block Insert: put(k, b)

When an application wishes to insert a new block, it calls the DHash put(k, b) procedure. The DHash code running on the application's node implements put as follows:

```
Void  put  (k, b)    // place one fragment on each successor
{    frags = IDAencode (b)
     succs = lookup (k, 14)
     for i (0..13)
     send (succs[i].ipaddr, k, frags[i])   }
```

Fig. 2-1. An implementation of DHash's put(k, b) procedure

2.4 Block Fetch: get(k)

In order to fetch a block, a client must locate and retrieve enough IDA fragments to reassemble the original block. The interesting details are in how to avoid communicating with high-latency nodes and how to proceed when some fragments are not available.

When a client application calls get(k), its local DHash first initiates a Chord call to lookup(k, 7), in order to find the list of nodes likely to hold the block's fragments. The lookup call will result in a list of between 7 and 16 of the nodes immediately succeeding key k. get() then chooses the seven of these successors with the lowest latency, estimated from their synthetic coordinates. It sends each of them an RPC to request a fragment of key k, in parallel.

```
 block get (k)
{  // Collect fragments from the successors.
frags = []; // empty array
succs = lookup (k, 7)
sort_by_latency (succs)
for (i = 0; i < #succs && i < 14; i++) {
// download fragment
<ret, data> = download (key, succ[i])
if (ret == OK)
frags.push (data)
// decode fragments to recover block
<ret, block> = IDAdecode (frags)
if (ret == OK)
return (SHA-1(block) != k) ? FAILURE : block
} }   return FAILURE  }
```

Fig. 2-2. An implementation of the DHash's get(k) procedure

3   Fragment Maintenance

A DHash system is in the ideal state when three conditions hold for each inserted block:

1. multiplicity : 14, 15, or 16 fragments exist.
2. distinctness : All fragments are distinct with high probability.
3. location   : Each of the 14 nodes succeeding the block's key store a fragment; the following two nodes optionally store a fragment; and no other nodes store fragments.

3.1 Global DHash Maintenance

The global maintenance protocol pushes misplaced fragments to the correct nodes. Each DHash node scans its database of fragments and pushes any fragment that it stores, but which fail the location condition, to one of the fragment's 14 successor hosts. For efficiency, the algorithm processes contiguous ranges of keys at once.

```
global_maintenance (void)
{ a = myID
while (1) {
<key, frag> = database.next(a)
succs = lookup(key, 16)
if (myID isbetween succ[0] and succ[15])
// we should be storing key
a = myID
else {
// key is misplaced
for each s in succs[0..13] {
response = send_db_keys (s, database[key .. succs[0]])
for each key in response.desired_keys
if (database.contains (key))
upload (s, database.lookup (key))
database.delete (key)
}   database.delete_range ([pred .. succs[0]])
a = succs[0]
} } }
```

Fig. 3-1. An implementation of the global maintenance protocol

the key. Otherwise, the DHash host is storing a misplaced fragment and needs to push it to one of the fragment's 14 successors, in order to restore the location condition.

4 Experiments and Their Interpretation

4.1 Fetch Latency

While we are mainly interested in throughput, the optimizations presented here also improve the latency of an individual block fetch. Figure 4-1 shows the latency of a block fetch with different sets of optimizations. Each bar represents the average of 384 fetches of different blocks, performed one at a time. The dark part of each bar indicates the average time to perform the Chord lookup, and the light part of each bar indicates the time required by DHash to fetch the fragments.

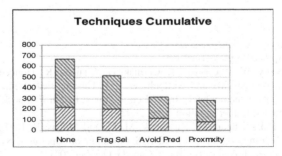

Fig. 4-1. The effect of various optimization techniques on the time required to fetch an 8K block using DHash

Adding fragment selection reduces the amount of time required to fetch the block by fetching fragments from the 7 nodes (of the 14 with fragments) closest to the initiator. This effect of this optimization is visible in the reduced size of the fetch time in the second bar (labeled `Frag Sel'). The lookup time is unchanged by this optimization (the slight variation is likely experimental noise). The third bar adds an optimization that terminates the Chord lookup on a node close to the target key in ID space, but also close to the originating node in latency. This optimization reduces the lookup time while leaving the fragment fetch time unchanged. It shows the importance of avoiding being forced to contact a specific node during the last stages of a lookup.

5 Related Work

DHash closely resembles a number of other storage systems in spirit. The systems include the original replication-based DHash, Tapestry/Pond, and Pas try/PAST. These systems store data in a DHT-like organization, aim to provide high reliability, and efficiency by exploiting proximity. DHash differs from these systems in its implementation approach: DHash's implementation techniques (proximity routing, server selection, congestion control algorithm) are based on a synthetic coordinate system and a protocol for efficient synchronization of data. The advantages of using the synthetic coordinate system are (1) proximity routing, server selection, and congestion control becomes simple and (2) reduces communication traffic, because nodes don't have to be probed.

6 Conclusions

This paper presented the DHash distributed hash table and the mechanisms it uses to provide robust and efficient operation. The design combined have techniques in a novel way. The techniques include erasure coding, replica synchronization, synthetic coordinates, proximity routing, and server selection to provided robust and efficient operation. The design centers around a storage representation which stores each block as a set of erasure encoded fragments. The fragment maintenance protocols restore any destroyed or misplaced fragments caused by system membership changes. The fragments combine with the synthetic coordinates to provide high-throughput and low-latency block fetch and store.

References

[1] Planetlab. http://www.planet-lab.org.
[2] Project Iris. http://www.project-iris.net.
[3] Adya, A., Bolosky, W. J., Castro, M., Cermak, G., Chaiken, R., Douceur, J. R., Howell, J., Lorch, J. R., Theimer, M., and Wattenhofer, R. P. Far-site: Federated, available, and reliable storage for an incompletely trusted environment.In 5th Symposium on Operating Systems Design and Implementation (Dec. 2002).
[4] Andersen, D., Balakrishnan, H., Kaashoek, M. F., and Morris, R. Resilient overlay networks. In Proceedings of the 18th ACM Symposium on Operating Systems Principles (SOSP '01) (Chateau Lake Louise, Ban_, Canada, October 2001).
[5] Anderson, R. J. The eternity service. In Pragocrypt 96 (1996).
[6] BitTorrent website. http://bitconjurer.org/BitTorrent/protocol.html.

DRWT: An Efficient Random Walk Algorithm for Unstructured P2P Networks*

Yiming Zhang, Xicheng Lu, Dongsheng Li, and Nong Xiao

School of Computer, National University of Defense Technology,
Changsha 410073, Hunan, China
ymzhang@nudt.edu.cn

Abstract. In this paper, we present a novel search algorithm called Dynamic Random Walk Team (DRWT), which achieves a better tradeoff between performance and overhead. The main difference between DRWT and the traditional Random Walk algorithms contains two aspects: (1) all nodes advertise their resource sharing information and maintain and broadcast the information with the EDBF-like manner, which discards the information dynamically when transmitted to neighbors; and (2) DRWT extends the concept of walker in traditional Random Walk to search team, which selects its search direction based on the resource location information at each intermediate node. Furthermore, each search team periodically contacts the requesting node and may be required to enhance its search intensity by sending out more walkers based on the distribution of the resource location information to accelerate the search process.

1 Introduction

Random Walk [1] algorithm, including its variations, retains the "blind" nature of query forwarding and then suffers a long delay when searching the resources in large-scale P2P networks. Recently, researchers proposed "informed search", with the main idea that the resource hosting nodes advertise their resource information first [2].

The maintenance and dissemination of the resource information consumes much storage space and bandwidth. To solve this problem, researchers propose schemes to compress the information with Bloom Filter (BF) technology [3,4]. These methods focus on different objectives and can achieve different trade-offs between delay and overhead respectively.

In this paper, we present a novel search mechanism called Dynamic Random Walk Team (DRWT), which achieves a better tradeoff between performance and overhead over previous methods. In DRWT, all nodes advertise their resource sharing information based on a EDBF-like manner, which discards the information dynamically when transmitting it to neighbors to reduce the overhead of the maintenance and dissemination. Each node maintains a neighbor information table to store the resource location information received from its neighbors to forward later queries more efficiently. To

---

* The work was supported by the National Basic Research Program of China (973) under Grant No.2005CB321801.

S. Chaudhuri et al. (Eds.): ICDCN 2006, LNCS 4308, pp. 169–174, 2006.

make sufficient use of the information maintained at each node, DRWT extends the concept of *walker* in traditional Random Walk to *search team*. When requesting resources, the requesting node sends out k query messages (search teams) and each team selects its search direction according to the resource location information at each intermediate node. Furthermore, each team periodically contacts the requesting node and may be required to enhance its search intensity by sending out more walkers (or descendent teams) based on the distribution of the resource location information to accelerate the search process.

2 DRWT Design

In this section, we will introduce the design of DRWT algorithm in detail.

2.1 Dissemination of Resource Information

In DRWT, each node maintains a neighbor information table to store the resource location information to guide queries more efficiently. To reduce the overhead of the maintenance and updating of the tables, we propose an extension of Exponentially Decaying Bloom Filter (EDBF) [3], called Proportional Discarding Bloom Filter (PDBF).

EDBF was proposed to discard some information by a predefined decay factor during the dissemination process [3]. To check if element x is in set S, EDBF returns a value representing the matching degree instead of a simple answer of yes or no. The algorithm to compute the matching degree is as follows. First, describe element x by a vector U of m bits initialized to all 0; second, Use k hash functions to compute $h_1(x)$, $h_2(x)$, ..., $h_k(x)$ and the bits indexed by these results in U are set to 1; third, compute the vector V representing set S by means of the traditional Bloom Filter; last, compute the matching degree of element x with set S by (1) (we use $A(x, S)$ and $A'(U, V)$ to represent it).

$$A(x,S) = A'(U,V) = \sum_{i=1}^{m} (U[i]*V[i]) / \sum_{i=1}^{m} U[i] \tag{1}$$

In EDBF, a node with degree d has a neighbor information table consisting of d entries, each of which is a Bloom Filter vector corresponding to one of its neighbors and maintaining the information of the accessible resources through that neighbor. All nodes advertise their resource sharing information based on an exponentially decaying manner, resetting a certain percentage of bits to 0 at each hop when transmitting to neighbors. The decay factor is predefined and won't change during the whole system lifetime. However, this static, uniform predefined parameter can't adapt to the dynamic and heterogeneous characteristics of P2P systems.

To solve this problem, we present an extension of EDBF, called Proportional Discarding Bloom Filter (PDBF). When disseminating the resource location information to neighbors, PDBF resets (discards) a dynamically selected percentage of bits which are set to 1 in traditional Bloom Filter. The percentage can be adjusted according to the limits such as storage, bandwidth, false positive rate, and so on.

In the rest of this paper, we (1) use $BF(x)$ to represent the Bloom Filter vector of the target resource x; (2) use $BF_{local}(A)$ to represent the Bloom Filter vector of the set of the local resources of node A; (3) use $BF(A, B)$ to represent the Bloom Filter vector of the set of the resources which can be accessed by node A through its neighbor node B (one entry of the neighbor information table of node A); (4) use $BF_{neighbors}(A)$ to represent the Bloom Filter vector of the set of all resources which can be accessed by node A through all of its neighbors; and (5) use $PDBF(A, B)$ to represent the updates which node A sends to its neighbor node B.

The algorithm for handling the updates received by a node (for example, node A) and generating new updates to its neighbors is shown in Fig. 1.

```
Procedure ReceiveAndCreateUpdate (Node A)
//Update NIT of node A and generate new updates //from
node A to each of its neighbors
1 for each U ∈ neighbors(A)
      //Update the entry of NIT related to node U
2     BF(A,U) ← BF(A,U)^ PDBF(U,A) ;
      //Clear the updates to node U
3     PDBF(A,U) ← 0 ;
4     for each V ∈ neighbors(A),V ≠ U
         // Take the union of all PDBFs received from
         // neighbors other than node U
5        PDBF(A,U) ← PDBF(A,U)|PDBF(V,A) ;
      //Add updates of local resources to PDBF(A, U)
6     PDBF(A,U) ← PDBF(A,U)|δ(BF_local(A)) ;
      // Only 1/d information survives
7     d = SelectDiscardProportion();
8     PDBF(A,U) ← PDBF(A,U)/d ;
```

Fig. 1. Algorithm for receiving updates and creating new updates

In order to reduce the bandwidth consumption of the dissemination of the resource location information, all updates are sent to neighbors periodically and created by taking the union (bitwise-OR) of all PDBFs received from neighbors other than the target neighbor and resetting a certain percentage of bits which are set to 1 in the union.

2.2 Dynamic Random Walk Team

To make sufficient use of the information maintained in the neighbor information tables and reduce the query delay, we present DRWT algorithm.

Traditional Random Walk forwards k query messages (walkers). The method of statically setting the value of k works well in small-scale networks, but it is difficult to choose a proper value of k to make a reasonable tradeoff between performance and overhead in large-scale P2P networks.

To solve this problem, we propose a scheme to adjust the value of k dynamically based on the resource location information distributed at intermediate nodes so as to get a better tradeoff between performance and overhead. Dynamic Random Walk Team (DRWT) extends the concept of *walker* in traditional Random Walk to *search team*. Unlike the walkers in traditional Random Walk, search teams have the ability to select the next direction to search and enhance its search intensity under some circumstances. Initially the requesting node sends out k query messages (search teams), and at the intermediate nodes each query is forwarded to the neighbors with the maximum matching degree computed by formula (2) of the target resource x with the accessible resources set S. Each team periodically contacts the requesting node and may be required to enhance its search intensity by sending out more walkers (or descendent teams) based on the distribution of the resource location information. Furthermore, the requesting node can limit the total number of the queries by terminating some uninformed teams.

```
Procedure ForwardQuery (Node B, Team T, Resource x)
// forwarding queries
1 if (HasSeenBefore (B, T))
       //If this query has been processed before
2      Terminate (T);
3      Return 0;
    // This query has not been processed before
4 if ( A'(BF(x),BF(B)) == 1 )
5      Return B;      //Target resource is found at node B.
6 MaxBF ← 0; //The max matching degree
7 CandidateSet ← {null} ;      //The neighbors with MaxBF
8 for each U ∈ neighbors(B)
9      if ( A'(BF(x),BF(B,U)) > MaxBF )
10         MaxBF ← A'(BF(x),BF(B,U)) ;
11         CandidateSet ← {U} ;      //Replace current set
12     if ( A'(BF(x),BF(B,U)) == MaxBF )
13         MaxBF ← A'(BF(x),BF(B,U)) ;
14         CandidateSet ← CandidateSet ∪{U} ;  //Add to current set
15 for each V ∈ CandidateSet
16     SendTeamTo (V);//Forward query to all proper nodes
    // Contact requesting node and send descendent search
    // team if asked
17 ContactRequestingNode(B, MaxBF, CandidateSet);
18 Return 0;
```

Fig. 2. Algorithm for forwarding queries

During the process of searching resource x, DRWT enhances the search intensity mainly in the following three cases.

(1) In large-scale P2P networks, the resource location information from the resource sharing node may decay to 0 long before reaching the questing nodes. Therefore, when

all search teams find nothing about the target resource in n continuous hops, i.e. exist node U, $A'(BF(x), BF_{local}(U)) = 0 \wedge A'(BF(x), BF_{neighbors}(U)) = 0$, each team will send out l new walkers (or descendent teams) to accelerate the search process. All the new walkers (teams) have the same initial TTL (T_{max}).

(2) The first team which finds some location information about the target resource $A'(BF(x), BF_{neighbors}(U)) > 0$ and contacts the requesting node, e.g. team ST at node U, will be required to send out l new walkers (or descendent teams) to enhance the search. Meanwhile, the total number of the queries in the network can be hold by terminating some uninformed teams. Furthermore, to avoid the influence of the bits which are set to 1 in the Bloom Filter vector by other resources, the requesting node may enhance the first m teams (not including the descendents of the enhanced teams) which find some location information.

(3) When a search team finds at a certain node (e.g. node A) that the probability of accessing resource x through one of its neighbor (e.g. node C) equals that through another neighbor (e.g. node D), i.e. $A'(BF(x), BF(A,C)) = A'(BF(x), BF(A,D)) > 0$, or the difference of the two probabilities is smaller than a certain threshold, the search team will send out a descendent team to each of the two neighbors.

The algorithm of DRWT for forwarding queries at a certain node (e.g. node B) is shown in Fig 2.

3   Analysis and Evaluation

We implement and evaluate DRWT in Neurogrid simulator [5].

3.1   Simulation Environments

Table 1 shows the simulation configurations.

Table 1. Simulation Configurations

Configurations	Value	Configurations	Value
common		DRWT	
No. of Nodes	2000	Width of Bloom Filter	64k bit
Average degree of all nodes	4	No. of hash functions	8
Distribution of the degrees	Random	DP (Discard Proportion)	50%
Size of the pool of resources	2000	No. of initial search teams	1
No. of resources per node	1	NH (described as follows)	2
Size of the pool of keywords	1000	NT (described as follows)	3
No. of keys per resource	1	Initial TTL	10

In DRWT, when disseminating the resource location information to neighbors, PDBF resets (discards) DP bits which are set to 1 in traditional Bloom Filter; and when all search teams find nothing about the target resource in NH continuous hops, each team will send out NT new descendent search teams to accelerate the search process.

3.2 Query Delay and Overhead

We carry out 10,000 searches for each algorithm and calculate the average delay and overhead. In DRWT, if there is at least one team finds $A(x,S) \geq 0.25$ according to (1), the requesting node terminates all the teams which find nothing about the target resource and stops the search enhancements, and while in DRWT', the requesting node does nothing to limit the total number of the queries.

Table 2 shows the average query delay and overhead of different algorithms.

Table 2. Average Query Delay and Overhead of Different Algorithms

	Delay (Hops)	Overhead (Messages)
DRWT	6.598	117.0
DRWT'	6.596	156.0
Gnutella	5.176	5990.4
RW	13.663	3607.2
Neurogrid	13.506	150.4

4 Conclusion

This paper present a novel search algorithm called Dynamic Random Walk Team (DRWT). DRWT extends the concept of walker in traditional Random Walk to search team, which selects its search direction based on the resource location information represented by PDBF which is published and disseminated before the search process. Experimental results show that DRWT achieves a better tradeoff between performance and overhead than any of the previous proposals.

References

1. C. Gkantsidis, M. Mihail, and A. Saberi, "Random walks in peer-to-peer networks," in Proceedings of IEEE Infocom, 2004.
2. B. Yang and H. Garcia-Molina. Efficient Search in Peer-to-Peer Networks. Proc. Of the 22nd IEEE International Conference on Distributed Computing Systems (ICDCS), Vienna, Austria, July 2002.
3. Abhishek Kumar, Jun (Jim) Xu and Ellen W. Zegura, "Efficient and Scalable Query Routing for Unstructured Peer-to-Peer Networks", in Proceedings of IEEE Infocom, 2005.
4. Deke Guo, Honghui Chen and Xueshan Luo, "Theory and Network Application of Dynamic Bloom Filters", in Proceedings of IEEE Infocom, 2006.
5. S. R. H Joseph. NeuroGrid: Semantically Routing Queries in Peer-to-Peer Networks. Proc. of International Workshop on Peer-to-Peer Computing, Pisa, Italy, 2002.

Stochastic Models of IEEE 802.11e Wireless Networks with Multimedia Applications*

Anurag Kumar

Department of Electrical Communication Engineering,
Indian Institute of Science, Bangalore 560 012, India
anurag@ece.iisc.ernet.in

Abstract. We provide a survey of some of our recent results ([9], [13], [4], [6], [7]) on the analytical performance modeling of IEEE 802.11 wireless local area networks (WLANs). We first present extensions of the decoupling approach of Bianchi ([1]) to the saturation analysis of IEEE 802.11e networks with multiple traffic classes. We have found that even when analysing WLANs with unsaturated nodes the following state dependent service model works well: when a certain set of nodes is nonempty, their channel attempt behaviour is obtained from the corresponding fixed point analysis of the saturated system. We will present our experiences in using this approximation to model multimedia traffic over an IEEE 802.11e network using the enhanced DCF channel access (EDCA) mechanism. We have found that we can model TCP controlled file transfers, VoIP packet telephony, and streaming video in the IEEE802.11e setting by this simple approximation.

Keywords: performance analysis of wireless LANs, QoS in WLANs, multimedia traffic performance over WLANs.

1 Introduction

Mathematical modeling has always been essential for the analysis and design of engineering systems. Particularly when dealing with systems involving a large number of entities that interact in complex ways, the experimental method is extremely limited. Good analytical models are necessary for sieving through the many design alternatives, and for providing general insights into phenomena. Ad hoc and mobile wireless networks present highly complex situations, as the devices have random and time varying relationships, and their interactions depend critically on the radio propagation environment and user behaviour. In this paper we will survey our work on some recent advances in the stochastic modeling of infrastructure wireless networks that adhere to the IEEE 802.11 standard. The complexity we tackle is that of multimedia traffic (voice, TCP controlled transfers, and streaming video) being carried on the service differentiation mechanisms of the IEEE 802.11e standard.

---

* This work was supported in part by a research grant from IFCPAR (Indo-French Centre for the Promotion of Advanced Research) under Project No. 2900-IT, and in part by a research grant from Intel (India).

S. Chaudhuri et al. (Eds.): ICDCN 2006, LNCS 4308, pp. 175–192, 2006.

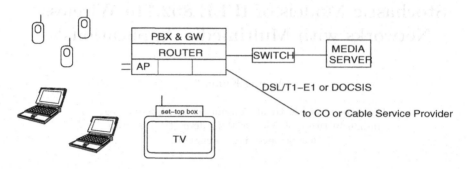

Fig. 1. An infrastructure wireless LAN carrying voice, video and TCP transfers; GW denotes a VoIP gateway

The original IEEE 802.11 medium access control (MAC) mechanism provided no means for differentiating the channel access provided to the contending devices. Such differentiation would be required in a situation such as that depicted in Figure 1, where different traffic types are carried on the WLAN. A new addition to the IEEE 802.11 suite of standards, IEEE 802.11e, now provides several access differentiation mechanisms within the distributed coordination function (DCF), a form of CSMA/CA. These mechanisms are collectively called EDCF (enhanced DCF). Access is differentiated by permitting devices (more precisely, queues within devices) to have different channel access parameters, such as the initial back-off window, the back-off multiplier, and the maximum back-off window. Another mechanism is that, after every channel activity, nodes with a lower access priority wait for a little longer than other nodes before reinitiating their back-off and attempt processes, thus giving the higher priority class nodes a better chance to access the channel. The time for which traffic classes wait after a channel activity is called an AIFS (arbitration interframe space).

We will begin by presenting some results on the saturation throughput analysis of single cell WLANs. By a single cell is meant that all nodes can decode each others transmissions, and hence only one successful transmission can take place at a time. Saturation throughput is the rate at which packets depart the nodes when every node has an unlimited number of packets to send. The standard technique for carrying out such saturation analysis is based on the seminal contribution of G. Bianchi ([1]), which was recently extended by us ([9]) via a more general fixed-point formulation. The fixed-point based saturation analysis has now also been done for IEEE 802.11e networks, thus paving the way for analysis of multimedia traffic in WLANs. In this paper we begin by surveying our work on the generalisations of fixed-point based saturation analysis of IEEE 802.11e networks ([13]).

Saturation throughput is an important measure, as in some situations the arrival rate being less than saturation throughput has been found to be sufficient for stability (see, for example, [10]). We have found that even when analysing WLANs with unsaturated nodes the following approximation works very well:

when a certain set of nodes is nonempty, their channel attempt behaviour is obtained from the corresponding fixed point analysis of the saturated system. In this paper, we survey our results on applying this approximation technique to analyse the performance and capacity of a single cell WLAN carrying constant bit rate VoIP telephone calls, TCP controlled file downloads, and streaming video ([11], [4], [6], [5], [7]).

2 Saturation Throughput Analysis of EDCF

2.1 The Case Without AIFS

There are n nodes, indexed by $i, 1 \leq i \leq n$. We begin with considering the case in which each node has one EDCA queue. We adopt the notation in [9], whose authors consider a generalisation of the back-off behaviour of the nodes, and define the following back-off parameters (for node i)

$K_i :=$ At the $(K_i + 1)$th attempt either the packet being attempted by node i
     succeeds or is discarded

$b_{i,k} :=$ The *mean* back-off (in slots) at the kth attempt for a packet by node i,
     $0 \leq k \leq K_i$

It has been shown in [9] that under the decoupling assumption, introduced by Bianchi in [1], the attempt probability of node i (in a back-off slot, and conditioned on being in back-off) for given collision probability γ_i is given by,

$$G_i(\gamma_i) := \frac{1 + \gamma_i + \cdots + \gamma_i^{K_i}}{b_{i,0} + \gamma_i b_{i,1} + \cdots + \gamma_i^{K_i} b_{i,K_i}} \tag{1}$$

In the exponentially increasing back-off case, with multiplier p (e.g., $p = 2$) $G(\cdot)$ becomes,

$$G(\gamma) = \frac{1 + \gamma + \gamma^2 + \cdots + \gamma^K}{b_0(1 + p\gamma + p^2\gamma^2 + \cdots + p^K\gamma^K)} \tag{2}$$

With the slotted model for the back-off process and the decoupling assumption, the natural mapping of the attempt probabilities of other nodes to the collision probability of a node is given by

$$\gamma_i = \Gamma_i(\beta_1, \beta_2, \ldots, \beta_n) = 1 - \prod_{j=1, j \neq i}^{n} (1 - \beta_j)$$

where $\beta_j = G_j(\gamma_j)$. We could now expect that the equilibrium behaviour of the system will be characterised by the solutions of the following system of equations. For $1 \leq i \leq n$,

$$\gamma_i = \Gamma_i(G_1(\gamma_1), \cdots, G_n(\gamma_n))$$

We write these n equations compactly in the form of the following multidimensional fixed point equation.

$$\gamma = \mathbf{\Gamma}(\mathbf{G}(\gamma)) \qquad (3)$$

Since $\mathbf{\Gamma}(\mathbf{G}(\gamma))$ is a composition of continuous functions it is continuous. We thus have a continuous mapping from $[0,1]^n$ to $[0,1]^n$. Hence by Brouwer's fixed point theorem there exists a fixed point in $[0,1]^n$ for the equation $\gamma = \mathbf{\Gamma}(\mathbf{G}(\gamma))$.

Definition 1. *We say that a fixed point γ (i.e., a solution of $\gamma = \mathbf{\Gamma}(\mathbf{G}(\gamma))$) is* **balanced** *if $\gamma_i = \gamma_j$ for all $1 \leq i, j \leq n$; otherwise, γ is said to be an* **unbalanced fixed point.** ∎

It is clear that if there exists an unbalanced fixed point for a *homogeneous* system (i.e., one for which all the nodes have the same back-off parameters), then every permutation is also a fixed point and hence, in such cases, we do not have a unique fixed point. In [13], it has been shown by simulation examples that, in general, there can exist unbalanced fixed points in the homogeneous case, and in such situations the balanced fixed point of the system does not characterise the average performance, even if there exists only one balanced fixed point. It is therefore of interest to determine conditions under which the system of fixed point equations has a unique fixed point. The following is a sufficient condition.

Theorem 1 (Ramaiyan et al. [13]). *If $G_i(\gamma)$ is a decreasing function of γ for all i and $(1 - \gamma)(1 - G_i(\gamma))$ is a strictly monotone function on $[0,1]$, then the system of equations $\beta_i = G_i(\gamma_i)$ and $\gamma_i = \Gamma_i(\beta_1, \ldots, \beta_i, \ldots, \beta_n), 1 \leq i \leq n$, has a unique fixed point.* ∎

Where nodes use exponentially increasing back-off, as in the IEEE 802.11 standard, the next result then follows.

Theorem 2 (Ramaiyan et al. [13]). *For a system of nodes $1 \leq i \leq n$, with $G_i(\cdot)$ as in (2), that satisfy $K_i \geq 1$, $p_i \geq 2$ and $b_{0_i} > 2p_i + 1$, there exists a unique fixed point for the system of equations, $\gamma_i = 1 - \prod_{j \neq i}(1 - G_j(\gamma_j))$, $1 \leq i \leq n$.* ∎

Remark 1. While Theorem 2 only states a sufficient condition, it does point to a caution in choosing the back-off parameters of the nodes. ∎

2.2   Analysis of the AIFS Mechanism

Our approach for obtaining the fixed point equations when the AIFS mechanism is included is the same as the one developed in [15]. However, in [13] we develop the analysis in the more general framework introduced in [9].

In legacy DCF, a node decrements its back-off counter and then attempts to transmit only after it senses an idle medium for more than a DCF interframe space (DIFS). However, in EDCA (Enhanced Distributed Channel Access; see

[12]), based on the access category of a node (and its AIFS value), a node attempts to transmit only after it senses the medium idle for more than its AIFS. Higher priority nodes have smaller values of AIFS, and hence obtain a lower average collision probability, since these nodes can decrement their back-off counters, and even transmit, in slots in which lower priority nodes (waiting to complete their AIFSs) cannot. Thus, *nodes of higher priority (lower AIFS) not only tend to transmit more often but also have fewer collisions compared to nodes of lower priority (larger AIFS).* The model we use to analyze the AIFS mechanism is quite general and accommodates the actual nuances of AIFS implementations (see [2] for how AIFS and DIFS differs) when the AIFS parameter values and the sampled back-off values are suitably adjusted.

2.3 One Traffic Class per Node

Let us consider two classes of nodes of two different priorities. The priority for a class is supported by using AIFS as well as b_0, p and K. All the nodes of a particular priority have the same values for all these parameters. There are $n^{(1)}$ nodes of Class 1 and $n^{(0)}$ nodes of Class 0. Class 1 corresponds to a higher priority of service. The AIFS for Class 0 exceeds the AIFS of Class 1 by l slots. For example, in the standard, the queues of Access Category 1 (AC 1) wait 1 extra slot beyond the queues of AC 3; i.e., $l = 1$ in this case. Thus, after every transmission activity in the channel, while Class 0 nodes wait to complete their AIFS, Class 1 nodes can attempt to transmit in those l slots. Also, if there is any transmission activity (by Class 1 nodes) during those l slots, then again the Class 0 nodes wait for another additional l slots compared to the Class 1 nodes, and so on.

As in [1] and [9], we need to model only the evolution of the back-off process of a node (i.e., the back-off slots after removing any channel activity such as transmissions or collisions) to obtain the collision probabilities. For convenience, let us call the slots in which only Class 1 nodes can attempt as *excess AIFS* slots, which will correspond to EA in the notation. In the *remaining* slots (corresponding to R in the notation) nodes of either class can attempt. Let us view such groups of slots, where different sets of nodes contend for the channel, as different *contention periods*. Let us define

$\beta_i^{(1)} :=$ the attempt probability of a Class 1 node for all $i, 1 \le i \le n^{(1)}$, in the slots in which a Class 1 node can attempt (i.e., all the slots)

$\beta_i^{(0)} :=$ the attempt probability of a Class 0 node for all $i, 1 \le i \le n^{(0)}$, in the contention periods during which Class 0 nodes can attempt (i.e., slots that are not Excess AIFS slots)

Note that in making these definitions we are modeling the attempt probabilities for Class 1 as being constant over all slots, i.e., the Excess AIFS slots and the remaining slots. This simplification is just an extension of the basic decoupling approximation, and has been shown to yield results that match well with simulations (see [15]).

Now the collision probabilities experienced by nodes will depend on the contention period (*excess AIFS* or *remaining* slots) that the system is in. The approach is to model the evolution over contention periods as a Markov Chain over the states $(0, 1, 2, \cdots, l)$, where the state s, $0 \leq s \leq (l-1)$, denotes that an amount of time equal to s slots has elapsed since the end of the AIFS for Class 1. These states correspond to the *excess AIFS* period in which *only* Class 1 nodes can attempt. In the *remaining* slots, when the state is $s = l$, *all* nodes can attempt. Analysis of this Markov chain provides $\pi(EA)$, the fraction of slots in which only Class 1 can attempt, and $\pi(R)$, the fraction of slots in which both classes can attempt. The transition probabilities of this Markov chain are functions of $\beta_i^{(1)}$, $1 \leq i \leq n^{(1)}$, and $\beta_i^{(0)}$, $1 \leq i \leq n^{(0)}$, defined above; see [13] for these details.

The average collision probability of a node is then obtained by averaging the collision probability experienced by a node over the different contention periods. The average collision probability for Class 1 nodes is given by, for all i, $1 \leq i \leq n^{(1)}$,

$$\gamma_i^{(1)} = \pi(EA)\left(1 - \prod_{j=1, j \neq i}^{n^{(1)}}(1 - \beta_j^{(1)})\right) + \pi(R)\left(1 - \left(\prod_{j=1, j \neq i}^{n^{(1)}}(1 - \beta_j^{(1)})\prod_{j=1}^{n^{(0)}}(1 - \beta_j^{(0)})\right)\right)$$

(4)

Similarly, the average collision probability of a Class 0 node is given by, for all i, $1 \leq i \leq n^{(0)}$,

$$\gamma_i^{(0)} = 1 - \left(\prod_{j=1}^{n^{(1)}}(1 - \beta_j^{(1)})\prod_{j=1, j \neq i}^{n^{(0)}}(1 - \beta_j^{(0)})\right)$$

(5)

Define $G^{(1)}(\cdot)$ and $G^{(0)}(\cdot)$ as in (1) (except that the superscripts here denote the class dependent back-off parameters, with nodes within a class having the same parameters). Then the average collision probability obtained from the above equations can be used to obtain the attempt rates by using the relations

$$\beta_i^{(1)} = G^{(1)}(\gamma_i^{(1)}), \text{ and } \beta_j^{(0)} = G^{(0)}(\gamma_j^{(0)})$$

(6)

for all $1 \leq i \leq n^{(1)}, 1 \leq j \leq n^{(0)}$. We obtain fixed point equations for the collision probabilities by substituting the attempt probabilities from (6) into (4) and (5) (and also into the expressions for $\pi(EA)$ and $\pi(R)$). We have a continuous mapping from $[0, 1]^{n^{(1)}+n^{(0)}}$ to $[0, 1]^{n^{(1)}+n^{(0)}}$. It follows from Brouwer's fixed point theorem that there exists a fixed point.

In the same manner as Theorem 2, the following result has been obtained in [13].

Theorem 3. *If $G^{(0)}(\cdot)$ and $G^{(1)}(\cdot)$ are of the form in (2), and if $K^{(i)} \geq 1, p^{(i)} \geq 2$, and $b_0^{(i)} > 2p^{(i)} + 1$, for $i = 0, 1$, then the fixed point will be unique.* ∎

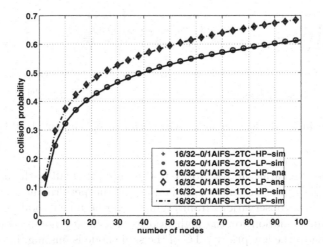

Fig. 2. Collision probability of high priority TC (HP) and low priority TC (LP) in a system of nodes with two TCs (see the plots with "2TC" in their legend). Both simulation (sim) and analysis (ana) are plotted. Also plotted is the collision probability (from simulation) of two classes of nodes when the two TCs of a node are considered as independent TCs in separate nodes (these are plots with "1TC" in their legend).

2.4 Multiple Traffic Classes per Node

The above fixed point analysis can be generalised to include the possibility of multiple traffic classes (or queues) per node. We consider n nodes and c_i traffic classes (TCs) per node i; the TCs can be of either AIFS class (for simplicity, we consider only two AIFS classes) and $c_i = c_i^{(1)} + c_i^{(0)}$ (the superscripts refering to the AIFS classes as before). The TCs in a node need not have the same $G(\cdot)$. Since there are multiple TCs per node, each with its own back-off process, it is possible that two or more TCs in a node complete their back-offs at the same slot. This is then called *virtual collision*, and is resolved in favour of the queue with the highest *collision priority* in the node. Unlike the single traffic class per node case where a collision is caused whenever any two nodes (equivalently, TCs) attempt in a slot, here, a TC sees a collision in a slot only when a TC of some other node or a higher priority TC of the same node attempts in that slot. A low priority TC of a node cannot cause collision to a higher priority TC in the same node. The details of the fixed point equations and their analysis are available in [14].

Figure 2 plots performance results for the multiple TCs per node case. We consider a set of nodes, each with two traffic classes. The higher priority TC has $b_0 = 16$ and AIFS = DIFS, while the low priority TC has $b_0 = 32$ and AIFS = DIFS + 1 slot; $p = 2$ and $K = 7$ for either case. Figure 2 plots the collision probability of the high priority TC and the low priority TC from simulation as well as the analysis. Also plotted is the collision probability for the two classes of nodes (from simulation) obtained by modeling the two TCs in a node as inde-

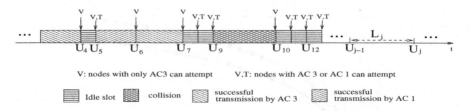

Fig. 3. An evolution of the channel activity with two ACs in 802.11e WLANs (From [6] © IEEE)

pendent TCs in separate nodes. Notice that except for small n, the performance of the multiple queue per node case is close to the performance of the single queue case. These observations from Figure 2 can be understood as follows. In the fixed point equation for the high priority TC in any node, only one term corresponding to the low priority TC of the same node is missing, in comparison to the case in which all the TCs are in $2n$ separate nodes. Hence, as n increases, the effect of this single TC in the same node diminishes, and the performance of the multiple queue per node case coincides with the performance of the single queue per node case each with one of the original TCs.

Remark 2. This observation is crucial for the analysis approach in Section 3, as it permits us to only work with an aggregate state variable for all the voice STAs and another aggregate variable for all the STAs that are downloading TCP controlled file transfers. Without the above observation we would have had to keep track of the state of individual queues in each node. ∎

3   CBR VoIP and TCP File Downloads over EDCF

We now provide a model that can predict the performance of a single cell infrastructure IEEE 802.11e WLAN, under a scenario where VoIP and TCP controlled file download traffic are carried over EDCA, over AC 3 and AC 1, respectively. Using the model, we find the maximum number of voice calls that can be carried with and without file downloads and the aggregate file download throughput for each number of admissible voice calls. We assume that there are no bit errors, and packets in the channel are lost only due to collisions.

3.1   The Modeling Approach

We follow the modeling approach of Kuriakose [11] and Harsha et al. [4], where only the IEEE 802.11 WLAN is analyzed for voice traffic and for TCP traffic separately. The following is the outline of the approach:

1. Embed the number of active nodes at *channel slot boundaries* (see Figure 3). Each channel slot begins with a system slot (20 μsec), during which nodes (that are allowed to attempt) count down their back-off counters. If no node

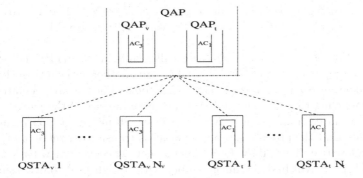

Fig. 4. An IEEE 802.11e WLAN model scenario where VoIP calls and TCP traffic are serviced on EDCA (From [6] © IEEE)

attempts at the end of the system slot, a new channel slot starts. If a node attempts at the end of this slot, then there is either a collision or a success, followed by a DIFS interval, at the end of which the next channel slot starts. If there is an idle channel slot, then in the next channel slot it is possible that a lower priority class may also be able to attempt (see Figure 3).

2. When a set of nodes are active (i.e., have nonempty queues) at a channel slot boundary, then the attempt probabilities of the nodes in the set are taken to be the same as if we had that set of *saturated* nodes. This saturation attempt probability is obtained from the fixed point analysis described above in Section 2.

3. Using these *state dependent attempt probabilities* we model the evolution of the number of contending nodes at channel slot boundaries as a discrete time Markov chain (DTMC). In conjunction with the random length channel slots, we obtain a Markov renewal process.

4. The stationary probability vector π of this DTMC is obtained, and then a Markov regenerative argument is used to obtain the performance measures.

Since VoIP traffic and TCP traffic could be handled at the same node we have multiple queues per node. However, as discussed earlier, in Section 2.4, the performance of the *multiple queues per node* case coincides with the performance of the *single queue per node* case, each node with one queue of the original system; basically the probability of virtual collision within a node is small. This observation leads to substantial reduction in the complexity of our analysis. We make use of this observation and consider the VoIP traffic and TCP traffic as originating from different nodes. Thus, let N_v be the number of full duplex CBR VoIP calls in the WLAN, involving N_v QoS enabled stations (QSTAs), each carrying one VoIP call. Similarly, let N_t be the number of QSTAs downloading TCP traffic in the WLAN, each having one session. The 802.11e AP (QAP) is viewed as two nodes: QAP_v having a queue for AC 3 VoIP traffic for all VoIP calls, and the other, QAP_t, having a queue for AC 1 TCP traffic to serve all TCP downloads. This model is illustrated in Figure 4. Note that at any time the WLAN in Figure 4 can be seen to consist of $N_v + N_t + 2$ nodes. We call the QSTAs with AC 3 as $QSTA_v$ and QSTAs with AC 1 as $QSTA_t$.

Modeling VoIP Phone Calls: Each VoIP call results in two RTP/UDP streams, one from a remote client to a wireless QSTA, and another in the reverse direction. We assume that each call uses the ITU G711 codec. Packets are generated every 20 ms. Including the IP, UDP and RTP headers, the size of the packet emitted in each call in each direction is 200 bytes every 20 ms. As a QoS requirement we demand that the probability that a packet is transmitted successfully within 20 ms is close to 1. Thus, if the QoS target is met, whenever a new packet arrives at a $QSTA_v$, it will find the queue empty with a high probability. Hence, the following three assumptions will be acceptable in the region where we want to operate: (1) the buffer of every $QSTA_v$ has a queue length of at most one packet, and (2) new packets arriving to the $QSTA_v$s arrive only at empty queues. The latter assumption implies that if there are k $QSTA_v$s with voice packets then, a new voice packet arrival comes to a $(k + 1)^{th}$ $QSTA_v$. (3) Since the QAP_v handles packets from N_v streams, there can be up to N_v packets of different calls in the QAP_v. Thus we expect that QAP_v is the bottleneck for voice traffic, and we assume that it will contend at all times (at least when N_v is large). This is a realistic assumption near system capacity.

As mentioned earlier, packets arrive every 20 ms in every stream. We use this model in our simulations. However, since our analytical approach is via Markov chains, we assume that the probability that a voice call generates a packet in an interval of length l slots is $p_l = 1 - (1 - \lambda)^l$, where λ is obtained as follows. Each system slot in 802.11b is of $20\mu s$ duration (hereafter denoted as δ). Thus in 1000 system slots there is one arrival. Therefore, for the 802.11b PHY we take $\lambda = 0.001$. This simplification turns out to yield a good approximation.

Modeling TCP Controlled File Downloads: Each $QSTA_t$ has a single TCP connection to download a large file from a local file server. Hence, the QAP_t delivers TCP data packets towards the $QSTA_t$s, while the $QSTA_t$s return TCP ACKs. Here we assume that when a $QSTA_t$ receives data from the QAP_t, it immediately sends an ACK, i.e., we do not model delayed ACKs here, though the delayed ACKs case can also be done (see [11]). We assume that QAP_t and the $QSTA_t$s have buffers large enough so that TCP data packets or ACKS are not lost due to buffer overflows. Since, by assumption, there are no bit errors, packets in the channel are lost only due to collisions. Also, we assume that these collisions are recovered by the MAC before TCP time-outs occur. As a result of these assumptions, for large file transfers, the TCP window will grow to its maximum value and stay there. As N_t is increased this assumption is close to what happens in reality.

We then adopt an observation made by Bruno et al. [3]. Since all nodes with AC 1 (including the QAP_t) will contend for the channel and no preference is given to the QAP_t, most of the packets in the TCP window will get backlogged at the QAP_t. The QAP_t's buffer is served FIFO, and we can assume that the probability that a packet transmitted by the QAP_t to a particular $QSTA_t$ is $\frac{1}{N_t}$.

Thus it is apparent that the larger the N_t, the lower is the probability that the QAP_t sends to the same $QSTA_t$ before receiving the ACK for the last packet sent. Then it is assumed that the probability that any $QSTA_t$ has more than one ACK is negligible. We can thus simply keep track of the *number* of $QSTA_t$ with ACKs. If there are several $QSTA_t$s with ACKs then the chance that QAP_t succeeds in sending a packet is small. Thus the system has a tendency to keep most of the packets in the QAP_t with a few nonempty $QSTA_t$s, each having ACKs to send back. This results in a closed system, wherein each time the QAP_t succeeds, it activates a $QSTA_t$ which then has an ACK packet, and each time a $QSTA_t$ succeeds, the number of non-empty $QSTA_t$s reduces by one.

Thus for the $QSTA_t$s that are downloading files, our modeling assumptions are: (1) a $QSTA_t$ has either 0 or 1 ACK packet waiting to be sent to the QAP_t, and (2) when the QAP_t sends a data packet it is assumed to be destined to a $QSTA_t$ that has no ACK queued.

3.2   The Analytical Model

We provide an outline of the mathematical model. The details are available in [6]. The evolution of the channel activity in the network is as in Figure 3. U_j, $j \in 0, 1, 2, 3, \ldots$, are the successive channel slot boundaries. Thus the interval $[U_{j-1}, U_j)$ is the jth channel slot. Let the time length of the jth channel slot be L_j (see Figure 3). Let $Y_j^{(v)}$ be the number of non-empty $QSTA_v$s, and $Y_j^{(t)}$ be the number of non-empty $QSTA_t$s at the instant U_j. Thus $0 \le Y_j^{(v)} \le N_v$ and $0 \le Y_j^{(t)} \le N_t$. Figure 3 shows the evolution of the channel activity when AC 3 and AC 1 queues are active; here the value of $l = 1$, i.e., the AIFS for AC 1 is one slot more than that of AC 3. Note that at the instants U_4, U_6, U_7 and U_{10}, only AC 3 nodes can contend for the channel, whereas AC 1 nodes have still to wait for one more system slot to be able to contend. At other instants, U_5, U_8, U_{11} and U_{13}, nodes with AC 3 or AC 1 can attempt. The AC attempt probabilities obtained from Section 2 above are conditioned on when an AC can attempt. Thus, we use the variable $Y_j^{(s)}$ to keep track of which ACs are permitted to attempt in a channel slot. Let $Y_j^{(s)} = 1$ denote that the preceding channel slot had an activity and so in the beginning of the jth channel slot, only nodes with AC 3 can attempt. Let $Y_j^{(s)} = 0$ denote that the preceding channel slot remained idle and hence, at the beginning of the jth channel slot any node can attempt. Thus $Y_j^{(s)} \in \{0, 1\}$.

In order to assess the voice capacity, we take the queue QAP_v to be saturated. However, to obtain the TCP throughput with different number of voice calls, we also need to model the number of voice packets in QAP_v. For this we introduce another variable, $X_j^{(v)}$, the number of voice packets in QAP_v.

Thus, for determining the voice capacity we work with the process $\{Y_j^{(v)}, Y_j^{(t)}, Y_j^{(s)}; j \ge 0\}$, and for studying TCP throughputs, for different number of voice calls, we work with the process $\{Y_j^{(v)}, Y_j^{(t)}, Y_j^{(s)}, X_j^{(v)}; j \ge 0\}$. In either case, in order to model the evolution of these processes we introduce the following approximation. We use the attempt probabilities obtained above in Section 2. Let $\beta_{n_v,n_t}^{(v)}$ be the attempt probability of a node with AC 3 and $\beta_{n_v,n_t}^{(t)}$ be the attempt probability of a node with AC 1, when there are n_v nonempty (and hence contending) VoIP nodes and n_t nonempty TCP nodes in a channel slot. These attempt probabilities are conditioned on the event that the corresponding ACs can attempt (which information we have taken care to keep in the state, via the variable $Y_j^{(s)}$)), and are obtained from saturation fixed point analysis above in Section 2 for all combinations of n_v, n_t. Our approximation is that the state dependent values of attempt probabilities from the saturated nodes case can be used for a WLAN where the nodes are not saturated, by keeping track of the number of nonempty nodes in the WLAN and taking the state dependent attempt probabilities corresponding to this number of nonempty nodes.

With the binomial distribution for voice packet arrivals assumed above, and the state dependent probabilities of attempt, it is easily seen that $\{Y_j^{(v)}, Y_j^{(t)}, Y_j^{(s)}; j \geq 0\}$ or $\{Y_j^{(v)}, Y_j^{(t)}, Y_j^{(s)}, X_j^{(v)}; j \geq 0\}$ form finite irreducible discrete time Markov chains on the channel slot boundaries and hence are positive recurrent. The stationary probabilities of the Markov Chains can then be numerically determined. Next the state dependent attempt probabilities are used to obtain the distribution of the channel slot duration. On combining the channel slot length analysis with the Markov chains above, we finally conclude that $\{(Y_j^{(v)}, Y_j^{(t)}, Y_j^{(s)}; U_j), j = 0, 1, 2, \ldots\}$, or $\{(Y_j^{(v)}, Y_j^{(t)}, Y_j^{(s)}, X_j^{(vAP)}; U_j), j \geq 0\}$ are Markov renewal processes. When analysing the voice capacity we let A_j denote the "reward" of value 1 in the process $\{(Y_j^{(v)}, Y_j^{(t)}, Y_j^{(s)}; U_j), j = 0, 1, 2, \ldots\}$ when the QAP_v wins the channel contention in jth channel slot. When analysing the TCP throughput, we let R_j denote a reward of value 1 in the process $\{(Y_j^{(v)}, Y_j^{(t)}, Y_j^{(s)}, X_j^{(vAP)}; U_j), j \geq 0\}$ when the QAP_t wins the channel contention in the jth channel slot. Writing $A(t)$ an $R(t)$ as the cumulative rewards until time t, a standard Markov regenerative argument ([8]), in each case, yields the reward rates $\Theta_{AP-VoIP}(N_v, N_t) := \lim_{t\to\infty} \frac{A(t)}{t}$, and $\Theta_{AP-data}(N_v, N_t) := \lim_{t\to\infty} \frac{R(t)}{t}$.

Since the rate at which a single call sends data to the QAP_v is λ, and the QAP_v serves N_v such calls, the total arrival rate to the QAP_v is $N_v\lambda$. This rate should be less than $\Theta_{AP-VoIP}(N_v, N_t)$ for stability. Thus, a permissible combination of N_v VoIP calls and N_t TCP sessions, while meeting the delay QoS of VoIP calls, must satisfy

$$\Theta_{AP-VoIP}(N_v, N_t) > N_v\lambda \qquad (7)$$

The above inequality defines the admission region for VoIP. Note that we are asserting that the N_v that satisfies Inequality (7) also ensures the delay QoS. This will be validated by simulation.

In our calculations we use the basic access mechanism for the TCP traffic. This will facilitate the validation of our analytical results through ns-2 simulations with the EDCA implementation of [16], which supports only the basic

Table 1. Parameters used in analysis and simulation of the EDCA 802.11e WLAN

Parameter	Symbol	Value
PHY data rate	C_d	11 Mbps
Basic (control) rate	C_c	2 Mbps
G711 pkt size	L_{voice}	200 Bytes
Videostreaming pkt size	L_{video}	1500 Bytes
Data pkt size	$L_{TCPdata}$	1500 Bytes
PLCP preamble time	T_P	$144\mu s$
PHY Header time	T_{PHY}	$48\mu s$
MAC - layer ACK Pkt Size	L_{ACK}	112 bits
MAC Header size	L_{MAC}	288 bits
Idle /system slot (802.11b)	δ	$20\mu s$

Parameter	Symbol	Value
AIFS(3) Time	$T_{AIFS(3)}$	$50\mu s$
AIFS(2) Time	$T_{AIFS(2)}$	$50\mu s$
AIFS(1) Time	$T_{AIFS(1)}$	$70\mu s$
SIFS Time	T_{SIFS}	$10\mu s$
Min. CW for AC(3)	$CW_{min}(AC(3))$	7
Max. CW for AC(3)	$CW_{max}(AC(3))$	15
Min. CW for AC(2)	$CW_{min}(AC(2))$	15
Max. CW for AC(2)	$CW_{max}(AC(2))$	31
Min. CW for AC(1)	$CW_{min}(AC(1))$	31
Max. CW for AC(1)	$CW_{max}(AC(1))$	1023

access mechanism. However, our analysis can be worked out for the RTS/CTS mechanism as well.

3.3   Numerical Results

In order to validate and show the accuracy of the model, we take two steps. Of course, we check if the performance measures predicted by our analysis match with those obtained from analysis. We also analytically obtain three auxiliary measures (namely, the attempt rate of AC 3 nodes, the attempt rate of AC 1 nodes, and the total collision rate in the WLAN (see [6]), and compare the analytical results for these with simulation. Here we only report the performance measures for VoIP and TCP; the other validations can be found in [6].

The simulations were obtained using ns-2 with an EDCA implementation [16]. The PHY parameters conform to the 802.11b standard. See Table 1 for the values used in our simulation.

In Figure 5, we show the analytical plot of the service rate applied to QAP_v vs. the number of calls, N_v for three different values of $N_t \in \{0, 1, 10\}$. We note that the QAP_v service rate crosses the QAP_v load rate after 12 calls for $N_t = 0$. This suggests that a maximum of 12 calls can be carried while meeting the delay QoS on an 802.11e WLAN when no TCP traffic is present on AC 1. When one TCP session is added to the WLAN (i.e., $N_t = 1$), the QAP_v service rate crosses below the QAP_v load rate after 10 calls. This implies that only 10 calls are possible when any TCP session is added to the WLAN. The same is the case even when 10 TCP sessions are added to the WLAN.

Remark 3. The analysis in Figure 5, assumes that the QAP_v is saturated. It is for this reason that the QAP_v service rate exceeds the load arrival rate for small N_v. The crossover point would however correctly model the value of N_v beyond which voice QoS will be violated.   ∎

From Figure 5, we observe that for each value N_v, with increase in the value of N_t from zero to a non-zero value, the service rate available to the QAP_v decreases. This is, of course, because the QAP needs to service the TCP traffic also. However, the curves of $N_t = 1$ and $N_t = 10$ are very close. The effect of one TCP transfer is the same as that of 10 TCP transfers. The reason is that the QAP_t queue is already saturated with 1 TCP. By adding more TCP transfers a few more QSTAs begin to contend, but this number does not change much with increasing N_t (see also Kuriakose [11]).

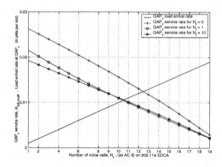
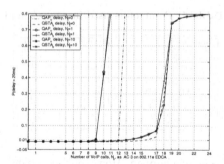

Fig. 5. Analysis results showing the service rate $\Theta_{AP-VoIP}$ applied to QAP_v, plotted vs. the number of voice calls, N_v for different number of TCP sessions N_t. Also shown is the line $N_v\lambda$. (From [6] © IEEE))

Fig. 6. Simulation results showing the probability of voice packet delay in QAP_v and $QSTA_v$ being greater than 20ms vs. the number of calls (N_v) for different values of N_t (From [6] © IEEE)

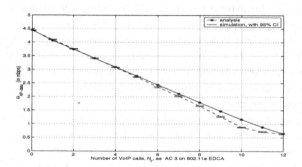

Fig. 7. Analysis and simulation results showing the total download throughput obtained by $QSTA_t$s for different values of N_v, and $N_t = 10$ (From [6] © IEEE)

Simulation results for the QoS objective of *Prob(voice packet delay > 20ms)* for the QAP_v and the $QSTA_v$s are shown in Figure 6. Note that the *Prob(voice packet delay : QAP_v > 20ms)* is greater than *Prob(voice packet delay : $QSTA_v$ > 20ms)* for each given N_v, and that the QAP_v delay shoots up before the $QSTA_v$ delay, *confirming that the QAP_v is the bottleneck*, as per our assumptions. It can be seen that with and without TCP traffic, there is a value of N_v at which the *Prob(voice packet delay > 20ms)* sharply increases from a value below 0.01. This can be taken to be the voice capacity. In the case of no data traffic, we obtain 12 calls, matching the analysis result and when there is data traffic, we get 9 calls, one less than the analysis result.

For a data packet length of 1500 bytes, using IEEE 802.11b PHY parameters, with PHY data rate of 11Mbps, we numerically calculate the total download throughput for TCP traffic, i.e., $\Theta_{AP-data}(N_v, N_t)$ (with $N_t = 10$) from our analytical model, for varying number of voice calls N_v. The analytical plot has

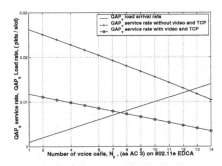 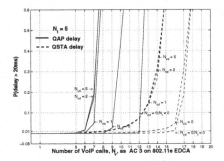

Fig. 8. Analysis results showing the service rate $\Theta_{AP-voip}$ applied to the QAP_v, plotted as a function of number of voice calls, N_v, without and with video and TCP sessions. When present, the QAP_{vd} is assumed saturated and $N_t = 5$. Also shown is the line $N_v\lambda$.

Fig. 9. Simulation results showing the probability of delay of at the QAP_v and $QSTA_v$, being greater than 20ms vs. the number of calls (N_v) for different values of N_t. The solid lines denote the delay of QAP_v and the dashed lines denote the delay of $QSTA_v$.

been given in Figure 7 and the figure also shows the simulated TCP download throughput with 95% confidence intervals. Figure 7 shows that the reduction of TCP throughput with increasing N_v is almost linear at the rate of $\frac{1}{3}$ Mbps per VoIP call.

Remark 4. Figure 7 can be used for admission control of VoIP calls in order to guarantee a net minimal throughput to the data traffic. For instance if at least 2 Mbps of aggregate TCP throughput is to be allotted to data traffic then Figure 7 says that only 7 VoIP calls should be admitted. ∎

4   CBR VoIP, Streaming Video and TCP File Downloads over EDCF

Finally, we briefly report on our results on modeling the complete situation depicted in Figure 1. To achieve this we need to add streaming video from the wired network into the QSTAs, via the QAP. The streaming video is handled in AC 2 in the QAP. We do not model any feedback traffic (e.g., RTCP packets) from the receiving QSTAs. Hence, the problem reduces to modeling one AC 2 queue in the QAP handling a video packet stream from the video server, thus yielding a model in which an AC 2 queue for video is added at the QAP in Figure 4. We follow an approach identical to that described in Section 3. The details of the analysis are provide in [7]. We present the results obtained from the analysis and simulation. The simulations were obtained using *ns-2* with EDCA implementation [16]. See Table 1 for the values used in the simulation.

In Figure 8, we show the analytical plot of QAP_v service rate vs. the number of calls, N_v for cases when only VoIP calls are present and when VoIP calls are present along with streaming video and TCP download sessions. From Figure 8,

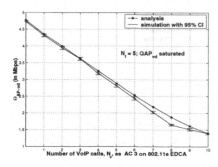
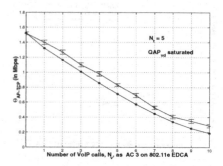

Fig. 10. The saturation throughput Θ_{AP-vd} applied to the QAP_{vd} is plotted as a function of number of voice calls, N_v

Fig. 11. Analysis and simulation results showing total download throughput obtained by $QSTA_t$s for different values of N_v and $N_t = 5$

as before (see Figure 5), we note that the QAP_v service rate crosses the QAP_v load rate, after 12 calls for $N_t = 0$ and no video sessions. When video streaming sessions and TCP download sessions are also present in the WLAN, the QAP_v service rate crosses below the QAP_v load rate after 7 calls. This implies that only 7 calls are possible when video and TCP download traffic are present.

Simulation results for the QoS objective of $Prob(voice\ packet\ delay > 20ms)$ for the QAP_v and the $QSTA_v$s are shown in Figure 9. Note that the $Prob(voice\ packet\ delay : QAP_v > 20ms)$ is greater than $Prob(voice\ packet\ delay : QSTA_v > 20ms)$ for given N_v and that the QAP_v delay shoots up before the $QSTA_v$ delay, *confirming that the QAP_v is the bottleneck*, as per our assumptions. It can be seen that with and without TCP traffic and video streaming traffic, there is a value of N_v at which the $Prob(voice\ packet\ delay > 20ms)$ sharply increases from a value below 0.01. This can be taken to be the voice capacity. When TCP and video traffic is present, we get a maximum of 6 calls, one less than the analysis result. When $N_t = 0$ and only VoIP and video traffic is present, we obtain a maximum of 8 VoIP calls.

We plot the analytical and simulation saturation throughput of video sessions vs. the number of VoIP calls in Figure 10. The number of TCP sessions, N_t, is 5. The video sessions are assumed to be using 1500 byte packets. The video queue of QAP in the simulation is saturated by sending a high input CBR traffic (more than 5Mbps). We observe that the analytical results match very closely with the simulation results for different number of VoIP calls. For instance, for $N_v = 4$, the analysis yields a video throughput of 3.25 Mbps while the simulation value is 3.26 Mbps. Note that the plot after $N_v = 6$ calls is not of any use because, from Figure 9 we already saw that the VoIP delay QoS breaks down after $N_v = 6$ calls. The error between the analysis and simulation then, is less than 5%, in the admissible region of VoIP calls. Suppose we consider actual SD-TV video streaming sessions with a rate of 1.5 Mbps between the server on the local network and the $QSTA_{vd}$s, then the results in Figure 10 imply that, with 4 VoIP calls and TCP download traffic, we can handle 2 video streaming sessions. How close we can go to the saturation throughput is answered by the QoS constraint of loss probability, which we have also analysed (see [5]).

The analytical and simulation results for aggregate TCP download throughput obtained by TCP sessions vs. the number of VoIP calls is shown in Figure 11. The number of TCP sessions, $N_t = 5$. The video sessions are assumed to be using 1500 bytes, with QAP_{vd} being saturated. For instance, for $N_v = 3$, the aggregate throughput obtained from analysis is 1.01 Mbps and that obtained from simulations is 1.10 Mbps. We note that though the analytical curve follows the shape of the simulation curve, it underestimates the aggregate TCP throughput by at most 100 Kbps when compared with the simulations.

5   Conclusion

In this paper we have surveyed some of our contributions to the modeling and performance analysis of IEEE 802.11 and 802.11e WLANs. We reviewed our extensions to the fixed-point based saturation analysis. Then we provided an analytical approach for obtaining the capacity of VoIP calls, streaming video and TCP controlled download throughput in EDCA 802.11e WLAN. The analysis proceeded by modeling the evolution of the number of contending QSTAs at channel slot boundaries. This yielded a Markov renewal process. A regenerative analysis then yielded the required performance measures. Our work provides the following modeling insights:

- Using saturation attempt probabilities as state dependent attempt rates yields a good approximation in the unsaturated case.
- Using this approximation, an IEEE 802.11e infrastructure WLAN can be well modeled by a multidimensional Markov renewal process embedded at channel slot boundaries.

We also obtain the following performance insights:

- Unlike the original DCF, the EDCA mechanism supports the coexistence of VoIP connections and TCP file transfers; but even 1 TCP transfer reduces the VoIP capacity from 12 calls to 9 calls. Subsequently the VoIP capacity is independent of the number of TCP transfers (see Figure 6). With a saturated video queue (handled as AC 2) the VoIP capacity drops to 6 calls.
- The AP is indeed the performance bottleneck in the case of packet voice traffic.
- For an 11 Mbps PHY, without video, the file download throughput reduces linearly with the number of voice calls at the rate of $\frac{1}{3}$ Mbps per additional voice call from 0 to 9 calls.

While a considerable amount of analytical modeling has been performed for small IEEE 802.11 networks, good models for larger networks, that capture spatial reuse and hidden nodes still remain elusive. This is an important area of ongoing work.

References

1. G. Bianchi. Performance analysis of the IEEE 802.11 distributed coordination function. *IEEE Journal on Selected Areas in Communications*, 18(3):535–547, March 2000.
2. G. Bianchi, I. Tinnirello, and L. Scalia. Understanding 802.11e contention-based prioritization mechanisms and their coexistence with legacy 802.11 stations. *IEEE Network*, 19(4), July/August 2005.
3. R. Bruno, M. Conti, and E. Gregori. Throughput analysis of TCP clients in Wi-Fi hot spot networks. In *Networking 2004*, LNCS 2042, pages 626–637. Springer, 2004.
4. S. Harsha, A. Kumar, and V. Sharma. Analytical model for an IEEE 802.11 WLAN using DCF with two types of VoIP calls. In *National Communication Conference (NCC), New Delhi*, January 2006.
5. Sri Harsha. Performance of multimedia applications on IEEE 802.11e wireless LANs. Master's thesis, Department of Electrical Communications Engg., Indian Institute of Science, August 2006.
6. Sri Harsha, Anurag Kumar, and Vinod Sharma. An analytical model for the capacity estimation of combined VoIP and TCP file transfers over EDCA in an IEEE 802.11e WLAN. In *Proceedings of the International Workshop on Quality of Service (IWQoS), 2006* 2006.
7. Sri Harsha, Anurag Kumar, and Vinod Sharma. An analytical model for the performance evaluation of packet telephony, streaming video, and TCP file transfers over EDCA in an IEEE 802.11e WLAN. in preparation, August 2006.
8. V. G. Kulkarni. *Modeling and Analysis of Stochastic Systems*. Chapman and Hall, London, UK, 1995.
9. Anurag Kumar, Eitan Altman, Daniele Miorandi, and Munish Goyal. New insights from a fixed point analysis of single cell IEEE 802.11 wireless LANs. In *Proceedings IEEE Infocom*, 2005. Also Technical Report No. RR-5218, INRIA, Sophia-Antipolis, France, June 2004, and to appear in IEEE Transactions on Networking 2007.
10. Anurag Kumar and Deepak Patil. Stability and throughput analysis of unslotted CDMA-ALOHA with finite numer of users and code sharing. *Telecommunication Systems*, 8:257–275, 1997.
11. G. Kuriakose. Analytical Models for QoS Engineering of Wireless LANs. Master's thesis, Indian Institue of Science, Bangalore, 2005.
12. Stefan Mangold, Sunghyun Choi, Peter May, Ole Klein, Guido Hiertz, and Lothar Stibor. IEEE 802.11e wireless LAN for quality of service. In *Proc. European Wireless (EW 2002)*, February 2002.
13. Venkatesh Ramaiyan, Anurag Kumar, and Eitan Altman. Fixed point analysis of single cell IEEE 802.11e WLANs : Uniqueness, multistability and throughput differentiation. In *ACM Sigmetrics*, June 2005.
14. Venkatesh Ramaiyan, Anurag Kumar, and Eitan Altman. Fixed point analysis of single cell IEEE 802.11e WLANs : Uniqueness, multistability and throughput differentiation. extended version, submitted, December 2005.
15. J.W. Robinson and T.S. Randhawa. Saturation throughput analysis of IEEE 802.11e enhanced distributed coordination function. In *IEEE Journal on Selected Areas in Communications, Volume: 22 , Issue: 5 , June 2004, Pages:917 - 928*. IEEE, 2004.
16. S. Wiethlter and C. Hoene. An IEEE 802.11e EDCF and CFB simulation model for ns-2, 2006.

Maintaining Information About Nearby Processors in a Mobile Environment

Faith Ellen*, Sivaramakrishnan Subramanian**, and Jennifer Welch**

Abstract. The problem of maintaining information about the location of nearby processors in a mobile adhoc network is considered. A new scalable, deterministic algorithm is presented, provided processors can only move along a line. Many open questions and directions for future work are discussed.

1 Introduction

In many algorithms designed for mobile adhoc networks, processors are assumed to know information (such as location) about the other processors that are located nearby [1,3,4,7,9]. However, as processors move, the information may change and the set of processors each particular processor needs to know about may change.

Updating information is not simply a matter of each processor broadcasting changes to its information when they occur. One problem is that nearby processors may not necessarily be within transmission range of one another. To handle this, processors have to relay some of the information they receive from their neighbours. For example, Calinescu [5] shows how processors can maintain information about the processors that are at most two hops away, assuming that broadcasts never interfere with one another.

A more significant problem is that there is interference when different processors perform concurrent broadcasts. In this case, the information contained in the messages will not be received by these processors. Furthermore, a processor that is in transmission range of two or more of these processors will also not receive any messages, even if it doesn't broadcast and the broadcasting processors are not within transmission range of one another.

One way to avoid interference is to employ time slicing. Each processor periodically gets allocated a time slot in which it can broadcast updates to its information. Unfortunately, the time between a processor's broadcasts depends on the total number of processors in the system and, hence, this solution is not scalable. In particular, if the number of processors is large, the information known about a specific processor will be out of date most of the time.

* University of Toronto, Canada, supported by the Natural Sciences and Engineering Research Council of Canada and the Scalable Synchronization Research Group of SUN Microsystems, Inc.
** Texas A&M University, USA, supported in in part by National Science Foundation grant 0500464 and Texas Advanced Research Program grant 000512-0007-2006.

Another approach to gathering and maintaining information about nearby processors and for communicating with them, popular in practice, is to settle for probabilistic guarantees on performance, by relying on random behavior of the processors. For instance, in the hello protocol [3], used to discover and maintain neighbor relationships in mobile adhoc networks, each processor periodically broadcasts a hello packet. When another processor receives such a message, it knows that the sender is currently its neighbor. It is assumed that the likelihood of missing more than a fixed number of such hello packets from a neighbor, due to collisions, is negligible. This likelihood can be reduced even further by adding some random jitter to the time when hello packets are sent.

In the IEEE 802.11 standard, the medium access control protocol resolves channel contention using randomization: a processor chooses a random "back-off interval" in some range, and waits this amount of time before performing the RTS/CTS protocol [2]. In this protocol, a few short control packets are exchanged, in which the processor requests to send (RTS). Once it has been cleared to send (CTS), the processor broadcasts the data. Since the control packets are short, the probability of collisions is assumed to be small. The use of a random backoff interval makes this probability even smaller.

The ability of processors to discover their neighbors and to communicate with them using these protocols is probabilistic. There always exists a (small) probability that a processor has incorrect information about its neighbors and that it is unable to transmit information to its neighbors. For some applications, such as real-time applications, which require stringent guarantees on system behavior, typically deterministic upper bounds on message delays, such probabilistic behavior is not acceptable.

In this paper, we consider how information about nearby processors can be maintained deterministically by processors as they move. Section 2 presents a model in which to study this problem. In Section 3, we give an algorithm for a restricted case in which processors move along a line. This case is a good model for one-dimensional environments such as highways and railroads. More importantly, the work in this section provides a good foundation for addressing various issues that arise in more general versions of the problem, discussed in Section 4. We also hope that the algorithm for the restricted case will provide insight to solutions for other versions.

2   Model

We consider a set of n processors moving in a Euclidean space, for example, on the plane or along a line. The motion of a processor can be described by its *trajectory*, a function that specifies the location of the processor as a function of time. There is an upper bound σ on maximum speed of a processor.

Because processors occupy space, there is also an upper bound on the density of processors. However, trajectory functions may be allowed to intersect. For example, a four lane highway can be modelled as a line on which at most four processors can occupy the same location at the same time.

Each processor is assumed to know its current location, for example, via GPS, and its future trajectory, for some period of time. We also assume the existence of a global clock, which can be read by all processors.

Processors communicate by wireless broadcast [10,8]. There are two important parameters related to the reception of broadcast messages, the *broadcast radius*, R, and the *interference radius*, $R' \geq R$. If a processor p is within distance R of another processor q during the time that q is broadcasting a message, then the message *arrives* at p. If, in addition, no other processor within distance R' of p transmits at any point during this period of time, then p *receives* the message broadcast by q. Collisions occur when a message arrives at a processor, but is not received. A processor broadcasting a message may or may not be aware of collisions that occur at processors within its broadcast radius.

Broadcasts occur during *broadcast slots*, which are disjoint unit intervals of time. They are sufficiently long so that a message which starts being broadcast at the beginning of a broadcast slot arrives at all processors within the broadcast radius of the sender by the end of the broadcast slot. Broadcast slots start every u units of time and each is followed by an interval of $u - 1$ time units that can be used by other algorithms. We assume that broadcast slot 0 starts at time 0. Then broadcast slot j starts at time ju.

3   An Algorithm for Maintaining Information on a Line

In this section, we present a scalable, deterministic algorithm for processors to maintain trajectory information about all nearby processors, provided processors can only move along a line. We make two simplifying assumptions. The first assumption is that each processor knows its entire trajectory function and can easily share this information with other processors. This means that trajectory functions must be representable in a relatively succinct way. The second assumption is that, at the beginning of the algorithm, each processor knows the entire trajectory of every nearby processor. This can be achieved by simply assuming that processors are initially sufficiently far apart from one another, so that no processors has any other processor nearby.

Our approach is to partition the line into *segments* of length G, starting at each multiple of G. The segments are coloured with the m *colours* $0, 1, \ldots, m-1$. Segment i is the half open interval $[iG, (i+1)G)$ and has colour $i \bmod m$. Segments with the same colour are assigned to the same broadcast slots and segments with different colours are assigned to different broadcasts slots.

Our algorithm proceeds in phases, consisting of $m - 1$ broadcast slots. The segments that are not assigned to any broadcast slot in a particular phase are assigned to the first broadcast slot in the next phase. During each broadcast slot, the only processors allowed to broadcast are those that were in a segment assigned to this broadcast slot at the beginning of the phase.

To avoid collisions between broadcasts performed by processors in the same segment, the processors in each segment at the beginning of a phase choose a *leader*. During each broadcast slot in that phase, only the leaders of segments assigned to the broadcast slot can perform broadcasts. Provided that all processors in the same segment know the locations of the processors that are currently in the segment, they can agree on the same leader, in some predetermined way, using only local computation. (Another possibility is to choose a leader of a segment immediately before a broadcast slot to which it is assigned. The problem with this approach is that a processor moving from one segment to another segment during a phase might entirely miss its opportunity to broadcast during a phase, even if both segments are scheduled.)

If segments of successively increasing colour are assigned to successive broadcast slots, then information propagates rightwards quickly, but may be slow to propagate leftwards. Similarly, if segments of successively decreasing colour are assigned to successive broadcast slots, then information propagates leftwards quickly, but may be slow to propagate rightwards. Instead, our assignment of segments to broadcast slots interleaves sequences of segments of successively increasing and successively decreasing colours.

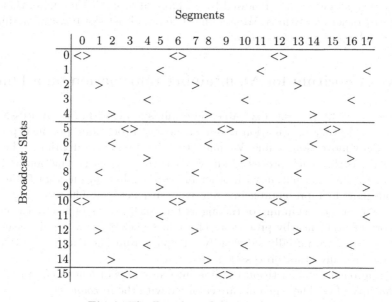

Fig. 1. The Broadcast Schedule for $m = 6$

The broadcast schedule for $m = 6$ is illustrated in Figure 1. A ">" indicates a segment that arises from the successively increasing sequence of segment colours, a "<" indicates a segment that arises from the successively decreasing sequence of segment colours, and a "<>" indicates a segment that arises from the intersection of both.

When m is odd, the broadcast schedule is slightly different. Specifically, in the second broadcast slot of an odd phase, the assigned segments are chosen according to the increasing sequence of segment colours, rather than the decreasing

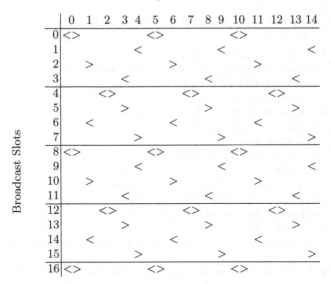

Fig. 2. The Broadcast Schedule for $m = 5$

sequence. For example, see the broadcast schedule for $m = 5$ that appears in Figure 2.

The complete algorithm is presented in Figure 3. The function `location()` returns the current location of the processor that called it.

There are two constraints we will impose on the parameters G and m. The first constraint,

$$(m - 1)u\sigma < G, \tag{1}$$

says that a processor cannot cross more than one segment boundary during a phase. The second constraint,

$$(m - 1)G - 2[(m - 2)u + 1]\sigma \geq R + R', \tag{2}$$

implies that every broadcast that arrives at a process is received. This follows from the facts that the distance between the end of a segment and the beginning of the next segment of the same colour is $(m - 1)G$, the time between the beginning of a phase and the end of its last broadcast slot is $(m - 2)u + 1$, and a processor can move at most distance $[(m - 2)u + 1]\sigma$ during this time.

If, in addition, there is a lower bound on the density of processors, then there is an upper bound on the time it takes for information to be propagated.

Lemma 1. *If there is never an interval of length $[R - 3(m - 1)u\sigma - 3G]/2$ that contains no processors, then the speed of information propagation is at least $G/2u$, (i.e. information travels at least one segment for every two broadcast slots), in the worst case.*

at time $\pi(m-1)u$, for any non-negative integer π,
%this is the beginning of phase π
    %determine the segment, i, in which processor p is located
    $i \leftarrow \lfloor \texttt{location}()/G \rfloor$
    if p is the leader of segment i then
        %determine the colour, f, of the segments which are
        %assigned to the first broadcast slot in phase π
        $f \leftarrow (\pi \bmod 2)\lfloor m/2 \rfloor$
        %determine to which broadcast slot, if any,
        %segment i is assigned in phase π
        $j \leftarrow (i-f) \bmod m$
        $offset \leftarrow (\pi \bmod 2) \ AND \ (m \bmod 2)$
        if $j=0$ then $slot \leftarrow 0$
        else if $j \leq \lfloor m/2 \rfloor - 1$ then $slot \leftarrow 2j-$ $offset$
        else if $j > \lfloor m/2 \rfloor$ then $slot \leftarrow 2(m-j) - 1 +$ $offset$
        %broadcast in the assigned broadcast slot
        if $j \neq \lfloor m/2 \rfloor$ then
            at time $\pi(m-1)u + slot$, broadcast trajectory information

Fig. 3. The Information Maintenance Algorithm for Processor p

Using this result, it is possible to prove that the algorithm enables processors to maintain trajectory information about nearby processors.

Lemma 2. *Suppose there is never an interval of length $[R-3(m-1)u\sigma-3G]/2$ that contains no processors, and all processors know the trajectory functions of the processors within distance $R + 2(m-1)u\sigma$ of themselves at the beginning of phase 0. Then all processors know the trajectory functions of the processors within distance $R + 2(m-1)u\sigma$ of themselves at the beginning of every phase.*

Theorem 1. *Suppose there is never an interval of length $[R-3(m-1)u\sigma-3G]/2$ that contains no processors, and all processors know the trajectory functions of the processors within distance $R + 2(m-1)u\sigma$ of themselves at the beginning of phase 0. Then all processors always know the trajectory functions of the processors within distance R of themselves.*

For these results, it is not necessary that each processor repeatedly broadcast all the trajectory functions it knows about. It suffices that processor p broadcasts the trajectory function of processor q only if, at the beginning of the phase, there is another processor q' that p knows about, but may not know about q (because q' is more than distance $R + 2(m-1)u\sigma$ away from q) and will come within distance $R + 2(m-1)u\sigma$ of q by the end of the phase.

Without the lower bound on the density of processors, but with a somewhat more stringent constraint between G and m, there is a similar result, but with the definition of nearby being closer.

Lemma 3. *Suppose that $R \geq 4(m-1)u\sigma + 4G$ and all processors know the trajectory functions of the processors within distance $R - G - 5(m-1)u\sigma$ of* *themselves at the beginning of phase 0. Then all processors know the trajectory functions of the processors within distance $R - G - 5(m-1)u\sigma$ of themselves at the beginning of every phase.*

The proofs of these results, including details about what information to include in broadcasts, appear in [11] and will appear in the full version of the paper.

The constraints on the relative values of the parameters are easy to satisfy. For example, suppose the broadcast radius, R, and the interference radius, R', are 250 meters and 550 meters, respectively, (which are their default values in the IEEE 802.11 standard), the length of a broadcast slot is 1 microsecond, and the time, u, between the beginning of successive broadcast slots is 100 microseconds. If $G = 30$ meters, $m = 31$ and $\sigma < 36,000$ km/hr, or if $G = 60$ meters, $m = 21$ and $\sigma < 4500$ km/hr, then all of the constraints are satisfied.

4 Directions for Further Work

There are many open questions that remain. Some of these address possible optimizations to the broadcast algorithm or the relaxation of various assumptions. Other questions are concerned with the model and various aspects of the problem.

In the previous section, a broadcast schedule was presented that avoids collisions and enables processors to quickly propagate information to other processors, provided the density of the processors never gets too small. Are there broadcast schedules that can propagate information faster? Are there broadcast schedules that can propagate information efficiently when processors can be further apart from one another? Perhaps an entirely different approach would be better. For example, allowing a small number of collisions might enable a more efficient algorithm to be obtained.

The density assumption ensures that processors moving towards one another will learn about each other's trajectory function before they are able to communicate directly, from processors located between them. However, if there is a large region containing no processors and the processors on the boundary of that region start moving towards one another, they cannot possibly get this information until the distance between them is less than the broadcast radius. Maybe the requirements for this situation should be relaxed so that processors only have to know about one another's trajectory functions until they have been close to one another for a sufficiently long period of time. However, this may have implications for the other parts of the algorithm and for applications that rely on knowledge of the locations of all nearby processors.

. Perhaps processors on a boundary should broadcast more frequently so that they can be guaranteed to have exchanged information by the time they are close together. Because processors can move at different speeds, processors can overtake one another and, consequently, which processor is on the boundary can change. In fact, if there are other processors close to the boundary, for example in the same segment as a processor on the boundary, it may not be best to have the actual processor that is on the boundary be responsible for performing these broadcasts, but instead have the leader of the segment perform them.

The assumption that each processor knows its entire future trajectory is probably the most unrealistic simplifying assumption we have made. It is more likely that a processor only knows its trajectory for some short period of time in the future, or that its trajectory function might change in response to events. Then processors would need to announce information about their trajectories either periodically or when they change.

It is also possible that a processor only has approximate information about its location. For example, a processor might not know its exact location, but only know the segment in which it is located at the beginning of the current phase, perhaps with some error in either direction.

How should processors announce movement between segments, updates to their trajectories, or other information (unrelated to their trajectories) that needs to be maintained, but can change at arbitrary times? One approach is to have the processors in a segment take turns being leader. Then they could announce any changes during their allocated broadcast slots. This could work well, provided the number of processors per segment is relatively small and care is taken to schedule processors when they change segments, so that they don't lose their opportunity to broadcast. If there are many processors in a segment, it might be better for the processors that have changes to announce to use a separate algorithm for transmitting this information to the leader of their segment, using an algorithm that adapts to the number of participating processors. For one segment, this problem is equivalent to broadcasting on a multiple access channel [6]. However, it is also necessary to avoid collisions with processors in nearby segments trying to do the same thing.

Our other simplifying assumption is that processors initially know the trajectories of all nearby processors. How can this be achieved, if processors are not initially far apart from one another? If processors have distinct identifiers in the range $\{1, \ldots, n\}$ and all processors begin at time 0, then it suffices for processor i to broadcast its trajectory information in broadcast slot i, for $i = 1, \ldots, n$. Then the broadcast schedule can begin with broadcast slot $n + 1$. Is it possible to perform the initialization more efficiently? For example, could it help to have the time at which processors broadcast be a function of both their identifiers and location? When processors can begin at arbitrary times, the problem may be more difficult.

The broadcast schedule relies on the existence of a global clock. Common knowledge of time enables processors to determine the current locations of other locations from their trajectory functions. A global clock also allows processors to agree on the beginning of broadcast slots and the beginning of phases. A weaker assumption is the existence of a heartbeat, a beacon that transmits ticks at regular intervals, but does not provide the time. In particular, this enables processors to construct local clocks that run at the same rate. If the ticks are sufficiently far apart, then our broadcast schedule still works. For example, when m is even, all even phases are the same and all odd phases are the same. If a tick occurs once every two phases, then processors can agree, for example, to start odd phases immediately after ticks. However, if ticks occur more frequently, then processors may need to rely on a clock synchronization protocol to agree on the number of each phase, when phases begin, or when broadcast slots begin. For processors on boundaries or during initialization, ticks that occur too frequently can be especially problematic, because there has been no communication and, hence, no synchronization. In these cases, one idea is for a processor to choose the length of time between successive broadcasts as a function of its location.

Most mobile ad hoc networks consist of processors moving on a plane or in space. Can the same approach that was used, in Section 3, to maintain trajectory information be extended from one dimension to two dimensions by appropriately colouring a tiling of the plane with squares or hexagons? What about in three dimensions?

Our model assumes omnidirectional antennas, which broadcast messages both to the left and right simultaneously. With directional antennas, the problem changes significantly. It is possible to avoid some interference, for example two nearby processors that want to broadcast away from one another. It also may be more energy efficient to use a directional broadcast if a message only has to be sent in one direction. However, if a processor wants to send the same information in both directions, it will need to perform two broadcasts instead of one. In two and three dimensional environments, this issue is even more complex, because one has to consider the conical broadcast regions where messages will arrive at other processors and the larger regions surrounding them where messages may cause interference.

Finally, it would be useful to implement our algorithm for maintaining trajectory information about nearby processors, to see how it performs experimentally and to find good choices for the parameters G and m. More generally, an experimental comparison of this algorithm with simpler approaches that rely on randomization would be interesting.

References

1. R. Bar-Yehuda, O. Goldreich, and A. Itai, On the Time Complexity of Broadcast in Multi-Hop Radio Networks: An Exponential Gap Between Determinism and Randomization, *Journal of Computer and System Sciences*, 45(1), pp. 104-126, 1992.
2. V. Bharghavan, A. Demers, S. Shenker, and L. Zhang, MACAW: A Media Access Protocol for Wireless LANs, *Proceedings of the ACM SIGCOMM'94 Conference on Communications Architectures, Protocols, and Applications*, pp. 212-225, Aug./Sep. 1994.
3. J. Broch, D.A. Maltz, D.B. Johnson, and J. Jetcheva, A Performance Comparison of Multi-Hop Wireless Ad Hoc Network Routing Protocols, *Proc. ACM/IEEE Intl Conf. Mobile Computing and Networking*, pp. 85-97, Oct. 1998.
4. D. Bruschi, M. D. Pinto, Lower bounds for the broadcast problem in mobile radio networks, *Distributed Computing*, 10(3), pp. 129-135, Mar. 1997.
5. G. Calinescu, Computing 2-Hop Neighborhoods in Ad Hoc Wireless Networks, *Lecture Notes in Computer Science*, Vol. 2865, pp. 175-186, Jan. 2003.

6. R. Gallager, A Perspective on Multiaccess Channels, *IEEE Transactions on Information Theory*, 31(2), pp. 124-142, Mar. 1985.
7. N. Malpani, Y. Chen, N. Vaidya, and J. Welch, Distributed token circulation in mobile ad hoc networks, *IEEE Transactions on Mobile Computing*, 4(2), pp. 154-165, Mar./Apr. 2005.
8. N. Vaidya, *Medium Access Control Protocols for Wireless Networks*, manuscript, 2006.
9. R. Prakash, A. Schiper, M. Mohsin, D. Cavin, and Y. Sasson, A lower bound for broadcasting in mobile ad hoc networks, *EPFL Technical Report. IC/2004/37*, Jun. 2004.
10. J. Schiller, *Mobile Communications*, Addison-Wesley, 2000.
11. Sivaramakrishnan Subramanian, *Deterministic Knowledge about Nearby Nodes in a Mobile One Dimensional Wireless Environment*, M.Sc. Thesis, Department of Computer Science, Texas A&M University, Sep. 2006.

Energy Aware Topology Management in Ad Hoc Wireless Networks

T. Shiv Prakash[1], G.S. Badrinath[1], K.R. Venugopal[1], and L.M. Patnaik[2]

[1] University Visvesvaraya College of Engineering, Bangalore 560 001, India
[2] Indian Institue of Science, Bangalore 560 012, India

Abstract. Topology control for ad hoc networks is needed to conserve energy and increase the network life time. In this paper we propose a Residual Energy Adaptive Re-Routing(REAR) scheme in conjunction with a Mixed Integer Linear Programming (MILP) model for prolonging the lifetime of the network. The approach is based on the multi-commodity flow which involves routing several requests from the sources to the sinks in a given network by splitting and re-routing the non-optimal flows over multiple paths. The REAR algorithm ensures uniform consumption of energy across all the nodes in the network thereby increasing the lifetime of the network. This algorithm is compared with earlier works and results observed show that the MILP algorithm in conjunction with the REAR algorithm perform better than the existing algorithms.

1 Introduction

Mobile ad hoc networks are multi-hop, wireless, infrastructure less collection of self organizing mobile hosts that form a temporary cooperative network without the aid of any base station. These networks can be created and used anywhere and anytime and are intrinsically fault-resilient as they do not operate under a fixed topology.

In ad hoc networks, nodes have limited battery power and these nodes have the capacity to modify the area of coverage with their transmitting power and thereby reduce energy consumption and increase the lifetime of the network. However, reducing the transmitting power leads to loss of connectivity. Hence, there is a need to maintain the connectivity of the network apart from reducing the redundant exchange of messages and extending the life time of the network. Since considerable amount of expensive energy is utilized to transmit packets over long distances, short multi-hops are preferred to reduce the average energy requirements, resulting in large delay in delivery of packets. Moreover inadequate security and poor quality of service add to the problems of ad hoc networks.

Motivation: The routing protocols in wireless ad hoc networks play a significant role in energy management and prolonging the lifetime of the network. If there is a large transmitting power at each node, then network connectivity is very high and delay is low, on account of smaller number of relay nodes between the source and destination. The number of nodes in the transmitting range being

S. Chaudhuri et al. (Eds.): ICDCN 2006, LNCS 4308, pp. 203–214, 2006.

high deteriorates the network capacity resulting in poor transmission quality as the nodes interfere with each other. Therefore, it is essential for the nodes to have an optimal transmitting power in the network.

Contribution: We have proposed a Multi Commodity Flow Model for maximizing the life time of the ad hoc wireless network by partitioning the load over multiple paths between a source destination pair using the Residual Energy Adaptive Re-routing Algorithm. This technique enhances the lifetime of the network. The rest of the paper is as follows: Section 2 presents related work and different power control schemes. Sections 3 and 4 presents the ILP and the MILP formulations and the *REAR* algorithm. Performance analysis and conclusions are presented in Sections 5 and 6 respectively.

2   Literature Survey

Bambos [1] has reviewed the developments in power control in wireless networks and identified the need for minimum power routing protocols. In [2], the authors suggest topology control of a multi-hop wireless network to minimize power consumption. Chang et al. [3] have proposed multi-commodity flow algorithms to select routes and corresponding power levels in a static wireless ad hoc network to maximize the life of the battery. Wieselthier et al. [4],[5],[6] have developed energy-efficient broadcast and multi-cast algorithms for wireless ad hoc networks.

Melodea et al. [7] have proposed a distributed topology control and geographical routing in ad hoc and sensor networks to improve energy efficiency. Li et al. [8] have analyzed localized topology control for heterogeneous networks with different power levels. Abhas et al. [9] have proposed a leader election and density based clustering algorithm for enhanced connectivity and maximizing life time. Shiva Prakash et al. [10], [11] have proposed an intelligent gateway selection heuristic which eliminates redundant gateways during passive clustering and reduce the number of rebroadcasts and have studied a number of peculiar cases of network topology, which are frequent in a mobile environment.

3   Problem Definition

Given an ad hoc wireless network $G_w(N, L)$ of a finite set of nodes, $N = \{ 1, 2, ..., n \}$ and a finite set of links $L = \{ (x, y) \mid x, y \in N \land x \neq y \}$; a link is said to exist between two nodes x and y if they are within the transmission range of each other. A node can either be a transmitter or a receiver or a relay node or all of the above. Consider the above defined graph $G_w(N, L)$, with N nodes and L links. The objectives are to,

- utilize the energy uniformly across all the nodes of the network.
- maximize the lifetime of the network by re-routing the flows optimally.
- reduce the load on the nodes of the network.

3.1 Assumptions

– The nodes are distributed uniformly in a two-dimensional area. The source and destination pairs are chosen randomly and multiple paths exists between the source and destination (*sd* pair).
– All the nodes are unaware of the topology. The network is not reconfigured during the computation.
– Each node is battery operated and has variable transmitting power and the battery is not recharged. The links between the nodes are bi-directional, that is two nodes can communicate using the same transmitting power.

4   ILP and MILP Models for Maximizing the Lifetime of the Ad Hoc Wireless Network

The objective is to formulate an Integer Linear Programming Model (ILP) to minimize the power consumption and maximize the lifetime of the network on a single fixed routing between a source destination pair. The following notations are used in the ILP formulation.

– l_{xy}, is the link between node x and node y.
– λ^{sd}, is the load between each (sd) node pair on a single path route.
– Λ^{sd}_{xy}, is the load between each (sd) node pair on a multiple path route.
– r, is the route between a (sd) pair.
– $r \in R$, is the set of all routes between any (sd) pair.
– h_{sd}, is the maximum number of hops allowed for any (sd) node pair.
– B, be the bandwidth of the node.
– B^x_{max}, be the maximum bandwidth at node x.
– T_{nl}, be the life time of the ad hoc wireless network.
– P_x, is the set of all nodes that are within the transmitting range of node x.
– E_{pmax}, is the maximum transmitting power of a node.
– E^x_{emax}, is the maximum energy at the node x.
– E^x_t, is the transmitting power of the node x.
– d_{xy}, is the distance between the nodes x and y.
– e_{xy}, is the energy required for the node x to transmit an information unit to its neighbor y.
– α, is the path loss factor.

The binary constraints defined below ensure that a link exists between the $s - d$ pair and a link exists between the two nodes x and y. Equation 1 describes that each edge corresponds to two directed links. Transmissions by a node can be received by all nodes within its transmission range; that is, if there is a link between the nodes x and y, and if $d_{xy} > d_{xk}$, then there is a link between x and k as in eqn. 2. This shows that the nodes have broadcast capability.

(i) *Binary constraints*:

$$l_{xy} = \begin{cases} 1 \text{ if a link exists between a node } x \text{ and node } y \\ \quad \text{ of the network} \\ 0 \text{ otherwise} \end{cases}$$

$$l_{xy}^{sd} = \begin{cases} 1 \text{ if a link } xy \text{ exists on} \\ \quad \text{a } sd \text{ pair path} \\ 0 \text{ otherwise} \end{cases} \tag{1}$$

(ii) *Topology constraints:*

$$l_{xy} = l_{yx} \qquad \forall xy \in N \tag{2}$$

$$l_{xk} = \begin{cases} 1 \text{ if } d_{xy} > d_{xk} \\ 0 \text{ otherwise} \end{cases} \tag{3}$$

The power model for adhoc networks states that if e_{xy} is the energy needed for a node x to reach node y, and d_{xy} is the distance between nodes x and y, then $e_{xy} = d_{xy}^{\alpha}$, were α takes a value ranging from 2 to 4. The nodes can adjust their transmitting power as shown in eqn. 4, where E_{pmax} is the maximum energy a node can expend for any transmission.

(iii) *Transmission range constraints:*

$$E_{pmax} \geq E_t^x \geq d_{xy}^{\alpha} l_{xy} \qquad xy \in N \tag{4}$$

$$2 \leq \alpha \leq 4$$

Each node has a maximum bandwidth B and a maximum transmitting power E_{pmax}. B of a node is the sum total of all the transmitted and received loads, i.e., their sum should not exceed the bandwidth capacity of the node as shown in the inequality 5. The first summation term represents all the outgoing packets at node x, and the second summation term represents all the incoming packets.

(iv) *Bandwidth constraints:*

$$\sum_{s,d} \sum_y l_{xy}^{sd} \lambda^{sd} + \sum_{s,d} \sum_y l_{yx}^{sd} \lambda^{sd} \leq B \qquad \forall x \in N \tag{5}$$

The flow constraints shown in eqn. 6 highlight the ILP problem where the flow over the $s - d$ pair is not splittable, l_{xy}^{sd} represents the entire flow between $s - d$ pair going through link $x - y$. The ILP problem is found to be NP-hard.

(v) *Flow constraints:*

$$\sum_y l_{xy}^{sd} - \sum_y l_{yx}^{sd} = \begin{cases} l^{sd} & \text{if } s = x \\ -l^{sd} & \text{if } d = x \\ 0 & \text{otherwise} \end{cases} \qquad \forall x \in N \tag{6}$$

$$l_{xy}^{sd} \leq l_{xy} \qquad \forall xy \in L \tag{7}$$

The constraint eqn. 8 ensures that the hop count for each node pair does not exceed the maximum count for any $s - d$ pair. An increased hop count will lead to a greater delay between the $s - d$ pair.

(vi) *Hop constraints:*

$$\sum_{xy \in r} l_{xy}^{sd} \leq h_{sd} \qquad \forall sd \in L \tag{8}$$

(vii) *Network Lifetime*: The lifetime of a node x is given by:

$$T_{max}^{x} = \frac{E_{emax}^{x}}{\displaystyle\sum_{y \in P_x} e_{xy} \sum_{sd} \lambda^{sd} l_{xy}^{sd}} \qquad x \in N \qquad (9)$$

The *lifetime* of the ad hoc wireless network T_{nl}, is defined as the active period of the network during which nodes are able to process and transmit data until a node fails due to exhaustion of its battery, resulting in the partitioning of the network. Therefore, the network lifetime T_{nl} under flow λ is the time when the first node in N dies out and the network is partitioned. Therefore, by minimizing the denominator in eqn. 9 the life time of the network can be augmented. We have,

$$T_{nl} = \min_{x \in N} T_{max}^{x} \qquad (10)$$

So,

$$T_{nl} = \min_{x \in N} \frac{E_{emax}^{x}}{\displaystyle\sum_{y \in P_x} e_{xy} \sum_{sd} \sum_{sd} \lambda^{sd} l_{xy}^{sd}} \qquad (11)$$

It is important to note that by routing the flow on to many shorter edges than few longer edges will invariably increase the energy consumed along that path. For a given request, the goal is to find a route that minimizes the maximum energy consumption. The modified MILP aims at finding this route and maximizing the life time of the network.

The Mixed Integer Linear Programming Model (MILP) is used for multiple path routing between a source destination pair. The notations used in MILP formulation are same as the ILP model except for the Bandwidth and Route Constraints which split the flow as shown in equations 12 and 13.

(i) *Bandwidth constraints*:

$$\sum_{s,d} \sum_{y} \Lambda_{xy}^{sd} + \sum_{s,d} \sum_{y} \Lambda_{yx}^{sd} \le B_w \qquad \forall x \in N \qquad (12)$$

(ii) *Flow constraints*:

$$\sum_{y} \Lambda_{xy}^{sd} - \sum_{y} \Lambda_{yx}^{sd} = \begin{cases} \Lambda^{sd} & \text{if } s = x \\ -\Lambda^{sd} & \text{if } d = x \quad \forall x \in N \\ 0 & \text{otherwise} \end{cases} \qquad (13)$$

The problem is to find a route within the hop-count h_{sd}, which minimizes the maximum transmitting power E_t^x for all nodes on the path, thus maximizing the network lifetime T_{nl}. We assume that each node can transmit signals to its neighbor in an error free way and the MAC layer protocols do not have signal interference in transmissions. Initially requests are routed on short edge paths (high energy consumption paths) in view of reducing transmitting power and later re-routed using *REAR* algorithm to reduce energy consumption. In the *RBAR* algorithm initially requests are routed on low energy consumption paths and later re-routed to reduce the total load flowing on a node. Both *REAR* and *RBAR* algorithms are compared in this paper.

4.1   Algorithm: Residual Energy Adaptive Routing(REAR)

The following notations are used in this algorithm.

- $Q = (s, d, \Lambda^{sd})$ is the set of requests.
- $k = |Q|$, is the total number of requests.
- W_x, is the weight of a node $x \in N$.
- $f_i(x)$, is the flow of request $i(1$ to $k)$ on node x.
- f_i^*, is the minimal flow for request i.
- C_i, is the cost of flow for request i.
- C_i^*, is the minimum cost of flow for request i.
- $\gamma(x)$, is the energy utilization at node x.
- γ^*, is the optimal value of γ(minimum possible maximum energy utilization).
- γ^0 is the energy utilization of the system at the start.
- ϵ, an error parameter greater that zero.
- η, is parameter in the exponent of the value W_x.
- σ, is the fraction of flow to reroute.

The aim is to find a scheme to route each request so that the maximum energy utilization is minimized. γ^* is the minimum possible maximum energy utilization. The flow is optimal if its utilization γ is atmost a factor $(1 + \epsilon)$ more than the minimum possible value γ^*, $\gamma \le (1 + \epsilon)\gamma^*$. It is either infeasible or feasible to give a flow for the problem, in which the utilization of each node is increased by a factor $(1 + \epsilon)$ where $\epsilon > 0$ be an error parameter. The input to a MILP may have some measurement error, by making ϵ small enough. A procedure for determining feasibility up to the precision of the input data can be obtained. ϵ is at most 1 and for $\epsilon > 1$ its value can be taken as 1.

Let W_x be a non-negative weight on node x. Then, the cost of the current flow for request i, using C_i as the cost function is shown in eqn. 14.

$$C_i = \sum_{xy \in L} W_x f_i(x) \qquad \forall i \in Q \tag{14}$$

For request i, C_i^* is the minimum cost function. Then the flow of the request is optimal if.

$$C_i - C_i^* = \epsilon C_i + \epsilon \frac{\gamma}{k} \sum_x W_x E_{emax}^x \tag{15}$$

else the flow is not optimal.

The algorithm $REAR$ takes a non-optimal input flow that has utilization γ^0 and error ϵ and returns a flow which is optimal or has an utilization at most $\gamma^0/2$. The procedure re-routes a fraction σ of the flow, of a non-optimal node onto a minimal flow of the request in order to reduce the energy utilization. [12]

A weight function $W_x = \frac{e^{\eta\gamma(x)}}{E_{emax}^x}$ has the property that the weight of a node x is a function of the energy utilization. It is a fraction of the energy of the node that is being used. By using the weight function, we penalize nodes with higher weights as nodes having higher energy utilization.

Table 1. Residual Energy Adaptive Re-Routing(REAR)

```
REAR()
begin
    γ = γ₀, η = 2(1+ε)/(γ⁰ε) ln(L/ε)

    While (γ ≥ γ⁰ / 2) and (γ ≤ (1 + 9ε)γ*)
do
    begin
        σ = ε/(8ηγ)
        For each node x, Wₓ = e^(ηγ(x))/E^x_emax
        Find max(Cᵢ) for rerouting
            i∈Q
        if Cᵢ - Cᵢ* = εCᵢ + ε(γ/k)Σₓ WₓE^x_emax then
        begin
            Find f*(x) a minimal flow for request i.
            fᵢ(x) = (1 - σ)fᵢ(x) + σfᵢ*(x)
        end
    end
end
```

The *REAR* procedure keeps finding flow requests with max(C_i) and repeatedly re-routes the flow so as to decrease the maximum flow on each node by setting $f_i(x) = (1 - \sigma)f_i(x) + \sigma f_i^*(x)$ and re-computes the weight function repeatedly producing an improved flow. Then the minimum energy utilization at the node x is as follows:

$$\gamma(x) = \frac{\sum_{y\in P_x} e_{xy} \sum_{sd} \lambda_{xy}^{sd}}{E_{emax}^x} \qquad (16)$$

$$\gamma(x) = \gamma^0 = \max_{x\in N}(\gamma(x)) = \frac{1}{T_{nl}} \qquad (17)$$

This results in maximizing the network life time T_{nl}, the *REAR* algorithm is shown in Table.I.

The *REAR* algorithm can be modified from energy utilization to bandwidth constraint. The values corresponding to $\gamma(x)$, γ^0, γ^*, E_{emax}^x can be changed to $\beta(x)$ bandwidth utilization at node x, β^0 is the bandwidth utilization of the system at the start, β^* is the optimal value of β(minimum possible maximum bandwidth utilization) and B_{max}^x (maximum bandwidth at node x) resulting in the expressions:

$$\beta(x) = \frac{\sum_{s,d}\sum_y \Lambda_{xy}^{sd} + \sum_{s,d}\sum_y \Lambda_{yx}^{sd}}{B_{max}^x} \qquad (18)$$

$$\beta(x) = \beta^0 = \max_{x \in N}(\beta(x)) \tag{19}$$

And, the algorithm is called Residual Bandwidth Adaptive Rerouting (RBAR). We observe that *REAR* performs better than *RBAR*. In *REAR* the fraction of the flow that is re-routed is proportional to the energy that is available at the node resulting in shorter edges allocated uniformly through out the network that leads to lower consumption of energy. In *RBAR*, the re-routing of flow is proportional to the bandwidth, and in cases of large bandwidth and low energy available at the node, hence longer edges are chosen independent of the energy available at the nodes thereby draining the nodes early. The earlier works have emphasized on bandwidth constraint solutions while we have used energy constraint solutions resulting in enhanced lifetime of the network.

In summary, the flow is routed on short edges, thus increasing the energy utilized at the end nodes of the short edges resulting in the depletion of battery and reduction in the life time of the nodes, which may result in the partitioning of the network. To increase the life time, we re-route the flow on the nodes which have low energy utilization. Nodes are penalized by assigning higher cost based on the energy utilization and we compute the cost of all the flows. The minimum cost route is computed for the maximum cost flow and the fraction(σ) of the same flow is re-routed on the minimum cost route. Cost of the nodes is recomputed and the above procedure is repeated until the flow is optimized.

5   Performance Evaluations

The performance of the proposed *REAR* algorithm and the *RBAR* algorithm are evaluated. The simulations are obtained using matlog a toolbox for MATLAB 6.5. In the simulation setup, the nodes are placed in a 30x30 two-dimensional region and are randomly and uniformly distributed within the workspace. All

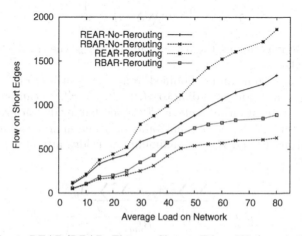

Fig. 1. REAR/RBAR: Flow on Shorter Edges VS Average Load

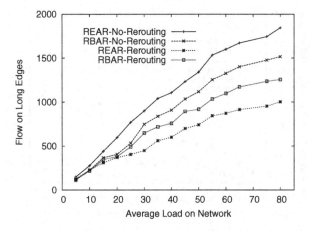

Fig. 2. REAR/RBAR: Flow on Longer Edges VS Average Load

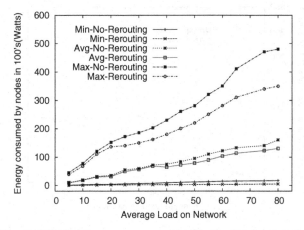

Fig. 3. REAR: Energy consumed by Nodes VS Average Load

nodes have the same maximum energy E = 20,000 units. The distance between two nodes is computed by *Euclidean distance*. The number of requests originating at a node is obtained using random Poisson function with mean value of $\mu = 1.5$ to generate a request of k. As mentioned earlier, the destination for these k requests are chosen randomly. The traffic between a sd pair is obtained by a random function of a normal distribution with variance of $0.75\mu_m$ where μ_m is the mean value of the normal distribution function. The maximum bandwidth is 500 units. The graphs are plotted for 5 to 80 units. The analysis of the results reveals that there is a reduction in energy utilization of the nodes using the *REAR* algorithm when compared with the *RBAR* algorithm.

The flow on shorter edges before and after rerouting for the *REAR* and the *RBAR* algorithms is shown in Fig. 1. There is a substantial increase of flow along the shorter edges before and after re-routing in the *REAR* algorithm.

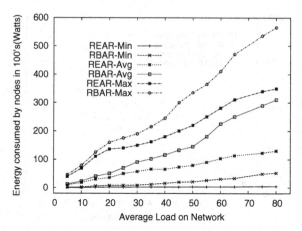

Fig. 4. REAR/RBAR: Energy consumed by Nodes VS Average Load

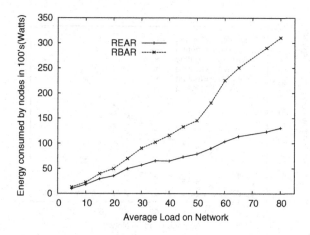

Fig. 5. REAR/RBAR: Average Energy consumed by Nodes VS Average Load

Redirecting the traffic on the shorter edges will invariably normalize the power consumption across the nodes of the network resulting in increased life time of the network. Using *REAR*, fraction of the flow retained along short edges is more than the fraction of the flow re-routed along to shorter edges using *RBAR*.

The flow along longer edges before and after rerouting for the *REAR* and the *RBAR* algorithms is shown in Fig. 2. There is a substantial decrease of flow along the longer edges before and after re-routing using our algorithm, avoiding traffic on the longer edges invariably helps in increasing the life time of the network, since longer paths necessitate the nodes to consume more energy. Even if the flow increases along the longer edges, the bulk of the flow continues to flow on the shorter edge paths, since this is the basic principle governing energy utilization for increasing lifetime. Using *REAR*, a fraction of flow re-routed along longer edges is less than the fraction of flow retained along longer edges using *RBAR*.

The energy consumed by the nodes for the minimum, average and maximum for the *REAR* algorithm before and after re-routing is shown in Fig. 3. There is a drop in the energy consumed after re-routing and larger at higher loads, especially when the network load is high.

Fig. 4 highlights the most important graph, it compares the energy consumed for the minimum, average and maximum cases after re-routing between the *REAR* and *RBAR* implementations. It can be clearly seen that *REAR* algorithm gives better performance in all the three cases and is significantly larger at higher loads. In Fig. 5 the average energy consumed at nodes after re-routing between the *REAR* and the *RBAR* algorithms is shown. The average energy difference is exponential with increase in the network load and is clearly evident.

6   Conclusions

In this paper we have proposed a topology control energy management to increase the lifetime of the network. In our approach, the flow requests are initially routed along short edges even though short edges utilize slightly higher energy. In addition, the REAR algorithm has been used to re-route a fraction of the flow along longer edges to normalize the average consumption of energy across all nodes of the network. The MILP algorithm in conjunction with the REAR algorithm ensures uniform energy utilization among the nodes of the network resulting in increased life span of the network. We have compared the MILP-REAR with the MILP-RBAR algorithms and it is observed that the average energy consumption in the MILP-REAR algorithm is closer to the minimum energy utilization at all the nodes and is much lower than that of the MILP-RBAR model. The energy utilization is significantly lower at high loads. The connectivity of the network and QOS utilization of shorter edges have contributed to increased life span of the network.

References

1. Bambos, N.: Toward Power-Sensitive Network Architectures in Wireless Communications: Concepts, Issues, and Design Aspects. IEEE Personal Communications, **vol 5** (1998) 50–59.
2. Lloyd E. L., Liu, R., Marathe, M., Ramanathan, R., Ravi, S.S.: Algorithmic Aspects of Topology Control Problems for Ad Hoc Networks. The Third ACM International Symposium on Mobile Ad Hoc Networking and Computing (MobiHoc), Laussane, Switzerland, (2002).
3. Chang, L., Tassiluas, L.: Energy Conservation Routing in Wirless Ad Hoc Networks. Proc. of IEEE INFOCOM 2000 Tel-Aviv, March (2000) 22–31.
4. Wieselthier, J., Nguyen, G., Ephremides, A.: Energy Efficient Broadcast and Multicast Trees in Wireless Networks. Mobile Networks and Applications (MONET), vol. 7 no. 6 (2002), 481–492.
5. Wieselthier, J., Nguyen, G., Ephremides, A.: Energy-aware Wireless Networking with Directional Antennas: The case of Session-based Broadcasting and Multicasting. IEEE Transactions on Mobile Computing, vol. 1 no. 3 (2002) 176–191.

6. Wieselthier, J., Nguyen, G., Ephremides, A.: Resource Management in Energy-Limited, Bandwidth-Limited, Transceiver-Limited Wireless Networks for Session-Based Multicasting. Computer Networks, vol. 39 (2002) 113–131.
7. Tommaso Melodia., Dario Pompili., Ian Akyildiz, F.: On the Interdependence of Distributed Topology Control and Geographical Routing in Ad Hoc and Sensor Networks. IEEE Journal on Selected Areas in Communication, vol. 23 no. 3 March (2002) 520–532.
8. Xiang-Yang Li., Yu Wang: Applications of k-Local MST for Topology Control and Broadcasting in Wireless Ad Hoc Networks. IEEE Transactions on Parallel and Distributed Systems, vol. 15 no. 12 December (2004) 1057–1069.
9. Ash Mohammad Abbas., Bijendra Nath Jain: Topology Control in Heterogeneous Mobile Ad hoc Networks. ICPWC, (2005) 47–51.
10. Shiva Prakash T., Arvinda C., Deepak A. P., Kamal S., Mahantesh H. L., Venu-gopal K. R., Patnaik L. M.: Efficient Passive Clustering and Gateway Selection In MANETs. Proc. of the 7th International Workshop on Distributed Computing, LNCS, (2005) 548–553.
11. Shiva Prakash T., Venugopal K. R., Patnaik L. M.: Efficient Gateway Selection for Passive Clustering in MANETs. International Journal of Computer Science and Network Security, vol. 5 no. 10. October (2005) 64–70.
12. Shiva Prakash T., Venugopal K. R., Patnaik L. M.: Energy Aware Topology Control in MANETs. Technical Report. Department of Computer Science Engineering, University Visvesvaraya College of Engineering, Bangalore University, Bangalore, December 2005.

On Maximizing Network Lifetime of Broadcast in WANETs Under an Overhearing Cost Model

Guofeng Deng and Sandeep K.S. Gupta

Arizona State University, Tempe, AZ 85281, USA
{guofeng.deng, sandeep.gupta}@asu.edu

Abstract. Absence of line power supplies imposes severe constraints on nodes in wireless ad hoc and sensor networks. In this paper, we concentrate on finding a broadcast tree that maximizes the network's lifetime. Previous studies showed that this problem is polynomially solvable when assuming receivers consume no energy or only designated receivers consume energy for receiving packets. Due to the broadcast nature of the wireless medium, however, unintended active nodes in the receiving range of a transmitting node may overhear the message and hence contribute to energy wastage. Under the overhearing cost (OC) model, the problem becomes NP-hard and the approximation ratio of the existing solutions, which are optimal under the non-overhearing cost (NOC) model, can be as bad as $\Omega(n)$. We investigate the problem by developing heuristic solutions. Simulation results show that our algorithms outperform the existing ones by up to 100%.

1 Introduction

Broadcast is an essential networking primitive in Wireless Ad hoc NETworks (WANETs) with a wide range of applications such as software updating, teleconferencing and on-line gaming. In particular, it is widely applied to command and query distribution in Wireless Sensor Networks (WSNs). However, the limited energy battery-powered wireless nodes impose severe energy constraints. This mandates efficient usage of energy resources for all the computation and communication tasks including a network-wide broadcast, as fast energy drain-out may lead to network partition and short network lifetime. Maximizing the lifetime of a broadcast operation is, therefore, imperative for improved availability of broadcast services.

One of the efficient and most widely used broadcast structure in WANETs is the tree-based structure. We adopt the definition of network lifetime of broadcast as the duration in which the source node is capable of transmitting broadcast packets to each node in the network. Approaches to maximizing tree based broadcast network lifetime fall into two categories: *static* [1] [2] [3] [4] [5] and *dynamic* [6] [7]. In a static approach, a single broadcast tree is used throughout the broadcast session, i.e. a broadcast tree is fixed once formed. In a dynamic approach, a series of broadcast trees is employed one after another, i.e. broadcast trees are updated during the broadcast session. Essentially, the latter may improve the fairness of battery utilization in each node and hence prolong the network lifetime. However, control overhead for frequent information exchange and network wide synchronization may impact the potential lifetime increment.

S. Chaudhuri et al. (Eds.): ICDCN 2006, LNCS 4308, pp. 215–226, 2006.

We concentrate on the static approach to the problem of maximizing network lifetime of broadcast, or equivalently *Maximizing Broadcast Tree Lifetime* (MaxBTL). The problem was addressed before by omitting receiving cost. In reality, however, a receiver's power consumption is not negligible [8] [9] [10] [11]. It was further studied in a model, which assumed that only designated receivers consume energy for receiving packets. In reality, however, this model relies on the synchronization among neighboring nodes, i.e. at any time only the transmitter and its designated receivers are active, but all other nearby nodes are switched off to avoid overhearing. We refer to the above model, under which receivers consume no energy or only designated receivers consume energy for receiving packets, as the *Non-Overhearing Cost* (NOC) model.

In this paper, we study the MaxBTL problem under a power consumption model in which a node consumes a certain amount of energy for receiving a packet either as a designated or non-designated receiver. This model is referred to as the *Overhearing Cost* (OC) model. While it is polynomially solvable under the NOC model, the MaxBTL problem becomes NP-hard due to the consideration of overhearing cost. We show that the two solutions, which are optimal under the NOC model, can perform $\Omega(n)$ times worse than the optimal solution under the OC model. We then propose two heuristic solutions, which take into account the overhearing cost when generating a broadcast tree. Simulation results show that they outperform the existing solutions. In particular, the performance of PRP is better than that of TPO and DRP by up to 100%.

The rest of the paper is organized as follows. Section 2 briefly summarizes related work. Section 3 introduces the network model and formulates the optimization problem. Section 4 investigates heuristic solutions to the MaxBTL problem under the OC model. Section 5 reports simulation results. Finally, Section 6 concludes the paper.

2   Related Work

Camerini proved that a Minimum-weight Spanning Tree (MST) minimizes the maximum link weight among all the spanning trees in an undirected graph [12]. Its application to a WANET, which is modeled as an undirected graph, includes that a MST minimizes the maximum transmission power among all the broadcast trees. In a special case, where homogenous nodes carry identical batteries, the lifetime of a node is inversely proportional to its transmission power and hence a MST is a maximum lifetime broadcast tree [3]. Das et al. extended the result to a network composed of nodes with various battery capacities and proposed a minimum decremental lifetime (MDLT) algorithm [4]. Lloyd et al. and Floréen et al. sought a subnetwork of maximum lifetime in which the source node is connected to all the broadcast group members [1] [2]. It is easy to see that any broadcast tree contained in such a subnetwork has the maximum lifetime. All the above solutions assume that the receiver consumes no energy for receiving packets. In [5], we proposed a polynomial optimal solution to the problem of MaxBTL under the assumption that only the designated receivers consume receiving power. In this paper, we take into account the receiving cost of non-designated receivers as well.

Recently, some topology control methods have been developed with the goal of minimizing interference [13] [14]. The interference of a link is evaluated in terms of the number of nodes that are affected by the bidirectional transmission between the two incident nodes in the resulting subnetwork; the interference of a node is defined as the maximum link interference of all the links incident to it. Interference-aware topology control techniques intend to minimizing the maximum or average interference of all links or nodes in the resulting subnetwork. In this paper, however, we are interested in minimizing the number of nodes than can be overheard along with the transmission cost. The two problems are different because a large amount of interference does not necessarily mean high overhearing cost and vice versa. For example, a subnetwork has a high level of interference if there is a link that covers all the nodes in the network. But if the covering-all link is incident to the source node, it involves no overhearing cost for broadcast, in which the source node directly transmits packets to all the nodes.

3   Preliminaries

3.1   Network Model

In WANETs, a node may act as a transmitter, a receiver or both. The *power consumption* in milliWatts (mW) of the transceiver of a node u, denoted by p_u, is the sum of transmission power (due to the amplifier in the transceiver), energy expenditure in the transmitter circuit electronics (e.g. multiplexing), and receiving power, denoted by p_u^{tr}, p_u^{ce} and p_u^{rc}, respectively, i.e. $p_u = p_u^{\mathrm{tr}} + p_u^{\mathrm{ce}} + p_u^{\mathrm{rc}}$. In particular, $p_u^{\mathrm{rc}} = 0$ if u does not receive any packet from other nodes; $p_u^{\mathrm{tr}} = p^{\mathrm{ce}} = 0$ if u does not forward any packet to other nodes, e.g. a leaf node in a multicast tree.

A signal can be successfully detected if the signal strength at the receiver is above a certain level after traversing the fading channel. For any pair of nodes u and v, we define $p(u, v)$ as the *transmission power threshold* (TPT) of u being successfully received by v. In other words, the transmission from u to v necessitates $p_u^{\mathrm{tr}} \geq p(u, v)$. Notice that we do not require that $p(u, v) = p(v, u)$. In the wireless medium, a single transmission can be received by multiple receivers. This effect that assists in conserving energy is referred to as *Wireless Multicast Advantage* [15]. To reach a set C of neighbors, p_u^{tr} of node u, which uses an antenna of appropriate directionality, is set to the maximum TPT to any node in C, i.e. $p_u^{\mathrm{tr}} = \max_{v \in C} p(u, v)$.

Motivated by [10], we present the OC model as follows. A node consumes a fixed amount of energy for receiving a packet from any other node. Hence, for each broadcast packet, the receiving cost of a node v is determined by the number of copies that v receives from its parent node as well as other neighboring nodes. Alternatively, we consider the receiving power p_v^{rc} of node v is proportional to the number of receivable neighbors around v, i.e. $p_v^{\mathrm{rc}} = \hat{p}_v^{\mathrm{rc}} \sum_{u \in N} X(u, v)$, where $\hat{p}_v^{\mathrm{rc}}$ is a node-dependent constant power cost for receiving packets by node v, N is the set of nodes in the network and $X(u, v) = 1$ if v receives packets from u, i.e. $p_u^{\mathrm{tr}} \geq p(u, v)$, otherwise $X(u, v) = 0$. For example, Fig. 1 depicts a broadcast tree rooted at the source node s in a WANET with symmetric TPT, i.e. the TPT of both directions is same between each pair of nodes. Under the OC model, node s can overhear the transmission by node a to b and c. Hence, $p_s = p(s, a) + p_s^{\mathrm{ce}} + \hat{p}_s^{\mathrm{rc}}$; while under the NOC model, $p_s = p(s, a) + p_s^{\mathrm{ce}}$.

We model a WANET as a directed and link-weighted graph $G = (V, A, p)$ called a *Transmission Power Graph* (TPG), where V is a set of nodes, A is a set of links and $p : A \to \mathbb{R}^+$ is a weight function. For each pair of nodes $u, v \in V$, there is a link in

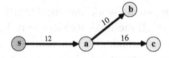

Fig. 1. A broadcast tree rooted at node s. An arrow that starts from a transmitter and ends in a receiver is associated with the transmission power threshold in milliWatts.

A joining u and v, denoted by (u, v), if $\mathcal{P}_u^{\mathrm{tr}} \geq p(u, v)$, where $\mathcal{P}_u^{\mathrm{tr}}$ is a node-dependent constraint called the *maximum transmission power*. The weight of a link (u, v) assigned by the function p is the TPT from u to v, i.e. $p(u, v)$. A node u is capable of adjusting its transmission power up to $\mathcal{P}_u^{\mathrm{tr}}$. While "broadcast tree" is a term used in networks, "spanning tree" is the counterpart in graph theory.

3.2   Battery Life

We denote the *battery capacity* in Watt-Hour (WH) of a node u by E_u, which may vary from node to node. A battery is treated as a linear storage of current and remains functional until the rated capacity of energy has been dissipated [8]. For example, the *lifetime* in hours (H) of a node u, denoted by ℓ_u, is the ratio between E_u and its power consumption p_u, i.e. $\ell_u = \dfrac{E_u}{p_u}$, since the transceiver is the dominant power consumer during the system operation in a wireless node [16]. We note that the lifetime computed under the linear model does not necessarily reflect the actual period of time in which the battery is functional [17]. However, the essence of maximizing network lifetime of broadcast is to balance the energy consumption at each node. In this sense, the linear model allows us to concentrate on how to improve the fairness. We put into our future consideration the effects of non-linear factors on the battery lifetime [18,19]. In the rest of the paper, we assume that a node is reliable in the sense that it dies only in the case of depletion of the battery energy.

3.3   Problem Statement

The *lifetime of a broadcast tree* T, denoted by $\mathcal{L}(T)$, is the period of time until the first node in T fails, i.e. $\mathcal{L}(T) = \min_{u \in T^{\mathrm{n}}} \ell_u$, where T^{n} is the set of nodes in T [3,4,1,2]. In this paper, given a WANET W, which consists of stationary battery-powered nodes, and a source node s, we investigate the problem of MaxBTL, which is to seek a broadcast tree T^* such that $\mathcal{L}(T^*) = \max_{T \in \mathcal{T}} \mathcal{L}(T)$, where $\mathcal{T}$ is the set of broadcast trees rooted at s in W. Notice that the network lifetime of simultaneous multi-session broadcast is more complicated and beyond the discussion in this paper.

Overhearing cost makes the problem difficult because considering transmission power level exclusively does not suffice. In some cases, a node which is not transmitting but only receiving packets from nearby nodes dies earlier than nodes that transmit packets. Actually, the MaxBTL problem under the OC model is NP-hard because a special case of the problem is equivalent to the minimum set cover problem, which is known to be NP-hard [20]. We omit the proof due to limited space.

It is easy to see that if each node has an identical level of battery energy, the MaxBTL problem is equivalent to finding a tree that minimizes the maximum nodal power consumption among all the broadcast trees. In this paper, we assume identical battery capacity for presentation simplicity. However, with minor modifications, e.g. replacing nodal power consumption by node lifetime as metric, the solutions presented in the rest of the paper are applicable to the non-identical battery cases.

4 Heuristic Solutions

In this section, we first summarize the two optimal algorithms, namely **Transmission Power Only** (TPO) and **Designated Receiver Power** (DRP), to the MaxBTL problem under the NOC model. Then, we propose two greedy heuristic solutions, **Cumulative Designated Receiver Power** (CDRP) and **Proximity Receiver Power** (PRP). Each of the algorithms iteratively grows a spanning that is rooted at the given source node. In each iteration, a link, which has the minimum "weight" all the links that join an on-tree node and a non-on-tree node, is included in the tree. All the four algorithms are greedy, but different definitions of the link weight contribute different performances.

4.1 TPO and DRP Algorithms

In TPO, the weight of a link (u, v), denoted by $w(u, v)$, only considers the power consumed for transmitting packets, i.e.

$$w(u, v) = p(u, v) + p_u^{\text{ce}} .\tag{1}$$

We present TPO in Algorithm 1. Tree T is initialized to the source node s. In each iteration of the *while* loop in Lines 2 through 8, a link is included into T until T spans every node in the network. The *for* loop in Lines 4 through 6 is used to choose a link (x, y), which joins an on-tree node and a non-on-tree node, that has the lowest weight. In a TPG consisting of n vertices and m links, the *while* loop and the *for* loop run $O(n)$ and $O(m)$ times, respectively. Therefore, the time complexity of TPO is $O(mn)$.

In contrast to TPO, which omits receiving cost, DRP takes into account the effects of receiving cost on the designated receivers. Specifically, the transmitting node consumes energy for receiving packets from its parent node in addition to the transmission power unless it is the source node; the designated receiver receives the packet by consuming some power. Hence, the weight of a link (u, v) is defined as the maximum of the power consumption between the transmitting node u and receiving node v, i.e.

$$w(u, v) = \begin{cases} \max\{p(u, v) + p_u^{\text{ce}}, \hat{p}_u^{\text{rc}}\}, & \text{if } u \text{ is the source node,} \\ \max\{p(u, v) + p_u^{\text{ce}} + \hat{p}_u^{\text{rc}}, \hat{p}_u^{\text{rc}}\}, & \text{otherwise.} \end{cases}\tag{2}$$

The time complexity of DRP is $O(mn)$ where n and m are the number of nodes and links respectively in a TPG. TPO and DRP are optimal solutions to the MaxBTL problem under the assumption of no receiver cost and designated receiver cost, respectively [12] [3] [5]. However, we show that they can perform as bad as $\Omega(n)$ times of the optimal value under the OC model in Theorem 1, where n is the network size.

Algorithm 1. Transmission Power Only (TPO) & Designated Receiver Power (DRP)

Input: A TPG $G = (V, A, p)$ and a node $s \in V$
Output: A spanning tree $T = (V', A')$
1: $V' \leftarrow \{s\}$; $A' \leftarrow \phi$
2: **while** $|V'| < |V|$ **do**
3:     $w(x, y) \leftarrow \infty$ {(x, y) is the link to be included in T}
4:     **for all** $u \in V'$ and $v \in V \backslash V'$ and $(u, v) \in A$ and $w(x, y) > w(u, v)$ **do**
5:         $x \leftarrow u$; $y \leftarrow v$
6:     **end for**
7:     $V' \leftarrow V' \cup \{y\}$; $A' \leftarrow A' \cup \{(x, y)\}$
8: **end while**
9: **return** T

Theorem 1. *Under the OC model, TPO and DRP have an approximation ratio that can be as bad as $\Omega(n)$, where n is the network size.*

Proof. Consider a TPG $G = (V, A, p)$ depicted in Fig. 2(a), where s is the source node and the rest are destinations. Each link is associated with its TPT. Let $\hat{p}_u^{\text{rc}} = t$ and $p_u^{\text{ce}} = 0$ for each node $u \in V$. Let ϵ be a sufficiently small positive real number. We first examine the result of TPO. Initially, s is the only node in T; then links (s, a) and (s, f) are picked because they both have the lowest TPT, i.e. $t - \epsilon$; in the third iteration, links that join an on-tree node and a non-on-tree node include (a, b), (f, b), (f, c), (f, d) and (f, e). Among them, (a, b) has the lowest weight t compared to the weight of all other links, which is $t + \epsilon$, and hence is included in T. Similarly, links (b, c), (c, d) and (d, e) are included in that order. In the resulting tree shown in Fig. 2(b), each node on the border, except for node e, is a transmitting node and is overheard by node f located in the center. Therefore, the maximum power consumption is $5t$ by node f in the resulting tree. Fig. 2(c) shows an optimal solution for the given TPG, in which the node in the center acts a transmitting node and forwards packets to all the nodes on the border. The maximum power consumption in the optimal solution is $t + t = 2t$ irrespective of the size of the network. In a generic network, we can enlarge the network depicted in Fig. 2(a) by allocating more nodes on the border. If n is the network size, then the maximum power consumption of a spanning tree constructed by using TPO is $(n - 2)t$. So, the approximation ratio of TPO is at least $(n - 2)/2$, i.e. $\Omega(n)$. A similar analysis will show that DRP has an approximation ratio of $\Omega(n)$ under the OC model.

4.2   CDRP Algorithm

A common problem of the above algorithms is that the effects of receiving power because of overhearing is neglected. We present CDRP, an extension to DRP, that takes into account the receiving power, possibly contributed by overhearing, of the transmitting node of a link. Apparently, a node that excessively overhears nearby traffic is not the transmitting node of an ideal candidate link. Therefore, the weight of a link (u, v) is defined as:

$$w(u, v) = \max \left\{ p(u, v) + p_u^{\text{ce}} + p_u^{\text{rc}}, \hat{p}_v^{\text{rc}} \right\} . \tag{3}$$

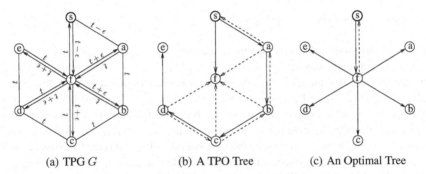

(a) TPG G (b) A TPO Tree   (c) An Optimal Tree

Fig. 2. Theorem 1. A solid line represents two directional link toward opposite directions. A dotted arc represents an overhearing transmission. In (a), each link is associated with its TPT.

We present CDRP in Algorithm 2. For each node u, p_u^{rc} and p_u^{tr} are initialized to be 0. Adding a link (x, y) increases the transmission power the selected transmitter x (see Line 14). On the other hand, it may cause overhearing by the nearby nodes. Specifically, a node k will have the additional cost $\hat{p}_k^{rc}$ for overhearing packets transmitted by u if k can hear u after (x, y) is included while it cannot before that (see Lines 11 through 13). This condition can avoid overcounting k's receiving power. In a TPG consisting of n nodes and m links, the *while* loop runs n times and each *for* loop runs $O(m)$ times. Therefore, similar to TPO and DRP, CDRP has the time complexity of $O(mn)$.

Algorithm 2. Cumulative Designated Receiver Power (CDRP)

Input: A TPG $G = (V, A, p)$ and a node $s \in V$
Output: A spanning tree $T = (V', A')$
1: $V' \leftarrow \{s\}$; $A' \leftarrow \phi$
2: **for all** $u \in V$ **do**
3:     $p_u^{rc} \leftarrow 0, p_u^{tr} \leftarrow 0$
4: **end for**
5: **while** $|V'| < |V|$ **do**
6:     $w(x, y) \leftarrow \infty$ {(x, y) is the link to be included in T}
7:     **for all** $u \in V'$ **and** $v \in V \backslash V'$ **and** $(u, v) \in A$ **and** $w(x, y) > w(u, v)$ **do**
8:         $x \leftarrow u$; $y \leftarrow v$
9:     **end for**
10:     $V' \leftarrow V' \cup \{y\}$; $A' \leftarrow A' \cup \{(x, y)\}$
11:     **for all** $z \in V$ **and** $(x, z) \in A$ **and** $p(x, z) \leq p(x, y)$ **and** $p(x, z) > p_x^{tr}$ **do**
12:         $p_z^{rc} \leftarrow p_z^{rc} + \hat{p}_z^{rc}$ {update receiving power if z was not reached by x before}
13:     **end for**
14:     $p_x^{tr} \leftarrow p(x, y)$
15: **end while**
16: **return** T

4.3 PRP Algorithm

In CDRP, the consideration of the overhearing cost is limited to the transmitting node of a link. We propose PRP that evaluates a link as the maximum power consumption in the subnetwork within its receiving range. So, the weight of a link (u, v) is defined as

$$w(u,v) = \max\left\{p(u,v) + p_u^{\text{ce}} + p_u^{\text{rc}}, p_x^{\text{tr}} + p_x^{\text{ce}} + p_x^{\text{rc}} + \hat{p}_x^{\text{rc}}, p_y^{\text{tr}} + p_y^{\text{ce}} + p_y^{\text{rc}}\right\}, \quad (4)$$

where k is any node to be covered by u, i.e. $p(u,x) > p_u^{\text{tr}}$ and $p(u,x) \leq p(u,v)$, and y is any already covered node by u, i.e. $p(u,y) \leq p_u^{\text{tr}}$. The nodes in the former category involve an additional overhearing cost as opposed to the latter. Specifically, v is one of the to-be-covered nodes and $p_v^{\text{tr}} = p_v^{\text{ce}} = p_v^{\text{rc}} = 0$ because v is not in the receiving range of any other node. We present PRP and the computation of the link weight, the *WEIGHT* function, in Algorithms 3 and 4, respectively. In Lines 11 through 13 in Algorithm 3, the receiving cost is updated for all recently covered nodes. In Line 14, the sender's transmitting power is calculated. In a TPG consisting of n nodes and m links, the *while* loop, the *for* loop in PRP, and the *for* loop in WEIGHT run n, $O(m)$ and $O(n)$ times, respectively. Therefore, the time complexity of PRP lis $O(mn^2)$.

Algorithm 3. Proximity Receiver Power (PRP)

Input: A TPG $G = (V, A, p)$ and a node $s \in V$
Output: A spanning tree $T = (V', A')$
1: $V' \leftarrow \{s\}; A' \leftarrow \phi$
2: **for all** $u \in V$ **do**
3:    $p_u^{\text{rc}} \leftarrow 0, p_u^{\text{tr}} \leftarrow 0$
4: **end for**
5: **while** $|V'| < |V|$ **do**
6:    $w(x,y) \leftarrow \infty$ {(x,y) is the link to be included in T}
7:    **for all** $u \in V'$ **and** $v \in V \setminus V'$ **and** $(u,v) \in A$ **and** $w(x,y) > WEIGHT(u,v)$ **do**
8:       $x \leftarrow u, y \leftarrow v, w(x,y) \leftarrow WEIGHT(u,v)$
9:    **end for**
10:    $V' \leftarrow V' \cup \{y\}; A' \leftarrow A' \cup \{(x,y)\}$
11:    **for all** $k \in V$ **and** $(x,k) \in A$ **and** $p(x,k) \leq p(x,y)$ **and** $p(x,k) > p_x^{\text{tr}}$ **do**
12:       $p_k^{\text{rc}} \leftarrow p_k^{\text{rc}} + \hat{p}_k^{\text{rc}}$ {update receiving power if z was not reached by x before}
13:    **end for**
14:    $p_x^{\text{tr}} \leftarrow p(x,y)$
15: **end while**
16: **return** T

Algorithm 4. Function: $WEIGHT(u,v)$

1: $weight \leftarrow p(u,v) + p_u^{\text{ce}} + p_u^{\text{rc}}$
2: **for all** $k \in V$ **and** $p(u,k) \leq p(u,v)$ **do**
3:    **if** $weight < p_k^{\text{tr}} + p_k^{\text{ce}} + p_k^{\text{rc}} + \hat{p}_k^{\text{rc}}$ **and** $p(u,k) > p_u^{\text{tr}}$ **then**
4:       $weight \leftarrow p_k^{\text{tr}} + p_k^{\text{ce}} + p_k^{\text{rc}} + \hat{p}_k^{\text{rc}}$
5:    **else if** $weight < p_k^{\text{tr}} + p_k^{\text{ce}} + p_k^{\text{rc}}$ **and** $p(u,k) \leq p_u^{\text{tr}}$ **then**
6:       $weight \leftarrow p_k^{\text{tr}} + p_k^{\text{ce}} + p_k^{\text{rc}}$
7:    **end if**
8: **end for**
9: **return** $weight$

It is worth noting that all the four algorithms have the same performance under the assumption of no receiving cost. This is because $\hat{p}_u^{\text{rc}} = 0$ and hence $p_u^{\text{rc}} = 0$ for each node u in the network and the link weight defined in (2), (3) and (4) is reduced to (1). Furthermore, when assuming designated receiver cost only, i.e. $\hat{p}_v^{\text{rc}} = 0$ for any node v as a non-designated receiver, we can easily verify that the link weight defined by (3) and (4) is same as (2) and hence CDRP and PRP are equivalent to DRP.

5 Simulation Results

In this section, we report the results of simulating the algorithms of TPO, DRP, CDRP and PRP under various scenarios. We conducted the simulations in networks consisting of 20 to 100 nodes, randomly deployed in a $100 \times 100 \ m^2$ field. The power consumption model and the battery model described in Section 3 were adopted. The TPT $p(u, v)$ between any pair of nodes u and v was set to $K d^{\alpha}$ mW, where K is a node-dependent constant, d (in meters) is the Euclidean distance between u and v, and α is a parameter that typically takes on a value between 2 and 4, depending on the characteristics of the communication medium [15]. We chose $\alpha = 2$. For each node u, we set $p_u^{\text{ce}} = 0$ for simplicity. The maximum transmission power was set to 1000 mW for all the nodes. Setting an identical level of battery energy for each node, we evaluated the performance of the algorithms by measuring the maximum nodal power consumption in the resulting broadcast tree, which is inversely proportional to the tree lifetime according to the discussion in Section 3.3. We considered symmetric or asymmetric transmission power thresholds for the two links connecting a pair of nodes in opposite directions. In the symmetric setting, for any pair of nodes u and v, we assigned $K = 0.5$ equally, i.e. $p(u, v) = p(v, u) = 0.5 \times d^2$; in the asymmetric setting, $K=1$ or 0.5, i.e. we randomly selected either $p(u, v) = d^2$ or $p(u, v) = 0.5 \times d^2$ independent of $p(v, u)$. We conducted simulations using various scenarios with three different receiver coss: constant non-zero receiver cost and node-dependent constant receiver cost. In the figures which record the maximum power consumption, each data point averages the results in 100 random deployments and is depicted with 95% confidence interval. The lower the maximum power consumption means the higher broadcast tree lifetime and vice versa.

5.1 Zero Receiving Power

Fig. 3 plots the simulation results for zero receiving cost. The four curves perfectly overlap because they become same algorithm under the assumption as discussed. In fact, they are all optimal in this case. The maximum power consumption reduced as the network size increased. This was because the average transmission power decreased in a denser network. With the same network size, each data point for asymmetric transmission power has a somewhat bigger value than the one for symmetric transmission power. This is because, on average, the transmission power threshold in the symmetric setting is smaller than that in the asymmetric setting.

5.2 Non-zero Constant Receiving Power

Fig. 4 shows the results when the receiving power was set to half of the maximum transmission power, i.e. 500 mW, equally for each node in the network. PRP dramati-

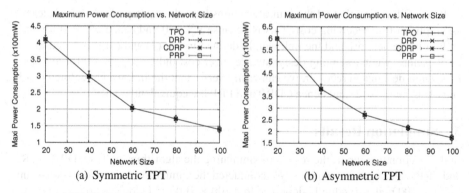

Fig. 3. Simulation results under the assumption of zero receiving power

cally outperformed TPO, DRP and CDRP. While the other 3 curves increased linearly as the network became denser, the one due to PRP was almost constant. The reason is that in general the overhearing cost of nodes in the broadcast trees generated by using TPO, DRP and CDRP is higher in a denser network. The cost was reduced by PRP which takes into account the effects of overhearing specifically. We also saw that CDRP outperformed TPO and DRP, although the difference was not as pronounced. The difference between the symmetric and asymmetric settings was not evident because the average transmission power was not as dominant as it was in the zero receiving power scenario. Furthermore, simulations with different receiving power values were conducted and the results showed the similar trends.

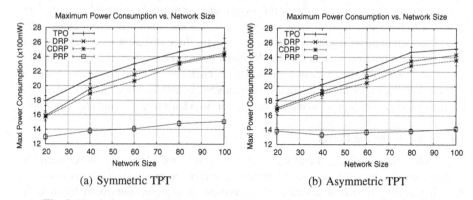

Fig. 4. Simulation results under the assumption of constant non-zero receiving power

5.3 Node-Dependent Constant Receiving Power

Fig. 5 depicts the results for node-dependent receiving power. For each node, the receiving power was randomly selected from $\frac{1}{3}$, $\frac{1}{4}$ and $\frac{1}{5}$ of the maximum transmission power, i.e. 1000 mW. We noticed the similar results to those in the constant receiving power experiments plotted in Fig. 4, except for smaller maximum power consumption values thanks to the reduced receiving power. No significant differences from Fig. 5 were observed in the additional experiments with different receiving power settings.

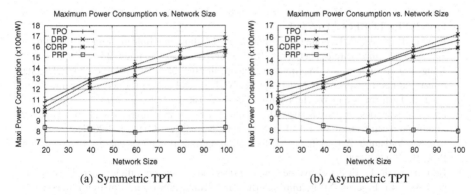

(a) Symmetric TPT   (b) Asymmetric TPT

Fig. 5. Simulation results under the assumption of node-dependent constant receiving power

6 Conclusions

In this paper, we investigated the problem of MaxBTL under the OC model that takes into account the overhearing cost. While it is polynomially solvable under the NOC model, MaxBTL becomes NP-hard under the OC model. We showed that the two solutions, TPO and DRP, which are optimal under the NOC model, can have an approximation ratio as bad as $\Omega(n)$ under the OC model. We proposed two new greedy heuristics, CDRP and PRP, by considering the effects of the overhearing cost when generating a broadcast tree. Simulation results showed that our solutions outperformed the existing solutions. In particular, PRP performed better than TPO and DRP by up to 100%.

This paper concentrated on the network lifetime maximization of a broadcast, which is a special case of the multicast problem. The latter is clearly a NP-hard problem, to which a possible heuristic solution is to prune the broadcast tree generated by CDRP or PRP such that only the necessary nodes for the multicast session are included. Performance evaluation of this prune-based approach is left for future work.

Acknowledgment

This work was supported by NSF grant ANI0196156.

References

1. Lloyd, E.L., Liu, R., Marathe, M.V.: Algorithm aspects of topology control problems for ad hoc networks. In: Proc. ACM MOBIHOC, EPFL lausanne, Switzerland (2002)
2. Floréen, P., Kaski, P., Kohonen, J., Orponen, P.: Multicast time maximization in energy constrained wireless networks. In: DIALM-POMC, San Diego, CA (2003)
3. Kang, I., Poovendran, R.: Maximizing static network lifetime of wireless broadcast adhoc networks. In: Proc. IEEE ICC. Volume 3. (2003)
4. Das, A.K., Marks, R.J., El-Sharkawi, M., Arabshahi, P., Gray, A.: MDLT: a polynomial time optimal algorithm for maximization of time-to-first-failure in energy constrained wireless broadcast networks. In: Proc. IEEE GLOBECOM. (2003)

5. Deng, G., Gupta, S.: Maximizing broadcast tree lifetime in wireless ad hoc networks. In: Proc. IEEE GLOBECOM. (2006)
6. Floréen, P., Kaski, P., Kohonen, J., Orponen, P.: Lifetime maximization for multicasting in energy-constrained wireless networks. IEEE J. Select. Areas Commun. 23(1) (2005)
7. Kang, I., Poovendran, R.: Maximizing network lifetime of broadcasting over wireless stationary ad hoc networks. ACM/Kluwer MONET Special Issue on Energy Constraints and Lifetime Performance in Wireless Sensor Networks 10(6) (2005) 879–896
8. Park, S., Savvides, A., Srivastava, M.: Battery capacity measurement and analysis using lithium coin cell battery. In: ISLPED, New York, NY, USA, ACM Press (2001)
9. Cui, S., Goldsmith, A.J., Bahai, A.: Modulation optimization under energy constraints. In: Proc. IEEE ICC. (2003)
10. Basu, P., Redi, J.: Effect of overhearing transmissions on energy efficiency in dense sensor networks. In: Proc. ACM the third international symposium on Information processing in sensor networks. (2004)
11. Vasudevan, S., Zhang, C., Goeckel, D., Towsley, D.: Optimal power allocation in wireless networks with transmitter-receiver power tradeoffs. In: Proc. IEEE INFOCOM. (2006)
12. Camerini, P.M.: The min-max spanning tree problem and some extensions. Information Processing Letters 7(1) (1978) 10–14
13. Burkhart, M., von Rickenbach, P., Wattenhofer, R., Zollinger, A.: Does topology control reduce interference? In: Proc. ACM MOBIHOC. (2004)
14. Moaveni-Nejad, K., Li, X.Y.: Low-interference topology control for wireless ad hoc networks. Ad Hoc & Sensor Wireless Networks (2005)
15. Wieselthier, J.E., Nguyen, G.D., Ephremides, A.: On the construction of energy-efficient broadcast and multicast trees in wireless networks. In: Proc. IEEE INFOCOM. (2000)
16. Raghunathan, V., Schurgers, C., Park, S., Srivastava, M.B.: Energy-aware wireless microsensor networks. In: IEEE Signal Processing Mag. Volume 19. (2002)
17. Rakhmatov, D., Vrudhula, S., Wallach, D.A.: A model for battery lifetime analysis for organizing applications on a pocket computer. IEEE Trans. VLSI Syst. 11(6) (2003) 1019–1030
18. Chiasserini, C.F., Rao, R.R.: Energy efficient battery management. IEEE J. Select. Areas Commun. 19(7) (2001) 1235–1245
19. Adamou, M., Sarkar, S.: A framework for optimal battery management for wireless nodes. In: Proc. IEEE INFOCOM. (2002)
20. Garey, M.R., Johnson, D.S.: Computers and Intractability, A Guide to the Theory of NP-Completeness. W. H. Freeman and Company, New York, NY (1979)

On Maximizing Residual Energy of Actors in Wireless Sensor and Actor Networks*

Ka. Selvaradjou and C. Siva Ram Murthy

Department of Computer Science and Engineering
Indian Institute of Technology Madras, India 600036
selvaraj@cse.iitm.ernet.in, murthy@iitm.ac.in

Abstract. We consider the problem of residual energy maximization of actors by optimal assignment of mobile actors in Wireless Sensor and Actor Networks (WSANs) to the event spots in real-time. Finding the optimal tour of multiple actors towards the reported events can be shown to be NP-Complete. We formulate the optimization problem as Mixed Integer Non Linear Programming and propose heuristics that find near optimal schedule of actors in a large scale WSAN. Maximizing the residual energy of actors leads to increased service time. We also study the impact of optimal positioning of actors at the end of their tour so as to cover up new events that might occur with stringent deadline constraints. From the simulations, we observed that the inter-zone deadline based scheduling performs fairly better than others by minimizing the overall movement required by the actors and reducing the deadline miss ratio. It is also observed from the simulations that proactive positioning of actors at the end of their schedule such that every zone is guaranteed to have at least one actor, performs better both in terms of increased lifetime and controlled deadline miss ratio.

1 Introduction

A Wireless Sensor Network (WSN) is a self-organizing ad hoc network with potential applications in autonomous monitoring, surveillance, military, health-care, and security [1]. It consists of a group of nodes, called sensor nodes, each with one or more sensors, an embedded processor, and a low power radio. Typically, these nodes are linked by a wireless medium to perform distributed sensing tasks. Sensor nodes are usually deployed in a large quantity to form an autonomous network. The data acquired by each node is sent to a base station or a sink node which uses this data for taking necessary actions.

Wireless Sensor and Actor Networks (WSANs) [2] are a new class of heterogeneous networks which include special nodes called as *Actuators* or *Actors* which are capable of acting on the environment. For example, in an application like intrusion detection, a set of sensors can relay the exact location and directional information of an intruder, to the sink node, which in turn can command the actors to pump gas on the intruders or otherwise to close the doors, thus preventing from further

---

* This work was supported by the Department of Science and Technology, New Delhi, India.

S. Chaudhuri et al. (Eds.): ICDCN 2006, LNCS 4308, pp. 227–238, 2006.

intrusion. These networks have widely differing sensor and actor node characteristics. While sensor nodes are small, inexpensive, usually static devices with limited computation, communication and energy resources, actor nodes are resource-rich and usually mobile. Also, the number of sensor nodes deployed may be in the order of hundreds or thousands. In contrast, actor nodes are smaller in number due to the different coverage requirements and physical interaction methods of actuation. Typically, a deployed WSAN is expected to operate autonomously in unattended environments. Real-time reporting of the events, scheduling of the actors such that actions are completed before deadline, coordination among the sensors and actors, and security are some important research issues in WSANs.

The rest of this paper is organized as follows. Section 2 gives an overview of related work. Section 3 gives the problem formulation for finding optimal schedule of actors in WSANs. Section 4 proposes the heuristics to achieve near optimal schedule in a distributed manner and outlines various policies for actor placement after carrying out the assigned tasks. Section 5 discusses the simulation results and compares with the solution obtained by the MINLP solver. Finally, Section 6 concludes the paper with a summary of its contributions and suggests scope for future work.

2   Related Work

Providing end-to-end real-time guarantees is a challenging problem in sensor networks. The routing protocol should be adaptive to avoid any congestion and coverage holes that might occur in the network. SPEED [3] is one such adaptive real-time routing protocol which reduces the end-to-end deadline miss ratio in sensor networks. In this protocol, every node maintains only the states of one-hop neighbors, hence scales well in sensor networks. RAP [4] is a multi-layer real-time communication architecture for sensor networks.

The authors of [5] formulated the problem of emergency vehicle routing and dispatching in real-time, as an integer programming model in which a dynamic shortest path algorithm is used. Emergency vehicles and incidents are divided into categories so that different constraints could be incorporated. The authors of [6], address two important issues of WSANs, viz., Sensor-Actor coordination and Actor-Actor coordination. In the latter case, it is assumed that sufficient number of actors are deployed so as to give enough coverage of the action range in the entire observation area. The problem is formulated as a *Residual Energy Maximization Problem* which finds, for each portion of the event area, the subset of actors that maximizes the average residual energy of all actors involved in the action, under the constraint of meeting the action completion bound. The work also proposed a localized auction control protocol in which actors coordinate among themselves so that a relatively resource rich actor is assigned to act on a selected overlapping area. This work assumes only static actors and does not consider the mobility of actors. Our work considers the case of mobile actors and finds optimum assignment of actors in order to minimize the energy consumed by the actors for mobility.

3   Problem Statement

In our work, we consider the problem of optimum assignment of actors to the
events reported by sensor nodes with the objective of minimizing the overall
movement of the actors required, guaranteeing the real-time deadline, and resource constraints of the events. Our model considers the case of mobile actors
such that they can move to the event area and act upon the environment. In
this work, we consider the problem of maximizing the residual energy of the
actors by utilizing the energy required for mobility at the minimum level possible. The problem has been formulated as a Mixed Integer Non-Linear Program
(MINLP) [7] optimization problem. This problem which is equivalent to the
Traveling Salesman Problem, can be shown to be NP-Complete. In this work we
propose heuristics that find near optimal scheduling of actors in a distributed
manner and investigate the effect of various policies by which actors are reposi-
tioned at the end of their schedules.

In this section, we present the system model, and then formulate the
problem of optimal assignments of actors in real-time sensor and actor network
applications.

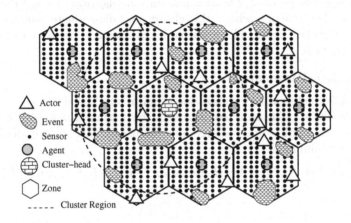

Fig. 1. Wireless Sensor and Actor Network Architecture

3.1   System Model

We consider the model of WSAN in which a large number of sensor nodes are
deployed randomly but without any sensing holes, and relatively a small number of actors distributed uniformly throughout the monitoring area. The entire
monitoring area is assumed to be divided into several zones such that every zone
is provided with at least one actor initially (Fig. 1). The actors are capable of
moving freely in the area and it is the energy required such as the battery in the
case of robots, fuel energy in the case of vehicles like trucks which we intend to
minimize, by way of optimal scheduling of events in the tour of actors such that
real-time constraints of the events are satisfied.

A relatively resource rich sensor node in every zone is elected to act as an agent which could schedule the actors for the tasks either individually (intra-zone), or by collaborating with its neighbor agents (inter-zone). All the sensor nodes within a zone report the events detected by them periodically to this agent node. This leads to a heterogeneous architecture in which multiple sink nodes are present in the network. This assumption simplifies the routing protocol to be static as the topology never changes. The actor(s) lying inside a zone get registered with their current position, and resource availability to the home agents. It is also assumed that the sensor nodes inform the position information of the detected event along with other parameters like deadline and resource constraints. The agent nodes periodically exchange the position of actors and events belonging to their zones. Thus, every agent node has a status information about its own and its neighborhood (one hop) actors and events. In the case of *intra-zone scheduling*, the agent nodes compute the optimal schedule of actors within their zone and disseminate the schedule to them. The actor(s) receives the schedule from the agent node and visit the events as per the schedule in order to take specified action to bring the events under control. In the case of *inter-zone scheduling*, the zones are further formed as clusters. One of the agent nodes is elected to be cluster-head which runs an algorithm to find the optimal schedule of all the actors within this cluster and disseminates the tour to the agents of respective zones. The agent nodes disseminate the tour to the actors of their own zone.

3.2   Problem Formulation

We formulate the following optimization problem as a Mixed Integer Non-Linear Program (MINLP). The objective is to find, the optimal assignment of actors to the events with deadline and resource constraints such that the overall movement of actors is minimized.

$$Given \; : A, E, S_{max}(A_i), RA(A_i, q, r), D(E_j), RR(E_j, q, r), P(A_i),$$
$$P(E_j), \forall i, \forall j \tag{1}$$
$$Find \; : \qquad\qquad T_{list}(A_i), \forall i \tag{2}$$

$$Minimize \; : \mathbb{Z} = \sum_{i=1}^{a} dist(P(A_i), P(T_{list}(A_i, 1))) +$$
$$\sum_{i=1}^{a} \sum_{j=2}^{|T_{list}(A_i)|} dist(P(T_{list}(A_i), j-1), P(T_{list}(A_i, j))) \tag{3}$$

Subject to:

$$T_{list}(A_i) \cap T_{list}(A_j) = \emptyset \; \forall i, \forall j \; s.t \; i, \; j \in \{1, 2, ..., a\} \; and \; i \neq j. \tag{4}$$

$$\sum_{i=1}^{a} |T_{list}(A_i)| = e \tag{5}$$

Table 1. Notations used in the MINLP

Notation	Description
A	Set of Actors - $\{A_1, A_2,\ldots,A_a\}$
E	Set of events - $\{E_1, E_2,\ldots,E_e\}$
$P(A_i)$	Position of the actor A_i
$P(E_j)$	Position of the event E_j
$D(E_j)$	Deadline of the event E_j
$T_{list}(A_i)$	List of events assigned to the actor A_i
$P(T_{list}(A_i,l))$	Position of the lth event in $T_{list}(A_i)$
$S_{max}(A_i)$	Maximum speed of movement of actor A_i
$RA(A_i,q,r)$	A_i has q units of resource type r
$RR(E_j,q,r)$	E_j requires q units of resource type r
T_c	Action completion time bound
$dist(P(A_i), P(E_j))$	Euclidean Distance between A_i and E_j

$$D(T_{list}(A_i, j)) \geq \frac{dist(P(A_i), P(T_{list}(A_i, 1)))}{S_{max}(A_i)} + T_c +$$

$$\sum_{k=2}^{|T_{list}(A_i)|} \left(\frac{dist(P(T_{list}(A_i, k-1)), P(T_{list}(A_i, k)))}{S_{max}(A_i)} + T_c \right) \tag{6}$$

$$if\ |T_{list}(A_i)| \geq 1.\ \forall i\ and\ \forall j,\ s.t\ i \in \{1,2,...,a\}\ and\ j \in \{1,2,\ldots,|\ T_{list}(A_i)\ |\}.$$

$$\sum_{j=1}^{|T_{list}(A_i)|} RR((T_{list}(A_i, j)), q, k) \leq RA(A_i, q, k) \tag{7}$$

$$\forall i,\ and\ \forall k,\ s.t\ i \in \{1,2,\ldots,a\}\ and\ k \in \{1,2,\ldots,r\}.$$

Table 1 explains the notations used in the formulation. In the formulation, the objective function $\mathbb{Z}$ (3) consists of two terms: The first term refers to the sum of distances between the current position of ith actor and the first task of A_i in its task list. The second term refers to the total sum of distances between the positions of successive tasks assigned for i^{th} actor. The individual terms and hence the total value of $\mathbb{Z}$ should be minimized.

The constraint (4) guarantees that the tasks are uniquely assigned for actors. It prevents from an event covered by more than one actor. The constraint (5) requires that the schedule of all the actors do not miss any events. The constraint (6) states that the actor A_i is able to reach and take action before the events miss their deadlines. It is to be noted that the action completion time, T_c, is added between every migration of the actor from an event to another. The constraint (7) states that the net resources required for every task assigned for a particular actor should be sufficient enough to carry out. That is, the availability of kth type of resource should be sufficient to carry out all the events that are scheduled for that actor.

4   Heuristics for Residual Energy Maximization of Actors

The problem finds tour of actors which visits the events exactly once, which is similar to the Traveling Salesman Problem. In case of TSP, the tour starts and completes at the same place, whereas in our problem, an actor visits the events in the schedule till the last event and does not return to the original position. Thus, the problem of finding optimal tour for the actors can be shown to be NP-complete. Moreover, the size of the sensor networks is typically larger. So, directing all the information about the tasks and actors for decision making process at a centralized sink node, will result in an unrealistic amount of time to find the optimal assignment which necessitates distributed computing in order to achieve real-time responses. Hence, we propose the following heuristics to find near-optimal assignments in a distributed manner which will minimize deadline miss ratio as well.

We assume that the entire monitoring area is divided into several zones (Fig. 1) in which a relatively resource rich sensor node acts as an agent and also as sink for that zone. Thus, all the sensor nodes within that zone will statically route their information regarding the events toward this agent/sink node. It is also assumed that the sink node has the knowledge of existence of actors in its zone and their related information such as position, and resource availability. We classify the heuristics into two broader categories: viz. Intra-Zone and Inter-Zone. In case of Intra-Zone, the assignment of actors is done locally within the zone while in the latter case, the assignment is done collaboratively by agents of neighboring zones. Thus, we propose and study the distance, deadline, and priority based heuristics with respect to intra and inter zone classifications. Here, we define priority, $\mathbb{P}$ of an event E_j as

$$\mathbb{P}(E_j) \propto \frac{1}{dist(P(A_i), P(E_j)) \times D(E_j)} \tag{8}$$

The schemes are described in the following subsections:

4.1   Intra-zone

In the following intra-zone heuristics, we assume that at least one actor is placed in every zone.

Distance based: The agent nodes compute the tour of their own actors such that the actors visit the *nearest event first*. While forming the tour of actors, if an event is found to be infeasible due to deadline or resource constraints, then it is dropped. As outlined in Algorithm 1, this heuristic aims to achieve the objective of minimizing the overall movement of the actor(s) by avoiding communication overheads among neighborhood agents.

Algorithm 1. Intra-Zone Distance based Task Assignment

1: **for** every actor inside the zone **do**
2:    Sort the *unassigned* events in non-decreasing order of their distances w.r.t actor.
3:    Assign the event to the actor, if and only if the event can be reached before its deadline AND the actor has enough resources for action.
4:    Append the event in the task list of the actor and update the new position of the actor.
5:    Mark the event as *assigned*
6:    Repeat steps 3 to 5 until all the events in the sorted list are examined.
7: **end for**
8: Transmit the schedule to all the actors within the zone.

The schedule of actors obtained by Algorithm 1 is disseminated by the agent node to all the actors within its zone. This and all the other intra-zone schemes have a potential demerit of not considering an event which might be closer to the current position of the actor, but located in the neighborhood zone.

Deadline based: In this algorithm, the events are first sorted in non-decreasing order of their deadlines and the actor(s) are assigned to the events with the earliest deadline. In forming the tour of the actor(s) within the zone of the agent node, the positions of the actor(s) are updated and feasibility of including the event in the tour is checked. The events are dropped, if found infeasible. The main focus of this, *'earliest deadline first'* heuristic is to minimize deadline miss ratio and accommodate as many events as possible in the schedule.

Priority based: The above algorithms either try to minimize the overall movement of the actor(s) or to keep the deadline miss ratio as low as possible. In order to address these dual objectives collectively, we propose *priority based* heuristic which captures both distance and deadline parameters. As mentioned in Equation 8, the priorities of the events are calculated at the agent node and sorted in decreasing order. The actor(s) within the zone are assigned to the events from this sorted list, provided they are feasible to schedule. Otherwise, they are dropped.

In all the above three schemes, the agent nodes schedule events to the actor(s) within their zone, independently. Though, it helps in finding the schedule quickly, the resulting assignment may not be significantly closer to the optimal assignment. Hence, we propose the following inter-zone heuristics in which an agent node collaborates with its one-hop neighbors in assigning the actors to the adjacent zones in an effective manner.

4.2   Inter-zone

This is similar to the intra-zone with the exception that a set of actors and events in the adjacent zones are also considered for schedule. The agent nodes form a *cluster* of one-hop region and one node is elected to be *cluster-head* which takes the responsibility of computing the feasible schedule for all the actors. The agent nodes in the cluster reveal the position of actors and events in their zone to the cluster head.

Distance based: Upon collecting this information from the neighborhood agent nodes, the cluster-head, in addition to its own zone, computes the schedule for all the actors with the distance metric, as discussed earlier in the case of intra-zone distance based heuristic. Infeasible events are dropped from assigning to the actors. The computed schedule of actors are then communicated to the other agent nodes in the cluster, which in turn, merely pass on this assignment to the actors of their own zones.

Deadline based: Similar to the above algorithm, the cluster-head sorts the events of all the adjacent zones (including its own zone) within the cluster in non-decreasing order of their deadlines. It then computes the feasible schedule for all the actors of its own zone and the neighborhood zones, such that the events from this sorted list are assigned to the nearest actors. The computed schedule is communicated to the other agent nodes which in turn, communicate to the actors of their own zones. The pseudo code of this scheme is outlined in Algorithm 2.

Algorithm 2. Inter-Zone Deadline based Task Assignment

Transmission (by agent nodes other than cluster-head):
Transmit the following parameters to the cluster-head
$P(A_i)$, $P(T_j)$, $S_{max}(A_i)$, $RA(A_i, r)$, $RR(T_t, r)$, and $D(T_j)$
Listen mode (by the cluster-head agent node):
Receive and store the above parameters from neighbor agents of its cluster area
Scheduling mode (by the cluster-head agent node):

1. Sort the events of its own zone and of neighboring zones in non-decreasing order of their deadlines.
2. Assign the event to a nearest actor only if the event can be reached before its deadline and the actor has enough resources for action.
3. Append the event in the task list of the actor and update the new position of the actor.
4. Repeat steps 2 and 3 until all the events in the sorted list are examined.
5. Transmit the schedule to all the actors within the zone.
6. Transmit the schedule of actors for neighborhood zones to the respective agent nodes.

Transmission (by the other agent nodes):
Transmit the schedule to all the actors within the zone

Priority based: In this algorithm, the priority lists of all the events are computed for all the actors within the zones covered by the cluster where the priority is defined as in Equation 8. This scheme has an additional computational overhead of re-computing the priority for every assignment of events as the current positions of the actors are updated.

Backtracking: In addition to the above mentioned heuristics, we have also attempted *backtracking* in scheduling algorithms. That is, when an actor A_i can not reach the event under consideration, say E_j, due to deadline constraint, then we backtrack up to k-past events in the schedule and try to accommodate this event. Here, the parameter k is the maximum allowed level of backtracking. While backtracking, care is taken to protect the deadline guarantee for the already assigned tasks, failing which this event is dropped from schedule. The intuition behind this backtracking is to minimize the deadline miss ratio further.

4.3   Actor Repositioning After Completing Tasks

The key idea behind residual energy maximization of actors at every instant of scheduling is to yield increased lifetime of the actors. That is, given a set of events, all the heuristics aim at arriving an optimum schedule that requires least energy possible and minimize the infeasible events. In all the above discussions, it is assumed that the tour of the actors start from the current position of actors and end at the last event in the schedule. This implies that over the period of time, it is possible that the distribution of actors in the terrain get changed. This might result in more number of actors moved to some part of the terrain leaving many other zones without having any actors. This is purely determined by the nature of the events occurring in the terrain. If new events are detected at such zones, then bringing in the actors from the zones that far away, may result in several tasks becoming infeasible in the schedule, due to their stringent deadline constraints. This necessitates the proactive schemes for optimal repositioning of actors at the end of their tour.

One possible proactive scheme would be to move back the actors to their home zones after completing all of their assigned tasks. This will guarantee that the actor distribution is not disturbed, but this happens at the expense of severe energy drain by the actors for movement. An equivalent approach to minimize deadline miss ratio but relatively with less energy consumption for moving would be to make sure that none of the zones are actorless. That is, if the schedule by any of the schemes outlined in the previous sections are such that none of the zones are actorless, then the actors remain at the place of last event. But, if any of the zone is left with no actor, then a good strategy may be to move an actor from a zone where redundant actors are available to this zone, but with energy constraint. We investigate the impact of three actor repositioning schemes viz. *Home, Stay,* and *One Guarantee*, on the lifetime of actors and deadline miss ratio. The *Home* strategy always moves back the actor to its starting position at the end of the tour. The *Stay* scheme is same as what has been discussed in the previous sections, i.e., actors remain at the last event's position. The *One Guarantee* strategy will move an actor to a zone only if the latter does not have one.

5   Simulation Results and Discussions

The algorithms mentioned in Section 4 are implemented in C++ for performance study. We considered the terrain dimension of 1000 m × 1000 m with 100 actors and 500 events placed randomly. We simulated 100 such scenarios, averaged the objective function value and the deadline miss ratio. The values of deadline parameters for the events were uniformly drawn between 10 and 500 seconds. The speed of all the actors was considered to be 5 m/s.

Simulation results in Fig. 2 compare the overall distance covered by all the actors according to the schedule generated by the heuristics mentioned in Section 4. The inner chart in the same figure shows the number of events missed in the schedule by these algorithms. In Fig. 3 normalized values of distance and infeasible events are plotted. Though the intra-zone distance heuristic seems to be giving least movement required, it happens at the cost of sacrificing more number of events due to deadline constraints. 3.5% of the events were not accommodated in the schedule by this heuristic.

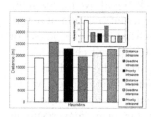 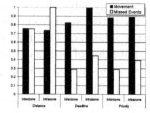 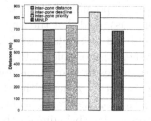

Fig. 2. Comparison of Heuristics w.r.t. Overall Distance Covered by Actors

Fig. 3. Comprehensive Comparison of Heuristics

Fig. 4. Comparison of MINLP Result with Inter-zone Heuristics

Similarly, the deadline miss ratio for intra-zone deadline and priority based heuristics was found to be 1.54% and 1.36%, respectively. The ratio for these heuristics in the case of inter-zone was found to be 2.6%, 1%, and 1%, respectively. With respect to deadline miss ratio, the inter-zone algorithms outperform the intra-zone. It can also be observed from this plot that with equal deadline miss ratio for inter-zone deadline and priority heuristics, the former gives better objective value which is 6.71% lower than that of priority based one. The reason for inter-zone deadline based heuristic performing better with respect to both the overall movement and deadline miss ratio is due to the fact that Algorithm 2 captures both deadline as well as distance together. Thus, this heuristic is equivalent to saying, *"assign the task with the earliest deadline, to the nearest actor with enough resources"*. The model of the MINLP problem was implemented in GAMS [8] and solved with the SBB solver available through NEOS optimization server [9] [10]. In solving the model, the problem size was restricted to have only 5 actors and 25 events, due to the time restriction imposed by the NEOS server. The results are compared with the schedule generated by all the *inter-zone* algorithms for the same scenario and results are shown in Fig. 4. As can be seen from this figure, all the schedules resulted in accommodating all the given events and hence, the distance heuristic gives the overall movement of the actors closer to the MINLP result. The objective function values of deadline and priority heuristics are found to be about 7% and 19%, respectively when compared with that of the optimum value.

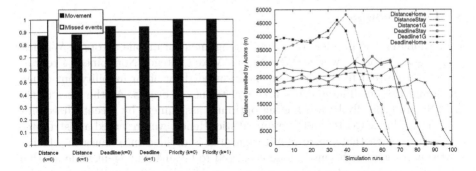

Fig. 5. Effect of Backtracking in Inter-zone Heuristics

Fig. 6. Distance Travelled by Actors

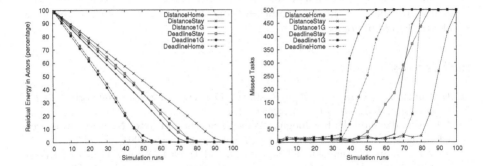

Fig. 7. Residual Energy of Actors

Fig. 8. Deadline Miss Ratio - A Comparison

As mentioned in Section 4, we attempted backtracking with window size, k with values of 0 (no backtracking) and 1. Observations from the Figure 5 reveal that significant improvement is seen in case of inter-zone distance based algorithm, while it shows only marginal improvement in the case of inter-zone deadline algorithm. This is due to the fact that unlike distance based algorithm, events with earliest deadlines are considered first in the process of scheduling, thus showing no further improvement in backtracking.

Figures 6, 7, and 8 give the plot of distance travelled by actors, residual energy of actors, and the deadline miss ratio respectively, over simulation runs. The results are plotted only for inter-zone distance and deadline based heuristics. As can be seen from these plots, the distance based heuristics with the "*stay at last event*" repositioning policy survives for longer duration. But, at every simulation run, the same trend as in Figures 2 and 3 can be observed. Thus, infer from these results that the *inter-zone deadline* would perform better than other heuristics if the events have stringent deadline constraints. The *stay* at last event repositioning policy fairs better with respect to increase in lifetime as far as the events happen at random places.

6   Conclusions

We formulated the problem of optimal assignment of mobile actors in Wireless Sensor and Actor Networks (WSANs) as Mixed Integer Non Linear Program (MINLP), in order to conserve the energy needed for actor mobility but otherwise fulfill the deadline and resource constraints of events. As the sizes of the WSANs are typically larger, finding optimum assignment by a centralized sink node using this MINLP would be unrealistic. Hence, we presented a distributed architecture such that entire monitoring area is divided into zones in which a relatively resource rich sensor node is elected to be sink and agent node for that zone. We presented intra-zone and inter-zone distributed algorithms to obtain near-optimal assignment of events to the actors and compared their performance. The impact of various schemes for actor positioning at the end of the schedule, on the lifetime of actors and deadline miss ratio is investigated. Future work will be focused on relaxing the constraint on proposed architecture such as the need for cluster heads in zones.

References

1. D. Culler, D. Estrin, and M. Srivastava, "Overview of Sensor Networks," *IEEE Computer*, vol. 37, pp. 41–49, August 2004.
2. I. F. Akyildiz and I. H. Kasimoglu, "Wireless Sensor and Actor Networks: Research Challenges," *Ad Hoc Networks*, vol. 2, no. 4, pp. 351–367, 2004.
3. Tian He, John A. Stankovic, Chenyang Lu, and Tarek F. Abdelzaher, "SPEED: A Stateless Protocol for Real-Time Communication in Sensor Networks," in *Proceedings of IEEE International Conference on Distributed Computing Systems*, pp. 46–55, 2003.
4. Chenyang Lu, Brian . Blum, Tarek F. Abdelzaher, John A. Stankovic, and Tian He, "RAP: A Real-Time Communication Architecture for Large-Scale Wireless Sensor Networks," in *Proceedings of IEEE Real Time Technology and Applications Symposium*, pp. 55–66, 2002.
5. Ali Haghani, Huijun Hu, and Qiang Tian, "An Optimization Model for Real-Time Emergency Vehicle Dispatching and Routing," in *Proceedings of TRB Annual Meeting*, pp. 1–23, January 2003.
6. T. Melodia, D. Pompili, V. C. Gungor, and I. F. Akyildiz, "A Distributed Coordination Framework for Wireless Sensor and Actor Networks," in *MobiHoc*, pp. 99–110, 2005.
7. J. Cyzyzk, M. Mesnier and J. More, "The NEOS server," *IEEE Journal on Computational Sceince and Engineering*, vol. 5, no. 3, pp. 68–75, 1998.
8. A. Brooke, D. Kendrick, A. Meeraus, Ramesh Raman, and Richard E. Rosenthal, *GAMS: A User's Guide and Tutorial.* GAMS Development Corporation, 1998.
9. NEOS Server. [Online]. Available: http://neos.mcs.anl.gov.
10. SBB Solver. [Online]. Available: http://neos.mcs.anl.gov/neos/solvers/minco:SBB/GAMS.html.

Locant: A Nature Inspired Location Service for Ad Hoc Networks

R.C. Hansdah and Prashant Khanna

Department of Computer Science and Automation
Indian Institute of Science
Bangalore-560012, India
{hansdah, khanna}@csa.iisc.ernet.in

Abstract. An efficient location service is a prerequisite to any robust, effective and precise location information aided Mobile Ad Hoc Network (MANET) routing protocol. Locant, presented in this paper is a nature inspired location service which derives inspiration from the insect colony framework, and it is designed to work with a host of location information aided MANET routing protocols. Using an extensive set of simulation experiments, we have compared the performance of Locant with RLS, SLS and DLS, and found that it has comparable or better performance compared to the above three location services on most metrics and has the least overhead in terms of number of bytes transmitted per location query answered.

1 Introduction

Location or position information based routing protocols for ad hoc networks have emerged as a class which has invited renewed research in the recent past. Location services provide position based routing algorithms with information about the positional information of other nodes. A node acquires information about its own position by a GPS[1,2] or some related service housed on itself. Essentially, there are two categories of location service, viz., *reactive* and *proactive*. In reactive location service(RLS)[3], a location query is generated when the need arises and no ready repository of location information is kept. In proactive location service, information about the location of nodes is either stored in a database or in all nodes of the network. Schemes like Dream Location Service (DLS)[3] and Simple Location Service (SLS)[3] fall in the category of proactive location service in which information is stored in all nodes of the network. Location services suggested so far in literature, depend explicitly on the routing protocol for which they have been designed since they make use of the routing protocol itself in the location service. Some of these location services append the node's location table to the location information packet being propagated and send the location information packet on previously stored paths. This leads to higher overhead per location query answered. In this paper we present Locant, a nature inspired location service based on the insect colony framework for position information based routing protocols in MANETs. The rest of the paper is organized as follows. In section 2, we briefly describe the insect colony framework. Section 3 contains the description of our algorithm. In section 4, we present the results of simulation experiments. Section 5 concludes the paper.

2 Insect Colony Framework

Ants moving between the nest and a food source deposit a volatile chemical called *pheromone* on the path traversed, and preferentially move towards areas of higher pheromone intensity. Future generation of ants hooked to the same source will travel on the same path thus reinforcing the goodness. Shorter paths can be completed quickly and frequently by the ants, and will therefore be marked with higher pheromone intensity. Changes in the environment, such as topological or path quality change, are accounted for by allowing pheromone to decay over time. This requires paths to be continuously reinforced with new information about the traffic in the network. This form of distributed control based on indirect communication among agents, which locally modify the environment and react to these modifications leading to a phase of global coordination among the agent is called *stigmergy*[3]. Locant derives inspiration from this insect colony framework to ensure optimal location service availability at all times with minimal overheads. The ingredients of ant colony behavior have been reverse engineered in the framework of the Ant Colony Optimization (ACO)[5].

3 Locant

3.1 Assumptions

The nodes are assumed to be equipped with a GPS or an allied service which provides it accurate position of itself. It is assumed that the location information provided by the GPS is accurate and without error. The universal time clock is also available which is synchronized in the network. The allocation of address to each node in the network is unique and is allotted prior to its initiation into the network.

3.2 Structure of Ants in Locant

There are three types of ants defined in Locant, viz., Normal Ant, Request Ant and Virtual Ant, the details of which are shown in Fig 1, Fig 2 and Fig 3 respectively. Fig 4 shows the entries of the location table hosted by each node in the network.

The Source ID is the unique address of the node, which is given to each node prior to its initiation into the network. The location of a node is characterized by the three dimensional coordinates in a Cartesian coordinate system derived from the information provided by the GPS. The velocity of a node is also recorded at the time of recording its location. The timestamp is the time instant when the current location and velocity information are recorded. The goodness of a node is the number of entries in its location table.

AntType =1	SourceID
Location	Velocity
Goodness	Timestamp

Fig. 1. Normal Ant

AntType =2	SourceID
Source Location	Source Velocity
Source Goodness	Source Timestamp
Destination ID	

Fig. 2. Request Ant

AntType =3	SourceID(v)
Location(v)	Velocity(v)
Goodness(v)	Timestamp(v)

Fig. 3. Virtual Ant

Node ID	Location	Velocity
Goodness	Timestamp	

Fig. 4. Location Table at Each Node

3.3 Algorithmic Description of Locant

On powering on, a node tries to find out activities of its neighbors. A node continues to check for activity of its neighbors after waiting for a random time interval t_{random} until it finds an active neighbor. Once the node detects that it is in the neighborhood of another active node, the Locant location service is initiated. After initiation, Locant broadcasts a normal ant to intimate the network of its existence. Three concurrent activities take place while Locant is active. These activities are as follows:

Location Information Update. Both the normal ant the request ant carries information about the source node. The virtual ant carries information about the node for which the corresponding request ant is supposed to gather information. On arrival of an ant at a node, this information is used to update the location table of the node.

Ant Creation. A normal ant is created proactively in Locant based on two metrics. The first one is on the occurrence of a timeout t_{resend} and the other after a node moves a distance d_{resend}. t_{resend} indicates the time interval after which we can assume that the location information regarding the node in the network is available on all nodes or can be found after a using a request ant. The second factor d_{resend} generates a normal ant when the node has moved a threshold distance from the previously recorded location. When a node need location information about another node, and the location information of this table is not in its location table, it generates a request ant and broadcasts the same. When a request ant reaches a node which has information about the destination node, this intermediate node generates a virtual ant carrying information about the destination node.

Destruction of Ants. All the ants are killed when they become stale. In addition, a request ant s killed when it finds information about the destination location.

The pseudocode for the algorithm is as given below:

```
while(!(received reply from neighbor))
{broadcast(HELLO);wait_random;}
```

```
Broadcast(Normal Ant);
while(1)
{
switch(event_occur_at_node)
{
        case(receive_location_request):
                {if(!loc_exist) broadcast(Request Ant);
                else send_loc_info_to_routing_protocol;
                break;}
        case(time_resend_exceed):
                {broadcast(Normal Ant);
                break;}
        case(distance_resend_exceed);
                {broadcast(Normal Ant);
                break;}
        case(receive Normal Ant):    // from other nodes
                {if (Timestamp>current_entry){
                    update_location_table;
                    rebroadcast(Normal Ant);}
                else drop(Normal Ant);
                break;}
        case(receive Request Ant):
                {if (Timestamp>current_entry){
                    update_location_table;
                    if(req_loc_exist){
                        send Virtual Ant;
                        drop(Request Ant);}
                    else rebroadcast(Request Ant);}
                 else drop(Request Ant);
                break;}
        case(receive Virtual Ant):
                {if(SourceID == self){
                    broadcast(Normal Ant);
                    drop(Virtual Ant);}
                else  if (Timestamp>current_entry){
                    update_location_table;
                    rebroadcast(Virtual Ant);}
                else drop(Virtual Ant);
                break;}
}}
```

4   Simulation Experiments

We have compared Locant to three other popular location services available
in literature, viz., SLS, DLS and RLS. A detailed comparison of these three
location services has been made in the much cited paper by Tracy et. al. in
[3]. The source code for the implementation of the location services mentioned
in [3] was obtained from the authors of [3] and has been partly used in this
simulation. NS2 [6], a popular network simulator was used for simulation of all
the four algorithms. The implementation of SLS, DLS and RLS were available
for NS version 2.1a7b. Locant was implemented on version 2.29 of NS. Effort
has been made to retain the same simulation environment for location services
studied in [3]. For Locant, the simulation details are presented in Table 5.

4.1   Simulation Results

The metrics used to compare Locant with other three location services are re-
sponsiveness, accuracy, convergence time, and control overheads. Figs. 5 and 6
give the overheads that each location service generates. Fig. 5 shows the number

Table 1. Simulation Parameters and Assumptions

Input Parameters	
Simulation Area	300x600, 500x500
Number of Nodes	50,100
Transmission Range	100m
Simulation Duration	200sec, 1000sec, 2000sec
Mobility Model	
Mobility Model	Random Waypoint Model (setdest : ns2)
Mobility Speeds	0,5,10,15,20 m/sec
Pause Time	10μ sec
Simulator Details	
NS2	ver 2.1a7b for SLS, DLS, RLS & 2.29 for Locant
MAC	802.11
Link Bandwidth	2Mbps
Number of trials per simulation	10

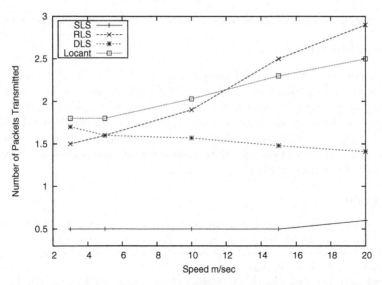

Fig. 5. Number of packets transmitted per Location Query Answered

of packets transmitted for each location query answered. In case of Locant, the metric is the number of ants produced per location query. Fig. 5 gives a perspective of the bandwidth requirements of each protocol. Locant having a flooding nature of propagation, transmits more packets, but consumes lesser bandwidth due to small size of ants. Overall, Locant provides a higher performance and lower overhead compared to a RLS and DLS and is comparable to SLS on most metrics of performance and scalability.

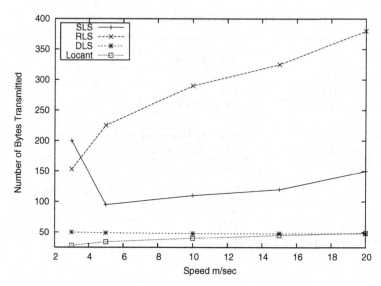

Fig. 6. Number of Bytes transmitted per Location Query Answered

5   Conclusions

In this paper, we have presented Locant, a nature inspired location service and have compared its performance to three other location services. Locant being a proactive location service during initiation, and reactive during location query phase scores favorably on most metrics. Overall, we conclude that Locant, a unique location service based on the insect colony framework and designed to work along a host of location information aided routing protocols scores favorably in its class of location service.

References

1. S. Căpkun, M. Hamdi, and J. Hubaux: Gps-free Positioning in Mobile Ad Hoc Networks, Proc. Hawaii Intl. Conf. System Sciences, Jan. 2001.
2. J. Hightower and G. Borriello: Location Systems for Ubiquitous Computing, IEEE Computer, vol. 34, no. 8, Aug. 2001, pages 57–66.
3. Theraulaz G, Bonabeau E.: A brief history of stigmergy, Artificial Life, Special Issue on Stigmergy, 1999; 5:97-116.
4. I. Stojmenovic: Home agent based Location Update and Destination Search Schemes in Ad Hoc Wireless Networks, In A. Zemliak and N.E. Mastorakis, editors, Advances in Information Science and Soft Computing, pages 611. WSEAS Press, 2002. Also Technical Report, University of Ottawa, TR-99-10, September 1999.
5. Goss S, Aron S, Deneubourg JL, Pasteels JM: Self-organized shortcuts in the Argentine Ant, Naturwissenschaften 1989; 76:pages 579-581
6. Baras JS, Mehta H: A Probabilistic Emergent Routing Algorithm for Mobile Ad Hoc Networks, In Proceedings of WiOpt03: Modeling and Optimization in Mobile, Ad Hoc and Wireless Networks, 2003.
7. Akaroa Research Group. Akaora-2 http://www-tkn.ee.tu-berlin.de/research/ns-2_akaroa-2/ns.html. Page accessed 01 May 2006

An Analytical Model for Capacity Evaluation of VoIP on HCCA and TCP File Transfers over EDCA in an IEEE 802.11e WLAN*

Sri Harsha, S.V.R. Anand, Anurag Kumar, and Vinod Sharma

Department of Electrical Communication Engineering,
Indian Institute of Science, Bangalore, 560 012
{harshas, anand, anurag, vinod}@ece.iisc.ernet.in

Abstract. In the context of the IEEE 802.11e standard for WLANs, we provide an analytical model for obtaining the maximum number of VoIP calls that can be supported on HCCA, such that the delay QoS constraint of the accepted calls is met, when TCP downloads are coexistent on EDCA. In this scenario, we derive the TCP download throughput by using an analytical model for the case where only TCP sessions are present in the WLAN. We show that the analytical model for combined voice and TCP transfers provides accurate results in comparison with simulations (using *ns-2*).

1 Introduction

The IEEE 802.11e [1] standard has been introduced in order to provide differentiated services to different traffic flows in an IEEE 802.11 WLAN. The 802.11e standard defines a new coordination function called hybrid coordination function (HCF). HCF has two modes of operation: enhanced distributed channel access (EDCA) which is a contention-based channel access function, and HCF controlled channel access (HCCA) which is based on a polling mechanism controlled by the hybrid co-ordinator (HC), which is normally resident in the QoS aware access point (QAP). EDCA and HCCA can operate concurrently in IEEE 802.11e WLANs. In this paper we provide an analysis of HCF with VoIP calls being carried on HCCA, and TCP file transfer downloads on EDCA. Each VoIP call comprises a wireless QSTA (QoS aware wireless STAtion) engaged in a VoIP call with a wired client via the QAP. In the case of TCP sessions, each STA engaged in a TCP transfer is downloading a long file from a server on the wired LAN via the QAP.

There have only been a few attempts to model and analyze the IEEE 802.11e MAC when subjected to actual Internet traffic traffic loads, e.g., TCP or VoIP traffic. Duffy et al. [6] and Sudarev et al. [15] propose models for the throughput of 802.11b WLANs in finite load conditions. Tickoo and Sikdar [16] obtain a delay and queue length analysis for an 802.11b WLAN assuming Poisson arrivals, and

---

* This paper is based on research sponsored by Intel Technology India.

S. Chaudhuri et al. (Eds.): ICDCN 2006, LNCS 4308, pp. 245–256, 2006.
© Springer-Verlag Berlin Heidelberg 2006

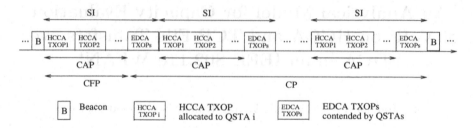

Fig. 1. HCF medium access pattern during a beacon interval in IEEE 802.11e WLANs

a decoupling approximation that is an extension of the one in [2]. Detti et al. [5] and Pilosof et al. [13] discuss throughput unfairness between TCP controlled transfers in 802.11 WLANs. Leith and Clifford [12] discuss how TCP unfairness can be removed using the QoS extensions in 802.11e. Bruno et al. [3] consider the scenario of STAs performing TCP transfers via an AP in 802.11 WLANs. Our modeling assumptions for TCP transfers on EDCA are drawn from this work. Our modeling approach follows [10] (see also [11]) and is a special case of the analysis we report in [7]. We discuss the relationship between this work and [10] and [3] in Section 3. Though performance evaluation of VoIP calls on HCCA has been done by Shankar et al. [14], they do not evaluate the throughput obtained by the background traffic they consider.

We provide a simple and yet accurate model to capture the performance when both EDCA and HCCA are used. First, we model the case when TCP file downloads are considered on the EDCA access category AC1. From this model we derive the total download throughput. Next, we consider the case where voice calls are serviced on HCCA and TCP download traffic is serviced on EDCA. We set a QoS objective that the WLAN delay does not exceed d (say 20 ms) (with a high probability) for voice calls. We show how many CBR VoIP calls can be accepted into the network, and also how the TCP throughput decreases with increasing number of voice calls up to the voice admission control limit. In related work, we have also provided an analytical model for IEEE 802.11e infrastructure WLANs, where voice and TCP downloads are handled on EDCA [7].

2   Overview of HCCA and EDCA

In the 802.11e standard, a superframe consists of two phases: a contention period (CP) and a contention free period (CFP); see Figure 1. EDCA is used only in the CP while HCCA can be used in both periods. Therefore a CP consists of controlled access periods (CAP), which refer to HCCA activity, alternating with EDCA activity.

HCCA is based on polling and is controlled by a hybrid coordinator (located in the QAP). In order to be included in the polling list of the HC, a QSTA must send a QoS reservation request using a special QoS management frame, and each individual traffic stream (TS) needs one reservation request. The QoS management frame contains traffic specification (TSPEC) parameters. The mandatory

Table 1. Parameters of the EDCA ACs as defined in 802.11e. "NA" means "not applicable."

AC	CW_{min}	CW_{max}	AIFS	TXOP	AC	CW_{min}	CW_{max}	AIFS	TXOP
AC(0)	31	1023	7	NA	AC(2)	15	31	2	6.016ms
AC(1)	31	1023	3	NA	AC(3)	7	15	2	3.064ms

TSPEC parameters include the mean data rate of the corresponding application, the MAC Service Data Unit (MSDU) size, the maximum service interval (the maximum time allowed between adjacent TXOPs allocated to the same station) and the minimum PHY rate (the minimum physical bit rate assumed by the scheduler for calculating transmission time). Basically, each TS first sends a QoS request frame to the QAP. Using these QoS requests, the QAP determines first the minimum value of all the maximum service intervals required by the different TSs that apply for HCCA scheduling. Then it chooses the highest submultiple value of the 802.11e beacon interval duration as the selected service interval (SI), which is less than the minimum of all the maximum service intervals. Thus, an 802.11e beacon interval is cut into several SIs and QSTAs are polled accordingly during each selected SI (see Figure 1).

EDCA defines a DCF-like random access to the wireless channel through access categories (ACs) [1]. At any node, the incoming traffic is mapped to one of the four ACs. Each AC executes an independent backoff process to determine the time of transmission of its frames. The backoff process is regulated by four configurable parameters: minimum contention window(CW_{min}), maximum contention window (CW_{max}), arbitration inter frame space (AIFS), and transmission opportunity (TXOP) limit. See Table 1 for the parameters of different ACs. It is through these ACs that the differentiation is achieved.

3   Modeling and Analysis of TCP File Transfers

We follow the modeling approach of Kuriakose [10] wherein the analysis has been done for the RTS/CTS mechanism. The approach of Kuriakose [10] is further based on the related work in [3]. Our approach is different from [3] since we incorporate the IEEE 802.11 DCF backoff procedure by using the saturation analysis from [2] and [9]; in particular, as against the constant attempt probability p in [3], the attempt probability in our model depends on the number of contending stations. Further, we extend the analysis of [10] to the basic access mechanism.

We use the TCP traffic assumptions of Kuriakose [10] and recall them here for sake of continuity. Each STA has a single TCP connection to download a large file from a local file server. Hence, the AP delivers TCP data packets towards the STA, while the STAs return TCP ACKs. It is assumed that when a STA receives data from the AP, it immediately sends an ACK, i.e., the delayed ACK mechanism is not modeled, though the delayed ACKs case can also be studied (see [10]). Further it is assumed that the AP and the STAs have buffers large enough so that TCP data packets or ACKS are not lost due to buffer overflows.

We assume that there are no bit errors and so packets in the channel are lost only due to collisions. Also, we assume that these collisions are recovered by the MAC before TCP time-outs occur. As a result of these assumptions, for large file transfers, the TCP window will grow to its maximum value and stay there.

We then adopt an observation made by Bruno et al. [3]. Since all nodes (including the AP) will contend for the channel and no preference is given to the AP, most of the packets in the TCP window will get backlogged at the AP. If there are M STAs (each involved with one TCP download session), we can assume that the probability that a packet transmitted by the AP is destined to a particular STA is $\frac{1}{M}$. Thus it is apparent that the larger the M, the lower is the probability that the AP sends to the same STA before receiving the ACK for the last packet sent. Thus, it is assumed that the probability that any STA has more than one ACK is negligible. We can thus simply keep track of the *number* of STAs with ACKs. If there are several STAs with ACKs then the chance that the AP succeeds in sending a packet is small. Thus, the system has a tendency to keep most of the packets in the AP with a few STAs having ACKs to send back. We observe that AP is the bottle-neck and hence can be considered saturated all the time.

3.1   The Analytical Model

In the case of the RTS/CTS mechanism, the transmission time of an RTS packet from the AP is smaller than the transmission time of an ACK packet from the STA. Therefore the total collision time when there is a collision between an RTS packet from the AP and an ACK packet from the STA is the same as when there is a collision between an ACK packet from one STA and an ACK packet from another STA. This is not true in the case of basic access mechanism. In basic access, the collision between an ACK packet from one STA and an ACK packet from another STA will result in a smaller collision time than the collision between the data packet from the AP and an ACK packet from an STA. This is because the data packet from the AP is larger than the ACK packet size. Thus we need to incorporate the two kinds of collisions in the analysis of Kuriakose [10].

In order to keep track of the kind of collisions as well, we need to embed the Markov chain in [10] at *channel slots* rather than at the end of successful transmissions. Figure 2 shows the evolution of the back-off process and the channel activity in the WLAN. Let the system slot length be δ (for IEEE 802.11b, $\delta = 20\mu s$). U_j, $j \in 0, 1, 2, 3, \ldots$, are the random instants that represent channel slot boundaries, where a channel slot could be an idle system slot, or a successful transmission, or a collision. Let the time length of the jth channel slot be L_j, i.e., $L_j = U_j - U_{j-1}$.

Let there be M stations that are downloading files using TCP. Let Y_j be the number of non-empty STAs, i.e., STAs with an ACK packet to be transmitted, at the channel slot boundary U_j. At most one departure can happen in any channel slot. Thus, $0 \le Y_j \le M$. Let $\eta(Y_j)$ be the probability of a channel slot being idle, $\sigma(Y_j)$ be probability that an AP transmission succeeds, $\alpha(Y_j)$

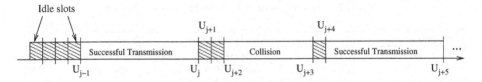

Fig. 2. An evolution of the back-off process and the channel activity. U_j, $j \in 0, 1, 2, 3, \ldots$ are the instants where j^{th} channel activity ends.

be the probability that a STA transmission succeeds, $\zeta_1(Y_j)$ be the probability that there is a long collision (involving an AP packet and a STA packet) and $\zeta_2(Y_j)$ be the probability that there is a short collision (not involving an AP packet), in the $j + 1^{th}$ channel slot. For determining these expressions, we use the following *state dependent attempt probability* model: let β_n be the attempt probability of any node in the network when there are n contending nodes. Our approximation is that β_n is obtained from the fixed point saturation analysis of [2] or [9] for each n. Then, since we have $Y_j + 1$ non-empty nodes (including the AP, that is always assumed saturated) at U_j, the probabilities defined above are as follows: $\eta(Y_j) = (1 - \beta_{Y_j+1})^{(Y_j+1)}$, $\alpha(Y_j) = Y_j\beta_{Y_j+1}(1 - \beta_{Y_j+1})^{Y_j}$, $\sigma(Y_j) = \beta_{Y_j+1}(1 - \beta_{Y_j+1})^{Y_j}$, $\zeta_1(Y_j) = \beta_{Y_j+1}\sum_{l=1}^{Y_j} \binom{Y_j}{l}\beta_{Y_j+1}^l(1 - \beta_{Y_j+1})^{Y_j-l}$, $\zeta_2(Y_j) = \sum_{l=2}^{Y_j} \binom{Y_j}{l}\beta_{Y_j+1}^l(1 - \beta_{Y_j+1})^{Y_j+1-l}$.

We now can write the evolution equation of the chain $\{Y_j, j \geq 0\}$, as follows:

$$Y_{j+1} = \begin{cases} Y_j + 1 \text{ w.p. } \sigma(Y_j) \\ Y_j - 1 \text{ w.p. } \alpha(Y_j) \\ Y_j \quad \text{ w.p. } \eta(Y_j) + \zeta_1(Y_j) + \zeta_2(Y_j) \end{cases}$$

With the state dependent probabilities of attempt, it is easily seen that $\{Y_j, j \geq 0\}$ forms a finite irreducible discrete time Markov chain on the channel slot boundaries and hence is positive recurrent. The transition probabilities, P_{ij}, $0 \leq i, j \leq M$ of the Markov Chain $\{Y_j, j \geq 0\}$ are given by

$$P_{ij} = \begin{cases} 0 & \text{for } j < i - 1 \\ \alpha(i) & \text{for } j = i - 1 \\ \eta(i) + \zeta_1(i) + \zeta_2(i) & \text{for } j = i \\ \sigma(i) & \text{for } j = i + 1 \\ 0 & \text{for } j > i + 1 \end{cases}$$

The stationary probabilities π_n of the Markov Chain $\{Y_j, j \geq 0\}$ can then be numerically determined.

We then use the state dependent attempt probabilities to obtain the mean of the channel slot durations. The channel slot duration, L_j can take five values (in number of system slots): 1 if it is an idle slot, T_{s-AP} if it corresponds to a successful transmission of AP, T_{s-STA} if it corresponds to a successful transmission of a station, T_{c-long} if it corresponds to a collision between an AP packet and

Table 2. Parameters used in analysis and simulation

Parameter	Symbol	Value	Parameter	Symbol	Value
PHY data rate	C_d	11 Mbps	AIFS (AC 1) Time	$T_{AIFS(AC1)}$	$70\mu s$
Control rate	C_c	2 Mbps	SIFS Time	T_{SIFS}	$10\mu s$
Data pkt size	$L_{TCPdata}$	12000 Bits	EIFS Time	T_{EIFS}	$384\mu s$
TCP/IP Header	L_{IPH}	320 Bits	PIFS Time	T_{PIFS}	$30\mu s$
PLCP preamble time	T_P	$144\mu s$	Min. CW (AC 1)	CW_{min}	31
PHY Header time	T_{PHY}	$48\mu s$	Max. CW (AC 1)	CW_{max}	1023
MAC ACK Pkt Size	L_{ACK}	112 bits	CF-Poll overhead	$T_{CF-Poll}$	$346\mu s$
MAC Header size	L_{MAC}	288 bits	Voice pkt size	L_{voice}	200 Bytes
TCP ACK pkt size	T_{TCPACK}	320 bits			

any STA packet, and $T_{c-short}$ if it corresponds to a collision between one STA packet and another STA packet. Then, the state dependent mean channel slot duration, $E_{Y_j}L$ is as follows:

$$E_{Y_{j+1}}L = \eta(Y_j) + T_{s-AP}\ \sigma(Y_j) + T_{s-STA}\ \alpha(Y_j) + T_{c-long}\ \zeta_1(Y_j) + T_{c-short}\ \zeta_2(Y_j)$$

where $T_{s-AP} = T_P + T_{PHY} + \frac{L_{MAC}+L_{IPH}+L_{TCPdata}}{C_d} + T_{SIFS} + T_P + T_{PHY} + \frac{L_{ACK}}{C_c} + T_{AIFS(AC1)}$; $T_{s-STA} = T_P + T_{PHY} + \frac{L_{MAC}+L_{TCPACK}}{C_d} + T_{SIFS} + T_P + T_{PHY} + \frac{L_{ACK}}{C_c} + T_{AIFS(AC1)}$; $T_{c-long} = T_P + T_{PHY} + \frac{L_{MAC}+L_{IPH}+L_{TCPdata}}{C_d} + T_{EIFS}$; $T_{c-short} = T_P + T_{PHY} + \frac{L_{MAC}+L_{TCPACK}}{C_d} + T_{EIFS}$; $T_{EIFS} = T_{SIFS} + T_P + T_{PHY} + \frac{L_{ACK}}{C_c} + T_{AIFS(AC1)}$.

In the above equations, C_d is the PHY data rate, C_c is the control rate, T_P is preamble transmission time, T_{PHY} is the PHY header transmission time, L_{MAC} is MAC header length, L_{IPH} is the length of TCP/IP Header, $L_{TCPdata}$ is the length of data packet, and L_{ACK} is length of MAC ACK packet. See Table 2 for values of these parameters.

On combining the channel slots with the above Markov chain, we find

$$P\left(Y_{j+1} = y, (U_{j+1} - U_j) \leq l \mid ((Y_0 = y_0, U_0 = u_0)\right.$$
$$(Y_1 = y_1, U_1 = u_1), ..., (Y_j = y_j, U_j = u_j)))$$
$$= P\left(Y_{j+1} = y, (U_{j+1} - U_j) \leq l \mid (Y_j = y_j, U_j = u_j)\right)$$

and conclude that $\{(Y_j; U_j), j = 0, 1, 2, ...\}$ is a Markov renewal process.

Throughput Calculation: Let A_j be the number of successes of the AP in successive channel slots, $j \in 0, 1, 2, 3, \cdots$. We see that A_j is 1 if the AP wins the channel contention and 0 otherwise. If there are n STAs active at the $j-1^{th}$ channel slot, then we have, $A_j = 1$ w.p. $\sigma(n)$ and 0 otherwise. Let $\Theta_{TCP}(M)$ denote the aggregate TCP download throughput (in bps). Applying Markov regenerative analysis [8], defining $E_n A = E(A_j|Y_{j-1} = n)$ and $E_n L = E(L_j|Y_{j-1} = n)$, we have

$$\Theta_{TCP}(M) = \left(\frac{L_{TCPdata}}{\delta}\right)\left(\lim_{t\to\infty}\frac{A(t)}{t}\right) \stackrel{a.s.}{=} \left(\frac{L_{TCPdata}}{\delta}\right)\left(\frac{\sum_{n=0}^{M}\pi_n\ E_n A}{\sum_{n=0}^{M}\pi_n\ E_n L}\right) \quad (1)$$

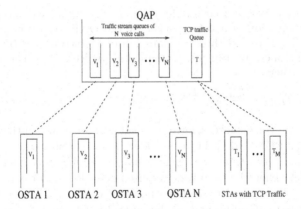

Fig. 3. An IEEE 802.11e WLAN scenario where voice calls are serviced on HCCA and TCP traffic is serviced on EDCA

and each TCP connection will obtain an equal share of the aggregate download throughput.

4 Voice on HCCA and TCP on EDCA

We use the reference scheduler [1] for the IEEE 802.11e Hybrid Coordination Function. We assume that there are no CFPs and we ignore the transmission time of the beacon frames. We do not consider voice activity detection and so the voice calls are considered as full duplex CBR packet streams. We assume that the calls use the G.711 codec. Therefore, we model the voice traffic as generating 200 (= 40 + 160) bytes per 20 ms, i.e. 160 bytes of voice payload + 40 bytes of header (IP + UDP + RTP). We assume that there are no transmission errors due to the channel.

We now consider the scenario where voice calls are serviced on HCCA and TCP transfers are serviced on EDCA as AC1. See Figure 3. We have N QSTAs with one voice TS each, and M QSTAs each performing one TCP download. At the QAP there are N queues for the N HCCA TSs, and one AC1 queue for EDCA TCP traffic.

Let the QoS constraint for VoIP calls be that the WLAN delay does not exceed d. Let T_{SI} denote the chosen service interval. Then, the T_{SI} assigned by the AP to the voice stream is $T_{SI} = d$. Each QSTA first sends a QoS request for inclusion into the polling list of the QAP. Since this is a one time affair, we can ignore this traffic. In a T_{SI}, each QSTA shall have one voice packet for uplink transmission to the QAP. As we are considering duplex voice calls, the QAP also has an equal number of voice packets to be sent downlink to the QSTAs. Thus, when the QAP seizes the channel, we can consider that the QAP first sends the voice packet to the QSTA. The QSTA after successful reception, sends an ACK packet to the QAP. The QAP then sends a QoS CF (QCF) Poll packet to the STA. In reply, the QSTA sends a voice packet to the QAP and this is followed by an ACK packet from the QAP. The QAP then starts a similar transmission for the next QSTA. We see that a bidirectional voice packet exchange of one call consists of transmission of a voice packet by the QAP, transmission of a QCF Poll packet by the AP and then transmission of a voice packet by the station. Let T_{voice} be the one way transmission time for a voice call packet, including all the overheads. Then

$$T_{voice} = T_P + T_{PHY} + \frac{L_{MAC} + L_{voice}}{C_d} + T_{SIFS} + T_P + T_{PHY} + \frac{L_{ACK}}{C_c} + T_{SIFS}$$

where L_{voice} is the voice packet length. See Table 2 for values of the parameters. For the 11 Mbps PHY and G711 voice codec, $T_{voice} = 630.2$ μs.

Let $T_{CF-poll}$ be the time for transmission of a QCF poll packet from the QAP to a QSTA. Then the total time required in each T_{SI}, for one bidirectional call is $2T_{voice} + T_{CF-Poll}$. In one T_{SI}, the QAP has to send voice packets and QCF poll packets to all nodes and all the nodes have to send their voice packets to the QAP. Hence in order that the QoS delay constraint is met, N calls are supportable if

$$N \leq \left\lfloor \frac{T_{SI}}{2T_{voice} + T_{CF-Poll}} \right\rfloor = \left\lfloor \frac{d}{2T_{voice} + T_{CF-Poll}} \right\rfloor =: N_{max}$$

where N_{max} is the maximum number of voice calls permissible with the delay bound d.

When voice calls are placed on HCCA along with TCP transfers on EDCA, the EDCA service takes vacations as in Figure 1. If T_{CAP} denotes the time of HCCA activity in one T_{SI}, it is as though, intermittently, the TCP download activity gets *frozen* and resumes again after the channel is again available after $T_{SI} - T_{CAP}$. Let the TCP download throughput when the whole of the time is available for the EDCA mechanism be Θ_{TCP}. The TCP download throughput, $\underline{\Theta}_{TCP}$ in the presence of HCCA voice activity can then be obtained as

$$\underline{\Theta}_{TCP} = \frac{(T_{SI} - T_{CAP})}{T_{SI}} \Theta_{TCP}$$
$$= \frac{(T_{SI} - N(2T_{voice} + T_{CF-Poll}))}{T_{SI}} \Theta_{TCP} \qquad (2)$$

Observation: When the EDCA activity resumes after the HCCA activity, there is a possibility of TCP activity spilling over into the next *SI* interval. This is because the STAs involved in EDCA TCP download activity are ignorant of any HCCA activity on the channel. When HCCA activity is going on, these STAs just sense that the medium is busy, freeze their back-off values and continue to sense the medium, until it is idle. Once found idle, all STAs wait for $T_{AIFS(AC(1))}$ and if the medium still continues to be idle, they start to decrement the back-off values. The STA which had the least frozen back-off value seizes the channel (assuming no other activity is there during the countdown on the medium and that no 2 STAs had the same least frozen back-off value). Once the medium is seized, the STA transmits one full packet, without regard to whether it might

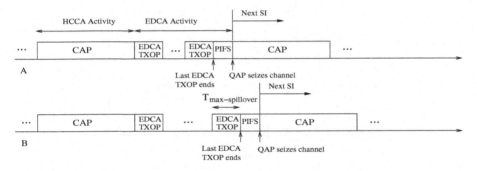

Fig. 4. Channel activity showing the start of a new SI. In A, the next SI starts as scheduled. In B, the next SI gets delayed by $T_{max-spillover}$ due to EDCA activity.

spill-over into the next T_{SI}. See Figure 4 that shows the activity of two scenarios. In Figure 4 A the last EDCA transmission finishes just $PIFS$ time before the next SI has to start. Thus the AP is able to grab the channel as scheduled, for beginning a CAP. At the other extreme, we show a possible scenario (in Figure 4 B) where the last EDCA transmission starts just PIFS before the start of the next SI. Now just when the AP was about to grab the channel, it finds it busy and so has to defer to the next SI. The channel remains busy until this EDCA transmission ends. Once this happens, the AP will grab the channel (by waiting for PIFS time that is smaller than the AIFS time of any QSTA) and thus start the SI. ∎

Equation 2 does not take into account the spill over time that can happen as explained above. Therefore it provides a lower limit of the obtainable throughput (hence the lower bar in the notation). Let the maximum spill over time be denoted by $T_{max-spillover}$. Depending upon whether the TCP sessions are using the basic mechanism or the RTS/CTS mechanism, we have different values of $T_{max-spillover}$. For the basic access mechanism, $T_{max-spillover}$ is the time length of one EDCA TXOP as seen from Figure 4 B. Therefore $T_{max-spillover} = T_P + T_{PHY} + (L_{MAC} + L_{IPH} + L_{TCPdata})/C_d + T_{SIFS} + T_P + T_{PHY} + L_{ACK}/C_c$
For a TCP download packet size of 1500 bytes, at 11 Mbps data rate, for IEEE 802.11b PHY, $T_{max-spillover}$ is 1.60 ms for the basic access mechanism. Utilizing this extra time gives the upper bound for the TCP download throughput

$$\overline{\Theta}_{TCP} = \frac{(T_{SI} - N(2T_{voice} + T_{CF-Poll}) + T_{max-spillover})}{T_{SI} + T_{max-spillover}} \Theta_{TCP}$$

Maximum Number of Voice Calls: If λ is the voice packet arrival rate, then in the time $T_{SI} + T_{max-spillover}$, due to N ongoing calls, $2N\lambda(T_{SI} + T_{max-spillover})$ packets arrive in the network. The multiplicative factor '2' is needed because each VoIP call corresponds to two streams: upstream and downstream. These packets need to be serviced in the next T_{SI}. The time required for the transmission of one packet is $\frac{2T_{voice} + T_{CFpoll}}{2}$. The QoS delay constraint is met if the time required for

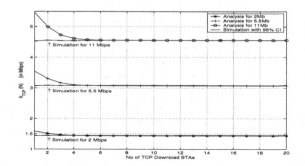

Fig. 5. Results from analysis and simulation: total download throughput Θ_{TCP} obtained as a function of the number of TCP downloads, M; the basic access mechanism is used for TCP transfers

the transmission of these packets by the HCCA mechanism does not overshoot T_{SI}. Thus for admission control, $N \leq N_{max}$ calls are permissible with

$$N_{max} = \max \{N : 2N\lambda(T_{SI} + T_{max-spillover})(T_{voice} + 0.5T_{CFpoll}) \leq T_{SI}\}. \quad (3)$$

5 Numerical Results and Validation

Due to the nonavailability of a simulator that implements both EDCA and HCCA functions concurrently, we modify the *ns-2* simulator to simulate our scenario as follows. First, we apply the HCCA patch [4] on *ns-2*. The HCCA patch [4] provides a simulation of HCCA on the 802.11 DCF WLAN; thus we can simulate VoIP calls on HCCA. However, in the time left over by the CAPs of HCCA, only channel access by DCF is possible. In order to simulate EDCA AC 1 activity in the remaining time, we configure the back-off parameters of AC 1 into the DCF of ns-2. Thus, we obtain the simulation scenario where the VoIP calls are on HCCA and the TCP sessions are on EDCA. Note that since DCF is designed for only one queue, at a time we can have only one AC of EDCA working with HCCA, which suffices for our purpose.

Figure 5 shows the total TCP download throughput vs. the number of TCP connections, as obtained from our analysis (using Equation 1), and also the simulation for different PHY data rates. The simulation results also show 95% confidence intervals. We see that the throughput obtained by analysis matches very closely with that obtained from the simulation for a number of STAs greater than 4. The analysis assumes that the AP is always saturated and the STAs have at most packet at any time. This assumption is not valid when the number of TCP sessions is small. For instance, in the case of 11 Mbps, when there is only one TCP session, there are only two nodes - the AP and one STA. In this case the queues behave symmetrically, i.e., the TCP window is split randomly between the two queues. This symmetry decreases with increase in the number of STAs. Thus our model is not valid for a small number of STAs, i.e., less than 5 (for 11 Mbps) as seen from Fig. 5.

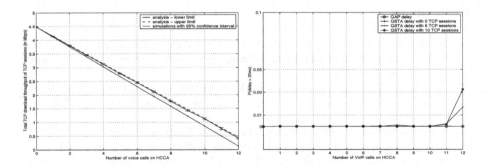

Fig. 6. Left: total download throughput Θ_{TCP} obtained as a function of the number of voice calls, N, on HCCA; bounds from analysis are also shown. Right: $Prob(delay \geq 20ms)$ for voice packets at the QAP and the QSTAs as a function of the number of voice calls, N, on HCCA; simulation results.

In the left panel of Figure 6 we show the simulated TCP download throughput as a function of the number of voice calls. We also calculate $\underline{\Theta}_{TCP}$ and $\overline{\Theta}_{TCP}$ using the value of Θ_{TCP} from Figure 5 for the 11 Mbps PHY (i.e., 4.5 Mbps). We notice that the two analytical values are indeed bounds, and the upper bound is closer to the simulation results, as the EDCA spill over occurs with a high probability.

Fig. 6 can also be used for admission control of voice calls in order to guarantee a net minimal throughput to the TCP sessions. For instance if at least 2 Mbps of total throughput is to be allotted to TCP sessions then the figure says that only 7 voice calls should be admitted on HCCA.

When only HCCA VoIP traffic is present, we obtain the maximum number of calls possible from Equation 3, as 12 calls, using the G711 codec, when the delay bound is 20 ms. In the presence of EDCA TCP download traffic, we obtain the analytical maximum number of voice calls, using Equation 3, as $N_{max} = 11$ calls. Thus, due to EDCA TCP traffic, the maximum number of VoIP calls decreases by 1, while guaranteeing the QoS delay constraint of 20 ms.

To validate the admission control region, we show the simulation results for the QoS measure, $Prob(delay \geq 20ms)$, for voice at the QAP and at the QSTAs in the right hand panel of Figure 6. This probability at the QAP is almost zero for all number of VoIP calls. This is because the QAP knows the VoIP packet arrivals at its queue and so schedules their transmission before polling the QSTAs. The probability of delay incurred by the VoIP packets at the QSTAs is also almost zero except at $N = 12$, where it suddenly increases when TCP traffic is added. Thus the delay QoS is not met when the number of calls is 12 and there is also TCP traffic on EDCA. This implies that a maximum of 11 calls are possible on HCCA when TCP traffic exists on EDCA. This confirms the analysis result. We observe that the maximum number of calls decreases only by one when the TCP streams are added in the WLAN. This can be attributed to the spill over of EDCA activity into the subsequent SI.

References

1. Wireless LAN Medium Access Control (MAC) and Physical Layer (PHY) Specification: Medium Access Control (MAC) Enhancements for Quality of Service (QoS), IEEE Std 802.11e, 2005.
2. G. Bianchi. Performance Analysis of the IEEE 802.11 Distributed Coordination Function. *IEEE Journal on Selected Areas in Communications*, pages 535–547, March 2000.
3. R. Bruno, M. Conti, and E. Gregori. Throughput Analysis of TCP Clients in Wi-Fi Hot Spot Networks. In *Networking 2004*, LNCS 2042, pages 626–637, 2004.
4. Claudio Cicconetti, Enzo Mingozzi, Luciano Lenzini, and Giovanni Stea. A Software Architecture for Simulating IEEE 802.11e HCCA. In *IPS-MoMe'05*, March 14-15 2005.
5. A. Detti, E. Graziosi, V. Minichiello, S. Salsano, and V. Sangregorio. TCP Fairness Issues in IEEE 802.11 Based Access Networks. preprint, 2005.
6. K. Duffy, D. Malone, and D. J. Leith. Modelling 802.11 Wireless Links. In *CDC-ECC '05*, volume 3, pages 6952 – 6957, 12-15 Dec 2005.
7. S. Harsha, A. Kumar, and V. Sharma. An Analytical Model for the Capacity Estimation of Combined VoIP and TCP File Transfers over EDCA in an IEEE 802.11e WLAN. In *Proc. IEEE IWQoS'06*, June 2006.
8. V. G. Kulkarni. *Modeling and Analysis of Stochastic Systems*. Chapman and Hall/CRC Press, 1996.
9. A. Kumar, E. Altman, D. Miorandi, and M. Goyal. New Insights from a Fixed Point Analysis of Single Cell IEEE 802.11 WLANs. In *IEEE INFOCOM'05*, pages 1550 – 1561, 13 - 17 March 2005.
10. G. Kuriakose. Analytical Models for QoS Engineering of Wireless LANs, *Master of Engg. Thesis*, ECE Department, Indian Institute of Science, Bangalore, April 2005.
11. G. Kuriakose, S. Harsha, A. Kumar, and V. Sharma. Analytical Models for Capacity Estimation of IEEE 802.11 WLANs using DCF for Internet Applications. submitted for publication, Apr 2006.
12. D. J. Leith and P. Clifford. Using the 802.11e EDCF to Achieve TCP Upload Fairness over WLAN Links. In Proceedings *WiOpt: Modeling and Optimization in Mobile, Ad Hoc and Wireless Networks*, pages 109–118, 2005.
13. S. Pilosof, R. Ramjee, Y. Shavitt, and P. Sinha. Understanding TCP Fairness over Wireless LANs. In *INFOCOM*, 2003.
14. S. Shankar, J. del Prado Pavon, and P. Wienert. Optimal Packing of VoIP calls in an IEEE 802.11 a/e WLAN in the Presence of QoS Constraints and Channel Errors. In *Global Telecommunications Conference, GLOBECOM '04*, volume 5, pages 2974 – 2980. IEEE, 29 Nov.-3 Dec 2004.
15. J.V. Sudarev, L.B. White, and S. Perreau. Performance Analysis of 802.11 CSMA/CA for Infrastructure Networks under Finite Load Conditions. In *LAN-MAN 2005*, volume 3, pages 1 – 6, 18-21 Sept 2005.
16. O. Tickoo and B. Sikdar. A Queueing Model for Finite Load IEEE 802.11 Random Access MAC. In *IEEE ICC, 2004*, volume 1, pages 175 – 179, 20-24 June 2004.

Developing Analytical Framework to Measure Robustness of Peer-to-Peer Networks

Bivas Mitra, Md. Moin Afaque, Sujoy Ghose, and Niloy Ganguly

Department of Computer Science and Engineering
Indian Institute of Technology, Kharagpur, India
{bivasm, moin, sujoy, niloy}@cse.iitkgp.ernet.in

Abstract. In peer-to-peer (p2p) networks, peer nodes communicate with each other with the help of overlay structure. As the peers in the p2p system join and leave the network randomly, it makes the overlay network dynamic and unstable in nature. In this paper, we propose *an analytical framework* to assess the robustness of different topologies adopted by these overlay structures, to withstand the random movement of peers in the networks. We model the dynamic behavior of the peers through degree independent as well as degree dependent node failure. Recently superpeer networks are becoming the most widely used topology among the p2p networks [8]. Therefore we perform the stability analysis of superpeer networks as a case study. We validate the analytically derived results with the help of simulation.

Keywords: peer to peer networks, complex networks, percolation theory, network resilience.

1 Introduction

Peer to peer (p2p) networks have recently become a popular medium through which huge amount of data can be shared. P2p file sharing systems, where files are searched and downloaded among peers without the help of central servers, have emerged as a major component of Internet traffic. Peers in p2p networks are connected among themselves by some logical links forming an overlay above the physical network. It has been found that these overlay networks, consisting of a large amount of peers are analogous to complex real world networks and can be modeled using various types of random graphs [15]. Generally the degrees of these random graphs are statistically distributed and become the characteristic feature of the topology of the overlay networks.

The topology of the overlay network is important from two aspects.

- The spread of information flow through the network is essential to perform efficient search in the p2p networks. The speed at which information spread is dependent on the topology of the network.
- As peers in the p2p system join and leave network randomly without any central coordination, overlay structures become highly dynamic in nature.

S. Chaudhuri et al. (Eds.): ICDCN 2006, LNCS 4308, pp. 257–268, 2006.

Frequently it partitions the network into smaller fragments which results in the breakdown of communication among peers.

In this paper we concentrate on understanding the stability[1] of the overlay structures which is a major challenge in front of the p2p network community. There is no formal framework available to measure the stability of various overlay structures modeled by random graphs. However different works in bits and pieces have been done mainly by the physicists which analyzes the dynamics of random graphs. Effect of random failures and intentional attacks in various kind of graphs are discussed by Cohen *et al.* in [1,2]. It has been observed from the results that Internet, which can be modeled by power law networks is more resilient to random failure than E-R graphs (Poisson random graphs). They also found both analytically and experimentally that scale free networks are highly sensitive to intentional attack leading support to the view of Albert [3]. In [4], Newman *et al.* developed the theory of random graphs with arbitrary degree distribution with the help of generating function formalism. Using this formalism, Callaway [5] found the exact analytic solutions for percolation[2] on random graphs with any degree distribution where failure has been modeled by an arbitrary function of node degree. In [7], researchers have addressed a more realistic scenario in which a network is subjected to simultaneous targeted and random attacks. This attack has been modeled as a sequence of "waves" of targeted and random attacks which removes fractions p_t and p_r of the nodes of the network. In all these works except [5], researchers have considered some particular types of networks like E-R, scale free or bimodal networks and analyzed the effect of a few specific kinds of failures like random, intentional or mixed upon them. In [5], researchers have dealt a more general case but failed to propose any generalized equation to measure the stability of random graphs. This paper utilizes many of aforesaid results and proposes a generalized equation to measure stability of p2p overlay structures against dynamic movement of peers.

As examples of random and frequent movement of peers, we model two kinds of node failures in random graph.

- The most common type of failures are denoted as *degree independent failure* where probability of removal of a node is constant and independent of degree of that node.
- In p2p networks, peers having higher connectivity (e.g. superpeers) are more stable in the network than the peers having lower connectivity because those loosely connected peers enter and leave the network quite frequently. These observation leads us to model a new kind of failure where probability of removal of a node is inversely proportional to the degree of that node. We denote this kind of failure as *degree dependent failure*.

---

[1] In this paper, we do not differentiate between the terms stability and robustness. They are therefore used interchangeably.
[2] Percolation indicates the existence of a critical probability p_c such that below p_c the network is composed of isolated clusters but above p_c, a giant cluster spans the entire network.

As example of topology, we consider superpeer networks. This is because, as most widely used overlay structures, considerable amount of interest has been recently generated in understanding the stability of these networks. We also verify the correctness of our theoretical model with the help of experimental results.

The rest of the paper is organized as follows. Section 2 models the generalized random graph for any kind of failures. It shows the condition for giant component disruption for any kind of disturbances in the networks. In section 3 we classify two different kinds of random failure and mathematically analyze their effect on the generalized random graph. Section 4 theoretically examines the stability of superpeer networks for degree independent and degree dependent failures. This section also compares the results derived from our mathematical model with experimental results. Section 5 concludes the paper.

2 Stability Analysis of Overlay Networks

In this section, we use generating function formalism to derive the general formula for measuring the stability of overlay structures undergoing failure. We formally model the overlay structures and various kinds of failures and define the stability metric which are the parameters of our analytical framework.

2.1 Topology of the Overlay Networks

The different types of overlay structure of the p2p networks can be modeled using the uniform framework of probability distribution p_k, where p_k be the probability that a randomly chosen node has degree k. So the degree distribution p_k signifies the topology of the overlay network which can be modeled as E-R graph, power law network, superpeer network or any other arbitrary topology. The most common overlay structures are the simple unstructured p2p networks where data are shared among peers in a naive fashion. In such a system like Gnutella [12], all peers have equal roles and responsibilities. Such topologies can be modeled by E-R graph with degree distribution $p_k = \frac{z^k e^{-z}}{k!}$ where z is the mean degree or power law network $p_k = ck^{-\beta}$ where β is a parameter and c is a constant.

Recently, the superpeer networks have become a potential candidate to model overlay structure where a small fraction of nodes are superpeers and rest are peers. Many popular p2p systems like KaZaA [13] have adopted superpeers in their design. A superpeer node having higher connectivity, acts as a centralized server to a subset of clients where client peers submit queries to their superpeer and receive results from it. However superpeers are also connected to each other to route messages over the overlay network and submit and answer queries on behalf of their clients and themselves. Superpeer networks can be modeled by bimodal degree distribution where a large fraction (r) of peer nodes with small degree k_l are connected with superpeers and few superpeer nodes ($1 - r$) with high degree k_m are connected to each other. Formally

$$p_k > 0 \quad if \ \ k = k_l, k_m; \quad p_k = 0 \quad otherwise$$

k_l & k_m are degrees of peers and superpeers respectively.

2.2 Different Kinds of Failure Models

Let q_k be the probability that a vertex of degree k be present in the network after the removal of a fraction of nodes. In our framework q_k is used to specify the various failure models.

- In degree independent random failure, the probability of removal of any randomly chosen node is constant, degree independent and equal for all other nodes in the graph. Therefore the presence of any randomly chosen node having degree k after this kind of failure is $q_k = q$ (independent of k).
- In degree dependent random failure, probability of failure of a node (f_k) having degree k is inversely proportional to k^γ. i.e $f_k \propto 1/k^\gamma \Rightarrow f_k = \alpha/k^\gamma$ where $0 \le \alpha \le 1$ and γ is a real number. Therefore probability of the presence of a node having degree k after this kind of failure is $q_k = (1 - \frac{\alpha}{k^\gamma})$.

2.3 Stability Metric

The stability and robustness of overlay networks are primarily measured in terms of certain fraction of nodes f_c called percolation threshold or critical fraction [10], removal of which disintegrates the network into smaller, disconnected components. Below that threshold, their exists a connected component which spans the entire network also termed as giant component[3]. The value of percolation threshold or critical fraction f_c signifies the stability of the network, higher value indicates greater stability against failure.

2.4 Generating Function Formalism

Based upon the above described model parameters, we use generating function formalism to find out the general formula to measure the stability of various overlay structures. In mathematics a generating function is a formal power series whose coefficients encode information about a sequence that is indexed by the natural numbers [4]. This generating function can be used to understand different properties of graphs. For example, the generating function $G_0(x)$ generates the probability distribution of the vertex degrees k. Therefore $G_0(x) = \sum_{k=0}^{\infty} p_k x^k$ where p_k is the probability that a randomly chosen vertex in the graph has degree k. Importance of the generating function lies in the convenient way the average over the probability distribution can be generated - for instance, the average degree z of a vertex in the case of $G_0(x)$ is given by $z = \langle k \rangle = \sum_k k p_k = G_0'(1)$. Higher moments can be calculated from higher derivatives also. Here we are using the generating function to explain a slightly more complicated concept.

---

[3] Giant component is a technical term which signifies the largest connected component in the network whose size is of the order of size of the network [11].

In our formalism q_k and p_k specifies the failure model and network topology respectively whose stability is subjected to examination. The formalism helps us to locate the transition point where the giant component breaks down into smaller components. $p_k.q_k$ specifies the probability of a node having degree k to be present in the network after the process of removal of some portion of nodes is completed. Hence

$$F_0(x) = \sum_{k=0}^{\infty} p_k.q_k x^k$$

becomes the generating function for this distribution. Distribution of the outgoing edges of the first neighbor of a randomly chosen node can be generated by

$$F_1(x) = \frac{\sum_k kp_k q_k x^{k-1}}{\sum_k kp_k} = F_0'(x)/z$$

where z is the average degree [5].

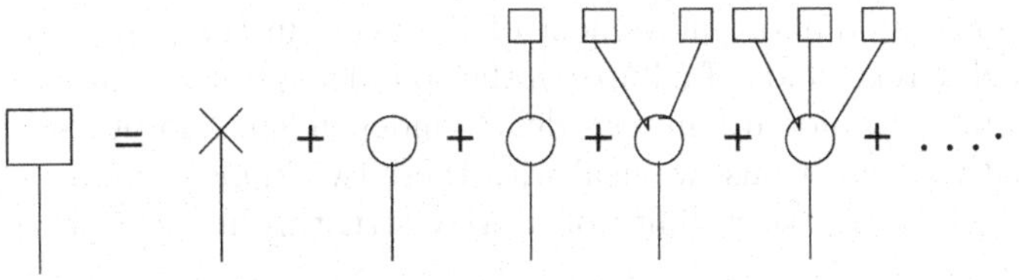

Fig. 1. Schematic representation of the sum rule for the connected component of vertices reached by following a randomly chosen edge. The probability of each such component (left-hand side) can be represented as the sum of the probabilities (right hand side) of having no vertex (which has been removed), only a single vertex, having a single vertex connected to one other component, or two other components, and so forth. The entire sum can be expressed in closed form as equation (1) and similarly (2).

Let $H_1(x)$ be the generating function for the distribution of the component sizes that are reached by choosing a random edge and following it to one of its ends. The component may contain zero node if the node at the other end of the randomly selected edge is removed, which happens with probability $1 - F_1(1)$, or the edge may lead to a node with k other edges leading out of it other than the edge we came in along, distributed according to $F_1(x)$. That means that $H_1(x)$ satisfies a self-consistency condition (Fig. 1) of the form [5]

$$H_1(x) = 1 - F_1(1) + xF_1(H_1(x)). \tag{1}$$

The distribution for the component size to which a randomly selected node belongs to is similarly generated by (Fig. 1) $H_0(x)$ where

$$H_0(x) = 1 - F_0(1) + xF_0(H_1(x)). \tag{2}$$

Therefore the average size of the components becomes

$$H_0'(1) = \langle s \rangle = F_0(1) + \frac{F_0'(1)F_1(1)}{1 - F_1'(1)}$$

which diverges when $1 - F_1'(1) = 0$. Size of the component becoming infinite implies that the entire network joins together forming one giant component.

$$F_1'(1) = 1 \Rightarrow \sum_{k=0}^{\infty} kp_k(kq_k - q_k - 1) = 0 \tag{3}$$

The equation (3) states the critical condition for the stability of giant component with respect to any type of graphs (characterized by p_k) undergoing any type of failure (characterized by q_k). Formulating this general formula is the primary contribution of the paper. In the rest of the paper, we investigate the stability situation under various special conditions.

3 Stability at Various Failure Scenario

We have seen that random movement of the peers in the p2p network can be modeled by different kinds of failures in the complex graph. As discussed, we address two kinds of random failures - degree independent and degree dependent. In the next two subsections, we deal with these two kinds of failures and investigate their effect on the stability of overlay structure modeled by generalized random graph.

3.1 Degree Independent Random Failure

In this section, we discuss the effect of degree independent random failure in generalized random graph. If $q = q_c$ is the critical fraction of nodes whose presence in the graph is essential for the stability of the giant component after this kind of failure then according to equation (3)

$$\sum_{k=0}^{\infty} kp_k(kq_c - q_c - 1) = 0$$

$$\Rightarrow q_c = \frac{1}{\frac{\langle k^2 \rangle}{\langle k \rangle} - 1}$$

Now if f_c is the critical fraction of nodes whose random removal disintegrates the giant component then $f_c = 1 - q_c$. Therefore percolation threshold

$$f_c = 1 - \frac{1}{\frac{\langle k^2 \rangle}{\langle k \rangle} - 1} \tag{4}$$

This is the well known condition [1] (derived differently) for the disappearance of the giant component due to random failure. Note that, we have reproduced it to show that it can also be derived from the proposed general formula (equation 3).

3.2 Degree Dependent Random Failure

In p2p networks, the peers (or superpeers) having higher connectivity are much more stable and reliable than the nodes having lower connectivity. Therefore probability of the presence of a node having degree k after this kind of failure is

$$q_k = (1 - \frac{\alpha}{k^\gamma}). \tag{5}$$

Using equations (3) and (5), we obtain the following critical condition for the stability of giant component after degree dependent breakdown

$$\langle k^2 \rangle - \alpha \langle k^{2-\gamma} \rangle + \alpha \langle k^{1-\gamma} \rangle - 2 \langle k \rangle = 0$$

where percolation threshold is

$$f_c = \sum_{k=0}^{\infty} \frac{\alpha}{k^\gamma} p_k.$$

Considering the value of $\alpha = 1$, where the fraction of nodes removed due to this kind of failure becomes maximum, the condition for percolation becomes

$$\langle k^{2-\gamma} \rangle - \langle k^{1-\gamma} \rangle = \langle k^2 \rangle - 2 \langle k \rangle \tag{6}$$

Thus the critical fraction of nodes removed is given by

$$f_c = \sum_{k=0}^{\infty} \frac{1}{k^\gamma} p_k. \tag{7}$$

where γ satisfies the equation (6).

Thus from the equations (6) and (7), we can determine the variation of percolation threshold f_c for various networks due to degree dependent random failure. We apply these formalism for superpeer networks and compare the results with experimental results in section 4.

4 Case Study: Stability of Superpeer Networks with Respect to Failure Models

In this section we study the robustness of the superpeer networks with the help of our analytical framework. We investigate the change of percolation threshold (f_c) due to the change of fraction of peers (r) and the connectivity of the superpeers (k_m) in the networks for various types of failure. To ensure fair comparisons, we keep *the average degree* $\langle k \rangle$ *constant for all graphs*. We verify our theoretical results with the help of experiments; the experimental setup is explained below.

4.1 Experimental Setup

The p2p overlay structure is represented by a simple undirected graph stored as an adjacency list. In order to generate the topology, every node is assigned a degree according to the topology being simulated. In the case of bimodal network the nodes are assigned the degrees depending on the k_l and k_m values and the fraction of these nodes in total. Thereafter the edges are generated using the "switching method" and the "matching method" referred to in [14]. However since these methods (as far as our knowledge goes, no better method exists) do not sample the total ensemble of all possible desired graphs (here bimodal) uniformly, the experimental results might vary a little from the theoretical results. Failure of a peer effectively means deletion of the node and its corresponding edges. In the case of degree independent failure, nodes are randomly selected using a time-seeded pseudo-random number generator and its edges removed from the adjacency list. In degree dependent failure, first the fraction of nodes having a certain degree that need to be removed is calculated, thereafter that many nodes are selected from the total set of all such nodes randomly and its corresponding edges are removed from the adjacency list.

4.2 Degree Independent Failure

Bimodal structure is mostly used to model superpeer networks. Let r be the fraction of peers in the superpeer networks having degree k_l and and rest are superpeers having degree k_m where $k_l << k_m$. Therefore bimodal degree distribution p_k becomes non zero only at k_l and k_m [6]. Mathematically $k_l p_{k_l} + k_m p_{k_m} = \langle k \rangle$ and $p_{k_l} + p_{k_m} = 1$ which provides

$$p_{k_m} = \frac{\langle k \rangle - k_l}{k_m - k_l} \qquad\qquad p_{k_l} = \frac{k_m - \langle k \rangle}{k_m - k_l}$$

$$\Rightarrow \langle k^2 \rangle = k_m^2 p_{k_m} + k_l^2 p_{k_l} = \langle k \rangle (k_l + k_m) - k_l k_m \text{ and using equation (4) we get}$$

$$f_c = 1 - \frac{\langle k \rangle}{\langle k \rangle (k_l + k_m - 1) - k_l k_m}$$

As the fraction of peers having degree k_l in the network is r therefore the average degree of the network $\langle k \rangle = k_l r + k_m (1-r)$ implies that $k_l = \frac{\langle k \rangle - (1-r)k_m}{r}$. Hence percolation threshold

$$f_c = 1 - \frac{\langle k \rangle r}{\langle k \rangle^2 - 2\langle k \rangle k_m + 2rk_m\langle k \rangle - r\langle k \rangle + k_m^2 - rk_m^2} \tag{8}$$

Using equation (8), we study the variation of percolation threshold (f_c) due to the change of the fraction of peers (r)(Fig 2(a)). Here we keep the average degree $\langle k \rangle = 5$ fixed and vary the superpeer degree $k_m = 25, 30, 40$ for each curve. The results for the same parameters are also deduced experimentally and shown in Fig 2(b). We first explain the features commonly observed in both theoretical

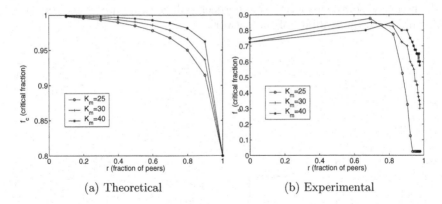

(a) Theoretical   (b) Experimental

Fig. 2. The above plots represent critical fraction (f_c) Vs fraction of peers (r) for various superpeer networks undergoing degree independent failure. Here X-axis represents the fraction of peer nodes (r) exists in the superpeer network and Y-axis represents the corresponding critical fraction or percolation threshold (f_c).

and practical results and then provide a comparative study between the two results.

General observations: It can be observed (in both theoretical and experimental results) that with the increase of the fraction of peers in the network, the percolation threshold decreases which indicates the increase of fragility of the network. That means increase of the fraction of superpeers in the network improves the stability of the network. When the fraction of superpeers is above 15% to 20% , the percolation threshold is quite high. But after that, there is a sharp fall of f_c thus drastically increases the vulnerability of the network.

Comparative study between theoretical and experimental results: It can be observed from the theoretical (Fig.2(a)) and experimental (Fig.2(b)) results that the behavior of critical fraction (f_c) with the change of the percentage of peers (r) is almost same for both cases. The only significant observation for the experimental result is when percentage of superpeers is quite high (80% to 90%), the value of f_c starts from a lower value. With the decrease of superpeers fraction, f_c goes up and reaches an optimum value. This indicates the optimum superpeer to peer ratio for which overlay network becomes most stable due to this kind of failure. The further decrease of superpeers again reduces the value of f_c. The initial increase of f_c cannot be captured by our analytical model. From the theoretical perspective, giant component size is the order of the network size and is intuitively considered same for all cases. But in practice, giant component is a finite fraction of size of the network which is not fixed for all cases but may vary (albeit slightly) from case to case. For the lower values of r (i.e. percentage of superpeers is high), some superpeers remain isolated in the network thus reducing the size of the giant component. This results in lower values of f_c. But with the decrease of percentage of superpeers, all the superpeers get connected which increases the stability of the network.

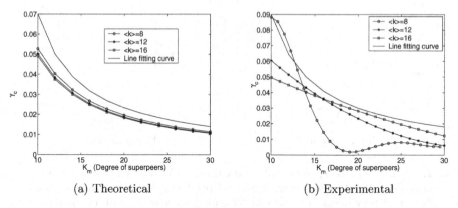

(a) Theoretical   (b) Experimental

Fig. 3. Change of γ_c with respect of superpeer degree k_m for superpeer networks undergoing degree dependent failure. Here mean degree $\langle k \rangle$ varies from 8 to 16. X-axis represents the superpeer degree(k_m) and Y-axis represents the corresponding γ_c.

4.3   Degree Dependent Failure

As introduced in section 2, in this case the probability of failure of a node is inversely proportional to the degree of that node. Mathematically the fraction of nodes removed $f = \sum_{k=0}^{\infty} \frac{\alpha}{k^\gamma} p_k$. According to equation (6), the bimodal network percolates if

$$\langle k^{2-\gamma} \rangle - \langle k^{1-\gamma} \rangle = \langle k^2 \rangle - 2\langle k \rangle.$$

If the value of $\gamma = \gamma_c$ satisfies this equation then removal of $f_c = \sum_{k=0}^{\infty} \frac{1}{k^{\gamma_c}} p_k$ fraction of nodes destroys the giant component. In most of the commercial superpeer networks like KaZaA [13], peers are only directly connected to the local superpeer making their degree $k_l = 1$. In that case, the value of γ_c which percolates the bimodal network can be derived from equation (6) and becomes

$$\gamma_c = 1 - \frac{\ln \frac{\langle k \rangle (k_m+1) - k_m - 2\langle k \rangle}{\langle k \rangle - 1}}{\ln k_m} \tag{9}$$

where lowest degree is assumed to be $k_l = 1$. We plot the variation of the γ_c that is required to percolate the bimodal networks with respect to the superpeer degree k_m for various average degree $\langle k \rangle$(Fig 3(a)). Like degree independent failure, the results for the same parameters are also deduced experimentally and shown in Fig 3(b). We first explain the features commonly observed in both theoretical and practical results and then provide a comparative study between the two results.

General observations: It can be easily identified from Fig 3, that with the increase of superpeer degree, the value of γ_c that percolates the network decreases.

These curves can be approximated by the polynomial $a/(x - b)$ ($0 < a < 1$ and b is some positive integer). Thus the decrease of γ_c follows hyperbolic trajectory. Another interesting observation is after a certain threshold k_m, the curves become parallel to the X-axis and never cuts it thus the value of γ_c is small but never becomes 0 (in that case $f_c = \sum_{k=0}^{\infty} \frac{1}{k^0} p_k = 1$). It implies that for any large value of k_m, although f_c becomes significantly large however it is required to remove only a part of nodes (and not all the nodes) from the network to dissolve the giant component.

Comparative study between theoretical and experimental results: In the case of degree dependent failure, the experimental results (Fig.3(b)) differ from theoretical (Fig.3(a)) for lower average degree $\langle k \rangle$ but matches quite well for higher values of $\langle k \rangle$. In both cases, initially γ_c decreases with the increase of superpeer degree (k_m). But after crossing a threshold value (which also reflects the optimum superpeer degree), further increases of k_m increases the value of γ_c which is not reflected by the theoretical analysis. The reason is almost same as explained in degree independent failure. Keeping average degree constant and increasing the superpeer degree leaves many of the superpeers isolated. This decreases the stability of the network thus increases the value of γ_c. This phenomenon becomes significant when the average degree of the network is low.

5   Conclusion and Future Work

The basic contribution of this work is the development of general framework to analyze the stability of various p2p overlay structures against dynamic movement of peers. We have modeled the behavior of these peers using degree independent and degree dependent random failure. As superpeer networks are currently most promising and widely used overlay structure, we perform stability analysis of these networks as a case study of our analytical model. It has been observed that when the fraction of superpeers in the network is less than 15%, the robustness of the network sharply decreases for degree independent failure. This result points to a zone where superpeer network is most vulnerable. Similarly for degree dependent failure, our analysis shows that increase of superpeer degree improves the stability of the network and the improvement follows a hyperbolic trajectory. Although our theoretical and experimental results have matched fairly, however the little differences between them result from the contradiction of the theoretical and practical concept of giant component. Difficulties to generate accurate graph with a given degree sequence are also responsible for the slight mismatch between theoretical and experimental results.

Deeper look into the differences between experimental and theoretical results is part of our future work. Similarly we have to perform a detailed comparative study of the stability of various overlay topologies like E-R graph, power law network, various kinds of superpeer networks like mixed Poisson and bimodal structure etc. In addition to the simple failure models discussed here, in future we will consider different kinds of attacks where nodes having more importance are been targeted and attacked to destroy the connectivity of the p2p network. Importance of a node can be determined by degree centrality, betweenness, eigenvector centrality etc. Moreover, comparative stability analysis of all these topologies with respect to combination of different attacks and failures will bring completeness to the work.

References

1. R. Cohen, K. Erez, D. Avraham, S. Havlin : "Resilience of the Internet to Random Breakdown", Vol. 85, No. 21 Physical Review Letters, 2000.
2. R. Cohen, K. Erez, D. Avraham, S. Havlin : "Resilience of the Internet under Intentional Attack", Vol. 86, No. 16 Physical Review Letters, 2001.
3. R. Albert, H. Jhong, A. L. Barabsi : "Error and Attack Tolerance of Complex Networks", Nature, 406, 2000.
4. M. E. J. Newman, S. H. Strogatz, D. J. Watts : "Random Graphs with Arbitrary Degree Distributions and Their Application", Physical Review , 2001.
5. D. S. Callaway , M. E. J. Newman, S. H. Strogatz, D. J. Watts : "Network Robustness and Fragility: Percolation on Random graphs", Vol. 85, No. 21 Physical Review Letters, 2000.
6. G. Paul, Sameet Sreenivasan, Shlomo Havlin, Stanley : "Resilience of the Internet to Random Breakdown", Phys Rev E, 72, 056130, 2005.
7. T. Tanizawa, G. Paul, R. Cohen, S. Havlin, H.E. Stanley : "Optimization of Network Robustness to Waves of Targeted and Random Attack", Physical Review E.,71,047101, 2005.
8. B. Yang, H. Garcua-Molina : "Designing a Super-Peer Networks ", Proceedings of the International Conference on Data Engineering (ICDE), Los Alamitos, CA, March 2003.
9. A. Valente, A. Sarkar, H. A. Stone : "2-Peak and 3-Peak Optimal Complex Networks", Physical Review Letters, 92: 118702, 2004.
10. M. Molloy, B. Reed : "A Critical Point for Random Graphs with a Given Degree Sequence", Random Structures and Algorithms 6, 161-179, 1995.
11. M. Molloy, B. Reed : "The Size of the Giant Component of a Random Graph with a Given Degree Sequence", Combinatorics, Probability and Computing 7, 295-298, 1998.
12. Gnutella website. http://www.gnutella.com
13. KaZaA website. http://www.kazaa.com
14. R. Milo, N. Kashtan, S. Itzkovitz, M. E. J. Newman, U. Alon : "On the Uniform Generation of Random Graphs with Prescribed Degree Sequences", eprint arXiv:cond-mat/0312028, 2003.
15. Q. Lv, P. Cao, E. Cohen, K. Li and S. Shenker : "Search and Replication in Unstructured Peer-to-Peer Networks", ACM International Conference on Supercomputing, New York, USA, 2002.

Design and Implementation of a Network Processor Based 10Gbps Network Traffic Generator

Sanket Shah, Tularam M. Bansod, and Amit Singh

Veermata Jijabai Technological Institute (VJTI), Mumbai, India
sanketshah5124@yahoo.com, tmbansod@hotmail.com,
vjti_amit@rediff.com

Abstract. Testing network processor based high throughput applications require high-speed traffic generator. Commercial traffic generators are very expensive and their internal working is proprietary. Hence, we have designed a network processor based network Traffic Generator (TG). The Control Plane (CP) takes care of the configuration of the traffic profile. The data plane (DP) is responsible for actual generation of the traffic. The TG requires another copy of TG or any other traffic generator for calibration. We explain the calibration methodology and the results of our experiments. Our system has been able to generate traffic up to 10Gbps.

Keywords: Traffic Generator, Network Processor, High Throughput, System Testing.

1 Introduction

General-purpose processors are ill suited for high speed networking applications where packets need to be processed at line-speed. These applications typically have very low memory reference locality, they have packet level parallelism instead of instruction level parallelism, and they generally do not use floating-point unit. Hence special purpose network processors [1, 8] (NP) are designed for high performance networking applications. Traffic generator must satisfy a number of requirements. It should generate various types of packet such as raw Ethernet frames, ARP packets, IPv4 datagrams, IPSec packets, and UDP datagrams. It should configure header part of all these protocols. It should also be capable of generating mixture of traffic at multiple ports. Given the cost and the proprietary nature of existing commercial traffic generators, we have decided to develop a Traffic Generator (TG) using the Network Processor itself. While our traffic generator uses a proprietary network processor, it has been designed as a general-purpose traffic generator capable of running on any network processor architecture. The organization of the rest of the paper is as follows. Section 2 describes the related work. Section 3 presents our architecture in detail and explains the functioning of the traffic generator. In Section 4, we describe the experiments required to calibrate the CP for traffic control purposes. Section 5 presents the future work, and Section 6 concludes the paper.

S. Chaudhuri et al. (Eds.): ICDCN 2006, LNCS 4308, pp. 269–275, 2006.
© Springer-Verlag Berlin Heidelberg 2006

2   Related Works

More details on the design and architecture of Network Processors can be found in [7, 8]. While routers were one of the earliest applications built on top of these processors [2], a large number of applications, including Intrusion Detection Systems [3], Stream Processing [4], High Capacity Link Emulators [15], Load-balancing of High Speed Links [14] etc. have been developed on top of network processors. An architecture that pushes application and middleware-level functionality to Network Processor has been proposed [13]. Schemes described in [11, 12] are specialized for generating UDP traffic. Other solutions like netperf [6] utilize general-purpose processors and hence are limited in speed. In contrast, using our approach, anyone developing applications for any Network Processor can use the very same NPs to develop a traffic generator. Our work only deals with how to generate traffic, given a traffic profile. It does not deal with what traffic profile should be used. This issue is discussed in [9, 10].

3   System Architecture

TG architecture is divided into two basic modules: CP and DP. The CP handles operations that do not need to be processed at wire speed like configuration of the traffic profile, and is responsible for the control and management of the network processor. The DP is responsible for the actual generation of the traffic. The operations performed by the CP are less time critical and have complex processing requirements. CP controls and configures various traffic profiles. It decides how many hardware threads are required to generate particular traffic profile at a given rate. It keeps information on DP resource consumption. User configures desired traffic profile using TCL scripts and passes it to CP. Output of the CP module is an intermediate data structure that is fed to DP. Hence any change in traffic profile is achieved by changing the CP code and the configuration file while the performance critical DP code stays unchanged.

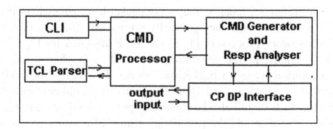

Fig. 1. CP Architecture

3.1   Control Plane Architecture

Figure 1 shows CP architecture. Command Generator and Response Analyzer generate actual command for DP and analyzes response packet that comes from DP. TCL parser is invoked when user wants to configure packets through a TCL file. A separate Command Level Interface (CLI) is also provided using which users can give explicit low level commands. Output of the Command Generator is encoded using an intermediate data structure. Intermediate data structure is designed in a way such that the DP only has to manipulate the offset values in the packet without having to know the packet. This makes the DP code independent of traffic profile. To add a new traffic profile, the needed module is plugged in CP side while DP stays untouched.

3.2 Data Plane Architecture

DP code runs on the network processor. It uses micro kernel services provided for the specific hardware. DP architecture is shown in Figure 2. It is divided into three sub modules: Control and Maintenance, Traffic Generation, and Traffic Receiver module. Control and Maintenance module (CMM) is responsible for communication with CP. Single request–response mechanism is implemented between CP and the CMM. CMM also maintains other threads and allocates job to available thread pool. It keeps track of resources of NP such as ports thread pool etc. Traffic generation threads act upon the intermediate data structure generated by the CP and make copy of a new packet and send it out on the specified port.

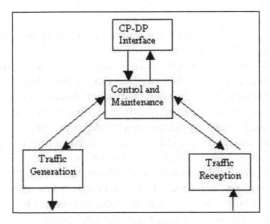

Fig. 2. DP Architecture

3.3 Traffic Generation Mechanism

The CP decides the number of threads required to generate packets at a particular port. A single thread generates packets on a single port at a time. Each thread has a predefined template area in on-chip memory. The pre-constructed packet for a thread is located in its template area that is the first packet to be generated by thread. Thread allocates same amount of memory in packet buffer area as the size of the pre-constructed packet. The thread then copies the pre-constructed packet into the packet buffer and writes it into the output queue of the desired port.

4 TG Calibrations

To generate traffic at a given rate, CP needs to know how much data can be generated by a single DP thread. The parameters affecting the overall throughput of a single thread are message size, and the number of fields to be modified from packet to packet. To check how these parameter variations affect the throughput, TG is calibrated using the IXIA [5] traffic generator. IXIA tool is able to measure the incoming traffic rate. Note that if one has another Network Processor available than one can use the TG in the 'receive' mode to profile itself.

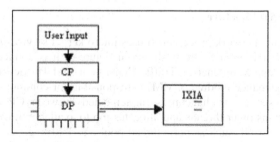

Fig. 3. Test Bed for TG calibration

4.1 Experiment 1

Objective: To decide single thread's capacity to generate traffic for a given packet size and the number of fields to vary.

Methodology: We use the test-bed shown in figure 3.The NP's port that is generating traffic is serially connected to the one of the IXIA's port. At receiving end, we can measure the rate at which packets are coming through that interface.

Discussion: The results of the experiments are shown in Figure 4. The throughput increases with the packet size. As the packet size increases, only the data payload section of each frame needs to be copied. No other instructions are required to process the payload. The overhead of header processing per packet gets reduced. With increase in the number of fields to modify, the throughput for a given packet size decreases. But the change is not linear. If the field that needs to be varied is on the boundary of the next buffer, then the whole of the next buffer needs to be written in the buffer pool again. This overhead decreases the rate slightly.

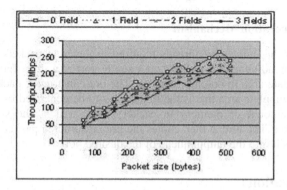

Fig. 4. Single Thread's throughput

4.2 Experiment 2

Objective: To determine the throughput variation with the number of threads and message sizes.

Methodology: Same as that of the Experiment 1. Each output port of the NP is connected to an input port of the IXIA. Here no field is varying from packet to packet.

Discussion: The results of the experiments are shown in Figure 5. Results are almost linear with periodic dips occurring when a new buffer is added to the payload. The average throughput per thread goes up as the number of threads increases. In general applications, scale-up due to multi-threading is typically sub- linear due to the contention between threads. In the current application, there is no contention between the threads and hence the shared overhead goes down with the increasing number of threads.

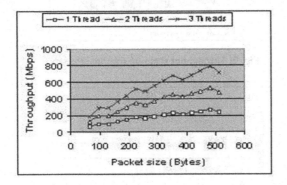

Fig. 5. Throughput variation

4.3 Configuring CP

Data from these experiments is used to configure the CP for deciding the number of threads to employ for a given traffic profile. We maintain a static table based on the results of the Experiment 1. This gives us the bandwidth of a single thread for a given message size and the number of fields to vary. We approximate the results of Experiment 2 by assuming linear scale-up of the throughput with the number of threads. To verify this assumption, we repeated Experiment 1 with two and three threads. Resulting throughput scale-up is shown in Figure 6 and Figure 7. This shows that the throughput

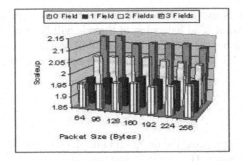

Fig. 6. Throughput scale-up for two threads

scales with the number of threads with a relative error of at most 6%. Dividing the desired throughput with the throughput for a single thread gives us the number of threads. To get the desired throughput, inter-packet delay is introduced appropriately in each thread.

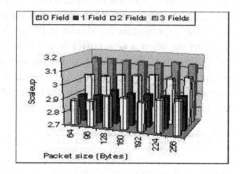

Fig. 7. Throughput scale-up for three threads

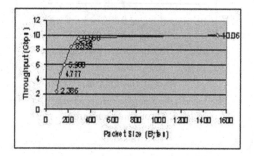

Fig. 8. T G Throughput with 60 threads

Figure 8 presents the result of running the traffic generator with all 60 threads in our NP. For packet sizes above 289 bytes, the Input-Output module is not capable of sending data at a rate more than 10 Gbps and becomes the bottleneck.

5 Future Works

At present TG design is using a static allocation of Traffic generation and receiving threads. In future dynamic load balancing of threads will be done. It requires some of the CP code to change but the main architecture will remain unchanged. TG supports 10 Gbps traffic. We plan to combine Multiple Network Processors to generate traffic at higher speeds.

6 Conclusions

In this paper, we have presented the design and implementation of a Network Processor based Traffic Generator. The architecture takes advantage of the control plane and data plane division found in NPs. The CP parses the given traffic profile and configures the threads of the DP for carrying out traffic generation task. An intermediate data-structure is employed so that DP code stays unchanged for changing a wide variety of traffic profiles. CP itself needs to be calibrated using another Traffic Generator. We have presented the experiment results and the methodology for calibrating CP. While we have worked with a proprietary processor, our design is generic and can be used with any Network Processor.

Acknowledgements. We thank anonymous reviewers for giving valuable suggestions.

References

1. M. Shorfuzzaman, M. Rasit Eskicioglu, and P. Graham: Architectures for Network Processors: Key Features, Evaluation, and Trends. Communications in Computing 2004: 141-146
2. T. Spalink, S. Karlin, L. Peterson, and Y. Gottlieb: Building a Robust Software-Based Router
3. H.Bose and K. Huang. A network intrusion detection system on IXP1200 network processors with support for large rule sets Technical Report 2004-02, LIACS, Leiden University, 2004
4. Fujitsu, Inc. Comet Stream Processor / FPGA. http://www.comet-can.jp
5. http://www.ixiacom.com, "IxLoad – Generating Traffic to test Content Aware Devices", IXIA
6. http://www.netperf.org/netperf/ training/Netperf.html - Netperf
7. http://www.intel.com/design/jvdssknetwork/papers/27905001.pdf
8. P. Crowley, M. A. Franklin, H. Hadimoglu, and P. Z. Onufryk, Network Processor Design: Issues and Practices Volume 1. San Fransisco, Ca: Morgan Kaufmann Publishers, 2003.
9. Heegaard, Poul E. GenSyn - a generator of synthetic Internet traffic used in QoS experiments. Proceeding of the 15th Nordic Teletraffic Seminar. 137–148, Sweden 2000.
10. B. A. Mah. An Empirical Model of HTTP Network Traffic. In Proc. InfoComm '97, April 1997.
11. S. Avallone, M. D'Arienzo, M. Esposito, A. Pescapè, S.P. Romano, and G. Ventre. Mtools. IEEE Network, 16(5):3, September/October 2002. Networking Column
12. http://www.citi.umich.edu/projects/qbone/generator.html - UDPGenerator
13. S. Avallone, A. Pescapè, G. Ventre, " Distributed Internet Traffic Generator (D-ITG): analysis and experimentation over heterogeneous networks ", in ICNP 2003 poster Proceedings, Intl Conf. on Network Protocols 2003 - Atlanta, Georgia (USA).
14. Ada Gavrilovska, et.al. "Network Processors as Building Blocks in Overlay Networks", 11th Symposium on High Performance Interconnects (HOT-I 2003), California, August 22-24, 2003.
15. G. Dittmann and A. Herkersdorf, "Network Processor load balancing for high-speed links", In Proc. International Symposium on Performance Evaluation of Computer and Telecommunication Systems (SPECTS), pages 727--735, San Diego, California, July 2002.
16. Abhijeet A. Joglekar, "High Capacity Network Link Emulation using Network Processor", Master's Thesis, January/May 2004.

Stochastic Spectral Density Analysis on Network Traffic Characterization

Abhik Das and S.K. Ghosh

School of Information Technology
Indian Institute of Technology, Kharagpur 721302, India
Phone: 91-3222-282332; Fax: 91-3222-282700
mail2abhikdas@gmail.com, skg@iitkgp.ac.in

Abstract. In the network traffic, the nature of the input output data/signal signals are used to demonstrate the statistical characterization of the traffic performance. Observations of traffic on network links typically reveal intensity levels (in bits/sec) averaged over periods of time periods which are relatively predictable from day to day. Systematic intensity variations occur within the day reflecting user activity. In this paper, the stochastic spectral analysis is performed on the input/output signal signals and the ratio of the spectral power of the output and input signals are taken as the characteristics of the statistical nature of the network traffic. For different time averaging schemes this characteristic ratio shows a bounded nature. In this paper the theoretical analysis is done on the boundedness of the characteristics ratio through the process of stochastic spectral density analysis.

Keywords: Network traffic, stochastic spectral power.

1 Introduction

Traffic theory currently plays an important role in the design of the network systems. Network provisioning is generally based on simple rules of thumb while considerable effort is spent on the design of a variety quality of service (QoS) mechanisms. It is necessary to apply the appropriate traffic-performance relation if the objective is to ensure that QoS [1-4] meets specific design targets for a given population of such users. The precise characteristics of this stationary process depend on the composition of Internet traffic [5]. It is well known that the arrival process of IP packets can exhibit extreme signal variations at multiple time scales forming the self-similarity phenomenon on network performance [6]. Yet more extreme variability (so-called multi-fractal behavior) occurs at smaller time scales due to the burstiness induced by TCP. It proves much simpler to describe traffic in terms of flows [7].

The analysis of traffic system of a network can be achieved by the process of the analysis of each node in the network. In this paper the concept of input/output bit signals are analyzed through stochastic power spectrum in which the characterization of the given node is done using the concept of spectral density of the bit signals.

S. Chaudhuri et al. (Eds.): ICDCN 2006, LNCS 4308, pp. 276–281, 2006.

2 Stochastic Spectrum Analysis of Traffic Characteristics

The network traffic is a time dependent discrete signal and hence, $\{X_t\}_{t=0}^{\infty}$ can be considered as the set of traffic such that $X_t \geq 0$ for $t \neq 0$ and without loss of generality we may assume that $X_0 = 0$ through out the process. Here $\{X_t\}_{t=0}^{\infty}$ can be assumed as a random process as the traffic input- output characteristics in the network due to uncoordinated actions of very large population of users but some analytical behavior can be represented through stochastic modeling. Let B represent the backwards shift operator, i.e., $BX_t = X_t$, and let $\nabla = 1 - B$ represents the differencing operator which acts on the discrete values of the network at different time steps. For a positive real value d the process $\{X_t\}$ can be said to be a d-dimensional traffic if $\nabla^d X_t = \varepsilon_t$, where the operator ∇^d can be defined through the binomial expansion of $(1 - B)^d$; $\nabla^d X_t = \varepsilon_t$ can be defined as d-dimensional changing parameter of the traffic. In reality, the network traffic can be considered as a non-stationary process due to its variability in the changing parameter, and can be assumed the spectral power density as [8],

$$I_{X,n}(\omega_j) = \frac{1}{n}\left|\sum_{t=1}^{n} X_t e^{-i\omega_j t}\right|^2 = \left(\frac{1}{\sqrt{n}}\sum_{t=1}^{n} X_t e^{-i\omega_j t}\right)\left(\frac{1}{\sqrt{n}}\sum_{t=1}^{n} X_t e^{i\omega_j t}\right) = F_X(-\lambda)F_X(\lambda) \qquad (1)$$

where $\lambda = \omega_j$.

Considering $\{X_t\}_{t=0}^{n} \subseteq \{X_t\}_{t=0}^{\infty}$ for $n < \infty$ be the n-sample set of the infinite domain traffic characteristics, we can state that

Theorem 1. Let $\{X_t\}_{t=0}^{\infty}$ is a random process with $\nabla^d X_t = \varepsilon_t$. Consider the realization sample $\{X_t\}_{t=0}^{n}$ and assume that $X_0 = 0$. Then $I_{X,n}(\lambda)$ of $\{X_t\}_{t=0}^{n}$ and $I_{\varepsilon,n}(\lambda)$ of $\{\varepsilon_t\}_{t=1}^{n}$ are related through the inequality

$$\left|1 - e^{-i\lambda}\right|^2 I_{X,n}(\lambda) \leq I_{\varepsilon,n}(\lambda) + n^{-1}X_n^2 - R_n(\lambda) \qquad (2)$$

where, for any fixed $\lambda \in (0, \pi)$, $E[R_n(\lambda)] \to 0$ as $n \to \infty$. $\qquad (3)$

Proof

Since $\nabla^d X_t = \varepsilon_t \geq X_t - X_{t-1}$, we get

$$F_{\varepsilon}(\lambda) = \frac{1}{\sqrt{n}}\sum_{t=1}^{n} \varepsilon_t e^{-i\lambda t} \geq \frac{1}{\sqrt{n}}\left(1 - e^{-i\lambda}\right)\sum_{t=1}^{n} X_t e^{-i\lambda t} + \frac{1}{\sqrt{n}}\left(X_n e^{-i\lambda(n+1)} - X_0 e^{-i\lambda}\right)$$

and $\left(1 - e^{-i\lambda}\right)F_X(\lambda) \leq F_{\varepsilon}(\lambda) - \frac{1}{\sqrt{n}}e^{-i\lambda(n+1)}X_n$.

Multiplying each side by its conjugate, $\left|1 - e^{-i\lambda}\right|^2 I_{X,n}(\lambda) \leq I_{\varepsilon,n}(\lambda) + n^{-1}X_n^2 - R_n(\lambda)$

$$R_n(\lambda) = F_{\varepsilon}(-\lambda)\frac{1}{\sqrt{n}}e^{-i\lambda(n+1)}X_n + F_{\varepsilon}(\lambda)\frac{1}{\sqrt{n}}e^{i\lambda(n+1)}X_n = G_n(\lambda) + G_n(-\lambda)$$

Since $\nabla^d X_t = \varepsilon_t \Rightarrow X_t - X_{t-1} \le \varepsilon_t \Rightarrow X_n \le \sum_{t=1}^{n} \varepsilon_t$,

Then $E[G_n(\lambda)] \le \dfrac{1}{\sqrt{n}} e^{-i\lambda(n+1)} E\left[\left(\dfrac{1}{\sqrt{n}}\sum_{t=1}^{n}\varepsilon_t e^{i\lambda t}\right)\left(\sum_{t=1}^{n}\varepsilon_t\right)\right] \le \dfrac{1}{\sqrt{n}}\sum_{t=1}^{n} e^{-i\lambda t}\sigma_\varepsilon^2$

Similarly, $E[G_n(-\lambda)] \le \dfrac{1}{\sqrt{n}}\sum_{t=1}^{n} e^{i\lambda t}\sigma_\varepsilon^2$ hence

$E[R_n(\lambda)] \le \dfrac{1}{\sqrt{n}}\sigma_\varepsilon^2 \sum_{t=1}^{n}\left(e^{i\lambda t} + e^{-i\lambda t}\right) = \dfrac{1}{\sqrt{n}}\sigma_\varepsilon^2 \sum_{t=1}^{n} 2\cos\lambda t$; for $\lambda \in (0,\pi)$ we have the upper bound,

$E[|R_n(\lambda)|] \le \dfrac{1}{\sqrt{n}}\sigma_\varepsilon^2 2\left|\sum_{t=1}^{n}\cos\lambda t\right| = \dfrac{1}{\sqrt{n}}\sigma_\varepsilon^2\left|\dfrac{\sin(n+1/2)\lambda}{\sin(\lambda/2)} - 1\right| \le \dfrac{1}{\sqrt{n}}\sigma_\varepsilon^2\left(\dfrac{\pi}{\lambda}+1\right)$

Hence for any fixed $\lambda > 0$, $E[R_n(\lambda)] \to 0$ as $n \to \infty$.

3 I/O Traffic Characterization

Theorem 1 gives the behavioral nature of the network traffic relating the traffic flow and the changing parameter of the network. For input output characteristics let us consider a characteristic parameter, which can be considered as characteristic ratio, $\rho_n(\lambda) = I_{X,out;n}(\lambda)/I_{X,in;n}(\lambda)$, and can be defined as the ratio of output traffic spectrum to the input traffic spectrum. It can be related with the changing parameter of traffic as follows.

Theorem 2. For d-dimensional traffic $(d \ge 1)$, $\rho_n(\lambda) \le I_{\varepsilon,out;n}(\lambda)/I_{\varepsilon,in;n}(\lambda)$ as $n \to \infty$.

Proof

$\left|1 - e^{-i\lambda}\right|^2 I_{X,in;n}(\lambda) \le I_{\varepsilon,in;n}(\lambda) + n^{-1}X_{in;n}^2 - R_{in;n}(\lambda)$

and $\left|1 - e^{-i\lambda}\right|^2 I_{X,out;n}(\lambda) \le I_{\varepsilon,out;n}(\lambda) + n^{-1}X_{out;n}^2 - R_{out;n}(\lambda)$ Hence

$\rho_n(\lambda) \le \dfrac{I_{\varepsilon,out;n}(\lambda) + n^{-1}X_{out;n}^2 - R_{out;n}(\lambda)}{I_{\varepsilon,in;n}(\lambda) + n^{-1}X_{in;n}^2 - R_{in;n}(\lambda)}$

From Theorem 1, $E[R_n(\lambda)] \to 0$ as $n \to \infty$; which implies that

$$\rho_n(\lambda) \le I_{\varepsilon,out;n}(\lambda)/I_{\varepsilon,in;n}(\lambda) \text{ as } n \to \infty. \tag{4}$$

Theorem 2 gives the realization of the bounded nature of characteristic ratio; it may be assumed that there must exist a strong bound for the characteristic parameter $\rho_n(\lambda)$. In reality the nature of network traffic can be assumed as a behavioral representation of Gaussian distribution. As d-dimensional changing parameter can be assumed as the noise pattern in the network traffic and may be positive or negative over the average traffic, the averaged squared nature of the changing parameter is taken into analysis.

Theorem 3. [9] Let $\{\xi_1,......,\xi_n\}$ be independent random variables such that $E[|\xi_i|^{2+\delta}]<\infty, 1\le i\le n$, for some $\delta\in(0,1]$. Let η be a zero-mean Gaussian random variable such that $E[\eta^2]=\sum_{i=1}^{n}E[\xi_i^2]$. Then for any $k>0$,

$$\left|\Pr\left(\left|\sum_{i=1}^{n}\xi_i\right|>k\right)-\Pr(|\eta|>k)\right|\le\frac{c}{k^{2+\delta}}\sum_{i=1}^{n}E[|\xi_i|^{2+\delta}] \tag{5}$$

where c is an absolute constant.

4 Time Averaging of Network Traffic

In network characterization different time slot averaging like 5 min averaging, 30 min averaging etc. is done on the network traffic $\{X_t\}_{t=0}^{\infty}$. Similarly different time slot averaging can be done on $\{\varepsilon_t\}_{t=1}^{\infty}$, where $\{\varepsilon_t\}_{t=1}^{\infty}$ be the independent random variable known as the changing parameter of the network traffic. If p-time slot averaging is considered then

$\varepsilon_1^p=(\varepsilon_1+.....+\varepsilon_p)/p$, $\varepsilon_2^p=(\varepsilon_{p+1}+.....+\varepsilon_{2p})/p$ and similarly on generalization of the network traffic $\varepsilon_t^p=(\varepsilon_{(t-1)p+1}+.....+\varepsilon_{tp})/p$ and hence $\{\varepsilon_t^p\}_{t=1}^{\infty}$ makes the p-time averaging changing parameter characteristics of the network. Then $F_\varepsilon^p(\lambda)=\sum_{t=1}^{n}\varepsilon_t^p e^{-i\lambda t}/\sqrt{n}$ for $\{\varepsilon_t^p\}_{t=1}^{n}\in\{\varepsilon_t^p\}_{t=1}^{\infty}$. Now $\left[F_\varepsilon^p(\lambda)\right]$ can be defined as

$$\left[F_\varepsilon^p(\lambda)\right]=\sum_{t=1}^{n}\left|\varepsilon_t^p\right|e^{-i\lambda t}/\sqrt{n}\ .$$

Lemma. If $\{\varepsilon_1,......,\varepsilon_n\}$ be independent random variables such that $E[|\varepsilon_t|^{2+\delta}]<\infty, 1\le t\le n$, for some $\delta\in(0,1]$. Let η be a zero-mean Gaussian random variable such that $E[\eta^2]=\sum_{t=1}^{n}E\left[\frac{\varepsilon_t^2}{n}\right]$ and if $I_{\varepsilon,n}^p(\lambda)$ be the power spectrum of p-th averaging traffic pattern then with high probability $I_{\varepsilon,n}^p(\lambda)\to I_{\varepsilon,n}(\lambda)$ as $n\to\infty$.

Proof

$$\left[F_\varepsilon^p(\lambda)\right]=\sum_{t=1}^{n}\left|\varepsilon_t^p\right|e^{-i\lambda t}/\sqrt{n}\ =\sum_{t=1}^{n}\left|(\varepsilon_{(t-1)p+1}+.....+\varepsilon_{tp})\right|e^{-i\lambda t}/p\sqrt{n}$$

$$\le\sum_{t=1}^{n}\left(\left|\varepsilon_{(t-1)p+1}\right|+.....+\left|\varepsilon_{tp}\right|\right)e^{-i\lambda t}/p\sqrt{n}$$

Hence for large n, $\left|\Pr\left(\left[F_\varepsilon^p(\lambda)\right]>k\right)\right|\le\left|\Pr\left(\left[F_\varepsilon(\lambda)\right]>k\right)\right|$ But using Theorem 3, which tells that $\Pr\left(\left[F_\varepsilon(\lambda)\right]>k\right)\to\Pr(|\eta|>k)$ as $n\to\infty$, and similarly

$$\Pr\left(\left[F_\varepsilon^p(\lambda)\right] > k\right) \to \Pr\left(|\eta| > k\right) \quad \text{as} \quad n \to \infty, \quad \text{then} \quad \text{for} \quad \text{large} \quad n,$$
$$\Pr\left(\left[F_\varepsilon^p(\lambda)\right] > k\right) \to \Pr\left(\left[F_\varepsilon(\lambda)\right] > k\right); \quad \text{which implies that with high probability}$$
$$I_{\varepsilon,n}^p(\lambda) \to I_{\varepsilon,n}(\lambda) \quad \text{as} \quad n \to \infty.$$

Using this lemma we can state the following statement,

Corollary. If ρ_n^p be the p-th average characteristic signal of input-output network traffic, then with high probability $\rho_n^p \to \rho_n$ as $n \to \infty$.

5 Experimentation

The following shows the 5 minutes time averaging input and output signal of a typical academic institute LAN; and their complex power spectrum is calculated. The power is calculated in dBc. Similarly we can get the characteristic ratio of the network traffic for different time averaging.

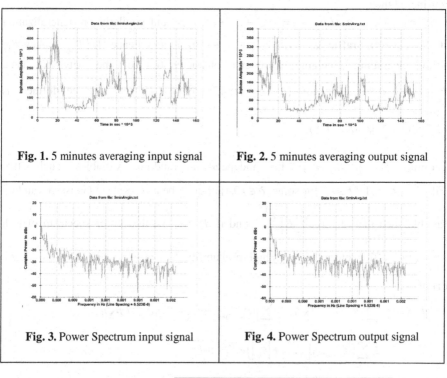

Fig. 1. 5 minutes averaging input signal

Fig. 2. 5 minutes averaging output signal

Fig. 3. Power Spectrum input signal

Fig. 4. Power Spectrum output signal

	5 min Averaging	30 min Averaging	2 hr Averaging
Charecteristic Ratio ρ	-1.79	-0.81	-1.29

Spectral Power (dBc)	Input Signal				Output Signal		
	5 min	30 min	2 hr		5 min	30 min	2 hr
	Averaging	Averaging	Averaging		Averaging	Averaging	Averaging
Total	13.23	14.5	16.5		11.47	13.69	15.21
Fundamental	0	0	0		0	0	0
Distortion	-3.82	-5.12	-1.12		-5.44	-4.12	-0.61
Noise	12.93	13.79	16.32		11.05	12.97	14.96
SNR	-11.42	-7.5	-13.84		-9.96	-7.43	-12.24

6 Conclusion

In this paper we are mainly concentrated on the statistical nature of network traffic and the theoretical characterization of its patterns. Though it is very much unusual to use analog signal processing parameters in the measure of network traffic, the use of statistical behavioral model enlightens the idea of probabilistic behavior randomness in network traffic pattern. The spectral analysis of input output traffic signals gives much scope to analyze the stochastic behavior of noise, distortion and signal to noise ratio in the particular node of network traffic unlikely other characterizations of network traffic. For a given network the value ρ can be taken as the characteristic value of the network traffic and hence can be used to measure the statistical nature of the network.

References

[1] B. Eklundh, Channel utilization and blocking probability in a cellular mobile telephone system with directed retry, IEEE Trans. Commun. COM-34 (1986) 329-337.
[2] D. Hong, S.S. Rappaport, Traffic model and performance analysis for cellular mobile radio telephone systems with prioritized and nonprioritized handoff procedures, IEEE Trans. Veh. Tech. VT-35 (3) (1986) 77-92.
[3] J. Misic, T.Y. Bun, On call level QoS guarantees under heterogeneous user mobilities in wireless multimedia networks, in: Proc. GLOBECOM'99, vol. 5, 1999, pp. 2730-2736.
[4] M. Cheung, J.W. Mark, Effect of mobility on QoS provisioning in wireless communication networks, in: Proc. IEEE WCNC, vol. 1, 1999, pp. 306-310.
[5] A.C. Lucas, D.E. Wreger, B.J. Dempsey, A.C. Weaver, Statistical Characterization of Wide Area IP Traffic, 6th International Conference on Computer, Communication and Networking,1997.
[6] W.E. Leland, M.S. Taqqu, W. Willinger, D.V. Weber, On the Self-similar nature of Ethernet, SIGCOMM 1993
[7] E.W. Nightly, H. Zhang, Traffic characterization and switch utilization using a deterministic bounding interval dependent traffic model, INFOCOM, 1995.
[8] Brockwell, P. J. , Davis, R. A., Time Series: Theory and Methods, Springer-Vorlag, New York, second edition, 1991.
[9] V. V. Buldygin, V. A. Koval, Convergence to zero and boundedness of operator normed sums of random vectors with application to autoregrassion process, Georgian Mathematical Journal, vol. 8 (2001), No. 2, 221-230.

Negotiating Monitoring Task Allocation for Orbiters

Doran Chakraborty[1], Sabyasachi Saha[1], Sandip Sen[1], and Bradley Clement[2]

[1] Department of Math & CS
University of Tulsa
Tulsa, Oklahoma, USA
{doran, saby, sandip}@utulsa.edu
[2] Jet Propulsion Laboratory
Pasadena, California, USA
bclement@aig.jpl.nasa.gov

Abstract. We are interested in the problem of coordination of ground-based control stations and orbiting space probes for allocating monitoring tasks for emerging environmental situations that have the potential to become catastrophic events threatening life and property. We assume that ground based sensor networks have recognized seismic, geological, atmospheric, or some other natural phenomena that has created a rapidly evolving event which needs immediate, detailed and continuous monitoring. Control stations can calculate the resources needed to monitor such situations, but must concurrently negotiate with multiple autonomous orbiters to allocate the monitoring tasks. While control stations may prefer some orbiters over others based on their position, trajectory, equipment, etc, orbiters too have prior commitments to fulfill. We evaluate three different negotiation schemes that can be used by the control station and the orbiters to complete the monitoring task assignment. We use utilitarian and egalitarian social welfare as the metric to be maximized and discuss the relative performances of these mechanisms under different preference and resource constraints.

1 Introduction

Recently there has been a research initiative to coordinate between Earth-based sensors (such as a video camera or devices on an ocean buoy) and orbiter missions for efficient monitoring and investigation of a large variety of natural phenomena [1]. Creating operation plans in such distributed settings is especially difficult when so many entities have input. Currently, the activities of a spacecraft are often planned weeks or months in advance for Earth orbiters; thus, these missions are practically unable to respond to events in less than a week. We study the problem of fully autonomous response to emerging, potential natural disasters that require coordination of control stations and earth orbiters for adequate monitoring. We are interested in expediting the response time and accuracy to different rapidly evolving natural phenomenon. Space orbiters are autonomous and have

S. Chaudhuri et al. (Eds.): ICDCN 2006, LNCS 4308, pp. 282–287, 2006.

prior commitments and resource constraints which may or may not allow them to take on additional monitoring load at short notice. We assume that orbiters can negotiate between themselves and with ground control centers and can evaluate the utility of an announced monitoring task based on their current schedule and resource constraints. An allocation of a monitoring task between multiple orbiters will have different utilities from the perspective of each of the orbiters and a ground-based control station. We are especially interested in the utilitarian (sum of utilities of all agents) and egalitarian (the utility of the least happy agent) metric of social welfare of such a system. Maximizing utilitarian social welfare in a system corresponds to maximizing the efficiency of the system while maximizing the egalitarian metric corresponds to maximizing fairness in the system.

2   Coordination Via Negotiation

For most of this paper, we restrict our discussion to one control station negotiating with two orbiters for allocating a fixed number of monitoring tasks given an impending emergency detected by a ground based network of sensors. The overall monitoring task can be divided among the two orbiters by partitioning the total time period into n non-overlapping sets. We now present three alternative negotiation mechanisms we have evaluated for task assignments and briefly discuss their merits and demerits.

Sequential auction: Auction mechanisms [3] can be used to find subtask allocations to maximize social welfare. Due to exponential time complexity of combinatorial auctions, a more feasible, simplified, auction scheme can be to auction each of the n time units sequentially. Suppose the utility to orbiter i for doing the jth unit task is u_{ij} and the corresponding utility to the control station is u_{ij}^c. The control station will award the jth unit task to the orbiter k, where $k = \arg\max_{i \in \mathcal{I}}\{u_{ij} + u_{ij}^c\}$, where $\mathcal{I} = \{1, 2\}$ is the set of negotiating orbiters.

Multi-issue monotonic concession protocol (MC): The orbiters arrange the possible task allocation agreements in decreasing order based on their utilities and propose allocations in that order. If one party finds that the utility of the allocation it is going to propose is as good as any proposal it has already offered, it accepts that proposal, A disadvantage of this protocol is the relatively slow exploration of different possibilities. This can, however, be improved by increasing the amount of concessions made at each step.

Mediator-based simulated annealing: Another distributed approach to task allocation is proposed by Klein et al. [2], where the negotiating parties try to improve on the current proposal. A simulated annealing scheme is used to search for better proposals where the current proposal is used as the starting point. In this approach, a mediator proposes an allocation offer[1], and the negotiating parties either accept, or reject the offer. If all of the parties accept the offer the mediator generates a new proposal by mutating the current offer. Otherwise, the

---

[1] The mediator initially generates this offer randomly.

mediator generates a new proposal by mutating the most recently accepted offer. The search terminates if any mutually acceptable proposal is not generated by the mediator for a fixed number of proposals.

3 Logistics of the System

Each orbiter is capable of sending pictures of different quality (q). We assume that u_i^τ, the utility that the orbiter receives in the form of payment for any time unit τ is proportional to the quality of service. Orbiters have a current schedule S_i, a vector of preassigned tasks for a finite horizon. We represent the vector S_i as $\{S_i^\tau\}^{l(S_i)}$ where $l(S_i)$ is the the total length of time for which the orbiter has preassigned tasks. The utility for S_i given by μ_{S_i} is a distribution of u_i^τ over $l(S_i)$ while the utility distribution of task t given by μ_t is a distribution of u_i^τ over $l(t)$. A proposal made by an orbiter is a vector $P_i \in \{P_i^\tau\}^{l(t)}$ where $P_i^\tau \in \{0,1\}$. Next, we need to define an allocation α as the set $\{\alpha^1, \ldots, \alpha^{l(t)}\}$, where $\alpha^\tau = i$ if the time unit τ of the monitoring task has been assigned to orbiter i. We assume that the utility of an allocation is characterized by the following factors: the orbiter prefers to allocate the same task for consecutive time periods; performing a new task (a task not allocated before) incurs a overhead cost which is half the value of the utility that the orbiter is supposed to receive for doing the task for that time unit; switching back to a task incurs a penalty that is proportional to the number of time units that elapsed in between. The control station maintains a tuple $V = < p_1, p_2 >$ where p_i denotes the preference of control station for orbiter i.

4 Experimental Section

In our experiments, we assume that μ_t and μ_{S_i} can be approximated by the function $f_\zeta(x) = \psi_\zeta \times 1/(\sqrt{(2 \times \pi)} \times d_\zeta) \times e^{-(x-m_\zeta)^2/2 \times d_\zeta^2}$ with parameters m_ζ, d_ζ and ψ_ζ, where $\zeta \in \{t, S_1, S_2\}$. The values of m_ζ and d_ζ are represented as fractions of $l(t)$. These parameters determine the shape of ζ and we vary them throughout our experiments to obtain different forms of μ_t and μ_{S_i}.

In the first series of simulations, we first tried to evaluate the performance of the three negotiation techniques when both the orbiters have similar light schedules (results in Figure 1): we use $m_{S_1} = m_{S_2} = 0.5$, $d_{S_1} = d_{S_2} = 0.5$ and $\psi_{S_1} = \psi_{S_2} = 0.5$. The values of m_t and d_t for all our experiments are chosen randomly for each run. From Figure 1 we see that for such schedules, the sequential auction approach dominates the other techniques when the metric is utilitarian social welfare while monotonic concession does better in terms of egalitarian social welfare. Under such a situation maximizing the utilitarian social welfare for each individual time unit leads to maximizing the metric for all the time units. The corresponding egalitarian social welfare is low as the bulk of the task is allocated to one orbiter to minimize the cost of switching between orbiters. The monotonic concession, does better on the latter metric as

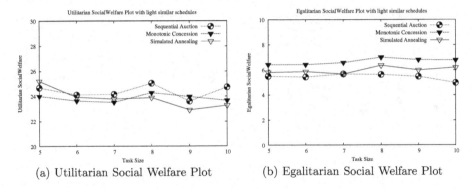

Fig. 1. Utilities obtained with different negotiating schemes when orbiters have similar light schedules

it supports a more fair allocation by requiring agents to make concessions until the allocation is mutually acceptable.

Next, we tried to evaluate the performance of the three negotiation techniques when both the orbiters have similar loaded schedules (results in Figure 2). For this scenario, we use $m_{S_1} = m_{S_2} = 0.5$, $d_{S_1} = d_{S_2} = 0.5$ and $\psi_{S_1} = \psi_{S_2} = 1.5$. Under such a situation, sequential auction is never a better solution which is reflected by its poor utilitarian and egalitarian social welfare values. In such resource constrained situations, the myopic approach of maximizing utility per subtask does not maximize the overall system utility. Mediator based simulated annealing performs best in terms of utilitarian social welfare while monotonic concession continues to provide the highest egalitarian social welfare. In the final simulation of the series, we tried to see the effect on performance of the three techniques when the orbiters schedules vary from being similar to being perfectly complimentary. We use $m_{S_1} = d_{S_1} = 0.25$ and vary m_{S_2} from 0.25 to 0.75 (results in Figure 3). The results show that sequential auction performs the best of the three mechanisms as long as the schedules are somewhat similar (for $m_{S_2} <= 0.5$). The other protocols produce better utilitarian social welfare with the increase in complementarity of the schedules. Monotonic concession continues to dominate in terms of egalitarian social welfare.

In another series of simulations, we tried to study the effect on the utilitarian social welfare of all the three mechanisms with varying m_{S_2} and p_2/p_1 keeping m_{S_1} fixed. Figure 4(a) plots the difference of the utilitarian social welfare of the sequential auction and monotonic concession mechanisms against m_{S_2} and p_2/p_1. Figure 4(b) plots the difference of the utilitarian social welfare of the sequential auction and simulated annealing mechanisms against m_{S_2} and p_2/p_1. In both the plots, it is clear that for a fixed schedule of orbiter 2 (fixed value of m_{S_2}), the value in the z axis shows an increase with increase in the value of p_2/p_1. This suggest that as the preference of control station for one orbiter increases, it is better to use the sequential auction mechanism if maximizing the utilitarian social welfare is the main criterion. The high utility received by

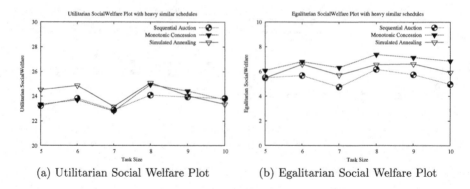

Fig. 2. Utilities obtained with different negotiating schemes when orbiters have similar loaded schedules

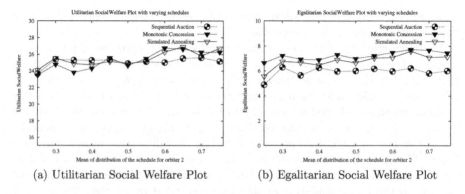

Fig. 3. Utilities obtained with different negotiating schemes by varying the schedule of the second orbiter

the control station for allocating most of the monitoring task to orbiter 2 is manifested in the high utilitarian social welfare of the system. The value in the z axis stabilizes for $p_2/p_1 \geq 2.5$ hinting that the control station can gain no more with further increasing in its preference for orbiter 2. This trend is true for all values of m_{S_2} (refer Figure 4). But the low value of egalitarian social welfare suggests that gain in total utility comes at the price of loss of utility of one agent. Such allocations will work in practice only if side payments are used by the control station to compensate the deprived orbiter.

To summarize our results, if the chief criterion of mechanism selection is high egalitarian social welfare, then monotonic concession should be the preferred choice. However, if the chief criterion is utilitarian social welfare maximization, then there is no single mechanism that can guarantee high value for all situations. When the allocations for each individual time unit are uncorrelated, maximizing the utilitarian metric for the entire monitoring task is achieved by maximizing the metric for each individual interval, sequential auction performs better. Unfortunately due to the dynamic nature of μ_{S_i} and μ_t, such a situation

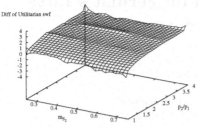

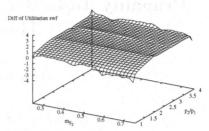

(a) Plot of difference of utilitarian social welfare of sequential auction and monotonic concession, varying m_{S_2} and p_2/p_1

(b) Plot of difference of utilitarian social welfare of sequential auction and simulated annealing, varying m_{S_2} and p_2/p_1

Fig. 4. Plot of difference of utilitarian social welfare

is not very common. Mediator based simulated annealing performs better under such circumstances as it provides fair approximations to the global optimum allocation through heuristic search over the entire search space.

5 Conclusion

In this paper we have studied the problem of fully autonomous response to emerging, potential natural disasters that require coordination of control stations and earth orbiters for adequate monitoring. We have compared three different negotiation mechanisms used by the orbiters and the control station to reach an efficient agreement on the allocation of the task. Our objective was to find a robust, fast and efficient negotiation mechanism that enables the orbiters and the control station to quickly reach an efficient and fair agreement. As part of our future work, we would also like to explore if the negotiating parties can adaptively choose the most suitable negotiation mechanism for different emergencies.

Acknowledgments. This work has been supported by a 2006 Oklahoma NASA EPSCoR Research Initiation Grant.

References

1. S. Chien, B. Cichy, A. Davies, D. Tran, G. Rabideau, R. Castano, R. Sherwood, D. Mandl, S. Frye, S. Shulman, J. Jones, and S. Grosvenor. An autonomous earth-observing sensorweb. *IEEE Intelligent Systems*, 20(3):16–24, 2005.
2. M. Klein, P. Faratin, H. Sayama, and Y. Bar-Yam. Negotiating complex contracts. *Group Decision and Negotiation*, 12:111–125, 2003.
3. P. Klemperer. Auction theory: A guide to the literature. *Journal of Economic Surveys*, 13(3):227–286, 1999.

Primality Tests Based on Fermat's Little Theorem

Manindra Agrawal

Department of Computer Science
Indian Institute of Technology, Kanpur
manindra@iitk.ac.in

Abstract. In this survey, we describe three algorithms for testing primality of numbers that use Fermat's Little Theorem.

1 Introduction

Pierre de Fermat, a 17th century mathematician, is famous for the *Fermat's Last Theorem*:

Theorem (Fermat's Last Theorem). *For any number $n > 2$, there is no integer solution of the equation $x^n + y^n = z^n$.*

Fermat did not give a proof of this theorem and it remained a conjecture for more than three hundred years. The quest for a proof of this theorem resulted in the development of several branches of mathematics. The eventual proof of the theorem is more than a hundred pages long [6]. A less well known contribution of Fermat is the *Fermat's Little Theorem*:

Theorem (Fermat's Little Theorem). *For any prime number n, and for any number a, $0 < a < n$, $a^{n-1} = 1 \pmod{n}$.*

Unlike Fermat's Last Theorem, this theorem has a very simple proof. At the same time, the theorem has had a great influence in algorithmic number theory as it has been the basis for some of the most well-known algorithms for primality testing – one of the fundamental problems in algorithmic number theory. In this article, we describe three such algorithms: *Solovay-Strassen Test*, *Miller-Rabin Test*, and *AKS Test*. The first two are randomized polynomial time algorithms and are widely used in practice while the third one is the only known deterministic polynomial time algorithm.

2 Preliminaries

The proofs in next section use basic properies of finite groups and rings which can be found in any book on finite fields (see, e.g., [2]). For numbers r and n, (r, n) equals the gcd of r and n. If $(r, n) = 1$ then $O_r(n)$ equals the order of

S. Chaudhuri et al. (Eds.): ICDCN 2006, LNCS 4308, pp. 288–293, 2006.

r modulo n, or, in other words, $O_r(n)$ is the smallest number $\ell > 0$ such that $n^\ell = 1 \pmod{r}$.

For number n, $\phi(n)$ denotes Euler's totient function which equals the number of a's between 1 and n that are relatively prime to n. If $n = p^k$ for some prime p then $\phi(n) = p^{k-1}(p-1)$.

3   Solovay-Strassen Test

The test was proposed by Solovay and Strassen [5] and was the first efficient algorithm for primality testing. Its starting point is a restatement of Fermat's Little Theorem:

Theorem (Fermat's Little Theorem, Restatement 1). *For any odd prime number n, and for any number a, $0 < a < n$, $a^{\frac{n-1}{2}} = \pm 1 \pmod{n}$.*

It is an easy observation that for prime n, a is a *quadratic residue* (in other words, $a = b^2 \pmod{n}$ for some b) if and only if $a^{\frac{n-1}{2}} = 1 \pmod{n}$. The *Legendre symbol* $\left(\frac{a}{n}\right)$ equals 1 if a is a quadratic residue modulo n else equals -1 for prime n. Therefore, for prime n,

$$\left(\frac{a}{n}\right) = a^{\frac{n-1}{2}} \pmod{n}.$$

Legendre symbol can be generalized to composite numbers by defining:

$$\left(\frac{a}{n}\right) = \prod_{i=1}^{k} \left(\frac{a}{p_i}\right)^{e_i}$$

where $n = \prod_{i=1}^{k} p_i^{e_i}$, p_i is prime for each i. This generalization is called *Jacobi symbol*. Jacobi symbol satisfies *quadratic reciprocity law*:

$$\left(\frac{a}{n}\right) \cdot \left(\frac{n}{a}\right) = (-1)^{\frac{(a-1)(n-1)}{4}}.$$

This, along with the property that $\left(\frac{a}{n}\right) = \left(\frac{a+n}{n}\right)$ gives an algorithm to compute $\left(\frac{a}{n}\right)$ that takes only $O(\log n)$ arithmetic operations.

For composite n, it is no longer neccessary that $\left(\frac{a}{n}\right) = 1$ iff a is a quadraric residue modulo n or that $\left(\frac{a}{n}\right) = a^{\frac{n-1}{2}} \pmod{n}$. This suggests that checking if $\left(\frac{a}{n}\right) = a^{\frac{n-1}{2}} \pmod{n}$ may be a test for primality of n. Solovay and Strassen showed that this works with high probability when a is chosen randomly. To see this, let n have at least two prime divisors and $n = p^k \cdot m$ with $(p, m) = 1$, p a prime, and k odd. (If every prime divisor of n occurs with even exponent then n is a perfect square and can be handled easily.) Let

$$A = \{a \pmod{p^k} \mid (a, p) = 1\}.$$

Clearly, $|A| = p^{k-1}(p-1)$ and exactly $\frac{1}{2}p^{k-1}(p-1)$ numbers in A are quadratic non-residues modulo p. Let $a_0 \in A$ be a quadratic residue modulo p and $b_0 \in A$ be a non-residue modulo p. Pick any number c, $0 < c < m$ and $(c, m) = 1$, and let a, b be the unique numbers between 0 and n such that $a = b = c \pmod{m}$ and $a = a_0 \pmod{p^k}$, $b = b_0 \pmod{p^k}$. Then,

$$\left(\frac{a}{n}\right) = \left(\frac{a_0}{p}\right)^k \cdot \left(\frac{c}{m}\right) = \left(\frac{c}{m}\right) = -\left(\frac{b}{n}\right).$$

If $a^{\frac{n-1}{2}} = \left(\frac{a}{n}\right) \pmod{n}$ and $b^{\frac{n-1}{2}} = \left(\frac{b}{n}\right) \pmod{n}$ then $a^{\frac{n-1}{2}} = -b^{\frac{n-1}{2}} \pmod{n}$. This implies

$$c^{\frac{n-1}{2}} \pmod{m} = a^{\frac{n-1}{2}} \pmod{m} = -b^{\frac{n-1}{2}} \pmod{m} = -c^{\frac{n-1}{2}} \pmod{m}.$$

This is impossible since $(c, m) = 1$. Hence, either $\left(\frac{a}{n}\right) \neq a^{\frac{n-1}{2}} \pmod{n}$ or $\left(\frac{b}{n}\right) \neq b^{\frac{n-1}{2}} \pmod{n}$. Therefore, for a random choice of a between 0 and n, either $(a, n) > 1$ or with probability at least $\frac{1}{2}$, $\left(\frac{a}{n}\right) \neq a^{\frac{n-1}{2}} \pmod{n}$.

The above analysis implies that the following algorithm works.

Input n.

1. If $n = m^k$ for some $k > 1$ then output COMPOSITE.
2. Randomly select a, $0 < a < n$.
3. If $(a, n) > 1$, output COMPOSITE.
4. If $\left(\frac{a}{n}\right) = a^{\frac{n-1}{2}} \pmod{n}$ then output PRIME.
5. Otherwise output COMPOSITE.

The test requires $O(\log n)$ arithmetic operations and hence is polynomial time.

4   Miller-Rabin Test

This test was proposed by MIchael Rabin [4] slightly modifying a test by Miller [3]. The starting point is another restatement of Fermat's Little Theorem:

Theorem (Fermat's Little Theorem, Restatement 2). *For any odd prime* $n = 2^s \cdot t$ *with* t *odd, and for any number* a, $0 < a < n$, *the sequence* $a^t \pmod{n}$, $a^{2t} \pmod{n}$, $a^{2^2 t} \pmod{n}$, ..., $a^{2^s t} \pmod{n}$ *either has all 1's or the pair* $-1, 1$ *occurs somewhere in the sequence.*

If n is composite, then the sequence may not satisfy the above property. Miller proved that, assuming Extended Riemann Hypothesis, for at least one a between 1 and $\log^2 n$, the above sequence fails to satisfy the property when n is composite but not a prime power. Miller proved that the same holds with high probability for a random a without any hypothesis. We will give Miller's argument.

Assume that n is composite but not a prime power. Let p and q be two odd prime divisors of n. Let k be the largest power of p dividing n. Let $p - 1 = 2^v \cdot w$ where w is odd.

We first analyze the case when there is a -1 somewhere in the sequence. Define set A_u as:

$$A_u = \{a \mid (0 < a < n) \wedge (a^{2^u \cdot t} = -1 \ (\text{mod } n))\}$$

for some $0 \le u < s$.

Then $a^{2^u \cdot t} = -1 \ (\text{mod } p^k)$ for every $a \in A$. Let

$$A_{p,u} = \{a \ (\text{mod } p^k) \mid a \in A_u\}.$$

Since the size of the multiplicative group modulo p^k is $p^{k-1}(p - 1)$, for every $a \in A_{p,u}$, $a^{p^{k-1} \cdot (p-1)} = 1 \ (\text{mod } p^k)$. Therefore, $a^{(p^k \cdot (p-1), 2^{u+1} \cdot t)} = 1 \ (\text{mod } p^k)$. Prime p does not divide t since otherwise it divides $n - 1 = -1 \ (\text{mod } p)$ which is absurd. Hence, $a^{(p-1, 2^{u+1} \cdot t)} = 1 \ (\text{mod } p^k)$. Since t is odd and $p - 1 = 2^v \cdot w$, $a^{2^{\min\{v, u+1\}} \cdot (w,t)} = 1 \ (\text{mod } p^k)$. If $v \le u$ then we get $a^{2^u \cdot t} = 1 \ (\text{mod } p^k)$ which is not possible. Hence, $v > u$ implying that $a^{2^u \cdot (w,t)} = -1 \ (\text{mod } p^k)$. It is easy to see that the equation $x^\ell = \pm 1 \ (\text{mod } p^k)$ for $\ell \mid (p - 1)$ has at most ℓ solutions. It follows that $|A_{p,u}| \le 2^u \cdot (w, t) \le 2^u \cdot t \le \frac{1}{2^{u-v}}(p - 1)$.

An identical argument shows that $|A_{q,u}| \le \frac{1}{2^{u-v'}}(q - 1)$ for $u < v'$ where $A_{q,u}$ is defined similarly to $A_{p,u}$ and $q - 1 = 2^{v'} \cdot w'$ for odd w'. By Chinese Remainder Theorem, it follows that $|A_u| \le \frac{1}{4^{u-v''}}(n - 1)$ if $u < v'' = \min\{v, v'\}$, 0 otherwise. Hence,

$$\sum_{0 \le u < s} |A_u| \le \sum_{0 \le u < v''} \frac{n - 1}{4^{u-v''}} = \left(\frac{1}{3} - \frac{1}{3 \cdot 4^{v''}}\right) \cdot (n - 1).$$

For the case when the whole sequence is all 1's, one can argue exactly as above to obtain that the number of a's giving rise to such a sequence is at most $\frac{1}{4^{v''}}(n - 1)$. Hence the probability that the sequence generated by a randomly chosen a satisfies either of the two properties is less than $\frac{1}{2}$.

The above analysis implies that the following algorithm works.

Input n.

1. If $n = m^k$ for some $k > 1$ then output COMPOSITE.

2. Randomly select a, $0 < a < n$.

3. If $(a, n) > 1$ output COMPOSITE.

4. Let $n - 1 = 2^s \cdot t$.

5. Compute the sequence a^t (mod n), a^{2t} (mod n), $\ldots$, $a^{2^s \cdot t}$ (mod n).

6. If The sequence is all 1's or has a -1 followed by a 1 then
      output PRIME.

7. Otherwise output COMPOSITE.

The test requires $O(\log n)$ arithmetic operations and hence is polynomial time.

5   AKS Test

This test was proposed by Agrawal, Kayal and Saxena [1]. It is the only known deterministic polynomial time algorithm known for the problem. The starting point of this test is a slight generalization of Fermat's Little Theorem.

Theorem (Fermat's Little Theorem, Generalized). *If n is prime then for any $r > 0$ and any a, $0 < a < n$,*

$$(x + a)^n = x^n + a \ (\mathrm{mod}\ n, x^r - 1).$$

On the other hand, if n is composite and not a prime power, then it appears unlikely that the above equation holds for several a's. This can be proven formally as follows.

Suppose that n is not a prime power and let p be a prime divisor of n. Suppose that $(x + a)^n = x^n + a \ (\mathrm{mod}\ n, x^r - 1)$ for $0 < a \le 2\sqrt{r} \log n$ and r is such that $O_r(n) > 4 \log^2 n$. Define the two sets

$$A = \{m \mid (x + a)^m = x^m + a \ (\mathrm{mod}\ p, x^r - 1), 0 < a \le 2\sqrt{r} \log n\},$$

and

$$B = \{g(x) \mid g(x)^m = g(x^m) \ (\mathrm{mod}\ p, x^r - 1), m \in A\}.$$

Clearly, p, $n \in A$ and $x + a \in B$ for $0 < a \le 2\sqrt{r} \log n$. Moreover, it is straight-forward to see that both sets A and B are closed under multiplication and hence are infinite. We now define two finite sets associated with A and B. Let

$$A_0 = \{m \ (\mathrm{mod}\ r) \mid m \in A\},$$

and

$$B_0 = \{g(x) \ (\mathrm{mod}\ p, h(x)) \mid g(x) \in B\}$$

where $h(x)$ is an irreducible factor of $x^r - 1$ over F_p such that the field $F = F_p[x]/(h(x))$ has x as a primitive rth root of unity.

We now estimate the sizes of these sets. Let $t = |A_0|$. Since elements of A_0 are residues modulo r, $t \le \phi(r) < r$. Also, since $O_r(n) \ge 4 \log^2 n$ and A_0 contains all powers of n, $t \ge 4 \log^2 n$.

Let $T = |B_0|$. Since elements of B_0 are polynomials modulo $h(x)$ and degree of $h(x) \le r - 1$, $T \le p^{r-1}$. The lower bound on T is a little more involved. Consider any two polynomials $f(x), g(x) \in B$ of degree $< t$. Suppose $f(x) = g(x) \ (\mathrm{mod}\ p, h(x))$. Then $f(x^m) = f(x)^m = g(x)^m = g(x^m) \ (\mathrm{mod}\ p, h(x))$ for any $m \in A_0$. Therefore, the polynomial $f(y) - g(y)$ has at least t roots in the field F (as x is a primitive rth root of unity). Since the degree of $f(y) - g(y)$ is less than t, this is possible only if $f(y) = g(y)$. This argument shows that all polynomials of degree $< t$ in B map to distinct elements in B_0. The number of polynomials in B of degree $< t$ is at least $\binom{2\sqrt{r} \log n + t - 1}{t - 1} \ge \binom{4\sqrt{t} \log n}{2\sqrt{r} \log n} > 2^{2\sqrt{t} \log n}$. This follows because B_0 has at least $2\sqrt{r} \log n$ distinct degree 1 polynomials assuming that $p > 2\sqrt{r} \log n$. Therefore, $T > 2^{2\sqrt{t} \log n}$.

With the above lower bound on T, we can now complete the proof. Since $|A_0| = t$, there exist $(i_1, j_1) \neq (i_2, j_2)$, $0 \leq i_1, j_1, i_2, j_2 \leq \sqrt{t}$ such that $n^{i_1} p^{j_1} = n^{i_2} p^{j_2} \pmod{r}$. Let $g(x) \in B_0$. Then

$$g(x)^{n^{i_1} p^{j_1}} = g(x^{n^{i_1} p^{j_1}}) = g(x^{n^{i_2} p^{j_2}}) = g(x)^{n^{i_2} p^{j_2}} \pmod{p, h(x)}.$$

Hence, the polynomial $y^{n^{i_1} p^{j_1}} - y^{n^{i_2} p^{j_2}}$ has at least $|B_0| = T > 2^{2\sqrt{t} \log n}$ roots in the field F. The degree of this polynomial is at most $n^{2\sqrt{t}}$, and therefore the polynomial is zero. This implies $n^{i_1} p^{j_1} = n^{i_2} p^{j_2}$ which means that n is a power of p. This is not possible by assumption.

The above argument shows that the following test works.

Input n.

1. If $n = m^k$ for some $k > 1$ then output COMPOSITE.

2. Find the smallest r such that $O_r(n) > 4 \log^2 n$.

3. For every a, $0 < a \leq 2\sqrt{r} \log n$, do

    If $(a, n) > 1$, output COMPOSITE.

    If $(x + a)^n \neq x^n + a \pmod{n, x^r - 1}$, output COMPOSITE.

4. Output PRIME.

The test requires $O(r^{\frac{3}{2}} \log^2 n \log r)$ arithmetic operations. An easy counting arguments shows that $r = O(\log^5 n)$ and hence the algorithm works in polynomial time.

References

[1] Manindra Agrawal, Neeraj Kayal, and Nitin Saxena. PRIMES is in P. *Annals of Mathematics*, 160(2):781–793, 2004.

[2] R. Lidl and H. Niederreiter. *Introduction to finite fields and their applications*. Cambridge University Press, 1986.

[3] G. L. Miller. Riemann's hypothesis and tests for primality. *J. Comput. Sys. Sci.*, 13:300–317, 1976.

[4] M. O. Rabin. Probabilistic algorithm for testing primality. *J. Number Theory*, 12:128–138, 1980.

[5] R. Solovay and V. Strassen. A fast Monte-Carlo test for primality. *SIAM Journal on Computing*, 6:84–86, 1977.

[6] A. Wiles. Modular elliptic curves and fermat's last theorem. *Annals of Mathematics*, 141:443–551, 1995.

Efficient Distributed Handshake Using Mobile Agents

Bilel Derbel

LaBRI, Université Bordeaux 1, ENSEIRB
351, Cours de la Libération, 33405 Talence France
LIF, Université de Provence
39 Rue Joliot-Curie, 13453 Marseille Cedex 13 France
derbel@labri.fr, derbel@cmi.univ-mrs.fr

Abstract. There is a handshake between two nodes in a network, if the two nodes are communicating with one another in an exclusive mode. In this paper, we give a mobile agent algorithm that allows to decide whether two nodes realize a handshake. Our algorithm can be used in order to solve some other classical distributed problems, e.g., local computations, maximal matching and edge coloring. We give a performance analysis of the algorithm and we compute the optimal number of agents maximizing the mean number of simultaneous handshakes. In particular, we obtain $\Omega(m\delta/\Delta^2)$ simultaneous handshakes where m is the number of edges in the network, and Δ (resp. δ) is the maximum (resp. minimum) degree of the network. For any almost Δ-regular network, our lower bound is optimal up to a constant factor. In addition, we show how to emulate our mobile agent algorithm in the message passing model while maintaining the same performances. Comparing with previous message passing algorithms, we obtain a larger number of handshakes, which shows that using mobile agents can provide novel ideas to efficiently solve some well studied problems in the message passing model.

Keywords: mobile agent model, message passing model, handshake, matching, random walk.

1   Introduction

Goals and motivations: This paper presents new efficient handshake algorithms in the distributed model of computation. Generally speaking, a handshake algorithm enables the establishment of safe communications between two nodes, which guarantees that both the two nodes are communicating with one another in exclusive mode. Distributed solutions of this problem are known in networks supporting message passing [1,2,3,4]. What happens if we consider a distributed system based on mobile agents? In particular, can we solve the problem while maintaining the same performances? More generally, the growing demand for distributed applications makes a case for the comparative study of the performances of systems based on mobile agents and systems based on more classical network communications. Many works in the last few years were intended to

S. Chaudhuri et al. (Eds.): ICDCN 2006, LNCS 4308, pp. 294–305, 2006.

understand the computational power of mobile agents and to solve new specific problems raised by their use. In this paper, we show how to *efficiently* solve the handshake problem by using mobile agents. Surprisingly, our mobile agent approach also leads to improved solutions and new ideas in the more classical message passing setting. Generally speaking, this work can be viewed as a part of a larger study concerning the complexity power of mobile agents and the benefit they may provide.

Models and notations: We model a network by a connected graph $G = (V, E)$ where V is the set of nodes and E the set of edges. We denote by Δ (resp. δ) the maximum (resp. minimum) degree of G and by $n = |V|$ (resp. $m = |E|$) the number of nodes (resp. edges). For each node $v \in V$, we denote by d_v the degree of v and by $\mathcal{N}(v)$ the neighbors of v, i.e, $\mathcal{N}(v) = \{u \in V \mid d_G(u, v) = 1\}$ where $d_G(u, v)$ is the distance between u and v in G.

In *the mobile agent model*, an agent (or robot) is an autonomous entity of computation able to move from a node to another and equipped with an internal memory. We assume the following:

- each node v is equipped with a white-board $\mathcal{WB}(v)$, which can be viewed as a memory place where agents can write and read information in a mutual exclusion manner.
- the outgoing edges around each node are labeled, that is each node has a numbering of the ports connecting it with its neighbors.
- each agent knows the port from which it is arrived in a given node.
- we only consider the synchronous case where agents have access to a global clock which generates pulses.
- agents can read and write in a white-board in negligible time.
- it takes one time unit to an agent to move from a node to a neighboring one.

For the clarity of our algorithm, we use a local generic function $\text{WRITE}(v) \in \{true, false\}$ which can be applied by each agent at any node v. At a given pulse, if many agents apply $\text{WRITE}(v)$ in node v, then $\text{WRITE}(v)$ returns *true* for only one agent and *false* for all others. In this case, the agent for which $\text{WRITE}(v) = true$ has instantaneously a read/write access to $\mathcal{WB}(v)$, i.e., it has access to $\mathcal{WB}(v)$ before the other agents.

In *the message passing model*, a node is an autonomous entity of computation that can communicate with its neighbors by sending and receiving messages. We assume that each node performs computations in negligible time. In the synchronous model, we assume that all nodes have access to a global clock that generates pulses. We assume that messages sent in a given pulse reach their destination before the beginning of the next pulse. In the asynchronous model, there is no global clock and a message delay is arbitrary but finite.

Problem definition: One can think of several formulations of the handshake problem depending on the distributed model. In this paper, we have based our work on the following general definition: "a handshake algorithm is a distributed procedure that enables a pair of adjacent nodes (u, v) to communicate *exclusively* with one another *at some time*". In other words, if a handshake occurs between nodes u and v at some time, then u (resp. v) has the guarantee that v (resp.

u) does not communicate with any other neighbors. In general, distributed algorithms solving the handshake problem works in infinitely many *rounds*. At each round, some handshakes occur between pairs of neighboring nodes. Then, communications take place between nodes where a handshake occurs. In practice, there are new rounds as long as some communication between pairs of nodes is required. The handshake problem can then be formulated more practically in terms of *matching: "Given a graph G, at each round, find a set of disjoint edges of E"*. It is clear that the set of these edges defines the nodes that can communicate with each others in an exclusive manner at each round. The number of edges computed at each round is called the *handshake number*. The handshake number is the ruling performance measure of a handshake algorithm. Our goal is to design an algorithm providing the highest possible handshake number.

Related works: All handshake algorithms in the literature use randomization and message passing. For instance, in the asynchronous message passing model and in the algorithm presented in [3,1,5], each node repeats forever the following three steps *(i)* choose randomly a neighbor, *(ii)* send him 1, and *(iii)* send 0 to all other neighbors. Then, there is a handshake if two neighboring nodes have sent 1 to each others, and a handshake between two nodes occurs with a given probability. The authors in [3] studied many probabilistic properties of the above algorithm for many graphs. In the general case, their handshake number is $\Omega(m/\Delta^2)$. Very recently, the authors in [6] gave a new efficient handshake algorithm. However, they assume a fully synchronous message passing model where nodes have access to a continuous real-valued global clock, and *communications take no time*. Therefore, the results in [6] are fundamentally different from ours.

Independently of its theoretical interest, the handshake problem can be applied in many settings. For instance, the authors in [4] use the handshake algorithm of [3] in order to efficiently solve the problem of broadcasting information under a restricted model of communication. In [2], the authors apply the handshake problem in order to practically implement well studied formal models based on local computations (see e.g., [7,8,9] for a quick survey).

The handshake problem is also tightly related to the fundamental problem of breaking the symmetry in distributed networks where nodes have to make decisions depending only on their local views. Typical problems where breaking the symmetry is essential are finding a maximal independent set (MIS), a coloring and a maximal matching. For instance, a maximal matching (see, e.g., [10] for a definition) can be computed using handshakes by deleting the edges computed at each round, and by iterating until the graph is empty. The same idea can be applied for distributed edge coloring by assigning a legal color to the edges computed at each round independently and in parallel.

Results and outline: In Section 2 of this paper, we give an efficient algorithm called AGENT HANDSHAKE for the handshake problem in the mobile agent model. Our algorithm is based on random walks of the agents. We give a probabilistic analysis of the performance of our algorithm. In particular, we compute the optimal (with respect to our method) number of agents that allows a maximal handshake number in expectation. We show that our algorithm is efficient for general graphs, and provides $\Omega(m\delta/\Delta^2)$ handshakes per round. It also becomes of special interest for many graph classes. For instance, for almost Δ-regular graphs, i.e., graphs such that $\delta = \Theta(\Delta)$, the handshake number is drastically reduced to $\Omega(n)$ which is optimal up to a constant factor.

In Section 3 we show how we can turn back to the asynchronous message passing model and emulate our algorithm to this model while maintaining the same performances. The technique is based on simulating agents using tokens. We obtain new improved message passing handshake algorithms. In additoin and since the simulation technique is independent of the handshake problem, our results show that solving a problem using mobile agents can provide new ideas to design new efficient algorithms in other distributed models. In Section 4 we discuss how to efficiently create the agents. In Section 5 we conclude the paper and raise some open questions.

2   Handshake Using Mobile Agents

In the rest of this section, we consider the mobile agent model and we assume that the white-board of each node v contains a single boolean variable b. We write $\mathcal{WB}(v) = true$ when $b = true$ and $\mathcal{WB}(v) = false$ when $b = false$. We assume that for every $v \in V$, $\mathcal{WB}(v)$ is initially equal to $false$ and that the network contains k agents. We do not make any assumptions on the initial positions of agents.

At pulse 0, each agent begins to execute algorithm AGENT HANDSHAKE (see Fig. 1). The algorithm consists of many rounds. At each round, agents in a node v first try to make a handshake randomly on a given edge. Once the handshake trial is finished, the agents in v move to an equally likely chosen neighboring node (see algorithm RANDOM STEP in Fig. 2). Then, a new round starts. Note that in Fig. 1, t_0 denotes the pulse at which a given round begins and it is not used by the agents in order to make any computation.

Let us consider a round which begins at pulse $t_0 = 3t$ (with $t \geq 0$) and let us consider an agent $\mathcal{A}$ at some node v. It may happen that many agents are in v at t_0. Only one agent in v is allowed to try to make a handshake. Hence, the agents first "fight" in order to mark the white-board of v. The agent who succeeds in marking $\mathcal{WB}(v)$ is chosen to try a handshake, i.e., line 2 of the algorithm. If agent $\mathcal{A}$ is not chosen to make the handshake, then it just waits (for two pulses) in v until the chosen agent come back (line 15). Otherwise, agent $\mathcal{A}$ moves to a neighboring node u (line 5). In this case, at pulse $t_0 + 1$ agent $\mathcal{A}$ arrives at u, and three cases arise:

1. $\mathcal{WB}(u) = true$: node u has been marked at pulse t_0. Thus, there was an agent in u at pulse t_0, and the handshake fails.
2. $\mathcal{WB}(u) = false$: no agents were in u at pulse t_0, and no other agents arrive at u in pulse $t_0 + 1$. Thus, WRITE(u) returns $true$ and the handshake succeeds.
3. $\mathcal{WB}(u) = false$: no agents were in u at pulse t_0, and at least another agent arrives at u in pulse $t_0 + 1$. Thus, if WRITE(u) returns $true$ then $\mathcal{A}$ succeeds the handshake.

Remark 1. It is important to note that once an agent in a node v executes line 14 of algorithm AGENT HANDSHAKE, the white-board of v verifies $\mathcal{WB}(v) = true$, i.e., there is an other agent for which WRITE(v) in line 2 returns *true*, and which instantaneously writes *true* in $\mathcal{WB}(v)$.

To summarize, when an agent is at some node v, we say that it succeeds a handshake, if it can firstly write the white-board of v and secondly the white-board of some unmarked node $u \in \mathcal{N}(v)$. In this case, we also say that a handshake is assigned to edge (u, v). It is clear that our algorithm is correct, that is at each round, the set of edges where a handshake is assigned are disjoint.

Line pulse	The Algorithm
$t_0=3t$	1: **while** *true* **do**
	2: **if** WRITE(v) **then**
	3: $\mathcal{WB}(v) \leftarrow true$;
	4: Choose at random (equally likely) an outgoing edge $e = (v,u)$;
	5: Move from v to u;
t_0+1	6: **if** WRITE(u) **then**
	7: **if** $\mathcal{WB}(u) = false$ **then**
	8: Handshake Success;
	9: **end if**
	10: **end if**
	11: Move back from u to v;
t_0+2	12: $\mathcal{WB}(v) \leftarrow false$;
	13: **else**
	14: **repeat**
	15: wait;
	16: **until** $\mathcal{WB}(v) = false$
	17: **end if**
t_0+2	18: execute algorithm RANDOM STEP;
	19: **end while**

Fig. 1. Algorithm AGENT HANDSHAKE: code for an agent at node v

```
1: choose randomly 0 or 1 with probability 1/2;
2: if 0 then
3:    do not move.
4: else
5:    choose at random (equally likely) an outgoing edge e = (v,v');
6:    move to v'.
7: end if
```

Fig. 2. Algorithm RANDOM STEP: code for an agent at node v

2.1   Analysis of the Algorithm: General Case

Let $\{\mathcal{A}_i\}_{i=\{1,\cdots,k\}}$ denotes the set of all agents. For every integer pulse $t \geq 0$ and for every integer $i \in \{1, \cdots, k\}$, let $\mathcal{A}_i(t) \in V$ denotes the position of agent

$\mathcal{A}_i$ at pulse $t \geq 0$. Let $\mathbb{P}_G(\mathcal{A}_i(3t) = v)$ denotes the probability that agent $\mathcal{A}_i$ is in node v at pulse $3t$, i.e., the beginning of a round.

From the description of the algorithm, each round takes 3 time units. Thus, each 3 time units, each agent makes a step of a random walk. A classical result from Markov chain theory [11] claims that there exists a unique stationary distribution for random walks on graphs (under some additional assumptions of aperiodicity which is satisfied by line 1 of algorithm RANDOM STEP). The stationary distribution is π the probability measure on G defined by:

$$\pi(v) = \frac{d_v}{2m}, \ \forall v \in V$$

In other words, if the starting point of a random walk is chosen according to π, then at each time the position of the random walk is still π-distributed. We recall that whatever is the distribution of the starting point, the random walk converges to the stationary distribution, that is, for every $i \in \{1, \cdots, k\}$, when $t \longrightarrow +\infty$, $\mathbb{P}_G(\mathcal{A}_i(3t) = v) \longrightarrow \pi(v)$.

In addition, we assume that each agent aims a proper random generator, and the agents execute algorithm RANDOM STEP independently. Hence, we use the following definition:

Definition 1. *We say that the k agents are under the stationary regime, if for every $v \in V$ and for every pulse t, we have:*

$$\mathbb{P}_G(\mathcal{A}_i(3t) = v) = \frac{d_v}{2m} = \pi(v)$$

and the positions of agents are independent: for any $(v_i)_{i\in\{1,\cdots,k\}} \in V^k$, we have:

$$\mathbb{P}_G\left((\mathcal{A}_i(3t))_{i\in\{1,\cdots,k\}} = (v_i)_{i\in\{1,\cdots,k\}} \right) = \prod_{i=1}^{k} \pi(v_i)$$

Let us consider a given fixed round and let us denote by N^v the number of agents in the node v at the beginning of the round.

Remark 2. It is easy to check that under the stationary regime, the r.v. $(N^v)_{v\in V}$ has a multinomial distribution that is, for any family of positive integers $(j_v)_{v\in V}$ such that $\sum_{v\in V} j_v = k$,

$$\mathbb{P}((N^v = j_v)_{v\in V}) = \frac{k!}{\prod_{v\in V} j_v!} \cdot \prod_{v\in V} \pi(v)^{j_v}$$

Notice also that the distribution of the $(N^v)_{v\in V}$ is preserved by a step of the random walks.

The handshake number depends on the graph G, on the number of agents k, on the round and on the initial position of agents. For the sake of analysis, we only assume the stationary regime and we focus on the expected handshake number $\mathbb{E}(H_k(G))$. We will see in Section 4 that assuming the stationary regime is more than of a theoretical interest.

We consider an edge $(u, v) \in E$, and we denote by ω_1 the event «*an agent moves from u to v in line 5*» and by ω_2 the event «*no agent moves from $\mathcal{N}(v)\backslash\{u\}$*

to v *in line* 5». We denote by $p(u \rightsquigarrow v) = \mathbb{P}(N^u \geq 1, N^v = 0, \omega_1, \omega_2)$ the probability that $\{N^u \geq 1\}$, $\{N^v = 0\}$, w_1 and w_2 arise altogether. Similarly, let $p_i(u \rightsquigarrow v) = \mathbb{P}(N^u = i, N^v = 0, \omega_1, \omega_2)$ for any $i \in \{1, \cdots, k\}$.

Fact 1. *The handshake number verifies:* $\mathbb{E}(H_k(G)) \geq \sum\limits_{(u,v) \in E} p(u \rightsquigarrow v) + p(v \rightsquigarrow u)$.

Lemma 1. *Under the stationary regime and at any round, the following holds:*

1. *For every edge* $(u, v) \in E$ *and for every* $i \in \{1, \cdots, k\}$, *we have:*
$$p_i(u \rightsquigarrow v) \geq \frac{1}{d_u} \cdot \binom{k}{i} \cdot \pi(u)^i \cdot (1 - \pi(u) - 2\pi(v))^{k-i}$$

2. *For every edge* $(u, v) \in E$, *we have:*
$$p(u \rightsquigarrow v) \geq \frac{1}{d_u} \cdot \left((1 - 2\pi(v))^k - (1 - \pi(u) - 2\pi(v))^k \right)$$

Using Fact 1 and Lemma 1, we obtain a general lower bound of $\mathbb{E}(H_k(G))$. In particular, we obtain the following:

Theorem 1. *Let* $G(m)$ *be a sequence of graphs such that* $G(m)$ *has* m *edges and* $\Delta/m \to 0$ *when* $m \to +\infty$. *Then, there exists* $k = \Theta(m/\Delta)$ *such that under the stationary regime* $\mathbb{E}(H_k(G(m))) = \Omega(m\delta/\Delta^2)$.

Remark 3. We note that the performance of the algorithm is not very sensitive to the value of k. For instance, if the value of k vary by a multiplicative constant close to 1, then the handshake number is up to a constant factor the same.

The previous theorem has to be compared with the previous best known handshake number which is $\Omega(m/\Delta^2)$ (in the asynchronous message passing model). For instance, if $\delta = \Theta(\Delta)$, then $\mathbb{E}(H_k(G)) = \Omega(n)$ for $k = \Theta(n)$ which is optimal up to a constant factor (the maximal theoretical handshake number is $n/2$). In the next section, we give a different approach to the problem which provides exact bounds for d-regular graphs.

2.2   Regular Graphs: Asymptotic Analysis

In this part, we consider a d-regular graph $G_n = (V_n, E_n)$ where d is fixed. For every $v \in V_n$, we suppose given an ordering of the neighbors of v from 1 to d. Let us consider a given fixed round. For every $j \in \{1, \cdots, d\}$, let the r.v. N_j^v be the number of agents in the j-th neighbor of v at the beginning of the round. Let $\mathcal{N}(v) \rightsquigarrow v$ be the event: «an agent moves from at least a node in $\mathcal{N}(v)$ to v in line 5». Let $\mathbb{P}_n (\mathcal{N}(v) \rightsquigarrow v, N^v = 0)$ the probability that $\{\mathcal{N}(v) \rightsquigarrow v\}$ and $\{N^v = 0\}$ in G_n. In the remainder, we make the following assumption:

$$\mathcal{Q} = \left(n \longrightarrow +\infty, \ k = k(n) \longrightarrow +\infty, \ k(n)/n \longrightarrow c \text{ and } c \in (0, +\infty) \right)$$

When G_n is regular and under the stationary regime, agents choose equally likely each node v. By symmetry of G_n, the distribution of $(N^v, N_1^v, N_2^v, \cdots, N_d^v)$ does not depend on v. Thus, in the following two lemmas, the node v may be seen as a generic node in V_n, or as the first node for any ordering on the nodes of G_n, or even as a node chosen randomly.

Lemma 2. *Assume $\mathcal{Q}$. Let v be a generic node in V_n. Under the stationary regime,*

1. *the following convergence in distribution holds*

$$(N^v, N_1^v, N_2^v, \cdots, N_d^v) \xrightarrow[n\to+\infty]{(law)} (X_0, X_1, X_2, \cdots, X_d)$$

   where the r.v. X_j are i.i.d and follow a Poisson distribution with parameter c, that is:

$$\mathbb{P}(X_j = \ell) = e^{-c}\frac{c^\ell}{\ell!}, \quad \forall \ell \geq 0$$

2. *for any round, we have*

$$\mathbb{P}_n\left(\mathcal{N}(v) \rightsquigarrow v, N^v = 0\right) \xrightarrow[n\to+\infty]{} e^{-c} \cdot \left(1 - \left(1 - \frac{1}{d} + \frac{e^{-c}}{d}\right)^d\right)$$

Theorem 2. *Assume $\mathcal{Q}$. For every d-regular graph G_n with d an integer constant, under the stationary regime, the handshake number verifies:*

$$\frac{\mathbb{E}(H_k(G_n))}{n} \xrightarrow[n\to+\infty]{} e^{-c} \cdot \left(1 - \left(1 - \frac{1}{d} + \frac{e^{-c}}{d}\right)^d\right) \tag{1}$$

One can numerically find the optimal constant c that maximize the limit given in Theorem 2. By taking $c = \log(2)$, the right hand side of (1) is larger than 0.196... for any d. Thus, our bound is optimal up to a small multiplicative constant factor ($\simeq 5/2$).

3   Application to the Message Passing Model

In this section, we show how to simulate our agent based algorithm in the asynchronous message passing model. The general outline of the method consists in using tokens to simulate agents. A similar idea appears in [12,13] in order to study the computational power of mobile agents.

Initially, we suppose that there are k tokens scattered at some nodes. Each time a node v has one or more tokens, v locally executes the algorithm that the agents are supposed to execute in node v. Each white-board can be simulated using the local variables of the corresponding node. The agent movements can be simulated by sending the tokens from a node to another (If many agents choose to move to the same direction, then the corresponding tokens are concatenated). Because we have only considered the synchronous mobile agent model, the above simulation method will automatically provide synchronous algorithms in the message passing model. However, following the technique of network synchronizer α [14] and using extra communication messages, we obtain algorithm DISTRIBUTED HANDSHAKE which works in the asynchronous case.

We assume that the function *sendTo* (resp. *sendAll*) allows to send a message to a specified (resp. all) neighbor(s), and the function *receiveFrom* allows to receive a message from a specified incoming edge (if there are no messages then the node waits until a message arrives). The variable #tokens(v) corresponds to

```
 1  while true do
 2  │   if #tokens(v) > 0 then
 3  │   │   Hs-trial ← false;
 4  │   │   choose an outgoing edge i at random;
 5  │   │   sendTo(i, 1);                              /* send a request to one neighbor */
 6  │   │   for j ∈ [1, d_v] and j ≠ i do sendTo(j, 0);      /* synchronization msg */
 7  │   │   for j ∈ [1, d_v] do
 8  │   │   │   receiveFrom(j);              /* receive request or synchronization msg */
 9  │   │   │   sendTo(j, 0);                /* send a reject or synchronization msg */
10  │   │   for j ∈ [1, d_v] do
11  │   │   │   Msg ← receiveFrom(j);               /* receive response of the request */
12  │   │   │   if j = i and Msg = 1 then Hs-trial ← true; /* handshake success */
13  │   │   #moves ← 0; move ← int [1, d_v];            /* tabular initialized with 0 */
14  │   │   for int ℓ = 1 to #tokens(v) do
15  │   │   │   choose 1 or 0 with probability 1/2;
16  │   │   │   if 1 then
17  │   │   │   │   choose randomly an outgoing edge i;
18  │   │   │   │   #moves ++; move[i]++;
19  │   │   #tokens(v) -= #moves;  /* update tokens: those who stay at the node */
20  │   │   for int ℓ = 1 to d_v do sendTo(ℓ, move.[ℓ]);       /* move other tokens */
21  │   else
22  │   │   sendAll(0);                                /* send synchronization msg */
23  │   │   request ← boolean [1, d_v];               /* tabular initialized with false */
24  │   │   for j ∈ [1, d_v] do
25  │   │   │   Msg ← receiveFrom(j);
26  │   │   │   if Msg = 1 then request.[j] ← true;   /* handshake request from j */
27  │   │   if ∃j such that request.[j] = true then
28  │   │   │   choose at random i ∈ [1, d_v] such that request.[i] = true;
29  │   │   │   sendTo(i, 1);                          /* accept request from neighbor i */
30  │   │   │   for every ℓ ≠ i do sendTo(ℓ, 0);          /* reject the others */
31  │   │   else
32  │   │   │   sendAll(0);                            /* synchronization msg */
33  │   │   for j ∈ [1, d_v] do Msg ← receiveFrom(j);  /* synchronization msg */
34  │   │   sendAll(0);                                /* synchronization msg */
35  │   for j ∈ [1, d_v] do
36  │   │   Msg ← receiveFrom(j);                      /* receive incoming tokens */
37  │   │   #tokens(v) += Msg;                         /* update the number of tokens */
```

Algorithm 1. Asynchronous DISTRIBUTED HANDSHAKE: code for a node v

the number of agents in node v in the original handshake algorithm. All tokens are given the value 1. When many tokens are sent to the same direction, we simply send their sum.

Theorem 3. *Algorithm* DISTRIBUTED HANDSHAKE *is correct and the number of handshakes at a given round is equal to the number of handshakes in algorithm* AGENT HANDSHAKE.

Using the previous theorem, it makes sense to compare the performance results of Section 2 in the mobile agent model and the performances of past algorithms [1,2,3] in the message passing model. Note that our algorithm can also be applied for implementing the edge local computation model [9] as in [2].

Moreover, compared with message passing solutions, our mobile agent algorithm allows to reduce the global number of computation entities in the network from n to only k. We think that this observation defines a new criterion allowing to compare different distributed solutions of a problem.

4   Distributed Initialization of Agents

In Section 2, we have assumed the stationary regime in our analysis. This is relevant if the agents have been moving randomly from a node to another in the network for a sufficiently long time before the computation of a task begins. For instance, this assumption can be realistic in the case of some distributed systems where the agents have been created in the past and have been waiting to do some tasks. In this case, the initial positions of agents do not matter and the previous analysis still holds.

If the computations begin before the stationary regime, our algorithms are still correct, only the analysis is different and depends on the initial positions of agents. For instance, if the agents have the same initial departure node, then the number of handshakes will be 1 at the first round and then it increases with time. In opposite, if the agents are well distributed over the network, then intuitively, there will be more handshakes at the first round and it will take less time to reach the stationary regime. In the following, we show how to create agents in such a way they are immediately under the stationary regime. The idea is to make the nodes start some agents locally and by they own such that the global number of agents is almost the optimal one since the first round.

First suppose that m is known and let k be the optimal number of agents computed in Section 2. Then, *at time* 0, *each node* v *creates a random number* N^v *of agents according to a Poisson law with parameter* $\frac{d_v}{2m} \cdot k$. Let K denotes the total number of agents effectively created by the nodes. Let us first describe the joint distribution of the N^v's knowing $K = \ell$. Let $(j_v)_{v \in V}$ a sequence of integers such that $\sum_{v \in V} j_v = \ell$. Thus, we have:

$$\mathbb{P}((N^v = j_v)_{v \in V} \mid K = \ell) \;=\; \frac{\mathbb{P}((N^v = j_v)_{v \in V}, K = \ell)}{\mathbb{P}(K = \ell)} \;=\; \frac{\prod_{v \in V} \mathbb{P}(N^v = j_v)}{\mathbb{P}(K = \ell)}$$

By a simple checking, conditionally on $K = l$, the r.v. $(N^v)_{v \in V}$ follows a multinomial distribution. Using Remark 2, we can conclude that agents are under the stationary regime. To be precise, there is a slight difference with the consideration of Remark 2, since there the agents were labeled.

Now, it is classical (and easy to show) that K follows a Poisson distribution with parameter $\sum_{v \in V} \frac{d_v}{2m} \cdot k = k$. Thus, the expected number of agents is $\mathbb{E}(K) = k$. Due to properties of concentration of the Poisson law, K is very close to k, i.e., $\mathbb{P}(|K - k| > k^{1/2+\epsilon}) \longrightarrow 0$ when $k \to +\infty$. Using remark 3, picking the number of agents at each node according to the Poisson law given above provides w.h.p., the same performances than in Section 2. In particular, we have the following:

Proposition 1. *For any graph G, if m is known, then there exists a distributed procedure for choosing the initial position of agents such that, w.h.p., at any*

*round, the handshake number is up to a constant factor the same than under the
stationary regime.*

In the case where neither m nor n are known, we give another distributed solution
which is efficient in the case of almost regular graphs. Let $x \in (0,1)$ be a parameter. Algorithm DIST_BERNOULLI depicted in Fig. 3 works in rounds. *At each
round,* each node creates *only one* agent according to a Bernoulli law with parameter x. If an agent $\mathcal{A}$ is created, then it tries to make a handshake with a neighboring node using the same technique than in algorithm AGENT HANDSHAKE.
Then, the agent $\mathcal{A}$ disappears, and a new round is started.

Input: *a constant parameter x.*
repeat for ever:
  1: create an agent $\mathcal{A}$ with probability x,
  2: agent $\mathcal{A}$ tries to make a handshake with a neighboring node chosen at random,
  3: agent $\mathcal{A}$ commits suicide.

Fig. 3. DIST_BERNOULLI: code for a node v

Notice that the total number K of agents created at each round using algorithm DIST_BERNOULLI is a r.v. following a binomial distribution with parameter n and x; and its mean is $n \cdot x$ (which matches up to a constant factor the
optimal number of agents in Section 2 in the case of almost regular graphs). In
the next theorem, the handshake number is simply denoted by $H(G)$. Inspired
by the analysis of Section 2, one can prove the following:

Theorem 4. *For every graph G, at any round of algorithm* DIST_BERNOULLI,
the expected handshake number verifies:

$$\mathbb{E}(H(G)) \;=\; \sum_{v \in V}(1-x) \cdot \left[1 - \prod_{u \in \mathcal{N}(v)} \left(1 - \frac{x}{d_u}\right)\right]$$

Corollary 1. *For every almost d-regular graph G, at any round of algorithm*
DIST_BERNOULLI, *the expected handshake number verifies:* $\mathbb{E}(H(G)) = \Omega(n)$.

5 Conclusion and Open Problems

We remark that, with some minor modifications, algorithm AGENT HANDSHAKE
works as well in an asynchronous mobile agent model. It would be very interesting
to give a performance analysis of our algorithm in this case. More precisely, it
would be nice to give a theoretical analysis in the case of a weighted graph
(where each edge has a weight which models the time needed to be traversed)
and weighted agents (where each agent has a weight which models its speed).
Hereafter, we discuss some other open problems:

1. For any graph G, how fast the stationary regime is reached, if initially each
   node creates a random number of agents according to a Poisson law (or even

a Bernoulli law) with some parameter possibly depending on its degree? It would be nice to create the agents using only local information in such a way the stationary regime is reached in polylogarithmic time for any graph.

2. Using our algorithms, can we improve the results of [4]? We conjecture that the answer is yes. Moreover, we are optimistic that our technique can help improving some other related applications such us maximal matching.

Acknowledgments. I am very grateful to J.F. Marckert for helpful discussions and comments, particularly on the probabilistic analysis. His suggestions have been extremely precious for writing this paper. I would also like to thank Y. Métivier, M. Mosbah and A. Zemmari for their helpful remarks.

References

1. Métivier, Y., Saheb, N., Zemmari, A.: Randomized rendez vous. In: Mathematics and computer science: Algorithms, trees, combinatorics and probabilities. Trends in mathematics, Birkhäuser (2000) 183–194
2. Métivier, Y., Saheb, N., Zemmari, A.: Randomized local elections. Information Processing Letters **82** (2002) 313–120
3. Métivier, Y., Saheb, N., Zemmari, A.: Analysis of a randomized rendez vous algorithm. Information and Computation **184** (2003) 109–128
4. Duchon, P., Hanusse, N., Saheb, N., Zemmari, A.: Broadcast in the rendezvous model. In: 21st Symposium on Theoretical Aspects of Computer Science. Volume 2996 of LNCS. (2004) 559–570
5. Reif, J., Spirakis, P.: Real time resource allocation in distributed systems. In: 1st Symp. on Principles of Distributed Computing, ACM (1982) 84–94
6. Hibaoui, A.E., Métivier, Y., Robson, J., Saheb-Djahromi, N., Zemmari, A.: Analysis of a randomized dynamic timetable handshake algorithm. Technical Report 1402-06, LaBRI (2006)
7. Litovsky, I., Métivier, Y., Sopena, E.: Graph relabelling systems and distributed algorithms. In: Handbook of graph grammars and computing by graph transformation. Volume 3. World Scientific (1999) 1–56
8. Chalopin, J., Métivier, Y.: A bridge between the asynchronous message passing model and local computations in graphs. In: Mathematical Foundations of Computer Science. Volume 3618 of LNCS., Springer-Verlag (2005) 212–223
9. Chalopin, J., Métivier, Y.: Election and local computations on edges. In: Foundations of System Specification and Computation Structures. Volume 2987 of LNCS., Springer-Verlag (2004) 90–104
10. Hanckowiak, M., Karonski, M., Panconesi, A.: On the distributed complexity of computing maximal matchings. In: 9th Symp. on Discrete Algorithms, ACM-SIAM (1998) 219–225
11. Loväsz, L.: Random walks on graphs: a survey. Combinatorics, Paul erdos is eighty **2** (1996) 353–397
12. Barrière, L., Flocchini, P., Fraigniaud, P., Santoro, N.: Can we elect if we cannot compare? In: 15th Symp. on Parallel Algo. and Architectures, ACM (2003) 324–332
13. Chalopin, J., Godard, E., Métivier, Y., Ossamy, R.: Mobile agent algorithms versus message passing algorithms. Technical Report 1378-05, LaBRI (2005)
14. Peleg, D.: Distributed computing - A locality-sensitive approach. SIAM Monographs on discrete mathematics and applications (2000)

Improved Distributed Exploration of Anonymous Networks

Shantanu Das[1], Shay Kutten[2], and Ayelet Yifrach[2]

[1] SITE, University of Ottawa, Ottawa ON K1N6N5 Canada
shantdas@site.uottawa.ca
[2] Faculty of Industrial Engineering and Management, Technion,
Israel Institute of Technology, Haifa, Israel
Kutten@ie.technion.ac.il, ayifrach@univ.haifa.ac.il

Abstract. The problem of constructing a labeled map of an anonymous and asynchronous network is addressed. We present an algorithm that explores and maps the network by using k identical agents that have no prior knowledge of the network topology. An algorithm of Das, Flocchini, Nayak and Santoro for mapping of the network requires that n and k are co-prime. Our improved algorithm, presented here, requires at most O($m \cdot \log k$) edge traversals, while theirs uses O($m \cdot k$) edge traversals (m is the number of edges in the network). The size of the whiteboard memory needed in our algorithm is the same as that used in DFNS algorithm O($\log n$). We employ techniques utilized in solutions to the Leader Election task, and introduce a modification to resolve issues of electing first "local leaders" among adjacent candidates, which otherwise may deadlock the process.

Keywords: anonymous network, unlabeled nodes, asynchronous distributed leader election, k agents, map construction.

1 Introduction

1.1 Labeled Map Construction and Related Work

Problems of exploring an anonymous and asynchronous network have been addressed extensively [3, 8, 11-16, 23]. Mapping an anonymous network and labeling its nodes by multiple agents was presented as the *Labeled Map Construction* (*LMC*) problem by Das *et al.* in [12]. The exploration of anonymous graphs requires the agents to label the nodes. We follow earlier works [12, 14, 20] in utilizing the whiteboard model (e.g. for labeling) and introduce improvements to the process by reducing the number of edge traversals.

In exploring the network by more than one agent (e.g. see [8, 12, 15, 16]) Das *et al* employ a group of k identical agents having no knowledge of the network's topology or of one another. The agents explore the network (consisting of n nodes), each starting from an arbitrary node, and executing identical algorithms. The objectives are to construct a map of the graph, and to label each node by a unique label, both map

S. Chaudhuri et al. (Eds.): ICDCN 2006, LNCS 4308, pp. 306–318, 2006.

and labels agreed upon by all the agents. The nodes in the graph have no identities[1]. The process eliminates all the agents but one, the elected *leader*, who maps the graph and labels the nodes. Based on [4, 6, 7, 19, 24], Das *et al.*[12] show that it is not possible, in general, to solve the *LMC* problem when n (the number of nodes) and k (the number of agents) are not co-prime, i.e. $\gcd(n,k)\neq1$. By introducing the requirement that an agent has the knowledge of either n or k and also that n is co-prime to k we ensure in our algorithm that an agent would always terminate successfully, solving the *LMC* problem. The *LMC* problem is closely related to other problems, such as *Leader Election* ([1, 2, 18, 20, 22, 28]), *Rendezvous* ([21, 23]) and *Labeling* ([17]). Solving one of these problems leads to solving all the others as well.

We consider a distributed solution to the *LMC* problem, as in [12], using k asynchronous agents exploring an undirected simple graph. A lower layer service (*traversal algorithm*) is used to transfer agents from one node to another. The traversal algorithm has rules for transfering the agent to another node, once called upon by the agent. Section 3.1 and [20] describe the interface between the agent algorithm and the lower layer service.

1.2 Our Results

Our solution of the *LMC* problem is deterministic and requires at most $O(m \cdot \log k)$ edge traversals compared to $O(m \cdot k)$ edge traversals in the algorithm of [12].

We modify techniques from solutions to leader election problem to resolve mistaken identification between neighboring candidates. Previous algorithms achieve efficiency by competing between neighboring candidates first, and between the far-away candidates only when a few remain. Such methods may deadlock in anonymous networks as nearby candidates may be indistinguishable. The main modification presented here is the addition of two search rounds beyond the per-phase used by the previous algorithm [20]. We show that this ensures that an agent encounters all nearby distinguishable agents and as a result, the algorithm solves the problem using at most $O(m \cdot \log k)$ edge traversals. We assume that an agent has the knowledge of either n or k and it also knows that n is co-prime to k. This ensures that an agent in our algorithm always detects termination.

The rest of the paper is organized as follow: In section 2 we describe the problem and the model for the algorithm, in section 3 we describe the full algorithm and finally, section 4 we present the proof of correctness and complexity analysis.

2 Model and Problem

The network is modeled as a graph $G= (V, E)$ with $|V|=n$ and $|E|=m$. The network is asynchronous, i.e. it takes a finite but unpredictable time to traverse an edge of the network. We assume that the edges of the network obey the FIFO discipline.

There are k mobile agents located in distinct nodes of the network. An agent is a mobile entity that can execute an algorithm and move through the edges of the graph. The operations of an agent at a node are atomic. Thus, only one agent can be active

---

[1] A similar situation that is solvable by this algorithm is one where the nodes do have identities but the identities are not unique. This case is not explicitly discussed.

(operating) at a node at any given time. An agent also has a storage that moves with it. Initially, the agents do not have any knowledge about the graph or its topology (except for the knowledge of n or k).

Each node contains a *whiteboard* - a memory area of the node used by agents to communicate with each other. An agent visiting a node v can write to the whiteboard of node v and also read any information written previously by another agent that visited node v.

The nodes and the agents in the graph are anonymous: they have no distinct identities. The edges incident to the nodes are labeled with port numbers providing a local orientation among the edges incident at a node. This allows the traversal algorithm at a node to distinguish between the edges incident to the node.

Formally, we re-state the *LMC* problem as follows: given an instance (G, λ, p) where $G(V,E)$ is a graph, λ is an edge-labeling defined on G, and $p: V \rightarrow \{0,1\}$ is a placement function defining the initial location of the $k = |\{v \in V : p(v) = 1\}|$ agents, the *LMC* problem is said to have been solved when one of the agents, designated as the "elected" agent, obtains a uniquely labeled map of the graph.

3 Presentation of the Algorithm

Our *LMC* algorithm proceeds in phases. The traversal algorithm is invoked by the agents several times in each phase. It moves an agent from one node to another, based on the agent's label. All agents' labels are initially identical but are later refined to distinguish agents from one another. Nodes and edges visited by an agent are marked with the agent's label (unless already marked by the same or larger label). An agent *territory* is the sub graph of G consisting of the nodes and edges marked by the agent.

3.1 Traversal Algorithm

The traversal algorithm used by the agents is a distributed version of the depth-first-search (*DFS*) algorithm ([25, 26] and its (serial but) distributed version [5, 9, 20]).

Each invocation of the DFS algorithm consists of the label of the agent, which is used for marking the ports of the nodes during the execution of the algorithm. Simultaneous invocations occur when more than one agent traverses the graph at a given time. As opposed to [20], not all are distinguishable. Hence, when an agent A enters a node v through an unvisited edge and one or more ports of node v are marked with A's label the DFS algorithm acts as if agent A visited this node. These ports may have been marked by the execution invoked by agent A or by an execution invoked by a different agent B with an identical label.

The operations agent A can execute at a node v (as a lower-level system call):

Go-To-Next(): Sends the agent to the next node to be visited.
Go-Territory(): Sends the agent to the next node to be visited in the A's territory.
Chase(): Sends agent A through the last port from which an agent (in the same phase) was sent (excluding a port which an agent in the same phase marked as *back edge*).

3.2   Informal Overview of the Algorithm

The message complexity improvement achieved over [12] is due to the usage of phases. This bounds the number of graph traversals through node v to $O(\log k)$. In each phase, an agent searches to find another agent in the same phase so that they can merge and become one agent in a higher phase. As we go to higher phases, fewer agents remain (there are at most $k \cdot 2^{-p+1}$ agents in phase $p>0$). The search is performed by agents, that annex nodes by writing the label of the agent to the node's whiteboard.

Phase 0 is different than all the phases that follow. Its goal is to initialize a label for the agent. An agent A wakes up and traverses the graph marking every unvisited node by turning on a "visited" flag in the node and destroying any sleeping agent in the node. Agent A maintains a node-counter which is increased by 1 after each node flagging. By the end of phase 0, each node of the graph would have counted by exactly one agent. After phase 0, agent A constructs a label out of its node-counter, its phase and the number of agents A annexed (at this point the phase equals 0 and the last field equals 1). Agent A then raises its phase to 1. Due to the assumption that $\gcd(n,k)=1$, there must be at least two agents with different labels after phase 0.

In all higher phases, the status of agent A can be in one of the following:

(i)   *Annexing status*: agent A tries to annex to its territory all the nodes (in lower phases) or to find another agent in the same phase.

(ii) *Chasing status*: agent A chases some other agent B in the same phase but with a lower label. Agent A attempts to reach B and merge, creating a single agent in the next phase.

(iii) *Candidate status*: agent A is waiting at a node to be merged or annexed.

Agent A in *annexing* status traverses the graph looking to encounter other agents. During the traversal, agent A annexes nodes by writing its label to the node's whiteboard. When agent A traverses a node that was traversed by another agent, agent A compares the label written in the node with its own and decides how to act. Agent A ignores labels of lower phase but becomes a candidate when the label is of a higher phase. However, if the label L is of the same phase then agent A will chase the agent that labeled the node if L is lexicographically smaller than its own label. On the other hand, agent A becomes a candidate if label L in the node is lexicographically bigger than its own label. When agent A encounters an agent B waiting in a node (B is in a *candidate* status), A will annex B if agent B is in a lower phase or *merge* with B if agent B is in the same phase. Agent A raises its phase only by a *merging*. When an agent recognizes it annexed all n nodes (or all k agents, if it knows k), it is the only agent left. At that time, it declares itself a leader. The leader traverses the graph, labeling the nodes with unique names and constructing a labeled map of the graph.

Definition. *Agents* A *and* B *are adjacent agents if there exists an edge connecting a node* v *labeled by* A *and a node* u *labeled by* B.

Our Modification. We now outline the modification (compared to [20]) that we introduce in order to deal with adjacent agents with the same label. This is the action an agent takes when it fails to merge with an agent in its own phase during its annexing traversal. First, if agent A completes an annexing traversal without encountering any agent at all (even in lower phases) then it enters the *candidate* status. Note that in [20] each agent has a unique label so when agent A completes an annexing traversal it either becomes a leader, or gets destroyed (at a node labeled with a higher phase or during the processes of creating an agent in a higher phase).

However, in our algorithm, if agent A encountered (and thus annexed) one or more agents in lower phases (thus A's label changed) A should take an action. If agent A updates its label during the traversal the nodes it already traversed would not be updated. If one of those nodes v is adjacent to a node marked by an agent B with the same label A had when it traversed v then A would not notice B (although the updated label of A is now different than that of B). Furthermore, when agent A during the current round enters a node labeled by it with the former label it would act as if it entered a node of another agent and start a chase. Hence, agent A cannot update its label during the traversal and should take an action after the termination of the current traversal. Notice that if agent A took any of the following options, that would fail to solve the problem:

- If agent A enters *candidate* status then this might have ended in a deadlock (see figure 1).
- If agent A raises its phase (without merging with an agent in the same phase) then the number of phases could be as high as $(k\text{-}1)$, thereby increasing the complexity of our algorithm.
- If agent A starts another annexing traversal (without raising its phase) then this might again end-up in a deadlock (see figure 2).

We solved the problem by the following mechanism, for which we prove that no deadlock arises and the complexity is still $O(m \cdot \log k)$. Let round I be the annexing traversal described above for a phase. We add two additional traversals per phase, termed *round II* and *round III*.

Round II: Agent A informs the nodes it annexed in *round I* about A's new label.

Round III: Agent A starts a new annexing traversal (the same as in *round I*). We will show that in this round the agent can only encounter agents from the same phase. An agent ends this round either by merging with another agent in the same phase (and thus starting a new phase) or, by becoming a candidate at a node.

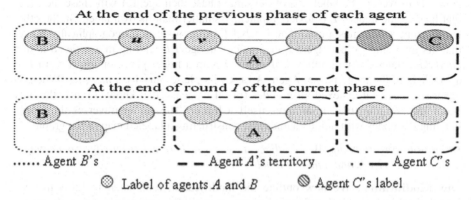

Fig. 1. Agents A and B have the same label at the beginning of phase p, hence when they visit nodes u and v during round I they do not know of one another. Agent C in phase q $(q{<}p)$ is annexed by agent A during round I. After round I, agents A and B have different labels. Thus, had A changed its status to candidate by the end of round I the algorithm would have had entered a deadlock (agent A waits for B and vice versa).

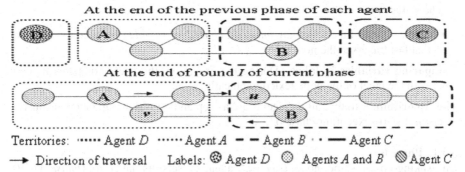

Territories: ······ Agent D ······ Agent A − − Agent B · · — Agent C
—→ Direction of traversal   Labels: ⊕ Agent D ⊗ Agents A and B ◎ Agent C

Fig. 2. Agents A and B have the same label at the beginning of phase p. Hence, during round I they cannot distinguish between themselves, and thus do not know of one another. During round I, agents C and D in phase q ($q<p$) are annexed by agent B and agent A respectively. After round I, agents A and B have different labels. Thus, had A and B started another annexing traversal without performing round II before that, then B would have had started chasing A from node v and A would have had started chasing B from node u. This would have had caused the algorithm to deadlock.

3.3 A More Formal Description

The data held by the agent
The label of the agent:

- *phase(A)* – The phase of agent A.
- *nodesAnnexed(A)* – The number of nodes marked at phase 0 by agent A itself and by the agents that were annexed by agent A.
- *agentsAnnexed(A)* – The number of agents annexed by agent A, including itself.

The status of the agent:

- *Status* – One of the following: *annexing, chasing, or candidate.*

Temporary variables:

- *tname(A)* – The value of *tname(A)* accumulates the values of *tname* of the agents that were annexed by agent A (during *round I* of the current phase). This value is initialized to *nodesAnnexed(A)* at the beginning of each phase.
- *agentsCounter(A)* – The value of *agentsCounter(A)* accumulates the values of *agentsCounter* of the agents that were annexed by agent A (during *round I* of the current phase). This value is initialized to 1 at the beginning of phase 0 and to *agentsAnnexed(A)* at the beginning of every other phase.
- *nodesCounter(A)* – The number of nodes annexed by agent A (initialized to 1).

Data written to a node v. The label of the node is equal to the label and the status of the agent that annexed it (*phase(v)* , *nodesAnnexed(v), agentsAnnexed(v)*).

The name of the node:

- *nodeName(v)* – The sequence number of the node (assigned by the last annexing agent).
- *visitFlag(v)* – Indicates whether the node was marked by an agent in phase 0.

The status of the node:

- *Status* – One of the following *annexed, chased,* or *round2* (assigned by the agent that last traversed the node).

Comparing variables in labels. During the execution, the agent compares its own label with the label of the node lexicographically.

The Algorithm. Initially, all the agents are asleep and on waking up (spontaneously), an agent A starts executing Phase 0.

3.3.1 Phase 0
On waking-up in some node (say u),[2] agent A sets its label to (*phase(A)* =0, *nodesAnnexed(A)*=0, *agentsAnnexed(A)* =1) and sets *agentsCounter(A)* to 1. Agent A marks node u as visited by turning on *visitFlag(u)*. Agent A then starts traversing the graph, using the traversal algorithm. When A reaches a node v it acts as follow:

- If v is unmarked then *(1)* A increments its *nodesCounter(A)* by 1; *(2)* marks node v as visited by turning on *visitFlag(v)*; *(3)* if a sleeping agent exists in the node then agent A destroys the agent; and *(4)* continues the graph traversal.
- If v is marked *visited* then A continues the traversal. Recall that the traversal algorithm acts as if A has been in node v before (which may or may not be the case), so it returns to the node from which A was last sent to node v and continues the traversal.

Upon termination of the traversal of phase 0, A raises its phase to 1 (*phase(A)* ← 1), sets values of nodesAnnexed (*nodesAnnexed(A)←nodesCounter(A)*), agentsAnnexed (*agentsAnnexed(A)← agentsCounter(A)*) and its status to *annexing*. If n is known and *nodesAnnexed(A)=n* or k is known and *agentsAnnexed(A)= k* (k=1) then agent A detects the successful termination and performs the *leader procedure* (described below). Otherwise, agent A proceeds to *Round I*.

3.3.2 Round I
Agent A starts an annexing process by starting a graph traversal with the label (*phase(A)*, *nodesAnnexed(A)*, *agentsAnnexed(A)*) and the *annexing* status. The following rules apply:

Whenever an annexing or a chasing agent A reaches some node v or raises its phase at some node v, agent A acts according to its label as follows:

Either annexing or chasing status
- If there is an agent C labeled (*phase(C)*, *nodesAnnexed(C)*, *agentsAnnexed(C)*) waiting in node v (as a candidate) then,
  • If *phase(A)* > *phase(C)* then agent A annexes agent C by adding the value of Cs *tname* and *agentsCounter* to its own *tname* and *agentsCounter* respectively. Agent A then continues the traversal. Agent A doesn't update its label till the end of the traversal. Thus agent A uses the variables *tname* and *agentsCounter* to collect the data from the annexed agents.

---

[2] We use a name such as u for the convenience of a description; note that the algorithm does not have an access to unique names such as u or A.

- • If $phase(A) = phase(C)$ then agent A merges with agent C to create a single agent B such that $phase(B) = phase(A)+1$, $nodesAnnexed(B) = tname(A) + tname(C)$ and $agentsAnnexed(B) = agentsCounter(A) + agentsCounter(C)$, with temporary variables $tname(B) = nodesAnnexed(B)$, $agentsCounter(B) = agentsAnnexed(B)$.
  - ○ If n is known and $nodesAnnexed(B)=n$ or k is known and $agentsAnnexed(B)= k$ then B detects the successful termination and performs the *leader procedure* (described below).
  - ○ Else: Agent B aborts its current traversal and starts *Round I*.
- • If $phase(A) < phase(C)$ then A changes its status to *candidate* and waits at node v (aborting its traversal algorithm).
- Otherwise agent A acts according to its status and label as follow:

Annexing status

- If the traversal has terminated and v is in the *annexed* status:
  - • If A annexed one or more agents during the traversal (that is $tname(A)>$ $nodesAnnexed(A)$) then agent A updates its label: $nodesAnnexed(A)\leftarrow tname(A)$ and $agentsAnnexed(A)\leftarrow agentsCounter(A)$.(This can happen only in round I)
    - ○ If n is known and $nodesAnnexed(A)=n$ or k is known and $agentsAnnexed(A)= k$ then agent A detects the successful termination and performs the *leader procedure* (described below).
    - ○ Else agent A proceeds to *Round II* (described below).
  - • In all the other cases A changes its status to *candidate* and waits at node v.

- If $phase(A) > phase(v)$ then A performs the *Annexing procedure* (described below) and then continues the graph traversal.

- If $phase(A) < phase(v)$ then A changes its status to *candidate* and waits at node v (aborting A's traversal algorithm).

- If $phase(A) = phase(v)$
  - • If v is in the *chased* status, agent A changes its status to *candidate* and waits at node v (aborting A's traversal algorithm).
  - • If v is in the *annexed* or *round2* status, agent A acts as follows:
    - ○ If $(nodesAnnexed(A),agentsAnnexed(A))=(nodesAnnexed(v),agentsAnnexed(v))$ and node v is with status *round2* then A performs the *Annexing procedure* (described below) and then continues the graph traversal.
    - ○ If $(nodesAnnexed(A),agentsAnnexed(A))=(nodesAnnexed(v),agentsAnnexed(v))$ and node v is with status *annexed* then agent A continues the traversal. Note that during this phase either agent A or an identical agent to A has visited node v before; in both cases, the edge through which agent A entered node v is now marked *back edge* for the label of agent A.
    - ○ If $(nodesAnnexed(A),agentsAnnexed(A))<(nodesAnnexed(v),agentsAnnexed(v))$ then agent A changes its status to *candidate* and waits at node v (aborting A's traversal algorithm). (Note that in [20] the agent is destroyed, here the label of the candidate is important to maintain at least one distinguishable agent).
    - ○ If $(nodesAnnexed(A),agentsAnnexed(A))>(nodesAnnexed(v),agentsAnnexed(v))$ then agent A *(1)* changes its status to *chasing*; *(2)* aborts the current traversal; *(3)* starts a new graph traversal in which it acts as described in (see section "chasing status").

Chasing status: When agent A labeled $(phase(A)$, $nodesAnnexed(A)$, $agentsAnnexed(A))$ in the *chasing* status, enters a node v labeled $(phase(v)$, $nodesAnnexed(v)$, $agentsAnnexed(v))$ with no agent in status *candidate* waiting at node v, agent A acts as follows:

- If v is in the *annexed* status and $phase(A) = phase(v)$ then A *(1)* changes node v's status to *chased*; *(2)* A then continues the graph traversal.
- In all the other cases: A changes its status to *candidate* and waits at node v (aborting A's traversal algorithm).

Note that the case where an agent in status *candidate* is waiting at node v was handled in the beginning of this paragraph in section "Either annexing or chasing status".

3.3.3 Round II

Agent A starts a traversal of its own territory (using operation *Go-Territory()* as explained earlier). Whenever agent A reaches node v:

- If node v is in status *annexed* and in the same phase as A then agent A assigns its own label to the label of the node and assigns the node the status *round2*.
- Else agent A changes its status to *candidate* and waits at node v (aborting A's traversal algorithm).

At the end of the territory traversal (if not aborted), agent A proceeds to round *III*.

3.3.4 Round III

Agent A starts an annexing process by starting a graph traversal with the label $(phase(A)$, $nodesAnnexed(A)$, $agentsAnnexed(A))$ and the *annexing* status and follows the rules applied in *Round I*. However, as we show later, an agent at the end of this round will not re-enter *Round II*.

Annexing procedure: Agent A annexes node v by assigning A's label to node v's label and changing node v's status to *annexed*.

Leader procedure: When A detects a successful termination, agent A acts as follows:

(1) Agent A sets $nodesCounter \leftarrow 0$

(2) Agent A invokes an execution of the graph traversal (using operation *Go-To-Next()* as explained in 3.1) to label every node with a unique name and to construct a map of the graph. Agent A labels node v by: *(a)* Incrementing the $nodesCounter$ by 1; *(b)* Naming node v by setting $nodeName(v) \leftarrow nodesCounter$.

The agent uses the labels of the nodes and the marks on the edges (the ports of the nodes) to construct a map of the graph.

4 Complexity and Correctness Proofs

Due to lack of space the proofs were omitted and can be found in http://iew3.technion.ac.il/Home/Users/kutten.html#part4

4.1 Correctness

All the lemmas concerning correctness are based on the assumption that $\gcd(n,k) = 1$ and the FIFO discipline behavior of the messages sent over the edges.

Definitions

(1) A *root* is the node from which an agent started the current graph traversal, if it is in the *annexing* mode.

(2) A *chase* is the action where an agent A in phase p changes its status to *chasing* as a result of entering a node labeled by some agent B, or agent A is in a *chasing* status, and continues to follow the traversal of agent B. We call agent A the *chaser* and agent B the *chased*.

(3) A *chase-route* is a sub-graph that consists of the nodes and edges traversed by the same chaser. The node at which the chaser ended the chase is termed as the *end* of the chase-route and the other brink of the chase-route is termed as the *beginning* of the chase-route. The chase-route is a directed path from the *beginning* to the *end*.

(4) A *sequence of chase-routes* is a maximal directed path in a sub-graph formed by the union of sub-graphs of chase-routes from the same phase, where the last node of each chase-route is a node that also belongs to another chase-route in the sequence.

Lemma 1. At any time after phase 0, when there are more than one agent, there are at least two agents with different labels (*phase, nodesAnnexed, agentsAnnexed*).

Lemma 2. The number of agents that ever reach phase $p > 0$ in an execution of the algorithm is at most $k \cdot 2^{-P+1}$.

Lemma 3. When agent A starts to chase agent B, agent A can enter only nodes labeled with the same phase of A or higher.

Lemma 4. When agent A chases agent B, agent A traverses a simple path in the graph, except possibly for the last traversed node.

Observation 1. If the last node v of the chase-route created by some chaser A creates a simple circle in the chase-route then the chased agent B became a candidate at v or merged with another candidate agent that waited at node v.

Lemma 5. A maximal sequence of chase-routes forms a simple path except possibly for the last traversed node.

Lemma 6. When agent A starts a chase after agent B in phase p, eventually, an agent in phase $p+1$ exists.

Lemma 7. In rounds *II* and *III*, agent A finds only nodes labeled with the same phase p or higher.

Lemma 8. If there is more than one agent at the highest phase p, then eventually there will be a chase in phase p.

Lemma 9. If there is more than one agent at a certain phase p, then an agent eventually raises its phase from p to $p+1$.

Lemma 10. In every execution of the algorithm, one and only one agent is left.

4.2 Complexity

The message complexity of an algorithm L acting on a graph G is the maximum number of edge traversals over all executions of L on G.

Lemma 11. The total number of edge traversals made by all agents in a given phase is $O(m)$.

Lemma 12. The total number of edge traversals performed in an execution is $O(m \cdot log k)$.

Bit Complexity: In our algorithm, the graph map is not carried by the agents but is constructed by the elected agent. The information carried by the agents during the election process consists of *phase(A)*, *agentsAnnexed(A)*, and *agentsCounter(A)*, each of size $log_2 k$, and *nodesAnnexed(A)*, *tname(A)*, *nodesCounter(A)* of size $O(log\ n)$. The size of *status* is a constant. The total number of edge traversals during the algorithm is $O(m \cdot log\ k)$. Thus, the bit complexity during the election is $O(m \cdot log k \cdot log n)$.

In [12] the map is carried by each agent thus the message size is $O(m \cdot log\ n)$ and $log n$ is the size needed to store the identity of a node or an edge. The agent traverses the graph using the map it carries. The total number of edge traversals during the algorithm is $O(m \cdot k)$. Thus, the bit complexity during the execution of the algorithm is $O(m^2 \cdot k \cdot log n)$. This bit complexity can be reduced to $O(m \cdot k)$ by marking the ports (with 'T' and 'NT') instead of carrying a map. The method of carrying the map by the agents at all times is more robust than the method of marking the port of the node.

Time Complexity: The time complexity in our algorithm is measured by the time it took the leader agent to traverse the graph in each one of the phases it passed. Thus, the time complexity of the algorithm is $O(m \cdot log k)$.

In the algorithm of Das *et al*, the time complexity is given by the total number of edge-traversals made by all agents together and this was shown to be $O(m \cdot k)$.

5   Conclusion

We used the method of separating the algorithm into two layers - the agent algorithm and the lower layer traversal. The traversal algorithm used here is the DFS algorithm intended for the family of undirected networks. It is possible to generalize the results to other families of networks by using other traversal algorithms. As we showed here for DFS- the fact that two identical agents may visit the same node does not cause the traversal to get "confused". If the algorithm is used for other families of graphs by using other traversals, care must be taken to make sure these traversals do not get "confused" when the routes of identical agents collide.

We addressed instances that are solvable because n and k are co-prime. Recall that there are other solvable cases [19, 24]. The algorithm can be used, with some modifications, to follow the ideas of [24] and solve some other possible cases.

Our algorithm constructs a map only when it can detect a successful termination since we included the map construction in the leader procedure. If desired, it is possible to have every agent construct a map as it goes. This will increase the bit complexity. However, it will ensure that a map is constructed by the last remaining agent also in the case that n and k are co-prime, but neither n nor k is known.

Finally, the model of the algorithm is based on the FIFO behavior of the edges. Communication protocols that do not guarantee the FIFO discipline do exist. Hence, it may be interesting to adapt our algorithm to deal with non-FIFO behavior.

References

1. Afek, Y., Gafni, E.: Time and Message bounds for Election in Synchronous and Asynchronous Complete Networks. SICOMP, Vol.20 No.2 (1991) 376-394.
2. Afek, Y., Matias, Y.: Elections in Anonymous Networks. Information and Computation, Vol. 113, Issue 2 (1994) 312 – 330.
3. Albers, S., Henzinger, M.R.: Exploring Unknown Environments. SIAM Journal on Computing, Vol. 29, No. 4 (2000) 1164-1188.
4. Angluin, D.: Local and global properties in networks of processors. Proc. ACM STOC (1980) 82–93.
5. Awerbuch, B.: A new distributed depth-first-search algorithm. Information Processing Letters, Vol. 20, No. 3 (1985) 147-150.
6. Barriere, L., Flocchini, P., Fraigniaud, P., Santoro, N.: Electing a leader among anonymous mobile agents in anonymous networks with sense-of-direction. Technical Report LRI-1310, Univ. Paris-Sud, France (2002).
7. Barriere, L., Flocchini, P., Fraigniaud, P., Santoro, N.: Rendezvous and Election of Mobile Agents: Impact of Sense of Direction. Theory of Computing Systems (2005).
8. Bender, M.A., Slonim, D.K.: The Power of Team Exploration: Two Robots Can Learn Unlabeled Directed Graphs. Proc. FOCS'94 (1994) 75-85.
9. Chlamtac, I., Kutten, S.: Tree-based broadcasting in multihop radio networks. IEEE Transactions on Computers, Vol. 36, No. 10 (1987) 1209 - 1223.
10. Cidon, I.: Yet another distributed depth-first-search algorithm. Information Processing Letters, Vol. 26, Issue 6 (1988) 301-305.
11. Cohen, R., Fraigniaud, P., Ilcinkas, D., Korman, A., Peleg, D.: Label-Guided Graph Exploration by a Finite Automaton. Proc. ICALP 2005 (2005) 335-346.
12. Das, S., Flocchini, P., Nayak, A., Santoro, N.: Distributed Exploration of an Unknown Graph. Proc. SIROCCO 2005 (2005) 99-114.
13. Dessmark, A., Pelc, A.: Optimal graph exploration without good maps. Theoretical Computer Science, Vol. 326 (2004) 343-362.
14. Diks, K., Fraigniaud, P., Kranakis, E., Pelc, A.: Tree exploration with little memory. Journal of Algorithms, Vol. 51 (2004) 38-63.
15. Fraigniaud, P., Gasieniec, L., Kowalski, D., Pelc, A.: Collective tree exploration. Proc. 6th Latin American Theoretical Informatics Symp. (2004) 141-151.
16. Fraigniaud, P., Ilcinkas, D., Rajsbaum, S., Tixeuil, S.: Space Lower Bounds for Graph Exploration via Reduced Automata. Proc. SIROCCO 2005 (2005) 140-154.
17. Fraigniaud, P., Pelc, A., Peleg, D., Perennes, S.: Assigning labels in unknown anonymous networks. Proc. ACM PODC 2000 (2000) 101–111.
18. Gallager, R.G., Humblet, P.M., Spira, P.M.: A Distributed Algorithm for Minimum-Weight Spanning Trees. ACM TOPLAS, Vol. 5 No. 1 (1983) 66-77.
19. Kameda, T., Yamashita, M.: Computing on Anonymous Networks: Part I-Characterizing the Solvable Cases. IEEE TPDS, Vol. 7, No. 1 (1996) 69-89.
20. Korach, E., Kutten, S., Moran, S.: A Modular Technique for the Design of Efficient Distributed Leader Finding Algorithms. ACM TOPLAS, Vol. 12, No. 1 (1990) 84-101.

318   S. Das, S. Kutten, and A. Yifrach

21. Kranakis, E., Santoro, N., Sawchuk, C., Krizanc, D.: Mobile Agent Rendezvous in a Ring. Proc. 23rd IEEE ICDCS'03 (2003) 592.
22. LeLann, G.: Distributed Systems - Towards a Formal Approach. Proc. IFIP Congress (1977) 155-160.
23. Panaite, P., Pelc, A.: Exploring unknown undirected graphs. Proc. 9th ACM-SIAM symposium on Discrete algorithms (1998) 316-322.
24. Sakamoto, N.: Comparison of initial conditions for distributed algorithms on anonymous networks. Proc. ACM PODC 1999 (1999) 173-179.
25. Sharir, M.: A strong-connectivity algorithm and its application in data flow analysis. Computers and Mathematics with Applications, Vol.7, No.1 (1981) 67-72.
26. Tarjan, R.E.: Depth first search and linear graph algorithms. SICOMP, Vol. 1, No. 2 (1972) 146-160.
27. Tel, G.: Introduction to Distributed Algorithms. Cambridge University Press (1994) 198-213.
28. Villadangos, J., Cordoba, A., Farina, F., Prieto, M.: Efficient Leader Election in Complete Networks. Proc. 13th PDP'05 (2005) 138-143.
29. Yifrach A.: Improved Distributed Exploration of Anonymous Networks. MSc Thesis, Faculty of Industrial Engineering and Management, Technion Israel Institute of Technology, Haifa, Israel (2006).

The Complexity of Updating Multi-writer Snapshot Objects

Hagit Attiya*, Faith Ellen**, and Panagiota Fatourou***

Abstract. This paper proves $\Omega(m)$ lower bounds on the step complexity of UPDATE operations for partitioned implementations of m-component multi-writer snapshot objects from base objects of any type. These are implementations in which each base object is only modifed by processes performing UPDATE operations to one specific component. In particular, we show that any space-optimal implementation of a multi-writer snapshot object from historyless objects is partitioned. This work extends a similar lower bound by Israeli and Shirazi for implementations of m-component single-writer snapshot objects from single-writer registers.

1 Introduction

An important problem in shared memory distributed systems is to obtain a consistent view of the contents of the memory while updates to the memory are happening concurrently. This problem can be formalized as the implementation of a snapshot object that can be accessed concurrently by different processes. A *snapshot object* [1] consists of a set of $m > 1$ components, each capable of storing a value. Processes can perform two different types of operations: UPDATE any individual component to have a specific value or atomically SCAN to obtain the values of all the components. A *single-writer* snapshot object is a restricted version in which there are the same number of updaters as components and only process p_i can UPDATE the i'th component. In a *multi-writer* snapshot object, there is no restriction on which processes may UPDATE a component.

It is often much easier to design fault-tolerant algorithms for asynchronous systems and prove them correct if one can think of the shared memory as a snapshot object, rather than as a collection of individual objects. This is why researchers have spent a great deal of effort on finding efficient implementations of snapshot objects from *base* objects that are provided in real systems, like registers or swap objects.

Many implementations of snapshot objects are known, most of them from registers [1,2,3,4,9,13,14], and several from stronger base objects [16,17]. However,

---

* The Technion, Israel, supported by the Israel Science Foundation (grant number 953/06).
** University of Toronto, Canada, supported by the Natural Sciences and Engineering Research Council of Canada, a Lady Davis Fellowship, and the Scalable Synchronization Research Group of SUN Microsystems, Inc.
*** University of Ioannina, Greece, supported by the Greek Ministry of Education's E.P.E.A.E.K. II programme for studies in informatics.

S. Chaudhuri et al. (Eds.): ICDCN 2006, LNCS 4308, pp. 319–330, 2006.
© Springer-Verlag Berlin Heidelberg 2006

320   H. Attiya, F. Ellen, and P. Fatourou

only a few lower bounds on the complexity of implementing snapshot objects
are known.

Jayanti, Tan, and Toueg [18] proved that any implementation of an m-
component single-writer snapshot object from historyless and resettable consensus objects requires at least $m - 1$ objects and SCANS take at least $m - 1$
steps. For multi-writer snapshot objects implemented from historyless objects,
Fatourou, Fich and Ruppert [7] improved the space lower bound to m, which
is optimal, since there are implementations from m registers. More importantly,
they proved that in any space-optimal implementation of a binary snapshot object from historyless objects shared by $n > m + 1$ processes, the worst case step
complexity of SCAN is in $\Omega(mn)$, which is asymptotically tight. This proof relies
on a number of structural lemmas which show that any space-optimal snapshot
implementation from historyless objects has a special form.

Israeli and Shirazi [15] proved a tight $\Omega(m)$ lower bound on the step complexity of UPDATE, for implementations of m-component single-writer snapshot
objects, under the assumption that only single-writer registers are used. No lower
bounds were known for the step complexity of an UPDATE operation when other
base objects, in particular, multi-writer registers, can be used.

In this paper, we prove that the worst case step complexity of UPDATE in
any implementation of an n-process m-component multi-writer snapshot object
from $m < n$ registers or $m < n - 1$ historyless objects is in $\Omega(m)$. We begin
by extending Fatourou, Fich, and Ruppert's structural lemmas [6,7] for space-
optimal implementations to show that any such implementation is *partitioned*.
Partitioned implementations can use any number of base objects, but each base
object can only be modified by processes performing UPDATES to one specific
component. Then we prove that, for any partitioned implementation of a multi-
writer snapshot object implemented from base objects of *any* type, the worst
case complexity of UPDATE is in $\Omega(m)$. We do this in two ways.

First, we observe that, if $n \geq 2m$, then any n-process partitioned implementation of an m-component multi-writer snapshot also gives an implementation
of an m-component single-writer snapshot object, shared by m updaters and m
scanners, from single-writer registers. Then the result follows from Israeli and
Shirazi's lower bound [15]. Their proof and, hence, this result, requires that the
number of possible values for each component is infinite.

Secondly, we give a direct proof of the lower bound for partitioned implementations. This proof even applies to binary snapshot objects (i.e. when each
component is only a single bit). Moreover, it does not rely on the existence of a
large number of processes: it suffices that there are three processes, two which
can perform UPDATES and one which can perform SCAN. This shows that it is the
number of components in a snapshot object, not the number of processes, that
is responsible for UPDATES taking a long time in partitioned implementations.

The best known multi-writer snapshot implementation is partitioned [1] and
has $O(mn)$ step complexity for both UPDATE and SCAN. There are also a number
of implementations which are not partitioned and have $o(m)$ step complexity
for UPDATE. They show that the lower bounds do not hold if the restriction to

partitioned implementations is removed. For example, there is a trivial implementation of a multi-writer snapshot object with $O(1)$ steps for UPDATE and SCAN. The implementation uses a single object that contains a *view* of the snapshot object: a SCAN simply reads this view; an UPDATE of component i atomically reads the view and modifies component i of the view.

Jayanti [16] uses an f-array to implement a multi-writer snapshot object with $O(\log m)$ steps for an UPDATE and one step for a SCAN. It uses $m - 1$ LL/SC objects, each containing a view, arranged in a binary tree. This implementation is not partitioned, since a process doing an UPDATE follows a path to the root from the leaf corresponding to the component, performing SC operations as it goes. The root contains the current values of all m components, so a SCAN can simply read the root.

Another implementation of a snapshot object has $O(1)$ steps for an UPDATE and an unbounded (but finite) number of steps for a SCAN. The implementation follows Kirousis, Spirakis, and Tsigas [19], and uses an $m \times \infty$ array of registers. Each row contains values written to a specific component of the snapshot object. The scanners also maintain a pointer, telling the updaters the column in which to put their value. An UPDATE to component i reads the pointer and writes its value in the corresponding place in row i of the array. A SCAN does fetch&inc on the pointer and then, for each component i, reads backwards in row i from the current value of the pointer (towards the beginning of the array) until it finds a non-empty entry. This implementation says that an $\Omega(m)$ lower bound does not exist if scanners can write to the same register or there is only one scanner, which can write to a single-writer register.

Fatourou and Kallimanis [8] recently presented two implementations of m-component multi-writer snapshot objects that support a single scanner and any number of updaters. One of these uses $m + 1$ registers and has $O(m^2)$ step complexity for both SCAN and UPDATE. Except for a single-writer register used by the scanner, this implementation is partitioned. The other implementation uses an unbounded number of registers, but has $O(m)$ step complexity for both SCAN and UPDATE. It is not partitioned. They also prove that any implementation from registers which supports a single-scanner must use at least m registers and the step complexity of SCAN is in $\Omega(m^2)$ if the implementation is space-optimal.

Riany, Shavit and Touitou [21] implement an m-component single-writer snapshot object, from $O(m^2)$ LL/SC objects. In their implementation, UPDATE has constant step complexity and SCAN has $O(m)$ step complexity. Their algorithm is based on a single-scanner snapshot object, which is a simplification of the algorithm by Kirousis, Spirakis, and Tsigas [19]. In their multi-scanner algorithm, scanners collaborate in collecting a view in order to reduce work and to guarantee that returned views are consistent. This algorithm is not partitioned: Although the updaters write only to a single object associated with their component, scanners write to multiple shared objects.

Jayanti [17] implements an m-component multi-writer snapshot object, with the same step complexity, from $O(mn^2)$ CAS objects. This algorithm also starts with a single-writer single-scanner snapshot object, and extends it in two steps. The algorithm is not partitioned.

2   The Model

We use a standard model of asynchronous shared-memory systems [5,20]. In this model, a set of n deterministic processes $P = \{p_1, \ldots, p_n\}$ communicate by accessing shared base objects. The system is totally asynchronous, so the order in which operations are performed by processes is assumed to be controlled by an adversarial scheduler. Algorithms must work correctly regardless of the schedule the adversary chooses.

A *configuration* is a complete description of the system at some point in time. It is comprised of the internal state of each process and the state of each shared object. A *step* of a process consists of a single operation accessing a shared object, the response to that operation, and some local computation that may cause the internal state of the process to change.

An *execution* starting from a configuration C is a sequence of steps, in which the steps performed by each process follow the algorithm for that process (starting from its state in C) and the responses to the operations performed on each object are in accordance with its specification (and the value stored in the object at configuration C). A configuration C is *reachable* if there is a finite execution that results in C starting from some initial configuration. An execution is *solo* if every step is performed by the same process.

An object is *historyless* [10] if all its non-trivial operations (i.e. operations which might change the value of the object) overwrite one another. The most familiar historyless object is a *register*, which is accessed either by a trivial *read* operation, which returns the value of the register without changing it, or by a non-trivial *write* operation with one parameter, which changes the register's value to the value of its parameter, overwriting its previous value. A *single-writer* register is restricted so that only one particular process can perform write operations; a *multi-writer* register can be written to by any process. Another type of historyless base object is a *swap* object, which supports *read* and *swap* operations. A process *covers* a historyless object in a configuration if the process will perform a non-trivial operation on that object, when it takes its next step. A set of processes $P' \subseteq P$ *covers* a set of objects $\mathcal{O}$ in a configuration if each process in P' covers an object in $\mathcal{O}$ and each object in $\mathcal{O}$ is covered by some process in P'.

A *(multi-writer) snapshot object* is an object with m components $1, \ldots, m$, each of which stores a value from a specified set. When this set is $\{0, 1\}$, it is called a *binary snapshot object*. A snapshot object supports two operations. The operation UPDATE(i, v) sets the value of component i to v. The SCAN operation returns a vector consisting of the values of the m components.

A *(wait-free) implementation* provides, for each process, an algorithm for performing UPDATE and an algorithm for performing SCAN. Every process executes only a finite number of steps to perform these operations, even if other processes run at arbitrary speeds or may crash. An UPDATE or SCAN operation by a process is *pending* after an execution prefix if the process has already executed the first step of this invocation of its algorithm, but has not yet finished performing the algorithm. A *serial-update execution* of a snapshot implementation is an execution in which UPDATE operations do not overlap; that is, in any configuration, there is at most one pending UPDATE operation.

We restrict attention to *linearizable implementations* [12]. This means that, in each execution, each simulated UPDATE or SCAN operation appears to take effect at some instant during the period of time it is pending. Thus, there is a linearization of the implemented operations which would produce the same responses for each operation as in the execution. Furthermore, if one simulated operation finishes before another simulated operation begins, the latter operation comes later in the linearization.

Consider any execution of a snapshot implementation that reaches a configuration C in which no process has a pending UPDATE to component i. Then there is a value v_i such that, for any SCAN starting at or after C and finishing before any subsequent UPDATE to component i begins, the value of component i returned by this SCAN is v_i. This is because all such SCAN operations must be linearized after all the UPDATES to component i that complete before C and before all the UPDATES to component i that start after C. We call v_i the *value of component i at configuration C*. If there are no processes with pending UPDATES to any component in configuration C, then the *value of the snapshot object at configuration C* is $(v_1, \ldots, v_m)$, where v_i is the value of component i at C.

3   Partitioned and Space-Optimal Snapshot Implementations

In this section, partitioned implementations of snapshot objects are defined and we prove that space-optimal implementations of multi-writer snapshot objects from historyless objects are partitioned.

Definition 1. *A snapshot implementation is* partitioned *if all of the objects can be partitioned into m disjoint sets $\mathcal{O}_1, \ldots, \mathcal{O}_m$ such that, in any serial-update execution from an initial configuration C_0, only processes performing UPDATES to component i can change the value of objects in $\mathcal{O}_i$.*

In particular, in any serial-update execution of a partitioned implementation, SCAN operations cannot change the value of any object. Any implementation of a single-writer snapshot object from single-writer registers in which SCAN operations do not write is partitioned.

Consider any n-process implementation of an m-component snapshot object from a set $\mathcal{H}$ of $m < n$ registers or $m < n - 1$ historyless objects. In the full version of the paper, we prove that this implementation is partitioned. The proof relies on structural lemmas from Fatourou, Fich, and Ruppert [6,7], which hold for such implementations.

Lemma 1. *Let C be a configuration with no pending* UPDATES. *Suppose that x is not the value of component i at C. Then the solo execution by any process, starting from C, in which it performs* UPDATE(i, x) *(after completing its pending* SCAN, *if necessary), must change the value of at least one shared object.*

Lemma 2. SCAN *operations do not perform non-trivial operations.*

For any configuration, C, without pending UPDATES, let $H(C, i, j, x)$ denote the first object that process p_j covers when performing a solo execution of UPDATE(i, x) starting from C (after completing its pending SCAN, if necessary). By Lemma 1, if x is not the value of component i at C, then this object exists.

Let C_0 denote the initial configuration in which the initial value of every component is 0. Let $H_i = H(C_0, i, i, 1)$ be the first object that process p_i covers when performing a solo execution of UPDATE$(i, 1)$ starting from configuration C_0.

Lemma 3. $H_i \neq H_j$ *for distinct $i, j \in \{1, \ldots, m\}$.*

Consider any serial-update execution α of the implementation starting from C_0. Let $C_0, C_1, \ldots$ denote the sequence of configurations without pending UPDATES that occur in α. We state two additional structural properties about this restricted execution. The proofs appear in the full version of the paper.

Lemma 4. *If x is not the value of component i at configuration C_k, then, for every process p_j, $H(C_k, i, j, x) = H_i$.*

Lemma 5. *In any serial-update execution starting from C_0, the only shared object to which non-trivial operations are performed during an* UPDATE *to component i is H_i.*

Together with Lemmas 2 and 3, Lemma 5 shows that space-optimal implementations of multi-writer snapshot objects from historyless objects are partitioned.

Corollary 1. *Any implementation of an m-component multi-writer snapshot object shared by $n \geq 3$ processes from $m < n$ registers or from $m < n - 1$ historyless objects is partitioned.*

4   A Simple Reduction

Israeli and Shirazi [15] proved the following lower bound for single-writer snapshot objects implemented from single-writer registers. Then a simple reduction extends this result to a lower bound for partitioned implementations of multi-writer snapshot objects from any base objects. With Corollary 1, this gives a lower bound on the step complexity of UPDATE operations for space-optimal implementations of multi-writer snapshot objects.

Theorem 1. *In any implementation of a single-writer snapshot object, over an infinite domain, shared by m updaters and m scanners, from single-writer registers, there is a serial-update execution in which some* UPDATE *operation takes $\Omega(m)$ steps.*

This lower bound can be extended to partitioned implementations of multi-writer snapshot objects from any base objects by observing that a partitioned implementation of a multi-writer snapshot object can be used to implement a single-writer snapshot object using only single-writer registers. Specifically, the objects that can be changed by processes performing UPDATES to component i are represented by different fields of the single-writer register of process p_i.

Theorem 2. *In any partitioned implementation of an m-component multi-writer snapshot object, over an infinite domain, shared by m updaters and m scanners, there is a serial-update execution in which some UPDATE operation takes $\Omega(m)$ steps.*

Note that the same reduction also works for implementations in which each process also has a single-writer register to which it can write at any time.

Combining Corollary 1 and Theorem 2 yields our first lower bound for space-optimal implementations.

Theorem 3. *Any implementation of an m-component multi-writer snapshot object, over an infinite domain, shared by $n \geq 2m$ processes, from m historyless objects, requires $\Omega(m)$ steps for an UPDATE, in the worst case.*

This theorem is true even if the implementation only works for serial-update executions. For this special case, there is a space-optimal implementation with $O(m)$ step complexity for both SCAN and UPDATE. The algorithm uses m registers, each containing a view plus a sequence number. A SCAN simply collects all m registers, picks one with the maximal sequence number, and returns its view. To perform UPDATE(i, x), a process collects all registers, picks one with the maximal sequence number, changes component i of its view to x, and writes this new view, together with a bigger sequence number, to the i'th register.

5 Partitioned Binary Snapshot Implementations

In this section, we give a direct proof of an $\Omega(m)$ lower bound on the number of steps to perform UPDATE in any partitioned implementation of an m-component snapshot object (from any base objects). Unlike the lower bounds in the preceding section, it does not require the set of possible values of the components to be infinite. In fact, this proof even applies to binary snapshot objects. Furthermore, the lower bounds in the preceding section required $2m$ processes: m scanners and m updaters. Here, the lower bound for partitioned implementations applies even when there are only two updaters and one scanner. We also get a lower bound for space-optimal implementations that applies when the *total* number of processes is greater than m (for implementations from registers) or $m + 1$ (for implementations from historyless objects).

The proof of our lower bound for partitioned implementations is similar in structure to the proof of Theorem 1 by Israeli and Shirazi [15]. Specifically, we prove that if all UPDATES take at most $m/6$ steps, then it is possible to construct an infinite serial-update execution consisting of a single SCAN operation with one complete UPDATE operation immediately before each step of the SCAN. This will contradict the assumption that the implementation is wait-free. To do this, we build successively longer executions of this form.

A *flippable execution of length* k is a finite execution $U_0 s_1 U_1 \cdots s_k U_k$ performed by two updaters, p_0 and p_1, and one scanner, q, starting from an initial configuration C_0, such that:

- U_j is a solo execution of a complete UPDATE operation performed by p_h, where $h \equiv j \bmod 2$, in which it complements the value of one component, for $j = 0, \ldots, k$,
- consecutive UPDATE operations are to different components,
- s_j is a single step of a SCAN operation performed by q, for $j = 1, \ldots, k$, and
- for any $f > 1$ and for any sequence $j_1 < \cdots < j_f$, where $1 \leq j_\ell + 1 < j_{\ell+1} \leq k$ for $1 \leq \ell < f$, the execution $U_0 s_1 U_1 \cdots s_{j_\ell - 1} U_{j_\ell - 1} s_{j_\ell} U_{j_\ell} s_{j_\ell + 1} \cdots s_k U_k$ starting from C_0 is indistinguishable (to all processes) from the flipped execution $U_0 s_1 U_1 \cdots s_{j_\ell - 1} U_{j_\ell} U_{j_\ell - 1} s_{\ell_j} s_{j_\ell + 1} \cdots s_k U_k$ starting from C_0 in which UPDATE U_{j_ℓ} is performed before $U_{j_\ell - 1} s_{j_\ell}$ instead of after $U_{j_\ell - 1} s_{j_\ell}$, for $\ell = 1, \ldots, f$.

When we say that an instance of an UPDATE operation complements the value of component i, we mean that it is an instance of UPDATE$(i, \overline{v_i})$, where $v_i \in \{0, 1\}$ is the value of component i of the snapshot object just before the operation begins.

Next, we show that a flippable execution cannot contain a completed SCAN operation, by showing that there is no place a SCAN operation can be linearized. This will allow us to extend the flippable execution to a longer one.

Lemma 6. *No* SCAN *operation in a flippable execution has terminated.*

Proof. Let $E = U_0 s_1 U_1 \cdots s_k U_k$ be a flippable execution starting from configuration C_0. To obtain a contradiction, suppose that process q has completed a SCAN by the end of E. Let $v = (v_1, \ldots, v_m)$ be the result of this SCAN. There might be many configurations during this execution at which there are no pending UPDATES and the value of the snapshot object is v. (If the domain of the snapshot object were infinite, this difficulty could be avoided by requiring every UPDATE to use a different value.) Let $j_1 < \cdots < j_f$ be a list of all indices $j_\ell \in \{1, \ldots, k\}$ such that v is the value of the snapshot object between $U_{j_\ell - 1}$ and U_{j_ℓ}, for $\ell = 1, \ldots, f$. Note that, since U_{j_ℓ} complements the value of some component, v is not the value of the snapshot object between U_{j_ℓ} and $U_{j_\ell + 1}$. Hence $j_\ell + 1 < j_{\ell+1}$.

Consider the flipped execution $F = U_0 s_1 U_1 \cdots s_{j_\ell - 1} U_{j_\ell} U_{j_\ell - 1} s_{j_\ell} s_{j_\ell + 1} \cdots s_k U_k$ starting from C_0 in which UPDATE U_{j_ℓ} is performed before $U_{j_\ell - 1} s_{j_\ell}$ instead of after $U_{j_\ell - 1} s_{j_\ell}$, for $\ell = 1, \ldots, f$. The executions E and F are indistinguishable to process q, so q returns the same result for its SCAN in both executions. Thus, in F, the SCAN by q must be linearized at some point where the value of the snapshot object is v.

Since the UPDATES do not overlap, they are linearized in the order $U_0, U_1, \ldots,$ U_k in E and in the same order in F, except that the order of $U_{j_\ell - 1}$ and U_{ℓ_j} are flipped, for $\ell = 1, \ldots, f$. Consecutive UPDATES are to different components, so the value of the snapshot object is the same after both have been performed, no matter which of the two is performed first. Hence, at all points in the linearization of F, except between U_{j_ℓ} and $U_{j_\ell-1}$, for $\ell = 1, \ldots, f$, the value of the snapshot object is the same as its value at the corresponding point in the linearization of E. Recall that, in E, the value of the snapshot object is not v between U_{j-1} and U_j, for $j \neq j_1, \ldots, j_f$.

Now consider the situation between $U_{j_\ell-1}$ and U_{j_ℓ} for any $\ell \in \{1, \ldots, f\}$. In E, the snapshot object has value v and U_{j_ℓ} is an instance of UPDATE$(i, \overline{v_i})$, where v_i is the value of component i of v. This implies that, between U_{j_ℓ} and $U_{j_\ell-1}$ in F, the value of component i of the snapshot object is $\overline{v_i}$ and, hence, the value of the snapshot object is not v.

Since the SCAN by q begins after U_0 in F, it must be linearized after U_0. If $j_f < k$, then the SCAN by q finishes before U_k in both E and F and, hence, must be linearized before U_k. If $j_f = k$, then the value of the snapshot object is v between U_{k-1} and U_k in E. This implies that the value of the snapshot object is not v either after U_k in E or after U_{k-1} in F. In this case, the SCAN by q must be linearized before U_{k-1} in F.

The value of the snapshot object is not v between U_0 and the last UPDATE performed in F. This contradicts the fact that the SCAN by q must be linearized at some point where the value of the snapshot object is v. □

Consider any partitioned implementation of an m-component binary snapshot object, shared by two updaters, p_0 and p_1, and a scanner q, in which serial UPDATES take at most $m/6$ steps. Suppose that UPDATES to component i only change the value of objects in $\mathcal{O}_i$. We show how to construct a flippable execution so that it can be repeatedly extended. The key idea is to choose the successive components to update so that the objects each UPDATE operation might change are not accessed during the previous or the next UPDATE operation nor during the step of the SCAN that precedes it. A counting argument shows that this is possible in each extension of the construction.

It is helpful to use a matrix to keep track of which objects a process accesses when it performs an UPDATE. For each $h \in \{0, 1\}$ and each configuration C without pending UPDATES in an update-serial execution, let B_C^h denote the $m \times m$ Boolean matrix where $B_C^h[i, j] = 1$ if and only if the solo execution of UPDATE$(i, \overline{v_i})$ by process p_h starting from configuration C accesses an object in $\mathcal{O}_j$, where v_i is the value of component i of the snapshot object in configuration C. In particular, $B_C^h[i, i] = 1$, since a process performing UPDATE$(i, \overline{v_i})$ must access an object in $\mathcal{O}_i$. (Otherwise, it changes the value of no objects and, hence, cannot affect the outcome of a SCAN that follows immediately afterwords.) We say that a column j of B_C^h is *light* if more than half of its entries are 0.

Lemma 7. *If process p_h takes at most $m/6$ steps to perform a solo UPDATE starting from configuration C, then there are at least $2m/3$ light columns in B_C^h.*

Proof. Process p_h performs at most $m/6$ steps in its solo execution of UPDATE$(i, \bar{b})$ starting from configuration C, where b is the value of component i of the snapshot object in configuration C. Hence, at most $m/6$ entries in row i of B_C^h are 1 and at most $m^2/6$ entries in B_C^h are 1. Let ℓ denote the number of light columns in B_C^h. Then, in each of the other $m - \ell$ columns, at least $m/2$ of the entries are 1. Thus at least $(m - \ell)m/2$ entries in B_C^h are 1. This implies that $m^2/6 \geq (m - \ell)m/2$ or, equivalently, $\ell \geq 2m/3$.   □

We now prove the main technical lemma, which shows the existence of a flippable execution, but with one additional property that makes the construction proceed more easily.

Lemma 8. *If every updater takes at most $m/6$ steps to perform a solo UPDATE, then, for all $k \geq 0$, there is a flippable execution, $U_0 s_1 U_1 \cdots s_k U_k$, such that U_k is an UPDATE to some component i_k by a process $p_{\bar{h}}$ starting from configuration C_k, where $h \equiv (k + 1) \bmod 2$ and column i_k of $B_{C_k}^h$ is light.*

Proof. By induction on k.

First consider the base case, $k = 0$. By Lemma 7, $B_{C_0}^1$ has at least $2m/3$ light columns. Let U_0 be a solo execution of UPDATE$(i_0, \overline{v_{i_0}})$ by process p_0 starting from configuration C_0, where i_0 is the index of a light column in $B_{C_0}^1$ and v_{i_0} is the value of component i_0 in C_0. Then the claim holds for $k = 0$.

For the induction step, suppose $E = U_0 s_1 U_1 \cdots s_k U_k$ is a flippable execution such that column i_k of $B_{C_k}^h$ is light, where U_k is a solo execution of UPDATE$(i_k, \overline{v_{i_k}})$ by process $p_{\bar{h}}$ starting from configuration C_k and v_{i_k} is the value of component i_k in C_k. By Lemma 6, process q has not completed its SCAN at the end of E. Let s_{k+1} denote the next step by process q and let C_{k+1} denote the configuration at the end of Es_{k+1}.

The component i_{k+1} for U_{k+1} to update will be chosen so that the resulting execution is flippable. But we must also choose it with some concern for the future, so that there is enough flexibility to choose the component to update in the following step of the induction.

To prepare for the future, we restrict i_{k+1} to be the index of a light column in $B_{C_{k+1}}^{\bar{h}}$. Let $I \subseteq \{1, \ldots, m\}$ be this set of indices. By Lemma 7, $|I| \geq 2m/3$.

Next, we ensure that it is possible to interchange $U_k s_{k+1}$ and U_{k+1}. To do this, we first restrict our choices for i_{k+1} so that process p_h will not access any object during U_{k+1} that might have changed value during U_k. Let $I' = \{i \in I \mid B_{C_k}^h[i, i_k] = 0\}$ consist of all indices $i \in I$ such that process p_h does not access any object in $\mathcal{O}_{i_k}$ when performing a solo execution of UPDATE$(i, \overline{v_i})$ starting from configuration C_k, where v_i is the value of component i in C_k. This ensures that U_{k+1} behaves exactly the same when performed starting from C_k as from C_{k+1}. By the induction hypothesis, column i_k of $B_{C_k}^h$ is light, so there are less than $m/2$ indices $i \in I$ such that $B_{C_k}[i, i_k] = 1$. Hence, $|I'| > |I| - m/2 \geq m/6$.

We further restrict our choices for i_{k+1} so that the other updater, $p_{\bar{h}}$, does not access any object during U_k whose value might be changed during U_{k+1}. Let $I'' = \{i \in I' \mid B_{C_k}^{\bar{h}}[i_k, i] = 0\}$ consist of all indices $i \in I'$ such that process $p_{\bar{h}}$ does not access any object in $\mathcal{O}_i$ during U_k, the solo execution of UPDATE($i_k, \overline{v_{i_k}}$) starting from configuration C_k. Then U_k behaves exactly the same when performed starting from C_{k+1} as from C_k. Row i_k of $B_{C_k}^{\overline{h}}$ contains at most $m/6$ entries with value 1. Since $B_{C_k}^{\overline{h}}[i_k, i_k] = 1 = B_{C_k}^{h}[i_k, i_k]$, at least one i with $B_{C_k}^{\overline{h}}[i_k, i] = 0$ is not in I'. Thus $|I''| \geq |I'| - m/6 + 1 > 1$. Let $i_{k+1} \in I''$ be such that q does not access an object in $\mathcal{O}_{i_{k+1}}$ during its single step s_{k+1}. Note that $i_{k+1} \neq i_k$, since $B_{C_k}^{\overline{h}}[i_k, i_k] = 1$. Let U_{k+1} be a solo execution of UPDATE($i_{k+1}, v_{i_{k+1}}$) starting from C_{k+1}, where $v_{i_{k+1}}$ is the value of component i_{k+1} of the snapshot object in configuration C_{k+1}.

It remains to prove that the execution $E' = U_0 s_1 U_1 \cdots s_{k+1} U_{k+1}$ starting from C_0 is flippable. Consider any sequence $j_1 < \cdots < j_f$ where $1 \leq j_\ell + 1 < j_{\ell+1} \leq k$ for $1 \leq \ell < f$. By the induction hypothesis, the execution $E = U_0 s_1 U_1 \cdots s_{j_\ell - 1} U_{j_\ell - 1} s_{j_\ell} U_{j_\ell} s_{j_\ell + 1} \cdots s_k U_k$ starting from C_0 is indistinguishable (to all processes) from the flipped execution $F = U_0 s_1 U_1 \cdots s_{j_\ell - 1} U_{j_\ell} s_{j_\ell} U_{j_\ell - 1} s_{j_\ell + 1} \cdots s_k U_k$ starting from C_0. In particular, the configurations at the end of these two executions are the same. Hence, executions $E' = E s_{k+1} U_{k+1}$ and $F s_{k+1} U_{k+1}$ starting from C_0 are indistinguishable to all processes.

If $j_f + 1 < k + 1$, we must also consider the sequence $j_1 < \cdots < j_f < j_{f+1}$, where $j_{f+1} = k + 1$. In this case, the flipped execution F' differs from $F s_{k+1} U_{k+1}$ in that U_{k+1} precedes $U_k s_{k+1}$ instead of following it.

F' is indistinguishable from $F s_{k+1} U_{k+1}$ to p_h because $i_{k+1} \in I'$ implies that p_h does not access any objects in $\mathcal{O}_{i_k}$ during U_{k+1} starting from configuration C_k. Since the implementation is partitioned, these are the only objects whose values can change during $U_k s_{k+1}$. F' is indistinguishable from $F s_{k+1} U_{k+1}$ to $p_{\overline{h}}$ because $i_{k+1} \in I''$ implies that $p_{\overline{h}}$ does not access any objects in $\mathcal{O}_{i_{k+1}}$ during U_k and these are the only objects whose values can change during U_{k+1}. F' is indistinguishable from $F s_{k+1} U_{k+1}$ to q because q does not access an object in $\mathcal{O}_{i_{k+1}}$ during its single step s_{k+1}. F' is indistinguishable from $F s_{k+1} U_{k+1}$ to all other processes, since they take no steps during $U_k s_{k+1} U_{k+1}$. By transitivity, F' is indistinguishable from E' to all processes and the claim holds for $k + 1$.   □

Our lower bounds follow from Lemmas 6 and 8 and Corollary 1. These lower bounds apply even if the implementation only works for serial-update executions.

Theorem 4. *In any partitioned implementation of an m-component multi-writer binary snapshot object, shared by at least two updaters and one scanner, there is a serial-update execution in which some UPDATE operation takes more than $m/6$ steps.*

Theorem 5. *Any implementation of an m-component multi-writer binary snapshot object, shared by $n \geq 3$ processes, from $m < n$ registers or $m < n - 1$ historyless objects, requires $\Omega(m)$ steps for an UPDATE, in the worst case.*

References

1. Yehuda Afek, Hagit Attiya, Danny Dolev, Eli Gafni, Michael Merritt, and Nir Shavit, *Atomic snapshots of shared memory*, JACM, vol. 40, no. 4, September 1993, pages 873–890.
2. James H. Anderson, *Multi-writer composite registers*, Distributed Computing, vol. 7, no. 4, May 1994, pages 175–195.
3. Hagit Attiya and Arie Fouren, *Adaptive and efficient algorithms for lattice agreement and renaming*, SICOMP, vol. 31, no. 2, October 2001, pages 642–664.
4. Hagit Attiya and Ophir Rachman, *Atomic snapshots in $O(n \log n)$ operations*, SICOMP, vol. 27, no. 2, April 1998, pages 319–340.
5. Hagit Attiya and Jennifer Welch, *Distributed Computing: Fundamentals, Simulations and Advanced Topics, 2nd edition*, Wiley-Interscience, 2004.
6. Panagiota Fatourou, Faith Ellen Fich, and Eric Ruppert. *A Tight Time Lower Bound for Space-Optimal Implementations of Multi-Writer Snapshots*, STOC 2003, pages 259–268.
7. Panagiota Fatourou, Faith Ellen Fich, and Eric Ruppert. *A Tight Time Lower Bound for Space-Optimal Implementations of Multi-Writer Snapshots*, manuscript, 2006.
8. Panagiota Fatourou and Nikolaos Kallimanis, *Single-Scanner Multi-Writer Snapshot Implementations are Fast*, PODC 2006, pages 228–237.
9. Faith Ellen Fich, *How Hard is it to Take a Snapshot?*, SOFSEM 2005, LNCS, vol. 3381, pages 27–35.
10. Faith Fich, Maurice Herlihy, and Nir Shavit, *On the Space Complexity of Randomized Synchronization*, JACM, vol. 45, no. 5, September 1998, pages 843-862.
11. Faith Ellen Fich and Eric Ruppert, *Hundreds of Impossibility Results for Distributed Computing*, Distributed Computing, vol. 16, no. 2–3, 2003, pages 121–163.
12. Maurice P. Herlihy and Jeannette M. Wing, *Linearizability: A correctness condition for concurrent objects*, TOPLAS, vol. 12, no. 3, July 1990, pages 463–492.
13. Michiko Inoue, Wei Chen, Toshimitsu Masuzawa, and Nobuki Tokura, *Linear time snapshots using multi-writer multi-reader registers*, WDAG 1994, LNCS, vol. 857, pages 130–140.
14. A. Israeli, A. Shaham, and A. Shirazi, *Linear-time snapshot implementations in unbalanced systems*, Mathematical Systems Theory, vol. 28, no. 5, September/October 1995, pages 469–486.
15. Amos Israeli and Assaf Shirazi, *The time complexity of updating snapshot memories*, Information Processing Letters, vol. 65, no. 1, 1998, pages 33–40.
16. Prasad Jayanti, *f-Arrays: Implementation and Applications*, PODC 2002, pages 270–279.
17. Prasad Jayanti, *An Optimal Multi-Writer Snapshot Algorithm*, STOC 2005, pages 723–732.
18. Prasad Jayanti, King Tan, and Sam Toueg, *Time and space lower bounds for nonblocking implementations*, SICOMP, vol. 30, no. 2, June 2000, pages 438–456.
19. L.M. Kirousis, P. Spirakis, and P. Tsigas, *Reading Many Variables in One Atomic Operation: Solutions with Linear or Sublinear Complexity*, IEEE Trans. on Parallel and Distributed Systems, vol. 5, no. 7, July 1994, pages 688–696.
20. Nancy Lynch, *Distributed Algorithms*, Morgan Kaufmann, 1996.
21. Yaron Riany, Nir Shavit, and Dan Touitou, *Towards a Practical Snapshot Algorithm*, Theoretical Computer Science, vol. 269, 2001, pages 163–201.

Simultaneous Consensus Tasks:
A Tighter Characterization of Set-Consensus

Yehuda Afek[1], Eli Gafni[2], Sergio Rajsbaum[3], Michel Raynal[4], and Corentin Travers[4]

[1] Computer Science Department, Tel-Aviv University, Israel 69978
afek@math.tau.ac.il
[2] Department of Computer Science, UCLA, Los Angeles, CA 90095, USA
eli@cs.ucla.edu
[3] Instituto de Matemáticas, UNAM, D. F. 04510, Mexico
rajsbaum@math.unam.mx
[4] IRISA, Campus de Beaulieu, 35042 Rennes Cedex, France
{raynal, ctravers}@irisa.fr

Abstract. We address the problem of solving a task $T = (T_1, ... T_m)$ (called $(m, 1)$-BG), in which a processor returns in an arbitrary one of m simultaneous consensus subtasks $T_1, ... T_m$. Processor p_i submits to T an input vector of proposals $(prop_{i,1}, ..., prop_{i,m})$, one entry per subtask, and outputs, from just one subtask ℓ, a pair $(\ell, \ prop_{j,l})$ for some j. All processors that output at ℓ output the same proposal.

Let d be a bound on the number of distinct input vectors that may be submitted to T. For example, $d = 3$ if Democrats always vote Democrats across the board, and similarly for Republicans and Libertarians. A wait-free algorithm that immaterial of the number of processors solves T provided $m \geq d$ is presented. In addition, if in each T_j we allow k-set consensus rather than consensus, i.e., for each ℓ, the outputs satisfy $|\{j \mid prop_{j,\ell}\}| \leq k$, then the same algorithm solves T if $m \geq \lceil d/k \rceil$.

What is the power of $T = (T_1, ..., T_m)$ when given as a subroutine, to be used by any number of processors with any number of input vectors? Obviously, T solves m-set consensus since each processor p_i can submit the vector $(id_i, id_i, ... id_i)$, but can m-set consensus solve T? We show it does, and thus simultaneous consensus is a new characterization of set-consensus.

Finally, what if each T_j is just a binary-consensus rather than consensus? Then we get the novel problem that was recently introduced of the Committee-Decision. It was shown that for 3 processors and $m = 2$, the simultaneous binary-consensus is equivalent to $(3, 2)$-set consensus. Here, using a variation of our wait-free algorithms mentioned above, we show that a task, in which a processor is required to return in one of m simultaneous binary-consensus subtasks, when used by n processors, is equivalent to (n, m)-set consensus. Thus, while set-consensus unlike consensus, has no binary version, now that we characterize m-set consensus through simultaneous consensus, the notion of binary-set-consensus is well defined. We have then showed that binary-set-consensus is equivalent to set consensus as it was with consensus.

1 Introduction

The Borowsky-Gafni simulation scheme relies on the realization that there is a read-write algorithm by which n processors involved in n simultaneous sub-consensus-tasks

S. Chaudhuri et al. (Eds.): ICDCN 2006, LNCS 4308, pp. 331–341, 2006.
© Springer-Verlag Berlin Heidelberg 2006

$T_1, ..., T_n$, can reach consensus in a wait-free manner in at least some T_k, though k is unknown a priori. Thus we can define the $(m, 1)$-BG task: processor p_i starts with some input value v_i and has to output a pair (ℓ, v_j) for some $1 \leq \ell \leq m$, and v_j is the initial proposal of some p_j in the participating set. All processors that output with first argument ℓ have to output the same value.

One can think of a variation of $(m, 1)$-BG in which the inputs are m-vectors and processors that output at T_k are to output the same k entry from one of the vectors. But it is easy to see that the vector problem solves the value problem by each processor p_i inputing $(v_i, v_i, ..., v_i)$, as well as the value problem solving the vector problem by associating vectors with values, and then for value v_i when output at k, a processor substitutes the kth entry of the associated vector. Henceforth the presentation proceeds with the value version.

In the BG simulation [3,4], we use n agreement protocols and rely on the fact that if the first agreement is not resolved then there is a processor "stuck" in the middle of the first agreement protocol and consequently we can proceed with one processor less. Here, when we have n proposals rather than n processors, we show a variant agreement protocol by which in each agreement protocol that does not terminate we, lose a proposal rather than a processor. Thus a sequence of n agreement protocols will solve the $(m, 1)$-BG task, $m \geq n$.

Now that we generalized the $(m, 1)$-BG task to any number of processors, we investigate the relationship between m and the power of the consensus that each task provides. Suppose that in each task T_j, we do not require consensus but rather k-set consensus. Thus, we have m subtasks $T_1, ..., T_m$ and processors output (ℓ, v_j) for some $1 \leq \ell \leq m$ and for each ℓ : $|\{v_j \mid (\ell, v_j) \in output \}| \leq k$. We call this task (m, k)-BG.

Our second result is that (m, k)-BG is read-write wait-free solvable for any number of processors, if the number of initial choices d satisfies $m \geq \lceil d/k \rceil$. Thus if we allow each T_j to solve 2-set consensus, then m can be half the number of initial choices. Alternatively, it can just be reduced to the consensus case: just solve $(m, 1)$-BG and group the outputs 1 to k, $k + 1$ to $2k$, etc.

Until this point we investigated what variation of BG tasks can be solved wait-free. We then turn to BG tasks with parameters that do not render it solvable and wonder about the power of these tasks.

Suppose we are given an $(m, 1)$-BG task as a subroutine. Since each subtask does consensus, it trivially solves m-set consensus by ignoring the subtask index. Can m-set consensus solve m-BG? Notice that $(m, 1)$-BG associates different output values with different subtasks. Our $(m, 1)$-BG algorithm answers this question on the affirmative. By using m-set consensus, the number of initial choices n becomes m, and then we can wait-free solve the $(m, 1)$-BG.

What if each subtask in the $(m, 1)$-BG task is a binary-consensus rather than consensus? We refer to this problem as m-BG-Binary. If $m = 1$ then we have our beloved consensus and it is known how to transform binary-consensus into consensus by repeated consensus on the binary representation of the eventual output value (A different approach is presented in [14].). But what if $m = 2$? When we try repeated binary-consensus, at the first invocation p_i may get a value from T_1 and in the second from T_2. How do you build a prefix under these conditions?

The question of the $(m, 1)$-BG task when each subtask is a binary consensus and the input is a binary vector with entry for each subtask was recently investigated in [10,11]. Thus, in subtask T_j if all input values to T_j are 0, only 0 can be returned for T_j. The problem was called the m-Committee-Decision problem as the connection to $(m, 1)$-BG was not realized. Obviously BG tasks encompass Committee-Decision as the proposed values are vectors and when returning a vector for T_j, one projects on the jth entry. Thus the interesting direction is to show that Committee-Decision encompasses BG tasks.

Using explicit topological arguments, it was shown in [10,11] that 2-Committee-Decision when used by 3 processors is equivalent to $(3, 2)$-set consensus. Here, as a simple corollary we show that $(m, 1)$-BG for n processors is equivalent to (n, m)-set consensus. Thus we show the equivalence between BG tasks and Committee-Decision.

The paper is organized as follows. We first outline the various tasks we deal with (section 2). We then outline the rather simple agreement algorithm that wait-free solves $(m, 1)$-BG for $m \geq n$ (sections 3 and 4). We then show a bit more involved construction that reduced $(m, 1)$-BG to m-Committee-Decision, or alternatively referred to as m-BG-Binary (section 5). We conclude with a discussion of the merits of characterizing set-consensus through simultaneous-consensus (section 6).

2 Problems Definitions and Preliminaries

In all the paper, we are interested in wait free algorithms [12].

2.1 Computational Model

Processor model. The system consists of an arbitrary number of processors [9,15] that we denote $p_1, p_2, \ldots$ In a run a *participating* processor p_i wakes up with some initial value $input_i$. The inputs value are taken from a set $Input$ of size n. It is important to notice that n denotes the maximal number of values participating processors wake up with. The number of processors that participate in a run is unknown to the processors.

A processor can crash. Given a run, a processor that crashes is said to be *faulty*, otherwise it is *correct* in that execution. Each processor progresses at its own speed, which means that the system is asynchronous.

Coordination model. The processors communicate and cooperate through atomic multi-reader/multi-writer registers. To simplify algorithm descriptions, *write-snapshot* objects [1,3] are also available to the processors.

A write-snapshot WS object provides the processors with a single operation denoted WRITESNAPSHOT(). It is a one-shot object in the sense that each processor can invoke WS at most once. A processor p_i invokes WS.WRITESNAPSHOT(v_i), and if it does not crash during the invocation, obtains a set of value s_i. The sets returned satisfy the two following properties:

- Self containment: $v_i \in s_i$,
- Comparability: $\forall i, j : i \neq j \Rightarrow s_i \subseteq s_j \vee s_j \subseteq s_i$.

Such an object can be implemented on top of multiple-reader/multiple-writer registers for an arbitrary number of processors [7].

2.2   The Problems

(m,1)-BG.   In the $(m, 1)$-BG problem, processors are trying to simultaneously solve m instances of the consensus problem. Each processor is required to decide in at least one of these instances. There are m consensus subtasks $T_1, ..., T_m$. Processor p_i wakes up with a private value v_i and is required to return a pair (ℓ, v_j) such that $1 \leq \ell \leq m$ and the value v_j has been proposed by some p_j. All processors that return first argument ℓ have to agree and return the same v_j. More precisely, each processor has to decide a pair (ℓ, v) such that:

- Termination: No processor takes infinitely many steps without deciding.
- Validity: If a processor p_i decides (ℓ, v_j) then $\exists j$ such that processor p_j wakes up with value v_j.
- Agreement: $\forall \ell, 1 \leq \ell \leq m : |\{v_j : (\ell, v_j) \text{ is decided by some processor }\}| \leq 1$.

(m,k)-BG.   The (m, k)-BG task is a generalization of the $(m, 1)$-BG problem. As in $(m, 1)$-BG, processors have to return a pair (ℓ, v). The processors that return first argument ℓ may return cumulatively at most k distinct values. The pairs returned have to satisfy the validity and termination properties of the $(m, 1)$-BG problem and the following agreement property:

- $\forall \ell, 1 \leq \ell \leq m : |\{v_j : (\ell, v_j) \text{ is decided by some processor }\}| \leq k$.

k-Set Consensus.   The k-set consensus problem is a generalization of consensus where processors must decide on at most k different values that have been previously proposed [5]. When $k = 1$, the problem boils down to the standard consensus problem [6]. Each processor is required to decide a value subject to the following conditions:

- Agreement: at most k distinct values are decided.
- Termination: no processor takes infinitely many steps without deciding.
- Validity: a decided value is an initial input value for some participating processor.

It is shown in [2,13,16] that in a system of $\alpha > k$ processors, the k-set consensus problem has no wait free solution when processors may have distinct input values.

m-Committee-Decision or m-BG-Binary.   In the binary consensus problem, processors start with either 0 or 1 and are required to eventually agree on one of their initial value. Suppose now that processors are provided with a collection of binary consensus objects $B_1, \ldots, B_m$ but are not guaranteed to obtain a response from each object, even if they propose a value in each binary consensus. A processor p_i is only guaranteed to obtain a response from one object B_j and j is not known a priori. Moreover, j may change from invocation to invocation.

More precisely, this coordination scheme is captured by the m-Committee-Decision problem [11]. In the m-Committee-Decision problem, processors are trying to solve m binary consensus instances called committees and each processor is required to make a decision for at least one of them. More explicitly, each processor p_i initially proposes a vector $V_i \in \{0,1\}^k$ (i.e., $V_i[c], 1 \le c \le k$ is p_i's proposal for the c-th committee) and decides a pair (c, v) such that:

- Termination: No processor takes infinitely many steps without deciding.
- Validity: If a processor decides (c, v) then $\exists j$ such that $v = V_j[c]$.
- Agreement: Let p_i and p_j be two processors that decide (c_i, v_i) and (c_j, v_j) respectively. $c_i = c_j \Rightarrow v_i = v_j$.

3   Wait-Free Solution to $(m, 1)$-BG, n Initial Values, $m \ge n$

Processor p_i marches in order through T_1 followed by T_2, etc. In T_i a processor writes an input value to its cell. The input to T_1 is the input it wakes up with. The input to T_j is adopted from T_{j-1}.

At T_j a processor writes its input, returns an atomic snapshot of input values and posts its snapshot in shared memory. If it then sees a snapshot of values of cardinality one, it returns this value for T_j and quits. Else, it adopts the minimum value from one of the posted snapshots (maybe its own) and proceeds with it to T_{j+1} (figure 1).

The observation is that the number of distinct values proposed to T_j is at most $n - (j - 1)$, thus a processor that arrives at T_n is guaranteed to get a snapshot of size one at T_n and to return.

---

in shared memory: $WS[1, \ldots, m]$; array of write-snapshot objects.
$\qquad\qquad\qquad SS[1, \ldots, m][1, \ldots, m]$ array of mwmr registers, initially $\perp$.

function $(m, 1)$-BG(v_i)
(01) $est_i \leftarrow v_i$;
(02) **for** $r_i = 1$ **to** m **do**
(03) $S_i \leftarrow WS[r_i].\text{WRITESNAPSHOT}(est_i)$;
(04) $SS[r_i, |S_i|] \leftarrow S_i$;
(05)   **for** $\ell = 1$ **to** m **do** $ss[\ell] \leftarrow SS[r_i, \ell]$ **enddo**;
(06)   **if** $ss[1] \ne \perp$ **then** return$(r_i, ss[1])$
(07)   **else** $est_i \leftarrow \min(ss[\ell])$ s.t. $(\ell \in \{1, \ldots, m\}) \wedge (ss[\ell] \ne \perp)$
(08)   **endif**
(09) **enddo**

Fig. 1. $(m, 1)$-BG algorithm, n initial value, $m \ge n$, code for p_i

4   Wait-Free Solution to (m, k)-BG, n Initial Values, $m \ge \lceil \frac{n}{k} \rceil$

At each T_i, a processor tries to choose a value that appears in a snapshot of size k or less. The observation is that going from T_j to T_{j+1} at least k values are left behind. The algorithm is described in figure 2.

```
in shared memory:  WS[1, ..., m]; array of write-snapshot objects.
                   SS[1, ..., m][1, ..., m] array of mwmr registers, initially ⊥.

function (m, k)-BG(v_i)
(01)  est_i ← v_i;
(02)  for r_i = 1 to m do
(03)      S_i ← WS[r_i].WRITESNAPSHOT(est_i);
(04)      SS[r_i, |S_i|] ← S_i;
(05)      for ℓ = 1 to m do ss[ℓ] ← SS[r_i, ℓ] enddo;
(06)      if ∃ℓ, 1 ≤ ℓ ≤ k : ss[ℓ] ≠ ⊥ then return(r_i, min(ss[ℓ]))
(07)                    else est_i ← min(ss[ℓ]) s.t. (ℓ ∈ {1, ..., m}) ∧ (ss[ℓ] ≠ ⊥)
(08)      endif
(09)  enddo
```

Fig. 2. (m, k)-BG algorithm, n initial values, $m \geq \lceil \frac{n}{k} \rceil$, code for p_i

4.1 Proof of the Protocol

In the following, we say that a value v is proposed at stage $r, 1 \leq r \leq m$ if it exists a processor p_i that starts stage r with $est_i = v$. For each $r, 1 \leq r \leq m$, let $I[r]$ be the set of values proposed at stage r.

Lemma 1. *(Validity) Let (ℓ, v) be a pair decided by some processor. v is a proposed value.*

Proof. Let p_i be a processor that decides (ℓ, v) at stage r. Let us observe v is taken from the set of input values of stage r, i.e., $v \in I[r]$. Moreover, $\forall r', 2 \leq r' \leq m$, $I[r'] \subseteq I[r' - 1]$ (line 07). As $I[1] =$ the set of values the processors wake up with and $v \in I[r] \subseteq I[1]$, validity follows. $\Box_{Lemma\ 1}$

Lemma 2. *(Termination) A correct processor eventually decides.*

Proof. We first observe that $\forall r, 1 \leq r \leq m : |I[r]| \leq n - k(r - 1)$ (Observation $O1$). Let us assume for contradiction that there is a correct processor p_i that does not decide. This means that p_i marches through stages $1, 2, \ldots, m$ without deciding. In particular, at stage m, p_i obtains a snapshot $S_i \subseteq I[m]$. It follows from $O1$ that $|S_i| \leq |I[m]| \leq n - k(m - 1)$. Moreover, as $m \geq \lceil n/k \rceil$, we obtain $|S_i| \leq n - k(\lceil n/k \rceil - 1) \leq k$, from which we conclude that p_i decides at stage m (line 06): a contradiction.

Observation O1. $\forall r, 1 \leq r \leq m : |I[r]| \leq n - k(r - 1)$.
Proof of O1. As there are at most n proposed values and these values are the input ones at stage 1, $|I[1]| \leq n$. Let us assume that the observation is true at stage $r, 1 \leq r < m$. Let p_i be a processor that proposes a value at stage $r + 1$. At stage r, p_i updates its estimate with a value picked in a snapshot of size $> k$. Moreover, there are at most $|I[r]| - k$ such snapshots and for each of them, only one value can be picked by the

processors (line 07). Consequently, at most $|I[r]| - k$ values can be proposed at stage $r + 1$, from which we obtain $|I[r + 1]| \leq |I[r]| - k \leq n - kr$. *End of the proof of O1*

$\square_{Lemma\ 2}$

Lemma 3. *(Agreement)* $\forall r, 1 \leq r \leq m : |\{v : \exists p_i \text{ that decides } (r, v)\}| \leq k.$

Proof. Let r be a stage number. The values decided by processors that return at stage r are picked in a snapshot of size k or less (line 06). Since these snapshots contain cumulatively at most k distinct values, at most k distinct values are decided at stage r.

$\square_{Lemma\ 3}$

5 $(m, 1)$-BG from m-BG-Binary

Let the number of initial values be $n > m$. We show how to use $(n - 1)$-BG-Binary to reduce the number of initial values by at least 1 to $n - 1$. Obviously m-BG-Binary implements j-BG-Binary for all $j \geq m$.

Thus the scheme is to start with the n initial values, reduce it to $n - 1$ then to $n - 2$ and until m. At this point we have at most m initial values and we can wait free solve $(m, 1)$-BG.

To reduce the number of initial values from n to $n - 1$, we go through $n - 1$ stages $T_1, ..., T_{n-1}$. In each stage we post initial value, snapshot, post snapshot, and then read snapshots. The algorithm is described in figure 3.

If a processor sees posted snapshot of size 1 containing some v_j but no snapshot of size 2, then it returns v_j. Otherwise it adopts the smallest value in some snapshot of size 2 or more and continues to the next stage.

If a processor finishes stage T_{n-1} without returning, it invokes the $(n-1)$-BG-Binary object. The observation to make is that in all stages there are posted snapshots of size 2. Otherwise 2 values would have been left behind at some stage and the processor should have terminated by the end of stage T_{n-1}.

Now come the voting step in which the processor goes to the $n-1$-BG-Binary object. At committee j it will observe the snapshot posted at T_j. There is a snapshot of size 2 containing two values. We associate the smaller value with 0 and the larger with 1. If the processor also sees a snapshot of size 1 posted, it votes for that value. Thus a processor that quits without voting is guaranteed that the value it choses for T_j will be voted for by all.

5.1 Proof of the Protocol

We first prove the observation stated in the algorithm description (Lemma 4). Wait-free termination directly follows from the protocol text. We use Lemma 4 in the proofs of validity (Lemma 5) and agreement (Lemma 6).

Lemma 4. *Let p_i be a processor that returns at line 18. When p_i reads $SS[1, 2]$, $SS[2, 2]$, ..., $SS[m, 2]$ at line 11, we have $\forall 1 \leq r \leq m : SS[r, 2] \neq \perp$.*

---

in shared memory: $WS[1, \ldots, m]$ array of write-snapshot objects
$SS[1, \ldots, m][1, \ldots, m+1]$ array of mwmr registers, initially $\perp$

function $(m, 1)\text{-BGFROMBGBINARY}(v_i)$
(01) $est_i \leftarrow v_i$;
(02) **for** $r_i = 1$ **to** m **do**
(03) $S_i \leftarrow WS[r_i].\text{WRITESNAPSHOT}(est_i)$;
(04) $SS_i[r_i, |S_i|] \leftarrow S_i$;
(05)   **for** $j = 1$ **to** m **do** $ss[j] \leftarrow SS[r_i, j]$ **enddo**;
(06)   **if** $(ss[1] \neq \perp) \wedge (ss[2] = \perp)$ **then** return$(r_i, ss[1])$
(07)   **else** $est_i \leftarrow \min(ss[j])$ s.t. $(j \in \{2, \ldots, m\}) \wedge (ss[j] \neq \perp)$
(08)   **endif**
(09) **enddo**
        % If p_i has not succeeded in $T_1, \ldots, T_m$, it uses m-BG Binary to decide %
(10) **foreach** $r \in \{1, \ldots, m\}$ **do**
(11)   **let** v_m (resp. v_M) be the smallest value (resp. greatest) value in $SS[r, 2]$;
(12)   **case** $(v_m \in SS[r, 1])$ **then** $V_i[r] \leftarrow 0$
(13) $(v_M \in SS[r, 1])$ **then** $V_i[r] \leftarrow 1$
(14)   *default*   **then** $V_i[r] \leftarrow 0$ or 1 arbitrarily
(15)   **endcase**
(16) **enddo**
(17) $(c_i, d_i) \leftarrow m\text{-BGBINARY}(V_i)$;
(18) **if** $d_i = 1$ **then** return$\big(c_i, \max(SS[c_i, 2])\big)$ **else** return$\big(c_i, \min(SS[c_i, 2])\big)$ **endif**

Fig. 3. $(m, 1)$-BG from m-BG-Binary, n initial values, $n = m + 1$, code for p_i

Proof. Let us assume for contradiction that the lemma is false. This means that it exists a process p_i that returns at line 18 and a stage number $R, 1 \leq R \leq m$ such that p_i does not see a snapshot of size 2 posted at stage R. More precisely, when p_i reads $SS[R, 2]$ in the second phase of the protocol (line 11), $SS[R, 2] = \perp$. Let τ be the time at which this occurs. As a processor can post in $SS[R, 2]$ only a snapshot of size 2 obtained at stage R (line 04), it follows that $\forall \tau' \leq \tau : SS[R, 2] = \perp$.

As p_i proceeds to the second phase of the protocol, it tries to decide in each T_r, $1 \leq r \leq m$. We show that that p_i decides in the first phase of the protocol (at line 06): a contradiction. The proof consider two cases according to the value of R.

- $m = R$. Let us observe that the first phase of the protocol is the (m, k)-BG protocol instantiated with $k = 1$ in which processors wake up with at most $n = m + 1$ values. Consequently, observation *O1* stated and proved in Lemma 2 is still valid. It then follows that at most $(m + 1) - (m - 1) = 2$ values can be proposed at stage m.

  As p_i proceeds to the second phase of the algorithm, it obtains a snapshot at stage m. Moreover, when p_i tries to decide at stage r, $SS[r, 2] = \perp$. Consequently, p_i obtains a snapshot of size 1 and does not see a snapshot of size 2, from which we conclude that p_i decides at line 06 in the first phase of the algorithm.

- $m > R$. Let us first remark that at most $m - R$ values can be proposed at stage $R + 1$ before time τ. The values proposed at stage $R + 1$ are taken among the smallest values in snapshots of size ≥ 2 posted at stage R. As at most $(m + 1) -$ $(R - 1)$ values are proposed at stage R (Observation $O1$ in Lemma 2), at most $(m + 1) - (R - 1)$ distinct snapshots can be posted in that stage. Moreover, as values proposed at stage $R + 1$ are picked in snapshots of size > 1 and no snapshot of size 2 is posted before time τ ($SS[R, 2] = \perp$ before time τ), it follows that at most $(m+1) - (R-1) - 2 = m - R$ values can be proposed in stage $R + 1$ before time τ.

We can think of stages $T_{R+1}, \ldots, T_m$ as a $(m - R, 1)$-BG protocol. It follows from the remark above that, before time τ, the size of the set of input values to this $(m - R, 1)$-BG protocol is at most $m - R$. As this protocol solves the $(m - R, 1)$-BG task if the number of distinct input values is $\leq m - R$ (section 3), a processor cannot marches through $T_{R+1}, \ldots, T_m$ before time τ without deciding. Hence, as p_i tries to decide in $T_{R+1}, \ldots, T_m$ before time τ, p_i decides in some T_r at line 06.

$$\square_{Lemma\ 4}$$

Lemma 5. *(Validity) Let (ℓ, v) be a pair decided by some processor. v is a proposed value.*

Proof. Let p_i be a processor that decides (ℓ, v). If p_i decides in the first phase of the protocol (at line 06), v is contained in a posted snapshot of size 1. If p_i decides in the second part of the protocol, it follows from line 18 and Lemma 4 that v is contained in a posted snapshot of size 2. In both cases, v belongs to some snapshot posted in the first phase of the protocol.

As already observed, the first part of the protocol is the $(m, 1)$-BG protocol. As the proof of validity in the $(m, 1)$-BG protocol does not depend on the number of values processors wake up with (Lemma 1), we can reuse it here. In particular, it is shown in Lemma 1 that all posted snapshots are included in the set of values processors wake up with, from which we conclude that v is a proposed value. $\square_{Lemma\ 5}$

Lemma 6. *(Agreement) $\forall \ell, 1 \leq \ell \leq m : p_i$ returns (ℓ, v_i) and p_j returns (ℓ, v_j) $\Rightarrow v_i = v_j$.*

Proof. In the following, we say that a processor p_i decides in slot ℓ if it returns (ℓ, v) at line 06 or at line 18. We show that for any slot $\ell, 1 \leq \ell \leq m$, at most one value is decided. Let D_ℓ be the set of processes that decide in slot ℓ. Let us consider a slot ℓ such that $D_\ell \neq \emptyset$. We consider three cases:

- Each processor p_i that belongs to D_ℓ returns at line 06. Due to the atomic snapshot properties, at most one snapshot that contains only one value can be returned by the object $WS[\ell]$. It then follows from lines 06-07 that processors $\in D_\ell$ decide the same value.
- Each processor that belong to D_ℓ returns at line 18. This means that each processor $p_i \in D_\ell$ gets back a pair (ℓ, d_i) from the m-BGBINARY object. Due to the agreement property of the object, $\exists d \in \{0, 1\}$ such that $\forall p_i \in D_\ell, d_i = d$.

Moreover, due to Lemma 4, when $p_i \in D_\ell$ reads $SS[\ell, 2]$ at lines 11 and 18, $SS[r, \ell] \neq \bot$. It then follows from line 18 and the fact that $\exists d$ such that $\forall p_i \in D_\ell$: $d_i = d$ that each processor that belongs to the set D_ℓ chooses the same value in $SS[\ell, 2]$ and agreement follows.

- Some processors that belong to D_ℓ return at line 06 and other processors at line 18. Let C be the set of processors that invoke the m-BGBINARY object (a processor in C does not necessarily decides in slot ℓ). Among them, let p_c be the first processor that reads $SS[\ell, 1]$. This occurs at time τ. If p_c sees a value v, every processor in C proposes v for committee ℓ (lines 12-13). Therefore, v is the only value that can be decided in slot ℓ through the m-BGBINARY object and agreement follows.

  Suppose that p_c does not see a snapshot of size 1 ($SS[\ell, 1] = \bot$) in slot ℓ. We claim that no process can decide at line 06 in slot ℓ: a contradiction with the case assumption. To prove the claim, let us observe that when p_c reads $SS[\ell, 1]$ (lines 12-12), $SS[\ell, 2] \neq \bot$ (Lemma 4). Thus, a process that subsequently reads $SS[\ell, 1] \neq \bot$ reads also $SS[\ell, 2] \neq \bot$ and cannot decide in slot ℓ at line 06.

$$\square_{Lemma\ 6}$$

6 Conclusion

Simultaneous consensus was first introduced in [10,11] where it was shown using explicit topological arguments that 3 processors two committees is equivalent to $(3, 2)$-set consensus. The approach of interpreting algorithms through the prism of simultaneous consensus was then followed in [8] where it proved beneficial in obtaining a clear proof of robustness. Here, we close the circle. We utilize the observation that the BG simulation [2,4] is also about simultaneous consensus, to adopt a completely algorithmic approach to the question. Through this algorithmic approach that adopts ideas from BGs, we show that simultaneous consensus in a clear way captures consensus and set consensus. Moreover, it is a stronger paradigm than set-consensus. It trivially implements set-consensus, but it took some work to show that set consensus implements it. We expect this new view of set-consensus to prove beneficial in the future.

Atomic-Snapshots Shared-Memory is a higher level construct than SWMR Shared-Memory, and yet equivalent to it. Later Immediate-Snapshot Memories were proved to be even a higher level construct than Atomic-Snapshots. There, when "higher level" can be interpreted precisely as "less executions" it is a consequence of [2,13,16] that Immediate-Snapshots is the end of the road. Is simultaneous consensus the end of the road for set-consensus? Will there be a sense in which one may find even a tightest characterization of set-consensus? While we leave this question open, we feel that at the least it is now easier to motivate set-consensus through simultaneous consensus. Simultaneous consensus comes across as a bit less of "an invention of bored theorists," than the question of "electing multiple values." Multiple fronts is natural in life while multiple-leaders is less so.

References

1. Afek Y., H. Attiya, Dolev D., Gafni E., Merrit M. and Shavit N., Atomic Snapshots of Shared Memory. *Proc. 9th ACM Symposium on Principles of Distributed Computing (PODC'90)*, ACM Press, pp. 1–13, 1990.
2. Borowsky E. and Gafni E., Generalized FLP Impossibility Results for t-Resilient Asynchronous Computations *Proc. 25th ACM Symposium on the Theory of Computing (STOC'93)*, ACM Press, pp. 91-100, 1993.
3. Borowsky E. and Gafni E., Immediate Atomic Snapshots and Fast Renaming (Extended Abstract). *Proc. 12th ACM Symposium on Principles of Distributed Computing (PODC'93)*, ACM Press, pp. 41-51, 1993.
4. Borowsky E., Gafni E., Lynch N. and Rajsbaum S., The BG Distributed Simulation Algorithm. *Distributed Computing*, 14(3):127–146, 2001.
5. Chaudhuri S., More *Choices* Allow More *Faults:* Set Consensus Problems in Totally Asynchronous Systems. *Information and Computation*, 105:132-158, 1993.
6. Fischer M.J., Lynch N.A. and Paterson M.S., Impossibility of Distributed Consensus with One Faulty Process. *Journal of the ACM*, 32(2):374-382, 1985.
7. Gafni E., Group-Solvability. *Proc. 18th Int. Symposium on Distributed Computing (DISC'04)*, Springer Verlag LNCS #3274, pp. 30–40, 2004.
8. Gafni E. and Kouznetsov P., Two Front Agreement with Application to Emulation and Robustness. *to appear.*
9. Gafni E., Merritt M. and Taubenfeld G., The Concurrency Hierarchy, and Algorithms for Unbounded Concurrency. *Proc. 21st ACM Symposium on Principles of Distributed Computing (PODC'01)*, ACM Press, pp. 161–169, 2001.
10. Gafni E. and Rajsbaum S., Musical Benches. *Proc. 19th Int. Symposium on Distributed Computing (DISC'05)*, Springer Verlag LNCS # 3724, pp. 63–77, September 2005.
11. Gafni E. and Rajsbaum S., Raynal M., Travers C., The Committee Decision Problem. *Proc. Theoretical Informatics, 7th Latin American Symposium (LATIN'06)*, Springer Verlag LNCS #3887, pp. 502-514, 2006.
12. Herlihy M.P., Wait-Free Synchronization. *ACM Transactions on programming Languages and Systems*, 11(1):124-149, 1991.
13. Herlihy M.P. and Shavit N., The Topological Structure of Asynchronous Computability. *Journal of the ACM*, 46(6):858-923, 1999.
14. Mostefaoui A., Raynal M.and Tronel F., From Binary Consensus to Multivalued Consensus in Asynchronous Message-Passing Systems. *Information Processing Letters*, 73:207-213, 2000.
15. Merrit M., Taubenfeld G., Computing with infinitely many processes. *Proc. 14th Int. Symposium on Distributed Computing (DISC'00)*, Springer Verlag LNCS #1914, pp. 164–178, October 2000.
16. Saks, M. and Zaharoglou, F., Wait-Free k-Set Agreement is Impossible: The Topology of Public Knowledge. *SIAM Journal on Computing*, 29(5):1449-1483, 2000.

Database Summarization and Publishing in Wireless Environments

Anshul Gandhi and R.K. Ghosh

Indian Institute of Technology, Kanpur - 208 016, India
{ganshul, rkg}@cse.iitk.ac.in

Abstract. Data dissemination in a mobile computing environment typically uses push based data delivery model. Processing queries under this scenario is challenging because we need to organize the broadcast data to efficiently process queries of an average mobile client. In this paper, we adopt the learning technique from [2] in order to learn the patterns of queries of the average mobile user. We then propose a method to create various summary databases from the main database available at server side, on the basis of these query patterns.

1 Introduction

In this paper we view query processing as the fundamental element for data requirements in broadcast channel from an average client's prospective. A client will be interested in some data items for which he/she would like to place a demand. So in trying to learn the data demands of an average client, the approach should be to analyze the pattern of queries originating from client devices. These patterns can be stored in a compressed trie like data structure much like the ones used in location prediction of mobile devices using subscriber mobility patterns [1, 2]. We, therefore, adopt the above technique for learning query patterns. We then form and analyse the Entity-Relationship graph (E-R graph) related to these queries by extracting the database attributes from them. Next we find a spanning subgraph of the E-R graph which can be used to construct the summary database by selecting appropriate database attributes and corresponding relationships from the main database at the server side. The server then intermixes summary data with an index before pushing it on broadcast channel which facilitates energy efficient retrieval by the mobile hosts.

2 Current Prediction Techniques

Two techniques, namely, LeZi update [1] and active LeZi [2] both based on Lempel-Zvi data compression algorithm [3] have been used in prediction of the location of a mobile node by learning its mobility pattern. We model the query prediction as an instance for the Active LeZi predictor with almost no overheads. The readers interested to know more about active LeZi may refer to the original paper [2]. In the database scenario, we keep track of queries received from various clients and record these in the trie.

Let the incoming queries be $q_1, q_2, \ldots, q_k$ at some time t. Every query makes references to a certain set of attributes from a database. We assume that the required set

S. Chaudhuri et al. (Eds.): ICDCN 2006, LNCS 4308, pp. 342–348, 2006.

of attributes can be extracted from the query. Once this set is available, every query will be identified with its attribute set and this distinct set of such attributes will be relabeled as q_1, q_2, ..., etc. This solves the issue of converting a query into a single element as required by Active LeZi. We then apply the Active LeZi technique to the input $Q = \{q_1, q_2, \ldots, q_k\}$, with q_i , $i \in \{1, 2, \ldots, k\}$, belonging to a domain of elements D. Note that here D is simply the powerset of all attributes in the given database. By looking at the output probability values from the Active LeZi scheme, we can pick the query with the highest probability and use this as our prediction for the next query (attribute-wise).

Despite its ease of implementation and simplicity, Active LeZi have some drawbacks when used as a query predictor which are revealed when we take a closer look at a query sequence. There is no concept of *aging* in active LeZi. Aging captures spatio-temporal locality. As the queries keep coming, they change trends. In other words, the query patterns change with time and/or location. If aging is not included, such patterns can never be captured.

3   Augmented Active LeZi

At the client side, there are two pieces of information that we plan to make use of, namely the location of the user and time at which the query has been sent. The client simply uses mobile device id or mobile cell id for the location. For the timestamp, a standardized clock for that region can be used. Hence, without much overhead in terms of uplink bandwidth, this extra information can be obtained from the client. We now have to change our trie accordingly.

From the Active LeZi, we see that the nodes simply contain the frequency of that particular pattern. We now change this node to include a pointer to a linked-list. Each node of this linked-list would be a 3-tuple with the following components: (i) the cell node id or the zone id, (ii) the date, and (iii) the time. No particular sorting within the linked list is required. Hence, as a new query comes in, we simply increment the frequency in the corresponding trie node and create a new node in the attached linked-list with information from the client. The trie would now look like the one shown in figure 1 (a).

Since aging is to be used for improving predictions, there is no need to run a check on aging at the server unless there is a need to predict; and also, we only need to check aging for those nodes of the trie that get affected by the input query. Consider a trie at time t; and suppose that we are interested in finding the probability of the next query being q_i. Then simply check aging for all those nodes in the trie that participate in computation of the cumulative probability value for q_i. We must, however, remove the aged entries before using the node for calculating the probability for q_i.

In the Active LeZi, we make use of all orders to calculate the probability for a prediction. We use the frequencies in the trie to get the final value. Using our linked list, we can calculate the average value of the time at which that particular node is accessed. Once we have the average value, we can compare it with the value of the current time and based on the deviation between the two, we can either add or subtract a factor from the total probability value. One can also choose to multiply the deviation value with

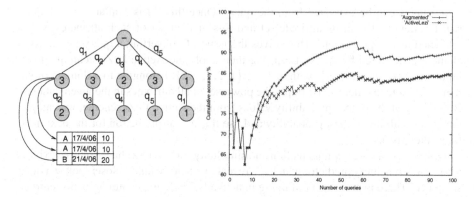

Fig. 1. Trie resulting from Augmented Active LeZi and comparison of Augmented Active LeZi with Active LeZi

the probability obtained from Active LeZi if the time factor is very significant for the database usage. In general, we can say that the probability function in the Augmented Active LeZi would be a function of the probability function used in the Active LeZi and the deviation between the average and observed values.

We tested augmented active LeZi for a simulated input data and compared its performance against active LeZi. Our test data was a set of 100 queries. From figure 1 (b), it is clear that the augmented predictor, which uses the hour of arrival of query to improve its prediction, outperforms the active LeZi by around 5% in our simulation. Since Active LeZi itself registers a success rate in the range of 80% in our case, the apparently small 5% increase in accuracy of prediction is indeed very significant. Though this simluation is in no way conclusive, it does show that there are cases where the Augmented Active LeZi will outdo the Active LeZi, especially if the incoming pattern tends to change its trends over time.

4   Constructing Summary Databases

4.1   Density of Prediction and Database Hierarchies

With the probability values at hand, we can now decide to use the highest-probability query to construct our database or we could decide to include more than one query into our summary database. We shall denote this number of queries by the parameter *density*. Note that higher the density, the larger would be the size of our database, which is not a very favourable requirement. But as the density goes up, so is the chance that the incoming query shall be answered by using the information contained in the summary database.

A prediction process is associated with an inherent chance of failure. In our case, a failure is exhibited when the client's query is not answered by the summary database. If the failure has resulted because of the low density value, then we can create another summary database which would now contain lower valued predictions which ccould answer the incoming query.

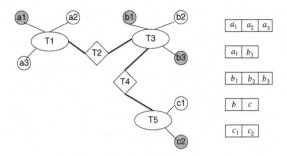

Fig. 2. E-R diagram corresponding to the example in section 4.2 and its tabular form

Assume that the predicted queries are sorted by decreasing cumulative probability values as $P = \{p_1, p_2, \ldots, p_k\}$ such that the set P contains all possible predictions (including the ones with zero probability). Say density = 3. Then, our summary database would answer queries p_1, p_2 and p_3. Let us assume that the incoming query is not in exact match with the predicted pattern and it corresponds to p_4. What we can do to avoid the loss of query is to create a second level of summary database which would have the power to answer queries p_4, p_5 and p_6. Note however that this level is at a lower priority than the first summary database. To tackle this issue, we could publish this level less number of times than compared to level 1. In fact, no matter how many such levels we have, we can publish them with a frequency which would be in a reverse ratio of their priorities.

4.2   Using E-R Modeling

We wish to ensure that we consider only those queries that are valid and reject those which are not. We also wish to do this as early as possible before updating the trie with the query. By using the E-R model corresponding to the database, we can model this issue in a different manner. Consider the E-R model shown in figure 2 and the corresponding tabular form of an arbitrary database which appears alongside.

Let the required attributes corresponding to an incoming query be the ones that are shaded in figure 2, namely, a_1, b_1, b_3 and c_2. Call these attributes as the set S. To ensure validity, all that is needed is to check whether there is a *marked path* between the required edges. A 'marked path' is a path that includes only those edges that are marked. Note that the E-R model is treated implicitly as a graph where the entities, relations and attributes are nodes and the edges are the edges of the graph. The outline of a simple algorithm to mark the edges is provided below.

```
i.  For all selected attributes, mark the edge connecting them to their parent
    entities.
ii. For an edge connecting a relation R to an entity E, mark it if the
    attributes of E included in R belong to S.
```

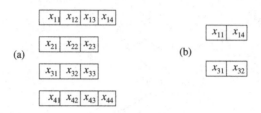

(a)   (b)

Fig. 3. Example

As an example consider the execution of above algorithm over the E-R graph shown in figure 2. After step 1, edges 1, 6, 8 and 12 gets marked in figure 2. Regarding step 2, we look at the attributes in the tabular form of R. Since R is connected to E, it must have attributes of E in its tabular form. If all these attributes belong to S, then the edge connecting R to E gets marked. So, after executing of step 2 over E-R graph of figure 2 edges 4, 5, 9 and 10 get marked. We, therefore, find that we have a marked path {1, 4, 5, 6, 8, 9, 10, 12} which touches all the attributes in S.

We can use the following steps to ensure validity of the query once the marking is done.

```
  i. Remove all unmarked edges.
 ii. Check whether we have a connected component of the remaining graph that
     connects all the nodes in S.
iii. If yes, return VALID; else return INVALID.
```

4.3 Construction Steps

After ensuring the validity of the query, our next task is to decode the queries back into their attribute requirements for the database construction. We shall collect all these attributes for each selected query into a set S. We now scan all the tables of the database and mark all those attributes of the database which belong to S. The algorithm is provide below.

```
initialize S:= null;
initialize D:= input database;
for (i ≤ 0, i < density, i++) do
   for each attribute x required by p(i) do
      S := SU{x}
   endfor
endfor
for each table T in database do
   for each attribute y of table T do
      if y belong to S mark y
      endif
   endfor
endfor
remove all unmarked components from D
for each table T in D do
   for every table T' in D such that (T∩T' = null)
   return D.
```

At this point, just by looking at the marked entries of the database, we can see what the desired output database would be like. It would be a collection of sub-tables of the original database. That is, if we delete all the unmarked attributes, then the remainder of the database would be our summary database.

Consider the following tabular schema in figure 3(a) for an input database. Here, the x's are attribute names (not necessarily distinct). Say our predictor marks attributes x_{11}, x_{14}, x_{31} and x_{32}. Our output would then be as shown in figure 3(b). Further, say x_{31} and x_{14} are actually from the same domain. That is, they share the same attribute name. We shall use the normal convention that if the attribute names are the same in a database, then these attributes belong to the same domain. We shall now save space by joining these two columns by using a *join* function call. We can simply modify the existing variants of the JOIN call to serve our purpose.

We require our JOIN to join the two tables that share any common attribute. The first common attribute found is selected and the JOIN is performed. Say, x_{31} is a subset of x_{14}. Then we would like to join T1 and T3 in such a way that no tuples are lost. We can use null values for the empty components of the tuples. Also, if x_{31} and x_{14} are disjoint, then we would simply have the output as one single table that would have as many tuples as there are in T1 and T3 combined and each tuple would be a 3-tuple in this case. One for x_{11}, one for x_{14}/x_{31} and one for x_{32}. In most cases, we would be saving considerable space by this method. However in cases where disjoint columns are operated on using JOIN, no space saving is achieved.

The extended algorithm including the JOIN appears below.

```
remove all unmarked components from D;
for each table T in D do
    for every table T' in D such that (T∩T'=null) do
      join T and T'; delete T'
    endfor
endfor
return D;
```

The resulting database for the previous case would be: T1 | x_{11} | x_{14}/x_{31} | x_{32} |

5   Conclusions

In this paper, we developed an idea to connect query prediction with the active LeZi predictor. We then proposed some augmentations to the active LeZi which has added advantages of aging and localizing the temporal behaviour of queries. We then gave a construction of summary databases for the mobile environment. Summary databases can be used to minimize the amount of data transfers over the network. As indicated at the beginning, the motivation behind this work was to reduce the size of data transmission on the broadcast channel. By reducing the size of data transmission we not only achieve better utilization bandwidth but also a substantial reduction in time for data transmission over wireless broadcast channel.

References

1. BHATTACHARYA, A., AND DAS, S. K. Lezi-update: An information-theoretic framework for personal mobility tracking in pcs networks. *Wireless Networks 8* (2002), 121–135.
2. GOPALRATNAM, K., AND COOK, D. J. Active lezi: An incremental parsing algorithm for sequential prediction. In *Proceedings of the Florida Artificial Intelligence Research Symposium* (2003).
3. ZIV, J., AND LEMPEL, A. Compression of individual sequences via variable-rate coding. *IEEE Transactions on Information Theory 24*, 5 (1978), 530–536.

Read-Write Reductions

Extended Abstract

Eli Gafni

Department of Computer Science, UCLA, Los Angeles, CA 90095, USA
eli@cs.ucla.edu

Abstract. The discovery, more than a decade ago, of the relation between Distributed-Computing (DC) and Algebraic-Topology (AT) raised the specter of requiring checking task solvability to be intimately connected to expertise in AT. Yet, in the area of Centralized Algorithms proving a problem to be NP or PSPACE complete requires more algorithmic expertise than complexity one. In analogy, we show that in DC the equivalent of polynomial-time reductions, is read-write reductions. We define the notion of read-write reduction between distributed tasks, and show that all interesting known read-write impossible tasks can be proven impossible via read-write reduction to a task called Symmetry-Breaking (SB). Discovering a read-write reduction requires solely algorithmic expertise.

1 Introduction

Since the introduction of topological arguments [2,20,21], they have been used among other uses, to argue the insolvability of a given task in a given model. Do we need now to run and study topology in order to make progress in this area of checking tasks for solvability?

We propose task called Symmetry-Breaking whose role in proving another task to be read-write insolvable is informally but usefully the analogue of the role of SAT in proving NP-completeness. To prove a problem NP-complete one does not need to be an expert in Turing Machine tricks. Once SAT was proven NP-complete from here on NP-completeness is proved by reduction. Similarly, we exhibit that all natural tasks to-date which are known to be insolvable wait-free in the shared-memory read-write model, can be proven so by reduction from the corresponding size SB task.

We do not claim that this analogy to be formal. I.e. we do not claim that if a task A is insolvable wait-free in the read-write model then there exits a reduction. In fact we know that to be false: SB is not solvable even when one is given the use of a Torus task [15] (or for that matter any orientable manifold), thus SB will not suffice to prove that the Torus task is insolvable. Yet we do not know how to pose a Torus task for arbitrary number of processors in a way that will not be "artificial." Thus, we conjecture that there exists a proper "natural" definition of "natural" families of tasks for which SB is the weakest task.

S. Chaudhuri et al. (Eds.): ICDCN 2006, LNCS 4308, pp. 349–354, 2006.

2 Definitions

A task is an input-output relation between sets of processors, each set called a *partici-pating set*, and output tuples, each specifying an output value for each processor in the participating set.

A task is solvable in certain model if there exists a protocol in the model, and a notion of when a processor participates in the protocol, such that for a run in the model with a participating set P, all processor output and halt so that the outputs constitute an allowed output tuple in the task.

The tasks we consider will be families of tasks, each parametrized by n, denoting the maximum size of the participating set. For each task we will consider two families: Non-Comparison, and Comparison. In the former the largest participating set is drawn out of $\{p_0, , p_{n-1}\}$. In the latter, the participating set is any set of processors of cardinality less or equal to n. It is known that the ability to draw the participating processors from a universe large enough is equivalent to the processor identifiers being used only via comparison [12].

Although the task definition is just a mapping from participating sets to output, it encompasses a processor that may wake up with different inputs by considering each input to be associated with different processor identifier and considering the comparison version of the task. Thus w.l.o.g. below we will refer to different inputs, albeit in that case only the comparison version makes sense.

We will say that a task A read-write *implements* B if given any numbers of copies of A and any number of read-write registers than we can wait-free solve B. We than will say that A is potentially stronger than B. If the opposite is also true than we say that A and B are *equivalent*. If we know that B is impossible to solve read-write wait-free, than such an implementation proves that A is insolvable read-write wait-free by *reduction from B*.

3 Task-Families

1. k-Set-Election: The task $SE(k, n)$ says that for all participating sets of size at most n each processor outputs an id of a processor from the participating set, and the number of distinct ids that appear in an output tuple is less or equal to k.
2. k-Strong-Set-Election: The task $SSE(k, n)$ is like Set-Election but in addition if p_i outputs p_j then p_j outputs p_j i.e. itself.
3. k-Set-Consensus: In the task $SC(k, n)$ each processor wakes up with an input tuple of size k, where at position i there is a 0 or 1. It returns as an output an index $1 \leq j \leq k$ and a single bit, 0 or 1. All processors that return the same index j return with it the same bit b. The non-triviality requires that b can be returned together with the index j only if there exist a participating processor who has b in the jth position of its input tuple.
4. k-Test-and-Set: In the task $TAS(k, n)$, $n > k$ participating processors output 0 or 1, and each output tuple always contains at least one 0, and at most k 0s. The largest participating set is of cardinality n

5. Symmetry-Breaking: In the task $SB(n)$ processors output 0 or 1. The largest participating set is of size n and the output tuples for this size correspond to all the possible n length bit strings, excluding the all 0s and all 1s strings.

6. n-Adaptive-Renaming: In the task $AR(f(k), m, n)$ processors return positive distinct integers in the range 1 o m. For $k < n$ they return in the range 1 to $f(k)$.

7. n-Renaming: In the task $R(m, n)$, $m \geq n$ processors return positive distinct integers in the range 1 to m.

4   Reductions

Below we first outline the sequence of reductions from $SB(n)$ that prove all the above tasks to be read-arite wait-free insolvable given that $SB(n)$. That $SB(n)$ is insolvable is a consequence of its equivalence to comparison $AR(2n-2, n)$. The latter was proved insolvable by direct topological arguments in [20].

In the subsection that follow the outline we elaborate on each item in the outline, respectively. Most of the reductions are almost at the level of folklore. Some are substantial, and then we reference them. No new reduction is introduced here and thus the contribution of the paper is just in organizing all these scattered related known items into a single place.

4.1   Outline of Sequence of Reductions

1. $SB(n)$ and $AR(2n - 2, n)$ are trivially solvable in the non-comparison model.

2. Below we show comparison $SB(n)$ and comparison $AR(2n-2, n)$ to be equivalent in the comparison model. The task $AR(2n - 2, n)$ was proved to be insolvable in the comparison model in [20].

3. If comparison $SB(n)$ is read-write wait-free solvable then comparison $SB(n + 1)$ is [16]. Thus $SB(n + 1)$ is weaker than $SB(n)$, but the reduction is white-box rather than black-box reduction. We do not know a black-box reduction for this fact.

4. Non-comparison $TAS(k, n)$ is equivalent to task $TAS(k, n + 1)$ and thus to $TAS(k, \infty)$. Below we show that non-comparison $TAS(k, k + 1)$ implements $SB(k+1)$, and obviously comparison $TAS(k, k+1)$ implements non-comparison $TAS(k, k + 1)$.

5. Non-comparison $SE(k, k + 1)$ is equivalent to $SSE(k, k + 1)$ which is equivalent to non-comparison $TAS(k, k + 1)$. Obviously the comparison versions implement their corresponding non-comparison ones. And obviously $SE(k, k+2)$ implements $SE(k, k + 1)$.

6. The non-comparison $SC(k, n)$ is equivalent to $SE(k, n)$.

7. The task $AR(2k - 1, 2n - 2, n)$ is equivalent to $TAS(n - 1, n)$.

4.2   Sketch of Reductions

1. Needs no further comment.

2. (a) Comparison $SB(n)$ implements comparison $AR(2n - 2, n)$: Processors use $SB(n)$ to break themselves into two disjoint groups each of which is

non-empty when the cardinality of the participating set is n. One group G_0 of cardinality n_0 consists of the processors that output 0 in $SB(n)$ and the other group is G_1 of cardinality n_1. Both groups now use the comparison renaming algorithm $AR(2k - 1, 2n - 1, n)$ in [?,8]. Only that G_0 renames from position 1 upwards, while group G_1 renames from position $2n - 2$ downward. We observe that $(2n_0 - 1) + 2n_1 - 1 \leq 2(n_0 + n_1) - 2 \leq 2n - 2$, where the first inequality is true iff both G_0 and G_1 are non-empty. It is easy to see that when the participating set cardinality is less than N the space is enough.

  (b) Comparison $AR(2n - 2, n)$ implements comparison $SB(n)$: Processors that obtain values from $AR(2n - 2, n)$ in the range 1 to n-1 output 0, while the rest output 1.

3. This was put in to raise the question whether any task A that can be shown to implement B *provided A was read-write wait-free solvable*, means that if B is not solvable than B can be reduced to A. We do not know the answer to this question but conjecture the answer to be positive. We challenge the reader to show that comparison $SB(n)$ implements comparison $SB(n + 1)$.

4. Trivially non-comparison $TAS(k, n + 1)$ implements non-comparison TAS (k, n). To see the reverse put processors p_0 to p_{n-1} through $TAS_1(k, n)$. At most k of them will obtain a 0. They then proceed some to $TAS_2(k, n)$ and some to $TAS_3(k, n)$. They proceed by renaming $AR(2k - 1, 2n - 1, n)$. Those that obtain values in 1 to $n - 1$ go to the corresponding ports in $TAS_2(k, n)$, and those that obtain a value j higher than $n - 1$ go to port $j - (n - 1)$ in $TAS_3(k, n)$. Processor p_n attaches to port n in $TAS_2(k, n)$. Processors that obtain values in $TAS_3(k, n)$ return as final output the negation of their output from $TAS_3(k, n)$, while processor with output from $TAS_2(k, n)$ retain their output. The idea of negation was proposed to us by Rafail Ostrovasky [17].

    To see that non-comparison $TAS(k, k+1)$ implements comparison $SB(n)$ take two copies $TAS_1(k, k+1)$ and $TAS_2(k, k+1)$. The n processors $AR(2k-1, 2n-1, n)$ rename into port of $TAS_1(k, k + 1)$ and $TAS_2(k, k + 1)$ where port i in the latter stand for the integer $i + (k + 1)$. processors out of $TAS_2(k, k + 1)$ negate their output.

5. (a) The task $SE(k, k + 1)$ is equivalent to $SSE(k, k + 1)$: Obviously SSE $(k, k + 1)$ implements $SE(k, k + 1)$. The reverse implementation appears in [2].

  (b) The task $SSE(k, k + 1)$ is equivalent to $TAS(k, k + 1)$: See [2].

6. Non-comparison $SC(k, n)$ is equivalent to $SE(k, n)$: In this issue [9].

7. The task $AR(2k - 1, 2n - 2, n)$ is equivalent to $TAS(n - 1, n)$:

  (a) The task $AR(2k - 1, 2n - 2, n)$ implements $TAS(n - 1, n)$: Processors that get values in 1 to $n - 1$ output 0, the rest output 1.

  (b) Processors do immediate snapshot [3]. Those that end up with snapshot of size n apply to $TAS(n - 1, n)$. They thus divide into three disjoint groups: Group $G_{<n}$ of those that obtain a snapshot of size less than n, Group G_0 of those that obtained 0 in $TAS(n - 1, n)$, and the rest are in G_1. Processors in $G_{<n}$ and G_1 $AR(2k - 1, 2n - 1, n)$ rename from 1 upward while those in G_0 rename from $2n - 2$ downward [8,14,18].

5 Conclusions

We have presented a sequence of reductions/implementations that show how all known interesting insolvable task can be deemed so by reduction from the family SB. This led to the speculation that any "interesting" task is at least as strong as SB. Indeed that speculation led to a renewed push to understand the relation between SB and TAS that has recently resulted in the conclusion that SB is strictly weaker than TAS. We also leave some interesting open problems. If it can be (white-box) shown that the read-write wait-free solvability of A, either by assumption of the existence of read-write code as in the BG-simulation [2,5], or by considering the topological ramification of such solvability, would imply the read-arite solvability of task B, does it necessarily implies that B can be reduced to A (black-box)? It will be elegant and satisfying if the answer is positive.

Finally, it will be of the utmost interest to capture rigorously what is informally considered a "natural" task family and show that any task of interest at the least breaks symmetry.

Acknowledgment. I am in debt to Sergio Rajsbaum who assigned me to give an invited talk at DISC 2004 Godel celebration session. An assignment that resulted in [8], where the idea of equating SB to SAT was first introduced.

References

1. Afek Y., H. Attiya, Dolev D., Gafni E., Merrit M. and Shavit N., Atomic Snapshots of Shared Memory. *Proc. 9th ACM Symposium on Principles of Distributed Computing (PODC'90)*, ACM Press, pp. 1–13, 1990.
2. Borowsky E. and Gafni E., Generalized FLP Impossibility Results for t-Resilient Asynchronous Computations *Proc. 25th ACM Symposium on the Theory of Computing (STOC'93)*, ACM Press, pp. 91-100, 1993.
3. Borowsky E. and Gafni E., Immediate Atomic Snapshots and Fast Renaming (Extended Abstract). *Proc. 12th ACM Symposium on Principles of Distributed Computing (PODC'93)*, ACM Press, pp. 41-51, 1993.
4. Borowsky E. and Gafni E., A Simple Algorithmically Reasoned Characterization of Wait-Free Computations (Extended Abstract). *Proc. 16th ACM Symposium on Principles of Distributed Computing (PODC'97)*, ACM Press, pp. 189–198, 1997.
5. Borowsky E., Gafni E., Lynch N. and Rajsbaum S., The BG Distributed Simulation Algorithm. *Distributed Computing,* 14(3):127–146, 2001.
6. Chaudhuri S., More *Choices* Allow More *Faults:* Set Consensus Problems in Totally Asynchronous Systems. *Information and Computation,* 105:132-158, 1993.
7. Fischer M.J., Lynch N.A. and Paterson M.S., Impossibility of Distributed Consensus with One Faulty Process. *Journal of the ACM*, 32(2):374-382, 1985.
8. Gafni E., DISC/GODEL presentation: R/W Reductions (DISC'04), 2004. http://www.cs.ucla.edu/˜ eli/eli/godel.ppt
9. Afek Y., Gafni E., Rajsbaum S., Raynal M. and Travers C., Simultaneous Consensus Tasks: A Tighter Characterization of Set-Consensus, This issue.
10. Gafni E., Group-Solvability. *Proc. 18th Int. Symposium on Distributed Computing (DISC'04)*, Springer Verlag LNCS #3274, pp. 30–40, 2004.

11. Gafni E. and Kouznetsov P., Two Front Agreement with Application to Emulation and Robustness. *to appear*.
12. Attiya, H., Bar-Noy, A., Dolev, D., Peleg, D., and Reischuk, R., Renaming in an asynchronous environment, J. ACM 37, 3 (Jul. 1990), 524-548.
13. N. Fredrickson and N. Lynch, Electing a Leader in a Synchronous Ring, JACM, January 1987.
14. Gafni E. and Rajsbaum S., Musical Benches. *Proc. 19th Int. Symposium on Distributed Computing (DISC'05)*, Springer Verlag LNCS # 3724, pp. 63–77, September 2005.
15. Eli Gafni, Sergio Rajsbaum, Maurice Herlihy, Subconsensus Tasks: Renaming is Weaker than Set Agreement, DISC06, Springer Verlag LNCS #4167, Stockholm, Sweeden, September 18-20 , 329-339, 2006.
16. Gafni E., In preparation.
17. Ostrovsky R., Private communication to the author.
18. Gafni E. and Rajsbaum S., Raynal M., Travers C., The Committee Decision Problem. *Proc. Theoretical Informatics, 7th Latin American Symposium (LATIN'06)*, Springer Verlag LNCS #3887, pp. 502-514, 2006.
19. Herlihy M.P., Wait-Free Synchronization. *ACM Transactions on programming Languages and Systems*, 11(1):124-149, 1991.
20. Herlihy M.P. and Shavit N., The Topological Structure of Asynchronous Computability. *Journal of the ACM*, 46(6):858-923, 1999.
21. Saks, M. and Zaharoglou, F., Wait-Free k-Set Agreement is Impossible: The Topology of Public Knowledge. *SIAM Journal on Computing*, 29(5):1449-1483, 2000.

Large Scale Voice over IP Experiences on High Performance Intranets

Francesco Palmieri

Università "Federico II" di Napoli, Centro Servizi Didattico Scientifico, V. Cinthia, 45,
80126 Napoli, Italy
fpalmieri@unina.it

Abstract. The goal of this paper is to provide some feedback on a VoIP pilot project developed over the Federico II University high performance metropolitan transport network, presenting an overview of the activities which have been taken since the pilot was started. The project was initiated in order to analyze the capabilities of VoIP technologies, figuring out their quality of service and interoperability requirements, the optimum call routing practices and to identify the challenges in building large voice over IP applications. As a result we realized, managed and tested a rather complex VoIP infrastructure transporting all the internal voice traffic between the three main aggregation areas grouping our University's sites in Napoli, which smoothly moved from a research system into an operational state.

1 Introduction

In earlier days, the Internet was mainly a collection of connected computers hosting and exchanging text-based or binary files based on the TCP/IP protocol suite. As the proliferation of Internet technology increased, the revolution shifting toward the convergence of data and voice networks sharing common transport facilities, is inexorably started and many network operators have to face the challenge of conveying real-time voice traffic together with traditional data flows, offering a viable and more efficient alternative to traditional switched circuit networks. But, in contrast with typical IP-based services, VoIP is characterized by stringent resources and Quality of Service (QoS) requirements, normally expressed in terms of available bandwidth and transfer delays, thus a proper design of network architecture, routing model and QoS controls (such as packet scheduling, bandwidth reservation mechanisms, traffic shaping or policing) is strongly required to ensure the efficient transport of voice traffic. The goal of this paper is to provide some feedback on a VoIP pilot project developed over the Federico II University high performance metropolitan transport network. During the last year we built up, managed and tested a large VoIP application transporting all the internal voice traffic between the three main aggregation areas, counting about 3000 phone users each one, grouping our University's sites in the urban territory. The primary goal of the pilot was to identify problems emerging in such large installations. We evaluated the quality of service requirements of VoIP transmission as well as examined the performance and interoperability features of the

S. Chaudhuri et al. (Eds.): ICDCN 2006, LNCS 4308, pp. 355–366, 2006.

different VoIP components in our network. Additionally, as a very main part of the investigations, the available QoS techniques, the call routing possibilities and fault-tolerance options were tested during a sophisticated and complete assessment. This resulted in a reconfiguration of the whole infrastructure performed several times until the optimal configuration has been reached. Our initiative changed in the last months from a research point of view to an operating telephony network with higher availability demands. Certainly, the VoIP infrastructure cannot be used as a testbed only anymore. Therefore, we considered it a very successful practice to evaluate the real voice over IP capabilities and to identify the challenges in building large interconnected VoIP installations working on high performance metro networks.

2   Operating Scenario

In this section we will give some useful details about the operating environment, such as the underlying transport network and the existing legacy telephony system, in which the VoIP pilot project has been developed. We also describe the architecture of the voice transport and IP telephony infrastructure that have been realized as the main building blocks of our evaluation and early technology deployment.

2.1   The Transport Network

The physical multi-ring fiber infrastructure, on which our network is based, is approximately 50 km long, consists of 156 9/125 G.652 single-mode fibers, connecting, in a multi-ring shape with differentiated ways, four ring-to-ring interchange and service aggregation centers, strategically placed on the metro area, which realize the main transport and access distribution infrastructure, serving actually more than 20 level-2 distribution sites providing access to end-users. The physical network layout is reported in the following figure 1.

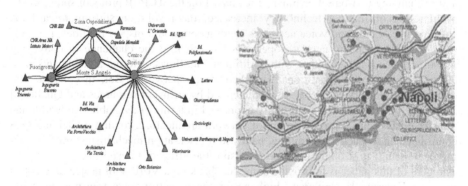

Fig. 1. Physical multi-ring layout and topology of Federico II fiber net

The backbone is built on a fully meshed MPLS core realized between three high performance Cisco routers (a 12410 GSR and two 7606 OSRs), each acting as an access aggregation point (or POP) in the metropolitan area. We realized two distinct independent rings between the core nodes using, for connecting each node to another both the primary and secondary branch on the ring. The links belonging to the primary ring are made on POS STM-16 (2.5 Gbps) interfaces and the links belonging to the secondary (or backup) ring and with the leaf access nodes are built on Gigabit Ethernet interfaces. All the connections between the routers are made with single mode optical fiber between long-range interfaces, STM-16 long reach (on the primary ring) and Gigabit Ethernet 1000baseLX/LH (on the secondary ring). The IS-IS protocol, extended with traffic engineering facilities, has been used as the IGP of choice for the propagation of link status and resource availability information in the whole MPLS domain. Multi-protocol BGP (with fully meshed sessions in the core and route reflectors at the edge) has been used to carry VPN information when the MPLS Layer 2 or Layer 3 VPNs are used for cooperating LAN isolation or security. In particular several virtual point-to-point connection have been realized between the "Monte S. Angelo" and "Centro Storico POPs" to offer pseudo-wire bandwidth guaranteed services, through *Any Transport Over MPLS* (ATOM) layer 2 tunneling and traffic engineered label switched paths, to external organizations.

2.2 The VoIP Pilot

Until an year ago, our university's telephony system was based on a classic private branch exchange (PABX) architecture, built on many Ericsson MD110 modules operating and manageable as a single integrated exchange, according to a classic hierarchical model based on three group switching points, located into the main area aggregation sites. The three switching points collecting all the satellite PABXes in their areas were connected each other in a ring shape through classic 2 Mbps leased data lines. Furthermore each group switching exchange was independently connected to the PSTN. In this scenario, the evolutionary pilot project has been conceived with essentially three main objectives:

- deploying VoIP between the existing PABX concentration areas to lower costs, by switching voice traffic on underutilized high speed MAN links.
- introducing and evaluating native IP telephony technologies to analyze their performance and functionality in a significant test bench for further new medium to large-scale realizations.
- figuring out the QoS requirements of VoIP, the interoperability with the available installations, the optimum routing properties of the transport network, and the inclusion of gateways between the different legacy and new technologies.

As the first step the three Ericsson MD110 group switching points (Monte S. Angelo, .via Mezzocannone, Fuorigrotta) have been connected to the high performance fiber ring with the introduction of IP voice trunk interface modules into each concentration exchange. Several redundant modules on each exchange have been connected via 100baseTX copper links to the Cisco 7606 OSR metro POP through the mediation of some Cisco Catalyst 3560 switches, collecting the copper links and performing fast to gigabit Ethernet conversion. This allowed the seamless migration of the legacy traffic between the PABX aggregations without any loss in terms of proprietary inter-exchange functionalities implemented through non-standard signaling.

Next we deployed a native IP telephony system built on devices from different vendors and performed several functionality and interoperability tests on them. IP phones from Cisco Systems and Ericsson have been deployed at multiple locations in the network and an MCS 7825H Call Manager from Cisco Systems has been installed in the Monte S. Angelo site to control the telephony functions of the Cisco phones and provide call routing facilities for all the standard H.323 clients. All our tests were based on the standard H.323 signaling protocol, with the call manager working as the top-level H.323 gatekeeper, and a full interoperability between all the devices has been achieved. It has also been shown that the different phones can be interconnected very easily to the network using the standard H.323 signaling protocol, this demonstrated that the process of integrating new devices can be considered as straightforward. Typically it just required the configuration of the IP address and the local numbering scheme to interconnect a new client. Also, there was no difference between using software based IP telephony applications such as Microsoft Netmeeting or Cisco IP Communicator and employing hardware-based IP phones.

Last, the IP telephony systems has been connected to the standard telephony systems on each of the three aggregation sites to allow calls from inside the VoIP domain to phones outside the IP world and vice versa. For this purpose we used three Cisco Systems 3745 multiservice routers with the role of voice gateways which were connected on the three group switching sites to the legacy PABX network and to the public telephone network using multiple channelized E1 interfaces, providing two separate channels for ongoing calls. The complete layout of the VoIP and IP telephony system deployed in the context of the pilot project is depicted in fig.2 below.

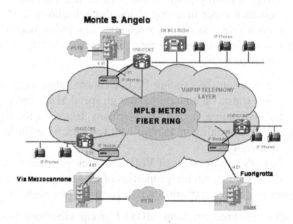

Fig. 2. The VoIP support infrastructure

3   Technical and Implementation Issues

We will now discuss some of the most important technological choices that have been adopted, after an extensive experimentation, to introduce adequate quality, robustness, and production-grade strength to our VoIP system.

3.1 Quality of Service Provisioning

It's unlikely that an arbitrary data network, even if a high performance one, is ready to handle good-quality VoIP traffic without the implementation of a proper QoS schema. This requires the cooperation of all logical layers in the IP network - from application to physical media - and of all network elements, from end to end. Given an IP network system's distributed nature, several highly interrelated optimizations tasks have to be performed simultaneously. Voice traffic is uniquely time-sensitive and it mixes very badly with the highly bursty Internet traffic. Even if huge bandwidth resources are available, VoIP traffic can't be queued or buffered too long, and if datagrams are lost, the conversation will be choppy or even incomprehensible. This led to a significant amount of effort aimed at enabling effective QoS support for voice traffic in our network. Our architecture has been designed to support three service classes, enforced by proper queuing strategies, traffic classification, call-admission controls, congestion avoidance mechanisms, traffic-shaping and policing techniques implemented according to the Differentiated Services model:

- *Premium Voice/Multimedia* – This service class is meant for voice calls that require excellent QoS to be used for very high quality voice or Voice/Video conferences. Each customer is guaranteed a certain amount of bandwidth for premium voice calls and a percentage of the upstream bandwidth is reserved for them. The number of premium calls that can be supported would depend on the codec used by the customer. Admission control is strictly enforced for calls belonging to this category. Premium calls are not allowed to borrow unused bandwidth that is reserved for other classes of service, since when the load offered by traffic belonging to other classes increases, each class must get the share of bandwidth reserved for it.

- *Regular Voice* – This service class is meant for voice calls that do not get admitted to the premium category. If we were to have only the premium category for voice calls, then some voice calls would get rejected if all the bandwidth reserved for the premium class were in use. Even if the bandwidth reserved for other classes of traffic were unused, we would be unable to take advantage of it, since premium traffic cannot borrow bandwidth from other classes. Such a strict fragmentation of resources leads to inefficient utilization. To address this issue, we introduce the concept of regular voice calls. Voice calls that cannot be admitted as premium can still be allowed to go through as regular calls. However, the regular calls are not given any strict QoS guarantees. Depending on the implementation, a portion of the upstream bandwidth may be reserved for them, or they may just share the bandwidth along with best-effort traffic. There is no admission control for the regular voice traffic. Under conditions of light load from best-effort traffic, the regular calls will receive acceptable performance. In the case of classic Internet traffic, the typical customer runs applications such as web browsing, email, file transfer, remote login and streaming multimedia, which offer low load on the transport link. Besides, the available bandwidth is usually quite high, so there is a reasonable chance of a regular call experiencing acceptable quality in a lightly loaded network.

- *Best Effort* – This service category is for non real-time traffic. Applications such as web browsing, email, FTP, telnet etc. fall under this category.

We served Premium voice class according to a strict priority queuing policy, implemented trough the *Low-Latency Queuing* (LLQ) paradigm. This mechanism forwards delay sensitive packets ahead of packets in other queues giving to delay-sensitive data, such as voice, preferential treatment over other traffic. This queuing strategy is policed to ensure that the other fair queues are not starved of bandwidth, by specifying the maximum amount of bandwidth available to the high priority traffic. When the interface is congested, the LLQ traffic is serviced until the load reaches the specified bandwidth value and all the excess traffic is dropped to avoid starvation on the lower priority queues. The Regular voice traffic class is served via the *Class-Based Weighted Fair Queuing* (CBWFQ) mechanism, by scheduling interactive traffic to the front of the queue to reduce response time, and allocating a specific amount of a queue to each class while leaving the rest of the queue to be filled in round-robin fashion, fairly sharing the remaining bandwidth among high-bandwidth flows. This essentially facilitates prioritizing multiple classes in queuing and allows a fine-grained control scheme providing, if useful, more differentiated traffic classes. In our architecture we also reserved a portion of bandwidth for Best Effort traffic in order to prevent starvation of these flows. Under the proper circumstances, these mechanisms, which are widely available in conventional packet-forwarding systems, can differentiate and appropriately handle time-sensitive isochronous traffic. We tested and evaluated the relative effectiveness of these mechanisms against other common QoS schemes in preserving the end-to-end subjective quality of voice streams in the presence of multiservice traffic and network congestion. Our tests revealed that QoS mechanisms that approximate per-stream assurances through classification, prioritization and careful forwarding techniques tend to perform better than mechanisms that simply reserve bandwidth and try to ensure low latency for forwarding without classification, or with too generic traffic classifications. Although this isn't a particularly surprising result, it is useful to compare the available technologies and examine some of the ancillary factors that heavily influence QoS provisioning in voice-grade transport services.

3.2 Call Routing Arrangements

Other terms of research in the project were the call routing facilities. In a very local VoIP installation this is a straightforward configuration step. Typically, all the local phones are hold in a database on the H.323 gatekeeper or SIP proxy. Long distance calls, or more precisely all the calls to non-IP phones, are routed to a single voice gateway which points to the POTS. The more flexibility is included into the VoIP installation the more complex is the resulting routing configuration. This applies even stronger to our VoIP network which interconnects multiple faculties, offices and research laboratories belonging to our university located on a very large urban area. We figured out different possibilities to implement such a distributed system. First, we started with a central approach. All the sites arranged their calls to go to a single gatekeeper and voice gateway located in the master site (in our case Monte S. Angelo). There we implemented a large routing table, which of course is always in a consistent state just because only one place exists where all modifications are applied. Secondly, to enable a much higher redundancy – for the routing core as well as for the availability of the network connections – we have already installed a voice gateway on each group switching site and we plan to move the routing decisions to a local gatekeeper (maybe another MCS 7825H Call Manager) placed in each area, realizing a gatekeeper hierarchy rooted on the "Monte S. Angelo" site. According to this schema we have three central core gateways containing the complete call routing information for their areas and referring to the upper layer gatekeeper for VoIP calls outside our IP telephony domain. Each core gateway statically route the VoIP calls associated to the other aggregation areas. This allows a high availability compared with a low complexity. Nevertheless, at the moment a central gatekeeper is installed to obtain the call routing table. All the calls are routed via this system. In case of a failure the calls are rerouted using the legacy telephone network.

3.3 Fault Tolerance During Backbone Outages

In our multi-ring shaped fiber network all the backbone faults were handled with redundancy and dynamic routing protocols that automatically updated the network topology and computed new routes around the failure. When we started to transport VoIP traffic we noticed that the switchover time due to the IGP convergence was not fast enough to prevent voice service disruption. We solved the problem by implementing for each site on the triangle-shaped VoIP infrastructure, a couple of explicit label switched paths on our MPLS backbone, namely the primary and backup paths, dedicated to the voice traffic, and implemented on them MPLS Fast Reroute protection to efficiently route traffic down the backup path in the event of an interface, node or link failure without any extra decision (IGP convergence) required. This setup significantly improved recovery times, reduced to less than 80 ms, which equates to noticeably higher network availability and performance.

4 VoIP System Performance Analysis

To complete our study about the VoIP capabilities and functional behavior in the pilot infrastructure a sophisticated and complete performance assessment has been performed. The methodological and implementation details, together with the most significant results are reported below.

4.1 Factors Influencing Voice Quality

The perceivable quality of voice transmission can be heavily influenced by several network dynamics originated by the link intrinsic properties, route and reachability fluctuations and congestion. These dynamics can be essentially characterized by three QoS metrics: delay, jitter and loss as described below. The end-to-end delay experienced by voice as it travels from source to destination has a significant effect on voice quality. It is recommended by [1] that delay bounds for the various grades of perceived performance in terms of human interaction can be defined as: Good (0ms-150ms), Acceptable (150ms-300ms), Poor (> 300ms). However most users find it inconvenient to carry out a conversation if the end-to-end delay is greater than 150 ms. Another factor influencing voice quality is the variation in delay (also called jitter). The source may send out voice packets in a uniform manner, but they may experience different delays across the network. Thus, the inter-arrival times of voice packets at the destination are variable, rather than constant. This delay variation results in unevenness in the reconstructed speech it the voice packets are delivered to the user as soon as they arrive. Several studies [2] suggest the following jitter values to be reasonably reliable estimates to determine the grade of perceived performance: Good (0ms-20ms), Acceptable (20ms-50ms), Poor (> 50ms). The fraction of voice packets lost during transit also affects the voice quality. Retransmission of voice packets is not feasible for real-time applications like voice, since they have very tight delay-bounds. As mentioned earlier, a packet that arrives too late is also considered lost. Though popular experience suggests loss levels greater than 1% can severely affect audio quality, there have not been well defined loss bounds in terms of the various grades of voice application performance. Current practice suggests the following loss values to be reasonably reliable estimates to determine the grade of perceived performance: Good (0%-0.5%), Acceptable (0.5%-1.5%), Poor (> 1:5%).

4.2 Methodology and Metrics

The real performance in a VoIP call is not measured by the classic network health parameters but on the perceptual speech quality. There are two popular methods to assess the audio quality in a typical VoIP call: Subjective and Objective quality assessment. A subjective factor is necessarily part of evaluating VoIP because a listener must be able to understand the received transmission, and both talkers must be able to tolerate the amount of delay between speaking and being heard, lost or fractured syllables, and echo that often impede the conversation. Subjective quality assessment involves letting a certain number of listeners to express their judgment about the speech quality, according to some standard guidelines and use it as a quality metric. Objective quality assessment does not rely on human judgment and involves automated procedures such as signal-to-noise ratio (SNR) measurements of original and reconstructed signals and other sophisticated algorithms to determine quality metrics. The problem with subjective quality assessment techniques is that human perception of quality is based on individual perception, which can vary significantly between a given set of individuals. The problem with objective quality assessment techniques is that they may not necessarily reflect the actual end-user experience. There have been studies [3] that show that when objective and subjective quality assessment are performed simultaneously, the results are comparable. In our study, we employ both the subjective and objective quality assessment methods to determine end-user perception of speech quality for VoIP calls traversing our network. To obtain subjective quality assessment scores from the users, we used the slider methodology presented in [4] on a sample of 10 individuals. All the participants to the subjective assessment ranked the audio quality on a scale of 1 to 5 for the various types of calls between the three main areas, characterized as PABX to PABX, PABX to IP prone, IP phone to PABX and IP phone to IP phone using what is basically the Mean Opinion Score (MOS) ranking technique. To obtain objective quality assessment scores we utilized the NetIQ VoIP Assessor tool [5] that provides a sophisticated implementation of the E-model and uses configurable VoIP traffic flows built on sample calls generated through the well-known Chariot technology as an input for its analysis. The E-model is a well established computational model, formally defined in the ITU Standard

G.107 [6], that uses transmission parameters to predict the subjective quality. It uses a psycho-acoustic R-scale whose values range from 0 to 100 and quantifies what is essentially a subjective judgment: a user's opinion of the perceived quality of voice transmission. After much study, the ITU determined which impairment factors produced the strongest user perceptions of lower quality. The E-model also includes factors for equipment and impairments and takes into account typical users' perceptions of voice transmissions. In more detail, the E-model rating factor R is defined as a linear combination of the individual impairments and is given by:

$$R = (R_0 - I_S) - I_d - I_e + A \qquad (1)$$

Where:

- R_0 groups the effect of noise, either background or circuit noise.
- I_s includes impairments simultaneous to the voice signal: due to quantization, too loud a connection, too loud side tone.
- I_d encompasses delayed impairments, included those caused by talker and listener echo or loss of interactivity.
- I_e covers the impairments caused by the use of special equipment; for example, each low bit rate codec has an associated impairment value. This impairment value can also be used to take into account the influence of packet loss.
- The term A is the expectation factor. It expresses the decrease in the rating R a user is willing to tolerate in favor of the "access advantage" over wire-bound telephony. As an example, the expectation factor for mobile telephony is 10.

The graphical relationship between the Rating Factor and the Mean Opinion Score, together with the correspondence table (taken from ITU G.107) between the MOS and user satisfaction are reported in fig. 3 below.

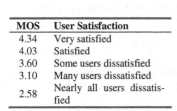

MOS	User Satisfaction
4.34	Very satisfied
4.03	Satisfied
3.60	Some users dissatisfied
3.10	Many users dissatisfied
2.58	Nearly all users dissatisfied

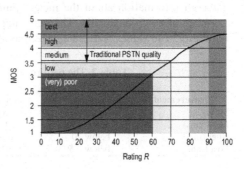

Fig. 3. MOS, Rating factor and user satisfaction taxonomy

Though the E-model fundamentally addresses objective quality assessment of voice, our collected data shows reasonable correlation of the subjective quality assessment scores for audio quality provided by the participants and the objective quality assessment scores provided by the VoIP assessor. This correlation between subjective results and objective measurements can yield significant insights into network performance. We collected these subjective rankings and objective measurements, categorized them by the network configuration under which they were collected, sorted them according to the user who produced the data, and stored them for later use in comparing the relative overall performance of the various network parameters. All the assessment measurements have been taken on a live network in several days and times. The variables that affect the MOS rankings are the dynamic network changes caused by route fluctuations and congestion, and the quality dynamics have been characterized by the metrics delay, jitter and loss as previously specified.

4.3 Assessment Setup and Configuration

To evaluate the performance of our VoIP pilot we realized several assessment sessions, each one hour long, consisting of 200 simultaneous simulated calls between the Monte S. Angelo (MSA) and Centro Storico (CS) sites, lasting for 5 seconds and then continuously restarting. The calls have been simulated between two Chariot performance endpoints, installed on Linux-based workstations and connected to the network trough Gigabit Ethernet interfaces, by using the most common codecs and divided in five 40-calls groups, as detailed in the following table.

Table 1. The objective assessment configuration

#	EP1	EP2	Codec	Calls
1	CS	MSA	G.723.1-MPMLQ (6.3 kbps)	40
2	CS	MSA	G.729 (8 kbps)	40
3	MSA	CS	G.711u (64 kbps)	40
4	MSA	CS	G.723.1-ACELP (5.3 kbps)	40
5	MSA	CS	G.729 (8 kbps)	40

We gathered information about the mean opinion score, packet loss, jitter, delay and the number of completed calls. The percentage of completed calls is our definition of reliability. The values were categorized as shown in the following table.

Table 2. The performance categories

Measurement	Good	Acceptable	Poor
MOS	Above 4,03	4,03 to 3,60	Below 3,60
Delay (ms)	below 150	150 to 300	above 300
Jitter (ms)	below 20	20 to 50	above 50
Lost Data (%)	below 0,50	0,50 to 1,50	above 1,50

4.4 Assessment Results

First of all we noticed that in all our tests there were no unsuccessful calls, so we measured a reliability percentage of 100%. Nevertheless, the measured loss, delay and jitter values were always very low, demonstrating the presence of well provisioned links in the underlying network. The MOS was calculated for each simulated call according to the E-model methodology and the average results obtained with and without QoS differentiation for voice traffic, together with impairment factor's contribution to the call quality are graphically shown in the leftmost graph in fig. 4.

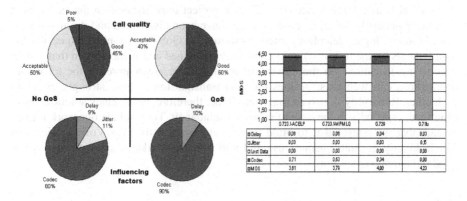

Fig. 4. Call quality evaluation results, with and without QoS

Here, observing each factor's contribution, shown as a percentage of all call quality impairments, we can notice that, when working on an high performance network, with plenty of bandwidth, the codec characteristics are the major impairment factor, followed by jitter and delay. This can be better observed from the rightmost graph that clearly shows how the lower speed codecs impair, also with their physiological delay, the quality of the audio signal much more than their high-speed counterparts such as those belonging to the G.711 family, essentially affected only from jitter. The MOS estimates calculated for all calls in the objective and subjective assessment, as reported in the comparison table below, indicate in both cases an acceptable call quality without QoS and a good quality when traffic differentiation is implemented.

Table 3. Objective and subjective analysis results

#	Call Group	Obj. w/o QoS	MOS QoS	Subj. w/o QoS	MOS QoS
1	G.711u	4,23	4,38	4,35	4,50
2	G.729	4,00	4,03	4,05	4,20
3	G.729	4,00	4,03	4,02	4,20
4	G.723.1 MPMLQ	3,79	3,82	3,48	4,02
5	G.723.1 ACELP	3,61	3,64	3,31	3,84

It is interesting to observe that the subjective MOS values reported by the 10 users sample nearly reflect the objective values calculated through the E-model implementation in the assessor, slightly improving the quality perception when QoS is provided and with some minor degree of satisfaction when the voice traffic is handled according to the best effort policy, especially for the lower-speed codecs, such as those in the G.723.1 family. This demonstrates that users are less sensible in the perception of signal impairments when the average quality is high and on the other side more sensible in presence of a poor speech quality.

5 Conclusions

This paper presented an overview of the activities and results which have been taken in the context of a large Voice over IP pilot project implemented on the Federico II metro ring network. Several technical issues have been discovered and discussed such as call routing, legacy telephony interoperability and QoS provisioning. Especially the requirements on the transmission quality were examined and it was shown that – even if some modifications on the current IP infrastructure are required – the telephony applications can well exist besides the data transmission without strongly effecting each other. Reliability is also an important issue; therefore, redundancy solutions were examined, especially in the case of routing redundancy. To conclude our work it must be said that we managed it to build up a really large testbed for VoIP applications which directly got into business use and will probably strike in a few time over the good old telephony system.

References

1. Black, U., "Voice over IP", Prentice Hall, 2000
2. ITU-T, "One Way Transmission Time", Recommendation G.114, 1996
3. Clark, A., "Modeling the effects of burst packet loss and recency on subjective voice quality", in Proceedings of IP Telephony Workshop, 2001
4. Mullin, J., Smallwood, L., Watson, A., Wilson, G., "New techniques for assessing audio and video quality in real-time interactive communications", IHM-HCI Tutorial, 2001
5. Pearsall, S., Walker, J. Q., "Doing a VoIP Assessment with Chariot VoIP Assessor", NetIQ Corporation, 2002
6. ITU-T, "The Emodel, a computational model for use in transmission planning," Recommendation G.107, 1998

Z!Stream: An Application Streaming System by Copy-on-Reference Block of Executable Files

Dongho Song

Dept of Computer Engineering, Hankuk Aviation University,
Hwajun Dong 200-1, Dukyang Ku,
412-791 Koyang City, Korea
dhsong@hau.ac.kr

Abstract. Application streaming is a deployment method of the software management, which is efficient in terms of time and space. However, there are difficult issues on dealing with streaming that replaces downloading, installation and execution of application programs. Application on-demand (AoD) streaming replies upon a copy-on-reference distributed virtual block system and virtualization of file, registry and others on the operating system level. The AoD system should be implemented without modifying operating system kernel and application codes to be streamed. Also it should be guaranteed that its performance is comparable to that of running the software locally installed. This paper presents a modeling of AoD based on copy-on-reference and pre-fetching based streaming to achieve concurrency between computation and communication.

Keywords: streaming, installation, deployment, virtualization.

1 Introduction

At the early stage of Internet, the use was limited to the delivery of web contents. A newly developing area is to deliver, deploy and execute complex application software over the Internet and Intranet. One of the common challenges faced by system administrators is how to deploy applications to many users rapidly, securely, and safely, without interfering with users' computers and keeping control of software delivered. There are a number of potential applications of the AoD streaming system: for system administrators to build a progressive deployment system with applications in a central software library, or to patch software across the enterprise while retaining central control.

PC users still face two fundamental problems in accessing application software: one is cost of installation time, and the other cost of keeping them all on their local disks: On the phase of installation, the program codes, made up of a main executable file, auxiliary executable files, registry files and other files including DLLs, are stored in a system directory, e.g., a Microsoft Windows directory and a user directory. On phase of storing the software on the local disks, a large storage space in the client's PC is required to store various software programs. It is undesirable to keep all these

S. Chaudhuri et al. (Eds.): ICDCN 2006, LNCS 4308, pp. 367–372, 2006.

applications on local hard-disks, though hard disks become huge and cheap. Trial software needs to be executed without full installation because once an application is fully installed on a local storage it may not be wiped out completely, especially if the application has some spy-wares or ad-wares. So, the installation prevents users from having mobility of application programs and motivates to adopt a virtual environment.

This paper tackles the mobility problems using application virtualization and streaming to maximize performance of the system through copy-on-reference and partial pre-fetching. The streaming [1] means the transfer of the application's bits to the target machine overlapped with its execution. Using the method, it is possible that an application starts execution before it has been completely downloaded. Unlike the linear sequences of data presented in audio and video streaming, the components of application programs may be executed in any order which varies with user inputs and other factors.

This paper is organized as follows. Section 2 discusses related work. Section 3 describes the architecture and its operations of our Z!Stream model. Section 4 discusses performance of Z!Stream system. Section 5 presents conclusions.

2 Related Work

IBM's PDS, recently published paper by Alpern [1], and other related work [2,3,4,5,6,7] are on execution environment and infrastructure designed specifically for deploying software on demand to a broken server machine at a server farm while enabling management from a central location. PDS intercepts a subset of system calls on the target machine to provide a partial virtualization at the operating system level. This enables an asset's install-time environment to be reproduced virtually on the target machine. Application blocks, called shards, are fetched as they are needed (or they may be pre-fetched), enabling the asset to be progressively deployed by overlapping deployment with execution. A framework is provided to intercept interfaces above the operating system (e.g., Java class loading), and to enable optimizations requiring semantic awareness not present at the operating system level. However, PDS can not stream conventional Windows desktop application programs to client PCs which has more complicated registry systems and other operating system environment that Z!Stream can support.

Zayas modified Accent at the kernel level to migrate processes using copy-on-reference virtual memory [8] and it was improved by integrating pre-fetching on object-oriented systems by Song[9]. When a process migrates, its memory image is initially left on the source machine, only the process's page tables, registers, and message channels need to be transferred immediately. As the process executes, it demands pages on its memory from the source. The copy-on-reference was adopted to Z!Stream to enhance the speed of streaming at the middleware level. However, copy-on-reference on Z!Stream is not a pure demand paging but a combination of demand files and their page blocks that are mapped by an indexing table. So, it can be called a copy of a group of blocks on a single reference.

3 Z!Stream AoD Streaming Model

The working scenario of Z!Stream AoD system is as follows: When a user goes to a host website and clicks on an application to run on his/her desktop, the user's access is redirected to the Control Server which designates Container Server. By the request of LaunchPad on the user's PC, the Container Server sends the blocks of the executable file that are necessary to load the application to the memory segment of the client PC.

Z!Stream intercepts messages related to a subset of system calls on the target PC to implement virtualization on the operating system level. While applications are running, various messages are generated to operating system for file accessing, I/O events and communications. These system calls need to be hooked, analyzed, filtered and further processed to replace local file requests from the applications to remote file block requests on the server machine in real-time and on-demand basis, i.e. copy-on-reference. During the operation of distributed virtual blocking, application processes can be suspended temporarily until the required blocks are delivered from the server or can be executed concurrently with the pre-fetched blocks.

To increase the speed of program initiation, copies of initial file blocks should be minimized; however, pre-fetching a group of blocks can improve the overall performance while interactive applications are running, if memory pollution is appropriately managed. Z!Stream allows the process to start executing if it has streamed about 5% of a whole executable code on a client machine, which is almost immediately after a click. It is expected that 20:80 rule is well applicable to the application program running, that is, less than 20% of executable codes encompass 80% of functionalities that users need. Fig. 1 shows a concept of the copy-on-reference with minimal pre-fetching based streaming protocol.

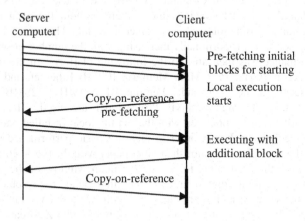

Fig. 1. Copy-on-referenced streaming protocol shows that the application process begins execution on the client computer and overlaps block downloading and execution

Virtualization of Windows files, registry and other operating system environments is another key functionality that realizes the AoD by eliminating the need of fully installing an application before the use. Thus, virtualization environment of an application program should be executed without any direct accessing Windows operating system. It makes those applications float on top of the real file and registry systems, and applications can be streamed, run and wiped out cleanly after use. The protocol in Fig. 1 shows overlapping of streaming of blocks of executable code and processing of computation. The degree of overlapping can be minimized by not pre-fetching, or maximized by heuristically managed rich pre-fetching pages related to a functional menu. There are some tradeoffs between not pre-fetching and rich pre-fetching in terms of performance and memory pollution. Details of management of pre-fetching are out of the scope of this paper.

4 Performance Evaluation

The Z!Stream system is fully implemented and optimized both on Microsoft Windows 2000, IIS and SQL Server, and on RedHat Linux, Apache, and MySQL. Launch Manager integrates with ActiveX components.

The main subsystems of Z!Stream actually affecting performance are the Container Server and the LaunchPad. Due to its distributed nature, it is difficult to predict the application-specific performance of the Z!Stream, but it is reasonable to conclude that the maximum number of streams simultaneously open, start-up time and execution overhead delays are good measure of overall system performance.

The performance would vary with the hardware and software specifications of the server, specifically, the amount of installed RAM, the power of the server's CPU, and the underlying operating systems on the client and servers. However, the result of tests shows that the number of sessions simultaneously connected is about 1000 per a server, i.e. 5 applications per user and 200 concurrent users are supported by a single Container Server. If several Container Servers are in use, the Z!Stream system is capable of handling load balancing among them without the need for a hardware-based load balancing function such as a Layer 4 Switch. Therefore, the throughput of the streaming server is proportionally increasing with the number of servers.

The performance was measured in the following platform: In the server side, Intel Pentium-IV Xeon 3GHz, 1GB Main Memory, 100MB Ethernet, and GNTOO Linux 2005.1 are used. In the client side, Pentium-III 650MHz, 128MB Main memory, 100MB Ethernet, and Windows-XP Professional are used. The execution time overhead on Z!Stream is compared with that on the local installed ones. Z!Stream has pre-fetching mechanism, but in order to measure basic performance this feature was not used for the tests. We will publish another paper with the pre-fetching in the future.

Start-up time (the time delay to pop up the main window of the application after clicking) and execution time overhead (the time delay to execute corresponding functions of the selected menu) are measured with two tests. We ran MS-Office 2003 (Word, Excel, PPT) and Adobe's Photoshop 7.0 both under Z!Stream and natively. In the first test, we measured the response time without the cashed blocks (the time to start up application program after a click at the first time without pre-cached files at all) to start up Office and Photoshop natively (local installed case has even a local cache on Windows XP). In the second test, we measured the same parameter with cached blocks as a normal operating mode, i.e. after the second trial. We measured performance using the standard benchmark for 20 clients and the data are shown in

Table 1. We found that this test ran slightly slower under Z!Stream than the native. The startup time averaged under Z!Stream is quite slower as opposed to the native mode. However, this delay is still tolerable if the full installation-time of the application is considered and the applications are running on a network.

In the third test, we tested with 200 concurrent users to the server with Winzip. Under this condition, the usage rates of CPU were 19.0% user and 23.5% system as shown in Fig.2. The response time is shown in blue and the number of virtual users in red. This figure shows the response time by increasing one concurrent user every second up to 200, using Compuware's QAload. After 100 users concurrently connected in 100 seconds, the average response time becomes 4 seconds; over 150 seconds, the average response time becomes 10 seconds.

Table 1. Measured Performance Data (time units: second)

Apps Name	Execution Environment		Startup Time	Functions	Execution Time overhead
Office 2003 (Word)	Z!Stream 3.0	no cache	32	Form->Font Menu Click	7
	Z!Stream 3.0	cached	21		4
	Local installed	no cache	6		1
	Local installed	cached	2		0.2
Office 2003 (Excel)	Z!Stream 3.0	no cache	15	Insert-> Function Window	1
	Z!Stream 3.0	cached	13		0.2
	Local installed	no cache	2		1
	Local installed	cached	1		0.1
Office 2003 (PowerP oint)	Z!Stream 3.0	no cache	16	Insert-> Chart	3
	Z!Stream 3.0	cached	13		1
	Local installed	no cache	3		2
	Local installed	cached	1		0.6
Photosho p 7.0	Z!Stream 3.0	no cache	65	File Filter-> Artistic-> Colored Pencil ··· Conversion	3
	Z!Stream 3.0	cached	38		2
	Local installed	no cache	27		2
	Local installed	cached	10		1.8

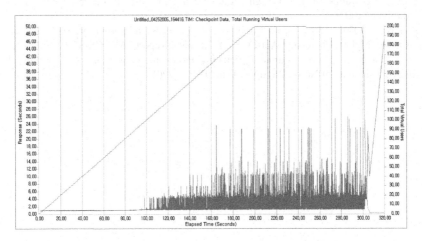

Fig. 2. Response time of 200 concurrent users on Z!Stream

5 Conclusions

As audio and video continuous media serviced on the Internet are generally based on a streaming technique, the contents industry has dramatically grown up. The same notion of streaming can be applied to shrink-wrap application software. However internal use of streaming is quite different in terms of processing: the former is in sequential accessing, and the latter in any order accessing. To support any order accessing in application streaming, Z!Stream adopts quite different technologies including virtualization, pre-fetching, and copy-on-reference streaming protocols.

Our evaluation with the Z!Stream shows that AoD streaming is quite an appealing technique of software deployment for users using rich client PCs by eliminating tedious installation and downloading. Application mobility with relatively reasonable performance has been achieved with the virtualization and streaming. We have experienced that average 30% of executable codes of a program seem enough for most of basic works. Z!Stream can support conventional shrink-wrap applications to be deployed, just like a web-based applications on the Internet.

References

1. Alpern B., Auerbach J., Bala V. Fraunhofer T., : PDS: A Virtual Execution Environment for Software Deployment, ACM VEE'05, June 11-12, (2005) Chicago, Illinois, USA. 175-185.
2. AppStream Inc. http://www.appstream.com/products-technology.html
3. Softricity Inc. http://www.softricity.com/products/technology.asp
4. DuBois, P. MySQL 2nd editon, Sams press. March (2005)
5. OSGi specification. http://www.osgi.org
6. Sapuntzakis, C., Brumley,D., Chandra, R., Zeldovich,N., Chow,J., Lam,M.S., Rosenblum,M. Virtual Appliances for Deploying and Maintaining Software. In Proceedings of the 17th Large Installation System Administration Conference, Oct (2003)
7. Kuacharoen P, Mooney V.J., Madisetti V.K., : Software Streaming via Block Streaming," IEEE Proceedings of the Design, Automation and Test in Europe Conference and Exhibition (2003)
8. E. Zayas, : The use of copy-on-reference in a process migration system, PhD. Thesis, Carnegie- Mellon University, April (1987) Technical Report CMU-CS-87-121.
9. Song, Dong Ho, : An Accurate Prefetching Policy for Object-Oriented Systems, PhD. Thesis, University of Newcastle-upon-Tyne, Dec. (1990)

Supervised Grid-of-Tries: A Novel Framework for Classifier Management

Srinivasan T.[1], Balakrishnan R., Gangadharan S.A., and Hayawardh V.

[1] Assistant Professor, Department of Computer Science and Engineering,
Sri Venkateswara College of Engineering, Sriperumbudur, TN, India 602 105
tsrini@svce.ac.in, bsrealm@msn.com,
{gangadharan, hayawardh}@gmail.com

Abstract. Packet classification is the problem of identifying which one of a set of rules maintained in a database is best matched by an incoming packet at a router and taking the action specified by the rule. This is a uniform enabler for many new network services like firewalls, quality of service and virtual private networks. These services require dynamic management of rules. While many algorithms recently proposed can perform packet classification at very high speeds, rule update times for these are not very fast. This paper presents an efficient classifier management algorithm, which effectively reduces the rule update time for the well known Grid-of-Tries classifier. To this end, we have devised a novel structure called Supervised Grid-of-Tries, which employs additional tracking pointers embedded into the trie to facilitate efficient rule updates.

Keywords: Packet classification, routing, grid-of-tries, supervised grid-of-tries.

1 Introduction

Packet classification is the underlying mechanism facilitating network services like quality of service, virtual private networks (VPN) and firewalls.

Several approaches to packet classification have been proposed. Traditional trie-based approaches to packet classification include the Hierarchical Trie, Set Pruning Trie and Grid-of-Tries with filter update complexities of $O(dw)$, $O(n^d)$ and $O(nw)$ respectively, where d denotes the number of dimensions, n the number of nodes and w the width of each dimension. This does not scale up well on large filter sets. Here, we present a structure that performs updates efficiently, even for large filter sets.

The paper is organized as follows. Section 2 describes the preliminaries. Section 3 portrays our proposed approach. Experimental results are displayed in Section 4. In Section 5, guidelines to choose between the schemes discussed in Section 3 are suggested. Concluding remarks are in Section 6.

2 Preliminaries

Here, the term "ancestor trie" refers to any trie which is under a first dimension node that is an ancestor of the first dimension node under which the current trie is present.

S. Chaudhuri et al. (Eds.): ICDCN 2006, LNCS 4308, pp. 373–378, 2006.
© Springer-Verlag Berlin Heidelberg 2006

The term "lowest ancestor trie" refers to the most immediate ancestor trie. In addition, we employ "links" to mean switch pointers and/or storedFilters.

Supervision Tree of Tries: A multi way tree representing the dependency hierarchy amongst the tries in the second dimension.

Supervision Tree of Nodes: A multi way tree representing the dependency hierarchy amongst the nodes in the second dimension.

Let A be a first dimension node (Fig. 1*a*). Let $S = \{B_1, B_2, ..., B_n\}$ be the set of nodes in A's sub tree reachable along paths $p_1, p_2, ..., p_n$ respectively, such that

1. B_i has a trie under it for $1 \leq i \leq n$
2. No node in path from A to B_i has a trie under it for $1 \leq i \leq n$
3. $p_i < p_{i+1}$ (lexicographically) for $1 \leq i \leq n - 1$
4. $B_i \neq A$ for $1 \leq i \leq n$

Then, S is the set of first dimension (*1d*) *st* children of A and there exists

1. A *1d* supervised trie child list begin (1d-st-cl(b)) link from A to B_1.
2. A *1d* supervised trie child list end (1d-st-cl(e)) link from A to B_n.
3. A *1d* supervised sibling next (1d-st-s(n)) link from Bi to B_{i+1} for $1 \leq i \leq n - 1$
4. A *1d* supervised sibling previous link from B_{i+1} to B_i for $1 \leq i \leq n - 1$.

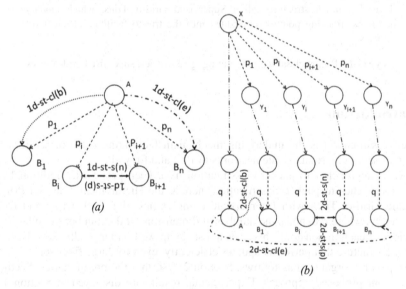

Fig. 1. *(a) st* First dimension child and sibling pointers. *(b) st* Second dimension child and sibling pointers.

Let A be a second dimension node (Fig. 1*b*) reached from the root of its trie along edges labelled q. Let this trie be under node X in the first dimension. Let $S' = \{ Y_1, Y_2, ..., Y_n \}$ be the set of nodes in X's sub tree reached along paths $p_1, p_2, ..., p_n$ respectively such that

1. Y_i has a trie under it that has a node reachable along edges labelled q for $1 \le i \le n$
2. No node from A to Y_i has a trie under it which has a node reachable along edges labelled q for $1 \le i \le n$
3. $p_i < p_{i+1}$ (lexicographically) for $1 \le i \le n - 1$
4. $Y_i \ne A$ for $1 \le i \le n$

Let $S = \{B_1, B_2, ..., B_n\}$ be the set of nodes such that B_i is reached from the root of the trie under Y_i along edges labelled q for $1 \le i \le n$. Then, S is the set of second dimension ($2d$) st children of A and there exists

1. A $2d$ supervised trie child list begin (2d-st-cl(b)) link from A to B_1.
2. A $2d$ supervised trie child list end (2d-st-cl(e)) link from A to B_n.
3. A $2d$ supervised sibling next (2d-st-s(n)) link from B_i to B_{i+1} for $1 \le i \le n-1$.
4. A $2d$ supervised sibling previous (2d-st-s(p)) link from B_{i+1} to B_i for $1 \le i \le n-1$

In the next section, we endeavor to present schemes resulting in efficient filter update for the Grid-of-Tries.

3 Proposed Approach

When inserting a rule into the Grid-of-Tries, there may be a need to set links from tries further below to the newly inserted trie or to have switch pointers or storedFilters emanating from the inserted trie itself to a trie above it. Unless we have a systematic method to track which tries need to be updated as a result of inserting or deleting a rule, it is tricky to perform incremental updates. We attempt to save on rule update time by modifying the existing Grid-of-Tries instead of complete reconstruction. During rule update, the Grid-of-Tries is modified in the first and second dimensions based on the rule. All other tries require amendment only if their lowest ancestor also does. Thus, there is a dependency hierarchy present among the tries and nodes. This hierarchy can be structured in the form of a supervision tree.

3.1 One Dimension Supervised (*1ds-SGOT*)

1ds-SGOT implements only the supervision tree of tries. In this algorithm, the first dimension nodes which have tries under them act as representatives of those tries. In order to insert a rule, we first traverse the first dimension. If a new node was created, we backtrack and update the supervision tree of tries. Next, the second dimension trie is traversed. If any new nodes were created in the second dimension, we set links from the current trie to the ancestor tries and to the current trie from tries in its st sub tree as necessary.

The worst case time complexity of this algorithm is $O(nw)$. However, occurrence of the worst case requires that several rare conditions be satisfied. Also, once the worst case has occurred, it cannot occur again until the rule that caused the worst case is removed. Memory requirements double for the first dimension in comparison to the Grid-Of-Tries algorithm due to the four additional pointers (*st*) that have to be maintained in addition to the existing four in each node.

3.2 Two Dimension Supervised (*2ds-SGOT*)

Performance can be further improved in certain environments at the expense of memory. The *2ds-SGOT* algorithm implements the supervision trees of nodes in addition to the supervision tree of tries.

The first dimension is handled as in *1ds-SGOT*. In the second dimension, if any new nodes are created, we set the *st* sibling and *st* child node pointers as appropriate. We then set switch pointers and storedFilters to corresponding nodes in the ancestor tries and to the current nodes from nodes in the sub tree of this node's supervision tree of nodes.

In *2ds-SGOT*, repeated access of nodes in the second dimension trie of the rule (that took place in *1ds-SGOT*) is avoided. All operations on a node are finished in a single visit. Also, nodes that do not require an update are skipped. Hence we stand to gain a reduction in worst case time, while the worst case complexity and conditions remain unchanged. In order to support the above features, extra processing is required through the maintenance of *st* pointers in the second dimension nodes. Memory requirements for the second dimension are approximately twice that of *1ds-SGOT* whereas the memory consumption of the first dimension is the same. Rule deletion can be performed along the same lines as insertion. With some modifications, the same approach can be used to perform supervised rule updates on extended grid of tries.

4 Experimental Results

The performance of *1ds-SGOT* is significantly dependent on the number of tries visited for updating. However, this is not the case with *2ds-SGOT* since, as stated previously, it avoids the access of nodes which are certain to not require updates. Besides, the number of times these nodes are visited is one as compared to the multiple times they are visited in *1ds-SGOT*.

We now proceed to analyze and compare the performance of our proposed algorithms against each other and the Grid-of-Tries method in different environments. The filter sets we utilize for our analysis are drawn from [4].

Our empirical results confirm that the time consumed by the conventional method for a rule update increases linearly with the number of rules (as the structure is completely reconstructed from the beginning with every new rule added) in the trie whereas it remains nearly constant for *1ds-SGOT*.

2ds-SGOT performs best in firewalls, which are most specific (and hence have the most number of tries), which is in conformance with the above deductions. Also, as expected, *1ds-SGOT* performs better than *2ds-SGOT* in the least specific environment of access control lists.

Table 2 shows the average update time for our algorithms on the various filter sets [6]. It is clear from the table that, as the specificity increases, the *2ds-SGOT* algorithm performs better than the *1ds-SGOT* algorithm.

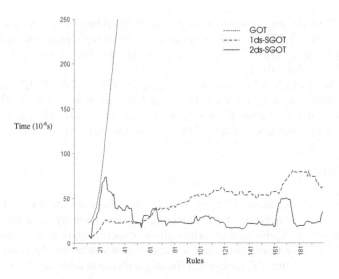

Fig. 2. Rule insertion times of the algorithms for sample filter set FW1

Table 2. Performance Comparison. Filter sets taken from [4].

Filter set	1ds-SGOT (10^{-6} s)	2ds-SGOT (10^{-6} s)
ACL1	41	61
ACL1_100	48	133
ACL1_1K	47	76
ACL1_5K	53	68
ACL1_10K	63	98
IPC1	69	51
IPC1_100	47	129
IPC1_1K	57	100
IPC1_5K	88	67
IPC1_10K	155	74
FW1	45	33
FW1_100	28	39
FW1_1K	109	38
FW1_5K	445	80
FW1_10K	1054	120

5 Selection of Optimal Scheme

We now discuss metrics that help in selecting the optimal scheme.

Specificity: We infer from the experimental results that as the specificity of the filter sets increases, the relative performance of *2ds-SGOT* improves over *1ds-SGOT* due to the increased number of tries. Thus it would be more advantageous to use *2ds-SGOT* in environments like firewalls. Conversely, *1ds-SGOT* should be preferred in environments like access control lists.

Scalability: With the impending transition to IPv6, the relative performance benefit for *2ds-SGOT* over *1ds-SGOT* would be amplified due to the significant increase in node accesses for rule updates. With increase in the number of rules, *2ds-SGOT* performs better than *1ds-SGOT*.

Reliability: In situations where the memory consumption of *2ds-SGOT* is about to exceed the available memory, there can be a seamless transition to *1ds-SGOT* which will enable the router to support as many rules as can *1ds-SGOT* while at the same time providing the performance of *2ds-SGOT* until no longer possible.

6 Conclusion

We have devised a novel method for efficient dynamic filter update for the Grid-of-Tries classifier. This is achieved by maintaining a supervision trees to track those parts of the trie which require updates. Through our experimentation, it is shown that our two techniques have nearly constant filter update times, whereas the conventional method has an update time which increases linearly with the number of filters.

References

1. V. Srinivasan, S. Suri, G. Varghese and M. Waldvogel. "Fast and scalable layer four switching," Proceedings of ACM Sigcomm, pages 203-14, September 1998.
2. T. Srinivasan, S. Prasad, B. Prakash, "Dynamic Packet Classification Algorithm using Multi-level Trie", Enformatika, Volume 3, pp.104-107, Transactions on Engineering, Computing and Technology, Dec 2004 (ISSN 1305-5313).
3. T. Srinivasan, Dhanasekar, M. Nivedita, B. Divya, Azeezunnisa Shakir "Scalable and Parallel Aggregated Bit Vector packet classification using prefix computation model", To appear in the proceedings of IEEE International Symposium on Parallel Computing in Electrical Engineering - PARELEC 2006, Bialystok, Poland, September 2006.
4. David E. Taylor, Jonathan S. Turner, "ClassBench: A Packet Classification Benchmark", IEEE INFOCOM 2005
5. T. Srinivasan, Azeezunnisa Shakir, Vijayalakshmi "PAFBV: A Novel Parallel Aggregated and Folded Bit Vector Packet Classification Scheme for IPv6 Routers", to appear in the proceedings of 6th IEEE International Conference on Computer and Information Technology - CIT 2006, IEEE Computer Society , Seoul, Korea, September 2006
6. Filter sets at http://www.arl.wustl.edu/~det3/ClassBench/

BGPSep_S: An Algorithm for Constructing IBGP Configurations with Complete Visibility*

Feng Zhao, Xicheng Lu, Peidong Zhu, and Jinjing Zhao

School of Computer, National University of Defense Technology,
Changsha 410073, Hunan, China
fengzhao1980@tom.com

Abstract. IBGP configurations based on the route reflection may violate the properties of complete visibility, thus leading to forwarding loops and sub-optimal paths. On the other hand, a router should not maintain too much BGP sessions because of performance reason. This paper presents an IBGP topology construction algorithm, called BGPSep_S, by taking into consideration the vertexes degrees, the vertexes separators and the shortest paths between vertexes in the underlying IGP graph. We prove that BGPSep_S guarantees complete visibility in normal situations. And the performance of BGPSep_S is evaluated on several real-world backbone topologies. Experimental results show that the maximum degrees of the IBGP topologies generated by BGPSep_S for these IGP topologies can be reduced by about 27%-68%, compared with full mesh and BGPSep.

1 Introduction

Border Gateway Protocol (BGP) [1] is the widely used interdomain routing protocol. BGP can be divided into two parts: External BGP (EBGP) and Internal BGP (IBGP). Full mesh IBGP configuration is often used for small ASes because it can guarantees correctness properties of complete visibility, loop-free forwarding. However, in large ASes, BGP route reflection [2] is often used in the IBGP topology design because of scalability reason.

However, IBGP configurations based on route reflection may lead to route oscillations, forwarding loops and sub-optimal paths [3]. These problems are hard to diagnose and debug, and networks with these problems are hard to manage.

M.Vutukuru et al. [3] present and analyze an algorithm, BGPSep, to construct an IBGP session configuration that is both correct and more scalable than a full mesh. They claim that to their knowledge, BGPSep is the first constructive algorithm to generate IBGP configurations with useful correctness guarantees, while scaling better than a full mesh. However, although the number of IBGP sessions is smaller than in a full-mesh configuration, BGPSep does not reduce the number of IBGP sessions of its top level route reflectors. That is, the maximum node degree of the IBGP topology

---

* This research was supported by the National Grand Fundamental Research 973 Program of China under Grant No. 2003CB314802 and the National High-Tech Research and Development Plan of China under Grant No. 2005AA121570.

S. Chaudhuri et al. (Eds.): ICDCN 2006, LNCS 4308, pp. 379–384, 2006.

remains the same as in a full-mesh configuration. A router should not maintain too much BGP sessions, because concurrent frequent updates on multiple peers may cause problems. So it is very meaningful to reduce the number of IBGP sessions a router needs to maintain.

This paper presents an IBGP topology construction algorithm, called BGPSep_S, which can generate an IBGP topology with much smaller maximum degree, compared with that generated by BGPSep or a full mesh configuration.

2   Complete Visibility and IBGP Configuration

To understand the idea and the characteristics of our algorithm, this section discusses the relationships between IBGP configurations, complete visibility, forwarding loops and sub-optimal paths.

We first describe some related notations, definitions and lemmas.

Consider the IGP subgraph G induced by the BGP routers of a network in an AS. Let V denote the set of BGP routers. Let d denote any destination. For every router A, let $Egress_d(A)$ denote the best egress router that A would have picked had it seen the best routes from every EBGP router in the AS.

We use the terms of *signaling chain, signaling chain of monotone increase, signaling chain of monotone decrease, concatenation* in Reference [4]. Still we need to define the following terms.

Definition 1. Given a signaling chain $S : A(= R_0), R_1, R_2, ..., R_r, B(= R_{r+1})$ and an IGP path P from A to B, if for $i = 0...r+1$, $R_i \in P$, then we say S *overlays* P, or P is *overlayed* by S.

Definition 2. For a signaling chain $S : A(= R_0), R_1, R_2, ..., R_r, B(= R_{r+1})$, if there exists a shortest IGP path P from A to B such that S *overlays* P, then we say S is a *shortest signaling chain* between A and B.

Then we can get the following theorem by using the *Claim 1* of Reference [4].

Theorem 1. An IBGP configuration guarantees that the property of complete visibility will be satisfied in the face of arbitrary IGP changes if, and only if, for any IGP path from a BGP router to another EBGP router, there exists a signaling chain that overlays this path.

3   The BGPSep_S Algorithm

One of our goals is finding an IBGP configuration that guarantees the complete visibility in the face of no IGP changes, thus avoiding forwarding loops and sub-optimal paths. According to the discussion of the previous section, we need to find an IBGP configuration such that there is a shortest signaling path from a router to any of its possible egresses.

In an IGP graph, for a vertex u whose degree is one, suppose that its adjacent vertex v has complete visibility. Then following the route reflection rules and the BGP route selection rules, vertex u will have complete visibility if we let u be the client of v.

In addition, if in the IGP graph we can find a graph separator, a set of vertexes whose removal partitions a graph into some connected components, then any shortest path beginning in a component and ending in a different component must pass through one or more routers in the separator. If we construct an IBGP topology by full meshing the routers in the separator, constructing a full mesh configuration within each connected component and setting up other necessary IBGP sessions such that there exist a shortest signaling between any router in a component and any other router in the separator, then there will be exist a shortest signaling between any two vertexes.

If we take away one or more vertexes from the components and add them into the set of vertexes in the graph separator, then we get a superset of the graph separator, which is still a graph separator. Obviously, the max degrees of the IBGP topologies based on different separators may be different. We hope that we can find an optimal separator such that the max degree of the generated IBGP topology is minimal. However, it is a very difficult task to find such an optimal separator for a large IGP graph in practice. Instead, after we get a separator we use a heuristic method to find a superset of the separator. We first find a shortest path from any router in the components to any other router in the separator. Then we add the vertexes in this path into the superset except the initial vertex.

3.1 The Algorithm Description

Our algorithm, BGPSep_S, is shown in **Algorithm 1.**

BGPSep_S takes the IGP graph $G = (V, E)$ formed by the BGP routers and produces the set I of IBGP sessions that must be established between the routers. Every element in I denotes an IBGP session and has the form (u, v, t), where u and v are the routers between which the IBGP session is established and t is the type of the IBGP session. If $t =$ "client", then the IBGP session between u and v is a client-route reflector session (with u being the client of route reflector v). If $t =$ "peer", then the IBGP session between u and v is a normal non-client IBGP session. The algorithm uses a procedure Graph-Separator, which is a graph partitioning algorithm that takes a graph G and returns a graph separator S. Also the algorithm uses another procedure Shortest-Path to find a shortest path between two vertexes.

Algorithm 1. BGPSep_S
Input: IGP Graph G, set V of BGP routers
Output: Set I of IBGP sessions
/* Step 1: removing the pendant vertexes gradually*/
$I = \varnothing$;
pending =**true;**
$G' = G$;

382 F. Zhao et al.

```
while pending == true do
  G = G';
  pending = false;
    foreach u ∈ G.V do
      if d_G(u) == 1 then /* d_G(u) is the degree of u in G */
        v = adj_G(u); /* v is the adjacent vertex of u */
        I = I ∪ {(u,v,client)}; /* let u be the client of v */
        G' = G' - {u};
        pending = true;
      end
    end
end
/* Step 2: Choose a graph separator S ⊆ G'.V . */
S = Graph-Separator(G');
G_1,...,G_m ← components of G'.V - S ;
/* Step 3:  find a superset S⁺ of S . */
S⁺ = S ;
foreach u ∈ G_i, v ∈ S do
  if u ∉ S⁺ then
    P = Shortest-Path(u,v);
    foreach w ∈ P do
      if w ≠ u then
        S⁺ = S⁺ ∪ {w} ;
      end
    end
  end
end
/* Step 4: Fully mesh the routers in S⁺ */
foreach u,v ∈ S⁺, u ≠ v do
  I = I ∪ {(u,v,peer)} ;
end
/* Step 5: Let every router in G'.V - S⁺ be a route
reflector client of some routers in S⁺  */
foreach u ∈ G'.V - S⁺, v ∈ S⁺ do
  P : u(= R_0), R_1, R_2, ..., R_r, v(= R_{r+1}) ← Shortest-Path(u,v);
  i = 1;
  while R_i ∉ S⁺ do
    i++;
  end
  I = I ∪ {(u,R_i,client)}
```

end

/* Step 6: full mesh routers in $G_i - S^+$ */

foreach $u, v \in G_i - S^+$ **do**

$\quad I = I \cup \{(u, v, peer)\}$

end

return I ;

3.2 Complete Visibility

We can prove that in normal conditions (i.e., the IGP graph is the same as the original graph when the BGPSep_S is running), the configurations generated by BGPSep_S will guarantees the properties of complete visibility. Because of page limitations, we just give the proof skeleton as follows.

We denote G_{sub} the subgraph G' that is generated after the *Step 1* of the BGPSep_S algorithm is finished. We can get the following two lemmas.

Lemma 1. In the IBGP configuration produced by BGPSep_S for the IGP graph G_{sub}, for any destination d, there exists a shortest signaling chain between every router $A \in G_{sub}.V$ and the egress router $Egress_d(A) \in G_{sub}.V$.

Lemma 2. In the IBGP configuration produced by BGPSep_S, for any destination d, there exists a shortest signaling chain between every router $A \in V$ and the egress router $Egress_d(A)$.

Then following from *Claim 1* in [4] and **Lemma 2**, we can know that the IBGP configuration output by BGPSep_S satisfies the property of complete visibility.

4 Implementation and Evaluation

We implemented the BGPSep_S algorithm in Matlab. The program reads the IGP graph from a file and writes the IBGP sessions to a file. In our implementation, the procedure Graph-Separator comes from the BGPSep implementation[1].

The performance of BGPSep_S is evaluated on the backbone topologies of 6 ISPs annotated with inferred link costs from the Rocketfuel project [5]. We compare the maximum degree of the IBGP topologies produced by the BGPSep_S algorithm with those produced by BGPSep or full mesh for these topologies. Also we assume conservatively that all the vertexes in the topology are external BGP routers, like [3].

The results are shown in Figure 1. We observe that the IBGP configuration produced by BGPSep_S results in a 27%-68% reduction in the maximum degree of the generated IBGP topologies.

---

[1] We thank Mythili Vutukuru et al. in the MIT Computer Science and Artificial Intelligence Laboratory for providing the source code of their BGPSep algorithm.

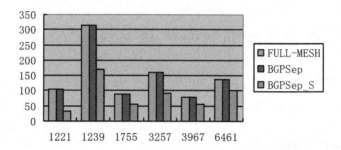

Fig. 1. The maximum degrees of the generated IBGP topologies: Rocketfuel ISP topologies

5 Conclusion

This paper discusses the relationship between the complete visibility and IBGP configurations and presents an IBGP topology construction algorithm, called BGPSep_S, by taking into consideration the vertexes degrees, the vertexes separators and the shortest paths between vertexes in the underlying IGP graph. We prove that BGPSep_S guarantees complete visibility in the face of no IGP changes. And the performance of BGPSep_S is evaluated on several real-world backbone topologies. Experimental results indicate that BGPSep_S can generate an IBGP topology with much smaller maximum degree, compared with that generated by BGPSep or a full mesh configuration.

References

1. Y. Rekhter, T. Li, S. Hares, Eds., "A Border Gateway Protocol 4 (BGP-4)", RFC 4271, January 2006.
2. T. Bates, R. Chandra, and E. Chen, BGP Route Reflection – An Alternative to Full Mesh IBGP, RFC 2796,Network Working Group, April 2000.
3. M. Vutukuru, P. Valiant, S. Kopparty, and H. Balakrishnan, How to Construct a Correct and Scalable IBGP Configuration, in Proceedings of IEEE INFOCOM, 2006.
4. F. Zhao, XC. Lu, PD. Zhu, JJ. Zhao, BGPSep_D: An Improved Algorithm for Constructing Correct and Scalable IBGP configurations Based on Vertexes Degree,HPCC 2006, in press. pp. 406-415.
5. R. Mahajan, N. Spring, D. Wetherall, and T. Anderson. Inferring Link Weights using End-to-end Measurements. In Proc. 2nd ACM SIGCOMM Internet Measurement Workshop, pages 231-236, Marseille, France, 2002.

Performance Enhancement in REM Using Adaptive Drop Policy for Protective and Best-Effort Traffic*

Hyon-Young Choi and Sung-Gi Min**

Dept. of Computer Science and Engineering, Korea University, Seoul, South Korea
{neongas, sgmin}@korea.ac.kr

Abstract. Adaptive REM(AREM) is proposed to support real time traffic from non real time traffic in routers. In AREM, we classify the traffics into real time flows and non real time flows and the marking probability of non real time traffic is increased proportional to the amount of protected real time traffic until the marking probability reaches its maximum limit. Our simulation result shows that AREM provides improved overall performance to real time traffic in a sense of low loss rate and bounded delay.

1 Introduction

With rapid growth of the Internet, the amount of real time traffic for multimedia applications such as internet phone or internet broadcasting has been increased. The requirements of real time traffic in the Internet are low loss rate and low end-to-end delay. Routers in the network have to reflect these requirements to support real time traffic.

Active Queue Management(AQM) such as Random Early Detection(RED) and its variances[1][2][3] is usually used to control congestion in a router. Interestingly, because end-to-end delay is primarily determined by the buffering, queuing and routing delay of routers, the same resources are related to end-to-end delay and congestion control. It means that AQM can be used both controlling congestion and supporting real time traffic in a router. But AQM only has considered the adaptiveness of traffic flow which is suitable for best effort flows, and they do not consider other characteristics of traffic such as delay and low packet loss rate for real time traffic.

Among AQM schemes, Random Exponential Marking(REM)[4] has a good feature to bound the queuing delay desired by adjusting the target queue length. But loss rate cannot be assured because REM treats all traffic to the same. And default parameters are not suitable for real time traffic because stabilized feature

---

* This work was supported by grant No.10016756 from the Growth Power Technology Development Project, funded by the Ministry of Commerce, Industry and Energy of Korea.
** Corresponding author.

S. Chaudhuri et al. (Eds.): ICDCN 2006, LNCS 4308, pp. 385–390, 2006.
© Springer-Verlag Berlin Heidelberg 2006

of REM takes a long time to reach steady state and has a large queue length before stabilized.

In this paper, we introduce Adaptive REM(AREM) for supporting real time traffic. AREM treats real time traffic differently from non real time traffic in dropping packets and uses optimized parameters to bound the queue length even before steady state reached. For calculating marking probability, we make a parameter varying pre-defined range. The amount of protecting real time traffic influences the variance of the parameter.

2 Adaptive REM for Congestion Control and Realtime Traffic Support

2.1 Random Exponential Marking(REM)

REM decouples the congestion measurement and performance metrics. The mean queue length in REM can be stabilized around the pre-defined target while the marking probability increases as the amount of traffic increases, so the queueing delay is not affected[4].

In REM, the degree of congestion based on mismatches is represented by 'price'. Eq. (1) shows how the price $p_l(t)$ can be calculated by mismatches for the queue l and the period t.

$$p_l(t+1) = [p_l(t) + \gamma(\alpha_l(b_l(t) - b_l^*) + x_l(t) - c_l(t))]^+ \quad (1)$$

where $\gamma > 0$ and $\alpha > 0$ are small constant and $[z]^+ = max\{z, 0\}$. And $b_l(t)$ is amount of buffer in period of t, b_l^* is target queue length, $x_l(t)$ is input rate and $c_l(t)$ is available link capacity.

In eq. (1), $x_l(t) - c_l(t)$ means the mismatch of input rate and $b_l(t) - b_l^*$ is the mismatch of queue length. α is weight factor between queue length mismatch and input rate mismatch. And γ is weighting factor of current price and previous price.

The marking probability is defined with exponential equation as eq. (2).

$$m_l(t) = 1 - \phi^{-p_l(t)} \quad (2)$$

2.2 Adaptive REM

Although REM has a possibility for supporting real time traffic, it still has some problems. Firstly, there is no discrimination for real time traffic because the main purpose of REM is congestion control in routers like other AQM. Secondly, there is big fluctuation of queue size with default parameters before it reaches the equilibrium state and the period of exceeding queue size than target queue size precedes steady state. In the un-stabilized period, real time traffic suffers from large queuing delay due to large queue length.

To support real time traffic with REM, we must protect real time traffic from non real time traffic. We can achieve this by artificially manipulating marking probability whenever we enqueue non-conforming real time packet. Following non real time packets are applied higher marking probability than usual one. The increased marking probability prevents the queue from increasing by enqueuing non-conforming real time packets.

In eq. (1), enqueuing real time packets increase $b_l(t)$, so queue length mismatch also increases. But the next price increase are limited by α and γ, so the next marking probability growth in eq. (2) is minimal. This causes steadily growth of queue size. To remedy this problem, we must change the marking probability artificially by changing ϕ in eq. (2). The ϕ was a constant value in REM.

To make ϕ change dynamically, we introduce new parameters, ϕ_{min}, ϕ_{max} and Δ. ϕ_{min} and ϕ_{max} are the minimum value and the maximum value of ϕ respectively. And Δ is an increasing or decreasing unit of ϕ. When a packet for the real time traffic is arrived, we increase ϕ by Δ until it is not over the ϕ_{max} after the packet is enqueued. And for the non real time traffic, we decrease ϕ by Δ while it is not below the ϕ_{min}.

To solve the second problem, we must adjust the REM's parameters to make un-stabilized period shorten. But because of REM's basic characteristic of stabilized feature, it is impossible to eliminate un-stabilized period entirely.

We make a strong restriction about exceeding target queue length to minimize un-stabilized period. If we applied the restriction based on target queue length, current queue length may have exceeded already target queue length. New parameter pq is introduced to estimate threshold value for applying the restriction. If the current buffer size exceeds $b^* \times pq$, we apply the restriction to prevent the queue from excessive growing by increasing ϕ value aggressively to ϕ_{max}. pq is a constant value between 0 and 1.

3   Simulation Studies

We investigate the performance of AREM for supporting real time traffic using ns-2[5] network simulator. We use two types of network, single link network and multilink network.

3.1   Single Link Network

We compare three types of schemes for single link network: S1, S2 and S3. S1 is original REM. S1 cannot aware whether the arriving packet is real time traffic and it applies same fixed ϕ for all incoming packets. S2 is REM with only protecting real time traffic. S2 has the ability to distinguish real time traffic, but S2 uses fixed ϕ like S1. S2 just enqueues every real time packet without dropping. And S3 is proposed AREM scheme.

Single link network topology is shown in Fig. 1. Link delay of all link is 10ms and link capacity is 2 Mbps except link between routers. And link between routers is 1 Mbps. There are total $n + m$ sources which are serving CBR service with 70 kbps. These are all UDP services, and only n sources consider as real time traffic reserved. Common parameters for S1, S2 and S3 are $\alpha = 0.1$, $\gamma = 0.001$ and $b^* = 25$. And S1 and S2 have same fixed ϕ as 1.005. For S3, we assign the parameters with $\phi_{min} = 1.005$, $\phi_{max} = 1.05$, $\Delta = 0.001$ and $pq = 0.7$.

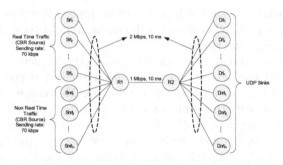

Fig. 1. Single (bottleneck) link network

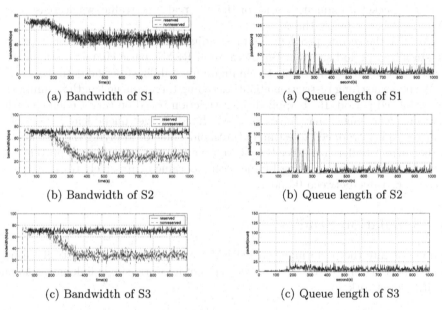

(a) Bandwidth of S1

(b) Bandwidth of S2

(c) Bandwidth of S3

(a) Queue length of S1

(b) Queue length of S2

(c) Queue length of S3

Fig. 2. Bandwidth of real time and non real time traffic with three schemes

Fig. 3. Queue Length of three schemes at router R1

We simulate with n=10 and m=10. All of non real time traffic started at 30 seconds, and real time traffic is starting at 60 seconds and one by one every 30 seconds.

Fig. 2 shows the bandwidth of three types of schemes respectively. With S1 in Fig. 2 (a), there is no difference between real time traffic and non real time traffic. So every traffic converges the fair shared bandwidth of the link capacity, 50 kbps. S2 in Fig. 2 (b) can distinguish the real time traffic from others. The real time traffic has fully serviced with its service rate 70 kbps and other traffic served with remain capacity. S3 in Fig. 2 (c) looks like all most same as S2's bandwidth allocation.

However, the queue length variation in Fig. 3 shows the difference of S2 and S3. S1 has big oscillation in queue length. S2 has same big oscillation and it goes up more than S1. This phenomenon is expected because the enqueued packet, which should be dropped, causes the queue length growth in short time. So the smoothed marking probability in REM cannot cope with rapid queue size growth. With S3, there is no such oscillation and almost all queue length is below the target queue length 25.

3.2 Multilink Network

Multilink network is used to verify the AREM's performance in various network traffic combined and traffic flowing through multiple AREM routers. Multilink network topology is shown in Fig. 4. There are three groups of flows, S to D, S_x to D_x and S_y to D_y. We can send three type of traffic for each group. In our simulation, the real time traffic flows from S to D. S_x to D_x and S_y to D_y are non real time traffic flows. Five real time traffic source and thirty UDP sources(CBR, fifteen each) are used. And all CBR traffic services with 70 kbps. Link delay of all link is 10ms and link capacity except link between routers is 2 Mbps. And link between routers is 1 Mbps. All parameters are the same as single link network topology with S3 scheme.

Fig. 5 shows the end-to-end delay from S1 to D1. The graph shows good example for end-to-end delay is bounded. In multilink network, Fig. 4, total link delay

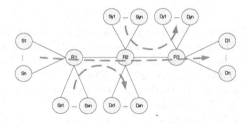

Fig. 4. Multilink(parking lot) network

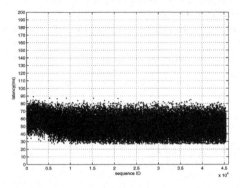

Fig. 5. End-to-end delay of S_i to D_i

from S to D is 40 ms. When a packet length is 1000 bytes and maximum queue size is 25 at link bandwidth 1 Mbps, the maximum queueing delay at an AREM router is 20ms. Therefore, theoretical maximum end-to-end delay is 80 ms. Note that last router R3 does not cause queueing delay. Fig. 5 shows the end-to-end delay of each packet arrived at D_i, which matches with the theoretical limit.

4   Conclusion

We have proposed AREM protocol for supporting real time traffic and shown that AREM does protect real time traffic with bounded queue length by modifying REM scheme. We have modified REM parameters to adapted to be more suitable to real time traffic. It turned out that parameter must be dynamically changed to reflect current router states. We achieve this by modifying marking probability equation and discriminating non real time traffic. In addition, excessive queue length problem in the un-stabilized period in REM is lessened by aggressive marking probability increase.

AREM displays suitable performance parameters such as the bandwidth usage, the queue length and the end-to-end delay for real time traffic. AREM is specially suitable for less strict QoS classes such as Controlled-Load service in Integrated Service[6] or Assured Forward(AF) service in Differentiated Service[7].

References

1. S. Floyd and V. Jacobson, "Random early detection gateways for congestion avoidance," IEEE/ACM Transactions on Netowrking, 1(4), Aug. 1993.
2. D. Lin and R. Morris, "Dynamics of Random Early Detection," Proc. of ACM SIGCOMM, SIGCOMM'97, pages 127-137, October 1997.
3. R. Mahajan, S. Floyd, and D. Wetherall, "Controlling high-bandwidth flows at the congested router," ICNP, November 2001.
4. S. Athuraliya, V. H. Li, S. H. Low, and Q. Yin, "REM: active queue management," IEEE Network, 15(3):48-53, May/June 2001. Extended version in Proceedings of ITC17, Salvador, Brazil, September 2001.
5. K. Fall and K. Varadhan, "ns Notes and Documentation," April 1998, http://www-mash.cs.berkeley.edu/ns/nsDoc.ps.gz
6. "Integrated Services in the Internet Architecture: an Overview," RFC 1633, April 1998.
7. "An Architecture for Differentiated Services," RFC 2475, December 1998.

A New Precomputation Scheme for MPLS Traffic Engineering Routing

Zhaowei Meng[1], Jinshu Su[1], and Vittorio Manetti[2]

[1] School of Computer, National University of Defense Technology,
Changsha 410073, P.R. China
{zwmeng, sjs}@nudt.edu.cn
[2] COMICS Lab, Dipartimento di Informatica e Sistemistica,
Università di Napoli Federico II,
Via Claudio 21, 80125 Napoli, Italy
vittorio.manetti@unina.it

Abstract. This paper presents a new precomputation algorithm for Multi Protocol Label Switching (MPLS) traffic engineering routing. The prior MPLS routing algorithms try to minimize the interference between different source-destination pairs by circumventing the critical links. But the process of identifying critical links is very computationally expensive. The main contribution of this paper is a new precomputation approach of route selection considering the interference. The proposed algorithm reduces online computing complexity through efficient precomputation. From the simulation results, the proposed algorithm outperforms prior algorithms in terms of efficiency and complexity.

1 Introduction and Related Works

Nowadays, the most frequently used routing algorithm in Internet is the Shortest-Path-First (SPF) algorithm. This algorithm may potentially cause some links being bottleneck and lead to poor resource utilization. So based on SPF, many algorithms which consider load balancing have been proposed, but MIRA [1] is the first algorithm which utilizes the knowledge of SD pairs and considers the interference phenomena. The problem of minimum interference routing is to find a path that maximizes the maxflow between all other SD pairs. This problem is shown to be NP hard. So M. Kodialam et al. give a heuristic algorithm - MIRA. The core notion of MIRA is "critical link". MIRA tries to avoid routing LSPs on such critical links of other SD pairs. So it performs better than former algorithms.

But MIRA also has some shortcomings. One shortcoming is that some links which are believed as non-critical by MIRA are shown to be indeed very important. S.Suri et al. illustrated this point by some special topologies [2]. Bin Wang et al. propose NewMIRA algorithm which utilizes maxflow value of SD pair and sub-flow value on the link to estimate its importance [3]. In [4], the authors provide an algorithm which divides the link criticality into multiple classes.

S. Chaudhuri et al. (Eds.): ICDCN 2006, LNCS 4308, pp. 391–396, 2006.
© Springer-Verlag Berlin Heidelberg 2006

The other shortcoming of MIRA is that the complexity of maxflow computation is very high. This limits MIRA's application in practical networks. W.S.S. et al. propose a new notion of interference [5] which uses the number of possible paths per link to denote link's criticality. W.S.S.'s approach reduces the complexity. In [6], the authors use the notion of criticality threshold to precompute more effectively.

This paper propose a new pre-computation approach for routing bandwidth guaranteed label switch path, which tries to consider influence resulted by all critical or "non-critical" links. Our approach reduces online computation complexity through efficient pre-computation. Extensive simulations were carried out to evaluate the performance of the proposed algorithm. The result shows that our approach performs better than former algorithms.

The rest of this paper is structured as follows. Section 1 reviews the main idea of MIRA and some related works. In Section 2 we propose a new pre-computation algorithm for routing bandwidth guaranteed flows, and describe it in detail. In Section 3, the efficiency of our new algorithm is evaluated and finally, Section 4 concludes our work.

2   Proposed Algorithm

2.1 System Model

Given a network represented by a directed graph (V,E) where V is a set of nodes and E is a set of links. The number of nodes is n and the number of links is m. The LSP setup requests are between specific source nodes and destination nodes. The SD pairs are $\{S_0,D_0\},\{S_1,D_1\},...,\{S_p,D_p\}$, where p is the number of SD pairs. We denote all these SD pairs by a set P. Each LSP set-up request arrives at ingress node. The requests arrive online, one by one, and there is no prior knowledge for future demands. Each ingress router knows the whole network's topology and state information of the links. The initial capacity of link l is denoted as $R(l)$, while the current available bandwidth is $r(l)$. The LSP request r_i is defined by a triple (s_i,d_i,b_i), where $(s_i,d_i) \in P$, and b_i is the amount of bandwidth required by the LSP. The objective is to find a feasible path (if exists) for LSP request r_i, otherwise the request will be rejected. In this paper, we focus on the routing of bandwidth guaranteed paths. No rerouting or request splitting is allowed.

2.2 Proposed Algorithm's Details

In this section, we will present our approach's details. We consider not only the critical links, but also "non-critical" links. The sum of sub-flows belong to different SD pairs traveling through the link will be used to estimate its interference degree. The residual bandwidth and hop counts are also considered. We will define a novel link weight function here:

$$w(l) = \begin{cases} \dfrac{b * \displaystyle\sum_{(a,b)\in P\backslash(s,d)} \alpha_{ab} f_{ab}(l)}{r(l) * \alpha_{sd} f_{sd}(l)} + C & \text{if } f_{sd}(l) \neq 0 \\[3ex] \dfrac{b * \displaystyle\sum_{(a,b)\in P\backslash(s,d)} \alpha_{ab} f_{ab}(l)}{r(l) * \alpha_{sd} r(l)} + C & \text{if } f_{sd}(l) = 0 \end{cases} \tag{1}$$

Where α_{sd} represents the relative importance of SD pair (s,d). And $f_{sd}(l)$ is the amount of sub-flow traveling through the link l when the maximum flow between (s,d) is achieved. The item C is a control constant.

In the link weight function, link's residual bandwidth $r(l)$ denotes the link's ability to hold future LSP requests. If the residual bandwidth is bigger, the link weight will be smaller and the algorithm will try to route LSP through such links. And if $\alpha_{sd} f_{sd}(l)$ is bigger and $\displaystyle\sum_{(a,b)\in P\backslash(s,d)} \alpha_{ab} f_{ab}(l)$ is smaller, we believe that routing request through link l will cause less impact on other SD pairs. So the algorithm will trend to route LSP on such links. Otherwise the algorithm will trend to avoid such links.

If $f_{sd}(l) = 0$, it shows that there is no flow traveling link l when the maximum flow is achieved. Because the way to achieve maximum flow is not distinct, it doesn't mean the request can't travel through link l. So we use $r(l)$ as a substitute for $f_{sd}(l)$.

Item C is a dynamic control constant. If constant C is chosen very big, the algorithm behaviors like SPF. If C is chosen relatively small, the algorithm trends to minimize the interference and balance the load.

But calculating this link weight still needs p maxflow computations. This is expensive for online routing. In order to reduce the online complexity, our algorithm adopts two phases - precomputation phase and online routing phase. Through effective precomputation, our approach could reduce online complexity successfully.

In the pre-computation period $t_k (k = 0,1,2,...)$, we compute maximum flow for each SD pair and record the sub-flow at that time $f_{sd}(l,t_k)$. These values will be used by online phase to predict the degree of link congestion. The pre-computation phase runs periodically, or anytime the topology and the SD pairs changed.

In the online phase, given an LSP request (s,d,b) to be routed, we try to estimate the impact of routing current request on the link to other SD pair by a link weight function as below.

$$w(l) = \begin{cases} \dfrac{b * \displaystyle\sum_{(a,b)\in P\backslash(s,d)} \alpha_{ab} f_{ab}(l,t_k)}{r(l) * \alpha_{sd} f_{sd}(l,t_k)} + C & \text{if } f_{sd}(l) \neq 0 \\[3ex] \dfrac{b * \displaystyle\sum_{(a,b)\in P\backslash(s,d)} \alpha_{ab} f_{ab}(l,t_k)}{r(l) * \alpha_{sd} r(l)} + C & \text{if } f_{sd}(l) = 0 \end{cases} \tag{2}$$

The algorithm's detailed pseudo code is listed below.

The Proposed Algorithm

INPUT: A residual graph $G = (V, E)$, a set P of all the source-destination pairs and LSP request r (s, d, b), which is a request for b bandwidth units between pair (s, d).
OUTPUT: A path from s to d with b bandwidth units.
PRECOMPUTATION PHASE:

At the pre-computation time point t_k $(k = 0, 1, 2, ...)$, $\forall (a, b) \in P$

1: Compute the maximum network flows,

2: $\forall l \in E$, record the amount of flow passing through the link- $f_{ab}(l, t_k)$.

ONLINE PHASE:
1: Compute the weight $w(l)$ for all $l \in E$ according to equation (2) .
2: Eliminate all the links whose residual bandwidth less than b.
3: Run Dijkstra algorithm using $w(l)$ as the weights in the reduced network.
4: Create an LSP from s to d with b bandwidth units and update the links' available bandwidth.

2.3 Complexity Analysis

In precomputation phase, computing maxflow for each SD pair using the highest label preflow-push algorithm needs $O(n^2\sqrt{m})$. There are p SD pairs, so the computation need totally $O(pn^2\sqrt{m})$. This is on the same level as MIRA and NewMIRA's $O((p-1)n^2\sqrt{m})$ .In online phase, Step 1 and step 2 both need $O(m)$. Step 3 needs $O(n^2)$. So the online computation complexity is only $O(n^2)$.

If the network state changes frequently, the algorithm will have to execute pre-computation more frequently and the total run time of algorithm will increase. But in the worst case, its complexity is no higher than MIRA and NewMIRA.

3 Performance Studies

The network topology and SD pairs used in the simulation are shown in figure 1. This topology was first used by M.S. Kodialam et al. in [1].

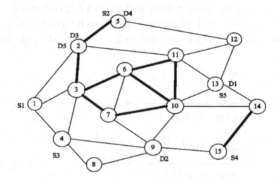

Fig. 1. The KL topology [1]

Lighter links have capacity of 1200 bandwidth units, while the darker ones have 4800 units. Links are bi-directional. Requests were randomly generated using the uniform distribution of bandwidth demand in the interval [1, 4]. The LSPs are long lives. 8,000 requests were randomly generated among the five SD pairs. Our algorithm runs at the intervals k=128. In this scenario, we assume the accurate resource availability information is available when selecting the route. And the constant C in the weight function is set to zero.

Figure 2 presents the number of rejected requests. From the figure we can see that both our proposed algorithm and NewMIRA rejected fewer requests than SPF and WSP all the time. And our algorithm rejected fewer requests than NewMIRA after 5000 requests, when the pre-computation period is 128.

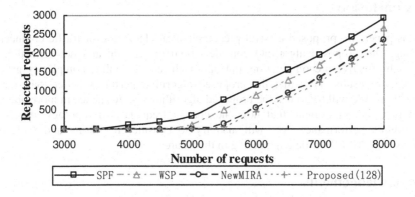

Fig. 2. Total rejected requests in KL topology

Figure 3 shows the amount of accepted bandwidth till up to total 8000 requests. After 7000 requests, the network is almost saturated. From the figure we can see that our proposed algorithm also accepts more bandwidth than NewMIRA when the precomputation period is 128. These two algorithms perform better than SPF and WSP.

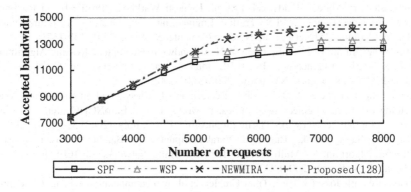

Fig. 3. Total accepted bandwidth in KL topology

From table 1, we can found that the total computation time of our proposed algorithm is much less than the NewMIRA algorithm, although a little higher than CSPF algorithm. When the precomputation period increases, the computation time will also decrease. But if the network status and traffic requests surge frequently, longer precomputation period (i.e. 512, 1024) will leads to worse performance. So there is a compromise to be considered when adjusting the precomputation period.

Table 1. Total computation time till 8000 requests in KL topology

Algorithm	CSPF	WSP	NewMIRA	Proposed(128)
Run time (sec)	0.80	0.80	4.68	1.02

4 Conclusion

In this paper, we proposed a novel precomputation algorithm for traffic engineering routing. Our proposed algorithm considers both the critical and non-critical links. Through effective precomputation, our approach reduces online complexity greatly. Simulation results show that the proposed algorithm performs better than former algorithms. We will try to test the proposed algorithm's performance in more practical scenarios, and investigate that how the change frequency of topology affects the algorithm's performance. We will also try to consider re-routing and multi-path routing with MPLS traffic engineering in the future.

Acknowledgements

This work is supported by the National Natural Science Foundation of China under Grant No.90604006.

References

1. M.S. Kodialam, T.V. Lakshman, Minimum Interference Routing with Applications to MPLS Traffic Engineering, in INFOCOM 2000, Tel Aviv, Israel, (2000) 884–893
2. Subhash Suri, Marcel Waldvogel, Priyank Ramesh Warkhede. Profile based Routing: A new Framework for MPLS Traffic Engineering. In: Quality of future Internet Services,Volume 2516 of Lecture Notes in Computer Science; (2001) 138-157.
3. Bin Wang, Xu Su, C. L. Philip Chen. A New Bandwidth Guaranteed Routing Algorithm for MPLS Traffic Engineering. In: IEEE International Conference on Communications 2002(ICC'02); New York, NY, USA; (2002) 1001-1005.
4. János Tapolcai, Péter Fodor, Gábor Rétvári, et al. Class-based minimum interference routing for traffic engineering in optical networks. In: 1st EuroNGI Conference on Next Generation Internet Networks Traffic Engineering; Rome, Italy; (2005) 31-38.
5. Wisitsak Sa-Ngiamsak, Ruttikorn Varakulsiripunth. A Bandwidth-Based Constraint Routing Algorithm for Multi-Protocol LabelSwitching Networks. In: IEEE ICACT 2004; Phoenix Park, Korea; (2004) 933-937.
6. Gábor Rétvári, József J. Bíró, Tibor Cinkler, et al. A precomputation scheme for minimum interference routing: the Least-Critical-Path-First algorithm. In: INFOCOM 2005; Miami, Florida, USA; (2005) 260-268.

A Mobility Aware Technique for Clustering on Mobile Ad-Hoc Networks*

Charalampos Konstantopoulos[1], Damianos Gavalas[2], and Grammati Pantziou[3]

[1] Research Academic Computer Technology Institute and
University of Patras, Greece
[2] Department of Cultural Technology and Communication,
University of the Aegean, Greece
[3] Department of Informatics, Technological Education Institution of Athens, Greece
konstant@cti.gr, dgavalas@aegean.gr, pantziou@teiath.gr

Abstract. Clustering for mobile ad-hoc networks (MANETs) has attracted the interest of many researchers as it offers enhanced scalability and performance improvement. The main challenge of the clustering algorithms is the formation of stable clusters despite the topological changes due to the host mobility. In this paper, we present a novel clustering algorithm, which first predicts the future host mobility and then uses this information to build a stable clustering structure over hosts that will probably exhibit low mobility in the future. In this way, long lifetime for the clustering structure is guaranteed, thereby eliminating the need for frequent reclustering. For predicting the future host mobility, we use provably good information theoretic techniques, which allow on-line learning of a reliable probabilistic model for future mobility.

1 Introduction

Clustering [1] is a promising approach for enhancing the scalability of mobile ad hoc networks (MANETs) in the face of frequent topology changes mainly due to the host mobility. Clustering not only makes a large MANET to appear smaller, but more importantly, it makes a highly dynamic topology to appear less dynamic [2]. In clustering, a representative of each cluster is elected as a cluster head (CH) and a mobile host (MH), which serves as intermediate for inter-cluster communication, is called gateway. Remaining members are called ordinary MHs. CHs hold routing and topology information while the boundaries of a cluster are defined by the transmission area of its CH.

The feasibility of a clustering method is determined by the stability of the cluster structure that it creates, despite network topology changes. Otherwise, frequent reclustering is required thereby creating a large volume of control messages which in turn consume considerable bandwidth and drain MHs' energy

---

* This work is co-funded by 75% from E.U. and 25% from the Greek Government under the framework of the Education and Initial Vocational Training II, programme "Archimedes".

S. Chaudhuri et al. (Eds.): ICDCN 2006, LNCS 4308, pp. 397–408, 2006.

quickly. As the main cause for topology changes in MANET is the host mobility, an efficient clustering method should seriously take the movements of MHs into account in order to form clustering structures resistant to the host mobility.

Many researchers [2, 3, 4, 5, 6, 7, 8] have acknowledged the importance of host mobility estimation for building clustering schemes more stable and less reactive to topological changes of ad-hoc networks. Authors in [2] propose the (a, t) clustering scheme, where MHs form clusters according to a path availability criterion. The network is partitioned into clusters of MHs, that are mutually reachable along cluster internal paths which are expected to be available for a period of time t with a probability of at least a. The parameters of this model are predefined. In addition, it is assumed that the movement of each MH is random and entirely independent of the movements of other MHs. However, this random walk model cannot always capture some host mobility patterns occurring in practice in MANETs.

MOBIC in [3] elects as CHs the MHs which exhibit the lowest mobility in their neighborhood. Each MH compares the receiving signal strength from its neighbors over the time and uses the variance in these values as an indication of how fast this MH is moving in relation to the neighboring MHs. MOBIC uses only the current mobility to determine the most suitable MHs for CHs. As an extension of MOBIC, MobDHop [4] also uses the variability in receiving signal strength as a hint of neighborhood mobility and builds variable-diameter clusters. It uses more samples of receiving signal than MOBIC to predict the future mobility but again the prediction model is rather simple since it is based on the assumption that the future mobility patterns of MHs will be exactly the same as those of the recent past.

DMAC in [5] and GDMAC in [6] proposed by Basagni are generic weight-based clustering schemes, where MHs with the highest weight among neighboring ones are elected as CHs. Basagni suggested to use the inverse of the speed of MHs as a weight in its scheme. However, he does not give any method for determining the speed of MHs. WCA in [7] is also a weight-based clustering technique which extends the work in [5,6]. The weight in this scheme is determined by considering various factors that affect the suitability of a MH as a CH. Among these factors is host mobility. Specifically, each MH measures its average speed by sampling its position coordinates at regular time intervals. This method of measurement requires the use of a GPS device on each MH, which is not always feasible. Furthermore, this method fails to capture the correlation that may exist among the movements of neighboring MHs as in the case of group movement.

Information theory based techniques for host mobility prediction have been first employed in [10], where the authors focused on the problem of mobile tracking and localization on cellular networks. Later, Sivavakeesar et. al [8] used the basic technique of [10] in their cluster formation algorithm for MANETs. A basic assumption in their work is that a geographical area is divided into circular-shaped regions named virtual clusters and each MH knows the virtual cluster where it is currently in. So, the ad-hoc network in their technique is very much like a cellular one and the ideas in [10] can be easily applied.

In this paper, we propose a novel mobility-aware technique for cluster formation and maintenance. The main idea in our technique is to predict the future mobility of MHs so as to select CHs that will exhibit the lowest future mobility in comparison to the other MHs. As a measure of host mobility rate, we use the probability of a MH having the same MHs in its neighborhood for sufficiently long time. A high probability value for a MH indicates a relatively immobile host or the existence of a group of MHs around this particular MH that exhibits the same mobility pattern. Whatever the case is, this MH is apparently a good candidate for a CH, because in all probability, it will serve the same neighbors for a long time. For predicting the future mobility of a MH, we make the realistic assumption for most MANETs that the movements of MHs are not random but demonstrate a regular pattern, which can be predicted provided that enough "historic" information has been gathered for the movements of each MH. For the organization of the historic record and the prediction of future mobility based on this record, we borrow context modelling [11] based prediction techniques from the field of data compression. Note also that we do not make any use of a fixed geographical partition in contrast to all previous works [10,8] and thus the notion of cells is irrelevant to our technique.

Besides the stability of the clustering structure, an important objective in cluster creation is to keep the number of elected CHs relatively low so that the virtual backbone built over these MHs will be of correspondingly small size and hence routing update protocols could be efficiently ran on this backbone. The well-known highest connectivity (degree) algorithm [1] promises the election of relatively few CHs. In this paper, we propose a new clustering algorithm named MobHiD, which combines the highest degree technique with our mobility prediction scheme and ensures a relatively small as well as stable virtual backbone despite host mobility. The performance of our technique was verified via simulation experiments, which compared our algorithm with other competitive techniques of the literature.

Note that our mobility prediction technique is of independent interest and may be combined with other clustering algorithms to enhance the stability of the derived clustering structure in the presence of frequent topology changes.

The paper is organized as follows. In Sect. 2, we discuss our mobility prediction method. In Sect. 3, we present our MobHiD clustering algorithm which uses the mobility prediction method. Section 4 addresses the details of the distributed implementation of MobHiD and then Sect. 5 discusses the simulation results about the performance of our clustering technique. Finally, Sect. 6 concludes the paper by summarizing the main contribution of our work.

2   Our Mobility Prediction Method

A MH is considered a good candidate for CH if its neighborhood is relatively stable in comparison to the neighborhoods of other candidate hosts. Let $neigh_{i,t} = (i_0, i_1, i_2, \ldots, i_{n_t-1})$ be the n_t neighboring MHs of MH i at time step t. Somehow, we have to estimate the probability of the stability of this neighborhood, i.e., the probability $P(neigh_{i,t})$ that this neighborhood will remain the same in the following time steps. By making the simplified assumption that the presence of a MH among the neighbors of MH i in the future is independent of the presence of any other host, we can equivalently write the probability $P(neigh_{i,t})$ as follows:

$$P(neigh_{i,t}) = P(i_0)P(i_1)\cdots P(i_{n_{t-1}})$$

where $P(i_j)$ is the probability of MH i_j being among the neighbors of MH i in the following time steps.

To estimate the above probability for each MH, we need a way to predict the movements of MHs after any given moment. This prediction should not involve complex calculations for this computation should be carried out on MHs with limited battery power and rudimentary processing capability. To this end, we can use prediction techniques, that have been successfully employed in the field of data compression. If we consider each neighborhood of a MH as a symbol of an alphabet, we can use this kind of techniques to predict the next symbol/neighborhood. Compression and decompression algorithms for images and video are routinely included in the software of new mobile phones and devices as their implementation does not have a prohibitive cost. Most successful compression methods use context-modelling techniques, which estimate the appearance probability of the next symbol in the text given that a substring (context) has already been seen. A digital-trie structure is typically used for organizing the contexts we meet as we are parsing the text. For updating this structure, we use an heuristic similar to that used in the LZ78 algorithm [12]. Specifically, a dictionary of common substrings found in the text is organized using a digital trie structure. Updating proceeds as follows:

1. Initially the dictionary is empty.
2. Examine the remaining input stream and search for the longest prefix which has appeared in the dictionary.
3. Add the prefix followed by the next symbol in the input stream to the dictionary.
4. Go to Step 2.

In our method, for a MH i, each symbol is the tuple of MHs that are neighbors of MH i at any given moment and the input stream is the sequence of neighbors of MH i over time. An example of our technique is illustrated in Fig. 1. Specifically, we see how a sequence of neighborhoods of MH 0 is parsed and inserted into the digital trie structure. The dashed lines on the left delimit the parsed subsequences of the neighborhood sequence. The cost of updating is minimal. Since, each new subsequence added to the dictionary consists of an already seen neighborhood subsequence followed by an extra neighborhood, the insertion of the new context in the dictionary requires only the addition of one leave at the end of the trie path corresponding to the longest prefix of step 2. Clearly, each trie node is associated with a neighborhood subsequence found during the parsing of the input neighborhood sequence and also has a counter, which shows how many times we have met the corresponding subsequence during this process.

For instance, the trie node labelled $\{(1,2,3,4),6\}$ shows that the sequence of neighborhoods $(1,2,3),(1,2,3,4)$ has been met 6 times in total during parsing. Note also this sequence includes all the node labels along the path from the root to the node $\{(1,2,3,4),6\}$. Also in step 2 above, as we follow down the path from the root to the leaves, we increase by one the counters of all the nodes we visit. After a while, this node counter accumulation builds reliable conditional probability estimates. Specifically, given that we have met a particular neighborhood subsequence and so we are at a particular node in the trie, the counter of each of the children of this node is a measure of the conditional probability of what neighborhood appears next in the input neighborhood sequence. Clearly, the skewer the probability distribution of the next possible neighborhoods, the better the prediction of what really follows.

Now, we are mainly interested in estimating the probability of a MH j appearing in the neighborhood of MH i given a particular sequence of recent neighborhoods, say $neigh_{i,t-r}, neigh_{i,t-r+1}, \cdots, neigh_{i,t}$. First, we count the number of appearances of MH j in all the nodes of the subtrie which has as a root the node corresponding to the neighborhood sequence $neigh_{i,t-r}, neigh_{i,t-r+1}, \cdots, neigh_{i,t}$. Then, we find the total number of neighborhoods that they have appeared after this particular sequence of neighborhoods by summing the counts of the nodes of the subtrie. Finally we get the appearance probability of MH j by dividing the first number with the second one. For example, given that the last two neighborhoods of MH 0 are the $(1,2,3),(1,2,3,4)$ (and so the current neighborhood is the $(1,2,3,4)$) we can easily see that the probability of MH 1 and 4 still being a neighbor of MH 0 from then on is $\frac{3+1}{2+3+1+1+1}(=\frac{4}{8})$ and $\frac{2+1+1}{2+3+1+1+1}(=\frac{4}{8})$ respectively while the same probability for MHs 2 and 3 is 1. So, the probability that MH 0 will keep having the current neighborhood $(1,2,3,4)$ in the following time steps is the product of the appearance probabilities of each MH, that is $\frac{4^2}{8^2}$

An interesting question about our technique is how much predictable the neighborhoods formed at each step really are. The formation of a particular neighborhood around a MH is not the result of the behavior of only this MH but it is the cumulative effect of the behaviors of a number of MHs at the same time. So the probability of the next neighborhood at a particular trie node may not be as biased as we would wish. Another difficulty is that each symbol in the trie now is a tuple of the ids that are neighbors of MH i. This could result in a large number of trie nodes and in addition many of the counts in the trie nodes may not have accumulate enough to be considered as statistically significant.

In order to alleviate these problems, we modify the basic scheme. We introduce the slack variable k and also allow each trie node to store a number of neighborhoods, where each neighborhood in this set differs in at most k MHs from all other neighborhoods in this set. Formally, neighborhoods $neigh_i$ and $neigh_j$ are stored in the same node only if $|neigh_i - neigh_j| + |neigh_j - neigh_i| \leq k$ where $-$ is the set difference operator. Now, as we go down the trie, the new neighborhood encountered at each step is checked against each of the possible children of the current trie node. We insert the new neighborhood to the first

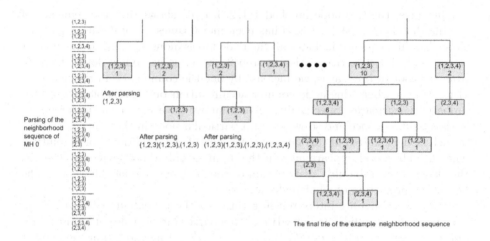

Fig. 1. An example of trie construction

child for which the condition above is not violated after that insertion. If none of the children satisfies the condition above, we create a new trie node as a child of the current trie node. This newly created trie node will contain only the new neighborhood. An important detail of this scheme is that we separately count the number of appearances of each individual neighborhood inside each trie node so that the neighborhood appearance probabilities can be accurately computed. With this modified scheme, we drastically reduce the number of trie nodes. This in turn allows the build-up of statistically significant counter values, which can be reliably used for the estimation of the appearance probability of MHs in the neighborhood of a particular MH.

3 Mobility Aware Highest Degree (MobHiD) Technique

The distributed implementation of our technique should create a stable clustering structure with minimal control overhead. As the CHs and gateways will form the virtual backbone through which messages will be routed on the ad-hoc network, the size of this backbone should be kept as small as possible so that the delay of message routing is correspondingly small. Also, we opt for one-hop clusters where each MH is one-hop away from its CH. In this way, the routing decisions inside each cluster are straightforward and there is no need for involved routing update protocols within each cluster.

The highest degree (HD) clustering algorithm [1] is a clustering scheme that creates a relatively small number of one-hop clusters and thus a small-size routing backbone. In this technique, each MH having the highest degree among all its neighbors is elected as CH. The degree of each MH is the number of one-hop adjacent MHs. The main weakness of the technique is the frequent CH changes due to host mobility. However, by combining the HD technique with our mobility prediction scheme, we substantially eliminate the instable behavior of the technique. More precisely, we define the weight w_i for each MH i as follows:

$$w_i = a_1 \cdot P(neigh_i) \cdot d_i + a_2 \cdot avg\_d_i \tag{1}$$

where $P(neigh_i)$ has been defined in the previous section and is the probability that the current neighborhood $neigh_i$ of MH i will remain the same in the future. Also, d_i is the degree of MH i, i.e., the number of neighbors in $neigh_i$, and avg_d_i is the average degree of the future neighborhoods of the MH i, which can be easily computed from the information contained in the subtrie having root the current neighborhood $neigh_i$. Finally, the coefficients a_1 and a_2 are used to give more weight to the first or the second term in the sum expression above.

A large value of weight w_i practically means that the MH i is surrounded by many neighbors that will remain in the vicinity for a long time with high probability. In addition, due to the second term in the weight expression, it is very likely that MH i will continue to be surrounded by a large number of neighbors in the future too. So, by electing as CHs hosts that have the largest weight value in their neighborhood, we can obtain a small-size virtual backbone, which will remain stable despite host mobility.

4   Distributed Implementation

In the proposed mobility prediction method, each MH i should compute its weight w_i according to the weight formula (1). Therefore, each MH should know its neighbors and how its neighborhood changes over time. This implies a periodic exchange of HELLO messages, namely messages HELLO($clusterhead?,w_i$) so that each MH i can inform its neighbors about its presence, whether it is a clusterhead or not and about its weight. The information carried by the two fields of the HELLO message proves useful when a MH wishes to affiliate another cluster or during reclustering.

Cluster Formation. With regard to the cluster formation, the distributed implementation should tolerate possible topology changes while cluster creation is in progress. Our method for cluster formation adopts some ideas of the distributed implementation of the DMAC clustering algorithm [5]. However, in our scheme the host weights are determined from the weight formula (1). Note that on the system startup, MHs have not yet gathered statistics in their trie structure and hence the initial CH election is carried out essentially according to the HD technique, i.e., in formula (1) we set $w_i = d_i$.

Cluster formation is done as follows: Each MH u that has the highest weight among its neighbors broadcasts the message CLUSTERHEAD(u) to its neighbors, thus declaring its decision of being CH. If the MH u does not possess the largest weight in its neighborhood, first it waits for the decision of all the MHs that have larger weight than its weight and then it decides its own role (CH or ordinary MH). More precisely, there are two cases. First, if MH u has received at least one CLUSTERHEAD message, it joins the cluster of the MH, say MH v, which has the highest probability of still being neighbor in the future in comparison to other MHs that sent CLUSTERHEAD messages. This information can be easily obtained from the trie structure of u. Then, MH u broadcasts the message JOIN(u,v) to communicate its decision to its neighbors. However, if MH u received only JOIN messages from all neighboring MHs with larger weights, this simply means that all these MHs have deferred to other CHs. Now, MH u is free to become a CH and thus it broadcasts the CLUSTERHEAD message to its neighbors.

Cluster Maintenance. Our method for cluster maintenance eliminates the problem of frequent CH changes, by allowing a MH to become a CH or to affiliate with a new cluster without starting a reclustering process. In addition, our method does not suffer from chain reaction effect [13] where local changes in clusterhead roles may propagate over the network. Indeed, in case of reclustering, the size of the affected area is effectively controlled by our method. In the following, we give a high-level description of the Cluster Maintenance.

First, if an ordinary MH u cannot connect to its CH anymore, it tries to find another neighboring CH v and then affiliates to the corresponding cluster by sending the message JOIN(u,v) to v. If more than one CHs exist in the neighborhood of u, it connects to the CH having the highest probability of still being neighbor in the future in comparison to other neighboring CHs. In the case that there is no CH in its vicinity, then u becomes a CH.

Reclustering may be initiated only by a CH. Specifically, reclustering is triggered, only when a CH realizes that the number of CHs having gathered in its neighborhood is above a particular threshold L. Due to the periodic exchange of HELLO messages, each CH can easily and rapidly check if the condition above for reclustering actually holds.

As said before, a difficult issue about reclustering is the extent of the area that will be affected by this reclustering. It is possible for a single local change in topology to trigger global reclustering with considerable control overhead. To avoid global reclustering in our scheme, we restrict reclustering locally around the CH that triggers the new reclustering. We introduce the parameter *cl_extent*, which determines the clusters around the triggering CH that will participate in the reclustering. Specifically, when a CH triggers a reclustering, it broadcasts the message RECLUSTER(*cl_extent*) to its neighbors. Then these neighbors receive the message, change their state from INACTIVE to ACTIVE and relay the message to their neighbors. When a CH receives the message, it first decreases by one the value of *cl_extent* and then sends the message. The last CH that reduces the value of *cl_extent* to 0 sends the message to its neighbors and the receiving MHs stop flooding the message any longer. After having received the RECLUSTER message, the MHs start executing the clustering algorithm. MHs which still remain in the state INACTIVE ignore any message CLUSTERHEAD or JOIN that arrives from neighboring MHs. However, all the MHs that will participate in a reclustering are not activated at the same time because the RECLUSTER message does not reach all relevant MHs instantly. So each MH

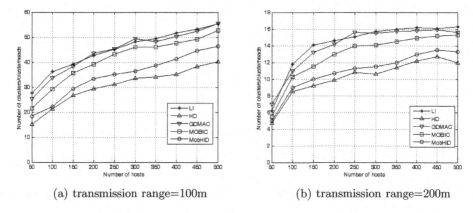

(a) transmission range=100m   (b) transmission range=200m

Fig. 2. Average number of CHs versus total number of MHs

waits for a while before starting the clustering algorithm so as to ensure that
all relevant MHs have been activated. Specifically, if the MH has been activated
by the receipt of the message RECLUSTER(cl_extent), then the MH needs to
wait for $(3 \cdot cl\_extent + 1) \cdot T$ seconds at most, where T is an upper bound of the
message transfer delay over a single link. Indeed, that much time is needed at
most for the RECLUSTER message to traverse the remaining cl_extent one-hop
clusters.

If a MH receives a new message RECLUSTER(cl_extent') while waiting for
starting the clustering algorithm, it extends its wait for another $(3 \cdot cl_extent' +
1) \cdot T$ seconds in order to accommodate the new reclustering request. After this
waiting period expires, the MH starts executing the clustering maintenance algorithm. Now, each MH that does not have the largest weight among its neighbors
should wait for a message, either CLUSTERHEAD or JOIN, from each active
neighbor with larger weight than its weight in order to take a decision, i.e.,
whether it becomes a CH or not. However, due to host mobility, a MH may not
be sure about which of its neighbors are actually active and hence whether it
should wait for them before reaching a decision. For this reason, each active MH
investigates the state of each neighboring MH with larger weight by sending the
message INVITE. On receipt of such message, each active MH sends the message
ACCEPT as an answer. Otherwise, when the MH is in the state INACTIVE, it
replies with the message DECLINE. So, a MH that receives one of these replies
from another MH knows whether it should wait for the decision of this particular
MH or not.

An invitation could also come from a MH executing a different instance of
reclustering. So, if more than one reclustering processes are concurrently in
progress, the exchange of INVITE/ACCEPT messages enables the fusion of
these processes into one. Now, the total affected network area is the union of the
affected areas of the initial concurrent processes.

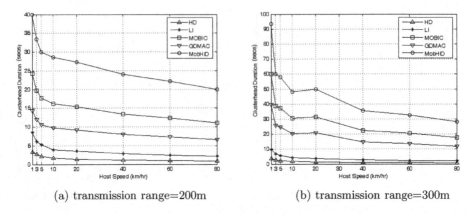

(a) transmission range=200m   (b) transmission range=300m

Fig. 3. Average CH duration versus maximum MH speed

A possible concern about the restricted reclustering is what happens on the boundary of the affected area. It may be the case that a number of CHs nearby the boundary have been elected and thus a CH outside the affected area may trigger again a reclustering. This chain reaction effect can be avoided by properly setting the L parameter which determines the number of CHs that can be adjacent to a CH before triggering reclustering. Note also that if the transmission range of each host is R, all the CHs that have been elected in the just finished reclustering are now at distance greater than R. Now, it can be proved [14] that in an area of radius R, there can exist at most 5 MHs whose mutual distance is greater than R and none of them occupies the center of the area. So at most 5 CHs inside the affected area can be neighbors with a CH which is outside the affected area. By setting $L > 5$ and assuming that only this specific reclustering event happens over the whole network, we can ensure that CHs outside the affected area do not unnecessarily trigger the reclustering process again.

5   Simulation Results

The performance of the MobHiD algorithm was tested through a series of simulations on the ns2 simulator. For comparison, we also simulated four other one-hop clustering algorithms, namely the Lowest ID (LI) [1], Highest Degree (HD), GDMAC as well as MOBIC. The simulation area was a terrain of 1000×1000 m^2. The hosts were moving according to the random waypoint model [9] with zero pause time. The speed of each host was selected randomly between 0 and a maximum value. The maximum value was set a value between 1 and 80km/hr.

Moreover, a number of parameters relevant to each technique were fixed before the experiments. First, for the MobHiD we set the a_1, a_2 coefficients to 0.7 and 0.3 respectively. We also set $k = 3$, $L = 6$ and $cl\_extent = 3$. As a context for determining the conditional host appearance probabilities in our mobility prediction technique, we used a maximum of 10 successive neighborhoods. Finally, we set the broadcast interval of HELLO messages to 1 sec. For GDMAC, by following the suggestion in [6], we set the weight of each host equal to $81 - speed$ where $speed$ is the host velocity. We also used $k = 6$ where k is the maximum number of neighboring clusters before triggering reclustering. We also set the parameter h equal to 30. This parameter in the algorithm leverages the frequency of reaffiliations. Finally for the MOBIC algorithm, we set the Clusterhead Contention Interval (CCI) parameter to 4 sec. The CCI determines how long two CHs can be neighbors before one of them gives up its role as a CH.

In the first set of simulations (Fig. 2), we studied the number of the formed CHs versus the total number of hosts for two values of transmission range. For the same parameter setting, we ran the simulation 50 times. The maximum speed of each host in these simulation runs was set to 70km/hr. Also, each simulation ran for 20 minutes and in each simulation we were sampling the number of CHs every 30 sec. Then we took the average of these samples for each simulation run. The values in Fig. 2 are the average of these values over the 50 simulation runs.

The LI technique, the MOBIC as well as GDMAC algorithm produce a higher number of CHs in comparison to MobHiD and HD algorithm. This is because the first three algorithms are not optimized for minimizing the number of resulting CHs in contrast to the last two techniques. Note also that MobHiD is close to the performance of HD. It is also clear that the number of CHs is much lower when the transmission range is relatively high. Indeed, in the second case the mobile hosts are more densely connected and thus more hosts gather in each cluster. This in turn results in much lower number of clusters and hence CHs.

In the second set of results (Fig. 3), we compared the techniques with respect to the duration of the elected CHs when the maximum speed of hosts increases. By doing so, we assessed the stability of the derived clustering structure with increasing host mobility. For these experiments, we used 50 hosts and ran each simulation with the same parameters 50 times. Each simulation ran for 10 minutes. The CH duration for a single simulation run was the average over all the CHs. Then we got the average of these values over the 50 simulation runs.

From the experimental results, we can see that MobHiD performs much better than the other techniques in the face of host mobility. Based on a more reliable prediction model, our technique ensures more stable clustering structure in comparison to other mobility-aware techniques. The HD and LI techniques do not consider the mobility of hosts in the CH election and hence their poor performance when the maximum speed of hosts is increasing. Again with larger transmission range, the host connectivity graph is more densely connected and the adjacency relations of hosts change less frequently despite the increased host mobility. So now, each CH serves for a longer period before giving up its role.

6   Conclusions

In this paper, we presented a mobility-aware clustering scheme which uses well known information theoretic techniques for reliably predicting the future mobility of MHs. The right prediction combined with the highest degree clustering technique yields a small number of clusters that are highly resistant to the topological changes of the ad-hoc network due to host mobility. For measuring the mobility, we do not use special purpose hardware such as GPS but the mobility of each MH is inferred from how different the neighborhood of the MH is over time. In this way, we take into account the strong correlation that usually exists among the movements of neighboring MHs, thereby achieving accurate prediction of future host mobility. Our results have been verified through simulation experiments, which showed the high performance of our technique in practice.

References

[1] M. Gerla and J. Tsai, Multicluster, Mobile, Multimedia Radio Network, *ACM-Baltzer Journal of Wireless Network*, vol. 1, no. 3, 1995, pp. 255–265.

[2] A. McDonald and T. Znatti, A Mobility-Based Framework for Adaptive Clustering in Wireless Ad Hoc Networks, *IEEE Journal on Selected Areas in Communications*, vol. 17, August 1999, pp. 1466–1487.

[3] P. Basu, N. Khan, and T. Little, A Mobility Based Metric for Clustering in Mobile Ad Hoc Networks, *Proc. of the 21st International Conference on Distributed Computing Systems Workshops (ICDCSW '01)*, 2001, pp. 413–418.

[4] I. Er, and W. Seah, Mobility-based d-Hop Clustering Algorithm for Mobile Ad Hoc Networks, *Proc. of IEEE Wireless Communications and Networking Conference (WCNC 2004)*, vol. 4, pp. 2359–2364.

[5] S. Basagni, Distributed Clustering for Ad-Hoc Networks, *Proc. of the 1999 International Symposium on Parallel Architectures, Algorithms and Networks (I-SPAN'99)*, June 1999, pp. 310–315.

[6] S. Basagni, Distributed and Mobility-Adaptive Clustering for Multimedia Support in Multi-hop Wireless Networks, *Proc. of IEEE International Vehicular Technology Conference*, September 1999, pp. 889–893.

[7] M. Chatterjee, S. Das, and D. Turgut, WCA: A Weighted Clustering Algorithm for Mobile Ad Hoc Networks, *Cluster Computing*, vol. 5, April 2002, pp. 193–204.

[8] S. Sivavakeesar, G. Pavlou and A. Liotta, Stable Clustering Through Mobility Prediction for Large-Scale Multihop Ad Hoc Networks, *Proc. of the IEEE Wireless Communications and Networking Conference (WCNC'2004)*, March 2004.

[9] D. Johnson and D. Maltz, Dynamic Source Routing in Ad Hoc Wireless Networks. In T. Imelinsky and H. Korth, editors, *Mobile Computing*, pp. 153–181, Kluwer Academic Publishers, 1996

[10] Amiya Bhattacharya and Sajal K. Das, LeZi-Update: An Information-Theoretic Framework for Personal Mobility Tracking in PCS Networks, *Wireless Networks*, vol. 8, March 2002, pp. 121–135.

[11] T.C. Bell, J.G. Cleary, and I.H. Witten, *Text Compression*, Prentice Hall, 1990.

[12] J. Ziv and A. Lempel, Compression of Individual Sequences via Variable-rate Coding, *IEEE Transactions on Information Theory*, vol. 24, no. 5, September 1978, pp. 530–536

[13] M. Gerla, T. J. Kwon, and G. Pei, On Demand Routing in Large Ad Hoc Wireless Networks with Passive Clustering, *Proc. of IEEE Wireless Communications and Networking Conference (WCNC'2000)*, September 2000.

[14] V. Marathe, H. Breu, H. B. Hunt III, S. S. Ravi and D. J. Rosenkrantz, Simple Heuristics for Unit Disk Graphs, *Networks*, vol. 25, no. 2, 1995, pp. 59-68.

Design and Analysis of Rate Aware Ad Hoc 802.11 Networks

G. Sandhya and K. Gopinath

Computer Science & Automation
Indian Institute of Science, Bangalore

Abstract. 802.11 WLANs are characterized by high bit error rate and frequent changes in network topology. The key feature that distinguishes WLANs from wired networks is the multi-rate transmission capability, which helps to accommodate a wide range of channel conditions. This has a significant impact on higher layers such as routing and transport levels. While many WLAN products provide rate control at the hardware level to adapt to the channel conditions, some chipsets like Atheros do not have support for automatic rate control. We first present a design and implementation of an FER-based automatic rate control state machine, which utilizes the statistics available at the device driver to find the optimal rate. The results show that the proposed rate switching mechanism adapts quite fast to the channel conditions.

The hop count metric used by current routing protocols has proven itself for single rate networks. But it fails to take into account other important factors in a multi-rate network environment. We propose transmission time as a better path quality metric to guide routing decisions. It incorporates the effects of contention for the channel, the air time to send the data and the asymmetry of links.

In this paper, we present a new design for a multi-rate mechanism as well as a new routing metric that is responsive to the rate. We address the issues involved in using transmission time as a metric and presents a comparison of the performance of different metrics for dynamic routing.

1 Introduction

The 802.11 physical layer is capable of operating at different rates. The rationale behind multi-rate support is the need to provide network coverage. Long distance transmissions are not possible at high data rates. Using lower data rates always is not a good idea either, since it leads to decreased throughput. It has been observed that the presence of even a single slow host in the system can degrade the overall throughput of the system to a level below the lowest rate. Keeping the data transmission rate fixed is thus not desirable. This motivates the need for a highly adaptive rate switching mechanism. Multi-rate support has a significant impact on higher layers such as routing and transport levels. In this paper, we present a new design for a multi-rate mechanism as well as a new routing metric that is responsive to the rate.

S. Chaudhuri et al. (Eds.): ICDCN 2006, LNCS 4308, pp. 409–420, 2006.
© Springer-Verlag Berlin Heidelberg 2006

Many WLAN products provide rate control support as part of their chipset. But certain chipsets (for eg., Atheros) do not allow automatic selection of transmission rate. An alternative is to do it at the device driver level using the statistics available. We discuss the design and implementation of an FER based approach, which could be used at the device driver for finding the optimal rate. We report on the performance of the proposed state machine using simulations and real world experiments. It is seen that the performance is quite close to that of manual configuration.

802.11 networks can operate in two different modes - infra-structure and ad-hoc mode. In an infra-structure mode, all the communication between the nodes go through a central entity called the access point. Hence routing has few implications in an infra-structure based network. Ad-Hoc networks are multi-hop wireless networks consisting of a collection of peer nodes communicating with each other without support from a fixed infrastructure. Packets might take a multi-hop path to reach the destination in such a network due to the lack of access points. Highly dynamic routing protocols are required to adapt the wireless system to the frequent changes in channel conditions and topology. These protocols exchange messages to decide the shortest path between the source and destination based on some metric.

The hop count metric used by current routing protocols proves to be good for single rate networks. But it fails to take into account other important factors in a multi-rate network environment. For example, the rate information provided by the lower layers can be used to drive the routing decisions. Consider the scenario in Figure 1. The hop count based metric routing protocols use the path A-B-C that consists of two slow links. But choosing the path A-D-B-E-C can boost the system throughput because the transmission time required is less at higher data rates.

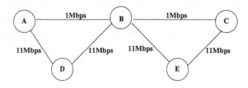

Fig. 1. Need for multi-rate aware routing

The two main performance measures that are substantially affected by the routing algorithm are throughput (Quantity of service) and average packet delay (Quality of service)[3]. Choosing high rate paths guarantee quantity of service. The issue is to provide a bound on the delay. Since high data rate links are shorter, it might be required to traverse more number of hops to reach the destination. The extra backoffs required and the congestion at intermediate nodes can add to the end-to-end delay experienced by the packet. The metric used for routing should strike a balance between throughput and delay. Another critical issue to be taken into account for routing in a wireless network is the asymmetry of links. The link characteristics in the forward direction may not be the same as that in the reverse direction. 802.11 MAC expects an ACK for each packet and hence the reverse path quality also has an impact on the successful transmission of a packet. It is desirable to come up with a metric that takes into consideration the transmission characteristics of link to aid the computation of optimal routes.

We propose transmission time as a better path quality metric. Transmission time is the amount of time between when a packet is sent and the time when the corresponding ACK is received. It incorporates the effects of the following factors: link rate, contention for the channel and asymmetry of links. We present a performance comparison of the various metrics that could be used for dynamic routing using real world experiments run on two testbeds (with 3-nodes and 5-nodes).

It is evident that the link rate characteristics of the system can be used to drive the different layers of the TCP/IP stack. Our work focuses on making the L2 and L3 layers of the protocol stack multi-rate aware. First, an analysis is presented for the design of the automatic rate switching mechanism and its performance is studied using simulations and experiments. The rate switching mechanism keeps track of the link status to its neighbors and this information is exported to the IP layer to guide the flows through optimal routes. We use two test-beds to study the effectiveness of using link quality as the metric for routing in wireless networks.

The rest of this paper is organized as follows. Section 2 gives the design for the proposed rate switching mechanism and discusses the result. The design and implementation details of the transmission time metric and the performance comparison of the different metrics are presented in Section 3. Section 4 discusses conclusions and future work.

2   Rate Switching Mechanism

2.1   Design

The IEEE 802.11 standard[1] does not specify the algorithm for switching the data rate. It is up to the vendors to design and implement such algorithms. Different approaches that can be used for rate switching include FER, SNR and throughput based methods. The SNR based method is not practically used, as the timely and reliable delivery of the SNR information, which is available at the receiver, cannot be guaranteed. It is also observed that the SNR information reported by most of the cards is not accurate. A better alternative is to go for FER based methods using the information available at the transmitter. This allows the design to be applicable even in systems where the interface does not provide SNR information.

Statistics available at the device driver. The driver reports either a frame error or successful transmission of the packet. In latter case, the number of ACK failures (retries) is reported. Rate switching is done based on the information provided by the driver. An unsuccessful transmission implies that even after 7 MAC-level retries (as specified in the 802.11 standard[1]), the packet is not delivered at the receiver end and hence the rate is to be brought down to a lower value. Another situation when rate is to be lowered is when transmissions are possible at higher rates but with more retries. We present the following analysis to study the effectiveness of down scaling the rate when packets are transmitted after retries. The transmission time for a packet requiring n number of retries (excluding contention for channel) is calculated as:

$effS_{BAS} = (S+\text{SIFS}+ACK) + n*(S+\text{AckTimeOut})$
$effS_{RTS} = (RTS+CTS+S+ACK+3*\text{SIFS}) + n*(RTS+\text{AckTimeOut})$ where
$effS_{BAS}$ = effective system time for sending a packet with BAS
$effS_{RTS}$ = effective system time for sending a packet with RTS/CTS
S = Time taken to send a data packet
n = number of retries; varied from 0 to 6.

Throughput is given by $pktsize/effS$ where $pktsize$ is the packet size in bits.

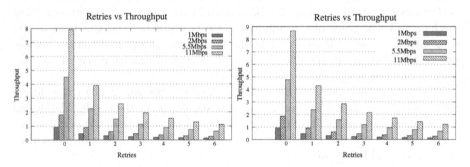

Fig. 2. Retries vs Throughput (BAS, Pktsize=512 and 1024)

Figures 2 and 3 show the throughput for Basic Access Scheme (BAS) and RTS/CTS Scheme (RCS). As can be observed from the graphs, even if multiple retries are required at 5.5Mbps or 2Mbps, throughput cannot be enhanced much by switching to lower rates. The results indicate that if the number of retries required at 11Mbps is greater than a threshold, say RETRY_THRES, it is beneficial to down scale the rate to 5.5Mbps. From, figure 2, we can find that the RETRY_THRES value is 0. From figure 3, the retry value at which the switching needs to be done is 1 for 512B pktsize and 2 for 1024B. We take the "optimal" value of RETRY_THRES to be 2, considering the different scenarios.

State Machine. The state machine (Fig 4) uses frame error for predicting the optimal rate for 802.11b networks. The various states are as follows:

1: <u>STATE_110.</u> When transmission is at the highest possible rate (11Mbps), the station is in STATE_110 state. If the number of retries required for a successful transmission is greater than RETRY_THRES, the rate should be lowered.

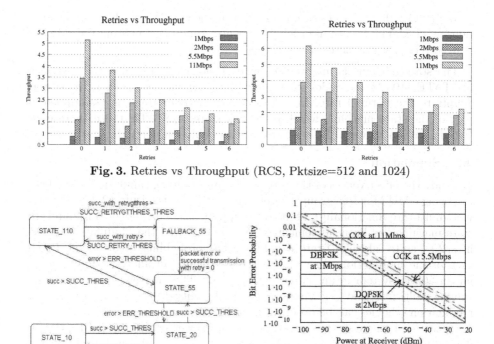

Fig. 3. Retries vs Throughput (RCS, Pktsize=512 and 1024)

Fig. 4. (a) Rate Switching state diagram (b) Receiver Power vs BER

Let succ_with_retrygtthres represent the number of consecutive successful transmissions requiring more than RETRY_THRES retries. If *succ_with_retrygtthres* is greater than a particular threshold, say SUCC_RETRYGTTHRES_THRES, we move on to the FALLBACK_55 state. A packet loss indicates that it has undergone 7 retries and it is a safe measure to decrease the rate. Let *error* be the count of the number of consecutive packet losses. If *error* is greater than ERR_THRESHOLD, the rate is reduced to 5.5Mbps and system goes to STATE_55.

2: <u>FALLBACK_55.</u> This is to check if transmission is possible at 5.5Mbps with no retries. A successful transmission in a single attempt takes the system to STATE_55. Otherwise, there is no advantage in down scaling the rate to 5.5Mbps. As in STATE_110, we monitor the number of successful transmissions requiring retry (*succ_with_retry*). When *succ_with_retry* is greater than the threshold, SUCC_RETRY_THRES, the system goes back to STATE_110. A packet loss causes the system to move to STATE_55 as in STATE_110.

3: <u>STATE_55.</u> Transmission rate is 5.5Mbps at this state. If the number of consecutive packet losses is greater than ERR_THRESHOLD, it decrements the rate to 2Mbps and goes to STATE_2. A count of the number of successful transmissions(*succ*) is maintained and when it reaches SUCC_THRES, rate is incremented to 11Mbps.

4: <u>STATE_20.</u> This state stands for transmission at 2Mbps. The same transitions as in STATE_55 are used for incrementing and decrementing the rate.

5: <u>STATE_10.</u> Transmission at 1Mbps.

The state machine is maintained for each neighbor. Initially, the system is in STATE_110. As the nodes start communicating with each other, the system adapts to the optimal rate. In addition, an inactivity timer is maintained as part of the state machine, which resets the state to STATE_110 if there is no communication between the nodes for a reasonably long period.

2.2   Simulation

To study the effectiveness of the proposed state machine, simulations have been run using CMU Monarch group's wireless extension to ns2. But ns2 does not provide multi-rate functionality. Multi-rate support has been added to ns2 and the state machine has been implemented. We implemented the Modulation classes in ns2 so as to add multi-rate capability. The probability of bit error, Pe for each of the modulation schemes is calculated using an analysis similar to [6] for an 802.11 system in an indoor environment. The analysis computes Pe assuming multi-path Rayleigh channel. The probability of bit error for the various modulation schemes can be observed from Figure 4.

Once Pe of the system is determined, the packet error rate (PER) can be determined as $PER = 1 - (1 - Pe)^n$ where n is packet size in bits. If PER is within acceptable limits (Pa), the packet is passed on to the higher layers.

The automatic rate control state machine has been added to ns2. A link table is maintained at each node which keeps track of the current state of the state machine and the transmission rate to all its neighbors.

Simulation. We have simulated the automatic rate control mechanism using the modified ns2 simulator. A two node set up is used and the distance between the two nodes are varied so that communication is possible at 11Mbps, 5.5Mbps, 2Mbps and 1Mbps. The experiments has been run with manual configuration (explicitly setting the rate) and with automatic rate control. Table 1 lists the various parameters used for the simulation.

Figure 5 shows the TCP throughput for the various transmission rates. It can be seen that the throughput for the proposed rate control mechanism is quite close to the manual configuration. The decrease in throughput is due to packet losses resulting from the attempts to increment the transmission rate. When transmissions are possible at 11Mbps but with multiple retries, automatic rate control outperforms manual configuration, the reason being that while manual configuration sends data always at 11Mbps, rate control mechanism switches to 5.5Mbps whenever required. At 11Mbps, throughput remains the same for both the schemes. The UDP throughput also shows similar behavior.

2.3   Implementation

To understand how the system adapts to the optimal rate under real-world situations, the rate control mechanism has been implemented in the device driver.

Table 1. Simulation Parameters for Automatic Rate Control

Parameter	Value	Parameter	Value
Number of Hops	2	Packet Size	1024
Routing Protocol	DSDV	SUCC_THRES	50
Propagation Model	Shadowing	ERR_THRESHOLD	1
Traffic (TCP)	FTP	SUCC_RETRYGTTHRES_THRES	2
Traffic (UDP)	CBR	SUCC_RETRY_THRES	2

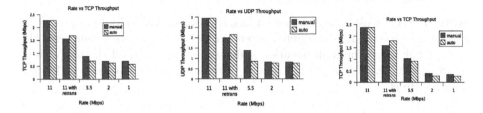

Fig. 5. Rate vs TCP and UDP Throughput (Simulation), and TCP Actual

A link table is maintained at each node, which keeps track of the current state of the state machine and the transmission rate to each of its neighbors. The same set of experiments as that of simulation has been done to analyze the performance. The experimental setup consists of one laptop equipped with a D-Link 650+ card and a desktop machine with a SparkLAN card. The distance between the machines has been varied so that transmission is done at 1Mbps, 2Mbps, 5.5Mbps and 11Mbps. Iperf traffic has been used to generate traffic and to collect the statistics. Figure 5 also plots the actual TCP throughput against the transmission rate. The results correlate with the simulation results.

3   Metrics for Ad-Hoc Routing

In an ad-hoc wireless network, each node acts as a router, forwarding packets for other nodes. Static routing may not be adequate for such networks because of the frequent changes in topology and channel conditions. The most widely used dynamic routing protocols include DSDV, DSR and AODV.

Current dynamic routing protocols like DSDV use minimum hop count as the metric for computing optimal path. We added transmission time and rate metrics into the Grid Ad-hoc networking project's DSDV implementation. Grid is a system for routing in wireless ad hoc mobile networks. It is implemented as part of the Click modular router and is written in C++. The Grid code is a set of Click elements that can be put together in various ways to run DSDV, DSR or geographic forwarding. It can be run at user level or kernel level in Linux. In addition to hop count metric, Click supports ETX[4].

To use the rate and Xtime metric, the following changes have been made to the original DSDV protocol. Suppose node X receives an advertisement from Y for destination D, which has a better metric m, an entry is made for destination D with next hop as Y. But instead of incrementing m by one as done for hop count metric, the cost of reaching Y is added to m. The cost of reaching Y is obtained from the link table maintained by each node. The link cost is calculated from the transmission rate to the next hop in the case of rate metric and from the transmission time in case of Xtime metric.

3.1   Computation of Link Cost

Rate metric. Cost assigned to each link is proportional to its link rate in the case of rate metric. It is computed as $metric = 1/r * 10$ where r represents the current link rate. The multiplication is done so as to round off the link cost to an integer value. Weights of 1, 2, 5 and 10 are assigned to link rates of 11, 5.5, 2 and 1 Mbps.

Xtime metric. The average transmission time taken by each packet is computed by measuring the time taken to get the ACK, after the packet is sent. This can be used as a measure of the link quality, since it takes into consideration the contention for the channel, the air time taken to send the packet and receive the ACK. Hence both the forward and reverse channel characteristics are taken into account for routing. The transmission time for each packet P_{xtime} is measured and the current transmission time per bit is given by $current\_xtime = P_{xtime}/packetsize$. Since the transmission time fluctuates, smoothening of the link cost is needed. This is done by computing new link cost as $link\_cost_{new} = w * link\_cost_{old} + (1 - w) * current\_xtime$. Higher weightage is given to the past history by choosing a higher value for the smoothing factor w. Experiments have been done to determine the right value of w and a value of 0.85 seems to be good. When there is no communication between the nodes, link cost is initialized to a value proportional to the current link rate, r: $link\_cost_{initial} = 1/r * 10$. As the nodes start communicating, the actual transmission time is learnt.

3.2   Implementation in Click

The Linux kernel module of the Click modular router has been used for the implementation. At kernel level, the Click module runs a separate kernel thread. Click code sits between the kernel's network stack and the device drivers. Click presents a pseudo-device to the kernel for sending and receiving packets to the kernel. Running Click in kernel provides more flexibility and eases the task of exporting the link cost information provided by the device drivers to the router.

The link table maintained at each node has an entry for the link cost. The link cost is computed from the current transmission rate or the transmission time and is stored in this field. An inactivity timer is associated with each link, which resets its cost to its initial value, if there is no data transfer through the

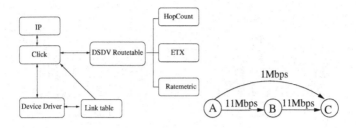

Fig. 6. (a) Click Design (b) Scenario 1

link for a reasonably long period. The timeout for the experiments has been set to 15 seconds. The metric used for DSDV routing is implemented as a different class in the Click modular router. Click has support for hop count and ETX metric. We added the Ratemetric class so as to support rate and Xtime metrics. The class is the same for both the metrics; only information about the link cost, which is used to compute the metric is different. The interactions between the different layers is shown in Figure 6.

The Grid implementation of DSDV has support for two options namely, USE_OLD_SEQUENCE_NUMBER and USE_GOOD_NEW_ROUTE. The first option essentially prevents the use of the current update until it is ready for advertisement. The second option is a modification of USE_OLD_SEQUENCE_NUMBER. It suggests the use of the new update, even if it is not ready for advertisement, as long as it has a better metric. These options were enabled for the experiments so as to prevent the use of a route with bad metric. Usually, new sequence numbers along one-hop path is heard first. There might exist a better multi-hop path, but if the above mentioned options are not used, packets are routed along the bad metric path. With those options enabled, it can be ensured that DSDV uses the previous best route until WST has expired and the best route for the new sequence number has been heard. In case the new update has a better route than previous one, new route is used without waiting for the expiry of WST.

3.3   Experiments

Experiments have been run for different scenarios to gain an insight into the performance characteristics of different routing metrics. The four metrics compared include minimum hop count (used by standard DSDV), ETX, rate and Xtime metric. We have used five machines running Click modular router. Two of the machines have been equipped with SparkLAN cards and three with D-Link 520+ cards. The TCP throughput and round trip delay for the packets have been measured for the following scenarios.

Scenario 1. A three node setup as shown in Figure 6 has been used for running the experiments. The TCP throughput and RTT has been measured with one connection (A to C) and three connections (A to B, B to C, A to C) (Fig 7). It

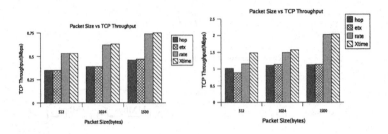

Fig. 7. TCP throughput: Scenario 1 (1 and 3 connections)

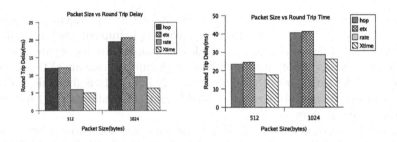

Fig. 8. Round Trip Time (Scenario 1 and 2)

can be observed that when the number of connections is one, the performance of rate and Xtime metrics is almost the same and is much higher than that of hop count and ETX metric. This is because, hop count metric does not take into consideration, the link rate of the path through which packet is routed. ETX uses the delivery ratio to compute the path. The reason for the decreased throughput for ETX metric can be the overhead due to link level probes and the use of single sized packets(134 bytes) for finding optimal path. Also, ETX metric is not designed for networks with links that run at a variety of bit rates. Experiments have been repeated with the same setup for three connections, A to B, B to C and A to C. The idea has been to load the high link rate path and Xtime metric is found to perform a bit better than rate metric. As in the previous case, hop count and ETX throughput is smaller.

The round trip time for the packets were measured using ping test for different packet sizes. It is seen that packets routed using rate and Xtime metric has less delay compared to the other metrics (Figure 8).

Scenario 2. A 5-node wireless testbed as shown in Figure 1 has been used for the next round of experiments. With one connection (A to C), it can be observed that rate metric throughput is less, because of the extra backoffs required for traversing more number of hops (Figure 9). In this case, the optimal path from A to C would be to follow the slow links from A to B and B to C. ETX metric and hop count metric performs well in such a case. Xtime metric performance is similar to that of ETX and hop count metric except when the packet size is

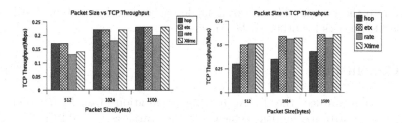

Fig. 9. TCP throughput: Scenario 2 (1 and 5 connections)

512 bytes. This deviation can be attributed to the route oscillations. The round trip delay for scenario 2 shows similar behavior as that of the three node setup (Figure 8).

We repeated the experiments with 5 connections (A to D, D to B, B to E, E to C and A to C). The four one-hop connections along the high throughput path (A-D, D-B, B-E, E-C) helps to build up the throughput in the case of rate metric. Throughput is less for hop count metric, since all traffic for the connection A-C goes only through the slow links and the slow hosts capture the channel for long period (Figure 9).

In addition to the above experiments, they were repeated with multiple flows from A to C; the behaviour/throughput was found to be about the same with respect to all the metrics considered. Due to lack of space, we omit discussion of these results here.

4   Related Work

[7] classifies the current approaches for rate switching into three main categories - throughput based, FER based and SNR based methods. ARF algorithm[12] used in Agere Systems uses the number of ACK misses as a parameter for rate control. [5] proposes the use of a combination of FER based method and Received Signal Strength (RSS). But RSS cannot be used for rate control at a node since the propagation characteristics of the forward link may not be equivalent to the reverse link.

Dynamic routing protocols proposed for use in wireless networks include DSR[9], DSDV[10], AODV and so on. Currently, research community has turned their attention towards utilizing the link characteristics as routing metric. The major works in the field of multi-rate aware routing protocols are MAS and MTM. [11] proposes the use of a thin layer, MAS (Multi-rate Aware Sub layer) in between IP and the link layer. Routing overhead is more in this case as both the IP and MAS layer flood the system with periodic broadcast messages. Another related work is MTM (Medium Time Metric) [2], which is independent of the routing protocol used. The metric takes into account the transmission rate as well as an estimate of the back off delay (310 us). But this estimate can be deceiving when the path is congested or under bad channel conditions. ETX[4] uses the delivery ratio to find optimal path. But the probe messages add more traffic into the system. The use of a single packet size for probing can lead to inaccurate metrics for other packet sizes.

5 Conclusions

This paper introduces the design and implementation of an FER-based automatic rate control mechanism, which uses the statistics available at the device driver. The results drawn from simulation studies and real world experiments show that its performance is comparable to the manual configuration. We propose transmission time as a metric to guide routing decisions. It accounts for the contention for the channel, air time to send the packet and the asymmetry of the links. Measurements done on two wireless testbeds show that transmission time metric performs consistently well across the different scenarios considered.

References

1. IEEE std 802.11b-1999. http://grouper.ieee.org/groups/802/11/
2. Baruch Awerbuch, David Holmer, Herbert Rubens. High Throughput Route Selection in Multi-rate Ad Hoc Wireless Networks. WONS 2004: 253-270
3. Dimitri Bertsekas and Robert Gallager. *Data Networks*. Prentice Hall, 1987.
4. Douglas S. J. De Couto, Daniel Aguayo, John Bicket, Robert Morris. A High-Throughput Path Metric for Multi-Hop Wireless Routing. In *Proc. of 9th Annual Intl. conference on Mobile Computing and Networking*, ACM Press, 2003.
5. del Prado Pavon J. and Sunghyun Choi. Link adaptation strategy for IEEE 802.11 WLAN via received signal strength measurement. In *IEEE International Conference on Communications*, pages 1108–1113, May 2003.
6. Michael Fainberg. A Performance Analysis of the IEEE 802.11b LAN in the presence of Bluetooth PAN Master's thesis, Polytechnic University, June 2001.
7. Ivaylo Haratcherev, Koen Langendoen, Inald Lagendijk, Henk Sips. Application Directed Automatic Rate Control, Telematica Instituut, Dec'02.
8. M. Heusse, F. Rousseau, G. Berger-Sabbatel, and A. Duda. Performance anomaly of 802.11b. In *Proceedings of IEEE INFOCOM*, San Francisco, USA, Mar 2003.
9. David B Johnson, David A Maltz. Dynamic Source Routing in Ad Hoc Wireless Networks. In Imielinski and Korth, eds., *Mobile Computing*, volume 353. Kluwer Academic Publishers, 1996.
10. Charles Perkins, Pravin Bhagwat. Highly Dynamic Destination-Sequenced Distance-Vector Routing (DSDV) for Mobile Computers. In *ACM SIGCOMM'94 Conf. on Communications Architectures, Protocols & Applications*.
11. Yongho Seok, Jaewoo Park, and Yanghee Choi. Multi-rate Aware Routing Protocol for Mobile Ad Hoc Networks. IEEE VTC 2003-Spring, Jeju, Korea, April, 2003.
12. A J van der Vegt. Auto Rate Fallback Algorithm for the IEEE 802.11a Standard. Referred in [7].

Tightly Packed IP Address Configuration (TPIA) Protocol in Small-Scale MANET[*]

Jin-Ok Hwang[1], Sung-Gi Min[1,**], and Young-Il Choi[2]

[1] Dept. of Computer Science and Engineering, Korea University,
Seoul, Korea
{withmind, sgmin}@korea.ac.kr
[2] Electronics and Telecommunications Research Institute, Korea
yichoi@etri.re.kr

Abstract. Configuring IP addresses is an important issue in ad-hoc networks without a centralized agent server. The previous configuration methods result in wasted IP addresses, and are unsuitable for assigning addresses in small-scale mobile Ad-Hoc networks (MANET). To address this problem, we propose a tightly packed IP address (TPIA) configuration protocol, which eliminates the IP address leaks characteristic of current addressing methods (Internet Protocol version 4, or IPv4).

1 Introduction

Mobile computing and wireless technology are increasingly popular topics in the network communications field. An Ad-Hoc wireless network is a diverse network, but it has little to no supporting infrastructure. Wireless data is transmitted via radio frequencies within a radius scope, which mobile nodes (MNs) identify by parameters, and the majority of routing protocols use the IP address as a unique identifier [1]~[3].

IP allocation is an important parameter, and is strongly associated with the routing protocol in the network layer. Currently, to get ad-hoc networks to communicate with external networks, such as the Internet, Mobile Nodes(MNs) are used connected using the IP stack. Consequently, IP address assignment is tightly coupled to the network layer for both routing protocol issues and accessing the Internet.

In the wireless network, the conventional method of IP assignment uses DHCP (Dynamic Host Configuration Protocol [4]). This method is based on a centralized agent server, which maintains the configuration information of all nodes in the network. However, this approach is not suited to ad-hoc networks, which are free to move randomly and organize themselves arbitrarily, and IP address assignment in

[*] This work was supported by grant No.10016756 from the Growth Power Technology Development Project, funded by the Ministry of Commerce, Industry and Energy of Korea.
[**] Corresponding author.

S. Chaudhuri et al. (Eds.): ICDCN 2006, LNCS 4308, pp. 421–429, 2006.

MANET remains unresolved. Therefore, IP address allocation must automatically configure without a centralized agent server in ad-hoc networks.

Previous studies [5]~[7] of automatic IP address configurations have several drawbacks. Among them, these methods lead to IP address leak, an issue that is important to resolve the practical application of IP addresses to current systems.

The wasted IP addresses are an undesirable byproduct of using IPv4 methods. To address this problem, we propose using tightly packed IP address (TPIA) configuration protocol. The TPIA protocol can assign an IP address without wasting IP space to join nodes in MANET. This paper is structured as follows. Section 2 introduces related work on automatic IP address assignment in ad-hoc networks. Section 3 describes the TPIA configuration protocol. Section 4 presents the algorithm for our strategy based on realized implementation. Section 5 compares the performance of TPIA with other methods. Lastly, Section 6 provides some concluding remarks.

2   Related Work

There are two fundamental ways to move nodes in MANET. In the first, an MN newly joins or abruptly departs within the freestanding MANET, and an unused IP address is allocated to the joining MN. This method is more difficult and complicated, due to a lack of a centralized controller for IP addresses. In the second case, if two split MANET configurations can be united, two separate nodes could be assigned the same address, leading to duplicate addresses and routing problems during communication.

Methods to address these problems have been proposed [5]~[7], but have several drawbacks to practical use.

In [5][6], the address pool 169.254/16 comprises two address sets, a temporary set and a legal set. The system assigns a candidate IP address from the temporary address pool to a newly joined node, which then performs duplicate address detection (DAD) for all participating MNs. If there is conflict with DAD, the process may be repeated a finite number of times until the system correctly chooses an unused IP address. One problem with this strategy is that splitting the addresses into two sets decreases the number of available IP addresses, wasting address blocks with temporary addresses. In addition, an MN is needed during the DAD time to receive an IP address. The DAD time in MANET incurs the communication overhead to receive an IP address.

In [7], the authors proposed an address allocation solution (the Prophet) without a centralized agent server for large-scale MANET. The method forecasts the IP address of the joining node using the assignment function, $f(n)$. This strategy has several advantages. For one, it does not require the DAD procedure to identify address conflicts, reducing overhead communication using $f(n)$.

However, the system requires much address space; if address space includes eight (small) spaces, the Prophet method can produce only four addresses, and the rest is leaked, creating wasted IP addresses.

In addition, the MANET has difficulty searching for a suitable assignment function $f(n)$ during network configuration. We can solve these problems with a TPIA configuration protocol, which will be suitable for small-scale MANET and prevent address leaks.

3   Tightly Packed IP Address Configuration (TPIA) Protocol

This section explains the TPIA protocol, which reduces IP address waste and overhead communication. We assume the following.

- We consider the current version of Internet Protocol (IPv4).
- The MANET commonly uses the 169.254/16 IP address zone [5],[6], for which Netid can be used. When we configure a MANET, the IP address should be assigned the continuous addresses, whose IP address zone is a pure address block without conflicts in the Hostid.
- An initialized MN recognizes the number of newly joined nodes, and defines the size of the address zone.

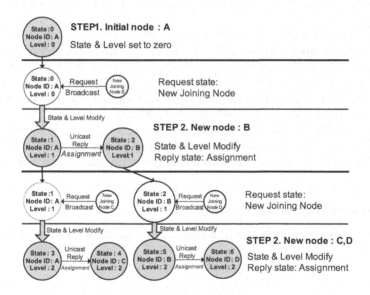

Fig. 1. The Example Model for Assignment of IP address

Consider the two conditions in MANET: MN is an existing node with an IP address (MN_A, including the initialized node) or a newly participating node without an IP address (MN_J). In Figure 1, MN_A is shown as a gray circle, and MN_J is represented by a dashed circle. MN_J sends the request message to MN_A to acquire an IP address.

For IP address allocation, the TPIA protocol uses the α, state and level called **Address Information (AI)**, represented as follows:

$$AI = [\ \alpha,\ \textbf{zone, state, level}]$$

where α is the starting IP address, and the zone represents the scope of the continues IP addresses starting from the α. In initialized mode, state and level are set to zero.

3.1 Initialization Protocol

When an MN enters the IP network, it searches the initialized node for the IP address using a broadcast message. If the MANET has not yet assigned a node (initialized node), the MN starts the initialization procedure by assigning the IP address set to itself, and gathering continuous IP addresses without conflict.

Here, the initialization procedure searches for the configured node to IP assignment. If the configured node cannot search, the MN is connected with an infra-network to obtain the IP address zone at the starting session.

Therefore, if an initialized node (e.g., node A in Fig. 1) exists in this MANET, it is able to make assignments for other nodes (new joining nodes) within a single hop distance.

Figure 1 illustrates the IP address assignment model. As mentioned above, if node A is configured successfully, and has the continues IP addresses without conflict, an MN (MN_A) can receive the IP request message from other MNs (e.g., MN_J), such as node B. The IP address request message sends the initial node to node A. If node A receives the message from node B, it changes the state and level to the IP assignment for node B (newly joining node).

Notice that MN_A (gray circle) changes the state and level, but the IP address of MN_A is not changed. The state and level are properties of the assignment, and MN_A sends the AI message with a changed state and level to a new joining node.

3.2 New Node Joining Protocol

When a new node requests the IP address, MN_A modifies the state and level as follows:

$$level = level + 1 \tag{1}$$

$$state = state * 2 + 1 \tag{2}$$

To assign the MN_J IP address, the state and level of MN_A is modified, but the IP address is not changed. Also, MN_A computes the state of MN_J, represented as follows.

$$state = (2) + 1 \tag{3}$$

MN_A then sends MN_J the **AI** message, which consists of the starting IP address, IP address zone, state (as calculated in expression (3)), and level (as calculated in expression (1)) of MN_J.

According to these equations, the node B(MN_J) receives the AI message. MN_J can then calculate the receiving message from the level and state of the AI message, and obtains the IP address as follows:

$$IPaddress = (3)/2 + \alpha \qquad (4)$$

where α is the starting IP address set by the initialized node. As addressed in expressions (1)~(4), a considerable MN can assign the IP address in MANET. If the MANET is large scale, we have algorithms to make it inefficient, but the majority of the MANET is small scale, so our system is adaptable to small-scale MANET.

3.3   Example of Protocol

When a node needs an IP address in MANET, the node searches for the initialized node. If one does not yet exist, the searching node becomes the initialized node.

In Figure 1, the initialized node A receives the starting IP address, α, and the zone. If the beginning IP address is 26 and the zone are 7, the effective area spans from 26 to 32. If a new joining node wants an IP address, node A prepares the AI information, as follows.

Node A's AI = [26, 7, 0, 0]

This AI information is a condition of node A. The new joining node B needs the AI information for node B. According to expressions (1) and (2), node A modifies the state and level. Therefore, if the state of node A is changed to 1, the level also becomes 1. Here, the IP address for node A is not changed; it maintains the starting address value of 26. Then, node A establishes the state of node B using expression (3). Therefore, the AI information of the new joining node B is expressed as follows:

Node B's AI= [26, 7 , 2, 1]

Then, node A sends the AI information to node B. If received, node B then calculates the IP address using expression (4). In our example, the IP address for node B becomes **27**.

If an ad-hoc node D joins the IP network, node B modifies its level to 2 and its state to 5, using expressions (1) and (2). Again, the IP address of node B does not change. Then, node B establishes the state and level of the newly participating node (node D), using expression (3), and sends the AI information to node D (MN_J). The reply message is contained in the level (2) and state (6) of node D in each case.

Node D's AI = [26, 7, 6, 2]

If begins at 26, the IP address of joining node D is **29**, using expression (4), which becomes node D's Hostid address. In the TPIA protocol, all nodes can allocate IP addresses without leaking addresses, and the DAD procedure is not needed.

4   The Algorithm

The following algorithm contains the pseudo-code of our system.

In Figure 2, the procedure of joining nodes is related to the number of requests, and the maxretry value is set to the maximum retry for the procedure.

```
Procedure MN_J ( )
    set const maxretry ← 3 ;
        bool configured ← false ;
        bool init_IPzone[ ]← 0 ;
        retry← 0 ;
        state← 0 ;
        getIP← 0 ;
    begin( )
        while (retry <maxretry) {
            broadcast request to other MN ;
                if (receive the AI message from MN_A) ;
                    state ← state_J ;
                    level ← level_J ;
                    get_IP ← (state/2) + α;
                    configured ← true ;
                else wait reply message ;
                }
```

Fig. 2. The procedure of joining node

The Boolean operation "true" is applied, and it assigns the IP address to a request MN. The MN_J sends the IP address request message to MN_A on broadcast, and MN_J begins the reply timer. If MN_A receives this message, it modifies the state and level for the IP address of the joining node, as above Figure 2.

If MN_A is the first initialized node, it configures the pure IP address for the number of joining nodes at the starting session in advance, like the comments in this pseudo-code.

In next page at Figure 3, the MN_A modifies the state and level using expressions (1) and (2), and then computes the state and level for a given IP address using expressions (1) and (3). In this process, expressed as "*procedure modify_ls*" the MN_A sends the AI message to the requested MN_J.

In Figure 3, the MN_J receives the reply message with the modified state and level, applies expression (4), and then obtains the new IP address. In this way, IP addresses will be assigned to all participating nodes without wasting IP addresses.

Procedure MN$_A$( )

            set *init_IPzone [n]* $\leftarrow$ *n* ; // variable address space ;

               state $\leftarrow$ 0 ;

               level $\leftarrow$ 0 ;

               IP $\leftarrow$ 0 ;

               $\alpha \leftarrow$ 0 ;

    begin

        if receive a request message from joining node **then** {

            execute the **procedure** *modify_ls (l , s)* ;

               begin

                   {

                       My_level $\leftarrow$ *level + 1* ;

                       My_state $\leftarrow$ **2 *** *state + 1* ;

                   }

                 save the new level, state **to** storage ;

               end

            execute the **procedure** *compute_IP (l , s)* ;

               begin

                   compute of **MN$_J$** *(l , s)* ; {

                       level_J $\leftarrow$ *My_level* ;

                       state_J $\leftarrow$ *My_state + 1* ;

                   }

               end

               make *the AI* { α , init_IPzone , *l , s* } ;

               send *the AI* **to** requested node ;

            }

      else

           wait *for response* ;

  end

Fig. 3. The procedure of Joining node

5   The Comparison of Performance

Table 1 compares our strategy with AAA[5],[6] and Prophet[7]. The first three rows are feature briefs of the three allocation solutions, and the performance evaluation focuses on unused IP addresses.

In our solution, conflicting IP addresses are not produced because MN_A computes IP addresses for MN_J in advance, using expressions (1)~(4). The computed IP addresses reduce overhead communication, and do not require the DAD procedure to detect IP address conflicts within the network.

Moreover, the unused IP addresses in our system represent a high level of efficiency. The IP address zone was tightly packed with MNs, and the wasted IP address zone was eliminated. In AAA[5],[6], the level of unused IP addresses is too high, due to this scheme's technique of splitting addresses into temporary and legal sets.

Therefore, if networks consist of eight nodes, this scheme uses the eight addresses in the address zone of 256, and the remaining addresses (248) are unused.

Table 1. Characteristics and performance comparison

Evaluation	AAA[5][6]	Prophet[7]	Our solution
Address conflict	Frequently Yes	No	No
Unused IP address	**High**	**High**	**Not exist**
Additional IP configuration	Change the Netid	Troublesome	Simpler
Communication Overhead	O((n+1) x k)	O(2l / n)	O(2l / n)

If all MNs (128 nodes) participate in the network, the unused IP zone is as much as 50% (temporary address pool).

The Prophet scheme[7] generates leak addresses (up to 37.5%) with the assignment function $f(n)$. For this reason, if many MNs participate in the MANET, a very broad address zone is needed. By contrast, if MNs are tightly packed, as they are in our solution, unused IP addresses cannot exist in the address space.

The maintenance of IP addresses induces the AODV routing protocol [3] to identify unused IP addresses. In Table 1, communication overhead is represented by O during the allocation time of the IP address, where n is the number of MNs, k is the retry time, and the number of links is l.

Our strategy is the quickest regarding communication overhead. The Prophet[7] and our scheme have the same efficiency, but the former generates a leak address zone. Our TPIA protocol resolves this issue and reduces communication overhead.

6   Conclusion

How to assign IP addresses in IPv4-based Ad-Hoc networks remains unresolved. We presented a very simple solution for automatic IP address assignment of participating nodes that does not waste IP addresses and reduces communication overhead compared to the AAA[5],[6] and Prophet [7] methods.

Therefore, the TPIA protocol offers an efficient way to resolve the problem of leak IP addresses for wireless mobile **Ad-Hoc** networks.

We have also some conspicuous security issues, network merging and splitting that are relevant to MANET protocols. These will be the focus of our future work.

References

1. C.Perkins and P.Bhagwat, "Routing over Multihop Wireless Network of Mobile Computers", in SIGCOM 1994.
2. D.B.Johnson and D.A.Maltz, "Dynamic Source Routing in *Ad-Hoc* Wireless Network", Mobile Computing 1996, Kluwer Academic Publishers.

3. C.Perkins, E.Belding-Royer, and S.Das,"Ad hoc On-Demand Distance Vector(AODV) Routing", RFC 3626, October2003.
4. R.Droms, "Dynamic Host Configuration Protocol", Network Working Group RFC 2131, March 1997.
5. C.E Perkins and Elizabeth M., "IP Address Autoconfiguration for Ad Hoc Networks", draft-ietf-manet-autoconf-01.txt, November 2001.
6. Yuan Sun, Elizabeth M.Belding-Royer and C.E Perkins, "Internet Connectivity for Ad hoc Mobile Networks", International Journal of Wireless Information Networks, Special Issue on MOBILE AD HOC NETWORKS(MANETs); Standards, Research Applications 2002.
7. Hongbo Zhou, Lionel M. NI,"Prophet Address Allocation for Large Scale MANETs", IEEE INFOCOM 2003.

TransMAN: A Group Communication System for MANETs

Kulpreet Singh, Andronikos Nedos, and Siobhán Clarke

Distributed Systems Group, Trinity College, Dublin, Ireland

Abstract. In mobile ad-hoc networks frequent topology changes and node failures increase the difficulty of providing reliability guarantees to applications. In traditional wired networks, group communication systems have been shown to be a useful middleware abstraction for providing strong reliability guarantees. A group communication system provides all its members with a consistent membership view while providing reliable and ordered communication between them. Existing group communication systems for MANETs do not provide consistent membership views. In this paper we describe TransMAN, a group communication system for mobile ad hoc networks that provide consistent membership views and a reliable broadcast communication between members. TransMAN relies on a reliable broadcast facility and uses implicit acknowledgements to maintain a graph capturing message relationships. This graph is used to implement important group communication properties such as non-blocking membership changes and virtually synchronous communication. We describe the various protocols that constitute TransMAN and provide an evaluation of our system using a real-world implementation. Experiments show that message delivery latency and the time required for group view changes are not adversely affected by network topology.

1 Introduction

Mobile ad-hoc networks (MANETs) are formed by nodes interacting with a short-range, wireless communication medium. Node mobility and the unreliability of the wireless channel pose a challenge while building applications that require reliable network communications, such as mobile multiplayer games or collaborative work applications. A group communication system (GCS) provides these guarantees in traditional wired networks. A complete GCS which provides deterministic reliable communication guarantees while addressing the challenges of MANETs is required.

To handle the dynamic nature of MANETs a GCS should support mergers and partitions of groups frequently caused by node mobility or poor wireless connectivity. A GCS should also not be adversely affected by transient connections in the network. Virtual synchrony [1] has been identified as a useful property to ease application development while using a group communication service that supports partitions [6]. Virtual synchrony enforces nodes that remain connected to deliver the same set of messages. Supporting virtual synchrony in MANETs will help ease the programmability of distributed applications for these networks.

S. Chaudhuri et al. (Eds.): ICDCN 2006, LNCS 4308, pp. 430–441, 2006.

Traditional techniques to support virtually synchronous communication [1], require applications to block during membership changes. With frequent network changes anticipated in MANETs, such an approach will result in applications blocking too often. Current solutions for group communication systems in MANETs are largely probabilistic [7] and do not provide consistent membership information; or assume a synchronous network [10]; or assume a location service [11]. There is a need for a group communication system for MANETs that can be used to develop reliable distributed applications.

In this paper we present a group communication service that provides totally ordered message delivery and supports group partitions and mergers along with virtual synchrony, without blocking client applications during changes in group membership. This is achieved by allowing multiple membership views to be proposed concurrently. Member nodes decide on a stable membership view through an agreement protocol, and the system handles transient connections and false suspicions with reduced extraneous message transmissions. We illustrate this with results from a real-world implementation of TransMAN.

TransMAN works best for applications that require a steady stream of many to many messages, such as multiplayer games and collaborative work applications. This is because TransMAN utilises these application messages to gather implicit acknowledgements, stabilise broadcast messages, detect failures and reach agreement on membership views. TransMAN utilises a reliable broadcast protocol to propagate the application messages to all nodes in the network. A number of mechanisms have been cited recently [14] that reduce redundant broadcasts in MANETs, and the use of any of these mechanisms will allow an efficient implementation of a group communication service. In this paper we use the counter based scheme [14] to reduce redundant broadcasts.

2   System Model and Architecture

We model a MANET as an asynchronous network where messages can get delayed and lost. The clocks on mobile nodes are assumed to drift with no bounded delays. Each mobile node communicates with other nodes using radio transmissions. A node communicates with nodes in its neighbourhood, and the nodes in its neighbourhood can change due to node mobility. We use the IEEE 802.11b MAC and assume it does not run into the fairness problem, an infinite set of nodes can participate in the MANET, the network can partition and various network partitions can merge, and finally nodes crash fail.

Figure 1 shows the TransMAN architecture diagram. The bottom layer implements a reliable broadcast protocol that is designed to suit the needs of our system. The protocol is described in [13].

Messages are received by the reliable broadcast layer and delivered to the higher layers only if certain conditions are satisfied. These conditions are described in [13]. Messages delivered by the broadcast layer are buffered in the message stability layer, where messages are kept until they are known to be delivered to all other nodes in the network. The membership agreement and the failure detection layers are notified when a message is being delivered. The failure detection layer uses the lack of regular notifications to suspect a failed node, while the membership agreement layer utilises these notifications to determine changes in the group membership. The membership layer also uses suspicion information from the failure detection layer.

The stream of application messages delivered by the broadcast layer at a node are utilised to determine failure suspicions and finally determine membership information without requiring special control messages or acknowledgements. Transient network connections are handled by initialising a new membership agreement which is either installed or later deleted if some other view is installed.

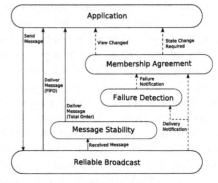

Fig. 1. TransMAN architecture

3   Message Dependencies

The membership service described in this paper builds on the message dependencies concept used to implement the reliable broadcast [13]used as a bottom layer in the TransMAN architecture. A message p_i has two kinds of dependencies. One the message sent by p before sending p_i, i.e., p_{i-1}, and second is the message last delivered by p before sending p_i. The dependencies are defined transitively and therefore are used for implicitly acknowledging messages, and also to determine messages stability. To provide these, the reliable broadcast protocol maintains a graph of messages, and these features allow the TransMAN membership service to be provided.

4   Failure Detection

Maintaining membership in an asynchronous network, even with a single partition, faces well known impossibility result [2] for implementing a group communication with consistent membership views. TransMAN targets a partitionable group membership service, avoiding this impossibility. Hence, we do not need a failure detector [2] to bypass this impossibility. However the membership service needs a way to start suspecting a node as failed so that it can initiate the view change protocol. For this purpose we include a failure detector in TransMAN.

To implement the failure detector, we utilise the notion that there is a stream of messages broadcast by each node in the group. Given that each node has a membership view and thus knows the size of the group, it has the necessary information to detect a member node as failed. A node detects another as failed if it does not receive a message from that node while receiving a dynamically determined number of messages from all remaining nodes.

Therefore, a node p detects a node q as failed if p does not receive a message from q while it receives w messages from all other nodes taken together. Such failures are termed "failure to broadcast". Further, a node p suspects another node q as failed if p broadcasts w messages, from p_n to p_{n+w}, and receives no message q_i such that $OPD(p, p_n, q_i)$ is true. That is to say, p has not received any message from q that acknowledges the reception of any of the last w message broadcast by p. Such failures are termed "failure to receive". We call the parameter w the wait length.

5   Membership Service

Before describing the membership service protocol we note the terminology used

- Group view, $\mathcal{G} = \{p_i, q_j, r_k, \ldots\}$ defined as a list of nodes and the sequence number of the message that was last delivered by each of these nodes.
- Current view, is the set of nodes that are members of the group at present.
- Tentative view, apart from including nodes from the current view also includes nodes that are not yet members but the broadcast layer has been receiving and delivering messages from these nodes. Further, each node uses the list of suspected members available from the failure detector to exclude any suspected nodes from the tentative view. Thus, the tentative view at a node captures the view that the node expects to install next.
- A group view $\mathcal{G}$ is said to "precede" $\mathcal{G}'$, written as $\mathcal{G} < \mathcal{G}'$, if $\mathcal{G}$ has at least one node with a last delivered sequence number lower than the one in $\mathcal{G}'$. Thus, view $\{p_i, q_j, r_k\}$ precedes the view $\{p_{i+1}, q_j, r_k\}$.
- Each node maintains a list of tentative views stored in *tviews*, that are awaiting agreement.

Changes in network connectivity initiate the membership agreement protocol. If such a change persists then the agreement is likely to terminate. If the change is transient, the agreement protocol doesn't terminate and is subsequently deleted in the future. This allows any applications using TransMAN to continue delivering messages uninterrupted by transient network conditions.

Schiper et al. [12] showed that a virtually synchronous membership service in an asynchronous environment can be reduced to solving agreement for the next proposed view. We follow a similar approach, where multiple proposed views are resolved, instead of one.

The membership service described is a best effort service. The service continuously strives to install group views reflecting the state of the MANET. If the network faces a high amount of churn, the nodes will work towards installing a group view. As the amount of churn reduces the nodes install a consistent group view reflecting the current state of the network.

5.1   Message Delivery During View Changes

We now describe how reliable message delivery and stabilisation are affected during group partition, merges and false suspicions of nodes. We examine three different network and node events, namely a merge between a number of groups, member failures and the false suspicion of a members —

1. *Merge:* The reliable broadcast protocol utilised by TransMAN allows delivery of messages from nodes that are not part of the current view. This supports FIFO delivery of messages *across* the merging groups.
2. *Failure:* If nodes fail or the network partitions, then messages are not stabilised as the failed or partitioned group members are unable to acknowledge the delivered messages. On the other hand, the reliability layer continues to deliver messages, which allows FIFO delivery of messages amongst nodes in each partition.
3. *False Suspicion:* In the case of false suspicions, a group view agreement is initiated but all messages are delivered and stabilised as governed by the reliable broadcast and stability protocols. This is possible because all members of the group continue to broadcast messages even if a node is falsely suspected. These members will eventually implicitly acknowledge all messages received from the falsely suspected node.

5.2 Membership Agreement Protocol

There are two phases involved in the execution of the membership agreement protocol. The first phase determines a group view that can be the next group view, and the second phase runs an agreement for this group view.

First Phase: View Determination. The first phase of the membership agreement is initialised when a node realizes the need for a view change. This can be caused by either 1. a node receiving a message from a non-member, 2. or a node suspecting a member. To initiate the first phase a node broadcasts a message containing its tentative view. We call this message the *init-view-change* message.

When a node receives an *init-view-change* message, it compares the tentative view that is included in the received *init-view-change* message to the one it maintains. Depending on the comparison between the two tentative views and the state of the membership agreement at the node, the node responds by either sending a new *init-view-change* message or it updates the state of the membership agreement.

A node sends a new *init-view-change* message in response to the received one if the received tentative view has some information that the receiving node's tentative view does not have. This new information is either a higher sequence number of the message last delivered by a node or the presence of a new node.

We denote with T the tentative view maintained at the receiving node and with T_{rcvd} the tentative view received. If $T < T_{rcvd}$ or $T \subset T_{rcvd}$, the receiving node updates T to T_{rcvd} and sends a new *init-view-change* message. Updating the view T to T_{rcvd} means updating the last delivered sequence numbers or including the new nodes in T_{rcvd}.

If $T > T_{rcvd}$ and $T \not\subset T_{rcvd}$ then the receiving node neither sends a new *init-view-change* message nor updates it tentative view.

If $\mathcal{T} \supset \mathcal{T}_{rcvd}$ then the $\mathcal{T}_{rcvd}$ is notifying the failure suspicion of a node at the sender. In this case the receiving node neither sends a new *init-view-change* message nor updates it tentative view. Instead the receiving node waits until it suspects the failed node and then sends a new *init-view-change*. This avoids the situation where false suspicions result in an initiation of extraneous membership agreements.

If the received tentative view is equal (both in nodes and their sequence numbers) to the one a node is maintaining, the node treats the received *init-view-change* message as a *view-acknowledgement* for the node's tentative view. The node maintains a list of these *view-acknowledgements* received for each membership agreement, as shown in Table 1.

Table 1. Example membership agreement at node p

	view-acks	OPD values		
		p	q	r
p_i, q_j, r_k	p_x	$OPD(p, p_x, mld[p])$	$OPD(p, p_x, mld[q])$	$OPD(p, p_x, mld[r])$
	q_y	$OPD(p, q_y, mld[p])$	$OPD(p, q_y, mld[q])$	$OPD(p, q_y, mld[r])$
	r_z	$OPD(p, r_z, mld[p])$	$OPD(p, r_z, mld[q])$	$OPD(p, r_z, mld[r])$

The first phase for a membership agreement at a node is completed when the node has delivered *view-acknowledgements* from all the nodes in the tentative view. If during the first phase any node detects a new node or a failed node, it sends an *init-view-change* with a new suggested view, resulting in the first phase being run again.

Second Phase: Agreement Termination. In the second phase, an agreement for the tentative view is initialised and the tentative view is pushed into *tviews*. The completion of this agreement for the tentative view finishes the second phase. At the end of the second phase all nodes will agree on the same view as the next view and then install the same view.

A membership agreement for a group with view $\mathcal{G} \equiv \{p_i, q_j, r_k\}$ terminates at node p when p determines that all other nodes in $\mathcal{G}$ have delivered the *view-acknowledgements* sent by all the nodes in $\mathcal{G}$. These *view-acknowledgements* were collected in the first phase of the protocol. Table 1 shows an example membership agreement run at node p, for a view p_i, q_j, r_k. The agreement shown will be complete at p when all OPD values shown in the table evaluate to true at p.

Requiring all nodes in a group view $\mathcal{G}$ to determine that all other nodes have delivered the same set of *view-acknowledgements* guarantees that all nodes have agreed on the same suggested view, and will eventually install the same view. This membership agreement protocol does not tolerate any failures. Instead, if any node fails, the membership service initiates a new agreement protocol.

Maintaining a list of tentative views for agreement in *tviews*, enables nodes to respond to multiple network events, i.e., node insertions or node failures, without the delay incurred by sequential processing of each such event. This is desirable in a dynamic environment such as MANETs. If an agreement for a tentative view does not terminate, the protocol ensures that it is deleted when a later[1] agreement terminates. This removes the transiently connected node from being considered as the next suggested new view.

The second phase for an agreement can finish in two ways. When an agreement protocol terminates or when an agreement later in the agreement list terminates. In the latter case, the membership protocol deletes all agreements in the agreement list which are ahead of the terminated agreement in the list of membership agreements. If during the second phase, a new suggested view is encountered and it finishes the first phase, it is also pushed into *tviews*. Next we show how this is useful in handling the frequent changes in a MANET and for implementing virtual synchrony.

Agreement State Machine. The state transition diagram in Figure 2 shows the states for the membership protocol. The STABLE state implies a view is installed, no changes in the view are suggested and no agreements are in the second phase. On receiving a message from a member node the state remains STABLE and the message is delivered and stabilised as per the reliable broadcast and stabilisation protocols.

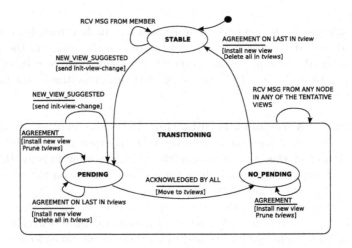

Fig. 2. State transition diagram for membership protocol

If a node receives a message from a new node, or it suspects a node in its view or it receives an *init-view-change* message it initiates the view change protocol. In the state transition diagram, these events are encapsulated by the NEW-_VIEW_SUGGESTED transition. On this transition, the protocol moves from the STABLE to the TRANSITIONING state.

The TRANSITIONING state has two sub-states, PENDING and NO_PEND-ING, which correspond to the presence of an agreement in the first phase or not.

---

[1] Later is defined in terms of the $<$ relationship.

The protocol is in the PENDING state if there is at least one agreement in the first phase. The protocol moves to NO_PENDING when the agreement for the tentative view moves to the second phase. At this point there is no agreement in the first phase, thus the state is called NO_PENDING. If in the NO_PENDING state a NEW_VIEW_SUGGESTED event occurs, the protocol moves back to the PENDING state.

5.3 Virtual Synchrony and Transitional Sets

The algorithm described in the previous sections delivers safe and totally ordered messages to the application. At the same time messages are delivered such that the set of nodes that survive a view change deliver the same set of messages.

Suppose a new view $\mathcal{G}$ is proposed, such that it is a merger of two partitions $\mathcal{G}'$ and $\mathcal{G}''$. The membership agreement ensures that all nodes in the proposed view $\mathcal{G}$ have delivered at least all messages that are prerequisites of the *view-acknowledgements* (from the relibale broadcast protocol). This requires that nodes in $\mathcal{G}'$ and $\mathcal{G}''$ deliver the same set of messages between them, before they install $\mathcal{G}$. Once the proposed view is installed, all nodes deliver the same set of messages. Thus all nodes that survive a view change deliver the same set of messages.

The approach to delivering and stabilising messages along with the current group view being sent with every *init-view-change* message allows a node to determine if the principle of virtual synchrony holds. This is achieved by calculating the transitional set [9] at every view install. The transitional set is easy to determine as described in [3] using the current view sent by each node with the *init-view-change* message.

The alternative to transitional sets, agreement on successors, is avoided as the latter requires installing a temporary view if overlapping groups merge. In a wireless medium without collision detection or fairness, nodes are often incorrectly suspected which leads to a higher number of potential merges with overlapping groups. This encourages us to support the transitional set approach to implement virtual synchrony.

6 Performance

In this section we present a performance study for an implementation of Trans-MAN. We evaluate the performance of TransMAN by measuring message latency and total number of transmissions between the time a message is transmitted and its delivery at all members. We measure these for both FIFO and totally ordered delivery. We also measure the system response to view changes when one node is added to or removed from the membership.

We study the average latency for message delivery while changing the network topology and group size. To isolate the evaluation from time based system parameters(such as heartbeat and optimiser buffer time), we also observe the system performance in terms of message transmissions.

6.1   Experimental Setup

Measurements are made by running the implementation of TransMAN on networks formed of up to 6 laptops using IEEE 802.11b. Each laptop runs Linux 2.4.27 on a Pentium III 1GHz processor with 256MB memory. The system implementation is developed in the Ruby programming language.

The broadcast layer at each node transmits a sequence of messages separated by randomly chosen time periods between the range of $500ms$ to $1500ms$. Each regular broadcast message is 200 Bytes in size. The counter based optimiser in the broadcast layer buffers each message before transmitting it for a time period. This time period is chosen randomly to be between $50ms$ and $200ms$. The maximum counter value is set to three, as [14] shows three to be the optimal value for reducing redundant broadcasts. If during the buffered period, a message is received for a third time, its transmission is cancelled.

Two network topologies are chosen, linear and clustered. For the linear case we set up a network of n nodes such that there are $n - 1$ hops between the furthest two nodes. To achieve this topology, we remove external antennas from the Cisco (aironet 350) IEEE 802.11b cards. Once the external antennas are removed each node has a transmission range of about 2 feet. This allows us to set up linear networks inside our lab.

Our most extreme network setup, a linear network with 6 nodes, has 5 hops. An IEEE 802.11b based MANET of 5 hops will extend to more than a Kilometre. We do not envision an application requiring the strong guarantees akin to those provided by TransMAN when the network is spread over a Kilometre. We use the linear 6 node network as an extreme case to observe the worst case performance of our system. For the clustered case, all nodes have their external antennas attached giving them a range of 250m. This results in a strongly connected network.

6.2   Message Delivery

We first analyse the delivery times for both FIFO and total order delivery. Figure 3 shows the delivery times for FIFO and total order message delivery. We observe that the average latency for FIFO delivering a message is less than $400ms$ and $200ms$ for linear and clustered topologies respectively. This shows that even while providing strong reliability guarantees TransMAN can be used for applications with latency tolerance of about $400ms$. Mobile mutliplayer games are a possible candidates.

From Figure 3, we see only a slight increase in the time required to deliver messages as the group size increases. An interesting result is that up to a group size of 5 nodes, the effect of topology on delivery times is not as adverse as expected. Due to the higher number of hops in the linear case we had expected much higher delivery times for the linear case.

Next we observe the number of transmissions between a message transmission and its delivery at all participating nodes. Figure 3 show the average number of transmissions required per node to deliver messages. The figure shows how in a clustered setup FIFO delivery is achieved by at most 2 transmissions.

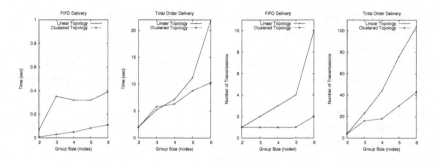

Fig. 3. Delivery times & Transmissions required: FIFO and totally ordered

The linear setup on the other hand shows a linear increase up to a network of 5 nodes. Again, the linear network of 6 nodes being an extreme example, shows a large increase in the number of transmissions required to deliver each message.

For total order delivery the linear case shows a steeper increase in the number of transmissions as compared to the clustered case. This is again due to the increase in the number of hops as the size of a linear network increases and the increase in the number of implicit acknowledgements required for total order message delivery.

Comparing the number of transmissions and time taken to deliver messages in total order from figures 3 we see that even though up to a network size of 5 nodes the latency of total order message delivery remains similar for linear and clustered setups, the number of actual transmissions required is much higher in the linear case. This is because even if in a clustered network total order delivery is achieved with fewer transmissions than in the linear case, the collisions and MAC layer backoffs result in similar message latencies as in a linear setup. This shows the affect of spatial reuse and how more transmissions are accommodated to provide similar latency.

Observing the clustered case for FIFO and total order delivery in Figure 3 we see that the number of transmissions required to deliver messages in total order grows more rapidly over the group size than in case of FIFO delivery. This is because as the group size increases each message has to be acknowledged by more and more nodes and this requires higher number of messages to be delivered, requiring higher number of transmissions.

6.3 View Changes

Finally we look at the system performance while responding to a view change. Figure 4 shows the number of message transmissions required to add and remove a node from a network of a given size. The x-axis shows the number of nodes in the network. For the graph showing node addition, the x-axis shows the group size before a new node is added. Correspondingly, for node removal, the x-axis shows the number of nodes before a node is removed. We observe latency in number of transmissions in the network to normalise the effects of varying heartbeats and buffering times.

Figure 4 clearly shows a linear increase in the number of transmissions required to respond to a change in group membership. This is because as the group size increases the number of messages required to reach an agreement also increases.

Another observation from Figure 4 is the similarity in the number of transmissions required to undergo a view change for the two topologies, until a network of 5 nodes. This is explained by the transitive nature of dependencies which allows each message transmission from a node to implicitly acknowledge a number of messages irrespective of the topology. Thus, each message transmission by a node contributes to progress towards membership agreements on all nodes. This effect of transitive dependencies on the number of

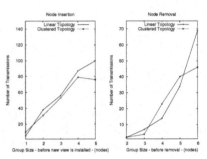

Fig. 4. View installation: adding and removing one node

transmissions required to install views shows that using a broadcast protocol is a good choice for implementing a virtually synchronous group communication.

7   Related Work

Group communication systems have long been a focus of study, with systems largely focussed on providing a solution in LANs [5] or WANs [4]. Group communication for MANETs has been under some study lately. Probabilistic system like [7] provide participating nodes with a randomised set of participating nodes as a group membership. Friedman [6] proposes using a fuzziness level attached to each node's membership information. The idea of geographical proximity is used in [8] to address the group membership problem. Using location information of nodes to determine a consistent group membership [11] has been studied and can provide a useful alternative to our system given a location service. Prakash and Baldoni [10] provide a group membership protocol for synchronous networks and is targeted towards channel allocation problems in wireless networks. Our system in contrast to these systems is a deterministic solution that supports virtual synchrony without requiring limits on clock drifts.

8   Conclusions

In this paper we presented TransMAN, a group communication system for mobile ad-hoc networks. TransMAN is a complete group communication stack offering comparable functionality and features as a group communication system for fixed-networks but is designed to cope with the challenges of dynamic MANETs.

At the core of the system is the technique of observing messages exchanges together with the exploitation of the broadcast nature of wireless communication. This reduces the acknowledgements and other control messages in the network. These protocols are combined to offer reliable, virtual synchronous group communication for MANETs.

An implementation of our system was developed in Ruby and we ran experiments with different group sizes and topologies. These results show a message delivery latency of $400ms$ for the worst case network setup and show that message latency increases linearly with network size.

References

1. K. Birman and T. Joseph. Exploiting virtual synchrony in distributed systems. In *Proceedings of the eleventh ACM Symposium on Operating systems principles*, pages 123–138. ACM Press, 1987.
2. T. D. Chandra and S. Toueg. Unreliable failure detectors for reliable distributed systems. *Journal of the ACM*, 43(2):225–267, March 1996.
3. G. V. Chockler, I. Keidar, and R. Vitenberg. Group communication specifications: A comprehensive study. *ACM Computing Surveys(CSUR)*, 33(4):427–469, 2001.
4. A. Das, I. Gupta, and A. Motivala. Swim: Scalable weakly-consistent infection-style process group membership protocol. In *DSN 2002*, pages 303–312, June 2002.
5. D. Dolev and D. Malki. The design of the transis system. Dagstuhl Workshop on Unifying Theory and Practice in Distributed Computing, September 1995.
6. R. Friedman. Fuzzy group membership. In *Future Directions in Distributed Computing*, volume 2584 of *Lecture Notes in Computer Science*, pages 114–118. Springer, 2003.
7. J. Luo, P. T. Eugster, and J.-P. Hubaux. Pilot: Probabilistic lightweight group communication system for ad hoc networks. *IEEE Transactions on Mobile Computing*, 3(2), April - June 2004.
8. R. Meier, M.-O. Killijian, R. Cunningham, and V. Cahill. Towards proximity group communication. In *Principles of Mobile Computing*, 2001.
9. L. E. Moser, Y. Amir, P. M. Melliar-Smith, and D. A. Agarwal. Extended virtual synchrony. In *The 14th IEEE International Conference on Distributed Computing Systems (ICDCS)*, pages 56–65, 1994.
10. R. Prakash and R. Baldoni. Architecture for group communication in mobile systems. In *Proceedings of the IEEE Symposium on Reliable Distributed Systems (SRDS)*, pages 235–242, October 1998.
11. G.-C. Roman, Q. Huang, and A. Hazemi. Consistent group membership in ad hoc networks. In *Proceedings of the 23rd international conference on Software engineering*, pages 381–388. IEEE Computer Society, 2001.
12. A. Schiper and A. Ricciardi. Virtually-synchronous communication based on a weak failure suspector. Technical report, LSR, EPFL, 1993.
13. K. Singh, A. Nedos, G. Gaertner, and S. Clarke. Message stability and reliable broadcasts in mobile ad-hoc networks. In V. Syrotiuk and E. Chávez, editors, *ADHOC-NOW*, pages 297–310. LNCS 3788, October 2005.
14. Y.-C. Tseng, S.-Y. Ni, Y.-S. Chen, and J.-P. Sheu. The broadcast storm problem in a mobile ad hoc network. *Wirel. Netw.*, 8(2/3):153–167, 2002.

On Fault Tolerance of Two-Dimensional Mesh Networks

Soumen Maity[1], Amiya Nayak[2], and S. Ramsundar[3]

[1] Department of Mathematics, Indian Institute of Technology Guwahati
Guwahati 781 039, Assam, India
soumen@iitg.ernet.in
[2] School of Information Technology and Engineering (SITE)
University of Ottawa, 800 King Edward Avenue
Ottawa, Ontario, K1N 6N5, Canada
anayak@site.uottawa.ca
[3] Computer Science & Engineering, Indian Institute of Technology Guwahati
Guwahati 781 039, Assam, India
sundark@iitg.ernet.in

Abstract. The catastrophic fault pattern is a pattern of faults occurring at strategic locations that may render a system unusable regardless of its component redundancy and of its reconfiguration capabilities. In this paper, we characterize catastrophic fault patterns in mesh networks when the links are bidirectional or unidirectional. We determine the minimum number of faults required for a fault pattern to be catastrophic. We consider the problem of testing whether a set of faulty processors is catastrophic. In addition, when a fault pattern is not catastrophic we consider the problem of finding *optimal* reconfiguration strategies, where optimality is with respect to either the number of processing elements in the reconfigured network (the reconfiguration is optimal if such a number is maximized) or the number of bypass links to activate in order to reconfigure the array (the reconfiguration is optimal if such a number is minimized). The problem of finding a reconfiguration strategy that is optimal with respect to the size of the reconfigured network is NP-complete, when the links are bidirectional, while it can be solved in polynomial time, when the links are unidirectional. Considering optimality with respect to the number of bypass links to activate, we provide algorithms which efficiently find an optimal reconfiguration.

1 Introduction

Mesh architectures consist of a large number of identical and elementary processing elements locally connected in a regular fashion. Each element receives data from its neighbors, computes and sends the results again to its neighbors. Few particular elements located at the extremes of the systems (these extremes depend on the particular system) are allowed to communicate with the external world. In this paper, we will focus on mesh architectures.

S. Chaudhuri et al. (Eds.): ICDCN 2006, LNCS 4308, pp. 442–453, 2006.
© Springer-Verlag Berlin Heidelberg 2006

Fault tolerant techniques are very important to mesh architectures [2]. Here we assume that only processors can fail. Indeed, since the number of processing elements is very large, the probability that a set of processing elements becomes faulty is fairly high. Without the provision of fault-tolerance capabilities, the yield of such an architecture would be so poor that it would be unacceptable. Thus, fault-tolerant mechanisms must be provided in order to avoid faulty processing elements taking part in the computation. A widely used technique to achieve fault tolerance consists of providing redundancy to the desired architecture [1,2]. In these systems the redundancy consists of additional processing elements, called spares, and additional connections, called bypass links. Bypass links are links that connect each processor with another processor at a fixed distance greater than 1. The redundant processing elements are used to replace any faulty processing element; the redundant links are used to bypass the faulty processing elements and reach others. The effectiveness of using redundancy to increase fault tolerance clearly depends on both the amount of redundancy and the reconfiguration capability of the system. It does however depend also on the distribution of faults in the system. There are sets of faulty processing elements for which no reconfiguration strategy is possible. Such sets are called catastrophic fault patterns (CFPs). From a network perspective, such fault patterns can cause network disconnection.

If we have to reconfigure a system when a fault pattern occurs, it is necessary to know if the fault pattern is catastrophic or not. Therefore it is important to study the properties of catastrophic fault patterns. Till today, the characterization of CFPs is known for linear arrays with the following results. The characterization has been used to obtain efficient testing algorithms both for unidirectional and bidirectional cases [13,14] with order of magnitude improvement over [3,4]. Efficient techniques has been obtained for constructing CFPs [12]. Using random walk as a tool, a closed form solution for the number of CFPs for uni- and bidirectional links has been provided in [8,10]. The knowledge of this number enables us to estimate the probability that the system operates correctly [11]. Recently, Maity, Nayak and Roy [9] characterize catastrophic fault patterns for two-dimensional arrays.

In this paper we completely characterize CFPs for mesh networks. We determine the minimum number of faults required for a fault pattern to be catastrophic. From a practical viewpoint, above result allow to prove some answers to the question about the guaranteed level of fault tolerance of a design. Guaranteed fault tolerance indicates positive answer to the question as: will the system withstand up to k faults always regardless of how and where they occur? We analyze catastrophic sets having the minimal number of faults. The paper also describes algorithm for testing whether a set of faults is catastrophic or not. In addition, when a fault pattern is not catastrophic, we consider the problem of finding optimal reconfiguration strategies for both unidirectional and bidirectional networks. Where the optimality is with respect to the number of processors in the reconfigured network or with respect to the number of bypass links. The reconfiguration is optimal if number of processing elements is maximized in the former case, while the number of bypass links are to be minimum in the latter case.

2   Preliminaries

In this paper, we will focus on *mesh networks*. The basic components of such a network are the processing elements(PEs) indicated by circles in Figure 1. There are two kinds of links : *regular* and *bypass*. Regular links connect neighboring (either horizontal or vertical) PEs while bypass links connect non-neighbors. The bypass links are used strictly for reconfiguration purposes when a fault is detected, otherwise they are considered to be the redundant links. We now introduce the following definitions:

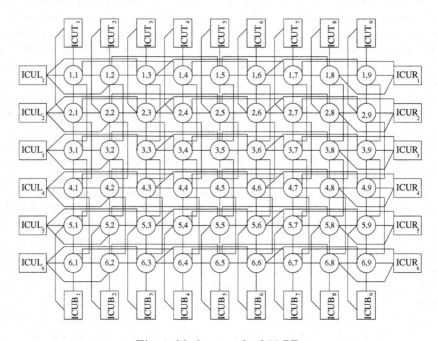

Fig. 1. Mesh network of 54 PEs

Definition 1. A mesh network $\mathcal{M} = (V, E)$ consists of a set V of PEs and a set E of links (where a link joins a pair of distinct PEs) satisfying the conditions listed below.

V is the union of five disjoint sets: the set $ICUL = \{ICUL_1, ICUL_2, \ldots, ICUL_{N_1}\}$ of left interface control units, the set $ICUR = \{ICUR_1, ICUR_2, \ldots, ICUR_{N_1}\}$ of right interface control units, the set $ICUT = \{ICUT_1, ICUT_2, \ldots, ICUT_{N_2}\}$ of top interface control units, the set $ICUB = \{ICUB_1, ICUB_2, \ldots, ICUB_{N_2}\}$

of bottom interface control units, and a two-dimensional array $A = \{p_{ij} : 1 \leq i \leq N_1, 1 \leq j \leq N_2\}$ of PEs. We sometimes refer to the processing element p_{ij} as (i, j).

E consists of the links obtained as follows. Fix integers $1 = g_1 < g_2 < \ldots < g_k \leq N_2 - 1$ and $1 = v_1 < v_2 < \ldots < v_l \leq N_1 - 1$. Join p_{ij} to $p_{i'j'}$ by a link if and only if (i) $i = i'$ and $j' - j$ is one of $g_1, g_2, \ldots, g_k$ or (ii) $j = j'$ and $i' - i$ is one of $v_1, v_2, \ldots, v_l$. Also join $ICUL_i$ to $p_{i1}, p_{i2}, \ldots, p_{ig_k}$ and join $p_{i,N_2-g_k+1}, p_{i,N_2-g_k+2}, \ldots, p_{iN_2}$ to $ICUR_i$ by links, for $i = 1, 2, \ldots, N_1$. Similarly join $ICUT_j$ to $p_{1j}, p_{2j}, \ldots, p_{v_lj}$ and join $p_{N_1-v_l+1,j}, p_{N_1-v_l+2,j}, \ldots, p_{N_1j}$ to $ICUB_j$ by links, for $j = 1, 2, \ldots, N_2$.

We assume that $N_2 > g_k$ and $N_1 > v_l$. We also assume N_1 and N_2 are multiple of v_l and g_k respectively.

Definition 2. We refer to $G = (g_1, g_2, \ldots, g_k \mid v_1, v_2, \ldots, v_l)$ as the *link redundancy* of $\mathcal{M}$. We call $g_1, g_2, \ldots, g_k$ the *horizontal link redundancies* of $\mathcal{M}$ and $v_1, v_2, \ldots, v_l$ the *vertical link redundancies* of $\mathcal{M}$.

Figure 1 shows a mesh network with $N_1 = 6$, $N_2 = 9$ and $G = (1, 3 \mid 1, 2)$. A link joining two PEs of the type p_{ij} and $p_{i,j+1}$ is called a *horizontal direct link* and a link joining two PEs of the type p_{ij} and $p_{i+1,j}$ is called a *vertical direct link*. Direct links are also called *regular links*. Links joining p_{ij} and $p_{i,\,j+g}$ with $g > 1$ are called *horizontal bypass links* and links joining p_{ij} and $p_{i+v,\,j}$ with $v > 1$ are called *vertical bypass links*.

The *length* of the horizontal bypass link joining p_{ij} to $p_{i,\,j+g}$ is g and the *length* of the vertical bypass link joining p_{ij} to $p_{i+v,\,j}$ is v.

Note that no links exist in the network $\mathcal{M}$ except the ones specified by G as in Definition 1. It is assumed that $ICUL$, $ICUR$, $ICUT$ and $ICUB$ always operate correctly and we are considering information flow from $ICUL \cup ICUT$ to $ICUR \cup ICUB$.

Definition 3. Given a two-dimensional array A, a *fault pattern* F for A is the set of faulty processors which can be any non-empty subset of A. An assignment of a fault pattern F to A means that every processing element belonging to F is faulty (and the others operate correctly).

Definition 4. A fault pattern is *catastrophic* for the mesh network $\mathcal{M}$ if $ICUL \cup ICUT$ is not connected to $ICUR \cup ICUB$ when the fault pattern F is assigned to A.

Definition 5. Let F be a fault pattern in a mesh network $\mathcal{M}$ with link redundancy $G = (1, g_2, \ldots, g_k \mid 1, v_2, \ldots, v_l)$. If we remove all faulty PEs, their adjacent links and all bypass links from $\mathcal{M}$ then a component of $\mathcal{M}$ will be called a *chunk*. Let $C_0, C_1, \ldots, C_n$ be the chunks of F where C_0 is connected with $ICUL \cup ICUT$, C_n is connected with $ICUR \cup ICUB$ and other C_i's are labelled arbitrarily.

Definition 6. A *path* from a working processor (i_0, j_0) to a possibly faulty processor (i_{s+1}, j_{s+1}) is a sequence of processors (i_0, j_0), (i_1, j_1), ..., (i_s, j_s), (i_{s+1}, j_{s+1}) such that, for each $k = 0, 1, \ldots, s$, processor (i_k, j_k) is a working processor connected by a link to processor (i_{k+1}, j_{k+1}) and a processor is used only once. The length of the path is $s + 1$. An *escape path* is a path form $ICUL \cup ICUT$ to $ICUR \cup ICUB$.

Our main contribution here is a complete characterization of catastrophic fault patterns for mesh networks. Let $\mathcal{M}$ be a mesh network with link redundancy $G = (g_1, g_2, \ldots, g_k \mid v_1, v_2, \ldots, v_l)$, and let F be a fault pattern. Then we prove that, F is catastrophic with respect to $\mathcal{M}$ implies that the cardinality of F, $|F| \geq \max \left\{ \frac{N_1}{v_l}, \frac{N_2}{g_k} \right\} v_l g_k$. We provide an algorithm to test whether a given F is catastrophic with respect to link redundancy $G = (g_1, g_2, \ldots, g_k \mid v_1, v_2, \ldots, v_l)$.

When a fault pattern is not catastrophic, we are interested in finding escape paths. Depending on the fault pattern there can exist several escape paths. We are interested in finding those escape paths that are *optimal* with respect to the size of the reconfigured network or the number of redundant links to be activated to reconfigure the network. Here optimality is achieved when the size of the reconfigured network is maximized, that is, when the number of processors in the escape path that reconfigured the network is maximized. In this case, an optimal escape path is called a *maximum escape path*, and a reconfiguration set that achieves a maximum escape path is called a *maximum reconfiguration set*. For example, consider the fault pattern $F = \{ (1,3), (1,4), (1,5), (2,1), (2,2), (2,3), (2,4), (2,5), (3,1), (3,4), (3,5), (4,1), (4,2), (4,3), (4,4)\}$ in a 4×5 mesh network $\mathcal{M}$ with link redundancy $G = (1, 2, 3 \mid 1, 2)$. The maximum escape path,

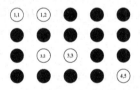

Fig. 2. A mesh with a fault pattern

having 4 processing elements, is given by $ICUL_1$ or $ICUT_1$, (1,1), (1,2), (3,2), (3,3) $ICUR_3$ or $ICUB_3$ for both bidirectional or unidirectional case. However maximum escape path is not unique always.

In the latter case, optimality is achieved when the number of redundant links that we have to activate in order to reconfigure the network is minimized. In this case, an optimal escape path is called *minimum escape path*, and a reconfiguration set that achieves a minimum escape path is called a *minimum reconfiguration set*. For example, consider the fault pattern in Figure 2. The escape path $ICUL_3$, (3,2), (3,3), $ICUR_3$ is a minimum escape path since it uses only two bypass links and there are no escape paths that use only 1 bypass link.

3   Characterization of Catastrophic Fault Patterns

In this section, we will characterize the catastrophic fault patterns for mesh networks and prove that the minimum number of faults in a catastrophic fault pattern is a function of N_1, N_2, the length of the longest horizontal bypass link and the length of the longest vertical bypass link.

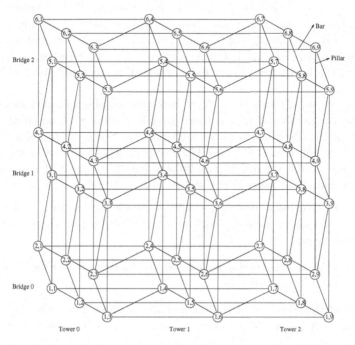

Fig. 3. Tower-Bridge representation of mesh networks of Figure 1

Theorem 1. *Suppose v_l divides N_1 and g_k divides N_2, then F is catastrophic with respect to $\mathcal{M}$ implies that the cardinality of F, $|F| \geq max\left\{\frac{N_1}{v_l}, \frac{N_2}{g_k}\right\}v_l g_k$.*

Proof: Suppose to the contrary that $|F| < max\left\{\frac{N_1}{v_l}, \frac{N_2}{g_k}\right\}v_l g_k$. Then partition the two-dimensional array A of PEs into blocks of v_l rows as $A = \left(A_1 \quad A_2 \quad \cdots \quad A_{\frac{N_1}{v_l}}\right)^T$ and again partition each block A_i into sub-blocks of g_k columns as $A_i = \left(A_{i1} \vdots A_{i2} \vdots \cdots \vdots A_{i\frac{N_2}{g_k}}\right)$. For example, sub-block $A_{12} = \{(1,4), (1,5), (1,6), (2,4), (2,5), (2,6)\}$ in Figure 3. We place the sub-blocks $A_{1j}, A_{2j}, \ldots, A_{\frac{N_1}{v_l}j}$ as consecutive floors to form tower j as shown in Figure 3. On the other hand, the sub-blocks $A_{i1}, A_{i2}, \ldots, A_{i\frac{N_2}{g_k}}$ form bridge i in between the towers. We will refer the sub-blocks as floors later. Observe that, each horizontal bypass link of the maximum length joins two consecutive elements in the same *bar* of a bridge. On the other hand, each vertical link of the maximum length joins two consecutive elements in the same *pillar* of a tower. For example, Figure 3 shows the bar $[(6,3), (6,6), (6,9)]$ and the pillar $[(2,9),(4,9), (6,9)]$. So, in this representation, going up along a pillar corresponds to using the longest vertical bypass links and going right along a bar corresponds to using the longest horizontal bypass links. Note that, there are $N_1 g_k$ bars and $N_2 v_l$ pillars. Now we consider two cases:

Case 1. $\frac{N_1}{v_l} > \frac{N_2}{g_k}$. That is $|F| < N_1 g_k$. Since the number of faulty elements $|F|$ is less than the number of bars, there must be a bar with no faulty element, regardless of the distribution of the fault pattern. Since the left and right of each bar are linked to ICUL and ICUR respectively, F cannot be catastrophic since we can use the horizontal bypass links of length g_k to avoid the faulty PEs, a contradiction.

Case 2. $\frac{N_1}{v_l} < \frac{N_2}{g_k}$. That is $|F| < N_2 v_l$. Since the number of faulty elements $|F|$ is less than the number of pillars, there must be a pillar with no faulty element, regardless of the distribution of the fault pattern. Since the top and bottom of each pillar are linked to ICUT and ICUB respectively, F cannot be catastrophic since we can use the vertical bypass links of length g_k to avoid the faulty PEs, a contradiction which proves the theorem.   □

This theorem gives us a necessary condition on the minimum number of faults required for blocking a mesh network when $v_l | N_1$ and $g_k | N_2$. In general we have the following result:

Theorem 2. *F is catastrophic with respect to $\mathcal{M}$ implies that the cardinality of F, $|F| \geq max\{N_1 g_k, N_2 v_l\}$.*

The proof of this theorem is similar to that of Theorem 1. This tells us that fewer than $max\{N_1 g_k, N_2 v_l\}$ faults occurring in A will not be catastrophic.

4   An Algorithm to Test Weather a Fault Pattern Is Catastrophic

4.1   Bidirectional Mesh

Let $\mathcal{M}$ be a bidirectional mesh network of $N_1 N_2$ processors with link redundancy $G = (1, g_2, \ldots, g_k \mid 1, v_2, \ldots, v_l)$, and let F be a fault pattern with m faults. A simple way to test if F is catastrophic for $\mathcal{M}$ is to consider a graph whose set of vertices is given by the chunks of working processors. More formally, we construct a graph $H = (V, E)$ as follows: The set V of vertices is $\{C_0, C_1, \ldots, C_n\}$, where C_i's represent chunks of F and $(C_i, C_j) \in E$ if and only if there are two processors, $p_{xy} \in C_i$ and $p_{x'y'} \in C_j$ such that $y = y'$ and $|x - x'| \in \{v_1, v_2, \ldots, v_l\}$ or $x = x'$ and $|y - y'| \in \{g_1, g_2, \ldots, g_k\}$, that is, such that these two processors are connected in $\mathcal{M}$ by a bypass link.

Fact 1. A fault pattern F is not catastrophic for a network $\mathcal{M}$, if and only if C_0 and C_n are connected in the graph H.

4.2   Unidirectional Mesh

Given a mesh network $\mathcal{M}$ and a fault pattern F, we construct a graph $G_0 = (V, E)$ as follows: The set V of vertices is the set of working processors and ICUs, and the set E of edges are the links between two working processors and the links between working processors and ICUs. In addition, there are two more vertices *source* and *sink*. We join *source* to each of the $ICUT$s and $ICULs$ and join each of the $ICURs$ and $ICUBs$ to *sink*. If $\mathcal{M}$ is unidirectional then G_0 is directed and undirected otherwise. For the directed graph we preserve the direction of the link, in the edge representing it. We call the graph G_0 the *auxiliary graph* of $\mathcal{M}$ for the fault pattern F.

Example 1. Consider the fault pattern $F = \{ (1,3), (1,4), (2,1), (2,2), (2,3), (2,4), (3,2), (3,4), (3,5), (4,1), (4,2), (4,4)\}$ in a 4×5 unidirectional mesh network $\mathcal{M}$ with link redundancy $G = (1, 2, 3 \mid 1, 2)$. Figure 4 shows the auxiliary graph.

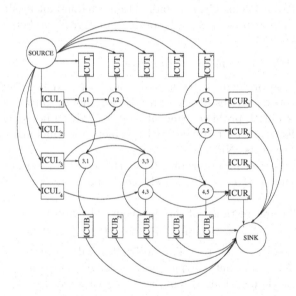

Fig. 4. Auxiliary graph G_0

Note that in the auxiliary graph $G_0 = (V, E)$, $|V| = 2N_1 + 2N_2 + w + 2$ and $|E| \leq 2N_1 + 2N_2 + w|G|$, where w is the number of working processing elements in the mesh. Also note that the auxiliary graph resulting from unidirectional mesh is directed acyclic in nature (See [5]). Time required to construct an auxiliary graph $G_0 = (V, E)$ is $O(2N_1 + 2N_2 + w|G|)$, that is, $O(N_1 + N_2 + w|G|)$.

To find out if the fault pattern is catastrophic or not, we assign weight 1 to all the edges in the auxiliary graph. Now, we can run the shortest path algorithm given in [5] for directed acyclic graphs and find out if there exists a path from *source* to *sink*. In a graph (V, E), the shortest path algorithm takes

$O(|V| + |E|)$ time. A fault pattern F is not catastrophic for mesh $\mathcal{M}$, if and only if *source* is connected with *sink* in the auxiliary graph. Thus the problem of testing whether a fault pattern is catastrophic for unidirectional mesh network requires $O(N_1 + N_2 + w|G|)$ time.

5 Maximum Escape Paths

In this section we consider the problem of finding maximum escape paths. We prove that the problem is NP-complete for a bidirectional mesh network, while for unidirectional mesh we provide an algorithm that finds a maximum escape path in $O(N_1 + N_2 + w|G|)$ time.

5.1 *MRL* Problem in the Case of Bidirectional Links

Consider the following *Maximuim Reconfiguration Length* (MRL for short) problem:

Definition 7. (MRL problem) Given a bidirectional redundant mesh $\mathcal{M}$, with link redundancy G, a fault pattern F and a positive integer K, is there an escape path of length at least K?

Theorem 3. *The MRL problem is NP-complete.*

Proof: We reduce the problem of testing whether there exists a hamiltonian path between two given vertices of a graph (HP for short), known to be NP-complete (see [6]) , to MRL problem. Since it is easy to give a non deterministic polynomial time algorithm that solves MRL problem we conclude that MRL problem belongs to the class NP.

Let $H = (V, E)$ be the input graph of the HP problem. Without loss of generality, assume that $V = \{1, 2, ..., n\}$ and that 1 and n are the vertices to be tested.

Consider the following instance of our problem. The mesh $\mathcal{M}$ has $N_1 = 3$ rows and $N_2 = \frac{(6n^3 - 3n^2 - 9n + 8)}{2}$ columns. For $i = 1, 2, ..., n$ define $a_i = (n + i - 2)n^2 + \frac{(n-1)(n-2) + (i-1)(i-2)}{2} + 1$. The horizontal link redundancies are for each edge $(i, j) \in E$, a horizontal bypass link of length $| a_i - a_j |$. Moreover there is an additional bypass link of length $g = a_1$ (it is easy to see that this is the longest horizontal link connecting $ICUL_2$ and PE $(2, a_1)$, and also PE $(2, a_n)$ and $ICUR_2$). The vertical link redundancy will be singleton $\{1\}$. The fault pattern F consists of all the processing elements in the first and the third rows and all the processing elements in the second row except those in the a_ith column, i.e., in the whole mesh only the processing elements $(2, a_i)$, $1 \le i \le n$, are working. Finally $K = n$.

Notice that the above MRL instance can be constructed in time polynomial in the size of the graph and all the integers occurring in the description of the instance are polynomially related to n.

We will prove that H has an hamiltonian path if and only if the above instance of the MRL problem admits a solution, i.e., if there is an escape path of size n. In order to prove this, we first need the following four facts.

a The only possible escape path connects $ICUL_2$ and $ICUR_2$. It is easy to notice that all other pairs of ICU's are already disconnected.

b Any escape path must traverse $(2, a_1)$ and $(2, a_n)$. Indeed, as the first and the last $g - 1$ processing elements are faulty and the length of the longest link is g.

c If $(2, a_i)$, with $1 < i < n$, is traversed by an escape path, then it must be traversed after $(2, a_1)$ and before $(2, a_n)$. Indeed, let d_{ij}, $1 \leq i \neq j \leq n$, be the distance between $(2, a_i)$ and $(2, a_j)$, i.e., $d_{ij} =\mid a_i - a_j \mid= n^2 \mid i - j \mid + \mid \frac{(j-1)(j-2)}{2} - \frac{(i-1)(i-2)}{2} \mid$. Since for $(i \neq j)$ it holds that $n^2 \mid i - j \mid < d_{ij} < n^2 \mid i - j \mid +n^2$, then (for $1 \leq i \neq j, u \neq v \leq n$), we have $d_{ij} = d_{uv}$ if and only if $\{i, j\} = \{u, v\}$.

d Graph H is isomorphic to the graph consisting of the non faulty elements $(2, a_i)$, $i = 1, 2, \ldots, n$ and their incident horizontal links. Indeed, since $d_{ij} < d_{1n} < g$, $1 \leq i \neq j \leq n$, processors $(2, a_i)$ and $(2, a_j)$ are connected by a bypass link, if and only if vertices i and j are connected by an edge in graph H. Moreover, since no other two working processors are at a distance d_{ij}, this bypass link connects only $(2, a_i)$ and $(2, a_j)$.

Now we can prove that there is an escape path of length at least $K = n$ if and only if there is an hamiltonian path between vertices 1 and n in the graph H. Assume that there is an escape path of size $K = n$. Since in $\mathcal{M}$ there is exactly K working processors, each processor is involved in the escape path. Since all the working processors are traversed, by **a, b, c, d**, we conclude that there exists a hamiltonian path between vertices 1 and n in H (recall that by the definition of path each processor can be traversed at most once).

Conversely, given a hamiltonian path between vertices 1 and n in H, by **d**, it corresponds to a path from $(2, a_1)$ to $(2, a_n)$, which traverses once all the non faulty processing elements of $\mathcal{M}$. This path can be easily extended to an escape path of size $K = n$ connecting $ICUL_2$ to $(2, a_1)$ and $ICUR_2$ to $(2, a_n)$, respectively, by means of the longest bypass link.

Therefore we can test if there exists a hamiltonian path between vertices 1 and n in H by testing if there exists an escape path of size at least K for the array $\mathcal{M}$.   □

5.2 *MRL* Problem in the Case of Unidirectional Links

When the mesh is unidirectional, the problem of finding a maximum escape path can be solved in $O(N_1 + N_2 + w|G|)$ time.

Definition 8. *An auxiliary escape path is a path from source vertex to sink vertex in an auxiliary graph.*

It is easy to note that if there are p edges in an auxiliary escape path then the corresponding escape path contains $p - 3$ processing elements.

Given a fault pattern F in an unidirectional mesh network, we first construct the corresponding auxiliary graph $G_0 = (V, E)$. To get the escape path with maximum processors, we assign weight -1 to all the edges in E. Now we run the

S. Maity, A. Nayak, and S. Ramsundar

single source shortest path algorithm for directed acyclic graphs (DAG) given in [5] on G_0 with the source vertex as the *source*. The shortest auxiliary path, if any, from *source* to *sink* is obtained. By shortest auxiliary path we mean that the sum of the edge weights in the path is least. This algorithm takes $O(|V| + |E|)$ time. The construction of the graph takes $O(N_1 + N_2 + w|G|)$ time. It takes $O(|E|)$ time to assign the weight -1 to each edge. So the total time spent to find out an escape path with maximum processing elements, if any, is $O(N_1 + N_2 + w|G|)$.

6 Minimum Escape Paths

In this section we consider the problem of finding minimum escape paths. We prove that the problem can be solved in $O(w|G| + (N_1 + N_2 + w) \log(N_1 + N_2 + w))$ time if the bypass links are bidirectional, and in $O(N_1 + N_2 + w|G|)$ time if the bypass links are unidirectional. First we consider the case of bidirectional links.

Given a fault pattern F in a bidirectional mesh network, we construct the auxiliary graph $G_0 = (V, E)$ and assign weight 1 to all the edges representing the bypass links (horizontal or vertical) in G_0 and 0 to all the remaining edges. Now run the Dijkstra's single source shortest path algorithm on G_0 with source vertex as the *source*. The shortest auxiliary escape path, if any, is then obtained. This algorithm requires $O(|V| \log |V| + |E|)$ time (using Fibonacci heap data structure, see [5]). The construction of the auxiliary graph takes $O(N_1 + N_2 + w|G|)$ time and it takes $O(|E|)$ time to assign weight to each edge. Thus the problem of finding minimum escape path for bidirectional mesh network requires $O(w|G| + (N_1 + N_2 + w) \log(N_1 + N_2 + w))$ time.

Now we consider the case of unidirectional links. Given a fault pattern F in a unidirectional mesh network, we construct the auxiliary graph $G_0 = (V, E)$ and assign weight 1 to all the edges representing the bypass links (horizontal or vertical) in G_0 and 0 to all the remaining edges. Now, repeat the shortest path algorithm for DAG, as in the subsection 5.2. The shortest auxiliary escape path, if any, is obtained. Thus the problem of finding minimum escape path for unidirectional mesh network requires $O(N_1 + N_2 + w|G|)$ time.

7 Conclusions

In this paper we have completely characterized catastrophic fault pattern for mesh networks. Before attempting any reconfiguration it is important to test whether the set of faults is catastrophic. We have presented testing algorithms to test whether a given fault pattern is catastrophic. When a set of faults is not catastrophic it is important to provide efficient reconfiguration algorithms that provide optimal reconfigurations. Optimality is considered either with respect to the size of the reconfigured network or with the amount of bypass links need to reconfigure the network. We have proved that when the links are bidirectional, the problem of finding optimal reconfiguration with respect to the size of the reconfigured network is NP-complete. In all the other three cases we give algorithms which efficiently find an optimal reconfiguration.

Acknowledgment. The authors like to thank the anonymous referees for important comments that improved the technical quality of the paper.

References

1. Balasubramanian, V. and Banerjee, P., A fault tolerant massively parallel processing architechture, *Journal of Parallel and Distributed Computing*, Vol. 4, 1987, pp. 363-383.
2. Bruck, J., Cypher, R. and Ho, C.T., Fault-tolerant meshes with minimal number of spares, *Proc. of 3rd IEEE Symposium on Parallel and Distributed Processing*, 1991, pp. 288-295.
3. De Prisco, R., Monti, A. and Pagli, L., "Efficient testing and reconfiguration of VLSI linear arrays", *Theoretical Computer Science*, Vol. 197, 1998, pp. 105-129.
4. De Prisco, R. and De Santis, A., Catastrophic faults in reconfigurable systolic linear arrays, *Discrete Applied Math.*, Vol. 75, 1997, pp. 105-123.
5. Cormen, T. H., Lierson, C. E, Rivest, R. L. and Stein, C., *Introduction to Algorithms*. MIT Press, Cambridge, MA.
6. Garey, M. and Johnson, D., *Computers and intractability*, Freeman, New York, 1979.
7. Kung, H. T., Why systolic architecture? *IEEE Computer*, Vol. 15, Jan. 1982, pp. 37-46.
8. Maity, S., Roy, B. and Nayak, A., Enumerating catastrophic fault patterns in VLSI arrays with both uni- and bidirectional links, *INTEGRATION: The VLSI Journal*, Vol. 30, 2001, pp. 157-168.
9. Maity, S., Nayak, A. and Roy, B., On Characterization of Catastrophic Faults in Two-Dimensional VLSI Arrays. *INTEGRATION, The VLSI Journal*, Vol. 38, 2004, pp. 267-281.
10. Maity, S., Roy, B. and Nayak, A., On Enumeration of Catastrophic Fault Patterns, *Information Processing Letters* Vol. 81, 2002, pp. 209-212.
11. Maity, S., Nayak, A., Roy, B., Reliability of VLSI Linear Arrays with Redundant Links. IWDC 2004, *Lecture Notes in Computer Science* Vol. 3326, pp. 326-337
12. Nayak, A., Pagli, L. and Santoro, N., Efficient construction of catastrophic patterns for VLSI reconfigurable arrays, *INTEGRATION: The VLSI Journal*, Vol. 15, 1993, pp. 133-150.
13. Nayak, A., Pagli, L. and Santoro, N., On testing of catastrophic faults in reconfigurable arrays with arbitrary link redundancy, *INTEGRATION: The VLSI Journal*, Vol. 20, 1996, pp. 327-342.
14. Nayak, A., Santoro, N., and Tan, R., Fault-Intolerance of reconfigurable systolic arrays, *Proc. of 20th Int. Symp. on Fault-Tolerant Computing*, 1990, pp. 202-209.
15. Leighton, T. and Leiserson, C. E., Wafer-scale integration of systolic arrays. *IEEE Trans. on Computers*, Vol. C-34, 1985, pp. 448-461.

Feedback Control with Prediction for Thread Allocation in Pipeline Architecture Web Server

Peng Shao-Liang[1], Li Shan-Shan[1], Liao Xiang-Ke[1], Peng Yu-Xing[1], and Ye Hui[2]

[1] School of Computer, National University of Defense Technology, ChangSha, China
[2] Hunan Science and Technology College, ChangSha, China
{pengshaoliang, shanshanli, xkliao, pengyuxing}@nudt.edu.cn

Abstract. With the sharply development of high-speed backbone network and phenomenal growth of Web applications, many kinds of Web server structures have been advanced and implemented to increase the serving ability of Web server. In this paper, we propose a pipeline architecture multi-thread web server open KETA which divides the requests processing into several independent phases. This architecture reduces parallelism granularity and achieves inner-request parallelism to enhance its processing capability. Furthermore, a combined feed-forward/feedback model is designed to manage thread allocation in this special architecture. The feed-forward predictor relates instantaneous measurements of queue length and processing rate of each pipeline phase to the thread allocation over a finite prediction horizon. The feedback controller deals with the uncertainty the predictor brings and improves open KETA's performance farther. Experimental results show the capability of open KETA and the effectiveness of the thread allocation model.

1 Introduction

The Internet has become an important medium for conducting business and selling & buying services. These applications require stringent performance guarantees from the web server. Some statistic shows that an e-commercial web site should guarantee its response in 7 seconds or it will lose more than 30 percent customers [1]. Measures suggest that web servers contribute for about 40% of the delay in a Web transaction and it is likely that this percentage will increase [2]. According to the Moore law, although end system's capacities will double every 18 months, network bandwidth would triple every year for the next 25 years. So the bottleneck is likely to be on the server side. In order to alleviate this pressure, some improvement should be made on web server. There are mainly three ways to achieve this [4]:

- Improve the performance of a web server node at the software level, namely software scale-up.
- Upgrade web server's hardware such as CPU, memory and network interfaces to improve processing capability. This strategy, referred to as hardware scale-up, simply consists in expanding a system by incrementally adding more resources to an existing node.

S. Chaudhuri et al. (Eds.): ICDCN 2006, LNCS 4308, pp. 454–465, 2006.

- Deploy a distributed web system architecture composed by multiple server nodes where some system component such as dispatcher can route incoming requests among different servers. The approach in which the system capabilities are expanded by adding more nodes, complete with processors, storage, and bandwidths, is typically referred to as scale-out.

In this paper, we concentrate on the first method --- software scale-up. Through comparison and analysis among the architecture of the mainstream web servers nowadays and their processing mechanism, we put forward a kernel pipeline web server — open KETA (KErnel neTwork geAr). This web server divides the processing of a request into four phrases, each of which has its own thread pool. Different phases of different requests can be executed concurrently like a pipeline on condition that there are no data and structure dependency. This architecture can reduce parallelism granularity effectively so that the resource of a web server can be utilized fully. Furthermore, a combined feed-forward / feedback model is designed to manage thread allocation in this special architecture. The feed-forward predictor adjusts thread allocation among all pipeline phases based on the instantaneous measurements of queue length and processing rate of each pipeline phase over a finite prediction horizon. The feedback controller deals with the uncertainty the predictor brings and improves open KETA's performance farther.

The rest of this paper is organized as follows. Section 2 briefly describes some related work. The framework of open KETA is introduced in Section 3. Section 4 presents the design of the feed-forward predictor and feedback controller. Section 5 describes the evaluation results.

2 Related Work

In view of the architecture, the mainstream web server can be classified into three categories: Single Process (SP), Symmetrical Multi-thread (SMT) and Asymmetrical Multi-thread (AMT) (or Symmetrical Multi-Process and Asymmetrical Multi-Processes).

In SP web server, a single process is responsible for the whole processing of all requests, including listening to the port, setting up connection, analyzing and processing requests, sending responses, etc. Some representative examples are μserver [5], Zeus[6] and kHTTPd[7]. This kind of web server always uses non-blocking systems calls to perform asynchronous I/O operation. SP server is able to overlap all the operations associated with the serving of many HTTP requests in the context of a single process. As a result, the overheads of context switching and process synch- ronization in the MT and MP architectures are avoided. However, relied on operating system's well support for asynchronous disk operations, SP web server may only provide excellent performance for cached workloads, where most requested content can be kept in main memory.

On workloads that exceed that capacity of the server cache, servers with MT or MP architecture usually perform best. SMT web server employs multiple threads to process requests. Some representative examples are KNOT [8] and Apache [9]. The capability and function of all threads are the same, which is the origin of the name

"Symmetrical Multi-Thread". SMT web server can overlap the disk activity, CPU processing and network connectivity concurrently so that it improves the server's parallelism capability. However, SMT web server ignores that the processing of a request also can be divided into several phases among which there are some potential parallelism.

AMT web server allocates different tasks to different thread. Flash [10] and Tux [11] are examples for this kind. They use one thread to process all connections and several helper threads to deal with the I/O operation. They decrease blocking time effectively and improve the efficiency of the service. However, it increases IPC cost between thread and helper threads and also can not utilize system resource fully like SMT architecture.

From the discussion above, we can see that most mainstream web servers have some parallelism capability and their parallelism granularity is request. Once a request is blocked on some operation, the thread will stop. It's well known that thread resource is limited and costly in web system so this paper tries to find a way to reduce parallelism granularity and achieve inner-request parallelism. Open KETA divides the processing of a request into four phrases. Thread in different phases performs different function and doesn't intervene with each other when running just like different pipeline phase. In this frame, even if a request is blocked in some special phase, threads in other phases still can process other requests. Utilization rate of threads is increased and the whole system performance is improved. In the following section, framework of open KETA is presented in Detail.

The application of control theory to software performance control has met much success in recent years. [12] presented a control theoretical approach to web server resource management based on web content adaptation. In [13, 14], control theory was used for CPU scheduling to achieve QoS guarantees on service delay. In [15], guarantees were made on delay control by applying control-theoretical techniques. This paper demonstrates that adding prediction to control loops can enhance feedback loop performance in a non-trivial way.

3   Framework of Open KETA

Open KETA is a kernel web server, the original developing intention of which is to improve web server performance by transferring the processing of static requests from user space to kernel space. When overloaded, performance of web server in user space is not so well because of much copy and syscall cost. Now many web servers are implemented in kernel space, such as kHTTPd and TUX. Considering system stability, kernel space web server only processes static requests instead of complex dynamic requests, and that dynamic requests are redirected to user space web server such as Apache. What's more, measurements [16, 17] have suggested that the request stream at most web servers is dominated by static requests. Serving static requests quickly is the focus of many companies. So we suppose that the implementation of open KETA will bring performance improvement. Figure 1 shows the processing

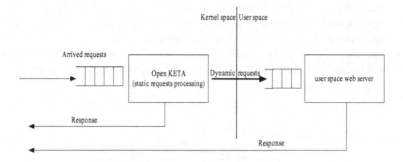

Fig. 1. Processing flow of open KETA

flow of open KETA. For Linux already has a kernel space web server TUX to accelerate requests processing, FreeBSD doesn't have yet, open KETA is implemented in FreeBSD kernel to improve its web performance.

As is introduced above, Open KETA divides the processing of request into four phrases: Accept Connection (accept), Socket Recv (receive), Data Process and Send Response (send) each of which has its own thread pool. Threads of different phases run in a pipeline-like manner. Partition of pipeline phases is not at random but with some principle. Firstly, coupling degree of different phase should be relatively low so that threads in different phases could run concurrently. Secondly, depth of pipeline should be proper because too flat can't bring much parallelism and too deep will cause much scheduling cost.

Open KETA uses a managed buffer (MB) to transfer some control structures among all the phases. Furthermore, a software cache data cache (DC) is used to cache objects to reduce the times of disk access. DC and MB are initialized by a main thread as open KETA is loading. The framework of open KETA is presented in Figure 2. Main task of each phase is stated as followed:

- Accept phase is responsible for listening to the port. Applied with HTTP 1.1, once it finds a new arrived request which doesn't belong to an existing socket it will create a new socket and set up connection, else if the socket is still keep alive, the request will stride over the accept phase and go to receive phase directly.
- Receive phase checks the completeness of http request and judges whether it's a static request. If not it will be redirected to web server in user space such as Apache. Here the socket the request belongs to is thrown to the socket list of user space web server directly in order to avoid the cost of recreating and destroying socket. If the arrived request is a static one, it is inserted to the task list of Data process phase.
- Data process phase first validates requests and then judges whether the object requested is in DC or not by a hash map, if yes the response message is generated. It is worth saying that the response head is stored in DC as long as the object is in DC so that the response message can reuse the response head. Once the object is not hashed in DC, get it from disk. If the conflict list of hash table is full or DC doesn't have enough space, some object will be

washed out from DC. The management of DC is based on the Buddy system but something different is a block chain which is used to manage the space effectively and avoid the forming of fragments.

● Just as its name implies, send phase sends the object back to clients. Open KETA utilizes Zero Copy which FreeBSD supports to reduce copy times and improve sending efficiency.

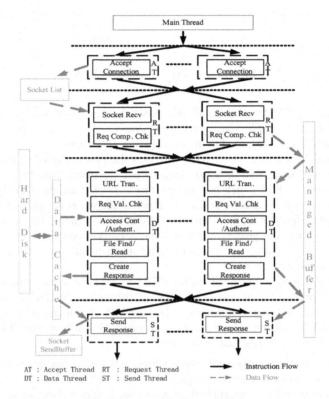

Fig. 2. Framework of open KETA

In order to guarantee the real time service, all thread pools are initialized by a main thread when open KETA is loading. The number of thread is set empirically in a configuration file. As to the activation of threads of each phase, there are two ways in common: One is that a scheduler is specialized in this work in each thread group. After the execution, thread in previous group passes the result to the scheduler in this group. The scheduler will choose a thread based on some special rule. This method is extendable in implementation but the scheduler may be the bottleneck. Another way is that thread chooses the next-phase thread itself based on some rule. The advantage of this method is that cost of copy and control can be reduced greatly but thread scheduling of each group is not transparent to other groups. Considering that open KETA is implemented in kernel, efficiency may be more important, so the latter is chosen and MB is used to transfer all control structures. When a thread has finished one task, it will check whether there are some unsettled tasks in task list, if yes the thread continues to process another task else it will sleep and not wake up until thread in previous phases activate it.

From what is afore-mentioned, thread number of each phase is set from a configuration file when open KETA is loading. Actually, this number many be varied to fit different load conditions. When size of requested objects is large and open KETA need disk access in high frequency, data process phase would be the bottleneck of the pipeline; when most objects can be cached in DC, send phase would be the bottleneck. So in order to smooth the running of the pipeline, more threads should be allocated to bottleneck phase. In our previous work [18], we use a feedback control approach to adjust thread number based on the queue length of each phase and server utilization rate. But these guidelines seem not sufficient; What's more, the drawback of pure feedback-based control is that it is a reactive approach, where corrections are made only after disturbances have had a chance to influence the system. Therefore, a feed-forward prediction is used to augment the feedback loop in this paper. The design of Feed-forward/Feedback Model will be presented in the following section.

4 Design of Feed-Forward/Feedback Model

The architecture of the feed-forward/feedback model is shown in Figure 3. The predictor is placed on the feedforward path to make estimates of per-phase thread allocation, it computes the thread number N^f for each pipeline phase from the processing rate and queue length of each phase regarding the past arrival pattern. Several feedback control loops adjust this allocation in response to measured per-phase processing delay deviation that due to inaccuracy of the predictor and compute a corrected value N^b. The objective of this model is to smooth the running of the pipeline. Since the more balanced the processing delay of all phases is, the more

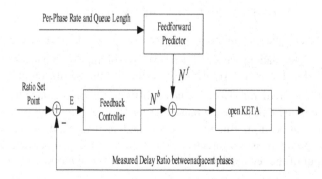

Fig. 3. The feedback control loop augmented with feedforward predictor

potential the pipeline have, all that the predictor and the feedback controller should do is to achieve this balance among all pipeline phases by adjusting the thread allocation. $N = N^f + N^b$ is the final value of the thread number. The design of the feed-forward predictor and the feedback controller will be described below in detail.

4.1 The Feedforward Predictor

In order to provide an efficient feed-forward prediction, it is important to have an accurate model of the processing delay of each phase. Consider there are four phases in the pipeline, the queue length and processing rate of phase i in the kth sampling time are $L_i(k)$ and $V_i(k)$, so the total number of requests that phase i need to process during the (k+1) th sampling time is $L_i(k)$ plus that phase i-1 will insert. $N_i(k)$ is the current thread number of phase I, by changing the thread number of phase i from $N_i(k)$ to $N_i^f(k+1)$, the processing rate may change from $V_i(k)$ to $\frac{V_i(k)}{N_i(k)}N_i^f(k+1)$. To achieve the balance afore-mentioned, the following equations should be satisfied.

$$\left.\begin{array}{c}
\frac{\lambda \Delta t}{\frac{V_0(k)}{N_0(k)}N_0^f(k+1)} = \frac{L_1 + \frac{V_0(k)}{N_0(k)}N_0^f(k+1)\Delta t}{\frac{V_1(k)}{N_1(k)}N_1^f(k+1)} \\
\frac{L_1 + \frac{V_0(k)}{N_0(k)}N_0^f(k+1)\Delta t}{\frac{V_1(k)}{N_1(k)}N_1^f(k+1)} = \frac{L_2 + \frac{V_1(k)}{N_1(k)}N_1^f(k+1)\Delta t}{\frac{V_2(k)}{N_2(k)}N_2^f(k+1)} \\
\frac{L_2 + \frac{V_1(k)}{N_1(k)}N_1^f(k+1)\Delta t}{\frac{V_2(k)}{N_2(k)}N_2^f(k+1)} = \frac{L_3 + \frac{V_2(k)}{N_2(k)}N_2^f(k+1)\Delta t}{\frac{V_3(k)}{N_3(k)}N_3^f(k+1)}
\end{array}\right\} \tag{1}$$

Accept phase is the first phase and does not have task list, so the requests it will process during the (k+1) th sampling time are $\lambda \Delta t$, Δt is sampling interval. Let M be the total capacity of the server, so

$$N_0^f(k+1)+N_1^f(k+1)+N_2^f(k+1)+N_3^f(k+1)=M \tag{2}$$

There are four equations in the four unknowns, $N_i^f(k+1)$, i=0, 1, 2, 3 (0 for accept, 1 for receive, 2 for data process, 3 for send). By solving these equations, we can get the desired value for $N_i^f(k+1)$, which describe the thread allocation of each phase suggested by the predictor. These values constitute the predictor output. Ideally, we hope the processing delay of each phase during the next sampling time will be equal through above allocation. But in the combined feed-forward/feedback model, the output of the predictor is not directly applied. Instead it is mathematically combined with the output of the feedback controller $N_i^b(k+1)$ whose purpose is to adjust for the deviation in resource allocation as described next.

4.2 The Feedback Controller

The main short-coming of the feed-forward predictor is the fact that the actual per-phase processing rates of the future requests are unknown. As mentioned above, all estimations are based on past measurement (per-phase processing rate). To deal with this uncertainty and to improve the performance of open KETA, several feedback controllers are added. These controllers use feedback from processing rate of each phase in last sampling point.

The control action is computed from the difference, E, between the measurements of the processing delay ratio between adjacent phases and the set-point 1. For one controller is used for every pair of adjacent phases, three controllers are needed for these four pipeline phases. At every sampling time k, the loop measures the deviation in the delay ratio $\frac{T_i(k)}{T_{i-1}(k)}$ (i = 1, 2, 3) from the ideal target 1.The performance error is therefore defined as $E_i(k) = 1 - \frac{T_i(k)}{T_{i-1}(k)}$. If the feed-forward predictor is ideal, the ratio $\frac{N^f_i(k)}{N^f_{i-1}(k)}$ of threads allocated to the two phases will be such that no error is observed. However, in general, the predictor is only approximate, causing a finite error to develop. The controllers are proportional, integral (PI) controller implemented according to the formula:

$$\frac{N_i^b(k+1)}{N_{i-1}{}^b(k+1)} = \frac{N_i^b(k)}{N_{i-1}{}^b(k)} + g_i(E_i(k+1) - r_i E_i(k)) \tag{3}$$

$$\frac{N_i^b(0)}{N_{i-1}{}^b(0)} = 1$$

where g and r are controller design parameters known as the controller gain and zero, respectively. To combine the predictor and the controller, we simple add their outputs:

$$N_i(k+1) = N_i^f(k+1) + N_i^b(k+1) \tag{4}$$

Together with the total capacity condition

$$N_0(k+1) + N_1(k+1) + N_2(k+1) + N_3(k+1) = M \tag{5}$$

From equation 3, 4, 5, all unknowns can be solved.

g_i and r_i were pre-calculated for different adjacent phases using simple step response experiments. Small changes of the server sped were applied. It was observed how the processing delay of each phase was influenced. These experiments help to compute g_i and r_i.

5 Experimental Evaluation

5.1 Comparison of Open KETA with Other Web Servers

Open KETA is implemented in FreeBSD 5.3 kernel. In order to compare its performance with other web servers, we have done some experiments under different loads. In view of open KETA's nature, all experiments are carried out only with static requests. The testing environment is made up of one server and three or five clients which are described next:

Server: SMP with two xeon 2.0G hz cpus,2GB memory, 36G SCSI hard disk and 1000M network card;
Clients: 2.4G hz cpu, 512M memory, 40GB 5400 rpm hard disk and 10-100M adaptive network card;

We use a testing tool SPECWeb99 to generate web work-loads in our experiments which is commonly used to evaluate the performance of web servers. Platforms for evaluated web servers are Apache, open KETA in FreeBSD 5.3, Apache, Tux, and Zeus in Redhat Enterprise Linux v3.0. Note that the results of Table1, 2, 3 for open KETA do not include the feed-forward/feedback model.

Table 1. Results of 300 concurrent connections (3 clients)

Tested object	Mean response time(ms)	Weighted bandwidth (bps)	Valid+ Invalid	Confor- ming	Opera- tions per second
Apache(freebsd)	410.0	303272.69	300+0	50	761
Apache(Redhat)	382.2	313600.49	300+0	56	765
Tux	320.4	373585.24	300+0	300	907
Zeus	342.5	357853.37	300+0	300	855
Open KETA	307.0	389930.76	300+0	300	954

When the concurrent connections are 1000, client may be the bottleneck (due to 10-100M network card), so more clients are used.

We can see from the results, the performance of open KETA is much better than the web servers listed above. A simultaneous connection is considered conforming to the required bit rate if its aggregate bit rate is more than 320,000 bits/second, or 40,000 bytes/second. Other guidelines can be easily understood by their name.

Table 2. Results of 600 concurrent connections (3 clients)

Tested object	Mean response time (ms)	Weighted bandwidth (bps)	Valid +Invalid	Confor-ming	Opera-tions per second
Apache (freebsd)	719.3	166083.41	600+0	0	771
Apache (Redhat)	758.2	157416.85	600+0	0	769
Tux	456.1	261535.11	600+0	600	1296
Zeus	536.1	228577.33	600+0	600	1100
Open KETA	352.4	356495.45	600+0	600	1702

Table 3. Results of 1000 concurrent connections (5 clients)

Tested object	Mean response time (ms)	Weighted bandwidth (bps)	Valid+ Invalid	Conforming	Opera-tions per second
Apache (freebsd)	1077.7	110974.79	983+17	0	773
Apache (Redhat)	1247.2	95514.28	989+11	0	750
Tux	791.1	150558.99	999+1	678	1244
Zeus	992.5	126145.36	996+4	565	987
Open KETA	437.7	290117.36	1000+0	35	2285

5.2 Experimental Results for the Feed-Forward/Feedback Model

The URL requests generating rate of SPECWeb99 is influenced by the server load. This character makes it unable to reflect the benefit adequately which the feed-forward/feedback model brings. So we use another testing tool Benchmark Factory to show the real performance of the model. Benchmark Factory allows to Specifies a predetermine rate to send transactions to a server without waiting for a response from a client. For example, if the InterArrival time is 1000ms, a transaction is sent to a server once every 1000ms, resulting in 1 TPS for that transaction.

The main thread of open KETA is responsible for the information collection and thread allocation in each sampling interval. Figure 4 and figure 5 present the TPS (Transactions per Second) comparison of open KETA without feed-forward/feedback model and with feed-forward/feedback model. The feed-forward/ feedback model helps to enhance open KETA's performance obviously.

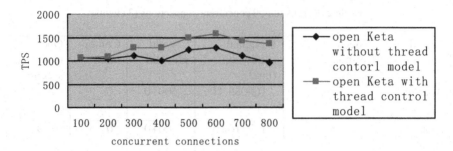

Fig. 4. TPS comparison (with VS without thread control model)

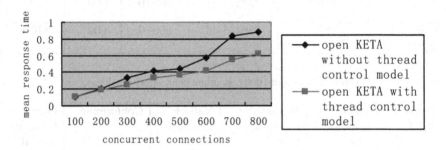

Fig. 5. Mean response time comparison (with VS without thread control model)

6 Conclusion

In this paper, we proposed the pipeline framework of a kernel web server open KETA. This architecture can reduce parallelism granularity effectively so that the resource of a web server can be utilized fully. Furthermore, we experimentally investigated the benefits of combing a feed-forward predictor with a feedback controller architecture in the context of achieving pipeline phases' balance of open KETA. The results showed in section 5 validate the predominance of open KETA and the effectiveness of the feed- forward/feedback model.

References

1. SHAN Zhi-Guang, LIN CHuang et. al. Web Quality of Service :A survey. JOURNAL OF COMPUTERS, Feb, 2004.
2. C. Huitema. Network vs. server issues in end-to-end performance. Keynote speech at Performance and Architecture of Web Servers 2000, Santa Clara, CA. http://kkant.ccwebhost.com/PAWS2000/huitema _keynote.ppt.
3. J. Gray and P. Shenoy. Rules of thumb in data engineering. In Proc. of IEEE 16th Int'l Conf. on Data Engineering, pages 3-10, San Diego, CA, Apr. 2000.
4. Valeria Cardellini, Emiliano Casalicchio. The State of the Art in Locally Distributed Web-server Systems. IBM research report, Computer Science, RC22209 (W0110-048) October 16, 2001.

5. Philippe Joubert, Robert King, Richard Neves, Mark Russinovich, andJohn Tracey. High-performance memory-baxde Web servers:Kernel and user-space performance. In Proceedings of the USENIX 2001 Annual Technical Conference, 2001.
6. Tim Brecht, David Pariag, Louay Gammo.In:Proceedings of the USENIX 2004 Annual Technical Conference:General Track, June,2004.
7. Arjan wan de Ven. kHTTPd Linux http accelerator. http://www.fenrus.demon.nl.
8. Rob von Behren, Jeremy Condit, and Eric Brewer. Why events are a bad idea for high-concurrency servers. In 9th Workshop on Hot Topics in Operating Systems (HotOS IX),2003.
9. The Apache Group. Apache http server project. http://www.apache.org.
10. Vivek S.Pai, Peter Druschel,and Willy Zwaenepoel. Flash:An efficient and portable Web server. In Proceedings of the USENIX 1999 Annual Technical Conference, Monterey,CA,June 1999.
11. Red Hat, Inc. TUX 2.2 Reference Manual, 2002.
12. T. F. Abdelzaher, K. G. Shin, and N. Bhatti. Performance guarantees for web server end-systems: A controltheoretical approach. IEEE Transactions on Parallel and Distributed Systems, January 2002.
13. C. Lu, T. Abdelzaher, J. Stankovic, and S. Son. A feedback control approach for guaranteeing relative delays in web servers. In IEEE Real-Time Technology and Applications Symposium, June 2001.
14. J. A. Stankovic, T. He, T. F. Abdelzaher, M. Marley, G. Tao,S. H. Son, and C. Lu. Feedback control scheduling in distributed systems. In IEEE Real-Time Systems Symposium ,London, UK, December 2001.
15. Dan Henriksson, Ying Lu, Tarek Abdelzaher. Improved prediction for web server delay control. In IEEE Real-Time Systems Symposium, 2004.
16. B. Krishnamurthy and J. Rexford. Web Protocols and Practices:HTTP/1.1, Networking Protocols, Caching, and Traffic Measurement. Addison-Wesley,2001
17. A. Feldmann. Web performance characteristics. IETF plenary. http://www.research.att.com/anja/feldmann /papers.html.
18. LI Shan-Shan, LIAO Xiang-Ke, LIU Jin-Yuan. Dynamic Thread Management in Kernel Pipeline Web Server. The IFIP Network and Parallel Conference, 2005.
19. Tarek F.Abdelzaher; Nina Bhatti. Web server QOS management by adaptive content delivery.

Variants of Priority Scheduling Algorithms for Reducing Context-Switches in Real-Time Systems

Biju K. Raveendran[*], K. Durga Prasad, Sundar Balasubramaniam[**],
and S. Gurunarayanan

BITS, Pilani,Rajasthan, India – 333031
{biju, f2001287, sundarb, sguru}@bits-pilani.ac.in

Abstract. In systems with power constraints, context switches in a task schedule result in wasted power consumption. We present variants of priority scheduling algorithms – Rate Monotonic and Earliest Deadline First - that reduce the number of context switches in a schedule. We prove that our variants output feasible schedules whenever the original algorithms do. We present experimental results to show that our variants significantly reduce the number of context switches. Our results also show that the number of context switches in the schedules output by these algorithms is close to the minimum possible number.

Keywords: Real time systems, scheduling, low power, preemption, and context switches.

1 Introduction

Power consumption is a limiting factor in most real-time embedded systems, due to limited battery life. This issue has been addressed at various levels – at the architectural level (e.g. DVS, DFS, caching), at the systems level (e.g. process management, memory management, compilation techniques), and at the applications level (e.g. data structures and algorithm design). At the operating systems level, there have been three primary approaches to address the power consumption problem: process scheduling techniques [1-13], paging systems [14], and performance tuning [15].

Various scheduling algorithms have been proposed to exploit energy-saving techniques at hardware level such as Dynamic Voltage Scaling and Dynamic Frequency Scaling [2, 3]. There are other scheduling algorithms that use support from memory hierarchy features [4], or compilers [5] to reduce power consumption. Most of these power-aware scheduling techniques are dependent on platform-specific features such as clocks, device characteristics, or memory technologies.

One architecture-independent factor that affects power consumption of a process schedule is the cost of pre-emptions (or context switches) [16]. Context switch

---

[*] Supported by Microsoft Research, India through a Ph.D. research fellowship.
[**] Supported by Microsoft Research, India through the Embedded Systems research grant 2004-06.

S. Chaudhuri et al. (Eds.): ICDCN 2006, LNCS 4308, pp. 466–478, 2006.

duration is a hidden, unproductive duration in a schedule. Context switch duration includes the time taken for saving the context of the current process / thread and loading the context of the next process / thread. Typically, the duration of a context switch between threads is less than that between processes but even the former is not insignificant. For the rest of the paper, we assume that we are referring to process contexts, but most of the issues related to context switching between processes are applicable for threads as well.

Various factors specific to the architecture and the operating system affect the context switch duration. For instance, the impact of register sets, floating point units, and caching schemes on context switch times have been reported in [17] and [18]. Gooch [18] also refers to the impact of the process queue on context switching time – in particular, the strong correlation between context switch time and the length of the run (process) queue. The direct impact of context switches in a schedule is the time spent in the act of context switching [15]. This time – dependent on the specific architecture and the operating system – is small but not insignificant. The number of context switches in a schedule may add up to a significant delay in the execution of a process and thus affect its schedulability. The total time spent in context switches would also result in wasted power consumption. An indirect but more significant impact of context switches could be due to data movement across the memory hierarchy i.e. cache block replacement and page replacement in RAM. In fact, the additional energy consumption due to this indirect impact has been reported to be significantly higher [6][15].

The amount of energy wasted due to context switches in a schedule is proportional to the product of the number of context switches in the schedule and the average impact of a context switch. A power-aware scheduling algorithm should account for the impact of context switches on power consumption. We address this issue through variants of priority scheduling algorithms (Rate Monotonic and Earliest Deadline First) that reduce the number of context switches in a schedule. Several scheduling algorithms have been designed to be preemption-aware, i.e. they reduce the number of preemptions or context-switches. We discuss these algorithms in Section 2. In Section 3, we describe our approach to reduce the number of context switches in a schedule and we present variants of well-known priority-scheduling algorithms – RM and EDF. In Section 4, we prove the correctness of our algorithms. In Section 5, we present experimental results to demonstrate the effectiveness of our algorithms in reducing context switches. In Section 6 we conclude.

2 Related Work

Various techniques have been proposed in the literature for reducing the number of context switches in a schedule. The techniques vary in complexity from simple, inexpensive heuristics to exhaustive search. Some techniques attempt to reduce the number of context switches while others address the indirect impact of context switches by reducing data movement in memory hierarchy.

In [7], Oh and Yang propose a variant of the Least Laxity First Algorithm to reduce context switches in a schedule. When there is tie in the laxity between two processes the modified LLF algorithm continues the execution of the active process while

3 Algorithms

Our approach to context switch reduction is similar to the one used in [7] and [12]: defer the preemption of an active process when it can be guaranteed that any process that is delayed will not miss its deadline. But the heuristics in MLLF and MMUF are weak. MLLF defers preemption only when there is a tie in the priority (i.e. laxity in this case) to begin with. The priority of the delayed process is frozen for the extension period. But if a higher priority process could have been delayed without missing the deadline, MLLF would not do this. MMUF uses the same heuristic as MLLF. Thus in the best-case scenario, MLLF and MMUF perform as well as EDF but no better.

We adopt a more aggressive approach that considers deferrals even in the presence of higher priority processes – without affecting the schedulability of the delayed processes. Our heuristic maximizes the extension period of the active process by considering the deadlines of all processes in the ready queue whose priority is same as or higher than the active process. Based on this heuristic, we present a scheduling algorithm (RCSS) parameterized by a priority function. By choosing the appropriate priority function, variants of EDF (named EDF_RCS) and of RM (named RM_RCS) are obtained from our algorithm. Schedulability of tasks is preserved by these variants i.e. the variant (say RM_RCS) is optimal if and when the original algorithm (say RM) is optimal. We present the algorithms below. We use the following notation in the algorithms:

readyQ(t) : the ready queue at time t ordered by priority.
deadline(J) : deadline of a job J.
period(J) : period of a job J (i.e period of task T, where J is an instance of T).
execution_time(J) : execution time of a job J.
remaining_time(J,t) : execution time of a job J still remaining at time t.
slack(J,t) : deadline(J) – t – remaining_time(J,t)

Algorithm Reduced Context Switches Scheduling (RCSS)
Input:
A list L of tasks *T1, T2, ... Tn*, their periods and execution times.
A priority function *priority*, that is job-level fixed.
Assumptions:
Arrival times for first instances of all tasks are assumed to be 0.
period(J) for a job *J* is the same as *period(T)* where *J* is an instance of task *T*.
For each job J, it is assumed that   *deadline(J) = arrival_time(J) + period(J)*.
Output:
A feasible schedule for L or failure.
begin
Let *Cur* be the job with the highest priority; **schedule** *Cur*;
For every time unit *t* when there is at least one **arrival** or a **departure** or a **deferred switch**:
Let *J* be the job with the highest priority in *readyQ(t)*
if (*Cur* is to depart)
    then *Cur = J* ; **schedule** *Cur*;
        else if (*priority(Cur) >= priority(J)*)
          then **continue** with *Cur*;
          else *ExtensionTime_Cur = extension_time(Cur, t)*;
                if (*ExtensionTime_Cur==0*)
        then **preempt** *Cur*; *Cur = J*; **schedule** *Cur*;
                else if (*ExtensionTime_Cur > 0*)
            then   mark a **deferred switch** at *t + ExtensionTime_Cur*;
                continue with *Cur* upto *t + ExtensionTime_Cur*;
else *fail*;
end RCSS

// This function computes the maximum time period up to which each of the queued
//jobs can be deferred; the minimum of these deferral times is the period for which the
//current job can be continued.

function int extension_time(current_job, t)
begin

Let $j1, j2, ..., jm$ be the jobs in *readyQ(t)* such that
$priority(j1) >= priority(j2) >= ... >= priority(jm) >= priority(current\_job)$
return $min_i[slack(j_i, t) - \Sigma_{k<i}(remaining\_time(j_k,t)+ceil((deadline(j_i)-$
$deadline(j_k))/period(j_k))*execution\_time(j_k))]$;

end extension_time

Variants of Rate Monotonic (RM) scheduling algorithm and Earliest Deadline First
(EDF) are easily obtained from the above algorithm (RCSS) by specifying the priority
function. They are given below:

Algorithm Rate Monotonic with Reduced Context Switches (RM_RCS)
Input: A list L of tasks $T1, T2, ... Tn$, their periods and execution times.
Assumptions: Same as in Algorithm RCSS
Output: A feasible schedule if L is RM-schedulable, failure otherwise.
  begin
          (1) Define the priority function as $priority(J) = H / period(T)$
      where T is a task in L, J is a job (instance) of T, and H is the hyper-period for L.
          (2) Execute RCSS.
end RM_RCS

Algorithm Earliest Deadline First with Reduced Context Switches (EDF_RCS)
Input: A list L of tasks $T1, T2, ... Tn$, their periods and execution times.
Assumptions: Same as in Algorithm RCSS
Output: A feasible schedule if L is schedulable, failure otherwise.
  begin
          (1) Define the priority function as   *priority (J) =   -1 * deadline(J)*   for any
job J
          (2) Execute RCSS.
end EDF_RCS.

Note on EDF_RCS
Observe that in this case the *fail* statement in Algorithm RCSS will never be reached
if the input L has a feasible schedule. Also, the extension time for any job may be
increased further by replacing the use of *ceil* with the use of *floor* in the function
extension_time(), without affecting feasibility.
End of Note.

We explain the working of our algorithm (EDF_RCS) with the help of an example.
  Consider the following list of tasks (Table 1):

Table 1. Task List **(L)**

Task	Arri. Time (for the first instance)	Period	Exec. Time
T1	0	4	1
T2	0	5	2
T3	0	20	7

Note
This job list is derived from Table 1 under our assumption deadline(J) = arrival_time(J) + period(J) for any job J. These jobs are arranged in the order of deadline and when the deadline is same, in the order of arrival – as this is the likely arrangement of a queue.
End of Note.

Table 2. Job list corresponding to L in Table 1 (Hyper-period = 20)

Job (Task)	Arri. Time	Exec. Time	Deadline
J1 (T1)	0	1	4
J2 (T2)	0	2	5
J3 (T1)	4	1	8
J4 (T2)	5	2	10
J5 (T1)	8	1	12
J6 (T2)	10	2	15
J7 (T1)	12	1	16
J8 (T3)	0	7	20
J9 (T2)	15	2	20
J10 (T1)	16	1	20

We illustrate the working of EDF_RCS with this list of jobs.

- At time t=0, the jobs in the ready queue are J1, J2, and J8 with priorities –4, –5, and –20 respectively. So, EDF_RCS schedules J1 for 1unit.
- At t=1, the ready queue has J2 and J8; J2 is scheduled.
- At t=3, J8 is the only process in the ready queue and is scheduled.
- At t=4, J3 arrives and has a higher priority (–8) than the active process J8 (–20). So EDF_RCS computes extension_time(J8,t) as follows:

extension_time(J8,t) = slack(J3, t) = deadline(J3) – t – remaining_time(J3)
= 8 – 4 – 1   = 3.

Thus EDF_RCS decides to continue J8 for up to 3 more units of time.

- At t=5, J4 arrives with priority (–10). EDF_RCS calculates the extension time as follows:

extension_time(J8,t) = min [slack(J3,t), slack(J4,t) –remaining_time(J3,t)– floor((deadline(J4)– deadline(J3))/period(J3))*execution_time(J3)]
= min[8 – 5 – 1, 10 – 5 – 2 – 1 – 0] = 2
So, J8 will be extended up to t + extension_time i.e. up to 5+2 = 7.

All subsequent decisions are EDF decisions. The final schedule for this example is as in Fig 1:

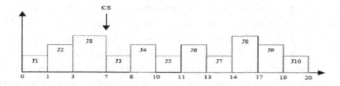

Fig. 1. Schedule by EDF_RCS (or RM_RCS) for task list in Table 1

Observe that EDF_RCS outputs a schedule with just one context switch. For this particular example, RM_RCS also outputs the same schedule i.e. the number of context switches is 1. As opposed to this RM produces the schedule in Fig. 2 (number of context switches = 5), EDF produces the schedule in Fig 3. (number of context switches = 3) and MLLF produces the schedule in Fig. 4 (number of context switches = 3). Furthermore, the minimum possible number of context switches in a feasible schedule is 1 for this task set (this can be verified easily). This example demonstrates that RM_RCS and EDF_RCS are aggressive in eliminating context switches whenever possible while the other algorithms are not. Our experimental results (shown in Section 5) confirm this argument.

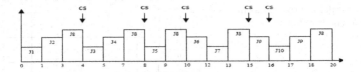

Fig. 2. Schedule by RM for task list in Table 1

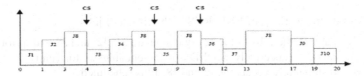

Fig. 3. Schedule by EDF for task list in Table 1

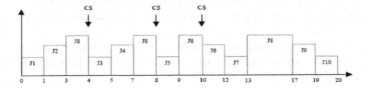

Fig. 4. Schedule by MLLF for task list in Table 1

4 Optimality of the Algorithms

We prove that our heuristic preserves optimality of scheduling decisions i.e. RM_RCS and EDF_RCS are optimal if and when RM and EDF (respectively) are optimal. For the purpose of the proofs we introduce some notations here.

- A schedule S is a sequence of runs of the form (id, start time, end time).
- When we want to identify some runs of a schedule but ignore others, we use:
  ((R1, t1, u1), S1, (R2,t2,u2), S2, …, Sn-1, (Rn,tn,un), Sn)
  where each triple (Ri, ti, ui) is a run starting at ti and ending at ti+ui whereas each Si is a sequence of runs – possibly empty – occurring between runs (Ri-1,ti-1, ui-1) and (Ri,ti,ui).
- We use NCS(S) to denote the number of context switches in a schedule S.

Theorem 1
If a task set is RM-schedulable, then RM_RCS outputs a schedule with no more context switches than the schedule output by RM.

Proof

Let S be the job set for the given task set. We show that the schedule generated by RM_RCS for S is feasible, if there is a feasible schedule generated by RM for S. We consider each branch of the *if* statement in an iteration of the loop in Step(2):

Branch 1 or 2 or 3: It is easily observed that RCSS agrees with RM in these cases.

Branch 4: *Cur* can be extended up to *extension_time(Cur,t)*. RCSS extends the execution of *Cur*. This leads to two possibilities:

(a) Some future runs of Cur are merged into the current run possibly including a partial run. In this case, **by Lemma 1**, feasibility is invariant under this transformation and NCS(U) <= NCS(S).

(b) All future runs of Cur are merged into the current run. In this case, by **Corollary 1**, feasibility is invariant under this transformation and NCS(U') <= NCS(S).

Branch 5: RCSS fails but in this case rest of the jobs would not be schedulable by RM either.

Now, *by induction on the number of iterations of the loop*, we conclude that RM_RCS outputs a schedule that is feasible if RM outputs a feasible schedule. Furthermore, each iteration of the loop in Step(2) of RCSS will introduce no additional context switches than RM would.

End of Proof.

The following lemma stated informally as: *the extension step in RCSS – the step that continues the active process – does not affect schedulability* is used in the proof above.

Lemma 1

Let S be a feasible schedule: $((R1,t1,u1), S1, (R2,t2,u2), S2, ..., Sm-1, (Rm,tm,um), Sm)$ where all Ri, $1 <= i <= m$ are runs of the same job B. Assume S was generated by a priority scheduling algorithm.

Let U be the schedule $(((R1,R2...Rk-1,Rk'), t1, u1+u2+...+uk-1+uk'), S1, S2, Sk-1, (Rk'',tk+uk', uk-uk'), Sk, ... (Rm,tm,um), Sm)$, where some runs of B at the beginning of S have been merged into a single run, and one run (Rk), has been partly merged.

Assume   extension_time(B, t1+u1) >= (u2+u3+...uk-1+uk')   **(AS)**

Then U is feasible and NCS(U) <= NCS(S)

Proof (omitted due to lack of space)

Corollary 1 is a special case of Lemma 1, where all the runs of a particular job are merged into one.

Corollary 1

Let S be a feasible schedule $((R1, t1, u1), S1, (R2,t2,u2), S2, ..., Sm-1, (Rm,tm,um), Sm)$ where all Ri, $1 <= i <= m$ are runs of the same job B. Assume S was generated by a priority scheduling algorithm.

Let U' be the schedule $(((R1,R2...,Rm), t1, u1+u2+...+um), S1, S2, Sm)$ where all runs of B in S have been merged into a single run.

Assume that   extension_time(B, t1+u1)>= (u2+u3+...um).

Then U' is feasible and NCS(U') <= NCS(S)

Proof
By Lemma 1, with k=m and uk = uk'.
End of Proof.

Theorem 2. If a task set is EDF-schedulable, then EDF_RCS outputs a schedule with no more context switches than the schedule output by EDF.

Proof
Similar to the proof for Theorem 1 but with priority(J) = -1*deadline(J) for any job J.
End of Proof.

5   Evaluation of the Algorithms

Algorithmic Complexity
Every scheduling decision of RCSS is either a priority decision or an extension decision. In the former case, the time taken for decision is O(logN) where N is the number of tasks. The O(logN) factor arises because the ready queue has to be kept prioritized. When the scheduling decision requires the computation of extension period, the time taken is O(logN + m*m) where m is the number of jobs of higher priority than the active job. The worst case value for m is O(N). Thus the worst case response time of our scheduling algorithm is O(N*N). But in practice, the value of m is likely to be less than N. Particularly for high priority jobs, the value of m will be much less than N.

Experimental Results
We demonstrate the effectiveness of our algorithms in reducing context switches using simulation results. We compare the performance of our algorithms (RM_RCS, EDF_RCS) with that of RM and EDF under three different conditions: number of context switches versus utilization, number of context switches versus hyper-periods, and number of context switches versus number of tasks. The details of these comparisons are described below in Experiments 1, 2, and 3. In addition, we also compare the performance of our algorithms against a context switch minimization algorithm (MIN_CS) that always returns a feasible schedule with the least possible number of context switches. MIN_CS is implemented as an exhaustive search algorithm that inspects all schedules and outputs the feasible schedule with the minimum number of context switches. The details of these comparisons are described in Experiments 4, 5, and 6. The following are the experiments and their results:

Experiment 1.   Comparison of RM_RCS with RM and comparison of EDF_RCS with EDF. Number of task sets: 7;   Invariants: Utilization (100%)
Comments: Experiment Duration = LCM of hyper-periods of the task sets.
Performance: (**Fig. 5**). Both RM_RCS and EDF_RCS show huge reduction in the number of context switches in comparison with RM and EDF respectively. In all cases, it can be observed that the number of context switches decreases with increasing number of tasks.

Experiment 2. Comparison of RM_RCS with RM and comparison of EDF_RCS with EDF. Number of task sets: 8; Invariants: Utilization (100%), Number of tasks (5) Performance: (**Fig. 6**). Again, both RM_RCS and EDF_RCS show huge reduction in the number of context switches in comparison with RM and EDF respectively.

Experiment 3. Comparison of RM_RCS with RM and comparison of EDF_RCS with EDF. Number of task sets: 10; Invariants: Number of tasks (5) Comments: Experiment Duration = LCM of hyper-periods of the task sets. Performance: (**Fig. 7 & 8**). RM_RCS and EDF_RCS show substantial reduction in the number of context switches in comparison with RM and EDF respectively: close to 100% for low utilization (less than 0.7), about 80% for medium utilization (between 0.7 and 0.9), and about 50 to 60% for high utilization (more than 0.9). We show these reductions as ratios of the number of context switches (e.g. N (EDF_RCS) / N (EDF)) in **Fig. 8**. In all cases, it can be observed that the number of context switches increases exponentially with increasing utilization.

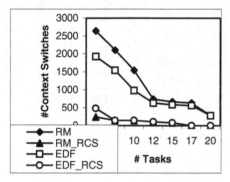

Fig. 5. # Tasks Vs # Context switches

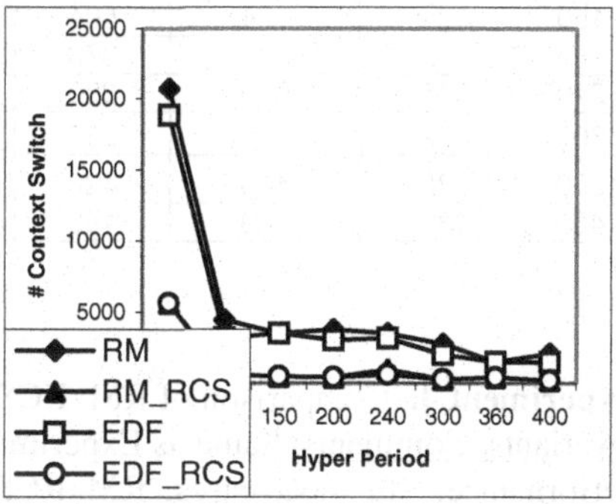

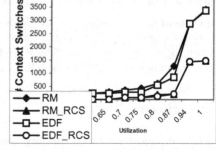

Fig. 6. Hyper-period Vs # Context switches

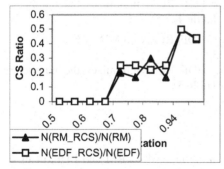

Fig. 7. Util. Vs Context switch Ratio

Fig. 8. Util. Vs # Context switches

476   B.K. Raveendran et al.

Table 3. Minimum # of Context switches (Varying number of tasks)

# Tasks	# Context Switches		
	RM_RCS	EDF_RCS	MIN_CS
5	240	480	240
8	140	140	140
10	140	140	140
12	105	105	105
15	84	84	84
17	0	0	0
20	0	0	0

Table 4. Minimum # Context switches

# Context Switches			
Hyp	RM_RCS	EDF_RCS	MIN_CS
40	5670	5670	5670
120	630	630	630
150	504	504	504
200	378	378	378
240	945	630	630
300	252	252	252
360	420	420	420
400	189	189	189

Table 5. Minimum # Context Switches

# Context Switches			
Util	RM_RCS	EDF_RCS	MIN_CS
0.5	0	0	0
0.55	0	0	0
0.6	0	0	0
0.65	0	0	0
0.7	70	70	70
0.75	70	70	70
0.8	180	120	120
0.87	210	210	210
0.94	1435	1435	1435
1	1470	1470	1470

Experiment 4. Comparison of RM_RCS and EDF_RCS with MIN_CS.
Invariants, Comments: Same as Experiment 1
Performance: In most cases, RM_RCS (or EDF_RCS) minimizes the number of context switches in a feasible schedule. (see **Table 3**).

Experiment 5. Comparison of RM_RCS and EDF_RCS with MIN_CS.
Invariants, Comments: Same as Experiment 2
Performance: In most cases, RM_RCS (or EDF_RCS) minimizes the number of context switches in a feasible schedule. (see **Table 4**).

Experiment 6. Comparison of RM_RCS and EDF_RCS with MIN_CS.
Invariants, Comments: Same as Experiment 3
Performance: In most cases, RM_RCS (or EDF_RCS) minimizes the number of context switches in a feasible schedule. (see **Table 5**).

6 Conclusion

We have designed variants of priority scheduling algorithms RM and EDF, using an aggressive preemption reduction heuristic. We have proved that these variants preserve the feasibility of schedules output by the original algorithms. Our experimental results show that our heuristic is highly effective in reducing context switches. Our variants not only vastly outperform other algorithms including other preemption reduction algorithms but also output schedules with the minimum possible number of context switches in most cases. The primary limitation of our algorithm is that the worst-case response time is quadratic in the number of tasks. We intend to experiment with tradeoffs in the computation time of the heuristic function – which is the bottleneck – with the reduction in the number of context switches. Our focus has been only on reducing the number of context switches. We would like to combine our approach with techniques for reducing cache impact of context switches so as to provide an effective approach to reduction in power consumed due to context switches.

References

1. H. Aydin, R. Melhem, D. Mosse, and P. Mejia-Alvarez, "Dynamic and aggressive scheduling techniques for power-aware real-time systems", Proceedings of the 22nd IEEE Real-Time Systems Symposium RTSS'01, Page: 95 – 105, Dec - 2001.
2. R. Xu, D. Mosse, and R. Melhem, "Minimizing Expected Energy in Real-time Embedded Systems", Proceedings of the 5th ACM international conference on Embedded software EMSOFT '05, Sep. 2005.
3. H. Chung-Hsing, U. Kremer, M. Hsiao, "Compiler-directed dynamic voltage/frequency scheduling for energy reduction in microprocessors", Proceedings of the International Symposium on Low power Electronics and Design, page 275-278, Aug. 2001.
4. M. Kandemir, G. Chen, W. Zhang, and I. Kolcu, "Data Space Oriented Scheduling in Embedded Systems", DATE'03, Proceedings of the conference on Design, Automation and Test in Europe , Page: 104-116, Mar. 2003.
5. D. Mosse, H. Aydin, B. Childers and R. Melhem, "Compiler-assisted dynamic power aware scheduling for real-time applications", In Workshop on Compilers and Operating Systems for Low Power, Oct. 2000.
6. C. G. Lee, J. Hahn, Y. M. Seo, S. L, Min, R. Ha, S. Hong, C. Y. Park, M. Lee, and C. S. Kim, "Analysis of cache-related preemption delay in fixed-priority preemptive scheduling", Proceedings of IEEE Transactions on Computers, page 700–713, Jun. 1998.
7. S. H. Oh, and S. M. Yang, "A Modified Least-Laxity-First Scheduling Algorithm for Real-Time Tasks", Proceedings of 5th International Conference on Real-Time Computing Systems and Applications, page 31 – 36, Oct. 1998.
8. W. Yun, and M. Saksena, "Scheduling fixed-priority tasks with preemption threshold", RTCSA'99, Proceedings of the 6th International Conference on Real-Time Computing Systems and Applications, page 328 – 335, Dec. 1999.
9. W. Yun, and M. Saksena, "Scalable real-time system design using preemption thresholds", Proceedings of the 21th IEEE Symposium on Real-Time Systems, page 25 – 34, Nov. 2000.
10. S. Lee, S. L. Min, C. S. Kim, C. G. Lee, and M. Lee, "Cache-Conscious Limited Preemptive Scheduling", Real-Time Systems, pages 257–282, Nov1999.
11. Z. Jianli and C. Chaitali, " System-Level Energy-Efficient Dynamic Tas Scheduling", Proceedings of the 42nd Annual Conference on Design Automation, page 628 – 631, Jun. 2005.
12. S. Vahid, T. Z. Saman, and N. Muhmoud, "A Modified Maximum Urgency First Scheduling Algorithm for Real-Time Tasks", Transactions on Engineering, Computing and Technology", page 19 – 23, Nov. 2005. http://enformatika.org/data/v9/v9-4.pdf

13. D. B. Stewart, and P. k. Khosla, "Real-Time Scheduling of Dynamically Reconfigurable Systems," *Proceedings of the IEEE International Conference on Systems Engineering*, page 139 – 142, Aug. 1991.
14. A. Lebeck, X. Fan, H. Zeng, C. Ellis, "Power Aware Page Allocation", *ACM SIGOPS*,Proceedings of the 9th International conference on Architectural support for programming languages and operating systems ASPLOS-IX ,page 105–116, Nov. 2000.
15. A. Acquaviva, L. Benini, and B. Ricco, "Energy Characterization of Embedded Real-Time Operating Systems", *ACM Computer Architecture News*, page 13-18, Dec -2001.
16. A.K. Mok, "Fundamental Design Problems of Distributed Systems for the Hard-Real-Time Environment," *Ph.D.Thesis*, Department of Electrical Engineering and Computer Science, Massachusetts Institute of Technology, Cambridge, Massachusetts, May 1983.
17. Bill Dittman "Strategied for Minimizing Context Switch Times in Large Register set Environment with Primary Focus on the PowerPC Architecture with Floating Point and AltiVec Extensions", Quadros Systems. http://www.rtxc.com/pdf/article_esd-conference_05-08-2004.pdf
18. Richard Gooch, "Linux Scheduler Benchmark Results", http://www.atnf.csiro.au/people/r gooch/benchmarks/linux-scheduler.html
19. Baldonado, M., Chang, C.-C.K., Gravano, L., Paepcke, A.: The Stanford Digital Library Metadata Architecture. Int. J. Digit. Libr. 1 (1997) 108–121.

Dynamic Path Shared Protection for Survivable Differentiated Reliable WDM Optical Networks

Lei Guo[1,2], Lemin Li[2], Jin Cao[2], Hongfang Yu[2], and Xuetao Wei[2]

[1] College of Information Science and Engineering, Northeastern University,
110004 Shenyang, China
[2] Key Lab of Broadband Optical Fiber Transmission and Communication Networks,
University of Electronic Science and Technology of China, 610054 Chengdu, China
`guolei@ise.neu.edu.cn`, `lml@uestc.edu.cn`, `caojin1981@163.com`
`yuhf@uestc.edu.cn`, `xuetao.wei@gmail.com`

Abstract. In WDM optical networks, the fiber links may share some common physical resources (e.g., cables, conduits) and the consequence is that they have the Correlated Link Failure Probability (CLFP), which denotes the probability of link l failure after link f fails. Based on $CLFP$, we propose a new dynamic survivable algorithm, called Differentiated Path Shared Protection (DPSP), to protect the double-link failures in WDM optical networks. In DPSP, each connection request can be assigned one working path and additional backup paths according to the differentiated reliable requirements of users. Compared to previous work, DPSP can obtain better performances in resource utilization ratio and blocking probability.

Keywords: WDM networks, differentiated reliability, Correlated Link Failure Probability (CLFP), double-link failures, path shared protection.

1 Introduction

In WDM optical networks, a wavelength channel has the transmission rate of over several gigabits per second [1]. If the fiber links fail, a lot of traffic may be blocked. Therefore, the protection design is very important for WDM optical networks. Previous works mostly investigate the single-link failure that is dominant in the WDM optical networks. The conventional protection schemes include dedicated protection, link shared protection, path shared protection, and segment shared protection [2-7], in which the path shared protection has the best resource utilization ratio.

With the size of networks keeps enlarging, the probability of risks become much higher, and thus the protection design for double-link failures has been considered in WDM optical networks [8-11]. In [12-14], the authors have investigated the double-link failures and presented the protection algorithms that is called Complete Path Shared Protection (CPSP). The basic idea of CPSP is to assign one working path and two link-disjoint backup paths to each connection

S. Chaudhuri et al. (Eds.): ICDCN 2006, LNCS 4308, pp. 479–490, 2006.

request. In the worst case, if the working path traverses a failed link and the first backup path traverses another failed link, the second backup path also can be available to transmit the traffic. It is obvious that CPSP is able to provide complete protection for double-link failures. In CPSP, the probability of link failure is assumed to be independent; that is, the failure of arbitrary link l and link t is not correlative. However, in actual networks the fiber links may have the relationships of correlated failures because they may share some common physical resources.

The relationship of correlated failures can be defined as Correlated Link Failure Probability (CLFP), written as:

$$CLFP(l|t) = F(l|t), \forall l, t \in L, l \neq t. \tag{1}$$

where L denotes the set of fiber links, and $F(l|t)$ denotes the probability of link l failure after link t fails, written as:

$$F(l|t) = F(l \cap t)/F(t) = F(l \cap t)/[1 - R(t)], \forall l, t \in L, l \neq t. \tag{2}$$

where $F(l \cap t)$ denotes the probability of simultaneous failure of link l and link t, and $R(t)$ denotes the reliability of link t. The probability $F(l \cap t)$ (between 0 and 1) can be obtained by the link failure detection based on the statistic experience. The link reliability $R(t)$ (between 0 and 1) can be determined by many environment factors (e.g., temperature, earthquake, humidity) and man-made factors (e.g., dredges up, fires). At the beginning period of the foundation of the network, $R(t)$ can be determined by the fiber component manufacturers. After several years, $R(t)$ can be estimated by the failure rate based on the past experience [15].

According to Eq.(1) and Eq.(2), we can observe that the value of $CLFP(l|t)$, $(l, t \in L, l \neq t)$ should be between 0 and 1. Bigger $CLFP(l|t)$ means higher probability of link l failure after link t fails, and smaller $CLFP(l|t)$ means lower probability of link l failure after link t fails.

Based on the idea of different Qualify-of-Protection (QoP) and users' requirements, previous works in [15-19] have investigated the differentiated reliable protection problem and proposed the corresponding algorithm to survive the single-link failure. The algorithm in [16] first computes a high reliable working path; if the reliability of the working path is not smaller than the users' requirement, the backup path is not needed; otherwise, the backup path should be needed. However, the algorithm in [16] assumes that there only exists the single-link failure and the link failure probability is independent; that is, $CLFP(l|t) = 0$, $(\forall l, t \in L, l \neq t)$. Therefore, the algorithm in [16] can not be suitable for double-link failures protection considering the relationships of correlated failures. However, the idea of differentiated reliability is sound and can be extended to our proposed algorithm in this paper, since the differentiated reliable protection can obtain better resource utilization ratio [16].

In [12-14], previous algorithm CPSP assigns one working path and two link-disjoint backup paths to each connection request. Although it can provide complete protection for double-link failures (i.e., 100% reliable protection), it has two main flaws (see subsection 2.2): 1) the assignment of two backup paths may lead to more reserved backup resources consumed; 2) if the degree of source node or destination node for a connection request is smaller than three (i.e., the network is not 3-connected), we cannot find three link-disjoint paths (one working path and two backup paths), and thus the connection request will be blocked [12-14]. Therefore, CPSP may have low resource utilization ratio and high blocking probability.

To overcome the two flaws of CPSP, in [20] the authors proposed a differentiated protection algorithm for double-link failures. However, the algorithm in [20] does not present some key issues in details, e.g., link-cost assignment with differentiated reliability, the policy of computing high reliable working and backup paths. Based on [20], in this paper we propose a new dynamic survivable algorithm, called Differentiated Path Shared Protection (DPSP), which considers the idea of differentiated reliable protection. DPSP can dynamically establish the connections according to the requirements of users, and thus compared to CPSP, it can save significant resources and reduce the blocking probability.

The rest of the paper is organized as follows. Section 2 is for problem statement. Section 3 proposes the procedures of DPSP in details. Section 4 presents the simulation results. Section 5 is for conclusions.

2   Problem Statement

2.1   Network Model

The network topology is $G(N, L, W)$ for a given survivable meshed WDM optical network, where N is the set of nodes, L is the set of bi-directional links, and W is the set of available wavelengths per fiber link. $|N|$, $|L|$ and $|W|$ denote the node number, the link number and the wavelength number, respectively. Connection requests arrive at the network dynamically, and there is only a connection request arrives at a time. We assume each required bandwidth is a wavelength channel and each node has the wavelength conversion (OEO) capacity. A minimal cost path algorithm, Dijkstra's algorithm, applies to compute the routes. The important notations and assumptions are introduced as follows.

$l \in L$: Bi-directional fiber link between a node pair in G.

$COST_l^*$: Dynamic cost of link l; it is determined by the current state of the network (e.g., free wavelengths, reserved wavelengths, paths' reliabilities).

WPn: Working path of connection n;

BP_n^1, BP_n^2: First and second backup path, respectively.

WW_l, FW_l, RW_l: Number of working wavelengths on link l, number of free wavelengths on link l, and number of reserved backup wavelengths on link l, respectively.

v_l^e : Set of connections whose working paths traverse link e and corresponding backup paths traverse link l.

$|S|$: Number of elements in set S.

482   L. Guo et al.

$R(l)$: Reliability of link l.
$CLFP(l|t)$: Defined as Eq.(1).
UR: Reliability required by users.

2.2 Routing Paths Selection

In this subsection, we present the routing paths selection of the previous scheme in [12-14] and our proposed scheme. The previous scheme does not consider the differentiated reliable protection, and it computes one working path and two link-disjoint backup for each connection request to provide complete reliable protection for double-link failures. Our proposed scheme considers the differentiated reliable protection based on $CLFP$, and it computes one working path, or one working path and one backup path, or one working path and two backup paths, for each connection request according to the reliabilities required by users. Therefore, our scheme can provide the satisfactory reliability to the users meanwhile it is able to save more resources. We give an illustration in Fig. 1, in which each link's reliability is assumed to be 0.98, all $CLFP$s are assumed to be 0.50, and UR is assumed to be 0.97.

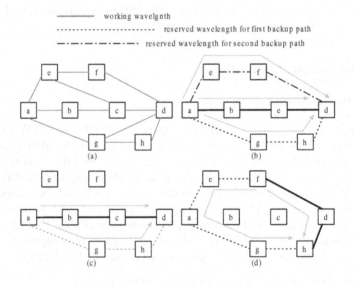

Fig. 1. Illustration for routing selection; assume reliability of each link is 0.98, all CLFPs are 0.50, and UR=0.97; a) network topology; b) routing selection without CLFP; c) routing selection with CLFP; d) a connection request with source node f and destination node h will be blocked by previous scheme, but it can be established by our scheme

Routing without differentiated reliable protection: For each connection request n, the previous scheme without differentiated reliable protection computes one working path and two link-disjoint backup paths. In Fig. 1(b), a connection with source node a and destination node d has been established. We can observe that the connection consumes nine wavelengths (three working wavelengths and six reserved backup wavelengths). Compare to our proposed scheme presented as follows, the previous scheme consumes more wavelength resources, and the consequence is that the resource utilization ratio will be low and the blocking probability will be high.

In Fig. 1(b), since the degree of nodes a and d is both three, there exists three link-disjoint paths (one working path and two link-disjoint backup paths). However, in Fig. 1(d), for the connection request with source node f and destination node h, since the degree of nodes f and h is both two, there only exists two link-disjoint paths ($f - d - h$ and $f - e - a - g - h$). Thus, the previous scheme cannot find three link-disjoint paths and this connection request will be blocked. Compare to our scheme presented as follows, this connection request can be established because the joint reliability of the working path and the backup path has already satisfied the users' requirements.

Routing with differentiated reliable protection: For an arbitrary lightpath denoted as LP_n (e.g., WP_n, BP_n^1, BP_n^2), the reliability can be written as:

$$R(LP_n) = \prod_{e \in LP_n} R(e). \tag{3}$$

The probability of LP_n failure can be written as:

$$F(LP_n) = 1 - R(LP_n) = 1 - \prod_{e \in LP_n} R(e). \tag{4}$$

Subject to double-link failures, the probability of BP_n^1 failure after WP_n fails (i.e., WP_n traverses a failed link and BP_n^1 traverses another failed link) can be written as:

$$F\left(BP_n^1 | WP_n\right) = \max_{t \in BP_n^1, e \in WP_n, t \neq e} [CLFP(t|e)]. \tag{5}$$

The probability of simultaneous failure of BP_n^1 and WP_n can be written as:

$$F\left(BP_n^1 \cap WP_n\right) = F(WP_n) \cdot F(BP_n^1 | WP_n) =$$
$$[1 - R(e)] \cdot \left\{\max_{t \in BP_n^1, e \in WP_n, t \neq e}[CLFP(t|e)]\right\}. \tag{6}$$

The joint reliability of BP_n^1 and WP_n can be written as:

$$R\left(BP_n^1, WP_n\right) = 1 - F\left(BP_n^1 \cap WP_n\right) =$$
$$1 - [1 - R(e)] \cdot \left\{\max_{t \in BP_n^1, e \in WP_n, t \neq e}[CLFP(t|e)]\right\}. \tag{7}$$

In this paper, we assume that there only exits double-link failures. In the worst case, if WP_n traverses a failed link and BP_n^1 traverses another failed link, BP_n^2

cannot fail simultaneously. Therefore, the probability of simultaneous failure of WP_n, BP_n^2, and BP_n^2 can be assumed to be zero, and the joint reliability of WP_n, BP_n^2, and BP_n^2 and can be written as:

$$R\left(BP_n^2, BP_n^1, WP_n\right) = 100\%. \tag{8}$$

Based on the above analysis, for a connection request n, we can compute the routing paths as follows:

Step1: Compute one working path. If and only if

$$R\left(WP_n\right) \geq UR. \tag{9}$$

accept the request and establish the connection; otherwise, go to Step 2.

Step2: Compute the first backup path. If and only if

$$R\left(BP_n^1, WP_n\right) \geq UR. \tag{10}$$

accept the request and establish the connection; otherwise, go to Step 3.

Step3: Compute the second backup path.

For the connection request with source node a and destination node d shown in Fig. 1(b), we first compute one working path $a-b-c-d$ and obtain $R(WP_n) = 0.94 < UR$, so that we need to compute the backup path. If the first backup path $a - g - h$ has been found, we can get $R(BP_n^1, WP_n) = 0.97 = UR$ in Fig. 1(c). Then, the reliability of the connection satisfies the users' requirement, and we need not compute the second backup path. We can find that, in Fig. 1(c), the connection only consumes six wavelengths (three working wavelengths and three reserved backup wavelengths). Compared to the previous scheme in Fig. 1(b), our scheme saves more wavelengths, and more free wavelengths can be used by the following requests, and the consequence is that the blocking probability can be reduced.

In Fig. 1(d), for a connection request with source node f and destination node h, since the degree of nodes f and h is both two, the previous scheme cannot find three link-disjoint paths and will block this connection. However, our scheme will not block this connection since $R(BP_n^1, WP_n) = 0.98 > UR$ if the working path $f - d - h$ and the first backup path $f - e - a - g - h$ have both been found. Compared to the previous scheme, in node-degree constraints, our scheme has lower blocking probability.

Comparison of two schemes: Comparing the two routing paths selection schemes, it is obvious that our scheme has tow advantages: 1) less backup paths assignment that will lead to fewer reserved wavelengths consumed and higher resource utilization ratio; 2) lower connections blocking probability in node-degree constraints. Therefore, our scheme has better resource utilization ratio and lower blocking probability than the previous scheme. We evaluate the performances in section 4 and find that the results are promising.

2.3   Reserved Backup Wavelength Assignment

For arbitrary link l, according to [14] the reserved backup wavelengths can be written as:

$$TRW_l = \max\{|v_l^t| + |v_l^t - v_l^e|, \forall t, e \in L, t \neq e \neq l\}. \tag{11}$$

The difference between TRW_l and RW_l is that TRW_l is the reserved backup resources on link l with n connections while RW_l is the reserved backup resources on link l with $(n-1)$ connections.

2.4   Link-Cost Assignment

Computing the working path: Assume connection request n arrives at a given time. We first adjust the cost of link $l(\forall l \in L)$ according to Eq. (12) and follow to compute a minimal cost working path WP_n that may be the maximal reliable path.

$$COST_l^* = \begin{cases} +\infty, if : FW_l = 0 \\ -\log R(l), otherwise \end{cases} \tag{12}$$

Proof: we compute the logarithm of both sides of Eq. (9), and obtain:

$$\log(WP_n) = \log R(1) + \log R(2) + ... + \log R(e) \geq \log UR. \tag{13}$$

Since $R(e)$ and UR are between 0 and 1, $\log R(e)$ and $\log UR$ have negative values. Multiplying both sides by -1 in Eq.(13), we obtain:

$$-\log(WP_n) = -\log R(1) - \log R(2) - ... - \log R(e) \leq -\log UR. \tag{14}$$

It is obvious that if the link-cost $COST_l^*$ is defined as such a function of its reliability (i.e.$-\log R(e)$), the cost is additive and the path with minimal cost may be the path with maximal reliability. Therefore, the standard shortest-path algorithm (i.e. Dijkstra) can be applied to compute the minimal cost path.

If the working path with maximal reliability has been found and the reliability of the working path is not smaller than UR, we know that the protection backup path is not needed. Thus, more wavelengths would be saved and the resource utilization ratio would be improved.

Computing the first backup path: If the reliability of the working path is smaller than UR, we know that the protection is needed. We first adjust the cost of link $l(\forall l \in L)$ according to Eq. (15) in which ε is a sufficient small constant (e.g., 10^{-2}) and follow to compute the first link-disjoint and minimal cost backup path BP_n^1 that may has high joint reliability with the working path.

$$COST_l^* = \begin{cases} +\infty, if : (l \in WP_n) \cup (FW_l + RW_l < TRW_l) \\ \varepsilon, else : 1 - F(WP_n) \cdot \max_{\forall e \in WP_n, e \neq l}[CLFP(l|e)] \geq UR \\ 1, otherwise \end{cases} \tag{15}$$

Proof: After the working path has been fixed, the reliability $R(WP_n) = \prod_{e \in WP_n} R(e)$ is a constant. To obtain high joint reliability $R(BP_n^1, WP_n)$, the $\max_{t \in BP_n^1, l \in WP_n, l \neq t}[CLFP(t|l)]$ in Eq. (7) should be small. If the link-cost is defined as Eq. (15), the minimal cost backup path will be favorite to traverse these links that will likely lead to satisfactory reliability (i.e., $1 - F(WP_n) \cdot \max_{t \in BP_n^1, l \in WP_n, l \neq t}[CLFP(t|l)]$). Therefore, the joint reliability $R(BP_n^1, WP_n)$ may be high.

If the working path and the first backup path have been both found and the joint reliability $R(BP_n^1, WP_n)$ is not smaller than UR, we know that the second backup path is not needed. Therefore, more reserved backup wavelengths can be saved and the resource utilization ratio can be improved.

Computing the second backup path: If the joint reliability $R(BP_n^1, WP_n)$ is smaller than UR, we know that the second backup path is needed. Since the joint reliability $R(BP_n^2, BP_n^1, WP_n) = 100\%$ according to Eq. (8), we need not focus on computing a high reliable route but focus on improving the reserved wavelengths sharing degree when computing the second backup path. We first adjust the cost of link $l(\forall l \in L)$ according to Eq. (16) and follow to compute the second link-disjoint and minimal cost backup path BP_n^2 that may use fewer new backup wavelengths.

$$COST_l^* = \begin{cases} +\infty, if : [l \in (WP_n + BP_n^1)] \cup (FW_l + RW_l < TRW_l) \\ \varepsilon, else : RW_l \geq TRW_l \\ 1, otherwise \end{cases} \quad (16)$$

Proof: we can see from Eq. (16) that, these links, which already have enough reserved wavelengths ($RW_l \geq TRW_l$) have less link cost. If the backup paths traverse these links, we need not reserve new backup wavelengths. Therefore, more wavelength resources can be saved and the resource utilization ratio can be improved.

3   Proposed Algorithm

3.1   Procedure and Complexity of the Algorithm

The procedures of our proposed algorithm, called Differentiated Path Shared Protection (DPSP), are presented as follows.

Step1: Wait for a connection request arrival.

If a connection request arrives, go to Step 2.

Else, update the network's state and go back to Step1.

Step2: Adjust the link-cost according to Eq. (12) and compute working path.

If succeed to find the working path, check the reliability of the working path according to Eq. (9).

If $R(WP_n) \geq UR$, record the routing and wavelengths assignment, update the network's state and go back to Step1.

Else, go to Step3.

Else, block the connection request, update the network's sate, and go back to Step1.

Step3: Adjust the link-cost according to Eq. (15) and compute the first backup path.

If succeed to find the first backup path, check the joint reliability of the working and backup paths according to Eq. (10).

If , record the routing and wavelengths assignment, update the network's state and go back to Step1.

Else, go to Step4.

Else, block the connection request, update the network's sate, and go back to Step1.

Step4: Adjust the link-cost according to Eq. (16) and compute the second backup path.

If succeed to find the second backup path, record the routing and wavelengths assignment, update the network's state, and go back to Step1.

Else, block the connection request, update the network's sate, and go back to Step1.

The above procedures of DPSP show that the time complexity mostly depends on running the times of Dijkstra's algorithm whose time complexity is approximately $O(|N|^2)$. In the worst case, DPSP will run one time of Dijkstra's algorithm to compute one working path, and run two times of Dijkstra's algorithm to compute two backup paths. Therefore, the time complexity of DPSP is approximately $O(3|N|^2)$.

3.2 Performance Parameters

The Resource Utilization Ratio (RUR) is calculated as:

$$RUR = \frac{\sum_{l \in L}(WW_l + RW_l)}{|E|}. \tag{17}$$

where E is the set of connections that are holding on the network. It is obvious that smaller RUR means that we need to assign fewer resources and also means a smaller bandwidth reserve on all the backup paths and a higher degree of backup capacity sharing; that is, a higher resource utilization ratio. Higher resource utilization will lead to lower traffic blocking because more free wavelengths can be used by the following requests.

The Blocking Probability (BP) is the ratio of $|R|$ to $|V|$, where R is the set of connection requests that are being abandoned by the network and V is the set of all connection requests that have arrived at the network. In the case of dynamic traffic, the BP can approximately reflect the effectiveness of resource utilization, and a smaller BP means a higher resource utilization ratio.

4   Simulation Results and Analysis

We simulate a dynamic network environment with the assumptions that the connection requests arrival according to an independent Poisson process with arrival rate β, and the connection holding time is negative exponentially distributed $1/\mu$. Then, the network load is β/μ erlang. In simulations, we assume $\mu = 1$ and each required bandwidth is a wavelength granularity. The test network topology can be found in [14], where each node-pair is interconnected by a bi-directional fiber link. The number of wavelengths for each fiber link is assumed to be five. All nodes are assumed to have wavelength conversion capacities.

According to [16-20], the reliability of each link is randomly distributed between 0.96 and 1, and the $CLFP$ of each link pair is randomly selected from 0.90, 0.50, 0.30, 0.20, 0.10. We compare the performances of DPSP to the previous $CPSP$ [12-14]. All simulation results are averaged by simulation of 10^6 connection requests.

We assume there are three different levels of users' requirements (i.e., 95%, 97%, and 99%). It is obvious that in Fig. 2(a) DPSP has smaller value of RUR than CPSP, and this means that DPSP has higher resource utilization ratio. The reason for this is that DPSP needs fewer backup paths and backup resources (see subsection 2.2), and then the resource utilization ratio of DPSP will be higher.

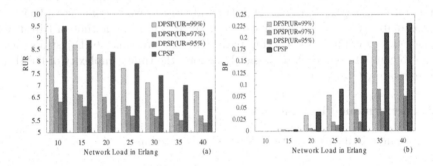

Fig. 2. Performance of DPSP and CPSP with different requirements of users: a) resource utilization ratio (RUR) versus network load; b) blocking probability (BP) versus network load

In Fig. 2(b), we can find that DPSP has lower blocking probability than CPSP. There are two reasons for this: 1) DPSP has higher resource utilization ratio, and then more free resources can be used by the following requests, and the blocking probability will be lower than CPSP; 2) DPSP can overcome the flaw of CPSP under node-degree constraints (see subsection 2.2) and can establish more connection requests, which results in lower blocking probability.

We also see that in Fig. 2(a), when the UR increases, the resource utilization ratio decreases. The reason for this is that, if the UR is higher, the connections need more backup paths and backup resources, and then the resource utilization ratio will be lower.

Fig. 2(b) also shows that, when the UR increases, the blocking probability increases. There are two reasons for this: 1) when the UR increases, the resource utilization ratio decreases, and then fewer free resources can be used by the following requests and the blocking probability will be higher; 2) when the UR increases, the connections need more backup paths, and then more connections will be blocked under node-degree constraints. Therefore, the blocking probability will be high when the UR increases.

We can thus conclude that the proposed DPSP can obtain better performances in resource utilization and blocking probability than previous CPSP.

5   Conclusions

In this paper, we have proposed a new dynamic survivable algorithm called Differentiated Path Shared Protection (DPSP) to protect the double-link failures in WDM optical networks. Considering the differentiated reliable protection, DPSP can assign one working path, or one working path and one backup path, or one working path and two backup paths to each connection request. The simulation results show that, compared to previous algorithm CPSP, DPSP can perform higher resource utilization ratio and lower blocking probability.

Acknowledgments. This work was supported in part by National Natural Science Foundation Grant 60302010.

References

1. Mukherjee, B.: Optical Communication Networks. Mc-Graw-Hill, New York (1997)
2. Ramamurthy, S., Sahasrabuddhe, L., Mukherjee, B.: Survivable WDM Mesh Networks. J. Lightw. Technol. **21** (2003) 870–883
3. Ho, P. H., Mouftah, H.: A Novel Survivable Routing Algorithm for Shared Segment Protection in Mesh WDM Networks with Partial Wavelength Conversion. IEEE J. Sel. Area. Comm. **22** (2004) 1548–1560
4. Wen, H., Li, L., He, R., et al: Dynamic Grooming Algorithms for Survivable WDM Mesh Networks. Photon. Netw. Comm. **6** (2003) 253–263
5. Ou, C., Zhang, J., Zang, H., et al: New and Improved Approaches for Shared-Path Protection in WDM Mesh Networks. J. Lightw. Technol. **22** (2004) 1223–1232
6. Ho, P. H., Tapolcai J., Cinkler, T.: Segment Shared Protection in Mesh Communications Networks with Bandwidth Guaranteed Tunnels. IEEE/ACM Trans. Netw. **12** (2004) 1105–1118
7. He, R., Wen, H., Li, L.: Shared Sub-path Protection Algorithm in Traffic-Grooming WDM Mesh Networks. Photon. Netw. Comm. **8** (2004) 239–249
8. Choi, H., Subramaniam, S., Choi, H.: On Double-Link Failure Recovery in WDM Optical Networks. In Proccedings of INFOCOM'02. **2** (2002) 23–26
9. Kim, S., Lumetta, S.: Evaluation of Protection Reconfiguration for Multiple Failures in WDM Mesh Networks. In Proccedings of OFC'03. **1** (2003) 210–211
10. Schupke, D., Prinz, R.: Performance of Path Protection and Rerouting for WDM Networks Subject to Dual Failures. In Proccedings of OFC'03. **1** (2003) 209–210

11. Zhang, J., Zhu, K., Mukherjee, B.: A Comprehensive Study on Backup Reprovisioning to Remedy The Effect of Double-Link Failures in WDM Mesh Networks. In Proccedings of ICC'04. **3** (2004) 1654–1658
12. He, W., Somani, A.: Path-Based Protection for Surviving Double-Link Failures in Mesh-Restorable Optical Networks. In Proccedings of GLOBECOM'03. **5** (2003) 2558–2563
13. Jozsa, B. G., Orincsay, D., Kern, A.: Surviving Multiple Network Failures Using Shared Backup Path Protection. In Proccedings of ISCC'03. **2** (2003) 1333–1340
14. Guo, L., Yu, H., Li, L.: Double-Link Failure Protection Algorithm for Shared Sub-Path in Survivable WDM Mesh Networks. Chin. Opt. Lett. **7** (2004) 379–382
15. Cao, J., Guo, L., Yu, H., et al: Dynamic Segment Shared Protection Algorithm for Reliable Wvelength Division Multiplexing Mesh Networks. Opt. Exp. **13** (2005) 3087–3095
16. Andrea, F., Marco, T., Ferenc, U.: Shared Path Protection with Differentiated Reliability. In Proccedings of ICC'02. **4** (2002) 2157–2161
17. Bolmie, N., Ndousse, T. D., Su, D. H.: A Differentiated Optical Service for WDM Networks. IEEE Comm. Mag. **4** (2000) 68–73
18. Saradhi, C. V., Murthy, C. S. R.: Routing Differentiated Reliable Connections in WDM Optical Networks. Opt. Netw. Mag. **3** (2002) 50–67
19. Yu, H., Wen, H., Wang, S., et al: Shared-Path Protection Algorithm with Differentiated Reliability in Meshed WDM Networks. In Proccedings of SPIE. **5282** (2003) 682–687
20. Guo, L., Yu, H., Li, L: A Dual-Link Failure Protection Algorithm with Correlated Link Failure Probability for Survivable WDM Networks (In Chinese). J. Electron. Info. Technol. **27** (2005) 1483–1487

A Time Model for Distributed Multimedia Applications

Winfried E. Kühnhauser[1] and Martin Süßkraut[2]

[1] Technical University at Ilmenau, Germany
[2] Technical University at Dresden, Germany

Abstract. The significant resource requirements of distributed real-time multimedia applications often push today's system platforms to their limits. As a consequence, efficient, economic and adaptive management of resources is a major issue in distributed multimedia systems.

This paper outlines a model-based time service encompassing three different aspects of time that are fundamental for sophisticated strategies within cross layer failure semantics, flow control, and synchronization.

1 Introduction

Distributed multimedia applications such as traffic control systems, video conferencing, or telemedicine systems exhibit communication patterns that in many ways differ from contemporary communication paradigms. Media streams are sequential, ordered infinite sequences of discrete typed data objects that continuously flow from some source to some destinations. In general, media streams also are quite voluminous, encompassing for example HDTV video streams with a bit rate of up to 2.8 GBit/sec. Media streams have real-time properties, using time to specify synchroneity, periodicity, ordering and timeliness. Last but not least, communication failures affecting single stream fragments are not fatal in general; they may be tolerated depending on the importance of the fragment as well as the application's quality requirements.

Contemporary communication models such as RPC or RMI do not apply well to such communication patterns. Distributed multimedia applications thus often build their own communication abstractions directly on top of low level transport protocols such as TCP, UDP, SCP, or RTP/RTCP.

This paper discusses a time model to support the design and implementation of stream communication abstractions. It focuses on four different aspects of time and evaluates how they can be exploited in communication failure semantics, flow control, and synchronization. The model has been implemented by the time service of the Noja middleware framework [1,2].

2 Time in Distributed Multimedia Applications

Time in distributed multimedia systems serves many different purposes.

Temporal Ordering. Objects in multimedia documents are ordered by their creation time. This time in general is relative to the begin of the document. For

S. Chaudhuri et al. (Eds.): ICDCN 2006, LNCS 4308, pp. 491–496, 2006.

example in a DV-coded PAL video document frame ordering is implemented by a time stamp carried by each frame. When media documents are communicated, media objects are wrapped into stream objects which may be ordered differently, depending on the order in which they are processed by the receiver.

Timeliness. In distributed real time multimedia applications arrival times of media objects are of major importance. Media objects arriving too early require buffer resources, while objects arriving too late may become useless. Here, time is used to synchronize stream processing with real time; incorrect synchronization may result in extensive resource usage or loss of media objects.

Synchroneity. Multimedia documents such as multi camera and multi audio track recordings consist of single media documents that are related to each other. Whenever the document is processed as a whole, interdependent streams have to be synchronized with respect to a common time base.

Periodicity. In many media document formats any two media objects have a fixed distance in time. PAL video documents for example consist of 25 frames per second, resulting in a frame distance of 1/25 second. Audio documents have a much smaller periodicity, e.g. 1/44.000 for a stereo document in CD PCM format. Periodicity of a media document for example allows to predict resource requirements and temporal ordering of future media objects in a media stream.

2.1   Model Requirements

This section discusses the role of time in four major building blocks of a communication model: failure semantics, flow control, synchronization and adaption control and summarizes the results in fig. 1.

A communication model's **failure semantics** specifies guarantees given to an application even in the presence of communication failures. Failure semantics simplify application level failure handling by providing easy-to-use abstractions restricting the visibility of complex low-level communication failures.

In order to detect timing failures, a failure semantics's implementation must compare the arrival deadline of a media object with its actual arrival time (question (1)). More sophisticated schemes also strive for predicting future timing failures (question (2)), thus allowing for failure prevention policies or for early discarding of media objects that are predicted to miss their deadline. Both, recovery and prevention policies will only be successful if they meet their objectives within the affected object's deadline (question (3)).

Flow control balances the flow of media streams between the components of a distributed multimedia application, including buffering of early stream objects (question (4)) as well as reordering stream objects that arrive in disarray (question (5)). Additionally, jitter compensation requires answering question (6).

Synchronization control manages the temporal relations between different media documents and/or different components of a distributed multimedia application. Questions (7) and (8) arise whenever multimedia documents encompassing more than a single media document are processed.

Adaptation control manages dynamic changes of application requirements, stream properties, or resource availability. Additionally to being triggered externally, adaptation control watches internal indicators such as variations of the total average media object processing time, the processing time within individual application components, or transmission times of communication channels (questions (9) - (11)).

(1) Is a given stream object in time?
(2) Can a given stream object reach its destination in time?
(3) Is there enough time for error recovery or prevention policies?
(4) Is a given stream object too early?
(5) What is the ordering of two given stream objects?
(6) What is the temporal distance between two given stream objects?
(7) What is the processing deadline for two given stream objects so that they will arrive synchronously at their destination?
(8) Which stream objects from different media streams must be processed synchronously?
(9) What is the average processing time of stream objects of one media stream in the multimedia application?
(10) What is the average processing time on one processor?
(11) What is the average transmission time on a given communication channel?

Fig. 1. Questions to be answered by the time service

3   The Model

The time model introduced in this section is a concise, precise and – with respect to the requirements summarized in figure 1 – complete foundation for exploiting and managing several different aspects of time in distributed multimedia systems. The heart of the model are three basic time types together with methods to handle corresponding time objects. This section introduces these time types and methods and illustrates how they are combined in order to provide answers to the question catalogue in figure 1.

3.1   Basic Sets and Functions

We model a distributed multimedia application by a directed graph, its node set P representing individual application components (processors), its edges ($\in P \times P$) modelling the flow of media streams among the processors.

Nodes as well as edges have attributes that describe time related dynamic properties such as current channel bandwidth, network load, or CPU and memory availability. In order to calculate and predict the timing behavior of an application, these attributes are monitored during application runtime.

Timing properties relate to observation points. Important observation points where streams enter and leave processors will be represented by the set $OP = \{In, Out\}$. As an example, the observation point at the output port of processor p where p connects to some processor q is denoted by (p, Out), while its counterpart at q is (q, In). At processors q with more than one incoming edge, each edge may have its individual observation point which then will be identified by (p, In, q); the same holds for outgoing edges, respectively.

When a multimedia document is wrapped into a media stream for communication, each *media object* is encapsulated by a *stream object*. The set of all stream objects managed by a multimedia application is represented by the set S, and the set of all media objects by the set M. Unwrapping a media object from a stream object is modelled by a function $mo : S \rightarrow M$.

Each stream object belongs to a media stream $ms \in MS$, MS denoting the set of all media streams of an application. Mapping a stream object to its media stream is modelled by $stream : S \rightarrow MS$. All stream objects of a media stream ms use the same path through the application graph: from the processor $source(ms)$ to the processor $sink(ms)$.

Time values are of type $T = \mathbb{R}$; negative numbers denote negative temporal distances. The end-to-end-time for a media stream is defined by $ete : MS \rightarrow T$.

3.2   Time Types

Media Time t_m. Any media document is an ordered sequence of media objects. Ordering is based on generation time stamps carried by each media object. In periodic document formats (such as PCM audio files) ordering may be implicit, given by the order objects appear within the document. Time stamps define temporal ordering as well as temporal distances. For each time stamped media object, the function $t_m : M \rightarrow T$ results in its media time. For each media object from the same document, t_m is strictly monotonous. For periodic documents with objects m_i and period $p \in T$, media time stamps compute by $t_m(m_i) = p * (i - 1)$.

Streaming Time t_s. Dynamic and proactive policies for adaptation, error correction and prevention require monitoring and prediction of the communication system's timing behavior. Error correction for example will ponder the time required for corrective actions against deadline misses (question (2)). To this end, stream objects take up time stamps at each observation point. For each stream object, the function $t_s : P \times OP \times S \rightarrow T$ results in its stream time at some observation point.

Stream-global Logical Clock t_g. In asynchronous distributed systems we cannot assume a global clock, and time stamps based on unsynchronized local clocks would not compare. However, clocks can be synchronized cheaply by an NTP-like synchronization scheme where the application graph serves as the NTP clock synchronization tree. A stream source serves as stratum-0 server, and explicit synchronization among stratum-0 servers becomes necessary only if more than a single source exists. Synchronization among lower strati then uses downstream synchronization by messages piggy-backed on the stream. Note that the resulting global clock is relative to the root of the synchronization tree and is global with respect to a given stream, only. By synchronizing the root node of the stream's synchronization tree with an NTP stratum-0 server the whole tree then becomes synchronized with UTC time. The function $t_g : MS \rightarrow T$ represents the stream-global logical clock within the model.

3.3   Questions and Answers

We now combine the time types t_m, t_s and t_g into functions answering the question catalog in fig. 1.

Failure Control. With respect to question (1), the boolean function $ontime(s)$ computes by comparing the expected *total processing time* tpt of s with the stream's end-to-end time: $ontime(s) \Leftrightarrow (tpt(s) = ete(stream(s)))$. If the observation point is the entry point of the sink for s, tpt computes easily by $tpt = t_s(sink, In, s) - t_s(source, In, s)$. However, in general an observation point is somewhere on the path between source and sink where $t_s(sink, In, s)$ is still unknown and has to be predicted. In this case, the more general form of tpt includes a *predicted remaining processing time* ppt related to $(p, op, q) : tpt(s) = t_s(p, op, s) + ppt(p, op, sink, In, s) - t_s(source, In, s)$. With ppt discussed below, *ontime* answers questions (1) and (2).

In order to answer question (3), the duration of the failure handling policy must be known. Policy-individual time-to-repair values are modelled by a policy-individual function $ttr : P \times OP \times P \times OP \times S \rightarrow T$ which any failure handling policy is required to provide. Then, the estimated arrival time eta for a stream object s, repaired at some observation point (p, op) with assistance of a node p' at observation point (p', op') is $eta(p, op, p', op', s) = t_g(stream(s)) + ttr(p, op, p', op', s) + ppt(p, op, sink, In, s)$. If $eta(p, op, p', op', s) \leq t_s(source, In, s) + ete(stream(s))$ holds, s can be repaired at p without violating end-to-end time guarantees.

Flow Control. We already know that a stream object is on time if $ontime(s)$ holds at observation point (p, op). For the same reasons, if $t_s(p, op, s) - t_s(source, In, s) + ppt(p, op, sink, In, s) < ete(stream(s))$ then s is too early, respectively if $t_s(p, op, s) - t_s(source, In, s) + ppt(p, op, sink, In, s) > ete(stream(s))$ then s is too late (question (4)); additionally, the difference between both sides of the equation quantifies punctuality.

The order of two stream objects $s, s' \in S$ (question (5)) at some observation point (p', In) is defined by the order s and s' left (p, Out), where (p, p') is an incoming edge at p'. Thus the relation $s \leq s'$ at observer point p is defined by $s \leq s' \Leftrightarrow t_s(p, Out, s) \leq t_s(p, Out, s')$. Note that due to stream object dependencies stream object order and media object order may differ.

For question (6), the temporal distance between two stream objects s and s' at observation point op on processor p computes by $distance_{t_s}(p, op, s, s') = t_s(p, Out, s') - t_s(p, Out, s)$. Note that $distance_{t_s}$ is a value relative to an observation point, suited for jitter compensation with respect to the last edge only. The absolute temporal distance $distance_{t_m}$ between two media objects computed by $distance_{t_m}(s, s') = t_m(mo(s')) - t_m(mo(s))$ can be used for (absolute) jitter compensation only if the difference between media and stream order is known.

Synchronization Control. For two stream objects s and s' to arrive at their destination synchronously (question (7)) their expected arrival times must be the same: $eta(p, op, sink, In, s) = eta(p, op, sink, In, s')$. The *optimum processing time* opt for each stream object is computed by $opt(p, op, s) = eta(p, op, sink, In, s) - ppt(p, op, sink, In, s)$. Because the processing time of any media object depends on its media time t_m, any two media objects s and s' from different streams have to be processed synchronously (question (8)) if and only if their media times are the same, i.e. the relation *dub* holds: s *dub* $s' \Leftrightarrow t_m(mo(s)) = t_m(mo(s'))$.

Adaptation Control. The *interim processing time ipt* of a stream object s between two observation points op, op' on processors $p, p' \in P$ is $ipt(p, op, p', op', s) = t_s(p', op', s) - t_s(p, op, s)$. Then, the *average processing time* $apt(p, op, p', op', S') = \sum_{s \in S'} ipt(p, op, p', op', s)(|S'|)^{-1}$ of stream objects between op, p and op', p' is computed based on statistical data collected from the observation of stream objects from some subset $S' \subseteq S$, which in an implementation will become stable only after a certain application runtime. This answers questions (9) - (11).

Predicted Processing Time ppt. Some of the above equations assume that stream times at both observation points are known. If we want to predict the *ipt* at some earlier processing stage, the more general *predicted processing time* $ppt(p, op, p', op', s) = apt(source, In, p', op', s) - apt(source, In, p, op, s)$ applies. *ppt* thus assumes that observations in the past allow to foretell the future. Within a given implementation environment, *ppt*'s quality will depend on the extent this assumption is honored.

4 Summary

The goal of our work was to develop a time model to support the design and implementation of stream communication abstractions in middleware frameworks for distributed multimedia applications. Our approach was to analyze the roles of time within a communication model's failure semantics, flow, synchronization and adaptation control components, and to develop a stringent time model in which many roles of time time are casted into a small set of well-defined time functions.

Implementing the formal model within the time service of the distributed multimedia framework Noja [1,2] was a straight-forward affair. For a description of the implementation and experimental results with respect to its resource requirements and real-time behavior we refer the reader to the long version of the paper available from the authors.

References

1. Eichhorn, A., Kühnhauser, W.E.: A Component-based Architecture for Streaming Media Applications. In: Proceedings of NET.OBJECTDAYS 2001 – 7th Workshop on Multimedia Information and Communication Systems. (2001) 273–286 ISBN 3-00-008419-3.
2. Eichhorn, A.: Modelling Dependency in Multimedia Streams. In: Proceeedings ACM Multimedia 2006, ACM (2006)
3. Hoffmann, M., Kühnhauser, W.E.: Towards a Structure-Aware Failure Semantics for Streaming Media Communication Models. Journal of Parallel and Distributed Computing **65**(9) (2005) 1047–1056

Destination Initiated Multi-wavelength Reservation Protocol (DIMRP) in WDM Optical Networks: Finding the Optimal Selectivity for Wavelength Assignment

Malabika Sengupta[1], Swapan Kumar Mondal[1], and Debasish Saha[2]

[1] Kalyani Government Engineering College, Kalyani, India
[2] Indian Institute of Management, Kolkata, India
sengupta.malabika@gmail.com, ds.calcutta@gmail.com

Abstract. In WDM optical networks, prior to data transfer, lightpath establishment between source and destination nodes is usually carried out through a wavelength reservation process. The two common approaches for this, namely Source Initiated Reservation (SIR) and Destination Initiated Reservation (DIR) use only one wavelength for reservation, and, under heavy load, it is often blocked due to outdated link information. The situation can be improved by increasing the number of wavelengths to be attempted for reservation concurrently. This idea, implemented on DIR in this paper, is termed as Destination Initiated Multiwavelength Reservation Protocol (DIMRP). DIMRP is analyzed to find that an optimum number named as selectivity (i.e., number of simultaneous wavelengths to be attempted for reservation) exists for a given value of mean connection requests and total number of wavelengths per link. DIMRP is compared with its peers and overall result appears quite promising to draw the attention of network providers.

1 Introduction

In wavelength division multiplexing (WDM) networks, when a connection request arrives at a source node, a dedicated path is required to be established between source and destination. This is realized first by determining a proper route between the source and the destination and then allocating a free wavelength to all the links of the route (wavelength assignment). Such an all optical path is commonly referred as a lightpath [2-3]. This work is restricted to wavelength assignment part only. It is considered that no wavelength converters are present at intermediate nodes.

Wavelength assignment protocols may be divided into two main categories based on number of wavelength(s) attempted to establish the lightpath. These are Single wavelength Reservation Protocols (SRP) and Multiple wavelength Reservation Protocols (MRP) Both SRP and MRP can again be classified as Source Initiated (SI) and Destination Initiated (DI), based on whether source or destination initiates the process of reservation [3] leading to four different types of protocols i.e., SISRP, DISRP, SIMRP and DIMRP. Different forms of SISRP, DISRP and SIMRP along with their modifications are studied in previous works [1-6]. It has been already established that DISRP in general is more efficient than SISRP and SIMRP in terms of blocking probability (bp) [3]. DISRP with retry is even better at the cost of a

S. Chaudhuri et al. (Eds.): ICDCN 2006, LNCS 4308, pp. 497–502, 2006.
© Springer-Verlag Berlin Heidelberg 2006

nominal increase in control overhead and average setup time. However, DIMRP is not attempted earlier, and, hence, no known results are available, to the best of our knowledge.

A connection request is blocked when no single wavelength is available for use throughout the chosen route between source and destination. Due to processing delays, when a control message actually tries to reserve a particular wavelength on route, that wavelength in the meanwhile may already been reserved by another contemporary connection request. This type of blocking is due to outdated global information. This motivates for reserving multiple free wavelengths (if available) instead of a single wavelength on every hop of the route, so that chance of getting at least one wavelength throughout the path may be improved considerably. However, this may cause the over reservation problem. In such cases some future requests may be blocked due to unavailability of wavelengths. In this work, the trade off between outdated information and over reservation in case of DIMRP is studied and compared with DISRP and DISRP with retry [3].

The paper is organized as follows. In section 2, DISRP is introduced while section 3 elaborates DIMRP. Results and discussions are presented in Section 4. Finally, Section 5 concludes the paper.

2 Destination Initiated Single Wavelength Reservation Protocol

In DISRP, a source node generates a PROB signal, which contains the information of the availability of wavelengths of the next link. The PROB gets updated as it strikes the nodes on the selected route and finally reaches the destination with a set of wavelengths available (say α). Now, if α becomes zero anywhere before the destination due to non availability of wavelength, the request is blocked and a control packet FAIL is sent in the reverse path to the source. On the other, if PROB reaches destination with a non-zero α, destination selects *one* from the available set of wavelengths and initiates a RES signal to reserve the wavelength hop by hop on the reverse path towards source. If it fails to reserve the wavelength (which may be reserved in the mean time by some other requests), a FAIL signal is sent to source and a REL signal is initiated towards destination to release the wavelength reserved up to that node and the request is blocked if no retry is attempted. In case of DISRP with retry, the destination after getting the REL signal, sends RES signal once again (retry) towards the source using another wavelength from PROB pool. This may be repeated for a number of retries till success or until all possible retries are exhausted. If all of them fail, a FAIL control packet is sent to the source.

3 Destination Initiated Multiwavelength Reservation Protocol

In case of DIMRP, control packets similar to that of DISRP are used. In DIMRP multiple number of wavelengths are attempted (if available) for reservation. When PROB signal reaches destination with number of available wavelengths (α) greater than 1, there is a choice on the number of wavelengths to be attempted concurrently for reservation, which may be termed as maximum wavelength permitted (mwp). The mwp should be less or equals to α and greater or equals to 1. If the RES signal reaches the source node successfully (i.e., at least one wavelength is reserved and lightpath is successfully established) then transmission is started. During transmission of first packet, all other reserved wavelengths if any, are released using REL. However before reaching the source node, if at any hop, no further wavelength is available for reservation due to outdated information, the reserved wavelengths up to that hop from the destination are released using REL signal. Also a FAIL signal is sent to the source and the connection is blocked. Finding an optimum value of mwp, termed as selectivity(s), is a challenging issue as over reservation may spoil the advantage of concurrency.

4 Results and Discussions

Extensive simulation experiments are done under various network conditions. Routing is assumed to be fixed and shortest path. Connection requests arrive to the network nodes following Poisson's distribution with mean rate of λ connections per second, and connection holding times are exponentially distributed with an average holding time of $1/\mu$ second. The number of wavelengths (w) on each optical fibre is varied from 30 to 80. NSFNet topology (16 nodes connected with 24 bidirectional links) is used in the simulations for which results are presented here.

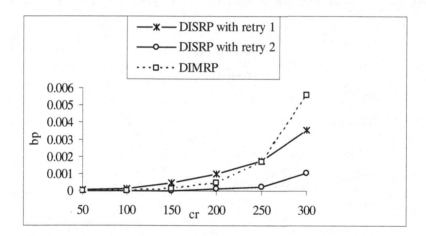

Fig. 1. Variation of bp with cr for DIMRP and DISRP (with retry) for w=70

DIMRP is first compared with DISRP (with retry 1 and retry 2) for w=70, which is shown in Fig. 1. Here DISRP without retry is not considered as it is already established that DIMRP performs better than DISRP without retry in respect of bp. From the figure it is observed that up to a certain value (250) of connection request (cr), DIMRP offers better result compared to DISRP with retry 1. DISRP with retry 2 is close to DIMRP for low values of cr (up to cr=150) and considerably better beyond that. It is obvious that DISRP with retry numbers more than two will be further better than DIMRP with respect to bp. But while choosing a protocol, the trade-off between bp, control packet and average setup time should be considered.

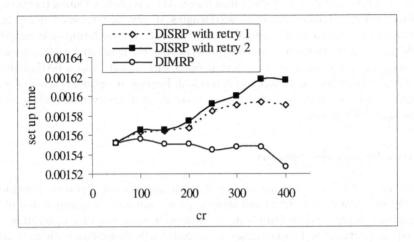

Fig. 2. Variation of set up time with cr for DIMRP and DISRP (with retry) for w=70

As average setup time is also an important parameter for a protocol, the average setup time of DIMRP and DIRSP with retries are studied and results are shown in

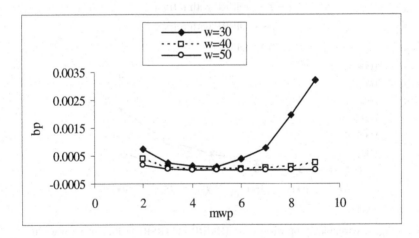

Fig. 3. Variation of bp with mwp for DIMRP for different wavelengths

Fig. 2. It can be observed from the figure that DIMRP is always better than DISRP with retries. This is because rate of success is more for more retries, but extra time is required to convert previous failure cases to success, thereby increasing the set up time. Another point may be noted that difference in set up time between DIMRP and

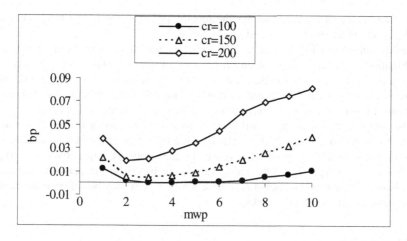

Fig. 4. Variation of bp with mwp for DIMRP for different cr

DISRP with retry also increases with increase in cr. This is due to the fact that at higher values of cr, more failure cases use retries to become successful taking more set up time.

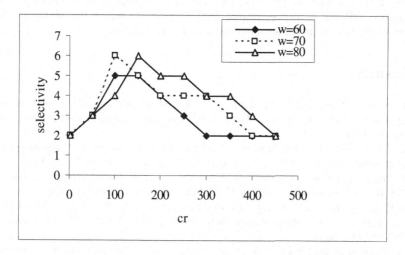

Fig. 5. Variation of selectivity with cr of DIMRP for different wavelengths

Another important parameter is the average number of control packets required in different protocols. In case of DIMRP number of control packets required is same as required for DISRP without retries. But for DISRP with retries, extra two control packets are required for each retry. Thus, if blocking probability, setup time and control packets are considered, then DIMRP appears to be the better choice.

Now, a relation among cr, w and mwp with bp is tried to find out in DIMRP. In this direction, first the variation of bp with mwp is studied for different values of w and a fixed value of cr. Fig. 3 shows the results. In Fig. 4, bp versus mwp are shown for different values of cr for a fixed number of w.

Results shown in Fig. 3 and Fig. 4 indicate that there must be a values for a combination of w and cr for which bp remains minimum. This information may be really useful for a given network. As w of a network remains fixed, depending on the status of cr (which can be studied at regular intervals), the system can switch over from one value of s to other to deliver better efficiency in terms of lower bp.

The relation of s with cr for different values of w is shown in Fig. 5. From the figure it can be observed that the system will deliver best result if s is selected as 5 when cr is 100 or 150 for w=60. However the same network will deliver best when s is selected as 2 when cr is 300. These values are based on the network considered here. However for different networks, these set of values may be different and can be found out by studying the networks.

5   Conclusion

In this paper, DIMRP is analyzed at length and selectivity is found out for different values of mean connection requests (i.e., arrival rate) and total number of wavelengths per link. From the results it can be concluded that, in a given network for which available wavelength is fixed, value of selectivity can be dynamically changed from time to time depending on the condition of connection requests to minimize blocking probability. DIMRP is also compared with its peers to report the advantages with respect to set up time and control overhead to justify its relevance.

References

[1] H. Zang, J.P. Jue and B. Mukherjee, "Review of routing and wavelength assignment approaches for wavelength-routed optical WDM networks", *Optical networks*, Vol 1, no 1, pp 47-60, Jan. 2000.

[2] I. Chlamtac, A. Ganz and G.Karmi, "Lightpath Communications: A Novel Approach to High Bandwidth Optical WANs", IEEE Trans. Commun., vol 40, no. 7, July 1992.

[3] D. Saha, "A Comparative study of distributed protocols for wavelength reservation in WDM optical networks", SPIE Opt. Netw. Mag., vol 3, no. 1, pp. 45-52, 2002.

[4] J. P. Jue and G. Xiao, "An Adaptive Routing Algorithm for Wavelength-Routed Optical Networks with a Distributed Control Scheme,"*Proc. IC3N'2000*, Las Vegas, Nevada, pp. 192-197, Oct. 2000.

[5] A. E. Ozdaglar and Dimitri P. Bertsekas, "Routing and Wavelength Assignment in Optical Networks", *IEEE/ACM Trans. On Networking.*, vol. 11, no. 2, pp. 259-271, April. 2003.

[6] F. Feng, X. Zheng, H. Zhang, and Y. Guo, "An efficient distributed control scheme for lightpath establishment in dynamic WDM networks," *Photonic Netw. Commun.*, vol. 7, no. 1, pp. 5–15, 2004.

A Hybrid Transformation Technique for Video Coding

M. Ezhilarasan[1] and P. Thambidurai[2]

[1]Assistant Professor, [2]Professor and Head
Department of Computer Science & Engineering and Information Technology
Pondicherry Engineering College, Pondicherry – 605 014, India
mrezhil@yahoo.com

Abstract. This paper proposes a hybrid transformation technique, where the intraframes of video sequence are coded by discrete wavelet transform and the interframes are coded with discrete cosine transform technique. It also proposes the selection of sequence of frames predicted from the reference intraframes. This proposal consistently minimizes the prediction error for the predicted frame for further processing. The experimental results show that the proposed hybrid transformation technique outperforms conventional transformation coding technique in terms of encoding time and prediction errors. The advantages of this approach include the potential for improving efficiency and ease of transmission.

Keywords: Transformation, video coding, discrete cosine transform, discrete wavelet transform.

1 Introduction

Transformation is the main module in any image and video coding standards. Spatial image data are inherently difficult to code effectively because neighboring symbols in the spatial domain are highly correlated and the energy is distributed randomly across the image. This necessitates the decorrelation of the symbols in the image. The desirable properties of the transformation module in image and video coding standards are energy compaction and suitable for practical implementation in software and hardware. The two most widely used transformation methods are Discrete Cosine Transform (DCT) [1] and Discrete Wavelet Transform (DWT) [2]. DCT is usually applied in small and equal sized blocks (8x8, 16x16) of image symbols and DWT is applied either on complete image or on large tiles of the image. Other alternatives of the transformations are 3-D transforms, variable block size transforms, fractal transforms and Gabor analysis.

DCT is best transformation technique for motion estimation and compensated predictive coding models. Due to blocking artifacts problems encountered in DCT, sub band coding methods are considered as an alternative for this problem. DWT is the best alternative method because of its energy compaction and preservation property. Due to ringing artifacts incurred in DWT, there is a tremendous contribution from the researchers, experts from various institutes and research laboratories for past two decades. In this paper, we have incorporated the advantages of DWT filter for

S. Chaudhuri et al. (Eds.): ICDCN 2006, LNCS 4308, pp. 503–508, 2006.

intraframes and DCT for interframes of motion compensated hybrid video encoder. However the intra frames are coded with wavelet transform, impact of this can be seen in both intraframe and interframe video sequence coding. With better quality anchor pictures are retained in frame memory for prediction, the remaining interframe pictures are more efficiently coded with discrete cosine transform.

The paper is organized as follows. Section 2 gives the basics of video coding, in which various redundancy minimization methods and motivation for hybrid transformation technique are briefly described. Section 3 discusses the proposed hybrid video encoder. Extensive experimental results and discussion have been provided for validation in section 4 and conclusion is given in section 5.

2 Basics of Video Coding

For any interframe video coding standards, the basic functional modules are motion estimation and compensation [3], transformation, quantization [4] and entropy encoder [5]. As shown in the Fig. 1, the temporal redundancies exists in successive frames are minimized or reduced by motion estimation and compensation module. The residue or the difference between the original and motion compensated frame is applied into the sequence of transformation and quantization modules. The spatial redundancy exists in neighboring pixels in the image or intraframe is minimized by these modules. The transformation module converts the residue symbols from time domain into frequency domain, which intends decorrelate the energy present in the spatial domain. This is so appropriate for quantization. Quantized transform coefficients and motion displacement vectors obtained from motion estimation and compensation module are applied into entropy encoding module, where it removes the statistical redundancy.

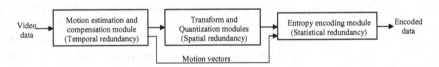

Fig. 1. Basic Video encoding module

In DCT-based MCP coding architecture [6], [7], previously processed frames are considered as reference frames to predict the future frames. Even though the transformation module is energy preserving and lossless module, it is irreversible in experiments. Subsequently the transformed coefficients are quantized to achieve higher compression leads further loss in the frame, which are to be considered as reference frames stored in frame memory for future frame prediction. Decoded frames are used for the prediction of new frames as per the MCP coding technique. JPEG 2000 [8] proved that high quality image compression can be achieved by applying DWT. This motivates us to apply DWT for intraframes and DCT for interframes of video sequence. In addition to the hybrid transformation technique, it is considered there will be memory constrained problem in the frame memory when conventional **I, P, P, P, P . . .** sequence applied. To resolve this problem, a new Group of Frames (GOF) sequence is also proposed in this paper, which minimizes the prediction error and also reduce the frame memory storage complexity.

3 Proposed Hybrid Video Encoder

Hybrid transformation technique incorporates the redundancy minimization techniques. In specific, the spatial redundancy is removed or minimized by incorporating the DWT for intraframes and DCT for interframes of video sequence. The advantage of the subband coding has been applied effectively by using Haar wavelet filter coefficients [0.707, 0.707] in intraframes. The main problem encountered by using DCT like blocking artifacts is over come by applying DWT for intraframes. However, DCT is the best transformation technique for block based motion estimation and compensation video coding. The first frame in a GOF [9] is intraframe coded. Frequent intraframes enable random access to the coded stream. Interframes are predicted from previously decoded intraframes. Hence, these briefly narrated in the following subsections.

3.1 Prediction of Frames

The GOF shows that every fifth frame is an intraframe as shown in Fig. 2. The two frames next to and before that intraframe are coded with reference to this intraframe. Thus errors are minimized since the maximum distance between intra and interframes is 2.

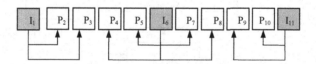

Fig. 2. Arrangement of Group of frames in proposed system

   In conventional motion compensated video coding architecture, the interframes are coded with respect to closest predicted frames or intraframes. In this proposal, interframes are coded only with the reference to intraframes. Hence, the previously processed decoded frames in the frame memory are wavelet coded. The propagation error incurred due to blocking artifacts in the case of DCT is significantly minimized in the subsequent frames. Bidirectional frames are not considered in this hybrid transformation video coding due to complexity. Hence, all the predicted frames are processed from intraframes. The sequence followed in this hybrid video coding is $I_1, P_2, P_3, I_6, P_4, P_5, P_7, P_8, I_{11}, P_9, P_{10}, \ldots$

3.2 Structure of Hybrid Transformation Video Encoder

Interframes are predictive frames that are effectively coded with respect to previously coded frames. At high frame rate, the correlations in the successive frames in a video sequence are more. Hence, reducing or minimizing the spatial correlations among the successive frames in a video sequence is to be effectively achieved by transformation techniques in interframe coding. The previously reconstructed frame is used to generate a prediction of the current frame. The difference between prediction and the current frame, the prediction error or residual, is quantized and encoded. Block based method is used for motion compensation. Full Search or exhaustive motion estimation algorithm is implemented for motion compensated prediction from closest intraframe. In this exhaustive search algorithm, every possible position in the search window is compared. Scalar quantization followed by arithmetic encoding is applied on transformed values and finally bit stream is generated and stored in video buffer. Fig. 3 shows the structure of the hybrid transform video encoder.

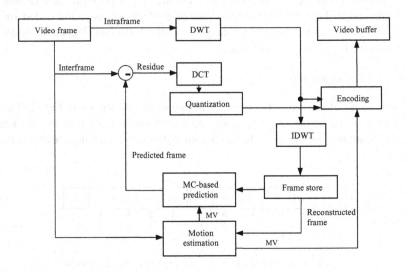

Fig. 3. Hybrid transform video encoder

4 Experimental Results and Discussion

The experiments were conducted for three video sequences "Usb" (316x128, 18 frames, 8 bpp), "Blur" (128x128, 8 frames, 24 bpp) and "Fishtank" (320x240, 96 frames). The experimental results show that the proposed hybrid transform coding technique outperforms over conventional DCT based video coding in terms of encoding time. Prediction error is greatly minimized by using the proposed method.

Table 1. Average PSNR (dB) comparisons of conventional and proposed GOF for DCT video coding

Sequence	Conventional GOF			Proposed GOF		
	Y-PSNR	U-PSNR	V-PSNR	Y-PSNR	U-PSNR	V-PSNR
Usb	31.9529	36.4677	36.6588	32.1638	36.7835	36.8897
Blur	34.1437	35.7634	35.7375	34.2945	35.7927	35.7906
Fishtank	31.5310	35.7282	35.2760	31.5677	35.7828	35.3384

Table 1 compares the Luminance and Chrominance values of various video sequences using conventional GOF and proposed GOF sequence for DCT based video coding. It is observed that 0.21 dB, 0.15 dB and 0.03 dB Y-PSNR [10] improvements in proposed GOF than the conventional GOF methods for "Usb", "Blur" and "Fishtank" video sequence respectively. A considerable improvement also achieved in U- and V-PSNR chrominance values.

Table 2. Average PSNR (dB) comparisons of conventional and proposed GOF for Hybrid video coding

Sequence	Conventional GOF			Proposed GOF		
	Y-PSNR	U-PSNR	V-PSNR	Y-PSNR	U-PSNR	V-PSNR
Usb	33.7759	35.3856	35.7582	33.8143	35.4151	35.7986
Blur	34.2633	34.8835	35.5948	34.3568	34.9086	35.6175
Fishtank	32.8396	34.7072	35.5448	32.8978	34.7449	34.5876

Table 2 compares the Luminance and Chrominance values of various video sequences using conventional GOF and proposed GOF sequence for hybrid based video coding. It is observed that 0.1 dB, 0.09 dB and 0.06 dB Y-PSNR improvement in proposed GOF than the conventional GOF methods for "Usb", "Blur" and "Fishtank" video sequence respectively. A considerable improvement also achieved in U- and V-PSNR chrominance values.

Table 3. Average PSNR (dB) comparisons and encoding time between DCT and Hybrid video coding

Sequence	DCT coding		Hybrid coding	
	Y-PSNR	Encoding time (ms)	Y-PSNR	Encoding time (ms)
Usb	32.1638	117328	33.8143	107000
Blur	34.2945	16531	34.3568	13407
Fishtank	31.5677	1205906	32.8978	1004703

Table 3 compares the Y-PSNR and Encoding time of various video sequences using proposed GOF sequence for both DCT and hybrid based video coding. It is observed that 1.65 dB, 0.06 dB and 1.33 dB Y-PSNR improvements in proposed hybrid coding for "Usb", "Blur" and "Fishtank" video sequence respectively. It is also seen that the encoding time of proposed hybrid coding is 1.09, 1.23 and 1.20 times faster than the conventional DCT coding for the video sequences taken for experiments.

5 Conclusion

In this paper, a hybrid transformation technique for video coding has been proposed. In which, the intraframes of video sequence are coded by DWT with Haar wavelet filter and the interframes of video sequence are coded with DCT technique. It also proposes the selection of sequence of frames predicted from the reference intraframes. These proposals consistently minimize the prediction error for the predicted frame for further processing. The experiments are conducted on three video sequences with different natures. The empirical results show that the proposed hybrid transformation coding technique is 1.09 to 1.23 times faster than conventional DCT transformation coding technique in terms of encoding time for the video sequences. It is also achieve 0.03 dB to 1.65 dB Y-PSNR improvement over the conventional transform coding methods.

Acknowledgments. The authors wish to thank S. Anusha, A. R. Srividhya and S. Vanitha undergraduate students for their valuable help.

References

1. N. Ahmed, T. Natarajan, K. R. Rao: Discrete Cosine Transform. IEEE Transactions on Computers, vol. C-23 (1974) 90-93
2. Marc Antonini, Michel Barlaud, Pierre Mathieu, Ingrid Daubechies: Image coding using wavelet transform. IEEE Transactions on Image Processing, vol. 1, no. 2 (1992) 205-220
3. Frederic Dufaux, Fabrice Moscheni: Motion Estimation Techniques for Digital TV - A Review and a New Contribution. Proceedings of IEEE, vol. 83, no. 6 (1995) 858-876
4. Allen Gersho: Quantization. IEEE Communications society magazine, (1977)
5. P. G. Howard, J. C. Vitter: Arithmetic Coding for Data Compression. Proceedings of the IEEE, vol. 82, no. 6 (1994) 857-865
6. Didier Le Gall: MPEG - A video compression standard for multimedia applications. vol. 34, no. 4 (1991) 47-58
7. Ming Liou: Overview of the px64 kbps video coding standard. vol. 34, no. 4 (1991) 60-63
8. B. E. Usevitch: A Tutorial on Modern Lossy Wavelet Image Compression - Foundations of JPEG 2000. IEEE Signal Processing Magazine, vol. 18, no. 5 (2001) 22-35
9. Joint Video Team Reference Software JM8.2 May 2004 [Online]. Available: http//bs.hhi.de/~suihring/tml/download.
10. Ze-Nian Li, Mark S. Drew: Fundamentals of Multimedia. Pearson Education, New Delhi (2004)

Location Verification Based Defense Against Sybil Attack in Sensor Networks

Debapriyay Mukhopadhyay and Indranil Saha

Honeywell Technology Solutions Lab Pvt. Ltd.
151/1, Doraisanipalya, Bannerghatta Road,
Bangalore 560 076, India
{debapriyay.mukhopadhyay, indranil.saha}@honeywell.com

Abstract. Security is a major concern for a large fraction of sensor network applications. Douceur first introduced the notion of sybil attack [4], where a single entity(node) illegitimately presents multiple identities. As the nodes in sensor networks can be physically captured by an adversary, sybil attack can manifest in a severe form leading to the malfunction of basic operational protocols including routing, resource allocation and misbehavior detection. In this study, we propose a location verification based defense against sybil attack for sensor network where we assume that the network is consisted of static sensor nodes. We report quantitatively about the probability of not being able to detect sybil attack. This probability is indicative of the usefulness of our proposed protocol.

Keywords: Sybil attack, Security, Wireless Sensor Network, Triangulation, Location Verification.

1 Introduction

Sensor networks are now being widely deployed in planned or ad hoc basis to monitor and protect different targeted infrastructures including life-critical applications such as wildlife monitoring, military target tracking, home security monitoring and scientific exploration in hazardous environments. The criticality of a large subset of applications triggers the need for providing adequate security support for them. Unlike in general data networks, the nodes of sensor networks may be physically captured by an adversary and thus can induce different modes of harmful attacks in addition to active and passive eavesdropping. This typical feature also makes the design of cryptographic primitives for sensor networks extremely challenging.

Douceur first introduced the notion of sybil attack [4], where a single entity illegitimately presents multiple identities. Physically captured nodes claiming superfluous misbehaving identities could control a substantial fraction of the system leading to malfunction of basic operational protocols including routing, resource allocation and misbehavior detection. An excellent taxonomy of sybil attacks in sensor networks and their detrimental effects are presented by Newsome *et. al.* in [8], along with some defense mechanisms. In their work, they have provided a definition of simultaneous sybil attack where an attacker tries to have his sybil identities all participate in the network at once.

S. Chaudhuri et al. (Eds.): ICDCN 2006, LNCS 4308, pp. 509–521, 2006.

Sybil attack could be prevented if each honest identity possesses an unforgeable certificate issued by some trusted Certifying Authority(CA) and it is mandated to produce that certificate as a proof of authenticity before the identity takes part in any network activity. This condition implies that for inducing sybil attack the adversary has to necessarily forge valid certificates. But since sensor nodes are resource constrained devices, so computationally expensive public key cryptography based certification schemes are not suitable to be applicable in sensor networks.

It has also been mentioned in [8] that location verification could be a promising approach to defend sybil attack. In this work, we aim to provide such a solution for defending simultaneous sybil attack. Our solution does not require to verify the exact physical position of a node, rather it works out by securely verifying whether the physical position of the node is within a region. The region is defined in terms of a new functional for planar triangulation which we have come up with and we call it as *Inner Core* of a triangulation. A lot of theoretical and algorithmic questions come along with this new functional, but in this paper we just try to show how this functional could be of use in defending sybil attack rather than delving into solving those problems. Lastly, our solution is mainly targeted for those sensor network based applications where it is required to deploy sensor nodes in a planned manner.

We organize our paper as follows. Section 2 describes prior art and also briefly reviews the merits and demerits of each. In Section 3, we formally define the problem by clearly mentioning network assumptions and security goals. Section 4 defines the new functional Inner Core for planar triangulation. In Section 5, we describe our solution and also provide a formal analysis of its security. Lastly, Section 6 concludes this work along with future directions of research.

2   Related Work

Sybil attack was first introduced by Douceur in [4], wherein a direct validation method of a node's identity based on resource testing was proposed. The basic idea of the scheme is to estimate the resource (*e.g.,* computation, storage and communication) associated with each identity and thereby deciding whether each identity possesses a dedicated hardware piece. Scheme proposed in their work applies for general P2P networks and is not suitable to be applicable in sensor networks where an adversary may bring in very powerful devices (in terms of computation, storage and communication) to defeat the scheme. Karlof *et. al.* analyzed different attacks including sybil attack in [7] for wireless sensor network and described some countermeasures against them. In their approach, each node is provided with a unique symmetric key which it shares with a trusted base station. Two nodes then can verify each other's identity through establishment of a shared key, via the base station, using symmetric Needham-Schroeder-like [2] protocol. The solution thus relies on the existence of a trusted third party. Again, there are some attacks [1] against Needham-Schroeder-like protocol in which case the proposed solution fails.

Wang *et. al.* [5] introduced the concept of trust graph in mobile ad hoc network, which facilitates in establishing trust relationship between communicating nodes and considers the possibility of having heterogeneous certifying authorities (CAs). Assumption here is that if a certifying authority CA_1 trusts another certifying authority CA_2, then CA_1 also trusts identities certified by CA_2. It is interesting to note here that this assumption and mechanism can safeguard against sybil attack as long as none of the CAs is compromised. Their scheme also demands each node to have moderately high storage and computational capability and also charges high communication cost and thus remains unsuitable for sensor networks. Newsome *et. al.* in their work [8] established a taxonomy of different kinds of sybil attack and provided two methods based on radio resource testing and random key predistribution to verify whether a node's identity is a sybil identity. Though their random key pre-distribution based scheme is very promising, but still its not mature enough to conceive the notion of certificate in the symmetric key domain. The scheme also has limitation in a typical scenario where the nodes of the sensor network come from different vendors.

Kong *et. al.* proposed a public key cryptography based distributed threshold certification scheme [3] which establishes trust relationship between communicating nodes via unforgeable, renewable and globally verifiable certificates carried by each node in the network. Its not explicitly mentioned that their work can stand against sybil attack as otherwise attacker has to guess valid certificate of the claimed identity. But, their work is based on public key cryptography and targeted to meet the needs of wireless ad hoc networks. It does not readily suit well in resource constrained sensor network architecture. Zhang *et. al.* in [10] have proposed an identity certificate based scheme to defend against sybil attack in sensor networks. Their method associates each node's identity with an unique identity certificate, where Merkle hash tree has been used as the basic means of computing identity certificates. Main drawback of the scheme is that it is not scalable as it does not allow nodes to join the network on the fly because of huge computational overhead. Method also requires a large number of messages getting exchanged to build a trust between a pair of nodes and also it can not stand against sybil attack launched by colluding nodes.

3   Problem Definition

Network Assumptions: The network is consisted of a large number of sensor nodes and is deployed by a single authority. We are considering here those sensor network based applications where it is required to deploy sensor nodes in a planned manner. We also assume the presence of a powerful setup server which configures the sensor network and is aware of the locations of all the sensor nodes being deployed. Once deployed, each node is static and can be thought of as placed in a plane with each node having a distinct position where it is placed / deployed. We also allow new nodes to join the network on the fly. But since its a planned deployment, so we only allow joining of new nodes within the convex hull of initial set of deployed nodes. This is not a very unrealistic assumption since for a planned deployment its not difficult to know a priori the region in which to deploy the sensor nodes and accordingly we can then deploy the initial set of sensor nodes. All the sensor nodes are capable of communicating using both radio frequency (RF) and sound channel and can only directly communicate with a limited number of neighboring nodes.

We also assume that both the transmission channels are perfectly secure, that is, any message being sent over any of these channels reaches the destination as unintercepted. All the sensor nodes trust the setup server and assume its behavior to be perfectly fare. Unlike in general data networks, nodes of a sensor network are susceptible to physical capture by an adversary and then can control them to attack the network. But the fraction of them will only be a small percentage of the overall network.

Security Goals: Our goal in this paper is to provide a mechanism to safeguard against simultaneous sybil attack where a malicious node simultaneously claims many identities of itself to defeat some of the well known protocols like data aggregation, routing, etc. An attacker who launches a simultaneous sybil attack will attempt to position the sybil identities in strategic locations of the network in order to defeat the above protocols. We thus choose to verify securely the position of any new node that pops up in the network, which in turn can act as a mechansim to defend against sybil attack.

4   Inner Core: A New Functional for Planar Triangulation

Definition 1. *Inner Core of a triangle (Figure 1) T with $v_i (i = 1, 2, 3)$ as vertices is defined as,*

$$IC(T) = \{\cap_{i=1}^{3} Disk(V_i, l_i)\} \cap T,$$

where $l_i = min$ {Length of the sides of the triangle T incident on V_i}, and $Disk(V_i, l_i)$ is the circular region with V_i as it's center and l_i as its radius.

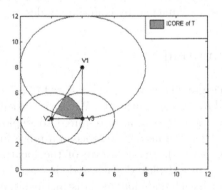

Fig. 1. Inner Core of Triangle T

Inner Core of triangulation Δ of a set $S \subset R^2$ of planar points is defined as the union of the inner cores of its constituent triangles, i.e.,

$$IC(\Delta) = \bigcup_{T \in \Delta} IC(T).$$

For a set S of planar points, the set $\mathcal{F}$ of all triangulations becomes exponential in size with the number of planar points. So, a natural and obvious question is to find out the triangulation for which Inner Core gets maximized, i.e., to find out $\Delta \in \mathcal{F}$ for which the area of $ConvH(S) - IC(\Delta)$ is minimized, where $ConvH(S)$ denotes the convex hull of the set of planar points S.

Delaunay triangulation D of a set of points $S \subset R^2$ forming a regular triangular lattice coincides with the lattice itself and hence $ConvH(S) - IC(D) = \phi$ and thus maximizes Inner Core. Getting started with this observation, we haven't been able to either prove or disprove that Inner Core achieves its maximum for Delaunay triangulation and hence we make the following conjecture.

Conjecture 1. *The functional $IC(\Delta)$ of a set of planar points S achieves its maximum if and only if Δ is the Delaunay triangulation of S.*

5 Protocol

In this section we describe the applicability of Inner Core in preventing sybil attack. We assume the presence of a software agent who is aware of the locations of all the deployed sensor nodes. Agent can get to know about the location of a sensor node either by consulting with the setup server or when a new node claims its location after joining the network. On joining the network when a new node claims its location, then agent applies our proposed protocol and tries to verify the claimed position. If it can verify the position then adds the claimed location in its list of deployed sensor nodes. Otherwise, it rechecks the claimed location with the setup server to get to know whether setup server has deployed any node in that location.

5.1 Basic Protocol

The agent starts this protocol by finding a triangulation Δ of the set of planar points S, where each point in S corresponds to a position of an immobile sensor node in the network. When a new node claims its position somewhere in the network, the agent identifies the triangle in which the claimed position of a new node is, and hands over the charge of the remaining part of the protocol to be executed by the sensor nodes in the positions of the vertices of the identified triangle. Agent does that by letting each sensor node representing a vertex of the identified triangle know about the claimed identity of the new node.

Remaining part of the protocol then goes as follows: Let, V_1, V_2 and V_3 be the nodes forming the triangle within which the new node claims its position.

Step 1: Each of the nodes V_i ($i = 1, 2, 3$), generates a random number R_i and attaches with it its own identity yielding a messages M_i where $M_i = R_i V_i$.

Step 2: Each of the nodes V_i ($i = 1, 2, 3$), then sends M_i to the new node X that claims its identity to be in the triangle.

Step 3: Node X receives three messages M_i ($i = 1, 2, 3$), one from each of the nodes and constructs $M_i' = R_i X$ and then sends it back to the node V_i ($i = 1, 2, 3$). Messages M_i are sent using radio frequency channel, and messages M_i' are sent using sound channel.

Step 4: Each node V_i ($i = 1, 2, 3$), then measures the elapsed time t_{ii} between the delivery of the message and the receipt of the corresponding message M_i' and reports back to the software agent by sending t_{ii}.

So, if we assume that the processing time in each node is almost close to zero, then,

$$t_{ii} = d(V_i, X)(1/c + 1/s) \qquad (1)$$

where $d(X, Y)$ denotes the euclidian distance between the nodes X and Y, and c and s are the distances traversed in unit time in radio frequency and ultra sound channel. The notion of using two channels for computing t_{ii} values has been borrowed from [6]. The reason why in Step 1, each node V_i ($i = 1, 2, 3$), generates a random number to compute the message M_i is straight forward. This is required to ensure that all the nodes V_1, V_2 and V_3 and also the newly claimed node X is actively participating in the protocol and thus is facilitating in correctly computing t_{ii} values. Otherwise, it could have been possible for a malicious node to defeat the protocol by replying early (if it knows in a priori these R_i's).

If the new claimed node X is a honest one, which claims its position within the Inner Core of the triangle defined by the nodes V_i ($i = 1, 2, 3$), then we could expect, for all the nodes V_i ($i = 1, 2, 3$), $t_{ii} \leq t_{ij}$, where t_{ij} is the total time required for a message to reach V_j from V_i and then getting back a response in turn from V_j, for all $j \neq i$ and $j \in \{1, 2, 3\}$. This time also we have the same assumption of using both radio frequency and ultra sound channel and hence t_{ij} values for $i = 1, 2, 3$ and $j \neq i$ where $j \in \{1, 2, 3\}$ can be calculated as

$$t_{ij} = d(V_i, V_j)(1/c + 1/s) \qquad (2)$$

It is to be mentioned here that since agent knows the locations of all the nodes V_1, V_2 and V_3 so it can easily compute the t_{ij} values at its side using (2).

So, if all the V_i's are honest, then the agent will consider the claimed node X to be an honest one if the above inequality holds for all $i = 1, 2, 3$, and for all $j \neq i$ where $j \in \{1, 2, 3\}$. If it is so, then it adds the node, location pair in its list of deployed nodes. This follows easily from (1) and (2) as for any vertex of the triangle, its distance from any point inside the Inner Core is less than or equal to its distance from the other two vertices of the triangle. This is the most ideal case which we could expect for the protocol to function properly.

Therefore, the agent is required to find a triangulation Δ of the set of planar points S such that the claimed location of the node is in the Inner Core of Δ. If no such triangulation exists then the software agent initiating the protocol consults with the setup server. If the setup server has deployed this node, then its possible for the agent to crosscheck it and in which case it allows the node to join the network otherwise rejects. Now given a point X within the convex hull of S, whether there exists any triangulation Δ of S such that X is in the Inner Core of Δ is not known to us. Even if it exists how to find out such a triangulation is also an open question. Hence as long as we do not have answers to these questions, agent can initiate the protocol by finding the *Delaunay triangulation* of S for which we conjecture that it maximizes Inner Core for a set of planar points.

The proposed protocol exhibits the following interesting properties. It does not require a large number of messages to get exchanged in order for the protocol to work. Agent contributes to the message complexity by sending three messages while delegating the charge of the protocol to the sensor nodes forming the identified triangle. Each of the three sensor nodes forming the triangle is required to send two messages, one to the new node and another to the Agent. The newly joined node requires to send three messages. From the protocol its also clear that messages are of short length. Also the protocol does not demand from any sensor to have stored a huge amount of information excepting only its own location in the plane. Protocol does not suffer from the problem of scalability as it allows new nodes to join the network on the fly. The only restriction here is that a new node will only be allowed to join the network if it is within the convex hull of initial set of deployed nodes.

5.2   Modified Protocol to Handle Processing Delay in the New Node

In Step 4 of the protocol, we have seen that each node V_i $(i = 1, 2, 3)$ computes the value of t_{ii} and the expression for t_{ii} in (1) assumes that processing time in each node (in particular, in the new node X) is almost close to zero. But in practice, this is not the case, as the new node X needs some time to process the packets (in Step 3 of the protocol) received from each of the nodes V_i $(i = 1, 2, 3)$. To handle this situation, we modify our protocol slightly. First we introduce a parameter called *minimum processing time* (Δ_{min}) for any sensor node and we also assume that a sensor node is capable of measuring the processing time for each packet. We now modify Step 3 of the protocol as follows. New node X constructs $M_i' = R_i \Delta_i X$, where Δ_i is the time spent in processing the message from node V_i $(i = 1, 2, 3)$. So, the elapsed time t_{ii}' between the delivery of the message M_i and the receipt of the corresponding message M_i' is given by,

$$t_{ii}' = d(V_i, X)(1/c + 1/s) + \Delta_i. \tag{3}$$

Because of the modification in Step 3 of the protocol, it is now possible for each node V_i $(i = 1, 2, 3)$ to be able to compute t_{ii}' instead of computing t_{ii} and in Step 4 of the protocol it reports back to the software agent by sending the pair t_{ii}' and Δ_i. The agent then checks for all $i = 1, 2, 3$ whether $t_{ii}' - \Delta_i \leq t_{ij}$, for all $j \neq i$ and $j \in \{1, 2, 3\}$, where t_{ij} retains the same meaning as has been described in the previous section, to verify the claimed location of the new node.

This above solution works fine when $\Delta_i = \Delta_{min}$. But, the problem arises when $\Delta_i > \Delta_{min}$. The new node X may maliciously claim its message processing time to be more than Δ_{min}, while the original processing time is very close to Δ_{min}.

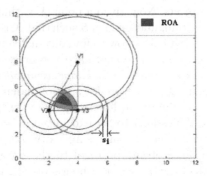

Fig. 2. Region of Acceptance of Triangle T

Doing this helps the node X to establish its location to be inside the Inner Core of the triangle, while actually being located somewhere outside the Inner Core. This is because, by choosing Δ_i's large enough node X can force $t'_{ii} - \Delta_i \leq t_{ij}$ for $j \neq i$ and $j \in \{1, 2, 3\}$ to get satisfied for all $i = 1, 2, 3$, and thus can defeat the protocol. The problem thus for the case $\Delta_i > \Delta_{min}$ can be solved as follows. The solution works by identifying a region included in the Inner Core of the triangle such that if the claimed location of X is inside this new region then its true location has to be within the Inner Core of the triangle. As malicious node can claim its message processing time as Δ_i ($> \Delta_{min}$) in order to make $t'_{ii} - \Delta_i$ to be less than equal to t_{ij}, similarly the verifying nodes V_i ($i = 1, 2, 3$) can adjust the values of t_{ij}'s accordingly to prevent the malicious node from defeating the protocol. How adjustments to these t_{ij} values can be made and how this relates to identifying a region included in the Inner Core of the triangle is discussed below.

When node X claims Δ_i as its message processing time for node V_i ($i = 1, 2, 3$) of the triangle, then the maximum distance which a message can traverse first in radio frequency channel and then in sound channel in time $\Delta_i - \Delta_{min}$ can be calculated as,

$$s_i = \frac{(\Delta_i - \Delta_{min})}{(1/c + 1/s)}. \tag{4}$$

We now define a new region called *Region of Acceptance (ROA)* relative to a triangle T with V_i ($i = 1, 2, 3$) as vertices as follows.

Definition 2. *Region of Acceptance of a triangle (Figure 2) T with $V_i (i = 1, 2, 3)$ as vertices is defined as,*

$$ROA(T) = \{\cap_{i=1}^{3} Disk(V_i, l'_i)\} \cap T,$$

where

$$l'_i = \begin{cases} l_i - s_i, & \text{if } l_i > s_i \\ 0, & \text{otherwise,} \end{cases}$$

and $Disk(V_i, l'_i)$ is the circular region with V_i as its center and l'_i as its radius.

Its now easy to see that, if the new node X claims Δ_i for node V_i ($i = 1, 2, 3$), then $ROA(T)$ is either fully included in $IC(T)$ or $ROA(T) = \phi$. To verify the location of the new node X, the agent then does the following.

1. On having received the t'_{ii} and Δ_i pair from each of the nodes V_i ($i = 1, 2, 3$), it first checks whether $ROA(T) \subseteq IC(T)$ or $ROA(T) = \phi$.
2. If $ROA(T) \subseteq IC(T)$, then agent computes the time t'_{ij} instead of t_{ij} for all $i = 1, 2, 3$, and $j \neq i$, $j \in \{1, 2, 3\}$ as

$$t'_{ij} = (d(V_i, V_j) - s_i)(1/c + 1/s)$$

$$\implies t'_{ij} = t_{ij} - (\Delta_i - \Delta_{min}) \text{ for all the nodes } V_i \ (i = 1, 2, 3).$$

Then it checks to find whether $t'_{ii} - \Delta_i \leq t'_{ij}$, for all $j \neq i$ and $j \in \{1, 2, 3\}$. If it is so, then the agent considers the new node X to be an honest one. This only applies, if the claimed location of the new node is within $ROA(T)$, which the agent can easily determine by calculating the values of s_i's from the Δ_i values. If the claimed location is somewhere inside $IC(T) - ROA(T)$, then to verify the location agent has to crosscheck it with the setup server.
3. If $ROA(T) = \phi$, then the agent verifies the location by crosschecking it with the setup server.

One interesting thing to note here is that, if $\Delta_i = \Delta_{min}$ for all $i = 1, 2, 3$, then $ROA(T) = IC(T)$ and as such the agent can verify the location anywhere within the Inner Core of the triangle.

5.3   Security Analysis

Let us now consider the case when all the nodes in the set S are not honest. These dishonest nodes can help a sybil node to establish its claim of being present in the Inner Core of a triangle. In this discussion we will assume that the message processing time of a sensor node is negligible, i.e., almost close to zero. We now define *Region of Vulnerability* of a triangle T as a region such that if a malicious node is physically present in this region then it can defeat the protocol by successfully inducing a sybil node within the Inner Core of T. Definition of *Region of Vulnerability* also takes into account the fact that either no node or any number of nodes forming the triangle T can be malicious. But since every node V_i has to report back to the agent by sending t_{ii} values, so a malicious node in the position of any vertex of a triangle can't help another malicious node to launch a successful sybil attack very easily by sending erroneous t_{ii} values. An attempt to do so may help the agent to be able to isolate the malicious nodes since it is computing the t_{ij} values at its side.

Region of vulnerability for a triangle can then be calculated for the following four cases.

Case A: All the vertices of the triangle are honest. *Region of Vulnerability* of T (Figure 3) can then be calculated as

$$Rov(T) = \{\bigcap_{i=1}^{3} Disk(V_i, l_i)\} - T,$$

where the notations l_i and $Disk(V_i, l_i)$ have been described earlier.

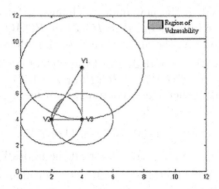

Fig. 3. Region of Vulnerability

Case B: Two of the nodes (V_i's) are honest, while the other one is not. We will see that in this scenario the protocol may fail, being unable to detect a valid sybil attack. Let us consider that in triangle T with vertices V_1, V_2, and V_3 node V_1 and V_3 are honest and V_2 is dishonest. The region of Vulnerability of triangle T is shown as shaded in Figure 4. Now, a malicious node actually being present in the shaded region and claiming a sybil identity within the region defined by the triangle T, can defeat the protocol in identifying the newly claimed node as a sybil node in association with another dishonest node V_2. Node V_2 represents the distance of the new node from itself by appropriately sending t_{22} such that the agent concludes that the new node is indeed in the Inner Core of the triangle. In this case the Region of Vulnerability can be formally written as

$$Rov(T) = \bigcap_{i \in V_{honest}} Disk(V_i, l_i) - T$$

where V_{honest} represents the set of honest nodes of triangle T and such that $|V_{honest}| = 2$.

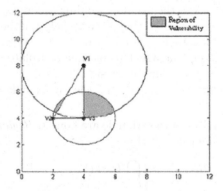

Fig. 4. Region of Vulnerability w.r.t. node V2

Case C: One of the nodes in T is honest, and the other two are not. This case is shown in Figure 5. Node V_3 is honest, and nodes V_1 and V_2 are dishonest. The region of vulnerability of triangle T with respect to the dishonest nodes V_1 and V_2 is shown as shaded in the figure. The Region of Vulnerability in this case can be formally written as

$$Rov(T) = Disk(V_i, l_i) - T,$$

where V_i ($i \in \{1, 2, 3\}$) is the only honest node of T.

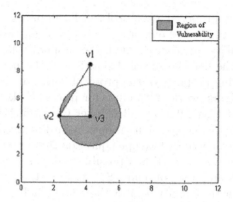

Fig. 5. Region of Vulnerability w.r.t. nodes V1 and V2

Case D: All the three nodes of the triangle are dishonest. In this case wherever the malicious node be physically present it can always launch a successful sybil attack and thus we have $Rov(T) = ConvH(S)$.

Region of Vulnerability for a triangulation Δ of a set of nodes S can be equivalently defined as the union of the region of vulnerabilities of its constituent triangles, i.e.,

$$Rov(\Delta) = \bigcup_{T \in \Delta} Rov(T).$$

Having defined the $Rov(\Delta)$ for any triangulation Δ of the set of nodes S, we will now calculate the probability that a sybil node will remain undetected by our protocol. This probability is simply the area of the region, the physical presence of a malicious node in which can help in successfully launching a sybil attack, divided by the area of the region inside the convex hull of the set of nodes S. This region, physical presence of a malicious node in which can help in successfully launching a sybil attack is essentially the intersection of $Rov(\Delta)$'s for all such Δ. So the probability that sybil attack remains undetected under the proposed protocol is given by,

$$\frac{\bigcap_{\Delta \in c} Rov(\Delta)}{ConvH(S)},$$

where $\mathcal{C}$ denotes the class of all triangulations of the set of planar points S. Since we don't have the answers to some of the questions related to Inner Core and as we have planned to use Delaunay triangulation $D \in \mathcal{C}$ for the time being, so the probability that sybil attack remains undetected is given by,

$$\frac{Rov(D)}{ConvH(S)}.$$

6   Conclusion

In this paper, we have proposed a protocol which can prevent simultaneous sybil attack in a sensor network and our protocol is meant for those sensor networks for which planned deployment of the nodes is required. The protocol works by securely verifying whether the physical position of the new node is within a region. One interesting property of the protocol is that its scalable as it allows new nodes to join the network on the fly. Our protocol takes the help of a new functional for planar triangulation called Inner Core which we have defined in this work. We have left three questions as open regarding this new functional and one in the form of a conjecture. Two open question that are of particular interest for the sake of the protocol are: (i) Is it possible to derive a characterization such that given a point X and a set of points $S = V_i : i = 1, 2,.... ,n$; we will be able to answer whether a triangulation Δ of the convex hull of S exists such that X is in Inner Core of Δ, and (ii) If yes, how can we find a polynomial time algorithm to find such a triangulation. Being able to answer these two questions will have significant impact on the performance of the protocol as it will help in minimizing the number of queries that an agent has to make to crosscheck the location of a node with the setup server.

References

1. R. Needham and M. Schroeder. "Using encryption for authentication in large networks of computers", In *Communications of the ACM*, pages 993 - 999, 1978.
2. D. Denning and G. Sacco. "Timestamps in key distribution protocols". In *Communications of the ACM*, 25:533-536,1982.
3. J. Kong, P. Zerfos, H. Luo, S. Lu, and L. Zhang. "Providing Robust and Ubiquitious Security Support for Mobile Ad-Hoc Networks". In *Proceedings of International conference on Network Protocols*, 2001.
4. J. R. Douceur. "The Sybil attack". In *Proceedings of IPTPS02 Workshop*, Cambridge, March 2002.
5. W. Wang, Y. Zhu, and B. Li. "Self-Managed Heterogeneous Certification in Mobile Ad Hoc Networks". In *Proceedings of IEEE Vehicular Technology Conference*, 2003.
6. N. Sastry, U. Shankar and D. Wagner. "Secure Verification of Location Claims". In *Proceedings of the ACM workshop on Wireless security*, pages 1 - 10, San Diego, CA, USA, 2003.
7. C. Karlof and D. Wagner. "Secure Routing in Wireless Sensor Networks: Attacks and Countermeasures". In *First IEEE International Workshop on Sensor Network Protocols and Applications*, May 2003.

8. J. Newsome, E. Shi, D. Song, and A. Perrig. "The Sybil Attack in Sensor Networks: Analysis and Defenses". In *Proceedings of Third International Symposium on Information Processing in Sensor Networks*, April 2004.

9. B. Parno, A. Perrig, and V. Gligor. "Distributed Detection of Node Replication Attacks in Sensor Networks". In *Proceedings of the 2005 IEEE Symposium on Security and Privacy*, May 8-11, 2005.

10. Q. Zhang, P. Wang, D. S. Reeves, P. Ning. "Defending Sybil Attacks in Sensor Networks". In *Proceedings of the International Workshop on Security in Distributed Computing Systems*, June 2005.

A New Scheme for Establishing Pairwise Keys for Wireless Sensor Networks

Abhishek Gupta, Joy Kuri, and Pavan Nuggehalli

Centre for Electronics Design and Technology
Indian Institute of Science, Bangalore
{agupta, kuri, pavan}@cedt.iisc.ernet.in

Abstract. This paper addresses the problem of secure path key establishment in wireless sensor networks that uses the random key pre-distribution technique. Inspired by the recent proxy-based scheme in [1] and [2], we introduce a *friend*-based scheme for establishing pairwise keys securely. We show that the chances of finding friends in a neighbourhood are considerably more than that of finding proxies, leading to lower communication overhead. Further, we prove that the friend-based scheme performs better than the proxy-based scheme in terms of resilience against node capture.

1 Introduction

In the last few years, wireless sensor networks (WSNs) have become a very actively researched area. The impetus for this spurt of interest were developments in wireless technologies and low-cost VLSI, that made it possible to build inexpensive sensors and actuators. Each such device has limited computational power, memory and energy supply. Nevertheless, because of the low cost, such devices can be deployed in large numbers, and can thereafter form a sensor *network*. Applications have been suggested in diverse areas, including surveillance, environmental monitoring, health care and crisis management systems.

In some application areas, security is a major concern. When sensor networks carry sensitive information, it is important to ensure privacy. For example, in a surveillance application, it would be very undesirable if intruders can access the information being carried by the network. To provide security, the well-developed public key cryptographic methods have been considered, but these generally demand excessive computation and storage from the resource-poor sensors [3]. This has led researchers to conclude that symmetric key cryptography, in which nodes share a secret key, is the only viable solution.

While cryptographically strong algorithms are available, the issue of *key distribution and management* is critical to the level of security actually achieved. At one end of the spectrum, we have a system in which all the sensors share a single secret key. But this makes the network very vulnerable; an adversary needs to capture just a single sensor node to access any information that the network carries. At the opposite end, we have a system where each node has a

S. Chaudhuri et al. (Eds.): ICDCN 2006, LNCS 4308, pp. 522–533, 2006.

distinct shared key for every other node. But for large sensor networks, such a scheme demands an excessive amount of on-board memory, which is again undesirable. It is also possible for nodes to securely generate keys on the fly using key exchange algorithms, such as the well-known Diffie-Hellman scheme. However, the computational and storage requirements for such schemes have also been deemed unacceptable for sensor networks [3].

In [4], Eschenauer and Gligor suggested a probabilistic solution to the problem of efficient key distribution. In this scheme, nodes have a secure link if they share a key in common and those which do not share a key undergo path key establishment phase to set-up a pair-wise key.A drawback of this scheme is that the secret key is known to all the nodes on the path from the source to the destination node during path key-establishment phase.

This 'per-hop key exposure' problem have been considered by several researchers. In [1], the authors proposed an elegant solution of using multiple node-disjoint paths between S and D for secure path key establishment. But the problem of discovering multiple node-disjoint paths is computationally hard, and too much overhead may be incurred in this process. In a later work [2], the authors relax the requirement of node-disjoint paths, and utilize multiple *proxies* for path key establishment. A proxy $\mathcal{P}$ is a node that shares one or more keys with the source node S and one or more keys with the destination node D.

In this paper, we propose a novel scheme to efficiently solve the 'per-hop key exposure' problem. It is based on nodes that are referred to as *friends* of the destination. A friend of the destination is simply a node that shares one or more keys with the destination. Each friend F in a neighbourhood of S sends *part-keys* back to the source, where a part-key is obtained by applying a hash function to all the keys shared between F and D. The source then chooses a number of these part-keys, say i, and uses a publicly known function to generate the shared key K_{SD} from them. S informs D about which i friends' part-keys were used, and this information is sufficient for D to generate K_{SD} using the publicly known function.

We compare our friend-based scheme with the proxy-based scheme reported in [2], and find several advantages. First, for a source-destination pair, the requirement for a node to be a friend is less stringent than for it to be a proxy. This implies that the computational and communication effort in finding a friend is less than in finding a proxy, making the friend-based approach more viable. Second, our friend-based scheme is able to achieve a level of security at least as good as the one based on proxies.

2 Related Work

The random key pre-distribution scheme was first proposed by [4]. We discuss this proposal in some detail in the next section. Based on this, several schemes with enhanced security features have been suggested. A q-composite-random key pre-distribution scheme is proposed by [5] which achieves strengthened security under small scale attack while trading off increased vulnerability in the face of a large scale physical attack on network nodes. It then uses multi-path key reinforcement scheme to update the communication key to a random value after key set-up phase.

In [6], a seed-based approach is used for assigning keys to each node. Each key is associated with a unique key identifier or key-id. Moreover, the key itself cannot be deduced from the knowledge of the key-id. For any node, a set of key-ids is generated from a common pseudo-random generator with the node identity acting as the seed. The corresponding keys are then stored in the node. This makes it possible for each node to identify the key-ids that another node has, and thereby find if they share any common keys. The seed-based approach reduces the communication burden in sharing key identifiers. For example, the source node can find out if it shares a common key with the destination node without having to communicate with the destination node. [7] uses similar technique for shared key discovery phase.

[8] gives a scheme where memory requirements can be reduced at the expense of pre-deployment knowledge. In this scheme, knowledge about which nodes are likely to be the neighbours of each sensor node is exploited such that the probability of any two neighbouring nodes sharing a common key is maximized without degrading the other performance metrics, such as security and memory usage.

The scheme in [9] exhibits a nice threshold property: When the number of compromised nodes is less than the threshold, the probability that any node other than these compromised nodes are affected is close to zero. Their scheme builds on Blom's key pre-distribution scheme [10] and combines the random key pre-distribution method with it.

Our work is closest to that reported in [1] and [2]. Both these papers consider the path key establishment problem. Let S and D be the source and destination between which a shared key is required. D generates a secret key and this key is securely passed to S. [1] proposes a scheme in which the key is broken up into l *nuggets*, and the nuggets are passed to D along node-disjoint paths. All nuggets are required to reconstruct the key. Therefore, an attacker has to capture at least one node along each of the node-disjoints paths to recover the key. In [2] , the authors note the following shortcomings of this scheme: *(a)* Finding l node-disjoint paths is an NP-hard problem, and too much overhead is required; further, in some cases it may not be possible to find l such paths, *(b)* A nugget is exposed to each intermediate node along its path to S; thus, contrary to intuition, increasing l does not necessarily improve the level of security, because the nuggets are exposed to more nodes, increasing the vulnerability of the scheme.

To address this drawback, [2] proposes a scheme in which no more than *one* node along a path knows the key nugget. This node is referred to as a *proxy*. Thus, D can securely pass a nugget to the proxy on the path, and the proxy can securely relay the nugget to S. Moreover, the paths used need not be node-disjoint any longer and, in fact, need not be composed of secure links either, because security is achieved by the shared keys between S and the proxy, and the proxy and D.

3   Path Key Establishment

We begin this section by reviewing briefly the basic scheme in [4]. We then discuss the path key establishment scheme given in [2]. This is followed by our friend-based scheme.

In [4], Eschenauer and Gligor suggested a probabilistic solution to the problem of efficient key distribution. In this scheme, each sensor node is assigned a *key-ring* consisting of k keys chosen at random (without replacement) from a pool of P keys. After deployment, two nodes within communication range exchange key-identifiers or challenges to discover common keys. Then, a common key is selected for secure communication. Node pairs without a common key establish a path key through a secure path.

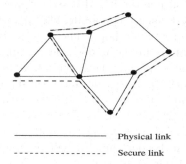

                                                    ——————————— Physical link
                                                    - - - - - - - - - - Secure link

Fig. 1. An example showing the network graph and the key graph

Figure 1 shows a wireless sensor network with 7 nodes. If two nodes are within radio range, they are joined by a solid line representing a link. The collection of nodes and links constitutes the "network graph." Further, a dashed line connecting two nodes indicates that they share one or more keys, *i.e.*, the link between them is secure. The sub-graph consisting of the nodes and the secure links is referred to as the "key graph."

A natural question that arises in this context is whether the key graph is connected. [4] makes use of fundamental results in the theory of random graphs, due to Erdös and Renyi [11], to determine the pool size P and the key-ring size k such that the key graph is connected with arbitrarily high probability.

Thus, two neighbours on the network graph can find, with very high probability, a secure path between them. This secure path is constituted by a sequence of links from the key graph. [4] suggests that this secure path be used to establish a key between the neighbours. In this approach, the key to be shared is successively encrypted and decrypted by the nodes along the secure path. The drawback is that the key to be shared is exposed to each node on the path, and if one of these nodes is compromised, the key is available to the adversary.

3.1   Proxy-Based Scheme

The solution to secure path key establishment given in [2] utilizes the notion of *proxies*. The idea is that D breaks the key into key nuggets and sends the nuggets securely to proxies by using one of their common keys. Next, each proxy $\mathcal{P}$, then forwards the key nugget securely to S using one of their common keys. Any path between D and $\mathcal{P}$, and between $\mathcal{P}$ and S can be used for this. The authors give two algorithms that D can use to discover proxies.

3.2   Friend-Based Scheme

The *friend*-based scheme we propose is similar in spirit to the scheme in [2], but has some further advantages. We will utilize the seed-based approach [6] for shared key discovery phase which reduces the communication burden in sharing key identifiers. We now outline the friend-based scheme.

S broadcasts a request packet containing the identifier of D and with the Time-To-Live(TTL) bit set to H hops. The request is sent to the nodes by using the broadcast support in the underlying routing protocol. Intermediate nodes receiving the request packet check their key-rings to find if they have any keys in common with D. If a node does not share a key with D, and if TTL is not zero, it simply forwards the request packet to others. If it does share a key, then it is a friend. All those friends which are proxies, send *part-key* back to S in encrypted form using the underlying encryption algorithm $E_e(.,.)$, with a bit in the header (hereby, will be called as HEB, the Header Encryption Bit) set to 1. Other friends, send part-key in clear text with HEB set to 0. A shortest path routing algorithm is used to route packets from F to S.

A part-key is simply an l-bit substring of a key shared between F and D. It is obtained by using a hash pre-specified function $h(.)$ on the key. In case F shares multiple keys with D, F performs an XOR operation on all the common keys and finally applies the function $h(.)$ to the result. This part-key is sent back to S.

On receiving part-keys from possibly multiple friends, source S randomly selects i of the part-keys, some of them(say, $n_e \geq 1$) should be one which were received in encrypted form. These i part-keys are then combined using a publicly known function $g(.)$ to obtain a full-length key K_{SD} to be used between S and D. Note that the n_e part-keys are first decrypted using the underlying decryption algorithm $E_d(.,.)$ and then are used as arguments for the function $g(.)$.

We note that only the identities of the friends are being sent to the destination D, not the part-keys. Moreover, these identities are sent securely to the destination by choosing one of the proxies, the information of which was already obtained during the broadcast-reply phase. Even if an adversary somehow manages to extract this information, he will not be able to generate the secret key. He will merely know the $key - ids$ of the friends involved and thus the common keys shared between every friend and D. Since it is computationally impossible to obtain keys from key-ids, the adversary will not have access to the keys themselves. Now, in addition to having node-ids' infomation, if the adversary also captures the communication between all the friends and S, he will not be able to generate the key K_{SD} as some of the part-keys involved were received in encrypted form. We note also that the method outlined here is independent of the specific functions $h(.)$ and $g(.)$ that are used. Pseudo-code for the friend-based scheme is supplied in the Appendix.

4 Comparative Analysis

In this section we first establish the viability of our friend-based approach as compared to the proxy-based approach. We show that in any collection of m nodes, the number of friends is statistically higher than the number of proxies. We then evaluate the security of our scheme in terms of the resilience of our scheme to node capture. We also show that the friend based scheme requires adversaries to expend much more computation effort than the proxy based scheme.

4.1 Feasibility Analysis

Suppose there are m nodes in the network excluding the source and destination nodes. Let r be a node other than the source and destination nodes. Let A be the event that r shares at least one key with the source node S, B be the event that r shares at least one key with the destination node D and C be the event that the source and destination nodes do not share a key.[1] We denote the complement of an event E by E^c.

Let p' be the probability that a node other than the source and destination nodes is *not* a friend, given that the source and destination do not share a key. If P is the key Pool size and k is the key ring size, then the probability p of a node being a friend is given by

$$p = 1 - p'$$
$$= 1 - P(B^c|C)$$
$$= 1 - \frac{\binom{P-k}{k}}{\binom{P}{k}} \qquad (1)$$

Let q be the probability that a node other than the source and destination nodes is a proxy, given that the source and destination not do not share a key. We have

$$q = P(A \cap B|C)$$
$$= 1 - P(A^c \cup B^c|C)$$
$$= 1 - P(A^c|C) - P(B^c|C) + P(A^c \cap B^c|C)$$
$$= 1 - 2\frac{\binom{P-k}{k}}{\binom{P}{k}} + \frac{\binom{P-2k}{k}}{\binom{P}{k}} \qquad (2)$$

[1] This is the event when the source and destination need to establish a secret key.

By comparing (1) with (2), we see that $p > q$. Therefore, in any collection of nodes it is easier to find friends compared to proxies. The complementary cumulative distribution function of the number of friend and proxies in a collection of m nodes is plotted in Fig. 2.

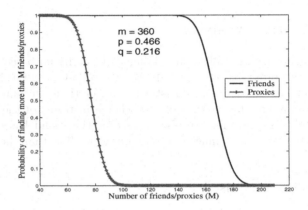

Fig. 2. The complimentary distribution function of the number of friends and proxies

4.2 Security Analysis

In analyzing the security properties of the friend-based and proxy-based schemes, we assume that S and D are never captured. In our threat model, we assume that once a node is captured, all of its keys become available to the adversary. Consequently, if S or D is captured then the secret key is revealed straight away. The more interesting case is when neither is captured.

Suppose that apart from S and D, there are m nodes in all. Let us now assume that x nodes (distinct from S and D) have been captured. It is possible for the adversary to find out which of these x nodes are friends or proxies. For this, knowing the node-id of D is sufficient. Then, the adversary can generate the key-ids in D's key-ring, as well as those in a captured node's key-ring and find out if there is a non-empty intersection. In this way, the number of friends or proxies in the x captured nodes can be obtained.

We now consider the i friends or proxies that were *actually used* to generate the key K_{SD}. Clearly, the x captured nodes can either include these i friends/proxies (let us call this event R) or not. If R^c occurs, then the adversary cannot obtain the secret key. If R occurs, the adversary can *possibly* obtain the key after some more effort, as we show below.

If R occurs, we know that the x captured nodes contain *at least* i friends/proxies, because the i friends/proxies actually used for K_{SD} are already present. Let the total number of friends/proxies present among the captured nodes be the random variable Z, taking values in $\{i, (i+1), \ldots, x\}$. In this situation, the adversary has to *guess* the right collection of i friends to obtain K_{SD}. Let us suppose that the adversary can make L attempts to get the key. Then, our basic measure of resiliency against node capture is the *probability of key recovery by the adversary in L attempts*. Clearly, as L increases, we expect the probability to increase.

Let H_L denote the event that K_{SD} is recovered by the adversary in L attempts. Then

$$P(H_L) = P(R^c)P(H_L|R^c) + P(R)P(H_L|R) \qquad (3)$$

Now, as noted before, $P(H_L|R^c) = 0$. So we need to obtain $P(R)$ and $P(H_L|R)$. $P(R)$ is given by

$$P(R) = \frac{\binom{m-i}{x-i}}{\binom{m}{x}} \qquad (4)$$

Also

$$P(H_L|R) = \sum_{k=i}^{x} P(H_L, Z = k|R)$$

$$= \sum_{k=i}^{x} P(H_L|Z = k, R)P(Z = k|R) \qquad (5)$$

$P(H_L|Z = k, R)$ can be found as follows. Given that there are k friends/proxies, the probability that the adversary finds the "correct" combination of friends/proxies in the first attempt is $\frac{1}{\binom{k}{i}}$. Similarly, using a standard combinatorial argument, the conditional probability that the correct combination of friends is found in the 2nd attempt is also $\frac{1}{\binom{k}{i}}$. In fact, this argument applies equally well to cases where the correct combination is found in the 3rd, 4th, ..., $\min(L, \binom{k}{i})^{\text{th}}$ attempt. In all cases, the conditional probability is $\frac{1}{\binom{k}{i}}$. Thus, we have

$$P(H_L|Z = k, R) = \frac{\min\left(L, \binom{k}{i}\right)}{\binom{k}{i}} \qquad (6)$$

The difference between the friend-based and proxy-based schemes appears when computing $P(Z = k|R)$. Recalling that p denotes the probability that a node is a friend and q the probability that a node is a proxy, we have from the binomial distribution:

$$P(Z = k|R) = \binom{x-i}{k-i} p^{k-i}(1-p)^{x-k} \qquad (7)$$

for the friend-based scheme and

$$P(Z = k|R) = \binom{x-i}{k-i} q^{k-i}(1-q)^{x-k} \qquad (8)$$

for the proxy-based scheme. Hence, from (3), (4) (5), (6), (7) and (8) we have

Theorem 1. *When x nodes are captured by the adversary, the probability of key recovery in L attempts in the friend-based scheme is*

$$\frac{\binom{m-i}{x-i}}{\binom{m}{x}} \sum_{k=i}^{x} \frac{\min(L, \binom{k}{i})}{\binom{k}{i}} \binom{x-i}{k-i} p^{k-i}(1-p)^{x-k}$$

and in the proxy-based scheme is

$$\frac{\binom{m-i}{x-i}}{\binom{m}{x}} \sum_{k=i}^{x} \frac{\min(L, \binom{k}{i})}{\binom{k}{i}} \binom{x-i}{k-i} q^{k-i}(1-q)^{x-k}$$

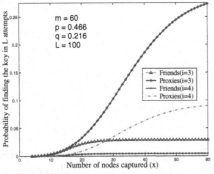

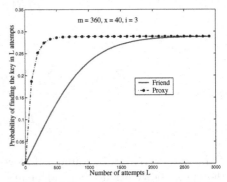

(a) Probability of key recovery within L attempts

(b) Probability of key capture with increasing L

Fig. 3. Security comparison between friend-based and proxy-based schemes

In Fig. (3(a)) we show how the probability of key recovery varies with x for the two schemes, for some values of m, i, p and q. It can be seen that the probability of key recovery is distinctly lower for the friend-based scheme.

We also note that as L tends to infinity, we obtain the probability that key recovery occurs *at all*. When both $L \to \infty$ and $x \to \infty$, the expressions suggest that the probability of key recovery in either scheme approaches $\frac{\binom{m-i}{x-i}}{\binom{m}{x}}$. This is intuitively meaningful, because *(i)* when many attempts are allowed, the difference between the two schemes is due only to the probabilities of finding a friend and a proxy (p and q), and *(ii)* when a large number of nodes is captured, practically the entire mass of the binomial distribution (in the expressions above) are being considered and the summation is very close to 1. Hence, the difference in performance between the two schemes vanishes as L and x become large, with the probability of key recovery being given by $\frac{\binom{m-i}{x-i}}{\binom{m}{x}}$. This can be seen in Fig. (3(b)).

The analysis above was carried out for a chosen number of attempts L. Alternatively, one may ask the question: Given that the i friends/proxies used to generate K_{SD} are included in the x captured nodes (*i.e.,* the event R), what is the *average* number of attempts required by an adversary to obtain K_{SD}? Letting N_F and N_P denote the random number of attempts required in the friend-based and proxy-based schemes respectively, we seek to obtain $E(N_F|R)$ and $E(N_P|R)$. This requires that the conditional probabilities $P(N_F = l|R)$ and $P(N_P = l|R)$, $l = 1, 2, \ldots,$, be obtained first; this can be done using the same approach employed above. We omit the details for brevity. Some representative values are given in Table 1.

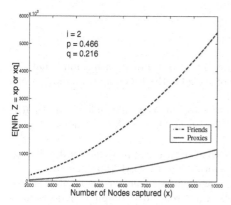

Fig. 4. Expected number of attempts required for key recovery in a typical scenario

Table 1. Comparison between friend-based scheme and proxy-based scheme

$m = 60,$	$i = 3,$	$P = 100000,$	$k = 250$
x	$P(R)$	$E[N_F|R]$	$E[N_P|R]$
29	0.1	256	46
35	0.2	435	72
41	0.3	682	106
45	0.4	890	133
48	0.5	1071	157
51	0.6	1274	184
53	0.7	1424	203
56	0.8	1669	234
58	0.9	1846	256
60	1.0	2037	280

It can be seen that as x increases, the difference in computation effort increases dramatically. To get some intuitive understanding of this phenomenon, we consider the friend-based scheme with large x. In this scenario, the number of captured friends will be very close to the expected number, namely xp, with high probability. Similarly, for the proxy-based scheme, the number of expected proxies is very likely to be around xq. Thus, we can make a first-cut comparison between the two schemes by considering the expected value of N_F and N_P, given that xp and xq nodes have been captured, respectively.

We plot these values in Fig. 4 and note that N_F is almost one order of magnitude greater than N_P.

5   Conclusion

Our friend-based scheme for secure path key establishment is inspired by the proxy-based scheme in [1] and [2]. We showed that because a friend needs to share one or more keys with *only* the destination, the chances of finding a friend in a neighbourhood are considerably greater than that of finding a proxy. This means that friends can be found with less communication overhead, and therefore, appreciable savings in energy can result.

Further, we showed that the friend-based scheme exhibits clear advantages with respect to resilience against node capture. This was proved by obtaining analytical expressions for the conditional probability of key recovery within L attempts by the adversary. For typical scenarios, the average computational effort for key recovery was also shown to be much larger for the friend-based scheme.

Our next step will be to carry out a detailed study of the energy expense incurred by the friend-based scheme and compare it with the proxy-based scheme.

References

1. Ling, H., Znati, T.: End-to-end pairwise key establishment using multi-path in wireless sensor network. In: Proceedings of the 2005 IEEE Global Communications Conference (GLOBECOM 2005). (2005)
2. Li, G., Ling, H., Znati, T.: Path key establishment using multiple secured paths in wireless sensor networks. In: Proceedings of ACM CoNEXT, Toulouse, France (2005)
3. Carman, D.W., Kruus, P.S., Matt, B.J.: Constraints and approaches for distributed sensor network security. In: Technical Report #00-010, NAI Labs. (2000)
4. Eschenauer, L., Gligor, V.D.: A key-management scheme for distributed sensor networks. In: Proceedings of the 9th ACM Conference on Computer and Communications Security (CCS). (2002)
5. Chan, H., Perrig, A., Song, D.: Random key predistribution schemes for sensor networks. In: Proceedings of IEEE Symposium on Research in Security and Privacy. (2003)
6. Zhu, S., Xu, S., Setia, S., Jajodia, S.: Establishing pairwise keys for secure communication in ad hoc networks: a probabilistic approach. In: Proceedings of the 11th IEEE International Conference on Network Protocols (ICNP). (2003)
7. Pietro, R.D., Mancini, L.V., Mei, A.: Random key assignment for secure wireless sensor networks. In: ACM Workshop on Security of Ad Hoc and Sensor Networks, George W. Johnson Center at George Mason University, Fairfax, VA, USA (2003)
8. Du, W., Deng, J., Han, Y.S., Chen, S., Varshney, P.K.: A key management scheme for wireless sensor networks using deployment knowledge. In: Proceedings of the IEEE INFOCOM. (2004)
9. Du, W., Deng, J., Han, Y.S., Varshney, P.K.: A pairwise key pre-distribution scheme for wireless sensor networks. In: Proceedings of the 10th ACM Conference on Computer and Communications Security (CCS). (2003)
10. Blom, R.: An optimal class of symmetric key generation systems. In: Advances in Cryptology: Proceedings of EUROCRYPT 84 (Thomas Beth, Norbert Cot, and Ingemar Ingemarsson, eds.), Lecture Notes in Computer Science, Springer-Verlag, 209:335-338. (1985)
11. Spencer, J. In: The Strange Logic of Random Graphs. Algorithms and Combinatorics 22, Springer-Verlag, ISBN: 3-540-41654-4 (2000)

Appendix: The Algorithm

Algorithm 1. The friend-based algorithm

Pseudo-code at S:
Input: Destination id D
Output: A pairwise key K_{SD}

Set TTL $= H$
Request packet (RP) contents: D
Receive part-keys
Randomly select:
n_e part-keys with HEB $= 1$ & $i - n_e$ with HEB $= 0$
for $j = 1$ to n_e **do**
    Part-key $j = E_d$(Selected part-key j, K_{SF_j}) $\{E_d(.,.) \rightarrow$ decryption algorithm$\}$
end for
for $j = n_e + 1$ to i **do**
    Part-key $j =$ Selected part-key j
end for
$K_{SD} = g$(part-key 1, part-key 2, ..., part-key i)

Pseudo-code at F_j (j^{th} friend of S):
Input: Destination id D
Output: Part key$_F$

Given D, generate key-ids $K_{D_1}, K_{D_2}, \ldots, K_{D_k}$
Given S, generate key-ids $K_{S_1}, K_{S_2}, \ldots, K_{S_k}$
Part-key$_F = 0$; flag$_s = 0$; flag$_d = 0$; HEB $= 0$
for $m = 1$ to k **do**
    for $l = 1$ to k **do**
        if $(K_{F_m} == K_{D_l})$ **then**
            Part-key$_F =$ XOR(Part-key$_F$, truncated K_{F_m})
            flag$_d = 1$
        end if
        if $(K_{F_m} == K_{S_l})$ **then**
            flag$_s = 1$
        end if
    end for
end for
if (flag$_s == 1$) and (flag$_d == 1$) **then** {Proxy node}
    Part-key$_F = E_e$(Part-key$_F$, K_{SF}) $\{E_e(.,.) \rightarrow$ encryption algorithm$\}$
    HEB $= 1$
end if
if (Part-key$_F \neq$ null) **then**
    Send Part-key$_F$ and identity F to S
else if (TTL $\neq 0$) **then**
    Broadcast request packet to neighbours
else
    drop the packet
end if

Distributed Location and Lifetime Biased Clustering for Large Scale Wireless Sensor Network

Biswanath Dey and Sukumar Nandi

Indian Institute of Technology Guwahati,
North Guwahati, Assam, India
{bdey, sukumar}@iitg.ernet.in

Abstract. Recent research in wireless sensor networks have shown in most of the WSN applications node positions are often known in priori, to be able to effectively assimilate data from the WSN deployment. Also expected lifetime of the network, ie. for how long the deployment should work, is often an important specification for a particular deployment. In this paper we proposed two novel protocols, we call, Location and expected Lifetime Biased Clustering (LeLBC) and a modification of it, with fully localized intra cluster chaining (LeLBC-ICC). Both the protocols utilize the location information and network lifetime requirement as the knowledge for scheduling cluster head selection expeditiously. Experiment results have shown that LeLBC outperforms widely quoted non deterministic cluster based protocol LEACH, while LeLBC-ICC gives comparable results with the near optimal solution PEGASIS. Both the protocols use only localized information and maximum numbers of nodes remain alive during entire lifetime of the network.

Keywords: Clustering, Energy efficiency, Network lifetime, Sensor Network.

1 Introduction

A wireless sensor network consisting of a large number of small irreplaceable battery powered sensors with low-power transceivers can be an effective tool for gathering data in a variety of environments[1,3,4]. The data collected by each sensor is communicated through the network to a single processing center called Base Station, usually having more resources in terms of energy and computing power. The base station uses all reported data to determine characteristics of the environment or detect an event[2,3,4]. Fig 1 shows a typical sensor network deployment. Such networks are deployed for numerous applications for unmanned data collection in uncongenial environments for a wide range of time eg. habitat monitoring, monitoring of sensitive environmental zones, biospheres, wildlife habitats etc., forecasting the trends related to weather, pollution, floods, structural wear and tear of buildings etc., smart home, smart office etc[1,2,3,4,6].

Sensor networks differ from conventional wireless ad hoc networks in certain ways [2]. The number of nodes in network is much higher with comparatively dense network topology. The nodes are highly resource constrained in terms of memory, processing power and battery life. Sensor networks are application specific i.e. they

S. Chaudhuri et al. (Eds.): ICDCN 2006, LNCS 4308, pp. 534–545, 2006.

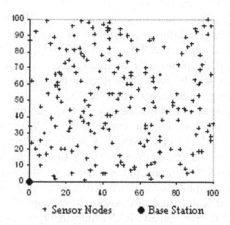

Fig. 1. A typical sensor network

are often designed and deployed with an end goal in mind, like for example data gathering in a region based on particular event over a specified period of time.

A sensor node is usually composed of four components [2], a processing unit, a power unit, one or more sensing unit and a transceiver. The processing unit is typically an 8-16 bit, 1-24 MHz microcontroller with 1KB-4MB onboard memory. The power unit usually consists of one or more batteries, providing 3V-4.5V, with a capacity ranging from 1700mAh-2700mAh. Due to limited and irreplaceable battery power of each sensor node, sensor networks are highly sensitive to energy usage. For any node, energy consumption is observed at three stages, sensing, processing and communication. While most of the energy is consumed in communication, optimizing these three stages leads to reduction in the energy consumed.

In large scale wireless sensor network, cluster based communication found to surpass the direct mode of communication in addressing scalability and energy efficiency [8,9,18,19]. Cluster based approaches tend to increase network lifetime by uniformly distributing the energy dissipation over the entire network. While in case of direct communication, nodes away from the base station tend to deplete more energy in communication and so dies more quickly, compared to the nodes nearer to the base station, thus creating energy imbalance in the network. This, in turn, causes network partitioning. Recent developments in sensor network research shows, in most of the WSN applications, node positions are known in priori, which is required, to be able to assimilate data effectively from the WSN deployment. While designing for a sensor network deployment, expected lifetime of the network, that is, for how long the deployment should work, is often an important criterion for a particular deployment, and needs to be approximated in advance for the successful deployment of the network [15,16].

In our protocols we have used these two parameters as the guiding factors for clustering. In LeLBC, we schedule the selection of cluster heads in a particular round of network operation based on its position in the network and the number rounds to be elapsed until the network should operate. Such scheduling of cluster heads is unlike non deterministic, randomized cluster head selection in LEACH[8,9]. In LeLBC-ICC, nodes within a cluster, forms intra cluster chains with purely localized information, to minimize the energy required due to transmission. However such chain formation is unlike the chaining scheme used in PEGASIS [11,12] which requires global knowledge of each node position. Experiments results has shown, both of our protocols performs relatively well than interesting data gathering protocols viz. LEACH and gives comparable results with PEGASIS.

This paper is organized as follows. Section 2 discusses the contemporary research reported in literature in clustering for sensor network. We emphasis on two highly quoted work LEACH [8] and PEGASIS [11] as the backbone idea of our protocols come from these two interesting protocols. Section 3 discusses the preliminary concepts in sensor network communication, regarding radio model used, performance metrics etc. The LeLBC protocol is discussed in section 4 followed by simulation setup in section 5 and results and discussions in sections 6. Section 7 presents the modification of LeLBC, viz. LeLBC-ICC which incorporates intra cluster chaining and the experiment results following intra cluster chaining. Finally in section 8 we conclude the paper detailing the future prospects and works still to be done.

2 Related Work

Routing and clustering is an intensely studied field in contemporary research in wireless sensor network [2,7,8,10,11,18,19]. In order to cope up with unique characteristics of sensor network described in previous section newer range of protocols had to be developed [2,3,4,5,17].

Low Energy Adaptive clustering hierarchy (LEACH)[8] is a hierarchical clustering protocol specific to sensor network first of its kind, which uses clustering for prolonging network lifetime. LEACH has four phases of operation viz. advertisement, cluster setup, schedule creation (TDMA) and data transmission. In the *advertisement phase* each node decides whether it can become a cluster head, based on a predetermined percentage P, of cluster head desired in the network with respect to total number of nodes in the network. With given cluster head probability P, during start of a network round r, a node that has not become cluster head in past $1/P$ rounds, tries to become the cluster head by generating a random number between 0 and 1, which is compared with a thresh hold $T(n)$, calculated as shown below. If the random number selected by a node is less than $T(n)$, the node becomes the cluster head. Each node that is elected to become a cluster head advertises itself using the medium access control based CSMA protocol and transmitting at the same energy.

$$T(n)=P/(1-P*(r \bmod (1/P)))$$

In *cluster setup phase* each non-cluster-head nodes decides which cluster to join based on the received signal strength from the cluster head advertisement. This process is repeated periodically with the aim so that every node in the network becomes cluster head and all nodes can equally share the responsibility of message transmission, ensuring longer life for all the nodes.

In *schedule creation phase* the cluster head builds a TDMA schedule for the member nodes and transmits the schedule to each member nodes and in *data transmission phase* each member nodes transmits its data to cluster head. At the end of every TDMA cycle cluster head aggregates all packets and sends as another set of messages to BS as CDMA packets.

Although LEACH is one of the most elegant protocol that is extensively studied by many researchers [10,11,13,17,18] the randomized nature of its cluster head selection has some limitations. There are ample scope for improvement as far as the network lifetime and energy efficiency is concerned as described in [10,11]. Efficient scheduling of cluster head selection biased by node location and expected network lifetime can increase the network performance which is the core focus of our research.

A major improvement over LEACH is achieved by PEGASIS[11] in terms of network lifetime, which is claimed to be the near optimal solution by its inventors. In PEGASIS, group heads are chosen randomly and each node communicates only with close neighbor(s) to form a chain leading to its cluster head. The randomization of the cluster heads guarantees that the nodes will die in a random order throughout the network thus keeping the density throughout the network proportional. PEGASIS assumes to have global knowledge of the network topology, allowing it to use a greedy algorithm while constructing the chain.

However in PEGASIS there are a few drawbacks. First the clustering is based on random cluster heads. The chain described in PEGASIS may not be an optimal routing mechanism, other approaches such as directed diffusion [7] appears to give better performance. Again each node knowing the location information of all other nodes is tremendously costly in terms of memory and scalability.

A possible solution to the above limitation would be to allow each cluster head making the best decision for the members of its cluster following a greedy algorithm which would result in a system that all nodes would be transmitting to the best neighbor in the cluster. We follow this scheme in LeLBC-ICC where as the nodes sends its location information to cluster head as part of its 'interest' to become the member of the cluster. Thus the scheme is fully localized with each node require to know only its own location information.

3 Preliminaries

A wireless sensor network, as shown in fig 1, can be viewed as a random deployment of N stationary nodes, over an $M*M$ area. The randomness of distribution can be uniform or skewed over the region[20]. The main sources of energy dissipation in sensor nodes are transmission and reception. With symmetric propagation channel[21], the energy required to send a packet of k bits from node u to node v, is same as sending the same packet from v to u.

The energy required to transmit a packet of k bits over a distance d is given by,

$$E_T = C_1 k + C_2 k d^\lambda + C_3$$

Whereas the energy dissipated to receive a packet of k bits is given by,

$$E_R = C_1 k + C_3$$

Where C_1 and C_2 are energy dissipated to run the transmitter circuitry and energy dissipation of the transmission amplifier respectively. These parameters depend on the selected radio model. For radio model used by inventors of LEACH, C_1 and C_2 are 50nJ/bit and 100 pJ/bit/m2 respectively. λ is the path loss component usually = 2. C_3

is a constant added in order to take in to consideration the overhead due to signal processing and minimum energy needed for successful reception and MAC control messages. For ideal MAC considerations we can ignore the constant C_3 (i.e. C_3=0).

In case of direct communication, each sensor node sends their packets directly to base station (BS). While in case of cluster based protocols, such as LEACH, nodes sends their packets to their nearest cluster heads (CH). The cluster head receive p k-bit packets from p neighbors, perform some aggregation operation and transmit the data to the base station in the form of q k-bit packets, where $q=cp$, with c (=1) being the compression coefficient.

The lifetime of a sensor network can be defined with three metrics [10] namely *first node dies* or FND, *half of the nodes alive* or HNA and *last node dies* or LND.

Given a particular network configuration we can determine the maximum number of rounds possible before the first node dies as shown in [11]. Likewise even if the approximate life time of a deployment is not specified in priory, it is possible to approximate it to some extent, locally at node level considering the initial energy level of each node, the energy cost for electronics and λ, the path loss component[15,16].

4   LeLBC: Location and Expected Lifetime Biased Clustering

At a round, our protocol, Location and expected Lifetime biased clustering (LeLBC), allows a node, to become CH based on its position and expected network lifetime in order to evenly distribute the energy dissipated throughout the network. This result in most of the nodes still remains reachable throughout the operating lifetime of the particular deployment.

Let us assume the sensor field in fig.2. Let us assume R to be the radius of the sensor field i.e. maximum distance of the farthest node from the BS. Let us assume a virtual circle with radius $R/2$ as shown and let E is the expected lifetime of the deployment.

Obviously during initial rounds, all the nodes have sufficient amount of remaining energy level to reach farthest node (CH or BS). But as more and more rounds get elapsed, remaining energy level as each node lowered and with that energy node can transmit to a shorter distance (We assume nodes can tune its transmitter based on energy level). Our target is to form cluster heads far from the half radius ($R/2$) circle during initial rounds and as the network ages, cluster heads are formed nearer to the circle of radius $R/2$.

With given network radius, R, the expected lifetime, E, finding the best feasible radius R' (lets call it as '*ideal radius*') for a cluster head at round r, involves a simple mapping depicted in fig 3.

The logic behind the working principle of the protocol is simple. During initial stages nodes (CHs) near the outer circle (radius=R), have sufficient energy to reach to BS. But with time, their energy will deplete and a stage will come, when with their remaining energy level they can not reach to BS but will still have sufficient energy to transmit up to the nodes nearer to the inner circle (radius=$R/2$). If during that stage

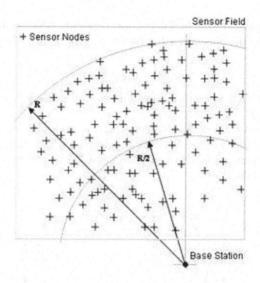

Fig. 2. A typical real world sensor network deployment

CHs are formed nearer to inner circle, distant nodes can still reach to BS through these CHs.

Again during initial rounds of network operation, nodes nearer to BS are favored to be the CHs than nodes nearer to inner circle (of $R/2$ radius). This will conserve the energy level of the nodes nearer to the inner circle, as in this case they are transmitting to a shorter distance than if they would have transmitted to BS. Considering uniform initial energy level for all the nodes, nodes nearer to BS will have sufficient energy to reach nodes nearer to the inner circle during later rounds of network operation. Thus all or most of the nodes will remain reachable from the BS, throughout the entire network lifetime, which is our prime objective. Different phases of the LeLBC protocol is enlisted below.

4.1 Cluster Head Selection Phase

The cluster head selection phase of LeLBC closely resembles with LEACH with some modifications taking into considerations of the two parameters viz. location of the node within the network and expected lifetime of the network as described above.

At any round 'e', once a node N is a candidate to become CH, first it is examined from its location where it is in the network, beyond the inner circle (radius=$R/2$) or below it (nearer to BS).

In the area beyond the half radius circle, based on the expected network lifetime E and present round 'e', ideal position of the node that should be the cluster head will be near the circle with radius, R_{out}^{ideal} where,

$$R_{out}^{ideal} = |(e-(R-R/2))/E|$$

Again in the area below the half radius line (nearer to BS), the ideal position of the node that should be the cluster head at round 'e', will be near the circle with radius, R_{in}^{ideal} where,

$$R_{in}^{ideal} = |(e*R/2))/E|$$

If the candidate node is on this radius line it will be selected as one of the cluster heads for this round.

Now as the nodes were randomly deployed, it is likely that the candidate may not lie in on this ideal radius line. We take a point P, on the circle with ideal radius, closest to the candidate node. Obviously this point lies on the straight line connecting candidate node and the BS.

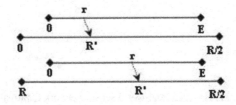

Fig. 3. Mapping to find most feasible CH position

We introduced a parameter we call, positional tolerance (P_T) here. If the candidate node is within the distance (P_T) from P, this node will be selected as one of the cluster heads for this round, other wise the node can not be the cluster head.

Note that if $P_T = 0$, it puts tight restriction on a node becoming cluster head, thus number of cluster heads will be very less, (may be even zero) as most of the candidate node will fail the test and thus the protocol behaves almost similar to direct transmission. On the other hand if $P_T = R$, LeLBC will behave similar to LEACH. Experimentally it is seen that a value near to $0.63*R$ for P_T gives best results.

4.2 Cluster Set Up Phase

Once some of the nodes become the CH, they broadcast advertisement packets, as in LEACH. A node, which is not a cluster head, selects the closest cluster head as its head. Election of cluster heads following the method stated above ensures that a non-cluster head node also conserves energy keeping network lifetime-wide communication in consideration. Once the cluster is set up, the cluster head then creates a TDMA schedule telling the member nodes when they can transmit; the schedule is broadcast to the non cluster nodes which requires only constant power for broadcasting the schedule.

4.3 Data Transmission Phase

All non-cluster head nodes send their data to their respective cluster heads in their respective TDMA slots. At the end of a TDMA cycle, the cluster heads aggregates the data and sends it to base station as CDMA frame.

5   Simulation Setup

We tested our protocol exhaustively, in MATLAB[22], for different network scenarios, with different parameters for network size, BS locations, node densities etc, as shown in table 1. For space constraint we present the performance characteristics of our protocol compared to existing ones for the most generalized parameters shown in bold face in the table. In all our simulations we have considered simple radio model, as in [8,11]. We have taken P_T =0.63R in all the cases.

6   Results and Discussions

Fig 4 and fig 5 shows the number of rounds elapsed when 1%, 25%, 50%,75%,100% of nodes dies for different protocols for scenario 1 and scenario 2 respectively. We have tested out protocols for different values of P_T ranging from 0-100% of Network Radius, R, and found the value nearly 0.63R for P_T gives the best results. So we have taken P_T =0.63R in all the cases in the simulations for scenario 1 and 2. Fig 6 plots characteristics depicting influence of P_T on different lifetime metrics.

Table 1. Simulation Parameter for different scenarios

Parameters	Scenario 1	Scenario 2
Network Size (In m*m)	**50m X 50m**	**100m X 100m**
Number of Nodes	50, **100**, 150	50, **100**, 200
Initial Battery Power of nodes (in J)	0.25, 0.50, **0.75**	0.25, 0.50, **0.75**, 1.0
Message length (in bits) [k]	2048, **4096**, 8192	2048, **4096**, 8192
Energy dissipation in T_x / R_x [C_1]	**50 nJ/bit**	**50 nJ/bit**
Energy dissipation in T_x amplifier [C_2]	**100** pJ/bit/m^2	**100** pJ/bit/m^2
Base station Location	(0,0), (25,25), **(25,150)**	(0,0), (50,50), **(50,300)**
Advertisement message length (in bits)	16, **32**, 64	**16**, 32, 64

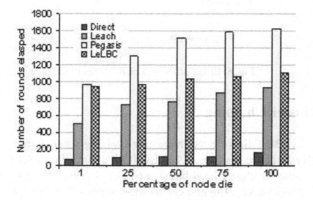

Fig. 4. Performance characteristics for scenario 1

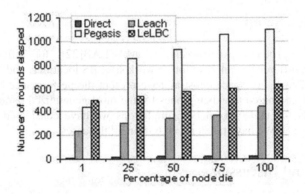

Fig. 5. Performance characteristics for scenario 2

We see that in both the scenarios LeLBC outperforms LEACH in terms of number of rounds. Also in LeLBC the nodes dies rather steadily with almost 100% of the nodes remain alive for 80% of the network lifetime. Fig 7 shows the rate at which nodes die with increasing number of rounds in all the protocols. However in both the scenario we see that, for LeLBC, the number of rounds for which the network operates is significantly less than that of chaining based protocol PEGASIS, which claimed to be near optimal[11]. In the following section we propose a modification of LeLBC, where we form intra cluster chaining but in a completely localized manner.

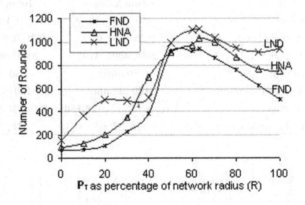

Fig. 6. Effect of P_T on LeLBC (scenario 1)

7 Intra Cluster Chaining

We modified LeLBC following the interesting chaining scheme proposed in [11] but in a completely localized manner. In LeLBC-ICC, during cluster set up phase a node that qualifies to be the cluster head broadcasts, as in LeLBC or LEACH, a strong but short advertisement packet. The non cluster head nodes select the closest cluster head and transmit a packet as its '*interest*' to become a member of the cluster. We modified

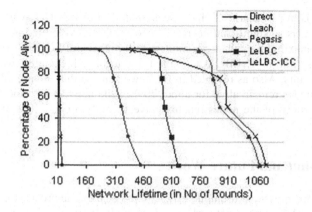

Fig. 7. Node dieing rate (scenario 2)

this interest packet. Now along with this interest packet, a non cluster head node also sends its location information to the intended cluster head.

Once the clustering is over, the cluster head will have the location information of all the member nodes. With this information the cluster head can calculate the best possible chain among the cluster members. Once such a chain is created, the cluster head broadcast the chain to the cluster members as part of the acknowledgement packet. The cluster members follow this chain for data transmission instead of following the TDMA schedule as in LEACH or LeLBC.

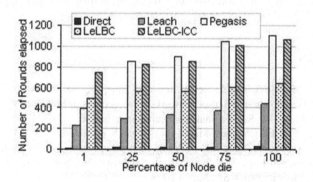

Fig. 8. Performance of LeLBC-ICC (scenario 2)

Note that no extra packet transmission is required than original LeLBC or LEACH. Such chaining saves energy during data transmission as described in [11,12]. However unlike PEGASIS, LeLBC-ICC is completely localized. Each node need to know only its own location. Again as the chain is formed by the cluster head, having implicitly obtained location information of all member nodes, it can determine the best chain possible, making it more efficient, unlike PEGASIS where individual nodes has equal influence over chain formation. Fig 8 shows the number of rounds elapsed when 1%, 25%, 50%,75%,100% of nodes dies in LeLBC-ICC compared to other protocols for scenario 2. It is seen that in LeLBC-ICC with intra cluster chaining, there is a significant increase in overall network lifetime performance. Although the maximum number of rounds is still higher in PEGASIS while 25-100% of nodes dies, but in LeLBC-ICC with fully localized chaining we are getting comparable results. Also as revealed in fig 7, we can see that in case of LeLBC-ICC 100% of the nodes remain alive for about 70% of the network lifetime while in case of PEGASIS 100% of the nodes remains alive for only around 40% of the network lifetime.

8 Conclusion and Future Work

In this paper we presented a unique efficient and scalable approach for clustering in large scale wireless sensor network based on node location and expected network lifetime. In both of our protocols we assumed only local and no global information available to individual nodes for cluster formation. Both the protocols have another unique characteristic where maximum number of nodes remains alive during 65-80% of network lifetime. This is very essential and required characteristics for any sensor network deployment in order to avoid network partitioning problem. This also aid to solve the problem of 'hole' formation in an uniformly deployed network. Its is seen that location and expected network lifetime information can be effectively used for efficient clustering in large scale wireless sensor network. We are working on extending the network simulator ns[23] to simulate LeLBC, LeLBC-ICC for sensor networks and thus obtain more empirical results that would help us establish the efficaciousness of our protocols and its applicability to other types of wireless networks.

References

1. D. Estrin, R. Govindan, J. Heidemann and Satish Kumar, "Next Century Challenges: Scalable Coordination in Sensor Networks", Proceedings in Mobicom'99, 1999.
2. I. F. Akyildiz, W. Su, Y. Sankarasubramaniam, and E. Cayirci, "A survey on sensor networks," IEEE Commun. Mag. , vol . 40, no. 8, pp. 102-114, 2002
3. V. Rajavivarma, Y. Yang and T. Yang, "An overview of wireless sensor network and applications," in Proc. 35th Southeastern Symposium on System Theory (SSST'03), pp. 432-436, Morgantown, USA, March 2003.
4. C. Y. Chong and S. P. Kumar, "Sensor networks: evolution, opportunities, and challenges," Proc. IEEE, vol 91, no. 8, pp. 1247-1256, 2003.
5. I. Chlamtac, M. Conti, and J. Liu, "Mobile Ad Hoc Networking: Imperatives and Challenges," Ad Hoc Networks, vol. 1, no. 1, pp. 13-64, 2003.
6. L. Clare, G. Pottie and J Agre, "Self-Organizing Distributed Sensor Networks," Proc. SPIE Conf. Unattended Ground Sensor Technologies and Applications, pp. 229-237, 1999.
7. C. Intanagonwiwat, R. Govindan, and D. Estrin, "Directed Diffusion: A Scalable and Robust Communication Paradigm for Sensor Networks," in Proceedings of the ACM/IEEE International Conference on Mobile Computing and Networking (MobiCOM '00), Boston, August 2000.

8. W.R. Heinzelman, A. Chandrakasan, and H. Balakrishnan, "Energy-Efficient Communication protocols for Wireless Microsensor Networks", Proc. 33rd Hawaiian Int'l Conf. on Systems Sciences HICSS'00, pp.1-10, Hawaii, USA, January 2000.
9. W.R. Heinzelman, A. Chandrakasan, and H. Balakrishnan, "An Application- Specific Protocol Architecture for Wireless Microsensor Networks," IEEE Transactions on Wireless Communications, vol. 1, no. 4, pp.660-670, October 2002.
10. M. J. Handy, M. Hasse and D. Timmermann, "Low energy adaptive clustering with deterministic cluster head selection," in Proc. 4th Int'l Workshop on Mobile and Wireless Communications Network (MWCN'02), pp 368-372, Sweden, Sept. 2002
11. S. Lindsey and C. Raghabendra, "PEGASIS: Power-Efficient Gathering in Sensor Information Systems", IEEE Int'l Conf. on Communications, 2001.
12. S. Lindsey, C. Raghabendra and K. M. Sivalingam, "Data gathering algorithms in sensor networks using energy metrics," IEEE trans. Parallel Distributed systems, vol 13, no. 9, pp 924-935, 2002.
13. Ioan Raicu, "Efficient Even Distribution of Power Consumption in Wireless Sensor Network", ISCA 18th Int'l Conf. on Computers and Their Applications, CATA'03, Honolulu, Hawaii, USA, 2003.
14. S. Basagni, "Distributed clustering for ad hoc networks", in Proc. 4th Int'l Symposium on Parallel Architectures, algorithms and Networks (I-SPAN'99) pp 310-315, Australia, June 1999.
15. D. M. Blough and P. Santi, "Investigating upper bounds on network lifetime extension for cell-based energy conservation techniques in stationary adhoc network", in Proc. Of the ACM/IEEE Int'l Conf. on Mobile Computing and Networking MOBICOM 2002.
16. M. Bhardwaj, T. Garnett, and A.P. Chandrakasan, "Upper bounds on the lifetime of sensor networks," In Proceedings of IEEE ICC, 2001
17. Katayoun Sohrabi, Jay Gao, Vishal Ailawadhi and Grefory J. Pottie, "Protocols for Self-Organization of a Wireless Sensor Network", IEEE Personal Communications, pp. 16-27, October 2000
18. J. N. Al-Karaki and A. E. Kamal, "Routing techniques in wireless sensor networks: a survey", IEEE Wireless Communications, Vol.11, no. 6, pp. 6-28, 2004.
19. Jamil Ibriq and Imad Mahgoub, "Cluster based routing in wireless sensor network: Issues and Challenges", Proc. of Int'l Symposium on Performance Evaluation of Computer and Telecommunication Systems SPECTS'04, pp. 759-766, San Jose, California, 2004
20. A. Conti and D. Dardari, "The effects of nodes spatial distribution on the performance of sensor networks," in Proc. IEEE 59th Vehicular Technology Conf. VTC'04, vol. 5, pp. 2724-2728, Italy May 2004.
21. T. S. Rappaport, "Wireless communications", Prentice Hall.
22. "MATLAB and Simulink for Technical Computing", http://www.mathworks.com/
23. "The network simulator-ns2", http://www.isi.edu/nsnam/ns

Power Aware Duty Scheduling in Wireless Sensor Networks

Umesh Bellur and Nishant Jaiswal

School of IT
IIT Bombay - India
{umesh, nishant}@it.iitb.ac.in

Abstract. Limited, non replaceable power supply to sensor nodes still remain the bottleneck for wireless sensor network applications. For many sensor network applications such as military surveillance, it is necessary to provide full sensing coverage to a security-sensitive area while at the same time minimize energy consumption and extend system lifetime by leveraging the redundant deployment of sensor nodes. In this paper we propose a new power aware sleep/duty scheduling scheme which maintains a full coverage of the region all the time and tries to increase the lifetime of the network by load balancing amongst the neighboring nodes.

Index Terms: Sensor Networks, Power Aware Duty Scheduling, Energy Conservation.

1 Related Literature Survey

In recent years quite a number of research interests have been towards finding duty/sleep scheduling scheme for wireless sensor networks. A few give deterministic approaches, like [1], others stay with randomized flavors[2]. Differentiated Surveillance[3] (Grid point approach) gives the best results in terms of power savings. We will try to come up with a duty scheduling scheme to improve upon Grid point approach.

Our problem definition: To come up with a duty scheduling scheme for wireless sensor networks which will provide a full coverage all the time and try to increase the lifetime of the network by load balancing amongst the neighboring nodes.

2 Proposed Region Based Scheduling Scheme

Regions. If we look at Figure 1, we could easily see that all the grid points which lie inside a area (e.g. r) have identical coverage. Such areas are called as *regions*. All these grid points inside a single region will lead to identical computation in Grid point approach[3]. If somehow these individual regions are found out "easily", such redundant identical computations could be eliminated.

S. Chaudhuri et al. (Eds.): ICDCN 2006, LNCS 4308, pp. 546–551, 2006.

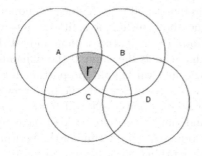

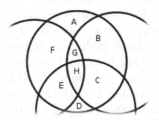

Fig. 1. Sensing Coverage to Region R   **Fig. 2.** Sensor Nodes sensing circumferences intersecting each other

There are two types of region, a border region and a non-border region. A border region is a region which has one edge as a border of the circle which defines the sensing region of the node in consideration. In Figure 2, regions A, B, C, D, E and F are examples of border regions. A non-border region is a region which has no edge common with the circle defining the sensing circumference of the node in consideration. In Figure 2 , regions G and H are non-border regions.

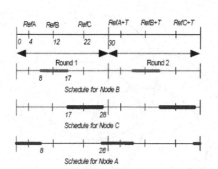

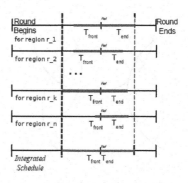

Fig. 3. Calculating node schedules for a single region   **Fig. 4.** The Process of Schedule Integration on a node

Individual Region Scheduling Calculation Phase and Schedule Merging Phase. In the initialization phase every node broadcasts a $PING$ message containing information about node's location, N randomly chosen time reference point $Ref[]$ from an interval $[0 - T]$, and current remaining power of the node. Consider node A and region r shown in Figure 1. Node A sorts time reference points in ascending order of all its neighbors who cover region r including its own reference point on a scale of $[0 - T]$, where T is the duration of a round (see Figure 3). Two consecutive reference points make an interval, T_{front} and

T_{end} of every node is set to left hand side midpoint and right hand side midpoint of the intervals respectively (Figure 3). The above technique splits the interval between the two reference points in half. In our scheme this is done only if the remaining power of consecutive nodes on this scale is the same. If the remaining power of these nodes are different then the interval is split proportionally to the remaining power of these nodes. This will account towards the power aware feature of our technique. A node which has more power left will tend to take more portion of the schedule each time and thus contribute to load balancing in the network which will eventually lead to increase in lifetime of the network. Since there is no overlap among the node's working schedules for region r and total coverage time equals the duration of the round, it is easy to conclude that at any time, all the points inside region r are covered by at least one node's schedule.

After each node calculates its schedules for regions it can cover, it creates an integrated schedule $(T, Ref, T_{front}, T_{end})$. The integrated schedule of each node is the union of its schedules for all the regions it can cover. Thus with the calculated integrated schedules of all the sensor nodes, at any time any region is covered by at least one awaken sensor node. To clarify this integration process further, refer to Figure 4.

Now that we have gone through the integrated schedule calculation phase, the question that still remains is, how to find such regions. Following subsections will explain the algorithms used to find these regions.

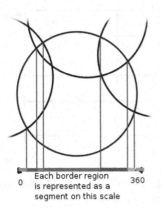

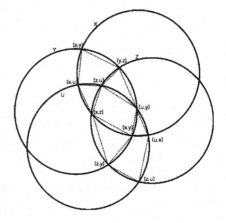

Fig. 5. Projection of Intersection points on scale of $[0, 2\pi]$

Fig. 6. Graph view of intersecting circles to find Non-border Regions

Border Region Discovery Algorithm. Border regions are relatively easy to find than the non-border region. Steps of the algorithm are as follows:

1. Find intersection points of my sensing circle with all my neighbor's sensing circles
2. Project all the intersection points on a scale of $[0, 2\pi]$. *(see Figure 5)*

3. Sort all these point of intersections. *on a scale of* $[0, 2\pi]$.
4. Each of these intervals will represent one border region.

Non-border Region Discovery Algorithm. Following are the steps involved in finding all the non-border regions:

1. Find all the intersections of all the circles (neighborhood nodes) with each other. *Each neighboring circle can intersect all the other $d - 1$ neighboring circles.*
2. Sort these d^2 intersection points. *Now view this intersection of circles as a graph (see Figure 6).*
3. Run a modified Breath First Traversal to find all the special cycles (non-border regions) in this graph.

When we view the intersection of circles as a graph (see Figure 6), intersection points will form the nodes. The circle segments will form the edges in the graph. We will do a modified BF traversal on this graph to find all the non-border regions. These non-border regions form a special type of cycle in the graph. These cycles do not have any edge dividing the region which it encloses into two parts. To find such cycles in the graph we only traverse the graph (Breath First Traversal) abiding by the following rule:

- Only children of a node (z,u) are (x,u) and (u,y) if the last node visited was (y,z) or (x,z).
- However if the last node was (x,u) or (u,y) then children are (y,z) or (x,z).

If we traverse in such a way we will only find cycles of type described above, which fortunately are the non-border regions. Region coverage calculation is simple, only those neighboring nodes completely cover a region which cover all the end points of that region.

Forecasting Energy Levels of Neighboring Nodes. Since our Power Aware Scheduling Scheme is using the power levels of nodes to determine the awake time in the Individual Region Schedule calculation phase, every node needs to know the current remaining power of all its neighbors at the start of every round. Each node keeps forecasting energy level of all its neighbors and also itself. If at any point of time a node finds out that the difference between its actual remaining power and its forecasted power is more than a threshold (*update threshold*), it send the actual power as a broadcast to all its neighbors.

Using different set of Reference Points. A new schedule is calculated every round. Awake time of nodes depend upon the selection of the reference points. If several sensor nodes, capable of sensing a particular region, select reference points very close to each other, there will result a extraordinarily long schedule for one of these nodes. To avoid such scenarios to repeatedly occur, we use a different set of reference points each time. A array of reference points is sent along with the *PING* message in the initialization phase itself.

3   Energy Conservation Results

Implementation of the above algorithm has been done on TOSSIM[4] (tinyos simulator). Ratio between message send energy and message receive energy is taken as 2.5 : 1. The ratio between node awake energy(sensing) and node sleep energy is taken to be 1000 : 1. The *update threshold* taken for experiments was $1/20^{th}$ of the full power. Graph (Figure 7) shows that at lower *update threshold* values the average remaining power of the network drops at a higher rate. This is due to more number of Update Remaining Power messages sent by nodes. When threshold value is increased lifetime of the network increases, however as we increase the value of this threshold the average remaining power of the network hits an optimum. This is because at very high threshold values nodes have inaccurate remaining power knowledge of neighbors and the power aware feature of our algorithm fails to load balance.

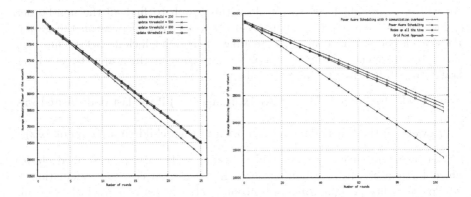

Fig. 7. Sensitivity of scheduling on update threshold

Fig. 8. Comparison between Region Based Scheduling and Grid Point Approach

    In Graph (Figure 8) the line which represents grid point approach plots average remaining power of the nodes when power unaware scheduling (Differentiated Surveillance[3]) was used. Power aware scheduling plots the average remaining power of the network when Region Based Approach was used. No communication overhead line represents the average remaining power if Regions Based approach was used with zero power being used to send and receive a message. This plots the best case performance of our algorithm, i.e. if our technique involved no communication overhead, how well would it had performed. The fourth line - Nodes up all the time is the worst case performance which we could achieve during a duty scheduling. This plots the average remaining power across round when all the nodes are up all the time. Figure 8 clearly shows that our algorithm performs

Figure 9 plots the Awake time of the nodes in the sensor network when Region Based Power Aware Scheduling is applied. It shows that most of the nodes are up for more than half of the round duration but less than 80% of it. Awake time greatly depends upon the topology and density of the network. These readings where taken on a grid topology. There still lies scope for reducing this uptime by applying some optimization techniques and this will be a part of our future work.

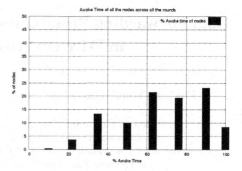

Fig. 9. Average Awake time of the Nodes

better than the Differentiated Surveillance technique and increases the lifetime of the network by load balancing amongst the neighboring nodes. Power aware technique incurs a one time initial setup costs which is evident from the fact that power aware graph starts much below the power unaware graph. However it catches up and surpasses the power unaware graph later after a few rounds.

4   Conclusion and Future Work

In this paper we looked at a new power aware, load balancing, and coverage preserving duty scheduling scheme for wireless sensor networks which does not leave any blind spot in the region and has reasonably low computational as well as communication complexity. There is scope for improvement in the forecasting method used to predict the remaining power levels of the neighboring nodes, since it directly affects the communication overhead incurred by this scheme. Also optimization techniques to reduce the average awake time of the nodes remain unexplored as of now.

References

1. Di Tian and Nicolas D. Georganas. A coverage-preserving node scheduling scheme for large wireless sensor networks. In *WSNA '02: Proceedings of the 1st ACM international workshop on Wireless sensor networks and applications*, 2002.
2. Chih fan Hsin and Mingyan Liu. Network coverage using low duty-cycled sensors: random & coordinated sleep algorithms. In *IPSN '04: Proceedings of the third international symposium on Information processing in sensor networks*, 2004.
3. Ting Yan, Tian He, and John A. Stankovic. Differentiated surveillance for sensor networks. In *SenSys '03: Proceedings of the 1st international conference on Embedded networked sensor systems*, 2003.
4. Philip Levis Sam Madden Joseph Polastre Robert Szewczyk Kalim Whitehouse Alec Woo David Gay Jason Hill Matt Welsh Eric Brewer and David Culler. Tinyos: An perating system for sensor networks.

Data Forwarding Protocol for Reliable Delivery Service in Wireless Sensor Networks

Joo-Sang Youn[1], Jihoon Lee[2], Seung-Joon Seok[3], and Chul-Hee Kang[1]

[1] Dep. of Electronics Engineering, Korea University, Seoul, Korea
{ssrman, chkang}@widecomm.korea.ac.kr
[2] Communication Lab, Samsung Advanced Institute of Technology San 14-1, Nongseo-Ri,
Kiheung-Eup, Yongin, Kyungki-Do 449-712 Korea
vincent.lee@samsung.com
[3] Dept. of Computer Engineering, Kyungnam University, Kyungnam, Korea
sjseok@kyungnam.ac.kr

Abstract. The end-to-end reliable data transport is one of important issues in large-scale wireless sensor networks (LS-WSNs). In this paper, the reliable data transport protocol, called the Data Forwarding Protocol (DFP), is proposed to improve the performance in wireless sensor environments consisting of mobile sensor nodes with low speed. The key idea of the protocol is that an Agent Host (AH), which plays rule of a source or a sink, estimates multi-split connections, to support reliable end-to-end deliver. Using AH nodes, the DFP locally performs local error control and flow control mechanism with low overhead in terms of an end-to-end connection. We evaluate the proposed DFP method using NS-2 simulator and prove that the performance of reliable delivery service can be increased to at least 30%, compared with that of traditional TCP-like end-to-end approach.

1 Introduction

Recent advances, microprocessor technology have enabled the deployment of the large-scale wireless sensor networks (LS-WSNs) where thousands or even tens of thousands of small sensors are distributed over a vast field to obtain high-precision sensing data [1]. There are frequent data losses due to the high link error rate over an end-to-end route beyond at least 6-hops. In the networks, the success rate of data deliver is under 50% [4]. Thus, in order to support a reliable data delivery service with low transport overhead, data forwarding protocol is necessary. In this paper, our work focuses on a reliable data transport in LS-WSNs. An error recovery in terms of hop-by-hop and end-to-end approaches, in existing work [2], is inconsistent at sensor networks because retransmissions may be frequently caused. In addition, wireless sensor networks based on event-based systems do not always need to achieve the data delivery up to 100%. Existing works (a hop-by-hop and end-to-end approaches), however, are implemented to achieve the guaranteed data delivery of 100%. Thus, traditional both approaches are inapplicable in such networks. In order to support only delivery rate required by sensor application, a Data Forwarding protocol (DFP) is

S. Chaudhuri et al. (Eds.): ICDCN 2006, LNCS 4308, pp. 552–557, 2006.

proposed. In the DFP, both hop-by-hop and end-to-end retransmissions are not performed. Instead, a local recovery mechanism at only joint node between split connections is performed.

The remainder of the paper is organized as follows. In section 2, we describe the data forwarding protocol. In section 3, we illustrate simulation results. Finally, Section 4 draws conclusions.

2 Data Forwarding Protocol (DFP)

The DFP performs a feasible local retransmission scheme with the minimum overhead of retransmission about data losses which result from link and congestion errors. The concept behind this protocol divides a source-sink connection into multi-split connections to compensate error accumulation. In the DFP, multi-split connections are estimated with an Agent Host (AH) agent that plays a role of a virtual source or a sink. Also, the AH performs local retransmission of loss data. It has a minimal temporary buffer which is used to store the data generated from a source. The stored data is used to retransmit loss data. Therefore, the AH are responsible to confirm that data have successfully delivered to next AH or a sink. In order to estimate optimal multi-split connection, the DFP need the values about the number of AHs and the hop-count between AHs over a source-sink route. Both values are determined according to the link error rate and target reliability required by a sensor application.

How to determine the position of the AH and the number of AH (N) is performed as follows; we firstly assume two parameters that are the target reliability (σ) and the prediction success rate (P_s) over a route between a nodes. Let e_p denote the error rate of one hop link and h denote the number of hops in the route. Here, we assume that e_p stays constant at least during the controlled time. Thus, P_S over the route with k retransmission can be defined as follows:

$$P_S = 1 - (1 - (1 - e_p)^h)^k \qquad (1)$$

Now, let AH_i be i th AH apart from the source (AH_0 is a source and AH_i is a sink) and P_{AHi} be the reliability from AH_i to AH_{i+1}. In order to determine hop-counter, h_i, between AH_i to AH_{i+1} target reliability (σ) must satisfy

$$\sigma \le P_{AH_i} \qquad (2)$$

where, P_{AHi} is obtained by equation (1).

The aim of the DFP provides the mechanism to provide target reliability with control overhead. Thus, N is minimized. The minimum N is derived as follows:

$$I = \left\lceil \frac{M}{h_i \le \dfrac{\log(1 - \sqrt[k]{\sigma - 1})}{\log(1 - e_p)}} \right\rceil \quad (1 < h_i < M) \qquad (3)$$

The DFP is composed of two parts; the configuration of multi-split connection and the local retransmission scheme between the AHs. Thus, it performs the procedure as follows; the connection estimation, the local error control (LEC), and the local flow control (LFC). In order to estimate multi-split connections, the DFP utilizes multiple AHs: < source, AH_0 >, < AH_i AH_i+1>, < AH_i-1, sink >. And the AH has the two controls such as the error control, called LEC, and the flow control, called LFC, to hide lost data from a source and then locally retransmit lost data over a split connection. The selected AH_i has the following information: {source ID, sink ID, AH_{i-1}, AH_{i+1}}. The AH are enabled at a connection establishment phase and released when a message is received from a source to close the connection.

- A multi-split connections establishment: On generating data, a source obtains a source-sink route, using routing protocol. Once an overall route is built, a source estimates values of the number of the AHs and hop-count between the AHs. Then, to indicate nodes which are selected as the AH, the source sends control message to the nodes with determined hop-distance interval. This procedure is repeated, by determining all AHs. When a sink receives the control message, to inform the end of split-connection establishments, a sink sends the active connection notification message to a source. On receiving the active connection notification message, a source forwards data. Also, to close this connection, close connection notification message is used by a source and a sink.
- Local Error Control (LEC) mechanism: the LEC is responsible for detecting data loss and retransmitting the lost data using a local buffer and a local buffer timer as retransmission timer. To perform error recover locally, all AHs keep all received data in its local buffer and forward the data towards next AH. To detect data loss, the LEC performs store-and-forwarding scheme like error detection scheme in traditional TCP. This mechanism not only decreases the burden of retransmission at a source and the generation of unnecessary control message from sink for requesting retransmission, but it also greatly contributes toward the data loss tolerance of the DFP against many data losses. However, this mechanism will give rise to a source-sink delay in low error-prone environments. Therefore, the LEC mechanism in the DFP has the tradeoff between reliability and delay. Hence, to consider this tradeoff, in the DFP, a Local flow control (LFC) is proposed. With the LFC, the DFP must operate in multi-data forwarding during periods of low-error condition to minimize end-to-end delay, while the DFP behaves more like store-and-forwarding communications [5] when the network state is high-error condition. Therefore,
- Local flow control (LFC) mechanism: a LFC decides the amount of transmitting data to avoid the buffer overflow of next AH or a sink. Thus, the LFC notifies a send window size to previous (upstream) AH. A send window size is included in each 'ACK' message. Whenever receiving ACK message, each AH chooses its send window size which is the smallest between the send window size depending on the current transmission state in physical layer and the residual size of the local buffer in itself. With the LFC, the overflow of the local buffer in (downstream) AH is prevented. If receiving ACK message with residual size of 0, which means high-error condition, the AH (the sender side) defers sending next data until next ACK with more than 1 arrives.

- The AH recovery mechanism: if the role of the AH_i is not played due to it's mobility before the connection closes, the AH_i has to select any node in its one-hop transmission range. Thus, in the situation, the AH_i sends the reset message to the AH_{i-1} (previous AH) and then the AH_{i-1} resends control message at the determined hop-interval to relay its AH_i (next AH). The selected AH also sends this message to the AH_{i+1} of the past AH_i for informing new AH.

3 Simulation Results

In this section, we evaluate the performance of the DFP, compared with end-to-end approach in scenarios with mobile multi-hop environments. Denoted as end-to-end approach, this approach uses traditional TCP. Thus, end-to-end approach represents the performance perceived in wireless sensor networks using existing scheme. The DFP is implemented in ns-2.28 [6]. The network configuration consists of 100 mobile nodes in 1000 x 1000m areas, where each node randomly moves according to the random way point model and a maximum speed varies from 1m/s to 3m/s. The transmission range is constrained to 40m. It is also assumed that the data length is 128 bytes and each query packet has 36 bytes. A basic transmission rate is 1Mbps. The energy model in [7] and S-MAC is applied. Dynamic Source Routing (DSR) [3] is employed. In the energy model, the transmission and reception power is assumed as about 0.66W, and 0.395W, respectively. The local buffer size is assumed to store 10 data. Three different scenarios were randomly selected and the simulation was run for 1000s. The simulation results show average value. A source generates five data per second and each event randomly chooses both a sources and a sink. The retransmission-count is set to 3. The hop-count between AH_i and AH_{i+1} and the number of AHs are determined by equation (3). The target satisfaction is set to 90 %. The Retransmission counter is set to 3 times. We assume the reliability over split connection is equal under the given total reliability.

3.1 End-to-End Latency

The results of average end-to-end delay are shown in Table 1. The delay is defined as the average time between the moment a source transmits a packet and the moment a sink receives the packet, also averaged over all source-sink pairs. In the results, as the

Table 1. The average end-to-end delay

Channel error rate	Average end-to-end delay (ms)					
	E2E approach			DFP		
	1 ms	2 ms	3 ms	1 ms	2 ms	3 ms
0.1	0.4	4.2	5.9	0.2	0.4	1.3
0.2	1.2	5.6	11.1	0.4	0.5	2.3
0.3	4.2	8.5	15.1	0.8	0.9	4.6
0.4	5.3	9.5	21.8	1.4	2.3	5.6
0.5	8.1	14.1	23.2	1.9	2.7	6.3

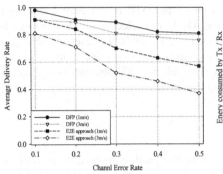

Fig. 1. The average delivery rate   **Fig. 2.** The communication cost

channel error rate and node mobile increase, the DFP has better end-to-end delay than that of end-to-end approach. Specially, the delay of the end-to-end approach increases exponentially, while the delay of the DFP increases linearly in the high-error rate region. The reason that the DFP shows better performance than the existing end-to-end approach in the large error region is caused by the fast error recovery in the LFC and LEC mechanisms. Consequently, the DFP provides the end-to-end delay assurance over the long hop situations.

3.2 Average Delivery Rate

To evaluate the performance of the DFP in both various link error conditions from 0.1 to 0.4 and mobile environments, the average deliver rate is evaluated. Fig. 1 shows an average delivery rate. As the channel error rate and speed of mobile node increase, the DFP achieves the average delivery rate of 0.87%, the end-to-end approach, however, achieves the average delivery rate of 0.39%. Thus, it has been proven from these results that the DFP can achieve the high average delivery rate under consideration of high-error conditions and mobility of sensor node. Moreover, it is verified that the LEC provides nearly an optimal average success rate regardless of variable channel error rate.

3.3 Communication Cost

Finally, we study the communication cost. The communication cost is defined as communication (transmitting and receiving) energy the network consumes; the idle energy is not counted because it does not indicate data forwarding. Fig 2 shows the simulation results under various channel error conditions over 6 hop route in static multi-hop networks. The channel error rate varies from 0.1 to 0.5. In the simulation, we force on measuring the retransmission cost to recover lost data. We separate the retransmission cost from the communication cost through calculating the number of retransmission data and ACK message. In simulation results, the DFP shows that the retransmission cost increases linearly, while a retransmission cost and a communication cost in the end-to-end approach increases more in the high-error rate region. Thus, these results show the DFP is sufficient to support the reliable data delivery in LS-WSNs.

4 Conclusion

This paper presents data forwarding protocol in LS-WSNs with mobile nodes. In our solution, two mechanisms are performed; local error control (LEC) and local flow control (LFC). The proposed protocol supports an efficient reliable delivery service with the low overhead of retransmission of data loss. LEC is the error control mechanism of both data loss detection and retransmission and LFC is the flow control with low overhead of a transmission rate. These mechanisms achieve the minimum energy expenditure for reliable transport. The simulation results show that the DFP has higher performance, compared with the end-to-end approach. We conclude that the DFP efficiently provides the reliable data delivery service.

Acknowledgement

This research was supported by the MIC(Ministry of Information and Communication), Korea, under the ITRC(Information Technology Research Center) support program supervised by the IITA(Institute of Information Technology Assessment).

References

1. Jerry Zhao and Ramesh Govindan, Connectivity Study of a CSMA based Wireless Network. Technical Report TR-02-774, USC/ISI, Los Angeles, CA, 2002.
2. Fred Stann and John Heidemann, "RMST: Reliable Data Transport in Sensor Networks," Proceedings of the First IEEE International Workshop on Sensor Network Protocols and Applications, 11 May 2003 Page(s):102 – 112.
3. D. Johnson, and D. Maltz, Dynamic Source Routing in Ad Hoc Wireless Networks in Mobile Computing, pages 153-181. Kluwer Academic, 1996.
4. C-Y. Wan, A. T. Campbell, and L. Krishnamurthy, "PSFQ: A reliable transport protocol for wireless sensor networks," in Proc. 1st ACM Int. Workshop Wireless Sensor Network Application, Atlanta, GA, Sep. 28, 2002, pp. 1-11.
5. M.R. Stervens, TCP/IP Illustrated, vol. 1, Addison-Wesley, Reading, MA, 1994.
6. Kevin Fall and Kannan Varadhan, editors. ns notes and documentation. The VINT Project, UC Berkeley, LBL, USC/ISI, and Xerox PARC, November 1997. Available from http://www-mash.cs.berkeley.edu/ns/.
7. W. Ye, J. Heidemann, and D. Estrin. Medium access control with coordinated adaptive sleeping for wireless sensor networks. IEEE/ACM Trans. Netw., 12(3):493-506, 2004.

Synchronous and Asynchronous Auction Models for Dynamic Spectrum Access

Shamik Sengupta and Mainak Chatterjee

School of Electrical Engineering and Computer Science
University of Central Florida
Orlando, FL 32816-2450
{shamik, mainak}@cpe.ucf.edu

Abstract. Recently, there is an urge to allocate chunks of the spectrum to the wireless service providers on a more dynamic basis rather than the current practice of static allocation. This shift in paradigm is a result of many studies that indicate the improper utilization of the spectrum by the service providers due to the static spectrum assignment. Also, the use of the spectrum has been found to be space and time invariant. In this paper, we investigate the dynamic spectrum allocation policy for optimal use of the spectrum band. We propose a dynamic spectrum assignment strategy based on auction theory that captures the conflict of interest between wireless service providers and spectrum owner, both of whom try to maximize their respective benefits. We compare two different allocation strategies – synchronous and asynchronous. It is demonstrated that synchronous strategy outperforms the asynchronous strategy. Through simulation results, we show how the optimal usage of spectrum band is achieved along with the maximized revenue for spectrum owner and higher probability of winning spectrum for the service providers.

1   Introduction

The presence of multiple wireless service providers in every geographic region is creating a competitive environment where the goal of every service provider is to maximize their profit and continue to enhance their service portfolio. Every wireless service provider buys spectrum from the spectrum owner (for example, Federal Communications Commission in the United States of America) with a certain price and then sells the spectrum to the subscribers (end users) in the form of services. In such a scenario, the aim of each service provider is to get a large share of subscribers and a big spectrum chunk from the spectrum band to fulfill the demand of these subscribers. As capacity of spectrum band is finite, the providers compete among themselves to acquire chunks of spectrum to offer services to a bigger customer base.

The competitive behavior for spectrum was initiated by spectrum auctions in most countries. Though the auctions were very successful in some countries (e.g., United Kingdom, Germany), they were open to criticism in others (e.g., Austria, Switzerland, Netherlands) [4]. Through the Federal Communications Commission (FCC), the spectrum for cellular services was auctioned in the United States.

S. Chaudhuri et al. (Eds.): ICDCN 2006, LNCS 4308, pp. 558–569, 2006.
© Springer-Verlag Berlin Heidelberg 2006

These spectrum allocations are long–term and any changes are made under the strict guidance of FCC.

This kind of static allocation of spectrum has several disadvantages because of being time and space invariant. It has been demonstrated through experimental studies that spectrum utilization is typically time and space dependent [7]. Thus static spectrum allocation may not be the optimal solution toward efficient spectrum sharing and usage. In static spectrum allocation, large parts of the radio bands are allocated to the military, government and public safety systems. However, the utilization of these bands are significantly low. One may argue that spectrum allocated to cellular and PCS network operators is highly utilized. But in reality, spectrum utilization even in these networks vary over time and space and undergo under-utilization. Often times, the usage of spectrum in certain networks is lower than anticipated, while there might be a crisis in others if the demands of the users using that network exceed the network capacity. Static allocation of spectrum fails to address this issue of spectrum sharing even if the service providers (with statically allocated spectrum) are willing to pay for extra amount of spectrum for a short period of time.

1.1   Dynamic Spectrum Access

With the dis-proportionate and time-varying demand and hence usage of the spectrum, it is intuitive that the notion of static spectrum assignment to providers is questionable. Though it might be argued that the implementation and administration is very easy, the fact remains that the current system is ineffective and deprives service providers and their end users. With the transition from 2G to 3G, the demand for bandwidth has been increasing. As a result, to better serve users, each of the service providers needs more spectrum in addition to the already allocated spectrum through static allocation.

As an alternative, the notion of *Dynamic Spectrum Access* (DSA) has been proposed and is being investigated by network and radio engineers, policy makers, and economists [2]. In DSA, spectrum is shared dynamically depending on demand of the service providers. In this new approach, parts of the spectrum band, which are no longer used or under–used, are made open to all the service providers as shown in figure 1. These parts of the band are known as the Coordinated Access Band (CAB) [2]. Whenever the total requested spectrum amount exceeds the spectrum available in CAB, then auction mechanism can be adopted. Spectrum is assigned dynamically from CAB for a certain lease period and again taken back after the lease period expires. Auction model in this case presents a simple way to depict the conflict among the service providers; and if designed properly, an auction will maximize the revenue also for the spectrum owner; thus providing incentive for spectrum owner to design and follow better auctions models. This method of spectrum sharing is efficient and will help service providers, users as well as FCC not to go through any artificial spectrum scarcity. At the same time, as service providers are ready to compete among themselves in a demand–supply world by paying more for the spectrum they need, this will provide FCC a better approach for maximizing its revenue.

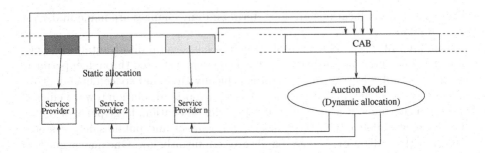

Fig. 1. Virtual merging and coordinated access band

1.2   Contributions of This Work

In this research, we deal with the process of dynamic spectrum allocation where service providers request for additional spectrum lease from the CAB in addition to the already allocated static spectrum. Upon expiry of the lease time, the additional amount of spectrum is returned to the CAB which is made available for reuse. Depending on time interval at which the allocation and de-allocation of spectrum is done form this common pool to the service providers, the spectrum allocation policy can be either *synchronous* or *asynchronous*. In this paper, we define both strategies and compare them. More specifically, the contributions of this paper are as follows.

• We formulate an auction theoretic model to address the DSA policy among the wireless service providers and depict the conflict among these service providers and spectrum owner.
• We devise a "Dynamic spectrum allocator knapsack auction" mechanism with the help of sealed bid, second price auction strategies that is used to dynamically allocate and de-allocate spectrum to competing wireless service providers.
• We investigate both the synchronous and asynchronous allocation policies and compare them in terms of average spectrum allocated, average revenue generated, and probability of winning spectrum after bidding is completed.
• With the help of extensive simulation study, we show that the proposed synchronous allocation strategy encourages the service providers and spectrum owner to participate in the auction. Synchronous allocation and de-allocation of spectrum at a shorter intervals generate average revenue more than the asynchronous allocation and de-allocation strategy. Also the probability of winning spectrum is greater for the synchronous strategy than the asynchronous strategy.

The rest of the paper is organized as follows. In section 2, we discuss the basics of auctions and their types. Our proposed auction methodology is presented in section 3. Synchronous and asynchronous allocation models are also discussed here. In section 4, we compare performances of both these models in regard to the dynamic spectrum access. Simulation model and results are presented in section 5. Conclusions are drawn in the last section.

2   Basics of Auctions

An auction is the process of buying and selling goods by offering them up for bid (i.e., an offered price), taking bids, and then selling the item to the highest bidder. In economic theory, an auction is a method for determining the value of a commodity that has an undetermined or variable price.

Auction types: There are several kinds of existing auction strategies. Depending on whether the bidding strategies of each of the bidders are disclosed in front of the other bidders, open and closed bid auctions are designed. In open auctions [1], [4], bids are open to everybody so that a player's strategy is known to other players and players usually take their turns one by one until winner(s) evolve. This auction game can be best known as the complete information game. Bids generated by players in open bid auction can be either in increasing (e.g., English and Yankee auction) [3], [4] or decreasing order (Dutch auction).

An important perspective of increasing auction is that it is more in the favor of bidders than the auctioneers. Moreover, increasing open bid auction helps bidders in early round to recognize each other and thus act collusively. Increasing auction also detract low potential bidders (bidders with low amount of spectrum request or low value bid) because they know a bidder with higher bid will always exceed their bids.

Closed bid auctions are opposite to open bid auctions and bids/strategies are not known to everybody. Only the organizer (spectrum owner in our case) of the auction will know about the bids submitted by the bidders and will act accordingly. Closed bid auctions thus do not promote collusion. Closed bid auctions are best generalized as the incomplete information game.

Spectrum auctions: Spectrum auction is more close to the multi–unit auctions. Multiple bidders present their bids for a part of the spectrum band, where sum of all these requests exceed the total spectrum band capacity thus causing the auction to take place. Moreover, unlike classic single unit auction, multiple winners evolve in this auction model constituting a winner set. The determination of winner set often depends on the auction strategy taken by the spectrum owner in this case.

Spectrum owner owns the coordinated spectrum band (CAB) and is the seller in the auction model. Service providers on the other hand are the buyers of this additionally created spectrum band. We assume that there are service providers who are already overloaded i.e., they have little or no spectrum left from their static allocation. To attract more users and to make more profit, these service providers request more spectrum from the CAB and advertise a price that they are willing to pay for that amount of spectrum for a certain period. Auction is then held by the spectrum owner depending on these advertised price and the requested amount of spectrum from the service providers in a dynamic basis.

3   Proposed Auction Model for DSA

Good auction design is important for any type of successful auction and often varies depending on the item on which the auction is held. The auctions held in Ebay [6] are typically used to sell an art object or a valuable item. Bidding starts at a certain price defined by auctioneer and then the competing bidders increase their bids. If a bid provided by a bidder is not exceeded by any other bidder then the auction on that object stops and final bidder becomes the winner.

There are two important issues behind any auction design. They are (i) attracting bidders (enticing bidders by increasing their probability of winning), and (ii) maximizing auctioneer's revenue. It is not at all intended that only big companies with high spectrum demand should have a chance at the new spectrum. The goal is to increase competition and bring fresh new ideas and services. As a result it is necessary to make the small companies, who also have a demand of spectrum, interested to take part in the auction. This way, revenue and spectrum usage maximization from the CAB can be made.

3.1   Auction Formulation

The situation described above maps directly to the 0-1 knapsack problem, where the aim is to fill the sack as much as possible maximizing the valuations of the items sacked. Here, we compare the spectrum bands present in CAB as the total capacity of the sack and the bids presented by service providers as the valuations for the spectrum amount they request. We propose this auction procedure as *"Dynamic Spectrum Allocator Knapsack Auction"*.

We formulate the above mentioned knapsack auction as follows. Let us consider that there are n service providers (bidders) looking for the additional amount of spectrum from the CAB. All the service providers submit their demand in a sealed bid way. We follow sealed bid auction strategy, because sealed bid auction has shown to perform well in all–at–a–time auction bidding and has a tendency to prevent collusion. Note that, each service provider has knowledge about its own bidding quantity and bidding price but do not have any idea about any other service providers' bidding quantity and price. We assume that the spectrum band available in CAB is W. Now, if the spectrum requests submitted by some or all of the service providers exceed the spectrum available in CAB then the auction is held to solve the conflict among these providers.

Let, $i = 1, 2, \cdots, n$ denote the bidders (service providers). We denote the strategy taken by service provider i as q_i, where q_i captures the demand tuple of this ith service provider.

$$q_i = \{w_i, x_i\} \tag{1}$$

where, w_i and x_i denote the amount of spectrum and bidding price for that spectrum respectively requested by ith service provider. Auction is best suited when the total demand is more than the supply, i.e.,

$$\sum_{i=1}^{n} w_i > W \tag{2}$$

Our goal is to solve the dynamic spectrum allocation problem in such a way so that earned revenue is maximized from the spectrum owner's point of view, by choosing a bundle of bidders, subject to condition such that total amount of spectrum allocated does not exceed W. Then, formally the allocation policy of the spectrum owner would be,

$$maximize_i \sum_i x_i, \quad \text{such that} \quad \sum_i w_i \leq W \qquad (3)$$

3.2   Synchronous and Asynchronous Auctions

Spectrum allocation with the help of proposed sealed bid knapsack auction can be done in two ways. In asynchronous allocation allocation and de-allocation of spectrum from and to the CAB are not done at fixed intervals. On the other hand, in synchronous allocation, allocation and de-allocation of spectrum from and to the CAB are done at fixed intervals.

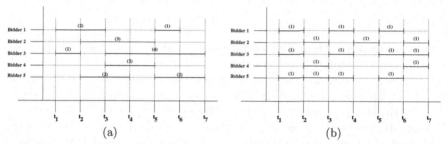

Fig. 2. a)Asynchronous allocation in different intervals of time; b)Synchronous allocation of spectrum in fixed intervals

Asynchronous allocation: As the name suggests, this allocation procedure of spectrum is asynchronous among the service providers as shown in figure 2(a). Whenever a service provider comes up with a request for spectrum from the CAB, the spectrum owner checks to see if that request can be serviced from the available pool of CAB. If the requested amount of spectrum is available, spectrum owner assigns this chunk to the service provider for the *requested time* (e.g., at time t_1, bidder 1's allocation time is 2 units while bidder 3's allocation time is 1 unit as shown in figure 2(a)) and declines if the spectrum requested is not available at that instant in the available pool. Similarly, if more than one service provider come up with requests for spectrum from the CAB, the spectrum owner checks to see if all the requests can be serviced from the available pool of CAB. If they can be serviced, the spectrum is assigned but if all the requests can not be granted, then the auction model comes into picture. We denote the strategy taken by service provider i as q_i^a, where q_i^a captures the demand tuple of this ith service provider in asynchronous allocation mode.

$$q_i^a = \{w_i, x_i, T_i\} \tag{4}$$

where, w_i and x_i denote the amount of spectrum and bidding price for that spectrum respectively requested by ith service provider and T_i is the duration for which the spectrum amount is requested. The numbers inside the parenthesis in the figure 2(a) denote the duration T_i of the spectrum lease allocated to the corresponding bidders from the CAB. As the decision about whether to allocate or not to allocate spectrum to a service provider is taken instantly in this allocation procedure by looking at the available pool only this allocation procedure is not very effective and may not maximize the earned revenue from spectrum broker point of view. It may easily happen that a service provider B is willing to pay a higher price than a service provider A who is willing to pay a lower price for the same demand and the available pool is such that only one request could be processed. But unfortunately B's request came up after A's request. In this allocation procedure, as the spectrum owner does not have any idea about the future, A's request will be processed and B's will be declined (assuming that the available pool does not change at the time of B's arrival. Thus revenue could not be maximized in this allocation procedure.

Synchronous allocation: The second allocation procedure that could be taken to encounter the situation presented in asynchronous allocation is to allocate and de-allocate spectrum chunks at fixed intervals (figure 2(b)). All the service providers with a demand from the CAB present their requests to the spectrum broker with their price which they are willing to pay. Spectrum broker takes all the requests, process them using some strategy and then allocate the spectrum bands to the providers at the same time for the *same lease period*. When the lease period expires, all the allocated spectrum chunks are returned to the common pool of spectrum for future use. For example, lease periods for all the bidders are indicated as 1 in the figure 2(b).

4   Performance Comparison

We analyze and compare the performances of synchronous and asynchronous allocation of spectrum with the help of knapsack auction.

Lemma. *Revenue generated in asynchronous allocation through knapsack auction procedure can not be better than revenue generated in synchronous allocation for a given set of biddings.*

Proof. We assume that there are n bidders competing for W amount of spectrum. In asynchronous allocation mode, the bid strategies taken by ith service provider is given by tuple q_i^a, while in synchronous mode, the tuples are represented by, q_i.

We prove the above proposition with the help of counter-example. We arbitrarily decide two time intervals, t_j and t_{j+1} for the asynchronous mode allocation. We assume that first deallocation(s) of spectrum (service providers returning the allocated spectrum to the CAB) and new allocation(s) are happening at time t_{j+1} after time t_j. Moreover, we assume that the asynchronous allocation at time t_j is maximal and provide us with maximum generated revenue from the CAB. Let, m be the number of bidders who were granted spectrum at time t_j. Then, the maximum revenue generated at time t_j can be given by,

$$\sum_i^m x_i \tag{5}$$

Now, we assume l of m bidders de-allocate at time t_{j+1} and rest $(m - l)$ bidders continue to use their spectrum. Then the revenue generated by these $(m - l)$ bidders is given by,

$$\sum_i^{m-l} x_i \tag{6}$$

Moreover, the $(n - m)$ bidders, who were not granted spectrum at time t_j, will also compete for the rest of the spectrum,

$$W - \sum_i^{m-l} w_i \tag{7}$$

Now, we need to find, whether the revenue generated in this asynchronous mode at time t_{j+1} can exceed the synchronous mode revenue at the same time by same set of bidders. For simplicity, we assume that the bidders do not change their bidding requests in time intervals t_j and t_{j+1}.

By the property of 0-1 knapsack auction, we know that the revenue generated by a subset (we denote this subset by Q) of $n - l$ set of bidders will be a local maxima, if only the revenue obtained from all the $(n - l)$ set of bidders are considered simultaneously, i.e., synchronous allocation of spectrum to $(n - l)$ interested bidders (note that l is the set of bidders de-allocating their spectrum at time t_{j+1} and are not taking part in auction at time t_{j+1}).

But on the other hand, in the asynchronous mode, $(m - l)$ bidders are already present and thus knapsack auction happens among $(n - m)$ bidders for the spectrum $W - \sum_i^{m-l} w_i$. Then, it can be easily said from the property of 0-1 knapsack auction that, this asynchronous mode will generate the same local maxima as the synchronous mode, if and only if all $(m - l)$ bidders (who are already present from the previous time interval) fall under the optimal subset Q. If any of the bidders out of $(m - l)$ bidders do not fall under the optimal subset Q, then it is certain that asynchronous mode allocation will not be able to maximize the revenue for that given set of biddings. Let us provide a simple example to clarify the proof.

An illustrative example: Let us consider that 5 bidders are competing for the CAB spectrum. We assume that the capacity of the CAB is 14 and the bid tuples generated by 5 bidders at time interval t_j are $(6, 10, 2)$, $(5, 9, 3)$, $(7, 14, 1)$, $(2, 8, 2)$ and $(3, 9, 3)$ taken arbitrarily. The first number of the tuple denotes spectrum amount requested, while the second and third number denote the price willing to pay for that spectrum request and time duration for which the spectrum request is done respectively. As we can see from the above tuples that bidder 3's request has duration 1, that means, bidder 3 will de-allocate first at time t_{j+1}.

We execute both asynchronous and synchronous knapsack auction. In asynchronous mode, the revenue generated at time t_j is 31 with the optimal subset of bidders given by bidder $2, 3, 4$. Now at time t_{j+1}, bidder 3 exits, while bidders 2 and 4 continue. Then rest of the spectrum left in the CAB is 7 for which the bidders 1 and 5 compete. Then the revenue generated at time t_{j+1} is given by 27 and the bidders granted are $1, 2, 4$.

On the other hand, in synchronous allocation, each of the providers are allocated and de-allocated at fixed time intervals. Then with the same set of bid requests of spectrum amount and price, it is seen that maximum possible revenue generated at time t_{j+1} out of the bidders $1, 2, 4$ and 5 (as bidder 3 is not interested to take part in auction at time t_{j+1}) is 28, while the optimal subset of bidders is given by $Q = \{1, 2, 5\}$. This shows that asynchronous auction may not provide the maxima depending on the bidders de-allocating and requesting.

5   Simulation Results and Interpretation

We simulate our dynamic spectrum allocator knapsack auction model and show how the synchronous allocation outperforms the asynchronous allocation. The factors that we consider for comparing the performance of the proposed synchronous knapsack sealed-bid auction with the asynchronous auction are the revenue generated by spectrum owner, total spectrum usage, and probability of winning for bidders. We consider the following for the simulation model:

- *Bid tuple:* The bid tuple q_i generated by bidder i in synchronous auction consists of amount of spectrum requested, w_i and the price the bidder is willing to pay, x_i. In asynchronous auction, the duration is also advertised in addition to the above two. Each bidder has a reservation or evaluation price for the amount of spectrum requested and the bid is governed by this reservation price. We assume that the reservation price of each bidder is considered sealed bid and is independent of other bidders' reservation prices.

- *Bidders' strategies:* We follow second price sealed-bid mechanism. We could have chosen the first price bidding policy; the only reason for choosing second price policy is that it has more properties than first price in terms of uncertainty [5]. After each round of auction, the only information bidders know is whether their request is granted or not. We assume that all the bidders are present for all the auction rounds; bidders take feedback from previous rounds and generate the bid tuple for next round.

- *Auctioneer's strategies:* Spectrum owner tries to maximize the revenue generated from the bidders. At the beginning of each auction round, spectrum owner collects the bid tuples and executes the dynamic programming knapsack solver and determines the winner(s). As we implemented synchronous allocation, the assigned band from CAB is taken back at the end of each round and reused for next round.

We compare the proposed synchronous sealed bid knapsack auction with the asynchronous sealed bid knapsack auction under the second price bidding policy, i.e., bidder(s) with the winning bid(s) do not pay their winning bid but pay the second winning bid. Simulation parameters are shown in table 1.

Table 1. Simulation Parameters

Parameter type	Parameter Value
Total amount of spectrum	125
Minimum amount of spectrum that can be requested	11
Maximum amount of spectrum that can be requested	50
Minimum bid for per unit of spectrum	25
Minimum time requested for spectrum leasing in asynchronous allocation	1
Maximum time requested for spectrum leasing in asynchronous allocation	5
Fixed time for spectrum leasing in synchronous allocation	1

Figures 3(a) and 3(b) compare revenue and spectrum usage for both the strategies (synchronous and asynchronous) with increase in auction rounds. The number of bidders considered in this simulation is 15. Note that, both revenue and usage are low at the beginning and subsequently increases with rounds. When auction starts, bidders always act skeptical, thus initial bids are always much lower than the true potential bids of them. With the increase in auction rounds, bidders get an idea of the bids of other bidders and thus try to increase or decrease their bids accordingly.

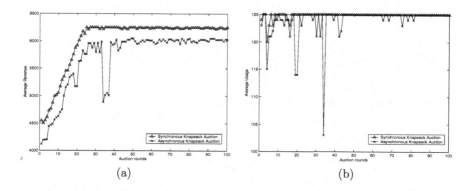

(a)   (b)

Fig. 3. a)Revenue generated and b)Spectrum usage with auction rounds

Figures 4(a) and 4(b) show the average revenue and spectrum usage with varying number of bidders for both the auction strategies. We observe that the proposed synchronous knapsack auction generates approximately average 10% more revenue compared to the asynchronous knapsack auction and also reaches steady

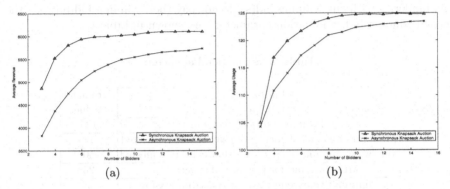

Fig. 4. a)Revenue generated and b)Spectrum usage with number of service providers

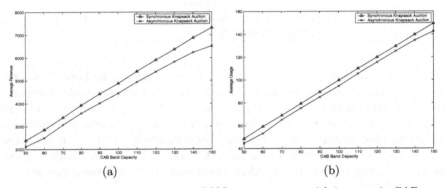

Fig. 5. a)Revenue generated and b)Spectrum usage with increase in CAB

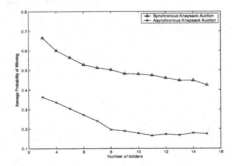

Fig. 6. Average probability of winning spectrum with number of bidders

state faster. The average spectrum usage is also more with the synchronous allocation policy. Figures 5(a) and 5(b) show the average revenue and spectrum usage with increase in capacity in CAB for both the auction strategies. It is clear that with increase in CAB, synchronous strategy provides more revenue and usage of CAB than the asynchronous strategy.

In figure 6, we look at the auction model from the bidders' perspective. Higher revenue requires high participation in number of bidders. We compare the two strategies in terms of the probabilities to win a bid. We observe that the proposed synchronous auction strategy has a significantly higher probability of winning compared to asynchronous auction strategy. This implies that providers will be encouraged to take part in the synchronous knapsack auction model thus increasing the competition among the providers and increasing the chance to generate more revenue.

6   Conclusions

In this paper, we proposed an auction mechanism for dynamic spectrum access that is based on the well known knapsack problem. The auction captures the conflict of interest between wireless service providers and spectrum owner. It is such designed that it maximizes the spectrum usage and the revenue of the spectrum owner. Both synchronous and asynchronous auction strategies are studied and compared. Through simulations it was found that it is in the best interest of both service providers and spectrum owner to adopt the synchronous auction. We also showed how the optimal usage of spectrum band is achieved and the revenue is maximized for the spectrum owner. The proposed mechanism yields higher probability of winning for the service providers and thus encourages the providers to participate in the bidding process.

References

1. R. Bapna, P. Goes, A. Gupta, "Simulating online Yankee auctions to optimize sellers revenue", Proceedings of the 34th Annual Hawaii International Conference on System Sciences, 2001.
2. M. Buddhikot, K. Ryan, "Spectrum Management in Coordinated Dynamic Spectrum Access Based Cellular Networks", Proc. of the First IEEE Intl. Symposium on New Directions in Dynamic Spectrum Access Networks, 2005, pp. 299-307.
3. S. Fatima, M. Wooldridge, N. R. Jennings, "Revenue maximizing agendas for sequential English auctions", Proc. of the Third Intl. Joint Conference on Autonomous Agents and Multi-agent Systems, 2004, pp. 1432 - 1433.
4. G. Illing and U. Kluh, "Spectrum Auctions and Competition in Telecommunications", The MIT Press, London, England, 2003.
5. W. Vickrey, "Couterspeculation, auctions, and competitive sealed tenders", J. Finance, vol. 16, no. 1, pp. 8-37, Mar. 1961.
6. http://www.ebay.com/
7. http://www.sharedspectrum.com/inc/content/measurements/nsf/NYC_report.pdf

A One-Pass Method of MIP Registration by WLAN Host Through GPRS Network

Sibaram Khara[1], Iti Saha Mishra[2], and Debashis Saha[3]

[1] Dept. of ECE, College of Engineering and Management, Kolaghat, Midnapur, India
sianba@rediffmail.com
[2] Dept. of ETCE, Jadavpur University, Kolkata, India
itisahamisra@yahoo.com
[3] MIS Group, IIM Calcutta, India
ds@iimcal.ac.in

Abstract. This paper proposes a new technique for Mobile IP (MIP) registration by WLAN host (WH) through GPRS network. The home agent (HA) of WH resides in external IP network. The gateway GPRS support node (GGSN) provides foreign agent (FA) functionality for WH in GPRS. After successful attach with GPRS network, WH needs two mandatory passes for MIP registration with HA. First it establishes PDP (packet data protocol) context in GPRS network and then it sends MIP registration request (MRR) to FA at GGSN. This causes a large delay for handoff from WLAN to GPRS. We propose a one-pass technique of MIP registration through GPRS network to reduce the handoff delay. We transport MIP-registration request of WH in the information field of activate-PDP-context request message to GGSN. Thus MIP registration message reaches GGSN before completion of PDP context establishment. This technique reduces the control signaling for handoff from WLAN to GPRS. We observed from simulated results that proposed one-pass technique reduces handoff delay by 18% compared to handoff delay in two-pass method.

Keywords: 3G, GPRS, loose coupling, MIP, tight coupling, UMTS, WLAN.

1 Introduction

The demand for high speed data transfer at user level for multimedia services is growing rapidly [1]. The bandwidth constraint has put a challenge of high data rate at user level for next generation wireless networks. The mobile networks (2.5G-GPRS/3G-UMTS) provide data transfer rate (144Kbps/2Mbps) much below required for multimedia services [2]. Other hand, WLAN can provide superior bit rate at user level (802.11b/802.11a, 11Mbps/54Mbps). Mobile networks provide best coverage and WLAN provides best bit rate [3]. Therefore, in WLAN/GPRS integrated network, a mobile station (MS) can avail the best services of both the networks. WLAN at hot spot can provide best bit rate and GPRS can provide always-connectivity out side the hop spots.

Design of dual mode terminal equipment [[4], [5]] and mobility management technique for vertical roaming are two key issues of WLAN/GPRS interworking network [6]. A user may be subscribed either to WLAN network or to GPRS network

S. Chaudhuri et al. (Eds.): ICDCN 2006, LNCS 4308, pp. 570–581, 2006.

or to both networks. WH is subscribed to only WLAN of external IP network and GPRS mobile station (GMS) is subscribed to only GPRS network. An MIP based mobility management is performed when WH moves within WLAN networks [7]. A GPRS mobility management technique is performed when GMS moves within GPRS network. An FA is required to be deployed at GGSN and HA at Gi interface for MIP based mobility management in roaming scenario [8]. GPRS network must provide FA functionality to WH when it moves from WLAN to GPRS network. In another roaming scenario GMS moves into WLAN and GPRS must provide HA functionality for MIP based signaling. In such case HA is deployed at same GGSN and an MIP based handoff procedure is performed between GMS and GGSN. Therefore, GMS's subscription and authority profile for WLAN service are stored at this entity.

WH must perform MIP based mobility management signaling through GPRS network with it's HA at external IP network [8]. The MIP based mobility signals are dealt like data packets by GPRS core networks. To transport these packets to GGSN, GPRS provides bearer service. To provide this service the PDP context establishment in GPRS network is mandatory [9]. When WH comes out from WLAN area and moves into GPRS coverage, it first performs the attachment signaling with GPRS network. Then, in first pass it creates PDP context and in second pass it sends MIP registration packet to FA. Therefore, MIP registration packet cannot be transported until the PDP context is created in GPRS network. This two-pass method of MIP registration in GPRS network increases handoff delay from WLAN to GPRS [8]. We propose a technique of combined PDP and MIP registration method. This technique helps to start MIP based signaling between FA at GGSN and HA at IP network before the complete establishment of PDP context. Both PDP context creation and MIP registration are feasible in one pass of signaling by inserting the MIP registration information in PDP request message. A faster handoff can be achieved as this technique reduces the control signals for handoff from WLAN to GPRS.

2 Review of Related Works

An operator's WLAN (OWLAN) system, based on loose coupling architecture of GPRS/WLAN integrated network, has been proposed in [10]. There the main design challenge was to transport the standard GSM subscriber authentication signaling from the terminal to the cellular site using IP framework. So OWLAN suggested implementing GSM SIM card reader, SIM authentication software module and roaming control module in MS. Network access authentication and accounting protocol (NAAP) was defined as alternative to EAP protocol at terminal. NAAP runs over UDP and it is capable of transporting GSM authentication messages through IP in WLAN access networks.

Although operator-oriented solution is useful for SIM based authentication and single subscription, but it covers only public WLANs at hot spots. To access private WLANs at office and residences, an MS needs frequent changes in its WLAN configurations. An internet-based roaming architecture has been implemented in [11], which cover private WLANs. Each mobile host gets a secure connection to corporate networks through SMG (secured mobility gateway), works as IPSec gateway and supports mobile IP for mobility management.

A tight coupling architecture of UMTS and WLAN integrated has been proposed in [12]. WLAN IP network is connected to SGSN through border router (BR). Intra-SGSN handoff from UMTS to WLAN is performed, and PDP context between SGSN and GGSN need not be upgraded. This technique provides a faster handoff. This system requires MSs to maintain complex states for mobility management, which requires dual contact with WLAN as well UMTS. Hot spot WLAN service cannot survive without UMTS availability.

An implementation technique of 3G based AAA server for UMTS/WLAN integrated network has been proposed in [13]. The 3G AAA server in the home PLMN terminates all AAA signaling with the WLAN and interfaces with other 3G components, such as the home subscriber server (HSS), home location register (HLR), charging gateway/charging collection function (CGw/CCF), and online charging system (OCS). AAA signaling uses EAP and DIAMETER protocol. In one architecture, WLAN routes data traffic directly to internet/intranet. In other architecture, WLAN traffic is routed to wireless access gateway (WAG) and WAG routes packet to Internet through packet data gateway (PDG). The PDG based architecture enables MS to access 3G packet-switched based services such as wireless application protocol, multimedia message service and IP multimedia services.

A critical review of the above works reveals that article abounds in efficient handoff from GPRS to WLAN area. As WLAN coverage is narrow, WH may frequently need GPRS service to sustain its IP connectivity. Therefore faster handoff mechanism from WLAN to GPRS is equally important. Hence in GPRS/WLAN integrated network, MIP based mobility management for WLAN subscriber through GPRS network still needs more focus. Our work attempts to address this space for faster handoff from WLAN to GPRS by introducing a one-pass method of MIP registration through GPRS network.

3   GPRS/WLAN Interworking Architecture

Figure 1 shows the interworking architecture for WLAN/GPRS integrated network. WLAN is directly connected to external IP network which may be Internet. GPRS network is connected to this IP network at GGSN through Gi interface. FA entity is deployed at GGSN and HA is implemented at Gi interface in stand alone mode. GGSN acts as foreign agent when WH goes outside the WLAN and enters in GPRS coverage. In this architecture, GPRS and external IP networks are owned by two different operators. GPRS operator has an agreement to provide the WLAN services of IP network to its own subscribers. Similarly, Internet promises the GPRS services to its own subscribers. The HA at Gi interface maintains the subscription and access profile of GMS for WLAN service. GPRS operator can maintain the agreement profile(s) for WH in HLR. Therefore, it can impose access control during GPRS attach procedure. In roaming scenario when GPRS terminal moves to WLAN area, it performs an MIP based mobility management with FA in access router (AR) and performs the registration with HA at Gi interface. The subscription and access profile of WH for GPRS service is maintained at it's HA in Internet.

4   The Handoff Management

The subscription and service profiles of GMS are maintained by GPRS network at two entities. Its GPRS profiles are stored at HLR and its WLAN profiles are stored at HA. The subscription and service profiles of WH are maintained by it's HA in Internet. In our proposed WLAN/GPRS interworking architecture, two type handoff procedures are performed.

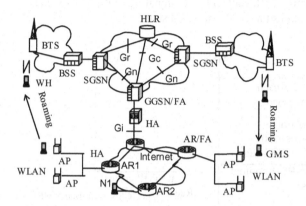

Fig. 1. Architecture of GPRS/WLAN interworking network

4.1   Handoff from GPRS to WLAN

We take the scenario, a GMS is initially in GPRS network and maintains a session with correspondent node (CN) N1 in Internet through GPRS network (Fig.1). The terminal's GPRS system is active and WLAN radio system is in passive scan mode. When it moves to WLAN, deployed at hot spot, its WLAN card is activated on receipt of beacon signals from WLAN access point (AP) [14]. The GPRS system is triggered off and terminal performs association with AP. Then it performs MIP based registration with HA at Gi interface through access router (AR/FA). After completion of MIP based handoff, the GMS can send packets to N1 through WLAN with much higher speed and packets are directly routed in Internet. Therefore, the HA maintains the anchor point of GMS while it is in WLAN area.

4.2   Handoff from WLAN to GPRS

Internet is the home network of WH [Fig 1]. The subscription and service profiles of WH are maintained at the HA in Internet. WH is the dual mode terminal and it has the capability to access GPRS network. GPRS operator must have agreement with Internet to provide IP connectivity through cellular network. The GPRS network may maintain the service profiles and QoS that such terminal can avail through GPRS network. The WLAN terminal may have subscriptions to access GPRS network from selected cells or routine area. When WH comes out of the hot spot area, they can be in cellular coverage. Therefore, their IP based sessions can continue through cellular network. These terminals will perform MIP based mobility and handoff management through GPRS network.

4.2.1 One-Pass Method

Following sequential operations are performed by WH and GPRS network for handoff management [Fig 2].

- WH performs GPRS attachment signaling with GPRS network and terminal equipment attains the GPRS-attached state.

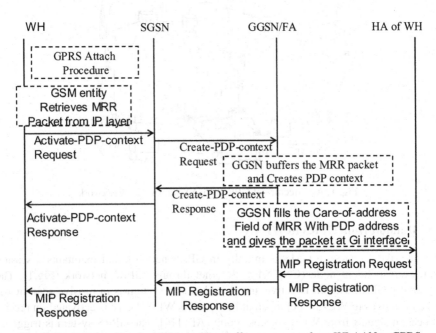

Fig. 2. Control signaling for MIP based handoff management from WLAAN to GPRS

- GSM sublayer of terminal retrieves the MRR packet from network layer.
- WH sends modified activate-PDP-context request message to SGSN and this message contains MRR packet.
- SGSN sends a modified create-PDP-context request to GGSN and it contains MRR packet.
- GGSN creates PDP context and it sends create-PDP-context response message to SGSN.
- GGSN fills the care-of-address field of MRR message with the PDP address and gives the MRR packet to FA.
- Now FA deals the MRR packet for MIP signaling with HA and simultaneously, create-PDP-context response message travels through GPRS network.

- FA receives the MIP registration response packet from HA and gives this packet to GGSN addressed to WH.
- Now PDP is already established. Therefore the MIP response packet is tunneled to SGSN using GTP and SGSN sends this packet to WH.

4.2.2 Service Access Point (SAP) and Protocol Stack for Retrieval of MRR Packet

We define new service primitives for MRR retrieval by GSM entity from network layer. A new network layer entity, WLAN/GPRS mobility agent (WGMA) is implemented in mobile terminal. The WGMA is developed in control management entity of network layer. This entity can use existing network layer SAP identifier (NSAPI) with SNDCP (subnet dependent convergence protocol) sublayer [15]. The SAP between sublayer SNDCP and sublayer GSM is defined as SNSM [Fig 3(a)]. This is an existing SAP in GPRS specifications. GSM entity can use this SAP for new services provided by SNDCP management entity.

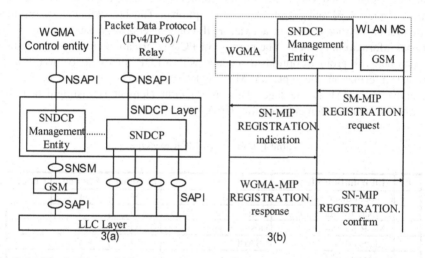

Fig. 3. (a) The interlayer SAP and protocol stack for retrieval of MRR packet by GSM entity from network layer and (b) the interlayer signaling for retrieval of MRR packet from network layer by GSM sublayer

- SM-MIP-REGISTRATION.request: This primitive is used by GSM sublayer before sending PDP activate request to network side [Fig. 3(b)]. This uses SNSM service access point to give information to SNDCP layer for retrieval of MIP registration packet from WGMA. The information contains NSAPI between packet data protocol entity and SNDCP. GSM sublayer gives this information to WGMA entity. Packet data protocol entity remembers this NSAPI through which it will receive the MIP registration accept packet from SNDCP sublayer in future.
- SN-MIP-REGISTRATION.indication: This is used by SNDCP layer to deliver the information given by SM entity for retrieval of MIP registration packet.

- MA-MIP-REGISTRATION.response: This service primitive is to be used by WGMA. This is already configured with the home address of terminal equipment, address of HA and FA. For whole GPRS network the only one FA functionality is implemented at GGSN. WGMA gives this information to SNDCP sublayer. WGMA remembers the NSAPI received from lower layer through which it expects the MIP registration accept after completion of PDP context establishment.
- SN-MIP-REGISTRATION.confirm: This is used by SNDCP sublayer. It gives the MIP registration packet from WGMA to GSM entity.

4.3 Format of Activate-MIP-PDP-Context Request (AMCR) Message

We define a modified format of activate-PDP-context request message to compose AMCR message. The AMCR message carries the MRR packet. The unused bit pattern such as 01010110 can be used in message type field (Table 1). First eight information elements in the packet have been kept same as in activate PDP context request message. First seven information elements are mandatory for activate-PDP-context request [16] and eighth element is optional. The last element was protocol configuration options (PCO) in activate-PDP-context request packet and which was optional information element. The purpose of PCO information element is to transfer external network protocol options associated with a PDP context activation. For this optional information element, an MIP registration request packet can be used alternatively in AMCR message. This information element is distinguished by a separate information element identifier (IEI).

Table 1. Format of AMCR message

IEI	Information Element	Type	Presence	Format	Length
	Protocol discriminator	Protocol discriminator	M	V	1/2
	Transaction identifier	Transaction identifier	M	V	1/2
	AMCR message identity	Message type	M	V	1
	Requested NSAPI	NSAPI	M	V	1
	Requested LLC SAPI	LLC SAPI	M	V	1
	Requested QoS	Quality of service	M	LV	4
	Requested PDP address	PDP address	M	LV	3 - 19
28	Access point name	Access point name	O	TLV	3 - 102
26	MRR packet	MRR packet type	M	LV	3 - 253

Maximum length of PCO information elements is 253 bytes. However in AMCR message this field can be specified for larger length if necessary. The unused hexadecimal value such as 26 can be used as IEI for MIP registration request followed by length of MIP registration request packet. WLAN MS sends AMCR message to network side. SGSN sends the MIP registration packet GGSN through create-PDP-context-request message.

4.4   Format of Create-MIP-PDP-Context Request (CMCR) Message

The CMCR is a new message type for GPRS tunneling protocol. Its format is similar to create-PDP-context request (CPCR) message except two information elements in the message. It's message type field bears new message identity for GTP. PCO is replaced by MIP registration packet. Therefore, all existing primitives can be used to process the information elements for CMCR message except PCO information.

4.5   Complete Handoff Procedure with Signaling in Layer Interfaces at Each Node

Four sublayers of WH terminal become active during handoff from WLAN to GPRS. GSM sublayer retrieves MRR packet from WGMA through SNDCP sublayer. Then, it sends a AMCR message to SGSN through LLC link. GSM sublayer of SGSN receives this message from LLC layer [Fig 4].

The interworking function at SGSN sends corresponding CMCR message through GTP to GGSN. The SNDCP sublayer in SGSN is used for only packet data transfer. After receiving CMCR message GGSN retrieves MRR message from PCO information field. The MRR is immediately not handled by the IP layer of GGSN at Gi interface. Rather it is buffered with a special mark that the care-of address field of this packet is to be filled after the completion of PDP context. GGSN creates PDP context and sends a response packet to SGSN. GGSN gives a PDP address (IP address) to WH through the response message. This PDP address is equivalent to care-of address in GPRS network. After receiving activate-PDP-context response message, the GSM entity of WH informs SNDCP layer that LLC connection has already been established for data packet. GSM also gives the SAPI to be used between LLC and SNDCP sublayers [[15], 16]].

Having transmitted the response of CMCR message, GGSN cares for MRR packet associated with it. The IP layer of GGSN at Gi interface is enhanced with FA functionality for WH. It has already provided a PDP address from its own address pool. The care-of address given by the GGSN is the foreign agent care-of address. This address can be put into the care-of address field of MRR message. The GGSN functionality can be enhanced so that after processing CMCR message it fills the care-of address field of MRR packet. It then gives the packet to IP layer of GGSN at Gi interface. Subsequently usual MIP based signaling performed between FA and HA. HA sends the MRR response packet usual way to GGSN. The address of FA is the IP address of GGSN at Gi interface. This packet is received by the FA at GGSN. FA gives this packet to GGSN for downward transmission.

After receiving MIP registration response packet from FA, GGSN deals it like an IP data packet. GGSN tunnels this packet to SGSN using PDP context. Finally it is received by WH from SGSN. The LLC layer at WH gives this packet to SNDCP sublayer through already configured SAPI. SNDCP gives this packet to network layer. Network layer does not take action for MIP registration packet rather it gives this packet to WGMA entity through its relay functionality.

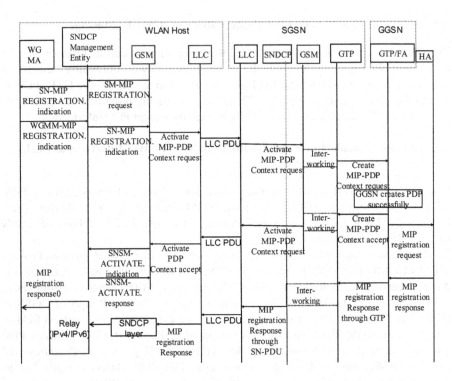

Fig. 4. The complete signaling for simultaneous PDP activate and MIP registration in one-pass method

5 Simulation

The network architecture [Fig. 1] has been simulated using NS-2.26 [Table 2]. We used WLAN as GPRS access network keeping the bit rate GPRS suite (144kbps) at user level. A WH is initially in its home networks. However the initial position of WH can be considered under any FA in IP network. The WH transmits packets to correspondent node (CN) at a bit rate 2Mb per sec. A wired node N1 connected to router AR2 is considered as correspondent node (CN). However, any WLAN host in IP network can be also considered as CN. When WH comes out of WLAN coverage, it initiates MIP based handoff signaling through GPRS network. We implement FA functionality at GGSN and HA functionality at AR1. The GTP based signaling for handoff management is developed at SGSN and GGSN node. All control and data packets between SGSN and GGSN are transported using GTP. The simulation is carried out for one-pass and two-pass methods for MIP registration when WH moves from WLAN to GPRS. After handoff, the WH transmits IP packets through GPRS network to CN at a bit rate of 144 Kb per sec.

Table 2. Values used for simulation

MAC	802_11
Interface Queue	DropTail/PriQueue
Link Layer	LL
Antenna	Omniantenna
Interface queue length	700
Adhocrouting	DSDV
Data packet size	500 bytes
Mean link delay	50us
Link layer over-head	25us
Receive Threshold power	3.625 x 10-10
Transmit Power	0.28183815
Bandwidth between any two wired node	50Mb 15Ms

6 Performance

Results obtained from simulation show that for a fixed packet size of 500 bytes, the handoff delay in one-pass method is reduced by 18.657% compare to handoff delay in two-pass method [Fig. 5(a)]. Figure 5(b) shows the variation in handoff delay in one-pass and two-pass methods while packet size varies from 100 bytes to 1000 bytes in steps of hundred. It is seen that for increasing packet size from 100 to 1000 bytes, handoff delay increases by 17.784% in one-pass method and by 21.852% in two-pass method.

We computed the inter arrival delay of received packets at CN before and after handoff from WLAN to GPRS in one-pass method [Fig. 6(a)]. The average inter arrival delay of received packets is 5.91ms before handoff and this corresponds to average throughput of 678.8Kb per sec. The average inter arrival delay after handoff is 27.78ms and it corresponds to throughput of 144Kb per sec. Figure 6(b) shows the bit rate received at CN before and after handoff in one-pass method. Handoff is initiated in 8th sec. During handoff signaling, the IP network still routes packets for CN already buffered in queue. Thus, CN still receives data packets during first phase of handoff session. We selected simulation parameters such that these packets do not flow beyond handoff session. Therefore, at the last stage of handoff session, throughput becomes zero. After handoff, WH transmits data at bit rate of 144Kb per sec through GPRS network. But, same session is continued although throughput goes very low. The simulation results for inter arrival delay of received packets and throughput are also observed in two-pass method of handoff [6(c), 6(d)]. It is seen that results are similar to those observed in one-pass method except increased handoff delay. Here, the duration for which CN does not receive any packet in handoff session is larger. Therefore, the duration for zero level of throughput is larger than that in one-pass method.

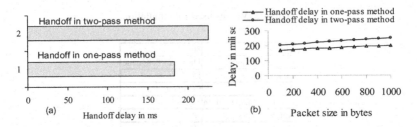

Fig. 5. Handoff delays in one-pass and two-pass methods 9b) Variation in handoff delays in one-pass and two-pass method with packet size

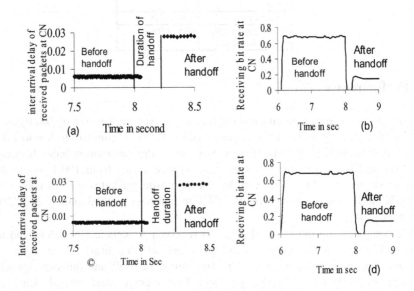

Fig. 6. (a) Interarrvial delay of received packet before and after handoff in one-pass method (b) throughput in Mbps before and after handoff in one-pass method (c) interarrival delay of received packet before and after handoff in two-pass method (d) throughput in Mbps before and after handoff in two-pass method

7 Conclusion

In the proposed architecture, the WLAN is loosely coupled to GPRS network. Both WLAN and GPRS networks converge to IP layer in integrated scenario. This architecture enables the GPRS subscriber to avail the WLAN service of Internet. This also facilitates the Internet subscribers to avail the internet service through GPRS. The Internet subscriber can maintain the session through GPRS network when they move from WLAN to GPRS. The proposed WLAN/GPRS architecture and handoff technique, support MIP based mobility management under roaming between GPRS and WLAN. The one-pass method of MIP registration by WH in GPRS network reduces the control signals for MIP based handoff management through GPRS. The handoff latency is reduced by 18% compare to two-pass method of handoff, although the through put in both methods are comparable with each other.

References

1. P. Mahonen, J. Riihijarvi, M. Petrova, and Z. Shelby, "Hop-by-Hop toward Future Mobile Broadband IP", IEEE Communication Magazine, Mar 2004, pp. 138-146.
2. S. M. Faccin, P. Lalwaney, B. Patil, "IP Multimedia Services: Analysis of Mobile IP and SIP Interactions in 3G Networks", IEEE Communication Mag, Jan 2004, pp. 113-120.
3. S. Simonens, P. Pellati, J. Gosteau, and K. Gosse, "The Evolution of 5 GHz WLAN toward Higher Throughputs", IEEE Wireless Communication, Dec 2003, pp. 6-13.
4. A. K Salkintzis, C. Fors and R.Pazhyannur, "WLAN-GPRS Integration for Next-Generation Mobile Data Networks", IEEE Wireless Communication, Oct 2002, pp-112-124.
5. S. Khara, I.S.Mishra and D.Saha, "An Alternative Architecture of WLAN/GPRS Integration", 63rd Vehicular Technology Conference (VTC'05) organized by IEEE at Melbourne, Australia from May 7-10, 2006, 0-7803-9392-9/06/$20.00 © 2006 IEEE.
6. S.-C Lo, G. Lee, W.-T Chen and J.-C Liu, "Architecture for Mobility and QoS Support in All-IP Wireless Networks", IEEE Journal on Selected Ares in Communications, Vol 22, No 4, May 2004, pp-691-704.
7. C. Perkins, "IP mobility support "IETF RFC 3220 Jan 2002.
8. H.-W. Lin, J-C. Chen, M-C. Hiang, C-Y Huang, "Integration of GPRS and Wireless LANs with Multimedia Applications", Proceedings of IEEE Pacific Rim Conference on Multimedia 2002, pp. 704-711.
9. 3GPP TS 04.07: "Mobile radio interface signalling layer 3; General aspects".
10. J. Ala-lLaurila, J Mikkonen and J. Rinnemaa, "Wireless LAN Access Network Architecture for Mobile Operators" IEEE Communications Magazine, Novmber 2001, pp-82-89.
11. H. Luo, Z. Jiang, B. Kim, N. K. Shankaranarayan and P. Henry, "Integrating Wireless LAN and Cellular Data for the Enterprise" IEEE Comp Soc, March-April 2003, pp-25-33.
12. M. Jaseemuddin, "An Architecture for Integrating UMTS and 802.11 WLAN Networks", Proceedings of IEEE Symp on Comp. and Communication.(ISSC-2003), pp. 716-723.
13. A. K. Salkintzis, "Interworking techniques and Architectures for WLAN/3G integration toward 4G Mobile Data Networks" IEEE Wireless Communication, June 2004, pp-50-61.
14. IEEE 802.11 Wireless LAN Medium Access Control (MAC) and Physical Layer (PHY) Specifications, 1999, http//standard.ieee.org/getieee802/download/802.11-1999.pdf.
15. 3GPP TS 04.08: "Mobile radio interface layer 3 specification (Release 1998)".

An Idea Bag Strategy to Discourage Selfish Behavior Under Random Token MAC Protocols for Wireless LANs

Jerzy Konorski

Gdansk University of Technology
ul. Narutowicza 11/12, 80-952 Gdansk, Poland
jekon@eti.pg.gda.pl

Abstract. Contention MAC protocols for a wireless LAN cannot count on selfish stations' adherence to the standard MAC. We consider anonymous stations in that a transmitted frame is only interpretable at the recipient(s). Two components of a MAC protocol are identified, a winner policy and a selection policy; by self-optimizing the latter, selfish stations can steal bandwidth from honest ones. We apply a game-theoretic framework to a protocol family called RT/ECD and design a repeated game strategy to discourage an invader – a station selfishly deviating from that strategy. We require that (R1) if there is no invader, or if an invader retreats to honest behavior, then ultimately all stations are honest, and (R2) an invader ultimately obtain less bandwidth than it would if behaving honestly. The proposed strategy fulfills (R1), while fulfillment of (R2) is examined via Monte Carlo simulation of heuristic invader strategies.

Keywords: wireless LAN, distributed MAC, random token, game theory.

1 Introduction

Contention MAC protocols for wireless LANs cannot count on network stations' adherence to the standard MAC if it runs counter their selfish interests. In this context it is appropriate for MAC design to meet game theory. Existing game-theoretic analyses extend to slotted ALOHA [1], [14] and CSMA/CA [2], [4] (as part of IEEE 802.11 [12]). The prevailing assumption is that the very principle of the contention is observed and only certain parameters may be configured selfishly. In this paper we model a class of contention mechanisms as follows: within each *protocol cycle* there is a finite *contention interval* to accommodate the stations' requests/attempts to transmit a data frame, and each station is free to select the instant within that interval where it makes its request/attempt. Such *Random Token* (RT) mechanisms [5] underlie slotted ALOHA and CSMA/CA, as well as HIPERLAN/1 [7] and some other known protocols. We allow the stations to be *anonymous* in that a transmitted frame is only interpretable at the recipient(s), all other stations perceiving it just as a burst of carrier. Anonymity is particularly justified in ad hoc systems, where stations are autonomous, likely to spoof on one another (their identifiers hardly being verifiable), and possibly use different data encoding/encryption schemes.

An RT protocol breaks up into two components: a *selection policy*, entirely within a station's discretion, determines the instant within the contention interval at which to make a request/attempt; a *winner policy*, common to all stations, defines the length of the contention interval, prescribes the rules of requesting to transmit a data frame, and determines a winner station in each protocol cycle (producing exactly one winner or none). We focus on a family of slotted-time protocols called RT/ECD (*RT with Extraneous Collision Detection*), where there are E contention slots in a contention interval, and a request to transmit a data frame has the form of a short pilot frame sent in a selected contention slot 1,..., E; it is expected to be reacted to with another short frame from the data frame's recipient. The mechanism is not unlike RTS/CTS access [12], although reaction frames need not be interpretable. Bandwidth utilization dictates that the earliest non-colliding pilot in the contention interval win: indeed, prolonging the contention beyond that does not increase the proportion of protocol cycles with a winner (hence, a collision-free data frame transmission), while increasing the contention overhead. Thus nontrivial winner policies only differ in how they account for the outcome of slots preceding the winning pilot. We compare two extreme cases: RT/ECD-0 and RT/ECD-∞, 0 and ∞ referring to the maximum allowed number of colliding pilots prior to the winning one (if any). Examples of protocol cycles under RT/ECD-0 and RT/ECD-∞ are shown in Fig. 1.

Two types of stations can be envisaged: *honest* and *selfish*. The former use some predefined standard selection policy e.g., uniform probability distribution over {1,...,E}, referred to as *Honest Randomizer* (HR). The latter are free to adopt any selection policy and self-optimize their bandwidth shares to the detriment of honest stations ("bandwidth stealing"). We assume that a selfish station is biased towards early contention slots, a selection policy referred to as *Selfish Randomizer* (SR).

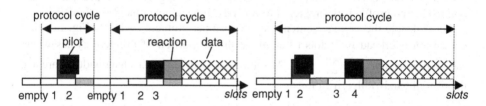

Fig. 1. Example protocol cycles; RT/ECD-0: slot 1 not selected, two stations select slot 2, lack of reaction terminates protocol cycle (*left*), RT/ECD-∞: lack of reaction after slot 2, reaction after slot 4 prompts the sender of the pilot to transmit data (*right*)

Given a winner policy, honest behavior should discourage any selfish deviation. Call a deviating station an *invader*. We require that (R1) if there is no invader, or if it retreats to honest behavior, then ultimately all stations use HR, and (R2) an invader ultimately obtain a lower bandwidth share than it would if behaving honestly.

We define one-shot RT/ECD games and look into their payoff structure under saturation load. We show that if SR is biased towards early contention slots heavily enough then under RT/ECD-0 the game resembles a multiplayer Prisoners' Dilemma (with a unique, fair, and Pareto non-optimal Nash equilibrium), whereas under RT/ECD-∞ falls into the class of *anti-coordination games* (with multiple unfair Nash equilibria at which exactly one station uses SR). Next we design strategies fulfilling (R1) and (R2) for a repeated RT/ECD game. In Sec. 2 we study one-shot RT/ECD-0 and RT/ECD-∞ games. In Sec. 3 related repeated games are defined, and a class of strategies are shown to fulfill (R1), while fulfillment of (R2) is examined via Monte Carlo simulation of heuristic invader strategies. Sec. 4 concludes the paper.

2 Binary RT/ECD Game

Consider N anonymous stations under RT/ECD-0 or RT/ECD-∞ with E contention slots. By choosing between HR and SR, each station pursues a maximum bandwidth share independently of the others. Thus an N-player *noncooperative game* arises, in which bandwidth shares are payoffs. In a one-shot game, choosing HR or SR is a single act performed simultaneously by all the stations.

Definition 1. (i) A binary *noncooperative game* [10] is a triple $(\{1,\dots,N\}, A, b)$, where $A = \{HR, SR\}$ is the set of feasible actions, and $b: A^N \rightarrow \mathbf{R}^N$ is a payoff function. Each station n chooses $a_n \in A$ and subsequently receives a payoff $b_n(\boldsymbol{a})$ dependent on the *action profile* $\boldsymbol{a} = (a_1,\dots,a_N) = (a_n, \boldsymbol{a}_{-n})$, where $\boldsymbol{a}_{-n}$ is the *opponent profile*. An action profile $(a,\dots,a)$ will be denoted all-a. (ii) A *Nash equilibrium* (NE) is an action profile $\boldsymbol{a} = (a_n, \boldsymbol{a}_{-n})$ at which $b_n(a_n, \boldsymbol{a}_{-n}) > b_n(a, \boldsymbol{a}_{-n})$ for all $n = 1, \dots, N$ and $a \neq a_n$. It is *Pareto optimal* if for any other action profile $\boldsymbol{a}'$ there exists an m such that $b_m(\boldsymbol{a}') < b_m(\boldsymbol{a})$, and *fair* if $b_1(\boldsymbol{a}) = \dots = b_N(\boldsymbol{a})$.

At a NE, each station plays the best reply to the opponent profile, hence no station deviates unilaterally – a likely outcome if the stations are rational (only maximizing own payoffs) and their rationality is common knowledge [10]. A fair and Pareto optimal action profile is desirable; unfortunately, it need not coincide with a NE.

Let O denote the average contention overhead per protocol cycle. (In Fig. 1 (right), contention overhead is 7 slots.) Let ω_n be the proportion of protocol cycles where station n wins, and $\Omega = \sum_{m=1}^{N} \omega_m$. At saturation load, station n's bandwidth share and the overall bandwidth utilization are:

$$b_n = \frac{\omega_n \cdot \tau_{\text{DATA}}}{\Omega \cdot \tau_{\text{DATA}} + O \cdot \tau_{\text{slot}}}, \quad b_\Sigma = \sum_{m=1}^{N} b_m = \frac{\Omega \cdot \tau_{\text{DATA}}}{\Omega \cdot \tau_{\text{DATA}} + O \cdot \tau_{\text{slot}}}, \tag{1}$$

where τ_{slot} and τ_{DATA} denote the slot and data frame duration, respectively. We write $b_{\text{HR}}(N, x)$ and $b_{\text{SR}}(N, x)$ for a station playing HR and SR, indicating the number x of stations playing SR. Similarly we write $\omega_{\text{HR}}(N, x)$, $\omega_{\text{SR}}(N, x)$, $\Omega(N, x)$, and $O(N, x)$.

Fig. 2 depicts the payoffs for RT/ECD-0 and RT/ECD-∞ obtained via Monte Carlo simulation ($N = 10$, $E = 8$, $\tau_{\text{DATA}}/\tau_{\text{slot}} = 20$, relative confidence intervals narrowed down to 5%), assuming $Pr[\text{SR selects slot } i] = p_{\text{SR}}(i) = const./\psi^{i-1}$ with $\psi = 10$. Arrows pointing northeast indicate incentives to switch from HR to SR; reverse incentives are indicated by arrows pointing northwest; lack of an outgoing arrow therefore indicates a NE at x. In both games, $x = 0$ is the only fair and Pareto optimal action profile. The RT/ECD-0 game is a multiplayer Prisoners' Dilemma [15] (always rewards playing SR and has a unique Pareto non-optimal NE at $x = N$); RT/ECD-∞ rewards "deep minority" stations (a single station using SR or the few using HR).

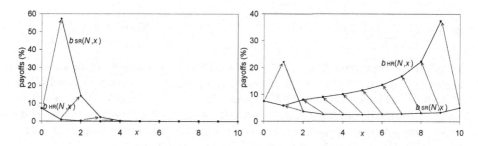

Fig. 2. One-shot game payoffs; RT/ECD-0 (*left*), RT/ECD-∞ (*right*)

A station inclines to a large ψ if it hopes that few other stations play SR. Assume that this is the case, a conservative approach since "bandwidth stealing" then becomes more painful. We will show that the layout of Fig. 2 is preserved for any p_{SR} that concentrates near $i = 1$. Both RT/ECD-0 and RT/ECD-∞ games then acquire a clear payoff structure: the former becomes a multiplayer Prisoners' Dilemma for any E, N, and τ_{DATA}/τ_{slot}, whereas, for any τ_{DATA}/τ_{slot} and under a mild restriction on E and N, the latter becomes an anti-coordination game with only unfair Nash equilibria.

Let $p_{SR}(i) = p_\psi(i)$, where $(p_\psi)_{\psi \in \mathbf{R}}$ is a family of probability distributions on $\{1,...,E\}$ continuous in ψ and such that $\lim_{\psi \to \infty} p_\psi(1) = 1$. Consider a *random* (N, E)-*arrangement* of N numbered objects in E boxes, obeying the Maxwell-Boltzmann statistic [8], and let $\Xi(N, E)$ be the probability of at least one box containing exactly one object. By the inclusion-exclusion principle [8] and with $0^0 = 1$ we have:

$$\Xi(N, E) = \sum_{l=1}^{\min\{N, E\}} (-1)^{l-1} \binom{E}{l} \binom{N}{l} \frac{l!}{(E)^l} \left(1 - \frac{l}{E}\right)^{N-l} . \tag{2}$$

Proposition 1. For sufficiently large ψ, (i) the RT/ECD-0 game is an N-player Prisoners' Dilemma with a unique, fair, and Pareto non-optimal NE at $x = N$ i.e.,

$$b_{SR}(N, x) > b_{HR}(N, x - 1), x = 1,...,N \tag{3}$$

$$b_{SR}(N, N) < b_{HR}(N, 0). \tag{4}$$

(ii) provided that

$$\Xi(N, E) > \frac{N}{N-1}\left[1 - \left(1 - \frac{1}{E}\right)^{N-1}\right], \tag{5}$$

the RT/ECD-∞ game has unfair Pareto optimal Nash equilibria at $x = 1$ i.e.,

$$b_{SR}(N, x) < b_{HR}(N, x - 1), x = 2,...,N \tag{6}$$

$$b_{SR}(N, 1) > b_{HR}(N, 0). \tag{7}$$

Proof. Let $P_\psi(i) = \sum_{j=i+1,...,E} p_\psi(j)$. $P_\psi(i)$ is nonincreasing in i and $\lim_{\psi \to \infty} P_\psi(i) = 0$. Hence, if ψ is large enough then $P_\psi(i) < 1 - i/E$ for all $i = 1,...,E - 1$. For RT/ECD-0,

$$\omega_{SR}(N,x) = \sum_{i=1}^{E} P_\psi(i)(P_\psi(i))^{x-1}\left(1-\frac{i}{E}\right)^{N-x}, \quad \omega_{HR}(N,x) = \frac{1}{E}\sum_{i=1}^{E}(P_\psi(i))^x\left(1-\frac{i}{E}\right)^{N-x-1}.$$

Therefore for large enough ψ, $\omega_{SR}(N, x) > \omega_{HR}(N, x-1) > \omega_{HR}(N, x)$ for $x \geq 1$, and $\omega_{SR}(N, x) < \omega_{SR}(N, x-1)$ for $x \geq 2$. If $\omega_{SR}(N, x) = \alpha\omega_{HR}(N, x-1)$ $(\alpha > 1)$ then $\Omega(N, x)$ $< \alpha\Omega(N, x-1)$ [since for $x = 1$, $\Omega(N, 1) = \omega_{SR}(N, 1) + (N-1)\omega_{HR}(N, 1) < \alpha\omega_{HR}(N, 0)$ $+ (N-1)\omega_{HR}(N, 0) < \alpha N\omega_{HR}(N, 0) = \alpha\Omega(N, 0)$, while for $x \geq 2$, $\Omega(N, x) = x\omega_{SR}(N, x)$ $+ (N-x)\omega_{HR}(N, x) < \alpha\omega_{HR}(N, x-1) + (x-1)\omega_{SR}(N, x-1) + (N-x)\omega_{HR}(N, x-1) <$ $\alpha(x-1)\omega_{SR}(N, x-1) + (N-x+1)\omega_{HR}(N, x-1)) = \alpha\Omega(N, x-1)]$.

The probability of at least $(i + 3)$-slot overhead (including synchronization, pilot and reaction slots) equals $(P_\psi(i))^x(1 - i/E)^{N-x}$. Summed over i, these probabilities yield O, and each of them decreases in x for large enough ψ. Thus $O(N, x) < O(N, x-1)$. Putting together the above findings along with (1), we prove (3) as follows:

$$b_{SR}(N,x) = \frac{\omega_{SR}(N,x)\cdot\tau_{DATA}}{\Omega(N,x)\cdot\tau_{DATA} + O(N,x)} = \frac{\alpha\cdot\omega_{HR}(N,x-1)\cdot\tau_{DATA}}{\Omega(N,x)\cdot\tau_{DATA} + O(N,x)}$$

$$> \frac{\alpha\cdot\omega_{HR}(N,x-1)\cdot\tau_{DATA}}{\alpha\cdot\Omega(N,x-1)\cdot\tau_{DATA} + \alpha\cdot O(N,x-1)} = b_{HR}(N,x-1).$$

To verify (4), observe that its left-hand side is arbitrarily close to zero for large enough ψ, whereas $\omega_{HR}(N, 0) = (1/E)\cdot\Sigma_{i=1,...,E}(1 - i/E)^{N-1} > 0$ implying $b_{HR}(N, 0) > 0$.

For RT/ECD-∞, the left-hand side of (6) is arbitrarily small for large enough ψ, whereas for $x = 2,..., N$, $\Omega(N, x-1)$ is arbitrarily close to $\Xi(N-x+1, E-1) > 0$ i.e., given that all the selfish stations are almost certain to select slot 1, an honest station wins if at least one of slots $2,...,E$ is selected by exactly one honest station. This implies $\omega_{HR}(N, x-1) > 0$ and $b_{HR}(N, x-1) > 0$.

It remains to prove (7) for $\psi \to \infty$ along similar lines as (4). Firstly, observe that $\omega_{SR}(N, 1) = (1 - 1/E)^{N-1} > \Xi(N, E)/N = \omega_{HR}(N, 0)$. The latter equality follows by symmetry and the left-hand side of the inequality represents the probability that at least one slot is left empty for a given station to select for a successful pilot – an event implied by, but not implying, that station winning the contention. Secondly, we have $(N - 1)\omega_{HR}(N, 1) < 1 - (1 - 1/E)^{N-1}$. Indeed, the right-hand side represents the probability that at least one honest station transmits a pilot in slot 1, where it is almost certain to collide with the selfish station's pilot; this is necessary, but not sufficient for one of the other honest stations to win. Thus (5) implies $\omega_{HR}(N, 1) < \omega_{HR}(N, 0)$. Finally, $\omega_{SR}(N, 1) = \alpha\omega_{HR}(N, 0)$ $(\alpha > 1)$ implies $\Omega(N, 1) < \alpha\Omega(N, 0)$, as can be shown by direct counting of random (N, E)- and $(N-1, E-1)$-arrangements.

Since all involved probabilities are continuous in ψ, one can expect a similar payoff structure for a large but finite ψ. Condition (5) is not too restrictive e.g., for $E = 8, 9$, and 10 it holds for $N \leq 16, 19$, and 23, respectively.

3 Repeated RT/ECD Game

Given that the desirable action profile $(x = 0)$ is not a NE of the one-shot RT/ECD games, one may ask if a *repeated* game admits a strategy fulfilling (R1) and (R2).

Definition 2. (i) A noncooperative *repeated game* [10] proceeds in stages, each consisting of a number of protocol cycles. In each stage $k = 1,2,\ldots$, a one-shot game $(\{1, \ldots, N\}, A, b)$ is played i.e., the stations each choose HR or SR, which they play consistently throughout the stage. If $a^k = (a_1^k,\ldots,a_N^k)$ is the action profile in stage k then the sequence $(a^1,\ldots,a^k)$ is the *play path* up to stage k.[1] In stage k station n receives a *stage payoff* $b_n^k = b_n(a^k)$. (ii) Player n's *strategy* is a function $\sigma_n \colon \Pi \to A$, where Π is the set of all play paths. That is, σ_n determines the action a_n^k to be taken in stage k given the play path up to stage $k-1$. By analogy with Definition 1, $(\sigma_1,\ldots,\sigma_N)$ will be referred to as a *strategy profile*, and all-$\sigma = (\sigma,\ldots,\sigma)$.

We are seeking a σ such that (R1) all-σ leads to all-HR regardless of initial conditions, and (R2) for an invader station n, $b_n^k < b_{HR}(N, 0)$ for sufficiently large k (that is, all-σ is a *subgame perfect NE* of the repeated RT/ECD game [10]). In our binary games, a sufficient characterization of a play path up to stage k is $(x^1,\ldots,x^k)$.

For the RT/ECD-0 game, a multiplayer Prisoners' Dilemma, one can use an honest strategy similar to SPELL [13] provided the x^k are observable despite the stations' anonymity. E.g., one may observe the proportion of protocol cycles with empty slot 1. Assuming $p_{SR}(i) = const./\psi^{i-1}$ with a large ψ, it is approximately $(1 - 1/E)^{N - x}/(\psi)^x$. Online estimation of this quantity in successive stages detects a clear maximum, revealing $x^k = 0$ and yielding N, as well as second- and subsequent-magnitude maxima, revealing respectively $x^k = 1, \ldots, x^k = x^*$, where x^* is a threshold. For example, with $E = 8$ and $\psi = 10$, the maxima differ by a factor of 8.75. The threshold x^* is dictated by statistical credibility: if the observed proportion is β ($\beta \ll 1$) then the relative width of a confidence interval is roughly proportional to $1/\sqrt{\beta}$. We take $x^* = 2$ i.e., a station can distinguish $x^k = 0, 1, 2$, and >2.

The same scheme works for the RT/ECD-∞ game, whose payoff structure calls for a novel honest strategy. Two candidates will be examined, *Nash* and *Idea Bag*.

3.1 Nash Strategy

The one-shot RT/ECD-∞ game admits a fair mixed NE, at which the stations play SR with the same probability P_{NE}. This symmetry permits to replace the routine linear system describing a mixed NE [3] by a single nonlinear equation in P_{NE}:

$$\sum_{x=0}^{N-1} B_{N-1,P_{NE}}(x)[b_{SR}(N, x+1) - b_{HR}(N, x)] = 0, \tag{8}$$

where $B_{K,p}(x) = \binom{K}{x} \cdot (p)^x \cdot (1-p)^{K-x}$. The Nash strategy recreates this NE in each stage, thus discouraging an invader playing SR with a different probability (e.g., always – hoping for $b_{SR}(N, 1)$, or never – hoping for $b_{HR}(N, N-1)$). For the parameter setting in Fig. 2 we get $P_{NE} = 0.1551$. Monte Carlo simulations of the repeated RT/ECD-∞ game for $N = 10$, $E = 8$ and $\psi = 10$ are illustrated in Fig. 3; stage payoffs are averaged over 1000 runs and normalized with respect to $b_{HR}(N, 0)$.

---

[1] Here k are superscripts; for powers we reserve the notation $(a)^b$ unless a is a numeral.

In Fig. 3 (left), a single invader always playing SR is unable to significantly outperform the stations playing Nash. However, the best (unrealistic) strategy of an invader station n is to predict the opponent profile $x_{-n}^k = |\{m \neq n \mid a_m^k = \text{SR}\}|$ prior to stage k, and play $a_n^k = \text{SR}$ when $x_{-n}^k = 0$, otherwise play $a_n^k = \text{HR}$. This is an *Ideal Invader* strategy. From Fig. 3 (right) one sees that it yields almost 40% above the fair bandwidth share – namely, $(1 - P_{\text{NE}})^{N-1} b_{\text{SR}}(N,1) + \sum_{x=1}^{N-1} B_{N-1,P_{\text{NE}}}(x) \cdot b_{\text{HR}}(N,x) \approx 1.391 \cdot b_{\text{HR}}(N,0)$. Thus if an invader can do better than randomize between HR and SR, the Nash strategy does nor prevent "bandwidth stealing." Neither does it ensure that x^k falls to zero in the absence of invaders (rather, x^k hovers around $N \cdot P_{\text{NE}}$).

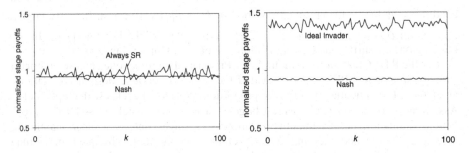

Fig. 3. Nash strategy; vs. Always SR (*left*), vs. Ideal Invader (*right*)

3.2 Idea Bag Strategy

A station may start with an "idea bag" – a set of possible substrategies to choose from. Each one prescribes an action in the next stage given the past play. As the game progresses, the station focuses on those that (would) have yielded the highest stage payoffs. Thus one arrives at various "meta-strategies" e.g., responsive learning [9] or virtual scoring [6]. In the latter, a virtual score is updated stage-by-stage for each substrategy. The station follows the currently highest ranking substrategy. At the end of a stage, it calculates the received stage payoff and increments the highest ranking substrategy's virtual score. It also examines the other substrategies and adds the stage payoffs they would have yielded to the respective virtual scores.

Consider an "idea bag" with two substrategies: σ_{HR} = "always play HR" and σ_{SR} = "always play SR." If $a_n^k = \text{HR}$ then σ_{HR} scores $b_{\text{HR}}(N, x^k)$ (real stage payoff) and σ_{SR} scores $b_{\text{SR}}(N, x^k + 1)$ (virtual stage payoff); if $a_n^k = \text{SR}$ then σ_{SR} scores $b_{\text{SR}}(N, x^k)$ and σ_{HR} scores $b_{\text{HR}}(N, x^k - 1)$. Let Δ_n^k = virtual_score(σ_{HR}) – virtual_score(σ_{SR}) at station n prior to stage k. The following specifies the Idea Bag (IB) strategy:

$$w_n^k = \begin{cases} \text{HR, if } \Delta_n^{k-1} \geq 0 \\ \text{SR, if } \Delta_n^{k-1} < 0, \end{cases} \tag{9}$$

$$\Delta_n^k = \Delta_n^{k-1} + \begin{cases} b_{\mathrm{HR}}(N, x^k) - b_{\mathrm{SR}}(N, x^k + 1), \text{if } w_n^k = \mathrm{HR} \\ b_{\mathrm{HR}}(N, x^k - 1) - b_{\mathrm{SR}}(N, x^k), \text{if } w_n^k = \mathrm{SR}. \end{cases} \quad (10)$$

IB has two drawbacks. First, it requires the knowledge of N and x^k to determine the virtual payoffs $b_{\mathrm{SR}}(N, x^k + 1)$ and $b_{\mathrm{HR}}(N, x^k - 1)$, while in fact x^k can only be distinguished up to the threshold x^*. Second, we want the game to converge to $x^k = 0$; unfortunately, under all-IB it turns out that either a one-shot NE is ultimately played ($x^k = 1$) or the play never converges to a particular action profile. The former is quite likely: once a one-shot NE is played in a stage, it is played forever (i.e., if there exists a k_0 such that $a_n^k = a_n^{k_0}$ for all $k \geq k_0$ and $n = 1,\ldots,N$ then $x^{k_0} = 1$ and vice versa; the proof relies on (6) and (7) in the spirit of fictitious play [11]).

It is easy to modify (10) so that under all-IB, $x^k = 0$ obtains for large enough k (a trivial modification would have Δ_n^k grow with k regardless of the play). The problem lies in ensuring that it still discourages persistent deviations from IB. We propose a heuristic called IB', with (10) replaced as follows. If $a_n^k = \mathrm{HR}$ then

$$\Delta_n^k = \Delta_n^{k-1} + \begin{cases} 0, \text{if } x^k = 0 \\ b_{\mathrm{HR}}(N,0) - b_{\mathrm{SR}}(N,1) - \mathrm{random}(D), \text{if } x^k = 1 \\ b_{\mathrm{HR}}(N,2) - b_{\mathrm{SR}}(N,3), \text{if } x^k = 2 \\ b_{\mathrm{HR}}(N,x^k) - b_{\mathrm{SR}}(N,4), \text{if } x^k > 2 \end{cases} \quad (11)$$

and if $a_n^k = \mathrm{SR}$ then

$$\Delta_n^k = \Delta_n^{k-1} + \begin{cases} b_{\mathrm{HR}}(N,0) - b_{\mathrm{SR}}(N,1), \text{if } x^k = 1 \\ b_{\mathrm{HR}}(N,1) - b_{\mathrm{SR}}(N,x^k), \text{if } x^k = 2 \\ b_{\mathrm{HR}}(N,2) - b_{\mathrm{SR}}(N,x^k), \text{if } x^k > 2, \end{cases} \quad (12)$$

where random(D) is a uniform random variable on $[0, D)$. Note that (11) and (12) attempt to mimic (10) i.e., retain the drive towards the one-shot NE. However, two features violate (10) and weaken the drive: when $x^k = 1$, Δ_n^k drops at *all* the stations (including the one playing SR), and when $x^k = 0$ it remains constant. (The latter feature is also of practical value as it prevents indefinite growth of Δ_n^k should the play converge to $x^k = 0$.) The other modifications account for observability of x^k up to x^* and pertain to the virtual payoffs (the b_{SR} terms in (11) and the b_{HR} terms in (12)). Finally, the presence of random(D) is vital to convergence to all-HR, as shown below. The following proposition states conditions under which all-IB' fulfills (R1).

Proposition 2. Assume that in the repeated RT/ECD-∞ game,

$$b_{\mathrm{HR}}(N, x) > b_{\mathrm{SR}}(N, x'), x = 1,\ldots,N, x' = 2,\ldots,N. \quad (13)$$

Then under all-IB' and with finite initial virtual scores, the play converges in probability to all-HR (the number of stages with $x^k > 0$ is finite with probability one).

Proof. If $x^{k_0} = 0$ for some k_0 then $x^k = 0$ for all $k \geq k_0$. Indefinitely long play with $x^k = 1$ is impossible, as is indefinitely long play with $x^k > 1$: in both cases, the Δ_n^k are all monotone in k. We now show that there exists a k_0' (finite with probability one) such that $x^{k_0'} = 0$. It suffices that for some k_0, the two smallest among the $\Delta_n^{k_0}$ are within an arbitrarily small $\varepsilon > 0$ of each other, implying that almost certainly they are both nonnegative (thus $x^{k_0} = 0$) or negative (thus $x^{k_0+1} = 0$). As an illustration, Fig. 4 (left) plots the Δ_n^k against k for a generic game scenario with random initial scores. Note that when $x^k > 1$, all stations playing SR increase Δ_n^k by the same amount, (dependent on x^k) and when $x^k = 1$, stations playing HR decrease Δ_n^k faster than those playing SR (due to the random term in (11)). Consider successive stages k_1, k_2, ... with $x^{k_i} = 1$. Suppose that $\Delta_{n_i}^{k_i}$ and $\Delta_{n_i'}^{k_i}$ are the smallest and second-smallest among the $\Delta_n^{k_i}$. Two cases are possible in the next stage: (a) $\Delta_{n_i}^{k_i+1}$ is the smallest among the $\Delta_n^{k_i+1}$, implying that the distance to the second-smallest among the $\Delta_n^{k_i+1}$ has shrunk, and (b) $\Delta_m^{k_i+1}$ and $\Delta_{m'}^{k_i+1}$ are now the smallest and second-smallest (with $m \neq n_i$), implying that they are within D of each other; consequently, there is a nonzero probability that $\Delta_m^{k_{i+1}}$ and $\Delta_{m'}^{k_{i+1}}$ will be within $\varepsilon > 0$ of each other. In either case the number of stages before that occurs is finite with probability one.

In our parameter setting, (13) is fulfilled for N up to 20. To illustrate the convergence of all-IB' to all-HR, a number of Monte Carlo simulations have been conducted with $D = 5$ and $N = 10$; all results are averaged over 1000 runs. Fig. 4 (right) depicts the number x^k of stations playing SR in successive stages. The dashed curve has been obtained for a fixed and large discrepancy between the stations' initial virtual scores, with $\Delta_1^0 = -b_{SR}(N, 1)$ and $\Delta_n^0 = b_{SR}(N, 1)$ for $n = 2,...,N$. This is an unfavorable setting, since it lessens the chances of all Δ_n^k quickly becoming nonnegative. Notice the lengthy plateau that corresponds to $N - 2$ stations constantly playing HR and the other two being stuck in a nasty pattern of the two lowest curves in Fig. 4 (left). One way of speeding up the convergence is to build in a firm upward drift of Δ_n^k in the initial stages; to this end, we have replaced each $b_{HR}(N, x)$ term in (12) by a linear combination of itself and $b_{HR}(N, N - 1)$, the latter component losing weight as the number of past stages with $x^k = 1$ grows. The convergence is now much faster (the solid curve) despite an even more unfavorable initial setting of virtual scores, with $\Delta_1^0 = -3 \cdot b_{SR}(N, 1)$ and $\Delta_n^0 = 3 \cdot b_{SR}(N, 1)$ for $n = 2,...,N$.

The problem with (R2) is to find a best reply to IB' (a worst-case invader), and next to establish that there is no better reply to that best reply than IB'. Compare Ideal Invader's performance against all-Nash opponent strategy profile – Fig. 3 (right) with that against all-IB' – Fig. 5 (left), for $N = 10$, $E = 8$, and $D = 5$, and with random initial scores set between $-3 \cdot b_{SR}(N, 1)$ and $3 \cdot b_{SR}(N, 1)$. The Ideal Invader station no longer enjoys a sustained advantage over $b_{HR}(N, 0)$, although it does enjoy a temporary

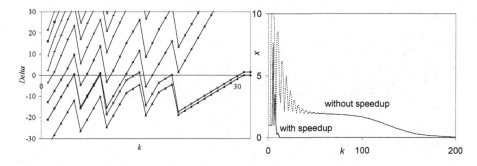

Fig. 4. IB' strategy; illustration for proof of Proposition 2 (*left*), convergence to all-HR (*right*)

advantage (in the initial 50 or so stages) when the IB' stations use the convergence speedup. The amount of bandwidth stolen from the honest stations is almost intangible, unlike in Fig. 3 (right) – apparently, IB' has a way with Ideal Invader. It is instructive to note that the best reply to an Ideal Invader station n is to confront it with an opponent profile with $x^k_{-n} = 1$ in each stage k. To preserve fairness, the IB' stations should therefore correlate their play and take turns at playing SR in successive stages. Fig. 5 (right) convinces that in most stages, the IB' stations manage to coordinate on $x^k_{-n} = 2$ instead, and only occasionally produce $x^k_{-n} = 0$ to the invader's advantage. Thus the little intelligence they use for virtual scoring permits them to perform distinctly better than Nash strategy stations facing a single Ideal Invader station.

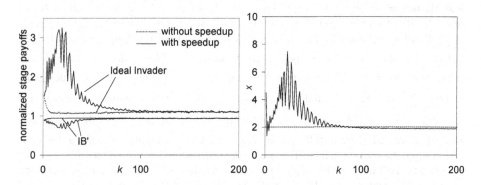

Fig. 5. IB' strategy vs. Ideal Invader; stage payoffs (*left*), number playing SR (*right*)

In reality, Ideal Invader might be approximated by sophisticated enough invader strategies. How would those perform against IB'? Two plausible approximations consist in: modifying (11) and (12) so that they more resemble (10) (thus the invader drives towards an unfair one-shot NE), or using a larger "idea bag" in the hope to outwit the honest stations, which only choose between σ_{HR} and σ_{SR}.

592   J. Konorski

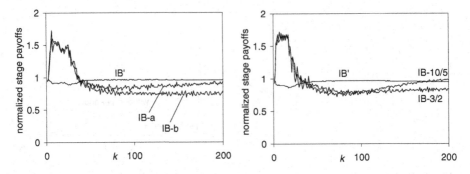

Fig. 6. IB' strategy; vs. IB-a and IB-b (*left*), vs. IB-Σ/H (*right*)

The approximation of IB, called IB-a, replaces the $x^k = 0$ and $x^k = 1$ entries in (11) by $b_{HR}(N, 0) - b_{SR}(N, 1)$ and $b_{HR}(N, 1) - b_{SR}(N, 2)$, respectively (the former difference is negative and the latter is positive). Fig. 6 (left) shows that an IB-a invader station does not enjoy a larger-than-fair bandwidth share except for a temporary advantage due to the convergence speedup used by the IB' stations. Interestingly, x^k tends to 0 as k increases: the drift toward SR at $x^k = 0$ is compensated by the drift away from SR at $x^k = 1$. To eliminate the latter, an invader might try another variation of IB, called IB-b, whereby the $x^k = 1$ entry of (11) is retained, creating a uniform drift towards SR. However, the IB-b curve in Fig. 6 (left) shows that this is in fact counterproductive.

Finally, an invader trying a larger "idea bag" must first constrain the set of substrategies. A wide class of substrategies consist in distinction of Q predefined stage outcomes, and mapping a sequence of H recent stage outcomes onto the set A of feasible actions in the next stage. There are therefore $2^{(Q)^H}$ different substrategies (e.g., $2.4 \cdot 10^{24}$ for $Q = 3$ and $H = 4$). Of this huge set, a modest number Σ are selected at random for inclusion in the "idea bag" [6]. We call the resulting strategy IB-Σ/H. Let o_n^k be stage k outcome perceived at station n. The action in stage k that substrategy $\sigma = 1,...,\Sigma$ prescribes for station n is obtained by first calculating $\alpha_0(\sigma) + \sum_{h=1}^{H} \alpha_h(\sigma) \cdot o_n^{k-h}$ and then taking $a_n^k = \text{HR}$ if this number is even, and $a_n^k = \text{SR}$ if it is odd. The $\alpha_h(\sigma)$ are random integers defining σ. The substrategy with the largest virtual score is followed in stage k; all substrategies prescribing the same action score the real stage payoff, whereas the other score the virtual payoff.

In our experiment, seven stage outcomes were distinguished at a station according to own action and x^k i.e., (HR, 0), (HR, 1), (HR, 2), (HR, >2), (SR, 1), (SR, 2), and (SR, >2), and assigned numerical values 0 through 6. Care was taken to include σ_{HR} and σ_{SR} in the "idea bag." Fig. 6 (right) presents the normalized stage payoffs for a single invader station playing IB-3/2 and IB-10/5 against $N - 1$ IB' stations. Again, after the initial surge due to the convergence speedup at the IB' stations, the invader finds its payoffs inferior to the fair bandwidth share and subsequently learns the game to achieve slightly higher payoffs. As expected, the learning process is the faster, the more intelligence (the larger Σ and H) the invader possesses. However, it does not lead to a distinct long-run advantage over IB'.

4 Conclusion

While adherence to a common winner policy is a prerequisite for using the network, there is room for adopting selfish selection policies. We have addressed this problem by studying one-shot and stage-by-stage repeated RT/ECD games. Under certain conditions, the one-shot RT/ECD-0 game is a multiplayer Prisoners' Dilemma, hence enables various cooperation enforcement strategies. However, RT/ECD-∞ gives rise to an anti-coordination game whose only Nash equilibria are unfair. A strategy IB' has been proposed for the repeated RT/ECD-∞ game, such that all-IB' fulfills (R1). Yet there is only partial evidence, based on examination of heuristic invader strategies, that (R2) is also fulfilled. As seen from Fig. 5 (left), an Ideal Invader station can "steal" a little bandwidth and never get punished. On the other hand, Ideal Invader is not realizable, which leaves the question about fulfillment of (R2) open.

Acknowledgment. This work was supported in part by the Ministry of Education and Science, Poland, under Grant 1599/T11/2005/29.

References

1. Altman E., El Azouzi R., Jimenez T.: Slotted Aloha as a Game with Partial Information. Computer Networks 45 (2004) 701–713
2. Altman E., Kumar A., Kumar D., Venkatesh R.: Cooperative and Non-Cooperative Control in IEEE 802.11 WLANs. INRIA Tech. Rep.5541 (2005)
3. Basar T., Olsder G. J.: Dynamic Noncooperative Game Theory. Academic Press 1982
4. Cagalj M., Ganeriwal S., Aad I., Hubaux J.-P.: On Selfish Behavior in CSMA/CA Networks. In *Proceedings of IEEE Infocom '05* (2005)
5. Chlamtac I., Ganz A.: Evaluation of the Random Token Protocol for High-Speed and Radio Networks. IEEE J. Select. Areas Commun. SAC-5 (1987) 969-976
6. Challet D., Zhang Y.-C.: Emergence of Cooperation and Organization in an Evolutionary Game. Physica A 246 (1997) 407
7. ETSI TC Radio Equipment and Systems: High Performance Radio Local Area Network (HIPERLAN); Services and Facilities; Version 1.1, RES 10 (1995)
8. Feller W.: An Introduction to Probability Theory and its Applications. J. Wiley (1966)
9. Friedman E.J., Shenker S.: Synchronous and Asynchronous Learning by Responsive Learning Automata. Mimeo (1996)
10. Fudenberg D., Tirole J.: Game Theory. MIT Press (1991)
11. Fudenberg D., Levine D.K.: The Theory of Learning in Games. MIT Press (1998)
12. IEEE Standard for Information Technology – Wireless LAN Medium Access Control (MAC) and Physical Layer (PHY) Specifications, ISO/IEC 8802-11 (1999)
13. Konorski J.: Playing CSMA/CA Game to Deter Backoff Attacks in Ad Hoc Wireless LANs, In: *Proceedings of AdHocNow 2005*. Lecture Notes in Computer Science, Vol. 1281. Springer-Verlag, Berlin Heidelberg New York (2005) 127–140
14. MacKenzie A.B., Wicker S.B.: Selfish Users in ALOHA: A Game-Theoretic Approach. In: *Proceedings of VTC Fall 2001* (2001)
15. Yao X.: Evolutionary Stability in the *n*-Person Iterated Prisoners' Dilemma. BioSystems 39 (1996) 189–197

A Signalling Technique for Disseminating Neighbouring AP Channel Information to Mobile Stations

Gurpal Singh[1], Ajay Pal Singh Atwal[1], and B.S. Sohi[2]

[1] Deptt of CSE & IT, BBSBEC, Fatehgarh Sahib, Punjab, India
[2] University Institute of Engineering and Technology, PU, Chandigarh, Punjab, India
{gurpal, ajaypal}@bbsbec.org, bssohi@yahoo.com

Abstract. Fast handoff is a major problem in the wireless networks and this problem is further aggravated due to limited range of 802.11 Access points. Scanning phase is the major contributor to 802.11 handoff delays; it can be decreased by reducing the number of channels that are scanned at the handoff time. Prior knowledge of the neighbouring Access points (AP) can help in reducing the number of channels to be scanned and thus can assist a mobile station (STA) in making a fast and accurate handoff decision. Dissemination of the neighbouring AP information to all the STA attached to a given AP is a challenging task and it needs to be accomplished without making major changes to the 802.11 standard or significant client/AP modifications. Low computational complexity and backward compatibility are the other issues which have to be taken into account while designing such handoff schemes. We have proposed a new method of providing neighbouring AP channel information to the STA. This method provides the neighboring channel information to the mobile nodes with the help of specially crafted Null CTS frames sent by the access points. We have shown that the overheads due to this scheme are well within the permissible limits.

Keywords: IEEE 802.11 networks, Handoff, Null CTS Frames, Signaling overheads.

1 Introduction

IEEE 802.11 based wireless and mobile networks [1] are experiencing a very fast rate of growth and are being widely deployed but they suffer from limited coverage range of AP, resulting in frequent handoffs, even in moderate mobility scenarios. 802.11 standards follow the "break before Make" approach at the handoff times. It is quite evident from [2][4][6] that the time taken by the STA to scan the neighbouring AP at the handoff time is a major contributor towards the handoff delay in 802.11 based networks. Long handoff delays can be decreased if numbers of channels to be scanned at handoff time are reduced.

In the scheme proposed by [4] all the channels have to be scanned. In [6] when using neighbour graphs, requires long time to build and is not suitable for fast changing topologies. In [2], a mechanism to reduce the handoff delay by staggering beacons, on different channels, in time, STA still have to run syncscan on all the

S. Chaudhuri et al. (Eds.): ICDCN 2006, LNCS 4308, pp. 594–599, 2006.

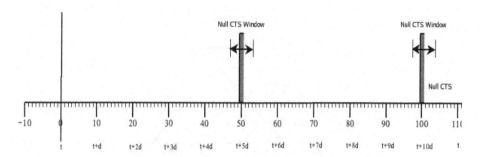

Fig. 1. Diagram shows scheduling of NULL CTS frames three non overlapping channels with beacon interval of 100ms

channels as STA have no method of knowing about their neighbours. This approach adds to high signaling overhead and strict timing constraints [2]. In [3] a technique where the strict timing requirements of syncscan have been removed, but still all channels need to be scanned.

In this paper we have proposed a scheme to disseminate accurate neighbouring AP channels information. This is accomplished while the STA is still connected to the current AP and without making modifications into the existing 802.11 standards. We have done analysis of this approach and have calculated the percentage signaling overheads due to this approach and provides excellent results if used in conjunction with the [2] or [3].

2 Basic Algorithm

Our algorithm proposes that all APs in the Distribution system (DS) know about the channel numbers on which their immediate neighbouring APs are operating. This Neighbour information is further disseminated to the STA's, by the current AP to which they are attached. One approach to gather neighbour information is to manually assign neighbour information, consisting of neighbouring AP channel numbers at the time of installation of DS. Another approach is to GPS enable all APs[7].

The task of disseminating this neighbour information to the STA attached to a given AP is a complex task and it needs to done with desirably no modifications to the existing standards, minimum modifications to client/AP software and minimum signalling overheads. To accomplish this task we exploit the existing CTS frames and tailor them for propagating neighbour information to associated STAs.

3 NULL CTS Frames

In this approach we have slotted the beacon interval into ten equal time division as shown in Fig 1. It is proposed that an AP sends specially crafted null CTS frames with duration field set to zero and destination address of self during the NULL CTS windows. Based on this, if null CTS frame is received by the STA at the interval $t+n*d$ (where n is the channel number, and t is the beacon interval, $d=t/10$), it is taken as indication of presence of an AP on channel n. It should be noted that Null CTS

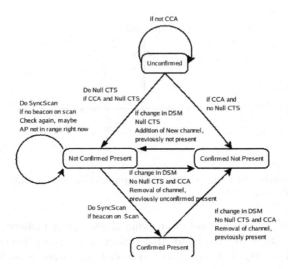

Fig. 2. State Machine Depicting how channels are selected for scan

transmission can be delayed in case, media is not available due to some ongoing transmission, this problem can be circumvented by using a window during which an AP can send a null CTS frame. By doing so the stringent timing requirements are taken care of (Fig 1).

All the null CTS for a given AP are sent during the time of associations/ reassociation or in case there is some change in the APINFO table. To ensure that neighbour information properly reach the STAs, the null CTS frames are repeated over the next beacon interval as well. Thus, the list of neighbouring channels is gathered by all the stations and is fed to the scanning algorithm, [2] or [3] or the classical scanning approach at the time of handoff, the scanning algorithm will run on limited number of channels as opposed to all the channels. We have defined the states into which a system can move and the State transition diagram is given in Fig 2.

- **Unconfirmed (UC):** Initially all the 802.11 channels for a STA are in this state.
- **Not Confirmed Present (NCP):** This state contains the channels for which null CTS was received from the currently associated AP. This state contains the list of neighbouring channels on which scanning algorithm will actually run to ascertain their signal strengths.
- **Confirmed Present (CP):** This state contains the list of channels from which the STA has received the beacons and measured their signal strengths. These channels will be used for making handoff decisions.
- **Confirmed Not Present (CNP):** This state will contain the list of channels for which channel was sensed to be clear at the time when null CTS was expected but no null CTS was received. These channels will never be used for handoff or scanning.

3.1 Overhead Due to Null CTS

In this section we calculate the overhead traffic due to the Null CTS frames in a given beacon interval and is represented in the form of percentage overhead of the normal traffic.

3.2 Calculation of Normal Throughput

For calculating the normal throughput we have adopted the model proposed by [8].

In a contention based environment as per [8] the probability p, of traffic of a given STA colliding with transmission of any of the other STAs can be approximated as:

$$p = 1 - \left[1 - \frac{2*(1-2p)}{(1-p-p(2p)^m)} \cdot \left(\frac{1}{W}\right) \right]^{(n-1)} \tag{1}$$

Where

n is the number of STAs	W is the minimum window size
m is the back off stage	max windows size is $2^m{*}W$
T_{slot} is slot time	$T_{payload}$ is time to transmit payload bits
T_{phy} is time to transmit packet	T_{cycle} is time between start of two packet.

Equation (1) can be solved for p by simplifying and applying Newton bisection method for various values of n, W and m. Table 1 shows the values of p for various values of n, with constant W and m. From (1) Success rate of transmission can be calculated which is given in equation (2)[8].

Table 1.

N	W	m	P
5	128	3	0.0625
10	128	3	0.119
15	128	3	0.168
20	128	3	0.231

$$r_{success} = \left(\frac{2*(1-p)}{(2-p)}\right) * \left(\frac{1}{T_{cycle}}\right) \tag{2}$$

$$T_{cycle} = T_{physical} + T_{SIFS} + T_{ACK} + T_{DIFS} \tag{3}$$

It is assumed that all packets are of uniform size and all the STAs are in saturated stage, i.e. they always have a packet to transmit.

In this case

packet payload	8184 bits	MAC Header	272 bits
PHY Header	128 bits	ACK Length	240 bits
Channel Bit Rate	1 Mbits/ sec	SIFS	28 microseconds
DIFS	130 micro sec	SLOT Time	51 microseconds
Channel Bit Rate	1 Mbits/sec	propagation delay	1 microsecond

The throughput is given by

$$Throughput = R_{success} * PayloadSize \tag{4}$$

$$Throughput = 2\frac{(1-p)}{(2-p)} * \left(\frac{PayloadSize}{T_{cycle}}\right) \tag{5}$$

Where units of T_{cycle} are taken in seconds and payload size is taken in bits and hence throughput is measured in bits per second. Now the throughput in a single beacon interval of 100ms duration is obtained as follows:

$$Throughput_{beaconInterval} = \frac{Throughput}{10} \tag{6}$$

3.3   Traffic Due to Null CTS

Let us assume that $T_{nullctswindow}$ is the size of Null CTS window and T_{cycle} represents the time to transmit a given packet. T_{cycle}, therefore represents the interval between the two packet transmissions. All the above intervals are taken in slot times.

Let $x = T_{nullctswindow} / T_{cycle}$ (7)

Eq. (7) represents the number of transmissions in a given null CTS window. In our calculations we take x=1 for $T_{Nullctswindow} \geq T_{cycle}$. AP will grab any transmission opportunity during Null CTS window to send Null CTS frame as it has highest priority.

$$Null\ CTS\ overhead = x * NullCTSlength * Neigbours \qquad (8)$$

Where size of null CTS MAC is 14 bytes and it contains the address of the AP which is sending it. Time taken to send a Null CTS frame is given below. This overhead is actually calculated on the basis of Null CTS frames sent in the beacon interval just succeeding the association/ reassociation request. It is expressed in number of bits used to send Null CTS frames corresponding to all the neighbours per beacon interval.

Length of Null CTS = SIFS + Physical header + (Null CTS MAC)
Where Size of null CTS MAC=14x8 bits   Physical Header size= 128 bits.

Number of neighbour depends on the deployment and available in APINFO table stored on AP.

$$overhead = \left[\frac{(Null\ CTS\ overhead)}{Throughput_{baeconinterval}} \right] * 100 \qquad (9)$$

Graph 1 shows the percentage overhead versus number of neighbours in a beacon interval for various numbers of STAs attached to a given AP.

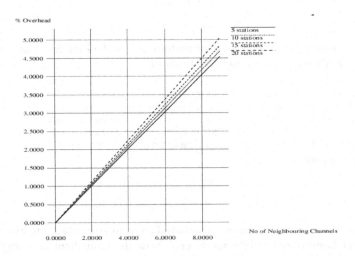

Graph 1. Overheads due to NULL CTS with varying number of neighboring AP

3.4 Backward Compatibility

Our approach is fully backward compatible with no modifications done to the base 802.11 standards. In case STA is not running the modified drivers it will simply ignore the Null CTS signaling frames and can use the original [2], [3] or standard scanning mechanism for handoff decision.

4 Conclusion

In this paper we have proposed a novel approach of providing neighbour information to the 802.11 wireless STA; that makes use of Null CTS frames for disseminating neighbour information using very small Null CTS frames and add very little to the signaling overheads. By providing neighbour information, number of channels to be scanned by the STA is reduced resulting in lesser number of scan operations. This approach is fully backward compatible and can be modified to suit both high mobility and low mobility scenarios. We have mathematically calculated the percentage overheads for the beacon intervals carrying the null CTS signaling elements and the results show that the overheads are within the permissible limits. Moreover, Null CTS signaling overheads are not continuous and are present only at the time of association/ reassociation requests.

References

1. IEEE. Part 11: Wireless LAN Medium Access Control (MAC) and Physical Layer (PHY) Specification. IEEE Standard 802.11, 1999.
2. I. Ramani, S. Savage, "syncscan :Practical Fast handoff for 802.11 Infrastructure Networks," IEEE INFOCOM 2005.
3. Yong Liao, Lixin Gao, "Practical Schemes for Smooth MAC Layer Handoff in 802.11Wireless Networks", Proceedings of the 2006 International Symposium on World of Wireless, Mobile and Multimedia Networks, WoWMoM 2006, June 26 - 29, 2006.
4. H. Velayos and G. Karlsson, "Techniques to reduce IEEE 802.11b mac layer handover time," Kungl Tekniska Hogskolen, Stockholm, Sweden, Tech. Rep. TRITA-IMIT-LCN R 03:02, ISSN 1651-7717, ISRN KTH/IMIT/LCN/R-03/02–SE, April 2003.
5. IEEE. Recommended Practice for Multi-Vendor AP Interoperability via an Inter-Access Point Protocol Across Distribution Systems Supporting IEEE 802.11 Operation. IEEE Draft 802.1f/D3, January 2002.
6. M. Shin, A. Mishra, and W. Arbaugh, "Improving the latency of 802.11 hand-offs using neighbor graphs," in Proceedings of the ACM MobiSys Conference, Boston, MA, June 2004.
7. Gurpal Singh, Atwal Ajay Pal Singh, Rajbahadur Singh, BS Sohi, IAPP modifications for a location based handoff technique in wireless Networks, SOFTWIM 2006, Proc of Workshop on Software for Wireless Communications and Applications Co-located with COMSWARE 2006, New Delhi, India, 2006.
8. Tay Y.C and Chua K.C., "A Capacity Analysis for the IEEE 802.11 MAC Protocol" in Wireless Networks vol 7 p159-171, Kluver Academic Publishers, 2001.Baldonado, M., Chang, C.-C.K., Gravano, L., Paepcke, A.: The Stanford Digital Library Metadata Architecture. Int. J. Digit. Libr. 1 (1997) 108–121

A Predictive Location Management Scheme by Extracting the Unique Sub-patterns from the Mobility Logs

Subrata Nandi[1] and Sanjib Sadhu[2]

[1] Indian Institute of Technology, Kharagpur,
[2] National Institue of Technology, Durgapur-9, West Bengal, India
sn_nitdgp@yahoo.co.in, sanjibsadhu411@yahoo.com

Abstract. We propose a predictive scheme, where the MT stores only current day movement log and sends this log to MSC during off-peak hours. The MSC performs offline computation to find unique sub-patterns and hot cells from pattern logs. The hot cells are downloaded in the MT which sends an update when it leaves a hot cell thus enables the MSC to identify the sub-pattern to be followed next. On arrival of a call the MSC performs selective paging Analytical study shows the total location management cost using the proposed scheme is far better than distance-based location management scheme.

Keywords: Predictive location management, mobility logs, sub-pattern.

1 Introduction

In cellular network a Location Area (LA) is controlled by a Mobile Switching Centre (MSC) consisting of Home Location Register (HLR) and Visitor Location Register (VLR). Location management (LM) involves two tasks: location update (LU) and paging. Several non-predictive LM strategies has been proposed in [4],[5]. Mobile terminal (MT) generally follows a regular pttern of cells. In predictive scheme, the location of MT can be predicted to some extent from the history of its movement stored in MSC database. Therefore the predictive LM schemes are preferred over non-predictive ones as prediction reduces paging cost drastically.

Among predictive LM schemes one proposed in [3] is based on the user mobility pattern. Here a MT stores several day movement logs and also patterns extracted from logs. There may be redundancy of some consecutive cells as patterns are concerned thus increasing storage requirement. Another scheme in [2] requires the regional route map to be downloaded in the MT. Here the pattern is identified by the MT. The above scheme expects the MTs to be very intelligent as it assigns huge computation load to it. In [6], the user mobility patterns (UMP) are derived from the users actual path (UAP) by sequential pattern mining method. The computation overhead of the algorithm is very high. Both [2], [6] assumes that a LA consists of single cell which is unrealistic. In this paper, we propose a predictive scheme which assigns more load to the MSC than MT. The MT stores only current day movement log and sends this log

S. Chaudhuri et al. (Eds.): ICDCN 2006, LNCS 4308, pp. 600–605, 2006.

to MSC during off-peak hours for computing the sub-patterns and hot cells. An analytical study considering semi-random mobility model estimated the LM cost.

Section 2 of this paper explains the proposed scheme with the algorithm to extract the unique sub-pattern and the paging procedure. The LU and paging cost is given in Section 3. Section 4 presents the results with discussion and Section 5 concludes.

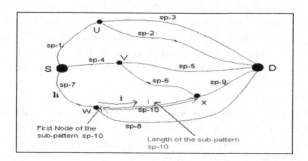

Fig. 1. Different sub-patterns extracted for a MT

2   The Proposed Predictive Location Management Scheme

Mobile Users generally follow regular trip routes from home (source) to office (destination) in morning and reverse route in evening. A node is defined as a tuple (c,t) with cell-id (c) and entry time (t) in the cell. The MT stores the node list (NL)of the current day. At the end of day each MT will send NL to the HLR via the VLR. For each MT the HLR will extract the patterns from the log of the different days some of which may have common sub-patterns. Here each pattern/sub-pattern is a sequence of consecutive cells. HLR will extract only the unique sub-patterns to store in database. The last cell of those sub-patterns is called hot cell whose next cell will determine the new sub-pattern that MT will follow. Fig.1 shows different sub-patterns (spi's) and hot cells generated in a MT trip from cell labeled S to D. The HLR will send the list of hot cells, source and destination cell ids to the corresponding MT. When the MT leaves its source cell or a hot cell the MT will send an update message and the HLR will determine from the log which sub-pattern the MT is going to follow. Whenever an incoming call arrives at time T, selective paging strategy is used i.e., the MT is searched in the predicted cell obtained from sub-pattern node list. If the MT is not found, it is searched in those cells where the probability of residence of the MT is non-zero at time T else the MT is searched exhaustively in the entire LA.

2.1   The Algorithm to Find the Unique Sub-pattern Followed by a MT

$S=\{ s_i : i \geq 1\}$ is set of all unique sub-patterns existing in database. Initially $S=\emptyset$. s_new is a new movement pattern obtained from a day's mobility log. Each s_i contains the beginning cell index (s_i.beg), last cell index (s_i.end), total no of cells(m) in it and the starting time(ST) of it.Here $m=(s_i$.end $-s_i$.beg $+1)$. The algorithm pattern() to identify the sub-patterns accepts s_new ,S and updates S if unique sub-patterns are found and is described below:

If(S=∅) then Add the entire new pattern s_new as a unique sub-pattern in S
Else {compare s_new with each s_i of S. If it exists, the algorithm is terminated, else call generate_sub_pattern() to generate unique sub-patterns to add in S and old s_i s' from which the new sub-patterns are generated, are deleted from S.}
The algorithm generate_sub_pattern ( ) is described as follows: Let H be the cardinality of the set S and n=length of s_new and Junction, initially 0, indicates the intersected cells in s_new by other s_i and each Junction has a flag "flag" whose 0&1 value indicates that 2 paths meeting it are different & same respectively.
For each s_i ∈ S Do   Begin j := 1;
   For i= s_i.beg to s_i.end Do Begin
     If(j^{th}cell of s_new = i^{th} cell of s_i) then /* s_i & s_new meets in junction-id j */
     Begin   H=H+1, get a new s_H and assign 0 to s_H.beg , (i - s_i.beg) to s_H.end   and update m of s_H and assign ST of s_i to ST of s_H and if this junction(j) is new, reset Junction.flag to 0,increase the junction by 1;
       For k : = 0 to s_H.end Do k^{th} cell of s_H := $(s_i$.beg + k$)^{th}$ cell of s_i;   /* EndFor */
       Update s_i.beg to (i+1), assign entering time(ET) of $(i+1)^{th}$ cell of s_i to ST of s_i.
Assign i to v and reset a flag "flag1" to 0 .
While((j<n)and(v<m)) Do   If($(j+1)^{th}$ cell of s_new = $(v + 1)^{th}$ cell of s_i) then
     increment both j, v by 1 and set flag to 1 Else   break; /* End While */
If((flag=0)and((j>n)or(v>m)))Then either s_new or s_i is terminated, so discard the current s_i ,exit from loop, select the next new s_i ,start the outermost for loop again.
Else if(flag1=1) then /* junction Cell id where s_i and s_new meets as j */
   Begin   H=H+1,get new s_H ,assign 0 to s_H.beg & (v - s_i.beg) to s_H.end, update m in s_H. Assign ST of s_i to ST of s_H ,1 to Junction.flag; if "j" is new, Junction=Junction+1;
     For k=0 to s_H.end Do k^{th} cell of s_H :=$(s_i$.beg + k$)^{th}$ cell of s_i; /* For end */
   s_i.beg := v;assign ET of vth cell of s_i to ST of s_i & v to i; Endif Else continue;   j++;
Endfor ;   Endfor /* End of outermost for loop */
Now assign "-1" value to the cell id of the Junction to denote it as last junction.
/*All s_i are checked. Now derive the new sub-pattern from the s_new */
t=0;
While(cell-id of the tth junction ≠ -1) do
If(the tth Junction.flag ≠ 1) then   Begin H=H+1, get a new s_H and assign 0 to s_H.beg;
If(t ≠ 0)then s_H.end:=(t^{th} junction-id)-($(t-1)^{th}$ junction-id)–1
else s_H.end:=t^{th} junction-id– 1 /* End of inner If */
update m of s_H and ST of s_H as ET of s_new. beg;
     For k:= 0 to s_H.end Do k^{th} cell of s_H := (s_new.beg + k$)^{th}$ cell of s_new;/*For end */
     Assign (the tth junction-id +1) to s_new.beg and t=t+1;
Endif

Now S is updated. If the cell-id of any junction obtained in the above algorithm is absent in the list of hot cell, that junction is added as a hot cell to the list. The worst case complexity of the above algorithm is O (H.m.n) where m is the length of longest unique sub-pattern and H, n are described as before. For a regular user the number of unique sub-patterns H is less, i.e. thus worst complexity of the algorithm is much better than [6].

2.2 The Procedure to Page a MT During Call Delivery

For an incoming call in a MT moving with average velocity V cells/hour, the sub-pattern being followed by it is obtained from the MSC database because when(at time t_2) the MT left the hot cell, the MT sent an update signal and at that time the MSC database tracked which sub-pattern is going to be followed by the MT. Now last update time (t_2) is compared with $ST(t_1)$ of the sub-pattern stored in the database and $\Delta t = (t_2 - t_1)$ sec. If $\Delta t=0$, then the MT is searched in the predicted cell from the mobility log. If $\Delta t >0$, the MT's entry time in the sub-pattern is late than actual time, so it is searched $C_1 = \left\lceil \dfrac{V}{3600} \times \Delta t \right\rceil$ cells behind the actual cell. If $\Delta t < 0$, the MT's entry time in the sub-pattern is before than the actual time, so it is searched C_1 cells ahead the actual cell. If it is not found, it is searched as described in section 2.

3 Analysis of the Proposed Scheme

For analyzing the LM cost of the scheme, we have assumed semi-random directional mobility model [1] and regular hexagonal cells.

3.1 Mobility Model and Traffic Model

In semi-random directional model [1] probabilities assigned to neighbors are estimated based on some criteria with more value assigned to a preferred neighbor (N_{PREF}) who takes the MT closer towards the destination. Let $S(0,0)$ and $D(x,0)$ be the source and destination of MT, h be the no of hops moved by the MT, at any instant from S and incoming call arrival follows a Poisson distribution with rate λ calls/hour.

3.2 Location Update and Paging Cost

Let h be the distance between the source and the 1st cell of the current pattern in cell units. The sub-pattern's length is l in cell unit that is being followed by the MT at that instant as shown in Fig 1. Let C be cost incurred to page a single cell. Since the call arrival follows the Poisson process, the expected no of calls in a particular time interval(I) will be required. We take this I as the time required to cover the pattern being followed at that instant. Let C_{avg} be average cost for a single call during this time interval I. The average paging cost, C_{pag} during the interval I is given by

$$C_{pag} = C_{avg} \times \sum_{n=0}^{\infty} \left\{ \frac{e^{-\lambda(l/V)} \times \left(\lambda \left(l/V \right)^n \right)}{n!} \times n \right\} = C_{avg} \times \left(\lambda \times \left(\frac{l}{V} \right) \right)$$

We assume that U be the cost of a single update. The average cost, U_{avg} for updating are given as three cases: if($ h \geq 5$) $U_{avg} = U$, if (($l < 5$) && ($1 \leq h \leq 5-l$))

$$U_{avg} = U \times \left(\frac{2^{l+1}-1}{l+1} \right) \times \prod_{i=0}^{l-1} \left(\frac{1}{7-h-i} \right) \quad \text{and} \quad \text{finally} \quad \text{if} \quad (l \geq 5 \,\&\&\, 5 > h \geq 1) \| (l < 5)$$

$$\&\&(5 > h > 5-l) \; U_{avg} = U \times \left(\frac{2^{6-h}-1}{6-h} \right) \times \left(\prod_{i=0}^{4-h} \left(\frac{1}{7-h-i} \right) \right).$$

4 Results and Discussion

We compare our scheme with the distance based location update (with distance threshold l hops which is generally 3 or 4 hops) scheme which performs the best among non-predictive schemes. Considering all types of cases it can be shown the total cost is $(2 \times l-1) \times \left(\frac{1}{5 \times 6^{l-1}} \right) \times U + \{ 3 \times l(l-1)+1 \} \times C$. The value of U and C is taken as 1.4 and 1 respectively. The graph in Fig. 2(c) shows the total cost against the different distance thresholds which is higher than that of our scheme. In distance based update case the total cost does not depend on the distance of LUC from the source cell of the MT. The total average cost $C_T = U_{avg} + C_{pag}$. In our scheme, we assume V=5 cells/hour. We have got the plot of LU, paging and total cost with respect to l for different values of h, in Fig 2(a), Fig. 2(b) and Fig. 2(c) respectively. Here h implies how far away the pattern is from the source cell S. So if h increases, the MT follows nearly optimal path. The graph in Fig 2(a) shows that the values of U_{avg}, for $h \leq 2$ decreases initially as the length of pattern increases because the probability to follow the exact current pattern decreases but in the latter stage of its trip becomes constant as it tends to follow optimal route with probability 1. As the probability to follow the path increases, the probability to send update message increases and the update cost will also increases and vice versa. For $h > 2$, the value of U_{avg} does not change with respect to length of pattern. It is quite obvious that when the MT moves far from the S, the MT follows the pattern having optimal route and therefore it is not required to send update message. The Fig 2(b) shows that the paging cost increases when the length of sub-pattern increases, but this rate of increase decreases if h or l increases as the MT will not deviate so much and try to follow optimal path and so paging cost is reduced. So for higher values of l the LU cost becomes constant, but the paging cost increases in slow rate. The Fig 2(c) shows that the total average cost of the MT decreases when the value of h increases.

5 Future Work

As a future work, the mobile users can be grouped into different categories according to their mobility pattern, which will reduce the storage overhead in MSC database, because the MTs will share some common sub-pattern among themselves.

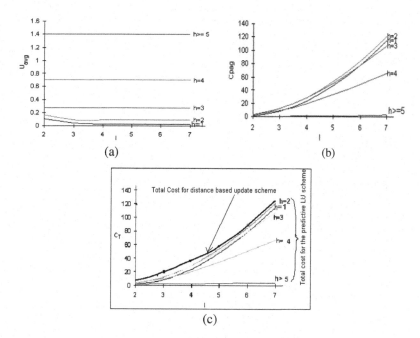

Fig. 2. (a) Updated cost vs length of sub-pattern (b) Paging cost vs length of sub-pattern
(c) Total cost(C_T) vs length of sub-pattern(l) of a MT

References

1. Nandi, S., et. al.: A Realistic Mobility Model for Simulation-Based Study of Wireless
   Cellular Networks. 2005 Workshop on Performance of Wireless Networks and
   Communication Systems (WiNCS '05) July 23-28 2005 Cherry Hill, Philadelphia, USA
2. Ghosh, R. K., Aggarwala, S., Mishra, H., Sharma, A., Mohanty, H,: Tracking of Mobile
   Terminals Using Subscriber Mobility Pattern with Time-bound Self Purging Indicators and
   Regional Route Maps. IWDC 2005, 27-30 December 2005. IIT Kharagpur, India,
   Proceedings in LNCS Vol. 3741, pp.512 – 523.
3. Cayirci, E., Akyildiz, I. F., User mobility pattern scheme for location update and paging in
   wireless system. IEEE Trans. On Mobile Computing. Vol. 1, No. 3, July-Sept. 2002.
4. Bar-Noy, A., et. al.: Mobile Users: Update or not to update? Wireless Networks, Vol.1, No. 2,
   July 1995.
5. Lee, B. K., Hwang, C. S.: A Predictive Paging Scheme Based on Movement Direction of a
   Mobile Host. IEEE VTC 1999.
6. Yavas, G., Katsaros, D., Ulusoy, O., Manolopoulos, Y.: A data mining approach for
   location prediction in mobile environments", in ELSEVIER , Data and Knowledge
   Engineering 54 (2005) p121-146.

Author Index

Lecture Notes in Computer Science

For information about Vols. 1–4246

please contact your bookseller or Springer